VIETNAM

An American Ordeal

GEORGE DONELSON MOSS

PRENTICE HALL
Englewood Cliffs, N.J. 07632

Library of Congress Cataloging-in-Publication Data

MOSS , GEORGE,
    Vietnam, an American ordeal / by George Moss.
       p. cm.
    Includes bibliographical references.
    ISBN 0-13-949918-0
    1. Vietnamese Conflict, 1961-1975. I. Title.
DS557.7.M66 1990   89-22798
959.704'3—dc20   CIP

> *For the young Americans
> who fought in the Vietnam war,
> and for those who opposed it.*

Editorial/production supervision and
interior design: JENNIFER WENZEL
Manufacturing buyer: ED O'DOUGHERTY
Cover design: RAY LUNDGREN GRAPHICS
Cover photos: COURTESY OF USMI PHOTO ARCHIVES
  AND NATIONAL ARCHIVES

 ©1990 by Prentice-Hall, Inc.
A Division of Simon & Schuster
Englewood Cliffs, New Jersey 07632

Printed in the United States of America

10 9 8 7 6 5 4 3 2 1

ISBN   0-13-949918-0

PRENTICE-HALL INTERNATIONAL (UK) LIMITED, *London*
PRENTICE-HALL OF AUSTRALIA PTY. LIMITED, *Sydney*
PRENTICE-HALL CANADA INC., *Toronto*
PRENTICE-HALL HISPANOAMERICANA, S.A., *Mexico*
PRENTICE-HALL OF INDIA PRIVATE LIMITED, *New Delhi*
PRENTICE HALL OF JAPAN, INC., *Tokyo*
SIMON & SCHUSTER ASIA PTE. LTD., *Singapore*
EDITORA PRENTICE-HALL DO BRASIL, LTDA., *Rio de Janeiro*

CONTENTS

FOREWORD

by
Stephen E. Ambrose

In 1975, shortly after the North Vietnamese Army overran Saigon, President Gerald R. Ford declared, "The lessons of the past in Vietnam have already been learned—learned by the President, learned by the Congress, learned by the American people—and we should have our focus on the future."

The American people responded gratefully to Ford's invitation to forget the whole nightmare. In 1978, when I offered a course on the Vietnam War at the University of New Orleans, six students signed up. Two of them dropped before the mid-term exam.

Over time, the national amnesia gave way to national curiosity. The subject no one wanted to talk about at the end of the seventies became the subject everyone wanted to about know at the end of the eighties. Publishers who would not touch a Vietnam War book suddenly could not find enough manuscripts to satisfy the market. In the seventies, the question most often asked of American history teachers by their students was, "Who killed Jack Kennedy?" In the eighties, it became "What happened in Vietnam?" Courses on the Vietnam War were the most popular history courses on campuses across the nation; at the University of New Orleans, when I offered such a course for a second time in 1989, the seating capacity of the auditorium, 250, was exceeded on the first day of registration.

Stephen Ambrose is a prominent military and diplomatic historian, acclaimed biographer of Dwight D. Eisenhower, and author of a biography of Richard Nixon. He teaches a course on the U.S. involvement in Vietnam at the University of New Orleans.

The surge of interest was inevitable. Young men have always wanted to know what the last war was like, why and how it was fought, what they missed (or escaped). They have the vague idea that the next war, their war, will be like the last one (it won't). Veterans of Vietnam, who once swore they never wanted to hear the word again, found that in their middle age, they were curious about what their leaders had been thinking when they sent them to Vietnam. They also wanted to correct the thousand-and- one misperceptions that those who did not serve had about the actions of American armed forces in Vietnam. Participants in the anti-war movement at home began to wonder about their dogmas. Doves and hawks alike realized that their predictions and assumptions had been proven wrong by events: the victory of the Communists in Vietnam did not lead to a victory by the Communists in Japan, Burma, the Philippines, much less to a Communist assault on San Francisco. Cambodia and Laos did fall to the Communists, but the damndest thing happened—as soon as the Americans were gone, Communist Vietnam was at war with Communist Cambodia and Communist China. The doves, meanwhile, had to face the fact that their assertion that the North Vietnamese were freedom-loving agrarian reformers was dead wrong, as the Communists imposed a dictatorship on southern Vietnam that was so extreme that tens of thousands of Vietnamese risked the extreme dangers of escaping in overloaded, un-seaworthy boats.

Clearly there was much to learn from a study of the Vietnam War. Clearly the American people wanted to know more, a great deal more, about what happened, and why. And they wanted to speculate on what could have been done differently, with what possible results. A hundred times a semester, and more, young students ask me, "Doc, we could have won that war, couldn't we?"

What they really mean is that in their view, the American armed forces were stabbed in the back by the cowardly politicians at home.

It is one of the many virtues of George Moss's solid and sensible study of the Vietnam War that he deals directly with this growing stab in the back legend. He has mastered the ever-growing literature about the war; he has thought long and hard about what he has read; and he has managed to escape the passions of the sixties and the seventies to see clearly and objectively what happened and why.

The result is a succinct assessment of America's longest war. If the subject is a painful one, so be it. We as a people must go beyond the "No More Vietnams" syndrome just as surely as we must eschew legends if we are truly to reach the point that President Ford said we had reached back in 1975. This book will help us get there.

PREFACE

OF BLACK MARBLE AND MEMORIES: EPIPHANY

Washington, D.C., April 4, 1987....A cold spring rain drenched clusters of visitors filing along the walkway bordering the Vietnam Veterans Memorial. From my vantage point in front of the Lincoln Memorial, I watched them descending slowly, occasionally stopping to read the names etched in the black marble slabs. Some may have sought a name they would remember, of a boy they had known, had loved, from among the 58,156 names of the dead stencilled in the bleak stone. I could feel the grief and anger welling inside a young woman as she reached out to touch an inscribed name. As I stood musing amid the afternoon shadows cast by Lincoln's brooding monument, the idea of writing the story of the long and disastrous American involvement in Vietnam first started to my mind. I wanted to answer the question that must have formed wordlessly in the young woman's mind that cold spring day: why? why Vietnam?

Vietnam....The word evokes a flood of horrid images and memories....A Buddhist monk incinerating himself, the head of the South Vietnamese police force summarily executing a Vietcong terrorist, a ditch near the hamlet of My

Lai-4 filled with the bodies of women and children, a screaming child, her naked body seared by napalm, racing down a road, plastic body bags lying on the tarmac at Tan Son Nhut Air Base awaiting a a flight home, Chicago police gassing and clubbing young people in the streets, the shootings at Kent State, and maimed Vietnam war veterans, opposed to the continuing conflict, angrily throwing their medals and ribbons onto the steps of the nation's capitol.

Questions about Vietnam arise: Why did the United States become involved for so long in the affairs of a seemingly small, poor, and insignificant country? Why did the world's richest and most powerful nation fight a long, losing war in Vietnam? What were the effects of this war effort on America and its people?

My book answers these questions and the other important concerns of those who have lived through the Vietnam war era and of those too young to have any direct experience of those traumatic years. Although it focuses on the American side of the story, my book provides the Vietnamese historical and political context in which the events of the U. S. intervention in that country occurred. I devote considerable attention to the political and military activities of both the Vietnamese Communists and a succession of governments in South Vietnam backed by the United States. It is important to remind ourselves that the outcome of the American Vietnam war was determined primarily by events occurring within the ill-starred nation of Vietnam, not by what happened within the United States.

America's longest war aroused the passions of most of its citizens, and divided them worse than any other conflict since the Civil War. Many people still harbor bitter feelings and memories about the war, whether they fought it or watched it on the evening television news. Knowing that such feelings persist, I have tried to write an objective account of the American Vietnam ordeal. My overriding concern always has been to tell the story as it actually happened, without taking sides. I don't think a valid history of the American Vietnam experience confirms either a hawkish or dovish view of the war. All Americans were complicit in a national tragedy. In my opinion, compassion and empathy are more appropriate responses to our nation's ordeal than righteous wrath or angry condemnation.

This is the history, from its genesis to its tragic denouement, of the failed American effort to determine the political destiny of the South Vietnamese people.

ACKNOWLEDGMENTS

It never ceases to amaze me that so many busy friends, colleagues, scholars, archivists, and editors have eagerly lent so much of their time and talent to my Vietnam project. I am exceedingly grateful for their words of support, for their many constructive criticisms, for their calling my attention to pertinent source materials, and for their genuine desire to see me produce the best book that I possible can,

I thank the National Endowment for the Humanities for supporting my participation in two recent Summer Seminars for College Teachers, which allowed me to think about and research particular aspects of the American Vietnam war. I thank Robin Winks, Yale University, who directed one of the seminars, for convincing me that Vietnam was an important story that I could write about. I also thank Michael Schudson, University of California, San Diego, who directed the other seminar, for helping me refine my thinking about the media coverage of history's first televised war. Daniel C. Hallin, Professor Schudson's colleague at UC, San Diego, shared his expert knowledge of media coverage of the war, and made many constructive suggestions that improved my manuscript.

Although I have relied mainly on secondary sources, I have made extensive use of primary sources, mostly declassified and published government documents. I have also had the opportunity to examine source materials located in various archival collections. In particular, I thank Charles Bryant of the Southeast Asia Collection at Yale University, and Richard J. Sommers and David Keough of the United States Army Military History Institute Archives at Carlisle Barracks, Pennsylvania for helping me access the archives. I am also grateful to the NEH for a travel grant which enabled me to visit some of the archival collections. I also thank City College of San Francisco for granting me a timely sabbatical leave that permitted me to devote all my time to the book for nearly a year.

I also thank many of my colleagues at City College of San Francisco, particularly Austin White, David Lubkert, Richard Oxsen, Ted Taylor, Francisco Wong, and Francine Foltz, who read parts of the manuscript, served as sounding boards for my ideas, and encouraged my efforts.

Special thanks go to several scholars who read the entire manuscript. Jack Colldeweih, Fairleigh Dickinson University, spent many hours subjecting every line that I wrote to rigorous criticism. He was both generous in his praise and unrelenting in his insistence that I write clearly, coherently, and accurately. Paul Conway, SUNY College at Oneonta, shared with me his extensive knowledge of all aspects of the American involvement in Southeast Asia and made numerous suggestions that improved the book. Kevin O'Keefe, Stetson University, helped me understand the complex events occurring in the Gulf of Tonkin the night of August 4, 1964, and made many other improvements. Stephen E. Ambrose, University of New Orleans, shared with me his vast knowledge of American military and diplomatic history of the Vietnam era.

I want to thank several people affiliated with my publisher, Prentice Hall. Special thanks go to the reviewers, Joseph St. Mark, St. Thomas Aquinas College; Patrick Hearden, Purdue University; Walter Capps, University of California at Santa Barbara; Roger Dingman, U.S. Air Force Academy, Colorado Springs; and William Duiker, Penn State University, for their helpful suggestions. I am most grateful to Steve Dalphin, Executive Editor, who manifested a remarkable faith in my ability to write the book about the Vietnam war that he wanted on schedule. It was a pleasure to work with Jennifer Wenzel as she directed the book production process through its various stages.

Special thanks go to my sister, Mary Chatelier, who put her historian's training to good use ferreting out many expressive photographs from the National Archives and other photographic collections for inclusion in the book. I am most grateful for the companionship of Bruno, who spent almost as much time on the word processor as I did; also for the love and support of my lovely wife Linda, and for her being, well, for her being just the way she is.

THE FALL OF SAIGON

The End as Prelude

As April 1975 drew to a close, South Vietnam faced extinction: 150,000 battle-hardened North Vietnamese troops surrounded Saigon, poised to launch a direct assault on the defenseless capital. Since January, when North Vietnamese forces launched what turned out to be the final offensives of the war, Communist troops had quickly swept through flagging South Vietnamese defenses. Now, they had positioned themselves for the kill.

They had been aided substantially on March 11 when South Vietnamese President Nguyen Van Thieu decided to surrender the strategic central highlands region to marshal his remaining forces for an all-out defense of Saigon. In the aftermath of Thieu's surrender of the northern half of his country, a disorderly retreat from the highlands turned into panicky flight. Leaderless soldiers, joined by frightened civilians, fled the central regions for the coastal city of Tuy Hoa. Thousands died during the two-week-long Convoy of Tears. The city proved to be only a temporary haven for the refugees because it too was soon surrendered to the advancing foes.

As North Vietnam applied increasing military pressure in the spring of 1975, President Thieu urgently requested increased American aid for his imperiled country. President Gerald R. Ford asked Congress to appropriate an additional $722 million dollars of emergency military aid for South Vietnam. But congressional leaders, knowing there was almost no public support for the aid bill, convinced that the United States would only be spending more money on a losing cause, refused Ford's request.

Thieu, who had counted on American aid to enable South Vietnam to survive the Communist onslaught, was angry at what he saw as an American betrayal of its commitments to his country. He believed that the United States had abandoned South Vietnam in its hour of desperate need. Thieu, knowing his armed forces could not fight effectively without American support, despairing of his country's fate, ceased to lead. Discredited, he resigned on April 21. Immobilized by pessimism and indecision at the top, the Saigon government was paralyzed. Its demoralized armies could not stop the Communist forces. Its equally demoralized citizenry awaited the end that they knew must come.

The sudden collapse of South Vietnam's defenses had caught American embassy officials in Saigon by surprise. Contingency planning for evacuations had been inadequate. U.S. Ambassador Graham Martin, a fervent supporter of the South Vietnamese cause, convinced that there would be an eleventh-hour decision by the United States to intervene and save South Vietnam, did not order evacuation procedures to begin until the third week of April.

In addition to evacuating remaining American military and civilian personnel and their dependents, U.S. officials removed thousands of South Vietnamese, many of whom had formerly worked for American military or civilian agencies and now feared for their lives. But for every South Vietnamese who had a coveted American connection or who could afford to purchase the proper credentials, there were many others who desperately wanted to leave but could find no way out.

On April 29, President Ford ordered Ambassador Martin to evacuate all remaining Americans. Helicopters from a U.S. fleet standing by about forty miles offshore made the final evacuations, sometimes under fire from North Vietnamese rockets and artillery. By now, order had completely collapsed in Saigon. Desperate mobs roamed the streets. Looters were everywhere, ransacking homes and apartments. During the evening, a large, angry crowd surrounded the U.S. embassy. Some were there hoping to find a way out; others came to jeer at the departing Americans. U.S. Marine security guards used tear gas and rifle butts to prevent hysterical people from climbing over the compound walls. Throughout the night, evacuees made their way to the rooftop heliport and their ride to safety. Ambassador Martin wearily boarded one of the last helicopters out of Saigon. By the early morning of April 30, all Americans and many of the eligible Vietnamese had safely departed the Saigon embassy. A few hours after the last Americans and their Vietnamese clients had departed Saigon, North Vietnamese tanks advanced into the heart of the city.

Just before noon, April 30, a column of North Vietnamese tanks rumbled up Thong Nhut Boulevard and rolled to a halt in front of Independence Palace. They formed a semi-circle in front of the capitol. Communist troops moved inside the building and arrested the Republic of South Vietnam officials whom they found there.   An announcement over radio Saigon proclaimed the triumph of the revolution. The bitter struggle for control of South Vietnam's political destiny that had consumed the energies of a generation had ended at last.

As memories of the Vietnam War recede, the time has come to seek answers to many questions: Who were the Vietnamese people, those inhabitants of a small, poor, seemingly unimportant country located on the other side of the world? How and why did the United States become involved for so long in their affairs? Why did the United States expend so much of its blood and treasure in Vietnam?

Why did so many Americans come to oppose that war? Why did America ultimately lose the Vietnam war? What was the experience of fighting the Vietnam war like for the men who fought? How have these men fared since their return to civilian life?

What effects did the long involvement have on the American political process? on the American economy? on American culture? What are the larger meanings of the Vietnam war experience for the conduct of U.S. foreign policy, for the use of U.S. military force, and for Americans' conceptions of themselves and the world?

A PLACE AND A PEOPLE

1

We must weaken [the enemy] by drawing him into protracted campaigns....When the enemy is away from home for a long time and produces no victories and families learn of their dead, then the enemy population at home becomes dissatisfied and considers it a Mandate from Heaven that their armies be recalled. Time is always in our favor. Our climate, mountains and jungles discourage the enemy; but for us they offer sanctuary and a place from which to attack.

Tran Hung Dao, a Vietnamese general
who defeated the Mongols in 1284

THE LAND

The Vietnamese say that their country resembles two baskets borne on the ends of a peasant's bamboo carrying pole. The baskets constitute two of the world's most densely populated rice-growing regions: to the north, the Red River delta, and to the south, the Mekong River delta. The pole represents the narrow and curving central part of the country composed of jungle-covered mountains and a fertile coastal strip. Vietnam's geographic area of 127,000 square miles makes it about the size of the state of New Mexico. When separated from northern Vietnam from 1954 to 1975, South Vietnam formed an elongated and sinuous country with a coastline about as long as California's.

Most of Vietnam's 63,000,000 (1988 est.) people cluster in the two alluvial deltas formed by the Red and Mekong rivers and in small coastal enclaves lying between them. The people inhabiting these regions comprise the 85 percent of the country's inhabitants who are ethnically Vietnamese. The sparsely populated mountainous regions north and west of the Red River delta and those of central Vietnam are home for a melange of ethnic minorities representing about 15 percent of the country's people. They are the people whom the French called "Montagnards," mountain people, inhabiting the mountainous terrain that constitutes three-quarters of the country's land mass. In addition to the Montagnards, about 800,000 Cambodians reside in the Ca Mau peninsula region and over 1 million ethnic Chinese live in Vietnam. In southern Vietnam about 80 percent of the people live on one-fourth of the land. Over 40 percent of the terrain is uninhabited. These unpopulated regions of South Vietnam, covered with jungle, elephant grass, and swamps, provided sanctuaries for the Vietcong guerrillas and avenues for invading North Vietnamese forces.

Vietnam lies entirely within the tropical zone. Its northernmost point is the same latitude as Key West, Florida; its southernmost extremity is the same latitude as the Panama Canal. Its climate is determined by monsoon cycles. From November to April, the winter monsoon, coming off the cold, dry steppes of Central Asia, dominates. During these months it does not rain much in Vietnam, and the climate is moderate throughout the northern half of the country. Between May and October, the summer monsoon blows in from the southwest, coming off the Indian Ocean, bringing with it high winds, heavy rains, and stifling heat and humidity. Vietnam's average annual rainfall is about six feet. The effects of the monsoons vary with the terrain. The Red River delta enjoys a mild winter; summertime temperatures rarely exceed 100 degrees. In the Mekong delta it is hot year-round. During the winter monsoon, it never rains in the south, then the summer monsoon brings torrential downpours. During some years it rains much more than the normal six feet, causing floods. During other years, far less than normal rainfall occurs, bringing droughts. Cycles of flooding, drought, and famine have afflicted the Vietnamese people throughout their long history.

French troops, and later Americans fighting in Vietnam, encountered serious obstacles posed by the summer monsoon. The heat, humidity, rain, and mud exhausted and discouraged young soldiers carrying 60-pound packs, struggling through elephant grass, jungle vines, and up mountainous terrain. The French and the Americans also discovered that they could not operate some of their sophisticated military equipment during the summer monsoon season. Highly mobile guerrilla forces often took advantage of the weather conditions to out-maneuver their Western enemies. Summer monsoons also meant special hazards for aviators. Pounding rains, dense ground fog, and treacherous winds caused many fatal aircraft accidents. Weather also determined the cycle of fighting for both French and American forces.

The heaviest fighting in southern Vietnam occurred during the dry season, from February through June, with combat intensity falling off from October through January.

THE FORGE OF HISTORY

The origins of the Vietnamese people are shrouded in the misty realms of prehistory. Thousands of years ago, people from China to the north, Thailand to the west, and Indonesia to the south settled in the Red River Valley. Over the centuries they intermingled. From their ethnological and biological fusion emerged an ethnically and racially distinct population, the Viets. A Viet culture based on rice cultivation and feudal principles of social organization was well-established by the second century B.C., when the Viets came into contact with their powerful neighbors to the north, the Chinese. The Chinese were destined to play a crucial role in shaping the evolving national culture and identity of the Vietnamese people over the ensuing centuries.[1]

Vietnamese history began in 208 B.C. On that date, recorded in Chinese annals, a Chinese war lord, Trieu Da, declared himself ruler of a large area encompassing southern China and Vietnam as far south as present-day Danang. He called these southernmost lands of his realm, "Nam Viet," meaning the land of the southern Viets. Trieu Da ruled his Vietnamese domains indirectly, content to leave Viet feudal lords in charge of affairs. A hundred years later, the great Han emperor, Wu-ti, conquered Nam Viet. It became a province within the Chinese empire; Chinese officials took over its governance. Wu-ti's conquest began an era of Chinese colonial domination of Vietnam that would last a millennium.[2]

For the next thousand years, the northern half of present-day Vietnam was controlled by the Chinese. During this long period of colonial rule, the Vietnamese adopted many features of Chinese culture. The elite Vietnamese classes embraced Confucian social and political values. They adopted the Chinese mandarinate, a hierarchical administrative system based on mastery of Chinese literary and philosophic works. To become a Mandarin, candidates had to devote years of study to the Chinese classics, then pass a series of rigorous examinations. Most mandarins came from elite backgrounds because only the wealthy could afford to allow their sons the years of study and training required to pass the demanding tests.

Although the Vietnamese admired many features of Chinese culture, and they doubtless benefited in many ways from their long, close association with the magnificent Chinese civilization, they fiercely resented Chinese political domination and economic exploitation. They also resented Chinese efforts to Sinicize them. In fact, Chinese efforts at forced Sinicization of the Vietnamese provoked the first of their many rebellions against Chinese rule. There occurred in A.D. 39 a rising, long-celebrated in Vietnamese history, led by two noblewomen, Trung Trac and her sister, Trung Nhi. The Trung sisters led an army that overwhelmed the Chinese garrisons stationed on Vietnamese soil and promptly proclaimed themselves queens of an independent Viet kingdom. Their rule was short-lived, however, for the emperor sent a strong army that restored Chinese rule in A.D. 42.[3]

Over the subsequent centuries of Chinese overlordship, the Vietnamese upper classes embraced much of the Chinese culture based on Confucian principles. But the vast majority of Vietnamese, the 90 percent of the population comprising the peasantry, remained relatively unaffected by this process of sinicization. They retained many of their traditional customs, a testament to the strength of their indigenous culture nurtured during their long pre-Chinese ethnic past as inhabitants of the Red River valley, the cradle of Vietnamese civilization.

There was one important Chinese cultural import enthusiastically embraced by the Vietnamese peasantry, the Buddhist religion. Originally founded by an Indian prince in the sixth century B.C., Buddhism reached the Vietnamese during the second century A.D. when Chinese Buddhist monks sought political asylum in the land of the Viets. Within a few centuries, Buddhism, particularly its Mahayana sect, had become a pervasive influence in the religious and political life of the Vietnamese peasants. Buddhist monks, living among the villagers, played prominent roles in community life.

Even though the Vietnamese elite were thoroughly Sinicized, they retained a strong sense of their Vietnamese identity and remained restive under Chinese rule. Between the sixth and tenth centuries, these Sino-Vietnamese notables led numerous rebellions against their Chinese masters. The Chinese suppressed them all. During most of this era of Chinese dominance, the empire was ruled by a mighty dynasty, the T'angs. Try as they might, Vietnamese nationalists could not rid themselves of Chinese control.

After the T'ang dynasty fell in 907, a series of uprisings in Vietnam eventually ended Chinese dominion. The crucial battle occurred in 939. In that year, a Vietnamese army, led by Ngo Quyen, confronted a far larger Chinese invasion force, led by the heir to the Chinese throne, along a stretch of the Bach Dang river, a tidal waterway in the vicinity of present-day Haiphong. Ngo, knowing that his troops were overmatched, resorted to a clever stratagem to defeat the more powerful Chinese. He had his troops drive pilings into the river bed so that at high tide the stakes would lie just below the water's surface, hidden from sight. Ngo then engaged the Chinese in battle and ordered his boats to feign retreat. The Chinese, sensing victory, pressed after Ngo's retreating ships, passing over the undetected pilings. He waited until the tide began to ebb. Timing the maneuver perfectly, Ngo ordered his ships to wheel about, and they drove the Chinese boats against the now-exposed pilings. With their ships impaled, the immobilized Chinese

Trung Hung Dao, a great Vietnamese military hero. Dao defeated an invading Mongol Army in 1284 to preserve Vietnamese national independence. Dao's guerilla warfare strategies were used by Vo Nguyen Giap, a history professor turned military commander, to defeat both the French and American invaders.
Source: Maurice Durand Collection, L'Ecole Française d'Extrême-Orient.

troops were slaughtered by Ngo's warriors. The imperial heir was taken prisoner and was later beheaded.[4] The Battle of Bach Dang, which destroyed Chinese colonialism in Vietnam, is commemorated by all Vietnamese as the beginning of Vietnamese national independence.

The Vietnamese maintained their independence for over 900 years. They successfully fought off Chinese invaders in the thirteenth century and thereafter stayed free of foreign rule except for a brief period during the fifteenth century when the Chinese, taking advantage of Vietnamese disunity, re-established a colonial regime of brief duration. For centuries it remained a constant of Vietnamese statecraft to be aware of the colossus to the north, to guard against Chinese intrusions upon their sovereign independence.[5] In modern times, this theme of Vietnamese independence from foreign conquerors has reasserted itself following the defeat of the French in 1954 and again following the withdrawal of the Americans in 1973. In Hanoi's Historical Museum today, a large room is devoted to celebrating the struggles of the Vietnamese people against Chinese invaders.[6]

Until the fifteenth century, Vietnamese expansion south of the Sixteenth Parallel was blocked by the kingdom of the Chams, a people of Indonesian origin. The Vietnamese eventually destroyed the Champa kingdom and pushed southward. Advancing colonies of Vietnamese peasant–warriors reached the Mekong delta region in the early seventeenth century, about the same time British colonists were settling the Atlantic seaboard of what would become the United States. Vietnam had attained its current geographic size by 1757. Political disunity hampered Vietnamese expansionism during the seventeenth and eighteenth centuries. During these centuries, Vietnam was ruled by separate, hostile governments, one located in the traditional capital of Hanoi, the other in a new city lying 400 miles to its south, Hue. Their armies clashed repeatedly, but neither was able to prevail over the other. With much of its energy absorbed in fighting the Hanoi regime, the Hue government was still developing the relatively underpopulated southern frontier region of the Mekong delta as the eighteenth century ended.

Vietnam was reunified early in the nineteenth century following decades of rebellions against both ruling houses. Eventually, Nguyen Anh, a nephew of the deposed ruler of the Hue kingdom, after a long series of military campaigns, defeated all foes, and emerged as the ruler of all Vietnamese in 1802. He proclaimed himself emperor, made Hue his imperial capital, and called his nation Vietnam.[7] He took the name Gia Long, founding the last Vietnamese imperial dynasty. Nguyen emperors were reduced to ruling in name only after 1883 because of the French conquest of Vietnam. Vietnam's last dynasty came to its end in 1955 when Bao Dai was defeated in a rigged election by Ngo Dinh Diem for the presidency of South Vietnam.

The reign of Gia Long lasted until 1820. During his years of power he re-established a traditionalist Vietnamese state administered by the Confucian mandarinate that had prevailed for centuries. According to Confucian theory and practice, Gia Long was an absolute monarch whose powers derived from a mandate of heaven. He was supreme lawmaker, the head of all civil and military institutions, and chief justice. The mandarins derived their authority solely from him. The despotism of the regime was modified in two ways. The emperor respected the authority of the head of a family, the most important Vietnamese social institution. Traditionally, submission to the head of one's family was the most important moral obligation facing every Vietnamese. Second, Gia Long partially observed the ancient Vietnamese proverb, "The law of the emperor ends at the village gate." He and his mandarins permitted a certain amount of village self-government. Local officials enforced village laws and customs, dealt with local problems, and collected taxes. Loyalty to one's village was a deeply rooted sentiment and profound civic obligation for all Vietnamese.[8]

The Vietnamese economy under Gia Long and his successors remained what it had been for ages, a static agrarian system based on the cultivation of rice. The great mass of the Vietnamese people remained peasants, tending their own fields or working as tenants and residing in villages and hamlets concentrated in the great rice-growing regions of the Red River and Mekong deltas. True to their Confucian principles, Gia Long and his mandarins discouraged all new economic developments, all modernizing trends. There was little industry, little commerce, and almost no foreign trade. No middle class of manufacturers and tradesmen emerged in nineteenth century Vietnam. Modern science and technology were forbidden. Few Vietnamese ever traveled beyond the confines of their native land or studied abroad.

Gia Long was succeeded in 1820 by his son, Minh Mang, who embraced a total Confucian orthodoxy in all matters of governance. He believed that Vietnam's national interest was best served by maintaining traditional institutions and ways of life based on the ancient Confucian way. He tried to isolate his country from all Western influences. He resisted all European efforts to open trade; he tried to suppress the activities of French Catholic missionaries who had been active in Vietnam since the seventeenth century. Because he and his mandarin advisers rejected all Western contacts, all efforts at modernization, Vietnamese officials found themselves virtually powerless by the mid-nineteenth century to defend themselves against aggressive European imperialists. When the French came to conquer them in the 1860s, about all the Nguyens could muster to resist them was a deep reservoir of nationalist feeling that had been nurtured on 2,000 years of Vietnamese struggles to retain their independence from foreign conquerors. But fierce patriotism and national pride proved to be no match against French military technology.

THE FRENCH COLONIAL ERA

The period of Vietnamese political unity achieved under the Nguyens ended with the French conquest of the 1860s. Fearing the political meddling of French missionaries working in his country, Minh Mang and his successors, Thieu Tri and Tu Duc, took strong measures to suppress them. These actions gave French officials a pretext to intervene in Vietnam. French officials, in the service of Emperor Napoleon III, had additional motives for intervention in Southeast Asia. Napoleon, activated by expansive dreams of imperial glory, wanted to acquire a colony in the region the French called "Indochina," to obtain markets for French manufactures, to provide raw materials for their factories, to expand their trade with China, and to gain a foothold in Southeast Asia to compete with the British who had conquered a vast colonial empire in the region stretching from India to the eastern half of New Guinea.[9]

Napoleon III sent a French naval expedition under Admiral Rigault de Genouilly to establish a French military base at Tourane (Danang) in 1858. Genouilly's forces occupied the port city, but could not reach the Vietnamese leaders residing in the imperial capitol at Hue, seventy-five miles to the north. Stalled at Tourane, the French were deluged by monsoon rains and stricken by disease. Realizing that his efforts to establish a French base at Tourane were failing, Genouilly sailed south. His troops occupied Saigon in early 1859. Another expedition arrived in 1861, enabling the French to add three provinces in southern Vietnam.

Vietnamese officials tried to drive them out of their country. But obsolete military technologies fatally handicapped Vietnamese efforts to resist French imperialism. Military deficiencies, not a lack of fighting spirit, forced the court at Hue to sign a treaty giving Saigon and the three southern provinces to the French in 1862. Even as they lost their lands, the proud Vietnamese told the French that while "disorder will be long…our cause will triumph in the end."[10] By 1867, growing military strength enabled France to conquer all of southern Vietnam, which they organized as a colony they called Cochin China.[11] The French required another sixteen years of political maneuvering and military action to complete their conquest of all of Vietnam. The imperial court at Hue was forced to sign a treaty with their conquerors in 1883 extending French authority over the whole country. Twenty-five years after sending a naval expedition to Tourane, the French had acquired control of all Vietnam. But the Vietnamese did not submit to French imperialism easily. It was not until the end of the nineteenth century that the French crushed all opposition and secured their hold on Vietnam.[12]

The French, during the years that they were conquering Vietnam, also imposed protectorates over neighboring Cambodia (1863) and Laos (1893). All these acquisitions were formally organized into the French Indochinese Union. After 1893, French Indochina constituted five administrative departments: a colony in southern Vietnam, Cochin China, and four protectorates, Cambodia, Laos, Annam (central Vietnam), and Tonkin (northern Vietnam). The French ruled their colony directly, initially using military personnel as administrators. In Annam and Tonkin, the French initially ruled through the Nguyen administrative apparatus, which they controlled. But as the years went by, French control over all its Vietnamese departments became more centralized and more pervasive. The imperial court at Hue and its mandarins were reduced in time to largely ceremonial functions. Hanoi served as the

capital of the entire Union, the French governor-general residing in that city. He was directly responsible to the Ministry of Colonies in Paris. Residents-Superiors governed each of the five departments. Most French nationals who emigrated to Vietnam settled in Cochin China. Saigon, its capital and commercial center, became known as the "Paris of the Orient." French economic and financial interests were concentrated in southern Vietnam. There they invested most of their capital and their administrative apparatus penetrated most deeply, down to the district and even village levels. Cochin China was the most profitable and therefore the most important department of the French Southeast Asian empire.

The French ruled solely by force, or the imminent threat of force, in Indochina. The Vietnamese never accepted French control as legitimate nor ceased resisting it whenever they could. Although French officials paid lip service to the goals of modernizing and "civilizing" the Vietnamese (what they called their *mission civilisatrice*), in practice French colonialism remained brutally exploitative. The French viewed Vietnam, its land, its natural resources, and its people as existing for the benefit of France, specifically for the enrichment of French economic interests with investments in that country. They expected Vietnam to generate valuable raw materials to feed into the French economy and to furnish a tariff-protected market for French manufactures. Many of the French regarded the Vietnamese as an inferior, child-like race, ideally suited for a life of hard work at low wages.

The French invested mainly in Vietnamese rice, rubber, and coal, which became the three leading Indochinese export commodities. The rich Mekong Delta become one of the world's leading rice-exporting regions. Rice growing in this region was dominated by a class of large landowners, many of them French, joined by a small class of Vietnamese landlords who cooperated with their colonial masters and enriched themselves in the process. During the 1920s and 1930s, rubber became the second most important Vietnamese export. Hundreds of rubber plantations, concentrated in southern Vietnam, all of them owned by the French, made Vietnam one of the world's leading sources of raw rubber. Vietnamese coal production was centered in Tonkin where two large French-owned mining companies accounted for more than 92 percent of the country's total coal output.[13]

Under French colonialism, the Vietnamese economy remained what it had always been, predominantly agricultural. The peasantry comprised about 90 percent of the national population, a vast labor force that paid taxes and bought cheap French imports if they could afford them. Industrial development of Vietnam was discouraged, being contrary to French neo-mercantilist policies. Some internal improvements were constructed during the first three decades of the twentieth century—railroads, highways, bridges, and harbors—and some local light industries evolved. But the French wanted short-run profits, having no interest in the long-run development of the Vietnamese economy.[14]

As a result of French colonial rule, aggravated by the world-wide depression of the 1930s, living standards for most of the Vietnamese people were lower on the eve of World War II than they had been a century earlier under the Nguyens. The concentration of land owning under the French brought the pauperization of millions of Vietnamese peasantry who lost ancestral lands formerly in their possession.[15] These landless families dropped into the ranks of tenants and day laborers entrapped in a vicious round of hard labor, low income, debt, usurious interest rates, and high taxes.

Before the French came, the Vietnamese prized a highly developed educational system. Literacy was widespread, and learning, according to the Confucian way, was revered. The French closed the Vietnamese schools, replacing them with schools modeled on the French system of education. The Chinese classics were abolished. The Chinese ideographic language was replaced with the Romanized "quoc ngu."[16] After 1878, the French declared that only "quoc ngu" and French could serve as official languages. But most Vietnamese children were excluded from the new French-style schools. On the eve of World War II, only about 15 percent of Vietnamese school-age children were attending schools of any kind.

In 1939, Vietnam had only fourteen secondary schools and one university serving a population of 20 million people. "About 80 percent of the population was illiterate after 60 years of French rule, in contrast to precolonial Vietnam where 80 percent of the people possessed some degree of literacy."[17]

In addition to creating a society made up mainly of landless, illiterate peasants ruled by a colonial bureaucracy and a small class of privileged Vietnamese who joined in the exploitation of their country, French colonialism also disrupted the traditional Vietnamese way of life based on the extended family and the village. French and Vietnamese bureaucrats violated the traditions of village autonomy. Traditional leaders, who neither understood the legal and political systems imposed by the French nor collected enough taxes, were replaced by Vietnamese middlemen. These brokers, chosen by French officials, often without roots or kin in the villages under their control, were an alien force against which there was no recourse nor appeal.

For the majority of Vietnamese families forced to endure three generations of French colonial rule, life became a daily struggle to maintain a miserable existence. The people were trapped within a socioeconomic system controlled by French officials and an elite class of Gallicized Vietnamese that allowed almost no opportunity for improvement or escape. The Vietnamese peasantry gradually realized that French colonialism was responsible for their oppression, but they also understood that they had two enemies: the French who ruled them and the privileged Vietnamese elite who exploited them. In time the struggle to achieve independence after World War II, common throughout Asia and Africa, throughout what would become known during the 1950s as the Third World, became for the Vietnamese a social revolution as well. This intertwining of nationalistic and revolutionary goals made the postwar history of Vietnam unique to Southeast Asia. Only in Vietnam did the struggle for home rule also become a struggle for who should rule at home.

THE RISE OF VIETNAMESE NATIONALISM

Vietnamese resistance to French rule began as the French were establishing their colony of Cochin China in the 1860s. Led by local mandarins, scholars, and officials from the emperor's court at Hue who detested the European intruders and whose own powers were threatened by the advent of the French, resistance took the forms of refusals to work, sabotage, and, most commonly, guerrilla warfare. Rebel mandarins appealed to the peasantry, in the name of the emperor and Confucian ideals drawn from Vietnam's precolonial heritage, to join them in efforts to regain their country's independence. A teenage emperor himself, Ham Nghi, joined one of these rebellions in Annam in 1885. He was later captured by the French, and was exiled to Algeria.

For decades, periodic revolts challenged the growing French colonial power. They all failed because of French military superiority and because the mandarin–rebels could offer the people only a return to the imperial past in place of French rule. But for many Vietnamese, the Nguyen dynasty had been discredited. The Court's short-sighted efforts to forestall all progress and to isolate Vietnam from Western forces in the first half of the nineteenth century had been responsible for the inability of the Vietnamese to keep the French out. Further, the catastrophe of the loss of political independence was proof to many patriots that the Nguyens had lost the mandate of heaven, the right to rule. In the eyes of many Vietnamese, the mandarin-led revolts were on behalf of discredited rulers and ideals. Other factors contributed to the defeat of the rebellions. No efforts were made to coordinate or unify the various risings. They were local, isolated insurrections, district uprisings, with no chance to inflict permanent defeat on the French or to drive them out of Vietnam. The French were also able to call on some segments of the Vietnamese populations for assistance in suppressing the rebellions. Catholic Vietnamese often sided with the French, remembering their persecution under the Nguyens. Various Montagnard tribes, for centuries neglected and despised by the lowland Vietnamese who regarded them as uncivilized, often joined French expeditions against the rebels.[18] The Vietnamese people paid a severe price for these risings; local economies were disrupted, taxes were increased to pay for the police forces required to suppress the insurrections, and thousands of Vietnamese were killed by the French. As the nineteenth century ended, the rebels were all dead, imprisoned, or exhausted. For a time, social peace settled on the land.

A new generation of Vietnamese nationalists came of age during the first decade of the twentieth century. Their leader was a scholar, Phan Boi Chau, recipient of a modern education. Although faithful to the idea of monarchy, Chau embraced Western philosophical rationalism, science, and constitutionalism. Detesting French suzerainty over his countrymen, he called for independence from France and for Vietnam to develop a constitutional monarchy. He hoped to place Prince Coung De, a descendant of Gia Long, on a restored, modernized throne.

An effective propagandist and organizer, Chau, working with the prince, formed the Association for the Modernization of Vietnam while both were living in Japan. For a time, Chau and the Prince hoped that Japanese liberals would support and finance their cause. In 1908, nationalistic followers of Chau staged mass demonstrations in cities throughout Vietnam protesting high taxes. The French responded by jailing thousands of demonstrators.[19] In the aftermath of the failure of the protests and disillusioned by lukewarm Japanese support, Chau moved to China where he became an enthusiastic follower of the Chinese revolutionary leader, Dr. Sun Yat-sen, founder of the Chinese Republic in 1911.

After World War I, Chau's movement declined. He was kidnapped by French agents, returned to Vietnam, and condemned to death. But the governor-general commuted his sentence to confinement for life at his home in Hue. Phan Boi Chau died in 1940, an obscure figure from Vietnam's turbulent political past. But Chau had been the first Vietnamese national leader to espouse modern political ideas and to call for the use of more sophisticated resistance tactics against French colonialism than the hopeless rebellions led by mandarin reactionaries.

French repression hindered the political activities of Vietnamese nationalists. Even moderates who tried to work for independence through legal political activity often found themselves in jail, under house arrest, or forced into exile to China or Japan. Nationalist organizations were forced to go underground to have any chance of political effectiveness. During the 1920s, the major underground organization was the Vietnam Quoc Dan Dang (VNQDD), the Vietnamese Nationalist Party. The VNQDD's goals were political independence and the creation of a Vietnamese republic. In early 1930, a garrison of Vietnamese soldiers stationed in northern Tonkin, influenced by VNQDD ideas, rebelled against French rule. They hoped that their revolt would start similar uprisings everywhere in Vietnam, creating a revolution. They were disappointed when French forces, moving quickly, suppressed their rebellion before it could generate any momentum. Afterward, French authorities destroyed the VNQDD organization; some of its leaders were able to escape to exile in China.

Following the destruction of the VNQDD, Marxist organizations took over the nationalist cause in Vietnam. In 1930, the Indochinese Communist Party was organized by a professional revolutionary and Vietnamese patriot calling himself Nguyen Ai Quoc (Nguyen the Patriot). The world would later know him as Ho Chi Minh.[20] He was born Nguyen Tat Thanh May 19, 1890, in Kim Lien, a small village in Nghe An province in central Vietnam, site of many rebellions against French colonial rule over the years. He was the son of a minor mandarin who had been dismissed from government service because of his nationalistic activities. As a youth, Ho attended Quoc Hoc lycee in Hue in order to prepare for a career in government service, but he left the school in 1911 without graduating. He shipped out on a French steamer determined to see the world. Ho Chi Minh would not set foot on Vietnamese soil again for almost 30 years. For the next several years he traveled widely and worked at a variety of jobs. He made a voyage to the United States, visiting Boston and New York. He later wrote about the abusive, brutal, and often lethal treatment of blacks by white Americans in the American South during the early twentieth century.[21]

Ending up in France during World War I, Ho became involved in the political activities of Vietnamese nationalists living in Paris. In 1919, while the victorious Allies were meeting at the Versailles Conference, Ho presented a petition to the Big Four demanding that the principle of self-determination embodied in Woodrow Wilson's Fourteen Points be applied to French Indo-china.[22] The leaders of the victorious great powers ignored the demands of this bold but obscure Vietnamese patriot. About the same time, Ho also joined the French Socialist Party and was a member of the faction that broke off to form the French Communist Party in 1920. He was to remain a committed Communist for the rest of his life.

Ho journeyed to Russia in 1923. He lived and studied in Moscow, becoming a specialist on colonial questions and a professional organizer. He went to China in 1925 as an assistant to the Comintern's adviser to the Koumintang during the years of cooperation between Moscow and the Chinese Nationalists. In Canton, Ho organized Vietnamese political exiles into the Vietnamese Revolutionary Youth Movement, a precursor of the Indochinese Communist Party. Here he met a brilliant Vietnamese nation-alist, Pham Van Dong, whose father had been a high-ranking mandarin involved in anti-French resistance activities. Dong would become prime minister of the People's Republic of Vietnam 30 years later.[23] After the Sino-Soviet split of 1927, Ho returned to Moscow for a time. He traveled to Hong Kong in 1930 where he organized the Indochinese Communist Party. Underground cells were established in Vietnam, and Haiphong became the center for Communist activities in the country.[24]

During 1930 and 1931, peasant rebellions erupted in several districts of central Vietnam, provoked by hard times and high taxes. The newly formed Indochinese Communist Party moved in to furnish leadership for the peas-ants in those regions. Communist leaders included Pham Van Dong and a brilliant young high school history teacher, Vo Nguyen Giap. Giap was destined to become a resourceful general who planned the campaigns that would bring the Vietnamese military victories over the French, the Ameri-cans, and the South Vietnamese forces. The Communists managed to set up people's "soviets" in two provinces of central Vietnam, Ha Tinh and Nghe An. They moved against large landlords and redistributed land to hard-pressed peasant farmers.[25]

But French forces moved into these regions quickly. Police and legion-naires instituted a reign of terror and crushed the peasant insurrections. Suspected agitators were given summary trials en masse and condemned. Thousands of Vietnamese—peasants, patriots, nationalists, liberals, and Communists—were destroyed.[26] Giap's wife and sister-in-law were exe-cuted by the French. The fledgling Indochinese Communist Party was badly damaged. A rumor spread that Ho himself had been killed by the secret police. During the 1930s, French prisons and penal colonies in Indochina bulged with thousands of political prisoners.

Despite these reversals, as World War II approached, the Indochinese Communist Party remained the best-organized, strongest, and most popular of the underground nationalist groups in Vietnam.[27] From 1936 to 1939, pressure on the Communists in Vietnam eased as a Popular Front government in France allowed the parties both in France and Indochina increased freedom for peaceful political activity. Both the French and Vietnamese Communists, following orders from Moscow, moderated their revolutionary programs and sought alliances with liberals and socialists. Many non-Communist nationalists were attracted to the Communist program, which emphasized democratic reform rather than revolution during the Popular Front years. The Indochinese Communist Party assumed unrivaled leadership of the Vietnamese drive for independence.[28] But the fall of the Popular Front government, followed by the signing of the Nazi-Soviet Pact in August 1939, brought renewed French attacks on the Vietnamese Communists. When World War II began with the German invasion of Poland on September 1, 1939, the Vietnamese Communists opposed the French war effort and resumed their revolutionary activity.

When World War II began in the fall of 1939, the French were firmly in control of Indochina. The French secret police suppressed the Communists and other radicals. But the events of war would break France's hold on its Southeast Asian empire and bring the liberation of the Vietnamese people from colonialism. The unique fusion of nationalism and Communism in Vietnam also imparted a social revolutionary thrust to the Vietnamese drive for self-determination. The war would also propel the United States into Southeast Asian affairs, inaugurating an entanglement in that region that would persist for thirty years.

WAR COMES TO INDOCHINA

In the late spring of 1940, Nazi armor rolled to an easy victory over French armies in a stunningly successful campaign, forcing France's surrender after only six weeks of fighting. Their German conquerors chose to occupy only northern France and turned over the government of the rest of the country to a collaborationist regime situated at Vichy. The Vichy government retained nominal control of French overseas territories, including Indochina. German victories over France and other European powers, British preoccupation with European threats to its interests, and the fact that the United States had declared its neutrality at the outset of war all created opportunities for Japanese expansionists to take over weakly defended European colonial possessions in Southeast Asia.

The Japanese, who had been waging war against China since 1937, quickly moved into Indochina after Germany had defeated France. Indochina was an important component of the expanding Japanese East Asian empire for several reasons. The Japanese wanted to stop the French from sending supplies to the Chinese via a route that wound through the mountains separating southern China from Tonkin. They also wanted to acquire airfields located in Vietnam that they could use to launch attacks against

Chinese targets. Further, Vietnam would serve Japan well as a rich source of raw materials such as rice and rubber. Vietnam's strategic location would also offer the Japanese a staging area for their expansion into Southeast Asian territories, principally the Dutch East Indies and British Malaya. Finally, Vietnam would be a basing area for Japanese troops and its harbors would serve as trans-shipment points for the resources the Japanese would be extracting from the southeastern territories whose conquests they were planning.

In August 1940, Japanese troops poured out of China into northern Vietnam. The Governor-General of Indochina, Admiral Jean Decoux, offered little resistance to the Japanese presence. By the end of 1941, the Japanese had acquired a free hand in Vietnam. Admiral Decoux granted them permission to station troops anywhere in the country and to use all the French naval and air bases. He also signed agreements guaranteeing that Japan would receive all Vietnam's exports. In return, the Japanese acknowledged French sovereignty over Indochina and permitted the French to maintain their administrative apparatus. Technically, the Japanese did not occupy Vietnam; the two countries agreed to joint control, a de facto dual sovereignty. Militarily and economically, the arrangement favored the Japanese. The French were saddled with the costs of administering territories whose riches were now going to Japan.[29]

The coming of the Japanese gave some Vietnamese nationalist groups unprecedented opportunities to achieve a greater role in political affairs because now both the French and the Japanese had to compete for the allegiance of the people. French administrators granted the Vietnamese additional political freedoms, upgraded the status of Vietnamese officials, and sought to organize young people into various groupings.[30] Some Vietnamese nationalists sought to work with the Japanese in the hopes of achieving independence from the French. These included adherents of two religious sects whose members mostly resided in southern Vietnam, the Cao Dai and the Hoa Hao. The Japanese encouraged these religious groups, playing on their Pan-Asian nationalistic and anti-French sentiments, but had no intention of granting the Vietnamese their independence.[31] In time Vietnamese enthusiasm for Japanese assistance in seeking liberation from the Vichy French cooled.

The new French-Japanese arrangement in Vietnam did not favor the Vietnamese Communists or other radical nationalistic groups. They suffered severe repression and were forced to seek sanctuary in southern China in order to survive. Here they benefited from the truce in China arranged between the Nationalists and the Maoists, who agreed to curtail their civil war in order to fight the Japanese invaders of their vast homeland. The Vietnamese Communists operated freely in southern China during the war. The Chinese government also worked with Vietnamese nationalists, both Communist and non-Communist, to hinder the Japanese war effort being mounted against China from Vietnam. The Chinese tried to unite all Vietnamese nationalists living in China within a front organization dedicated to carrying on sabotage and espionage activities against the Japanese in Vietnam.[32] But only the Vietnamese Communists proved capable of carrying out these dangerous tasks and the Chinese turned to them.

Ho Chi Minh, still known as Nguyen Ai Quoc to his followers, the leader of the Communist remnants, was residing in southern China in 1941. He understood that the French defeat in the European war and its forced acceptance of the Japanese presence in Vietnam offered his cause a great opportunity if he could exploit it. Ho knew that these revelations of French weakness had encouraged many Vietnamese, including businessmen, landowners, and urban workers, to join the peasants supporting independence. He also knew that these groups needed leadership; they had to be organized and given direction. Further, he knew that he had to establish a political base in Vietnam. Independence from both Japan and France could not be achieved by emigres living in China.

Ho set out to achieve both objectives. Vietnamese Communist leaders met May 10, 1941, on Vietnamese soil in the village of Pac Bo in Cao Bang province with Ho chairing the meeting. It was the first time in thirty years that he had set foot in his native land. The participants agreed that the party's main goal was to organize all Vietnamese—peasants, workers, middle class elements, and landlords—to achieve independence. The social revolution would have to wait. The Communist leaders played down their revolutionary goals of land redistribution and the nationalization of industries. To organize all these groups, a new organization was created: the Vietnam Doc Lap Dong Minh (Vietnamese League for Independence). The French and the Americans would come to know this group as the Vietminh. Under the Vietminh umbrella there gathered organizations of peasants, workers, students, intellectuals, women, and landlords. These associations were organized at the village level. There were also pyramids of associations that paralleled the political jurisdictions of the country, including district and provincial associations. At the top stood the Central Committee, controlled by Ho and his lieutenants, all of whom were Communists. All associations were also controlled by party members, but many non-Communist participants joined the associations because the Vietminh represented the largest and most effective anticolonial movement in Indochina. Ho and his associates had created the Vietminh as a national-front organization controlled by the Indochinese Communist Party to attract Vietnamese patriots of all political persuasions to a common cause, the struggle to rid their country of Japanese and French rule.[33]

In addition to forming the Vietminh front organizations, Ho and his associates began organizing guerrilla bases in Cao Bang. Following Maoist strategies, Ho's goal was to liberate this remote mountainous northern province and to replace the colonial administration with their own party apparatus.

Within six months they had succeeded. A training site for guerrillas established near Pac Bo was turning out battle-ready soldiers at the rate of 125 a month as the year ended.

When Chinese officials selected the Vietminh to take charge of anti-Japanese espionage and guerrilla campaigns in Vietnam, a Chinese general, Chang Fa-K'uei, upon learning of Nguyen Ai Quoc's Communist past, urged him to change his name lest the Nationalist leaders reject him. To oblige his Chinese sponsors, Nguyen selected the name Ho Chi Minh (he who enlightens) sometime in early 1943.[34] With Chinese sponsorship, the Vietminh automatically qualified for funding from the U.S. Mission in China that was bankrolling the entire Chinese war effort against the Japanese. Thus, American involvement in Vietnam reaches back to the days of World War II, when the American China mission found itself bankrolling Communist guerrillas engaged in resistance activities against the Japanese in Tonkin while American pilots bombed and strafed Japanese installations in various parts of the country. These wartime experiences provided U.S. officials with a sense of Vietnam's significance: as a source of foodstuffs and raw materials, and its strategic location astride major shipping lanes linking India, the islands of the southeast Pacific, China, and Japan.

THE ROOTS OF AMERICAN INVOLVEMENT

The fall of France in June 1940 created serious diplomatic problems for the United States. President Franklin Roosevelt despised and distrusted the collaborationist Vichyites, but granted them diplomatic recognition in order to forestall a German occupation of their colonies in North Africa and to try to prevent, unsuccessfully, Japanese occupation of Indochina. American officials were angered by French acquiescence in the Japanese penetration of Vietnam. They resented the fact that French officials made little effort to resist Japanese demands and appeared to settle comfortably into a joint occupation with them. American officials were also unhappy that possession of Indochina gave the Japanese strategic leverage in Southeast Asia and its continuing war with China. They later attributed many of the Japanese successes in conquering Southeast Asian territories, including the Philippines, in 1941–1942, to their ability to use Indochina as a base of operations.

It was the Japanese move into all of Indochina in the summer of 1941 that probably made war between the United States and Japan inevitable. Roosevelt viewed Japanese entry into that strategic region as a clear sign that the Japanese planned further imperialistic moves into the southeast Pacific region. The American response to Japan's takeover of all Indochina was to cut off Japan's supply of oil. The oil cutoff created a crisis for the Japanese leaders. With only six weeks of oil reserves on hand, the Japanese would have to get the oil embargo rescinded quickly or else find new sources of supply to prevent their war machine and industrial economy from grinding

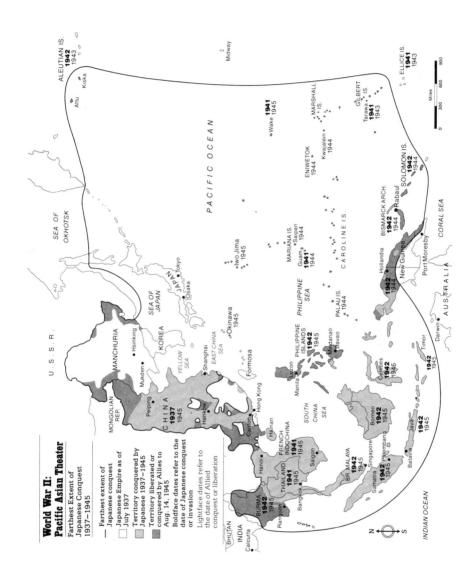

World War II: Pacific Asian Theater

Farthest Extent of Japanese Conquest 1937–1945

— Farthest extent of Japanese conquest

☐ Japanese Empire as of July 1937

▨ Territory conquered by Japanese 1937–1945

▧ Territory liberated or conquered by Allies to Aug. 14, 1945

Boldface dates refer to the date of Japanese conquest or invasion

Lightface dates refer to the date of Allied conquest or liberation

ALEUTIAN IS. **1942** 1943

Kiska

Attu

Midway

ELLICE IS. **1941** 1943

Wake **1941** 1945

MARSHALL IS.

GILBERT IS. **1941** 1943

Tarawa **1941** 1943

Kwajalein 1944

ENIWETOK 1944

SOLOMON IS. **1942** 1944

BISMARCK ARCH. **1942** 1944

Rabaul

MARIANA IS.

Guam **1941** 1944

Saipan 1944

CAROLINE IS.

PALAU IS. 1944

Hollandia

New Guinea **1942** 1944

Port Moresby

CORAL SEA

AUSTRALIA

Darwin

Timor **1942** 1945

PACIFIC OCEAN

SEA OF OKHOTSK

U.S.S.R.

MONGOLIAN REP.

MANCHURIA

Hsinking

Mukden

Peiping

CHINA **1937** 1945

Hankow

Shanghai

YELLOW SEA

EAST CHINA SEA

KOREA

SEA OF JAPAN

JAPAN

Tokyo

Osaka

Okinawa 1945

Formosa

Iwo Jima 1945

PHILIPPINE SEA

PHILIPPINE ISLANDS **1942** 1945

Luzon

Manila

Mindanao

Davao

Celebes **1942** 1945

SOUTH CHINA SEA

Hong Kong

Canton

Hainan

FRENCH INDOCHINA **1941** 1945

Hanoi

Saigon

Borneo **1942** 1945

BR. MALAYA **1942** 1945

Singapore

Sumatra

Palembang **1942** 1945

Java **1942** 1945

Batavia

THAILAND **1941** 1945

Bangkok

Rangoon

BURMA **1942** 1945

BHUTAN

INDIA

Calcutta

INDIAN OCEAN

N

S

0 300 600 900

Miles

to a halt. U.S. and Japanese negotiators met through the summer and fall of 1941 to try to resolve their conflicts. As a price for restoring Japan's oil supplies and other trade goods that had been embargoed, Washington demanded that the Japanese get out of China and Indochina. These terms proved unacceptable to Japan, who would not consider abandoning their expansionist ambitions. The Japanese response came December 7, 1941, at Pearl Harbor, which brought America into the Asian war. Soon afterward, the Japanese, using Vietnam as a staging area, occupied the East Indies and began extracting oil from this former Dutch colony. The Japanese also made use of Vietnamese ports as depots for the oil and other resources that they were getting from their newly conquered empire in the southeast.

The Japanese move into Indochina also brought the first U.S. military intervention into Vietnam in early 1942, about a month after America had entered the war. Cutting the Japanese lifeline from Southeast Asia and denying the Japanese use of air bases in Vietnam for continuing attacks on China became major tactical objectives of the American Volunteer Group, famed as the "Flying Tigers" under the command of General Claire L. Chennault. The Flying Tigers operated under the control of the Chinese Nationalist Army. Flying out of bases in southern China, the Flying Tigers, in early 1942, began attacking Japanese air fields in northern Vietnam. On May 12, 1942, John T. Donovan, a former Navy pilot, was shot down and killed by Japanese anti-aircraft fire while flying his P-40 on a strafing mission over Hanoi. Donovan was the first American to be killed on Vietnamese soil.[35]

As the war progressed, the future political status of Indochina became a diplomatic problem among the wartime Allies. It was tied to a larger issue, the postwar fate of the European Asian empires. On the one hand, U.S. officials, faithful to Atlantic Charter war aims, firmly opposed the restoration of colonial imperialism in Asia. Liberation from Japanese occupation was to be followed by independence. On the other hand, President Roosevelt had an understanding with the British prime minister, Winston Churchill, that the Atlantic Charter did not apply to British colonial possessions, particularly the vast Southeast Asian subcontinent, India. But Roosevelt made clear early in 1944 the kind of future he envisioned for Indochina:

> France has had the country for nearly one hundred years, and the people are worse off than they were at the beginning....France has milked it for one hundred years. The people of Indochina are entitled to something better than that.[36]

Charles De Gaulle, the leader of the Free French government-in-exile, whom Roosevelt disliked intensely, joined with Churchill in an effort to thwart FDR and forestall the loss of Indochina after the war. Churchill, linking De Gaulle's attempts to retain France's Asian colonies with his own efforts to cling to empire, supported De Gaulle. The colonial issue created fissures in the wartime alliance's conduct of the war in the Far East. The

British tried to claim wartime jurisdiction of Indochina, which the Americans had assigned to the China theater, in order to restore the colony to France at the conclusion of the war. Roosevelt, perceiving Churchill's strategy, circumvented British efforts by ordering that no U.S aid would go to French forces in Indochina and forbidding the British to conduct military operations in the region without clearance from the American China command.[37]

Pursuing efforts to prevent a return of French colonialism in Vietnam, Roosevelt asked Chiang Kai-shek, the Nationalist leader of China, if he wanted to govern Indochina. The answer he got was an emphatic no. Chiang, aware of Vietnam's long history of resistance to Chinese colonialism, told Roosevelt that the Vietnamese were "not Chinese. They would not assimilate into the Chinese people."[38] Following Chiang's rejection, Roosevelt proposed the idea of an international trusteeship for Indochina until the people were ready for independence. Churchill strongly opposed Roosevelt's proposal, which he saw as implicitly threatening to British imperial interests.[39]

THE AUGUST REVOLUTION

While international leaders were quarreling over the political future of Indochina, Vietminh guerrillas carried out espionage missions and guerrilla raids on Japanese forces occupying northern Vietnam. The Vietminh also used their wartime guerrilla activities and the prestige gained from their American connections to strengthen their leadership of the Vietnamese nationalist movement. In December 1944, in Cao Bang province, Ho ordered the creation of a military division of the Vietminh, the Vietnamese Liberation Army. During the winter of 1944–1945, under the leadership of Vo Nguyen Giap, Vietminh guerrillas gained control of three northern provinces and engaged Japanese forces in sporadic combat.[40] Starting in 1945, the Vietminh received support from an Office of Strategic Services (OSS) contingent operating out of the U.S. China Mission at Kunming. The Vietminh helped OSS commandos rescue downed U.S. pilots and provided them with information on Japanese troop movements in Vietnam. OSS officers came to know many of the Vietminh leaders, including Ho Chi Minh, and assisted them in their struggle for national independence

By 1945, U.S. and British forces had reclaimed many of Japan's wartime Southeast Asian conquests. They had liberated important territories including the Dutch East Indies, Malaya, and the Philippine archipelago. Confronted with their rapidly shrinking assets in Southeast Asia, Japan made a determined effort to hold their vital Indochina positions. American planes from carriers operating with the U.S. Third Fleet in the Tonkin Gulf began attacking Japanese shipping in Saigon harbor. Army Air Corps bombers from Clark Field in the Philippines carried out raids on Saigon and Danang, destroying Japanese warships and freighters. Within a few months, American planes had closed Japanese supply lines from Vietnam to China and their home islands. In May 1945, U.S. bombers from the Philippines knocked out all railway linkages between Vietnam and China. Indochina was cut off from the remaining Japanese theaters of war.[41]

U.S. air raids signalled that the end of the Japanese presence in Indochina was fast approaching. Many of the French in Vietnam, who had collaborated with the Axis for years, prepared to join the fight for Vietnam's liberation from Japan. Sensing the changed French attitudes, the Japanese moved to prevent French action against them in their hour of approaching defeat. On March 9, 1945, the Japanese brought the eighty-year-old French rule over the Indochinese people to an end. In a series of lightning raids that took the French by surprise, Admiral Decoux and many French officials were arrested, and most French soldiers were disarmed and interned. Thousands of French nationals were also interned. Only a few hundred managed to escape to the hills. Some joined the Vietminh guerrillas; others fled to China. Japanese officials took charge of running Indochina.[42]

In their efforts to retain control of Vietnam, the Japanese also installed a Vietnamese government headed by Emperor Bao Dai, who, prior to the war, had been the French-controlled ruler of Annam for ten years from his palace in Hue.[43] Japanese officials informed Bao Dai that he was the ruler of an "independent" nation that had been "liberated" from the French imperialists. In reality, the Japanese were going through a desperate charade. The new government had neither the resources nor the power to command. Japanese Army officers remained in control of Vietnamese affairs. Bao Dai also understood that Japan would soon be defeated and his shadow government would be discredited because of its association with the Japanese, who were no more loved by the Vietnamese people than the French.

With the French removed from power and the Japanese on the verge of defeat, the Vietminh moved quickly to position themselves to take control of their country. General Giap took command of the Vietnam Liberation Army. Vietminh forces now controlled much of Tonkin, and their influence was spreading rapidly over the country and reaching into the cities.[44] They were harnessing the vast energies of a people who were sensing that their moment of liberation from both Japanese and French dominion was fast approaching. Vietminh elements continued to work with OSS teams, gathering intelligence on Japanese troop movements, harassing Japanese outposts, and rescuing downed American flyers. Other U.S. groups, including military intelligence units, also worked with Vietminh guerrillas in various parts of Vietnam.

Japanese forces in Vietnam surrendered to Vietminh forces in mid-August, a few days after U.S. planes had dropped atomic bombs on the Japanese cities of Hiroshima and Nagasaki, abruptly ending World War II. Vietnam rapidly underwent a nationalist revolution that summer of 1945. Everywhere, Vietminh associations took control of local, district, and provincial governments.[45] A provisional council in Saigon comprising religious sectarians, various Communist splinter groups, and several non-Communist nationalist groups, declared their support for the Vietminh. Because they headed the only well-organized political and military movement in Vietnam, the Vietminh were able to supplant the deposed French and the beaten Japanese and take power without any significant opposition.[46] On August 29, The Vietminh formed a national government they called the Provisional Government of the Democratic Republic of Vietnam, with its capital in Hanoi. On September 2, 1945, Ho Chi Minh made a public declaration of Vietnamese independence before 500,000 people assembled in Hanoi's Ba Dinh Square.[47] Ho, who admired the United States because it had defeated the Japanese and because of its official commitment to self-determination for Asian peoples following the war, and who hoped for American support of Vietnamese independence, began his speech with words taken from the American declaration of 1776:

> We hold truths that all men are created equal, that they are endowed by their Creator with certain unalienable Rights, among these are Life, Liberty, and the pursuit of Happiness.[48]

Americans joined the festivities later in the day that celebrated Vietnam's independence. A flight of U.S. aircraft overflew the city. U.S. Army officers stood with Giap and other Vietminh leaders on the reviewing stand as Vietminh forces passed in review. A Vietnamese band played the "Star Spangled Banner."[49]

For the first time in eighty years, Vietnam was united and independent, under a government controlled by the Communist-led Vietminh. They had quickly taken control of the entire country. Their revolution represented a remarkable merging of a people and a movement that gave expression to the deep yearning of nearly all Vietnamese citizens to be rid of foreign control. In the rush to achieve national independence, factional conflicts and ideological differences among Vietnamese political parties, which were sharpest in southern cities, were temporarily submerged. Soon after Ho's declaration of independence, Emperor Bao Dai abdicated, promising to support the new provisional government, conferring legitimacy upon it, and linking it to Vietnamese political traditions. Most Vietnamese, Communist and non-Communist alike, accepted Ho Chi Minh as the leader of the revolution that had retrieved Vietnamese independence. The Communist revolutionary and devout Vietnamese patriot also symbolized Vietnam's revived nationhood.

But the peaceful Vietnamese national revolution was not destined to endure. As U.S. Army officers joined with Vietminh leaders in Hanoi to celebrate the rebirth of Vietnamese independence, American leaders in

Washington were clearing the way for the return of the French to Vietnam. Before he died, Roosevelt had retreated from his support of Vietnamese nationalism. Concerned to maintain good relations with important European allies at Yalta, Roosevelt did not actively oppose France's announced intention to return to Indochina.[50] Secretary of State Edward Stettinius told the French foreign minister that the United States had never questioned, "French sovereignty over Indochina."[51] Roosevelt's successor, Harry S Truman, a more parochial nationalist than the cosmopolitan statesman he replaced, having no interest in Asian self-determination, supported the French goal of reimposing colonialism on the Vietnamese people.[52] Truman and other Allied leaders, meeting at Potsdam a few weeks before Ho made his declaration of independence, had determined that Vietnam would be divided temporarily at the 16th parallel. North of that boundary, Chinese Nationalist troops were to handle the surrender of Japanese forces, to arrange for their repatriation to Japan, and to obtain the release of all prisoners of war and Allied internees. South of that line, British troops would take charge of these matters. As the Potsdam conferees made these secret agreements, they did not specify the shape the political future of Vietnam would take, but, in effect, they granted the French a free hand to return to Indochina and to reimpose colonialism on the Vietnamese people.[53]

As the Vietnamese nation made its reappearance, French forces planned their re-entry into Vietnam. The revolution of the summer of 1945 that ended the French colonial era of Vietnamese history also began thirty years of conflict that eventually claimed more than a million Vietnamese lives and tens of thousands of French and American lives. For Vietnamese patriots, a moment of celebration would be followed by decades of conflict.

NOTES

1. Duiker, William J., *Vietnam: Nation in Revolution* (Boulder, Colo.: Westview, 1983), p. 13.
2. Le Thanh Khoi, *Le Viet-nam: Histoire et Civilization* (Paris: Editions du Minuit, 1955), pp. 88–97.
3. Duiker, *Vietnam: Nation in Revolution*, p. 15.
4. Hall, Daniel G. E., *A History of Southeast Asia*, 2nd ed. (New York: St. Martin's, 1955), pp. 199–200.
5. Cady, John F., *Southeast Asia: Its Historical Development* (New York: McGraw Hill, 1964), pp. 103–106; Duiker, *Vietnam: Nation in Revolution*, pp. 18–19.
6. Kahin, George M. and Lewis, John, *The United States in Vietnam: An Analysis in Depth of the History of America's Involvement in Vietnam* (New York: Delta, 1967), p. 5.
7. Duiker, *Vietnam: Nation in Revolution*, pp. 22–23. Although during the war, Americans often referred to Hue as the "ancient imperial capital" of Vietnam, it only became the capital in the early nineteenth century and its eminence lasted for less than a century. Hanoi is the ancient capital of Vietnamese civilization; it

has been the seat of government for Vietnam for most of its 2,000-year history and is today the capital of Cong Hoa Xa Hoi Chu Nghia Viet Nam (The Socialist Republic of Vietnam).

8. Buttinger, Joseph, *The Smaller Dragon: A Political History of Vietnam* (New York: Praeger, 1958), pp. 283–294.

9. Cady, John F., *The Roots of French Imperialism in Eastern Asia* (Ithaca, New York: Cornell University Press, 1954), pp. 97–102, 136–159, 178–180, and 186–191.

10. Buttinger, Joseph, *A Dragon Defiant: A Short History of Vietnam* (New York: Praeger, 1972), p. 60; also his *Vietnam: A Dragon Embattled*, vol. 1 (New York, Praeger, 1967), p. 495.

11. Hall, Daniel G. E., *The History of Southeast Asia*, pp. 560–570. Cochin China, Annam, and Tonkin are the Western names given to the three regions of Vietnam. The French also called Vietnam "Annam" and referred to the Vietnamese people as "Annamites" or the "Annamite people," names that the Vietnamese despised and rejected. The Vietnamese have never thought of their country as divided into distinct regions; they think in terms of the whole nation, at the same time recognizing distinctive regional characteristics. During the colonial period, they called the three regions mentioned above Nam Viet, Trung Viet, and Bac Viet, that is, South Vietnam, Central Vietnam, and North Vietnam.

12. Buttinger, *Vietnam: A Dragon Embattled*, vol. 1, pp. 138–144; Duiker, *Vietnam: Nation in Revolution*, pp. 23–26.

13. Doyle, Edward, Lipsman, Samuel, and the editors of Boston Publishing Company, *Setting the Stage* (Boston, Boston Publishing Co., 1981), pp. 119–120. The first volume of a multi-volume history of Vietnam called *The Vietnam Experience*. The volumes are illustrated and generally well written.

14. Thompson, Virginia, *French Indochina* (London: Allen & Unwin, 1937), pp. 228–234; Cady, John F., *SE Asia: Its Historical Development* (New York: McGraw-Hill, 1964), part 5, chap. 18, pp. 406–434.

15. Lancaster, Donald, *The Emancipation of French Indochina* (London: Oxford University Press, 1961), pp. 65–66.

16. The Vietnamese language is monosyllabic. Words are invariable. Verbs are not conjugated, and nouns are not declined. Different meanings of the same word are expressed by different levels of pitch. For most of Vietnamese history, Chinese ideographs were used in writing the language. In the seventeenth century, Portuguese and French missionaries invented a system of writing Vietnamese in the Latin alphabet called "quoc Ngu." In "quoc Ngu," syllabic tone is indicated by diacritical marks above, below, or through a letter. During their colonial tenure, the French made "quoc ngu" an official language along with French. Currently, "quoc ngu" is in general use throughout Vietnam.

17. Buttinger, *A Dragon Defiant*, p. 68.

18. *Ibid.*, pp. 111–144.

19. *Ibid.*, pp. 151–156.

20. The man the world knows as Ho Chi Minh employed numerous pseudonyms until 1943 when he adopted his final, famous name. Many aspects of his life remain mysterious, for he never kept diaries, wrote a memoir, nor dictated his biography to anyone. From the time he left his native land in 1911 until he returned during the second World War, he traveled continually.

21. Lacouture, Jean, *Ho Chi Minh: A Political Biography*. Translated from the French by Peter Wiles. Translation edited by Jane Clark Seitz. (New York: Random House, 1968), pp. 13–21; Fall, Bernard B.(ed.), *Ho Chi Minh on Revolution, Selected*

Writings, 1920–1966 (Boulder, Colo.: Westview, 1984), pp. 43–51. Ho Chi Minh wrote essays about lynching and the Ku Klux Klan, both of which were published in France in 1924. A pamphlet, bitterly critical of U.S. racial practices, "La Race Noire," was published in Moscow in 1924.

22. Doyle and others, *Setting the Stage,* pp. 156–157. Ho's petition is entitled "Revendications du Peuple Annamite." It begins: "Depuis la victoire des Allies, tous le peuples assujettis fremissent d'espoir devant la perspective d'lere de droit et du justice qui doit s'ouvrir pour eux en vertu des engagements formeis et solennels, pris devant le monde entier par les differentes puissance de L'Entente dans la lutte de la Civilisation contre la Barbarie."

23. Duiker, William J., *The Communist Road to Power in Vietnam* (Boulder, Colo.: Westview, 1981), pp. 17–18.

24. *Ibid.,* pp. 32–33.

25. Hammer, Ellen J., *The Struggle for Indochina* (Stanford, Calif.: Stanford University Press, 1954), pp. 84–86; Duiker, *The Communist Road,* pp. 33–40.

26. Duiker, *The Communist Road,* pp. 40–43.

27. Duiker, *Vietnam: Nation in Revolt,* pp. 37–38.

28. In 1935, Stalin became alarmed at the growing power of Fascist states in Europe, concluding that they posed a grave threat to Soviet interests. He instructed Communist parties in Western democracies to abandon their revolutionary tactics and form coalitions, "popular fronts," with liberal and socialist parties to combat the Fascist menace. A Popular Front governed France from 1936 to 1939. The Indochinese Communist Party under Ho's leadership responded to Comintern directives. It moderated its revolutionary program and formed alliances with liberal and socialist groups within Vietnam. The Popular Front strategy ended in August 1939, with the signing of the Nazi–Soviet Non-Aggression Pact. Communist parties in France, Vietnam, and elsewhere resumed their revolutionary postures as war began in Europe and intensified in Asia.

29. Lancaster, Donald, *The Emancipation of French Indochina* (London: Oxford University Press, 1961), chap. 6, pp. 98–104.

30. Buttinger, *Dragon Embattled,* vol. 1, pp. 244–50; Hammer, *Struggle,* p. 31.

31. Buttinger, *Dragon Embattled,* vol. 1, pp. 250–253.

32. Chen, King C., *Vietnam and China, 1938–1954* (Princeton, N. J.: Princeton University Press, 1969), pp. 44–48.

33. Devillers, Philippe, *Histoire du Vietnam de 1940 a 1952* (Paris: Editions du Seuil, 1952), pp. 96–113; Duiker, *The Communist Road,* pp. 64–72; Chen, *Vietnam and China,* pp. 51–55; and Pike, Douglas, *History of Vietnamese Communism, 1925–1976* (Stanford, Calif.: Hoover Institution Press, 1978), pp. 30–51.

34. Lacouture, *Ho Chi Minh,* pp. 78–79.

35. Doyle and others, *Setting the Stage,* p. 176.

36. Quoted in *ibid.,* p. 177.

37. LaFeber, Walter, "Roosevelt, Churchill, and Indochina, 1942–1945," *American Historical Review,* vol. 80 (December 1975), pp. 1277–95.

38. Quoted in Pettit, Clyde Edwin, *The Experts* (Secaucus, N. J.: Lyle Stuart , 1975), p. 13.

39. Hess, Gary R., "Franklin D. Roosevelt and Indochina," *Journal of American History,* vol. 59 (September 1972), pp. 353–68.

40. Patti, Archimedes L., *Why Vietnam? Prelude to America's Albatross* (Berkeley, Calif.: University of California Press, 1980), pp. 55–56. The Office of Strategic Services

(OSS) was a wartime intelligence agency whose agents also engaged in commando operations behind enemy lines. They committed sabotage and aided resistance forces, which often included Communists within their ranks, in both the European and Asian theaters of war. See "Instructions By Ho Chi Minh For Setting Up of the Armed Propaganda Brigade for the Liberation of Vietnam," December 1944, printed in Porter, Gareth, ed., *Vietnam: The Definitive Documentation of Human Decisions* (Stanfordville, N. Y.: Earl M. Coleman Enterprises, 1979), vol. 1, pp. 14.

41. Devillers, *Histoire*, p. 152; Chen, *Vietnam and China*, pp. 113–4. Chen points out that the Chinese Nationalists only helped the Vietnamese Nationalists, particularly the VNQDD and Dong Minh Hoi. He finds no evidence that the Vietminh ever received any help from the Chinese Communists. The Soviets displayed no interest in the Vietminh revolution. The Vietminh were on their own except for some help from their American friends in the OSS.

42. Hammer, *Struggle*, pp. 36–45.

43. *Ibid.*, p. 46–47.

44. Buttinger, *Dragon*, vol. 1, pp. 292–5; Duiker, *The Communist Road*, pp. 94–100.

45. Buttinger, *Dragon*, pp. 296–8; Duiker, *The Communist Road*, pp. 94–100; Porter, ed., *Vietnam Documents*, vol. 1, "Resolutions of the Vietminh Conference to Establish a "Free Zone," June 4, 1945, pp. 47–49.

46. Duiker, *The Communist Road*, pp. 98–99; Chen, *Vietnam and China*, pp. 102–14 is a good brief account of the Vietminh August Revolution; Porter, *Vietnam Documents*, vol. 1, "Appeal By Ho Chi Minh for General Insurrection," August 1945, pp. 60–61.

47. Chen, *Vietnam and China*, pp. 11–112.

48. Smith, R. Harris, *OSS: The Secret History of America's First Central Intelligence Agency* (New York: Delta, 1973), pp. 351–55; Ho's Declaration is printed in Porter (ed.), *Vietnam Documents*, vol. 1, pp. 64–6.

49. Herring, George C., *America's Longest War: The United States and Vietnam, 1950–1975*, rev. ed. (New York: Knopf, 1986), p. 3; quoted in Kahin, George McT., *Intervention: How America Became Involved in Vietnam* (New York: Knopf, 1986), pp. 14–15.

50. Kahin, *Intervention*, p. 5.

51. Gardner, Lloyd C., *Approaching Vietnam: From World War II Through Dienbienphu* (New York: W. W. Norton, 1988), pp. 46–63; Lafeber, "Roosevelt, Churchill, and Indochina," p. 1289.

52. Kahin, *Intervention*, pp. 19–20; Arnold A. Offner, "The Truman Myth Revealed: From Parochial Nationalist to Cold Warrior," March, 1988, unpublished paper presented at the Organization of American Historians convention; and Herring, George, "The Truman Administration and the Restoration of French Sovereignty in Indochina," *Diplomatic History*, vol. 1 (Spring 1977), pp. 97–117.

53. Kahin, *Intervention*, pp. 15–16; Tuchman, Barbara, *The March of Folly: From Troy to Vietnam* (New York: Ballantine, 1984), pp. 239–240.

THE ELEPHANT
AND THE TIGER

2

It will be a war between an elephant and a tiger. If the tiger ever stands still, the elephant will crush him with his mighty tusks. But the tiger will not stand still....He will leap upon the back of the elephant, tearing huge chunks from his side, and then he will leap back into the dark jungle. And slowly the elephant will bleed to death. That will be the war of Indochina.

Ho Chi Minh

THE RETURN OF THE FRENCH

British and Chinese troops entered Vietnam in September 1945 to carry out the Potsdam directives issued the previous month by the victorious Allied powers. In the train of the British troops entering southern Vietnam came French forces, determined to reimpose colonialism on Indochina in the aftermath of the Japanese defeat. Insertion of these outside military forces triggered a series of conflicts that engulfed Vietnam for decades, delaying the emergence of an independent, unified Vietnamese state for more than thirty years.

The French were driven by a mix of motives to reimpose their rule on the Vietnamese, Cambodian, and Laotian peoples after the war. Economic considerations were important, especially in Cochin China, where the French financial and commercial interests were concentrated. The French also had a politico-psychological motive for returning to Indochina. The quick Nazi conquest of France in 1940, followed by the rigors and humiliations of the German occupation, had dealt French national esteem serious blows as had Japanese occupation of Indochina and other French possessions in the South Pacific. Permanent loss of their Southeast Asian colonies in the wake of wartime humiliations would be more than the French national psyche could bear. But the most important reason for the French drive to regain control of their former Southeast Asian possessions transcended Indochina and concerned the political cohesion of France's entire overseas empire. French officials had a view of colonialism resembling the subsequent American domino theory: If one colony won its independence, others would then be tempted to stage similar breakaways from French control. If the Vietnam domino fell, not only would the Cambodian and Laotian dominoes follow quickly, but, far worse in the French view, their much more valuable North African possessions, Morocco, Tunisia, and— the most valuable of all French overseas territories—Algeria, would rise in rebellion against French colonialism. To safeguard the interests of their one million Algerian "colons," the French prepared to reconquer 24 million Vietnamese.[1]

The advance wave of British and Indian troops under the command of General Douglas D. Gracey reached Saigon in mid-September 1945. General Gracey, who favored the French returning to Indochina, in reaction to the political disorder he encountered within a country in the throes of revolution after a disruptive war, declared martial law and gave orders to disarm all Vietnamese forces. But he released and rearmed about 5,000 French troops that the Japanese had interned. These French forces, armed with U.S. weapons, joined by newly arriving French troops carried to Indochina in U.S. and British ships, overthrew the Vietminh government in Saigon on September 23, 1945. The French had forced their way back into Vietnam. The Tricolor once again flew over public buildings in the "Paris of the Orient." The Saigon takeover, engineered by the French with British and U.S. support, triggered a thirty-year war for control of Vietnam that ended only when the DRV troops captured Saigon April 30, 1975.[2]

The Vietminh leader in Saigon, Tran Van Giau, ordered a general strike and also ordered counterattacks against the French. Nearly all Vietnamese, determined to prevent a return of the French, joined the resistance, including the religious sectarians and a criminal organization, the Binh Xuyen, the Cochin China "mafia." General Gracey responded to these actions by releasing and rearming Japanese soldiers. A multinational force of British, Indian, French, and Japanese forces, many armed with American weapons, undertook the pacification of southern Vietnam in the fall of 1945. For the British, what has been called First Indochina War, 1945–1946,[3] proved to be short. As more French troops arrived, and as the British completed their assigned task of supervising the repatriation of Japanese troops, their troops were withdrawn. As spring came to southern Vietnam in 1946, the British soldiers were gone.

Most Americans were not aware of the complex political developments taking place in a remote corner of the world at the end of World War II. American media gave little attention to these events or to the role Americans played in helping the French return to Vietnam. Americans would have been astounded to learn that Allied political maneuvering in Vietnam in the fall of 1945 was preparing the ground for a long U.S. entanglement in that country. But one American knew what was happening in Vietnam and he did not like it. General Douglas MacArthur, preeminent hero of the Pacific war and newly appointed American pro-consul in Japan in charge of the occupation and reconstruction of America's recent enemy, passionately denounced the Allied intervention in southern Vietnam: "If there is anything that makes my blood boil, it is to see our allies in Indochina deploying Japanese troops to reconquer the little people we promised to liberate."[4]

By February 1, 1946, French forces under the command of General Jacques Phillipe LeClerc[5] had brought Cochin China under their control. But Leclerc's troops controlled only the cities, towns, and main roads. Vietminh forces effectively contested French authority in the countryside, where most Vietnamese lived. Ho Chi Minh and his Vietminh associates in Hanoi supported these resistance efforts, but they could not control events in the South where Vietminh strength and popularity was thinner than in the north. While concerned about the French presence in southern Vietnam, Ho remained focused on the Tonkin region because once again Chinese forces had invaded northern Vietnam.[6]

To carry out his part of the Potsdam bargain, Chiang Kai-shek sent an army of 150,000 troops commanded by General Lu Han into Tonkin. The Chinese forces brought along some Vietnamese nationalist politicians, remnants of the VNQDD, the Dong Minh Hoi, and other groups, who had been living in exile in China since the 1930s. As the Chinese troops marched through hamlets and villages, they replaced Vietminh officials with the Vietnamese political leaders that they had brought with them. Chiang appeared to be using Chinese troops to destroy the Vietminh revolution in the northern half of Vietnam and to install a government headed by Vietnamese nationalists who would look to China for guidance and protection. By the end of September, Dong Minh Hoi and VNQDD officials, backed by Chinese troops, controlled the countryside.[7] Posing a further problem for the Vietminh, the Chinese troops behaved more like bandits than soldiers, systematically looting the Vietnamese villagers as they marched through the countryside. The Vietminh, powerless to stem the invasion of the huge Chinese army, remained in power only in Hanoi. Facing a French takeover in the south and Chinese occupation in the north, Ho and his colleagues maneuvered desperately to save their imperiled revolution.

The Vietminh bribed the Chinese generals in order to keep themselves in power. Requisitioning gold and currency from the Vietnamese people, Ho made Lu Han and his friends rich men. In return, the Chinese were content to leave his fledgling government in power and to avoid conflict with the Vietminh leaders. Ho also appointed VNQDD leaders to positions in the Vietnamese Provisional Government. Soon afterward, the VNQDD split, with half joining the Vietminh coalition. In addition, Ho dismantled the Indochinese Communist party apparatus and introduced a range of democratic reforms that brought Vietnamese Catholic and other non-Communist groups over to his government. Most important, Ho called for elections to elect delegates to a National Assembly in order to draft a constitution and to establish a permanent government for Vietnam. To save his revolution, Ho was forced to softpedal it.

The first national elections in Vietnamese history took place January 6, 1946. Voter turnouts were massive. Over 90 percent of eligible voters participated, and Vietminh candidates scored an overwhelming victory, winning 206 of the 254 elections.[8] But Ho allowed nationalist delegates seventy slots to guarantee them an important role in his new government. His deft maneuvering had bought off the Chinese generals, co-opted the political threat posed by the Vietnamese nationalists that the Chinese had brought with them, and broadened the popular base of support for his Vietminh-controlled government among non-Communist elements who made up the large majority of the Vietnamese population.

The Chinese Nationalists, resuming their civil war with the Maoists in the aftermath of the Japanese defeat, were less interested in taking control of northern Vietnam or restoring Vietnamese nationalist political groups to power than in using their temporary occupation of the country to wrest concessions from the French. U.S. officials, committed to the restoration of French sovereignty in Indochina, also pressured the Chinese to "facilitate the recovery of power by the French."[9] But the Chinese refused to permit French troops to enter northern Vietnam until they had extracted major concessions from France.

French and Chinese negotiators concluded a series of political and military agreements in February and March 1946. The French agreed to give up all their pre-war trading rights and concessions in China in exchange for China's permitting their re-entry into northern Vietnam. But the return of French troops to the north would require Vietminh permission in the spring of 1946 because the French were not strong enough at the time simply to walk in and overpower Ho's forces without absorbing considerable casualties if the Vietminh chose to resist them. There was also the possibility of the Chinese backing the Vietminh to keep the French out if Ho refused to accept the return of the French.

For his part, Ho Chi Minh was willing to seek a compromise with the French in order to rid his country of the rapacious Chinese whom he believed to be a greater long-range threat to Vietnamese sovereignty than the French.[10]

Delicate negotiations between the French and Vietminh officials took place at the same time as the French-Chinese talks. Ho headed the Vietminh team of negotiators dealing with the French. Jean Sainteny, the commissioner-delegate for Tonkin, headed the French delegation. Sainteny offered many concessions to obtain Vietminh acceptance of their reoccupation of northern Vietnam. The two sides reached a preliminary understanding signed on March 6, 1946. By its terms, France appeared to be taking its first steps toward decolonizing Indochina. Ho's government was declared to be "a free state within the French Union." France also agreed to hold a national referendum to determine whether the colony of Cochin China would rejoin Annam and Tonkin in a reunited Vietnam or would remain a separate French territory. In return, the Vietminh agreed that French troops would replace Chinese forces north of the 16th parallel and they could remain for five years. The Chinese accepted these arrangements, agreeing to withdraw all their troops by June 16, 1946. For a hopeful moment it appeared that moderation and statesmanship had averted both war and colonialism in Vietnam.[11]

But the March 6 agreement soon proved to be a sham. French officials refused to hold the promised plebiscite in Cochin China and construed the new status of Vietnam as a "free state within the French Union" to be only a facade for continuing French colonial domination of the country. Meanwhile, 15,000 French troops re-entered Tonkin, with Chinese and U.S. acceptance.

While these crucial events that set the stage for the subsequent French and U.S. involvements in Vietnam were taking place, the Soviet Union ignored Vietnam, having no interest in Indochinese nationalism in particular nor in the larger issue of Asian nationalism in 1945 and 1946. Soviet priorities at the time were oriented toward Europe. Stalin favored French Communist officials over a minor Communist leader in Southeast Asia who appeared from Moscow's perspective to be a Vietnamese nationalist first and Communist second. Stalin had hopes that the French Communist Party, the largest political party in France, might win the 1946 elections and take control of the French government legally. Although they did not win that election, the Communists came out of it with several cabinet positions, and their leader, Maurice Thorez, became deputy premier. Fearful that they would lose electoral appeal if they supported anticolonialism, Communist leaders in the government supported the French drive to reimpose colonialism on Indochina, a popular cause in France in 1946 and 1947. Stalin backed the French Communists, leaving Ho and the Vietminh to fend for themselves.

From his vantage point in Hanoi in the spring of 1946, Ho felt isolated and vulnerable. The major powers were either backing or accepting French efforts to reimpose colonialism in Indochina. The Vietminh had no allies in either the Communist or Western camps as they prepared to face the French alone.[12]

Ho and his associates tried to negotiate agreements with the French to avoid a war and to preserve a measure of autonomy. French and Vietminh officials met at Dalat, a mountain resort in the Central Highlands, to try to define the March 6 agreement. Giap led the Vietminh delegates. At Dalat, the French representatives made clear that their interpretation of the phrase "free state within the French Union" meant continuing French colonialism in Vietnam. Ho refused to accept the outcome of the Dalat conference as final and called for further negotiations in France. In the summer of 1946, French and Vietnamese delegates met for a series of talks at Fontainebleau near Paris. Ho himself journeyed to France to head the Vietminh contingent. These talks also failed because the French refused to budge from their Dalat interpretation of the March 6 accords. Ho then met with the French prime minister, Georges Bidault, and other top officials. He pleaded with them to make some concessions that he could take back to his people. He also warned the French leaders: "If we must fight, we will fight. You will kill ten of our men and we will kill one of yours. Yet, in the end, it is you who will tire."[13]

Even though Ho had conceded most of the French demands, they would only offer him the promise to hold the Cochin China referendum and to agree to more negotiations at a later date. They never made good on either commitment. Sick at heart, Ho had to return to Hanoi in October 1946, bringing only a flimsy *modus vivendi* to show for his extensive diplomatic efforts.[14]

The fragile peace in Tonkin was broken the following month. On November 20, French and Vietminh customs collectors quarreled over who had the right to collect customs duties at the port of Haiphong. That night, squads of French and Vietminh soldiers exchanged fire in city streets. "These were the opening shots in the eight-year war between the French and the Vietminh,...."[15] In the aftermath of these skirmishes, French officials decided to teach a hard lesson to the Vietnamese who did not seem to know their place in the colonial scheme of things. On November 23 the Vietminh were given two hours to vacate the Chinese quarter of Haiphong. At the end of two hours, a French cruiser shelled the sector, killing 6,000 Vietnamese civilians. On November 28, the French commander, General Morliere, issued an ultimatum demanding that the Vietminh yield control of the city, its suburbs, and the main highway between Haiphong and Hanoi to the French military. The Vietminh refused these demands. On December 18, the French moved troops into Hanoi and occupied several government buildings. On the 19th, General Morliere ordered General Giap to disarm his forces.[16] Giap defied the French leader and refused to obey his command.

That night the Vietminh leaders held a plenary meeting. General Giap ordered a war of national resistance to begin. Later that same evening, Vietminh guerrillas destroyed the Hanoi power plant, plunging the city into darkness. Other guerrilla forces attacked the homes of French civilians and planted mines in the streets of Hanoi. All over northern Vietnam, French installations were hit by guerrilla raiders. As these attacks took place, Ho removed himself from Hanoi and set up a temporary government at Ha Dong, six miles to the south.[17]

The war that had begun in Saigon in September 1945 had spread north, engulfing all Vietnam. In retrospect, the conflict, which Ho had tried hard to avoid, appears inevitable because the French were determined to reimpose colonialism on a people who absolutely refused to accept it, who were ready to fight to preserve their revolution if they must, and who had the means to resist French imperialism. Vietnamese nationalists had been dreaming of an independent, unified Vietnam for eighty years. French efforts to shear off Cochin China from the rest of Vietnam also threatened to unbalance the national economy in which southern Vietnam exchanged surplus food for industrial products from densely populated northern Vietnam.

As the war that was destined to last eight years and to end in French humiliation began, confident French officials predicted that the conflict would last three months at most. Their modern army faced a native militia force that was both poorly armed and poorly trained. French officials, assuming an easy victory over the forces they contemptuously called "the barefoot army," regretted only that their soldiers would not be home for Christmas.

THE FRANCO-VIETMINH WAR

When the war began, the Vietminh could field about forty thousand troops, more than the French had in Vietnam in December 1946. But the poorly prepared Vietminh soldiers could not hope to defeat "a serious French effort to restore colonial rule in Vietnam."[18] The Vietminh also had to face French armed might alone. The early phase of the Franco-Vietminh war tested Ho's claim that the Vietnamese tiger could survive the French elephant's efforts to crush it.

The Vietminh looked to Maoist doctrines of guerrilla warfare for strategic guidance as they planned their campaigns against the French forces. On December 22, 1946, the revolutionary government announced that the struggle against the French imperialists would advance through three stages. Applying Maoist precepts to their struggle, the revolutionaries stated that the first stage of the war would be defensive, during which the Vietminh guerrillas would abandon the urban areas if they had to and retreat into the countryside and to the mountains of northern Vietnam. During this stage, the Vietminh would avoid major battles with the French forces, concentrate on building up their own main force units, and continue political organizing in the villages. The second stage would be one of equilibrium, in which the revolutionary forces would be growing in strength and the imperialist forces would be declining. The third stage would feature a general offensive by the revolutionary forces, stronger than their enemies, that would defeat the imperialist armies and drive them from the country.[19] No specific time frames were mentioned in the December 22 announcement; there were no indications how long they expected each phase to last. But it was clear that the Vietminh planned for a protracted war against the French, a war that could go on for years, and one that they were evidently confident they would ultimately win.

Already controlling Cochin China, the French forces in the early months of 1947 occupied the major cities and towns of Annam and Tonkin. The Vietminh main force units avoided combat with the more powerful invaders, and what resistance the French encountered in these early campaigns came mostly from local guerillas. The Vietminh put up their stiffest resistance in Hanoi, and it took the French forces three months to take the city. Beyond the cities, the Vietminh remained in control of much of the countryside. Viet Bac, the mountainous northern provinces, remained a revolutionary stronghold and haven. Near the remote mountain village of Bac Can, fifty miles from the Chinese border, Ho established his headquarters.[20]

In October 1947 the French launched a major offensive designed to destroy the Vietminh main forces and to capture the revolutionary leaders in their Viet Bac sanctuaries. The French sent a powerful force of twelve infantry battalions, reinforced by armored units and air support, deep into the northern countryside. French paratroopers staged a surprise raid on Vietminh headquarters located in a cave near Bac Can. They missed capturing Ho and other Vietminh leaders by less than an hour.[21] Although they failed to capture the revolutionary leadership, the French military campaign scored major successes. They killed an estimated 10,000 Vietminh main force personnel and forced the rebels to abandon large areas of Viet Bac.

At the same time that they launched their military offensive in the north, the French, convinced that they could not defeat the Vietminh by force alone, moved to undercut the Vietminh politically by forming alliances with Vietnamese groups that would cooperate with them against the revolutionaries. The heart of the French political strategy involved forming a Vietnamese government in Saigon and persuading former emperor Bao Dai to head it. The French plan was to create a non-Communist Vietnamese state that would offer a political alternative to the Vietminh revolutionary regime and provide a rallying point for non-Communist Vietnamese nationalists. Such a government could pose a threat to the Vietminh. If Bao Dai succeeded in uniting the various non-Communist political factions into a cohesive force, he could create "a serious alternative to the Vietminh Front for the loyalty of the Vietnamese people."[22]

The French political strategy in 1947 failed for two main reasons. The first, a perennial problem of Vietnamese politics, especially southern urban Vietnamese politics, was the inability of various non-Communist nationalist factions to form a stable coalition government. The second was the French refusal to grant the proposed government anything resembling independence. It promised to be only a puppet regime that most Vietnamese regarded as a cover for French colonialism, and they made a point of shunning it.

Although the French had seized both the military and political initiative in the fall of 1947, they had failed to either destroy the Vietminh army or to create a viable political alternative to Ho's revolutionary nationalism. French leaders failed to realize it then, but their effort to reimpose colonialism on the Vietnamese had reached its highwater mark. Vietminh prospects improved markedly in 1948. The Russians began to support them politically, and the Chinese Communists were fast gaining the upper hand against Chiang Kai-shek's Nationalist armies. Maoist victory in China, which now appeared to Ho and his associates to be only a matter of time, offered the promise of significant economic and military assistance, and also political support for the struggling Vietnamese revolutionaries.

Emboldened by developments in the Soviet Union and China, and by a sense that the French campaign to destroy their revolution had already reached its limits, General Giap announced that the Vietnamese struggle against the French had progressed to its second stage, the stage of equilibrium. No longer would the rebels be content to remain on the defensive; they would henceforth move to expand both the geographic area and population under their control and to wear down the French main forces. During the second phase of their struggle, they relied mostly on guerrilla tactics, but occasionally they deployed main force units in swift mobile assaults on French forces.[23] During 1948, both the Vietminh military forces and their party apparatus doubled in size. They regained most of the territory they had lost in the north the previous year and expanded the area in Cochin China under their control. As the year ended, the Vietminh controlled about 55 percent of all Vietnamese villages. The French, who found themselves bogged down in a "quicksand war," mainly controlled the cities and coastal enclaves.[24]

French officials in Vietnam, having failed to defeat the rebels militarily, tried again to outmaneuver them politically. The French were also concerned to attract direct United States military support for their increasingly expensive efforts in Indochina that were quickly losing favor with the French public. After a series of negotiations, the French finally persuaded Bao Dai to head a new government that was given the status of "an associated state within the French Union." According to the Elysee Agreement signed March 8, 1949, the French agreed to "independence" for a "Vietnamese state" that included all of the country. But the new state was to be incorporated into the French Union without most of the attributes of sovereignty. The French retained control over the new government's foreign affairs, defense forces, and any taxes levied on French properties. The new political order constituted a sham, a facade for continuing French domination, and failed to attract the support of most Vietnamese nationalists.[25] For most Vietnamese there were only two real political choices available in 1949: One could either support the French effort to reimpose colonialism on Indochina, or one could support the revolutionary nationalists resisting the French efforts to reimpose colonialism. The vast majority of the Vietnamese, whatever their politics, opted to support or at least accept the Vietminh.

Perceiving that Bao Dai's government had little authority and only a narrow base of support, the Vietminh forces in the south escalated their revolutionary activity in Saigon and vicinity. They also infiltrated the new government's police force and its civil service bureaucracies and launched a series of assaults on provincial capitals in the Mekong delta. But French troops routed the guerrillas in the delta and they were forced to seek refuge in the Plain of Reeds, a huge area of swamps, waterways, and rice paddies fifty miles southwest of Saigon.[26]

By far the most important political event of 1949 influencing the course of the Franco–Vietminh war and the growing U.S. involvement in Vietnam was the Maoist victory in China. The People's Republic of China (PRC) was established in November 1949 as Chiang Kai-Shek, accompanied by remnants of his government and army, fled the Chinese mainland for the island of Formosa (Taiwan). A month later, Chinese Communist forces appeared at the Vietnamese border. In January 1950 the new Chinese government extended both military assistance and diplomatic recognition to Ho's government, the Democratic Republic of Vietnam (DRV). Moscow soon followed suit, formally recognizing the DRV.[27]

The new relation between China and the Vietminh transformed the Franco–Vietminh conflict both politically and strategically. Until now, Ho had waged his battles with France alone. Now he had a powerful friend next door. Ho's government also threw off its Front trappings. It became openly Communist, and many non-Communist elements were purged. The Indochina Communist Party, which had been dissolved in 1945, reappeared as the Dang Lao Dong Viet Nam (the Vietnamese Worker's Party, or VWP, a.k.a. the Lao Dong). For the first time since the formation of the Vietminh in 1941, the Vietnamese revolution was cast within a Marxist–Leninist framework.[28] Henceforth, the Vietnamese revolution would be led openly by the Lao Dong. The revolutionaries also made it clear that the socialist revolution, which for so long had been played down for the sake of national unity, would commence as soon as the French were driven out of Vietnam.

Although the political consequences of the new alliance with China were significant, the most important result of the new relationship was to strengthen the Vietnamese Communist military forces tremendously and to give them the option of moving to the general counteroffensive, the projected third stage of their struggle against the French.[29] In April 1950, Ho Chi Minh journeyed to Beijing where he concluded a "lend–lease arrangement" with the Chinese.[30] The Chinese sent the Vietminh artillery, mortars, and modern rifles. In addition, Chinese instructors and technicians arrived in Viet Bac to train the Vietnamese in the use of more effective weapons and tactics. By the fall of 1950, General Giap had 60,000 regulars, organized into five infantry divisions. His soldiers were all indoctrinated, disciplined, well-trained, and armed with modern weapons. The Vietminh army had become a formidable military force.

While the Vietnamese revolutionaries were being strengthened immensely by their Chinese friends, the French effort in Vietnam was sagging, hampered by declining popular support. In the eyes of many of the French back home, the Indochina war had become too expensive; they did not like it and they did not want it. The French government refused to send conscripts to fight in the war for political reasons, and it also reduced the number of French troops in Vietnam by nearly 10,000. When Giap took the offensive in 1950, the French forces found themselves with fewer troops having to face the newly enhanced Vietminh units.

Giap's objectives were to clear out a string of French garrisons that reached into the northern countryside along the Chinese frontier. The principal garrison was at Dong Khe. It fell to the aggressive assaults of the Vietminh after two days of tough fighting on September 16, 1950.[31] After Dong Khe had fallen, the French evacuated two other sites, and the Vietnamese battered the retreating columns from these garrisons.

Dong Khe was a major military disaster for the French. It exposed all the other outposts to attack. They were either overrun or evacuated, and the retreating troops were often hammered by the mobile, aggressive Vietminh units that were using artillery, mortars, grenades, and machine gun fire. French losses were heavy, some 6,000 were either casualties or captured by the Vietminh. The French also abandoned a huge stockpile of valuable weapons, ammunition, medical supplies, and foodstuffs, all eagerly confiscated by the victorious Vietminh troops.[32] Giap's forces drove the French out of northern Tonkin and confined them to the coastal enclaves.

Giap's border offensive during the fall of 1950 constituted a major turning point in the Franco-Vietminh war. For the first time the Vietminh had attacked and defeated sizeable units of a modern European army. Giap's troops were now positioned to invade the strategic Red River delta with its large population and rich rice harvests. They also had unrestricted access to China and its resources, and growing prospects for aid from the USSR and the Eastern Bloc countries. Most of all, the Vietminh could now seize the tactical initiative in the war.[33] French morale sank, and, for the first time, worried French officials had to confront the unthinkable possibility that they could be defeated by their former colonial subjects.

COLD WAR, COMMUNISM, AND CONTAINMENT

Although the Truman administration had supported the return of the French to Indochina following the defeat of the Japanese, Washington was nevertheless alarmed by the outbreak of the Franco-Vietminh war in 1946. Because the Indochina conflict was only one of several national revolutions occurring simultaneously in Southeast Asia, that economically and strategically significant region, from Washington's vantage point, appeared to be one of the globe's most volatile areas.[34] The State Department was leery of the United States overtly aligning itself with French colonialism. Further, by the end of 1947, Washington officials were skeptical that the French could ever defeat the Vietminh militarily, that Vietnamese nationalism could be subdued by force. They believed that the French would have to make some accommodation to satisfy the nationalist aspirations of the Vietnamese people.

But if they were unhappy with French efforts to retrieve their Indochinese empire, State Department officials were positively appalled at the prospect of an independent Vietnamese nation under the control of the Communist revolutionary Ho Chi Minh. Although they had no evidence linking Ho to Moscow nor any sign that he was carrying out Soviet policies in Indochina, and they knew that he was both the leader and personification of the powerful Vietnamese drive for self-determination, State Department officials operated on the assumption that Communism and nationalism were incompatible ideological forces. They could not believe that Ho could be what he in fact was: both a committed Communist and a dedicated Vietnamese patriot. They could not accept political reality—that the Vietnamese Communists expressed and represented the nationalistic aspirations of most Vietnamese whatever their politics. State Department officials therefore assumed that Ho Chi Minh and his chief associates were Stalinist agents. They believed that it was in the best interests of the United States to prevent a Communist revolution in Indochina that they equated with advancing the imperial interests of the Soviets.[35]

In short, U.S. policy makers confronted a dilemma in Indochina. On the one hand, they rejected imposing colonialism as neither desirable nor possible; on the other hand, they rejected a French military withdrawal that would leave "chaos and terroristic activities" in its wake and open the way to a Communist takeover in Vietnam. Not wanting the French either to win or get out, and unable to implement or even conceive of an alternative policy, State Department officials shrugged their shoulders and followed a passive policy that amounted to accepting the French effort to reimpose colonialism in Indochina.[36]

America's Indochina policy in 1946 and 1947 was distinctly secondary to U.S. interests in Europe. The Truman administration pursued a Euro-centered foreign policy premised on the view that Soviet expansionism across war-torn Europe represented the principal threat to American vital interests in the postwar world. In March 1947 the president had proclaimed the Truman Doctrine, which committed the United States to a policy of containing Communism in Europe. Within western Europe France was the focus of U.S. concerns in the late-1940s because it had a war-shattered economy, an unstable government, and a powerful and popular Communist party. American officials feared that the Communists could come to power in France, given its shaky economic and political status.

Committed to keeping France within the Free World orbit, the United States provided France with political, economic, and moral support during the late-1940s. Part of this support took the form of leaving the French a free hand in Indochina. Between 1946 and 1949, the official U.S. position on the Franco-Vietminh war was one of neutrality. Covertly, the United States furnished the French with substantial amounts of financial and military assistance.[37] Marshall Plan funds earmarked for rebuilding the French industrial infrastructure got siphoned off for the Indochina War effort.[38] The American Indochina policy during the late-1940s was hostage to the much more important commitment of building up postwar France in order to prevent a possible Communist takeover in that crucial European country.

Just as it profoundly altered the political and strategic situation in Indochina, the Chinese revolution induced major changes in America's Indochina policy that, in turn, were components of a general reorientation of U.S. global foreign policy during 1949 and 1950. The French, facing both a much more formidable foe armed and trained with Chinese assistance and the loss back home of popular support for their colonial war, starting in late 1949, began requesting more aid from the United States. France warned U.S. officials that without greater amounts of American military and economic assistance, they could lose the war and have to leave Indochina. They found a receptive audience in Washington, where President Truman and his advisers were reappraising American foreign policy in the light of two global disasters that had occurred in the fall of 1949: the Soviet's successful testing of an atomic device that fractured the American nuclear monopoly and the fall of China to the Communists that took 600 million people behind the "Bamboo Curtain."

In the aftermath of these two major blows to American prestige and power, President Truman and his advisers, convinced that the principal goal of Soviet foreign policy was to dominate the world and that the recent Chinese revolution accorded with Stalinist ambitions for imposing Communism worldwide, looked at a world divided into two hostile camps. Truman interpreted this political bipolarity in highly charged moralistic terms. He saw the forces of freedom engaging the forces of tyranny. In Truman's simplistic, Manichaean view, the complex conflicts of interest between the Western powers and the Communist nations pitted the forces of light against the forces of darkness in a mortal struggle for control of the political future of the planet and the destinies of all its people.[39] Fearing a shift in the balance of power in favor of the Communists, dreading the prospect of global war, "the Truman administration initiated plans to increase American military capabilities, shore up the defense of Western Europe, and extend the containment policy to the Far East."[40]

Convinced that Europe faced grave danger from an expansionist Soviet Union now empowered with nuclear weapons, the United States moved to shore up French defenses and to propose rearming West Germany. Fearful lest the French not approve the creation of a European Defense Community (EDC), a plan for integrating French and West German forces into a multinational army, the United States met French demands for direct American support for their Indochina campaign. The Truman administration implemented a program of direct military and economic assistance for the French colonial war in Indochina in the hopes that such support would induce the French to cooperate with U.S. strategic designs for Europe and would also free up French resources for NATO.

At the same time that the United States was committing itself to underwriting the security of western Europe, Washington came to the conclusion that, in the aftermath of the Chinese revolution, the strategic security of Southeast Asia had become an important United States interest. From the American perspective, it appeared that Southeast Asia, with its explosive mix of declining European imperial powers and unstable newly independent states, was vulnerable to pressure from both China and the USSR, especially China because of its geographic propinquity. Loss of these rich former European colonies to the Communists would close western Europe out of major markets. Cutting off sources of vital raw materials such as rubber, tin, and oil would retard Europe's, particularly Britain's, postwar recovery and would also set back the economic recovery of America's principal Far Eastern ally, Japan.

From within the framework of the new American Southeast Asian policy calculus, American officials regarded Indochina, particularly Vietnam, as the key to the security of the entire region. If Ho's revolution, now backed by both the Chinese and the Soviets, succeeded in driving the French out of Vietnam, it would open the rest of Southeast Asia to Communist penetration.[41] It was this application of the domino theory to the Franco–Vietminh war in the aftermath of the Maoist triumph in China that greatly raised the American stake in Indochina and transformed what had been a comparatively minor appendage of the U.S. Euro-centered goal of shoring up France after World War II into a major foreign policy concern in its own right. The domino theory reflected the American ignorance of the profound differences among Asian nations and societies, ignorance of the power of Asian nationalisms, and perhaps a racist fallacy that because all Asians look alike, all Asian nations will act alike.

Another factor, in addition to developments in Europe and Asia, drove Washington to invest the outcome of the Franco-Vietminh war with enhanced strategic significance in 1950. American internal political considerations, particularly the growth of domestic anti-Communism, exerted a strong influence on the Truman administration's new foreign policy design. Conservative Republicans accused Truman's liberal Democratic administration of being "soft on Communism," that is, they accused these officials of not taking the tough, effective measures that they insisted were needed to contain the spread of Communism abroad and to squelch "Red" subversion at home.[42]

The Maoist triumph in China gave the domestic practitioners of the politics of anti-Communism an enormous boost. Many conservative Republicans, and some Democrats, charged President Truman, Secretary of State Dean Acheson, and other high administration officials, with the "loss of China." Chiang fell, these critics asserted, because the Truman administration did not provide the Chinese Nationalists with enough military and economic support, that they, in effect, sold them out to the Communists. Senator Robert Taft of Ohio led the Republican onslaught against the Truman administration for "losing China."

In the aftermath of the fall of China to the Communists, Truman feared that if his administration did not energetically back the French in Vietnam and then they subsequently lost their war, the conservative senatorial wolf pack would be after him again, this time for the "loss of Indochina." Such an outcome would cost both him and the Democrats popular support and the next election. This domestic political factor that bedeviled Truman and Acheson became "one of the most powerful and enduring factors shaping American policy toward Vietnam."[43] During the early and mid-1960s, the domestic politics of anti-Communism strongly influenced the decisions of the Kennedy and Johnson administrations that gradually committed the United States to its longest war.

Washington also feared that if Vietnam fell to the Communists, so would Laos, Cambodia, Thailand, Burma, and Malaysia. Perhaps Indonesia, possibly even the Philippines and the Indian subcontinent, would be vulnerable. Ultimately, American security itself could one day be imperiled by the expansionist Communist monolith. What Washington perceived to be at stake in Vietnam by 1950 was no longer merely the outcome of a regional colonial war. Indochina had become one of the front lines in the global Cold War between Communism and Freedom. In American eyes, the French were no longer merely fighting to reimpose colonialism on the Vietnamese, they were part of the Western world's concerted effort to contain Chinese and Soviet Communism in Europe and Asia.

Whatever lingering anticolonial scruples American officials may have held were quickly overmastered by the application of the containment doctrine and its domino correlative to Southeast Asia in the aftermath of the Chinese revolution and the Soviet acquisition of a nuclear capability. For the Truman administration, supporting the French war in Indochina had become an urgent necessity, a strategic imperative, vital to the security interests of the United States and its allies. A regional conflict between Asian nationalists and French imperialists that had begun in 1945 had by 1950 become enmeshed in the global Cold War struggle between East and West.[44]

The French made it easier for the United States to directly support its Indochina war by creating the Bao Dai puppet regime in 1949. Although the Bao Dai government possessed few attributes of sovereignty and few Vietnamese supported it, it enabled the French to claim, disingenuously, that they were fighting to preserve a non-Communist Vietnamese nation from the forces of international Communism intent on pulling Indochina into the Russian–Chinese orbit. Although the Bao Dai ploy attracted few Vietnamese, American officials apparently convinced themselves that the French were offering the Vietnamese people a genuine nationalistic alternative to the revolutionary cohorts of Ho Chi Minh. Even if U.S. officials were not certain that the French, with American help, could defeat the Vietminh, they feared that if they did not lend assistance, the French would surely lose and that outcome would be ruinous to U.S. interests in Southeast Asia. In February 1950, the United States extended diplomatic recognition to Bao Dai's "Associated States of Vietnam." By backing the Bao Dai regime, the United States hoped to "avoid the appearance of being an accomplice of French imperialism."[45]

By backing French imperialism and its Vietnamese puppets, the United States had aligned itself with the losing side in the Franco–Vietminh war. By the time America committed itself to directly supporting the French military effort, the Vietminh armed forces had gained the strategic initiative and had taken the offensive. The revolutionary nationalists controlled two-thirds of the land and the people of Vietnam. The Chinese were providing Giap's forces with substantial amounts of modern weaponry. The French were on the defensive, clinging to the cities and coastal enclaves. The war had become unpopular in France, and the French government was wavering in its support of the war. Bao Dai himself acknowledged that his pseudo-government was merely a French tool.[46]

The outbreak of the Korean War that occurred in late June 1950, when North Korean armies suddenly invaded South Korea in order to try to unify Korea under Communist control, confirmed the Truman administration's belief that the Soviet Union was an expansionist power intent on dominating all of Asia. Truman assumed that the North Korean troops were Soviet proxies and that Beijing also marched to Stalin's orders. Chinese intervention in the Korean War in late November 1950 raised the specter in Washington and Paris that Chinese troops could also invade Vietnam. These developments reinforced President Truman's and Secretary of State Acheson's sense of the importance of Vietnam and the vital need for the French to continue their war to prevent Communist expansion into Southeast Asia. In the summer of 1950, the first U.S. aid package for the French Indochina war was implemented and a unit of U.S. military advisers, designated the Military Assistance and Advisory Group (MAAG), was sent to Vietnam. MAAG officials were to coordinate the aid program and to instruct the French, and, later, the Vietnamese, in the use of American weapons and tactics. At the same time, U.S. officials inaugurated a program of economic and technical assistance for the Bao Dai government. During 1951 and 1952, the United States provided increasing amounts of military and economic aid to the French war effort.[47] With America backing the French and China backing the Vietminh, the Franco-Vietminh war had become an international affair.

The French also feared a Chinese invasion of northern Vietnam akin to the Chinese intervention in Korea. Knowing that their forces could not cope with the Chinese should they come in, the French sought to get Washington's assurances that American troops would be sent to Indochina to fight the Chinese if they entered Vietnam. President Truman, wary of getting into another land war in Asia after Korea, made it clear to French officials that under no circumstances would American ground troops be sent to Indochina.[48]

The Americans found themselves repeatedly frustrated by their French partners. Despite receiving large amounts of U.S. military aid, the French forces could never reverse the course of the war. The French never seriously considered fighting for a truly independent Vietnam. They paid lip service to the cause of Vietnamese nationalism, but they kept the Bao Dai regime tightly under their control, thus preventing it from ever becoming a credible alternative to the revolutionary nationalists. The French also hampered the U.S. aid programs that furnished economic and technical assistance to the Vietnamese people because they did not want the Vietnamese people to know that the Americans were helping them. Any efforts by Americans to pressure a series of weak French governments to fight harder or to consider a grant of independence to the Vietnamese were met by French arguments that they could not approve the EDC, or that they might have to leave Vietnam and let the United States confront the results of a Communist takeover. Rather than risk such possibilities, Washington acquiesced in the face of these French threats, continued to provide ever increasing amounts of aid, and let them call the shots.[49] Consequently, in the eyes of most Vietnamese, the Americans appeared to be supporters of French colonialism, not Asian nationalism, and the French position in Indochina continued to deteriorate.

The Truman administration, by intervening on the side of French imperialism in Vietnam in pursuit of American ideologically driven foreign policy objectives in Southeast Asia, committed serious errors in geo-political judgment. Erroneously elevating a minor concern to a vital interest, they exaggerated the strategic significance of Vietnam. They also consistently misread the nature of Vietnamese revolutionary nationalism. They failed to understand that its causes were indigenous, they failed to understand that Ho Chi Minh and his Communist associates represented the cause of Vietnamese nationalism, they failed to understand the powerful and widespread appeal that the drive to regain independence from European colonialism had with nearly all Vietnamese regardless of their politics, and they failed to understand that Ho was not controlled by either the Soviet Union or China. Truman and Acheson's flawed Indochina policies, based on false premises and faulty judgments, laid the groundwork for the American ordeal in Vietnam.

THE ROAD TO DIEN BIEN PHU

As the Truman administration, in response to the Soviet possession of nuclear weapons, the Chinese revolution, and the Franco-Vietminh war, devised its expanded foreign policy based on containing Communism around the world, the war in Indochina also expanded. The Vietminh offensive during the fall of 1950 forced the French to face a hard choice. They could either increase their military forces substantially and seek a military victory over the Vietminh or they could try for a negotiated settlement with their stubborn foes. Neither choice appealed to French officials, and they tried to avoid the dilemma by calling on the United States for military aid and by creating a Vietnamese national army to supplement the French forces; the French called this latter move "the yellowing of the army." American aid was soon forthcoming, and "the new Army of the Republic of Vietnam began to take shape."[50] In addition, the French brought in their best field commander to take charge of the war, General de Lattre de Tassigny. De Lattre soon infused the French forces with new determination and confidence. He viewed the Red River delta as the key to winning the war, and he built up French defenses in that region by stringing a series of concrete forts along the boundaries of the delta to prevent infiltration of this strategic region by Vietminh forces.

General Giap, having concluding that the time had come to launch the third stage of the protracted war against the French imperialists, opened a general offensive in January 1951 in the western end of the delta. Two Vietminh infantry divisions, 22,000 troops altogether, attacked the provincial capital of Vinh Yeh, which was defended by a force of 10,000 French. In two days of hard fighting in which Giap employed a series of human wave attacks, the outnumbered French beat off the Vietminh and inflicted heavy casualties on them by using superior firepower and air attacks. During the ensuing months, the Vietminh attacked other towns at the edges of the delta, and the outnumbered French fought them off every time and usually inflicted heavy casualties. Giap called off the failed offensive in June after having lost about 15,000 troops either killed or wounded.[51]

Clearly, Giap's decision to take the offensive had been premature. The campaigns against de Lattre's soldiers showed that the French were still full of fight and revealed serious weaknesses in the DRV army's ability to conduct large-scale conventional warfare. The Vietminh troops had tried to run before they could walk. But the failed Vietminh offensive in 1951 did not alter the basic military situation. DRV forces significantly outnumbered the French; they could marshal 225,000 troops against about 150,000 French main forces deployed throughout Indochina.[52] The French remained in an essentially defensive position. Substantial amounts of American military aid, the creation of ARVN, the presence of General de Lattre, and the bloody losses inflicted on the Vietminh troops could not turn the tide of war in favor of the French.

Between 1951 and 1953, the Vietminh launched several attacks primarily in northern Vietnam. There was correspondingly little fighting in central and southern Vietnam. French pacification efforts were relatively successful in Cochin China, and, consequently, the Vietminh forces had a much thinner base of popular support in Saigon and vicinity. In the north, the DRV forces retained the strategic initiative; the French remained in defensive positions, although occasionally de Lattre would send out a strike force to hit the Vietminh. The normal pattern was for the Vietminh to chose the time and place for an assault. Their strategy was to probe the French for weak spots, attack in force, inflict as many casualties as they could, and then break off the engagement and retreat to their mountain sanctuaries in Viet Bac. Their goals were to wear the French down, to keep pressure on them, to undermine their morale, and to weaken their political support back in France.

One of the major campaigns fought during this phase of the war took place at Hoa Binh in November 1951. Hoa Binh was a town located about fifty miles west of Hanoi, outside the de Lattre line of defense. It sat astride a major supply and communications route of the Vietminh in the hills to the west of the delta. It was inhabited by the Muouong tribe, a Montagnard people loyal to France. If the French could hold Hoa Binh, it would seriously hamper the ability of Vietminh main forces to mount attacks in the Red River delta and it would extend the French defense perimeter twenty-five miles west. The French occupied the town without meeting much resistance from the Vietminh initially.

Giap, determined to drive the French out of the strategic site, committed several divisions to the battle. The Hoa Binh campaign lasted three months with many intense battles as Giap sent wave after wave of attackers against the French positions. Both sides were now using modern American weapons. The weapons had been furnished to the French under the U.S. aid program; the Vietminh had acquired them from the Chinese and through theft and capture. The DRV attacks gradually wore the French down, and they were forced to withdraw from Hoa Binh in mid-February.[53] Meanwhile, General de Lattre, who had become seriously ill during the battles for Hoa Binh, returned to France, where he died on February 11, 1952, of cancer.

Hoa Binh was a major victory for the Vietminh. Six months after their victory, Vietminh political cadres had organized most of the villages of the western delta. More important, the victory at Hoa Binh gave Ho Chi Minh, General Giap, and the other DRV leaders a growing confidence that defeating the French was within their grasp.

During the years 1951 to 1953, as the war raged on, the Vietminh political cadres continued their efforts to organize the Vietnamese people in the cities and coastal enclaves still under French control. DRV leaders had always emphasized the crucial role that political organizing played in their revolution to rid Vietnam of the French presence and to implement Communism. They hoped to foment popular uprisings in the cities that would further weaken the declining French grip on Indochina. But Vietminh organizers found little support for their cause among the urban populations.[54] Among the urban classes that they assumed might share an affinity for their movement—students, workers, and intellectuals—they often encountered either opposition or indifference. Disappointed, Vietminh leaders concluded that the major political base of the Vietnamese revolution would have to remain in the countryside.

To solidify their support among the poorer classes of peasants and to strike against landlords who opposed their program, the Vietminh implemented land reform in areas under their control. They modeled their land reform after the Maoist program implemented during the Chinese Civil War. In Tonkin and Cochin China, thousands of peasants received land.[55] Land reform strengthened the Vietminh political base in the countryside, weakened the landlord classes, advanced the Vietminh social revolution, and foreshadowed the large-scale land reform programs undertaken in North Vietnam during the mid-1950s.

In April 1953, General Henri Navarre assumed command of the French forces in Indochina with orders to win the war. Given the assets available to him, he knew that he had been assigned an impossible mission. The DRV forces now totalled 350,000 armed troops, organized into eight infantry and one armored division, and the size of the Vietminh army increased daily as new troops arrived from China where they had been undergoing training.[56] French force levels, deployed over the whole of Vietnam, were not sufficient to counter this large DRV army. The new Vietnamese national army (ARVN) had not developed as expected; its troops had little incentive to fight for the Bao Dai government, which they knew to be French controlled; there was wholesale avoidance of military service in that army, and the quality of its recruits was low. Navarre knew that the ARVN could not supplement the French expeditionary forces. In France, by the spring of 1953, public opposition to the war was widespread; many politicians were openly calling for negotiations to end the conflict that its critics called *la guerre sale* (the dirty war). Washington, fearing the loss of Indochina to the Communists, was putting pressure on the French government, headed by Premier Joseph Laniel, to step up its war effort.

Under pressure both from his government and the Americans, General Navarre developed a plan to try to improve the French military position in Indochina before any negotiations began. The first phase involved regaining control of the Red River delta. Navarre attacked Vietminh strongholds in the western delta. Following a strategy that had been worked out the previous January, Giap did not challenge the French forces. His troops retreated in the face of Navarre's assaults. French troops regained delta provinces that had fallen under Vietminh control. While French forces reoccupied parts of the delta, Giap's forces ranged widely over northwest Vietnam and into Laos where Vietminh forces threatened a French-supported regime in that land-locked country.[57]

General Navarre, concerned for the safety of Laos and wanting to disrupt the Vietminh offensive in northwest Tonkin, decided to take a strategic gamble. In mid-November 1953, he sent his paratroopers to occupy strong points blocking a major Vietminh invasion route into Laos and also cutting off one of their supply routes from China. He also intended to tie down a sizeable number of Giap's forces in order to keep them out of the Red River delta. He chose a site by a village lying 170 miles northwest of Hanoi just ten miles from the Laotian border. The town was located near two airstrips in a broad valley surrounded by hills and mountains. Navarre assumed that Giap would be forced to attack the new fortress. Navarre believed that he, having control of the air and possessing superior firepower, would be able to send enough troops to make the French position invulnerable to Vietminh assaults. Navarre intended to force the Vietnam to fight at a place of his own choosing and then inflict a significant defeat on them that would improve the French military position. The site General Navarre selected to make his stand would soon become famous as a symbol of French futility in Indochina. It was called Dien Bien Phu.

The DRV did not respond immediately to the French thrust into Dien Bien Phu, and they continued their campaign in northwest Tonkin and Laos. Navarre, while building up his defenses at Dien Bien Phu, also launched the second phase of his plan to regain the military initiative in Indochina, a series of operations in northern Annam called "Operation Atlante."[58] These attacks were designed to clear the Vietminh forces out of north-central Vietnam to permit the pacification of this major rice-growing region. Giap chose not to commit any main force units to challenge Operation Atlante, relying instead on local guerrillas to disrupt French efforts to pacify these key coastal provinces. Giap also countered Navarre's move into northern Annam by sending Vietminh main force units into the central highlands regions to the west. Their attacks on French outposts in Kontum Province forced Navarre to disperse his forces and prevented the French from consolidating their position in Annam.

While the DRV and French forces battled each other throughout northern and central Vietnam during the fall of 1953, both sides also moved toward negotiating a settlement. Laniel indicated his interest in finding a compromise solution to the conflict.[59] Ho said that he would like to hear the French proposals. In February 1954, the foreign ministers of the major powers scheduled an international peace conference to convene in April in Geneva to consider proposals for the unification of Korea in the aftermath of the armistice agreement that had ended the Korean war the previous August. The foreign ministers added the settlement of the Indochina War to the conference agenda.

Shortly after the announcement that a peace conference would be meeting in May to settle the Franco-Vietminh war, General Giap decided to attack Dien Bien Phu. He had several reasons for doing so: (1) He wanted to inflict a major military defeat on the French that would coincide with the opening of the Geneva Conference in order to maximize the DRV's leverage at the bargaining table. (2) Dien Bien Phu was the key to the Navarre strategy. If the garrison were taken, the French plan would fail and the Vietminh would retain the military initiative. (3) A defeat at Dien Bien Phu could finish the French in Indochina. Such a devastating defeat just might destroy the remaining French will to continue the war.[60]

Giap was confident that he and his staff had devised a strategy that would bring the Vietminh forces victory. He planned a siege of the French positions. He also planned to destroy the airstrips to cut off French supply sources and to prevent them from bringing in reinforcements. He would use artillery and mortar barrages to wear down the French. Infantry assaults would seize their strong points one by one until their center was taken.[61]

For the battle, Giap deployed over 50,000 main force troops, another 50,000 support forces, and over 100,000 workers to man his supply lines. The Vietnamese were also joined by an estimated 20,000 to 30,000 Chinese workers, technicians, mechanics, truck drivers, advisers, and artillerymen. The Chinese made a crucial contribution to the Vietminh campaign at Dien Bien Phu. In addition to personnel, the Chinese supplied ammunition, weapons, gasoline, and foodstuffs. Chinese officers also helped Giap plan and implement his tactics. The Soviets furnished trucks and artillery and also established a Soviet Bloc aid pool to support the DRV war effort.[62]

The French had a scant 12,000 troops under Colonel De Castries dug in at Dien Bien Phu to face Giap's battle-ready hordes. The French had arrayed themselves in a coordinated series of strongly defended areas. The main ones were clustered around the larger airstrip. Away from these main points there were four other defended areas, each guarding an approach to their center.[63]

The Battle of Dien Bien Phu began on March 13, 1954, at sunset, when Vietminh artillery placed in the surrounding mountainsides opened fire on the French positions below. Vietminh infantry also assaulted one of the outlying strong points that first night. Fighting was fierce, and the Vietminh sustained heavy losses. Within two days, Vietminh artillery and mortars had shut down the airstrips. Thereafter, the French defenders could only be reinforced and supplied by parachute drop. Vietminh artillery continually shelled the French positions. Navarre, victimized by faulty military intelligence, had not anticipated that the Vietminh could bring in the firepower that they did. He had counted on his air force silencing the enemy's artillery.

French soldiers in combat at Dien Bien Phu, April 1954. The Vietminh victory at Dien Bien Phu brought to an end French efforts to reimpose colonialism on Indochina. *Source*: USMI Photo Archives.

But the French planes could not destroy the Vietminh guns because they had been placed in camouflaged tunnels dug into mountains and they were moved around constantly.[64]

In early April, Giap launched a series of all-out infantry assaults in an effort to overrun the outer defenses. The French fought them off and inflicted heavy losses on the attacking Vietnamese. Following the failure of his assault tactics, Giap resorted to tunneling. Vietminh sappers tunneled their way toward the French positions. Night and day they dug. Miles of trenches zigzagged toward the strong points. The French perimeter steadily shrank in the face of this ant-like labor. French artillery, mortars, explosive charges, and counter-attacks delayed but could never halt the tunneling process.

As Giap's sappers slowly tightened the noose, Navarre realized that Dien Bien Phu was doomed. But with the airstrips closed down, he could not extract his soldiers from what had become a trap that he had set for them. Neither could he adequately reinforce and supply his beleaguered force nor evacuate his wounded. He concluded that only massive air strikes by American bombers could save the defenders. High French officials urged the Americans to intervene and to save them. The United States refused.

Giap ordered a series of assaults beginning May 1. Night and day the Vietminh soldiers attacked the French positions. They came in waves, unrelentingly. The French defenders, gallant to the end, fought hard, even heroically. They made the Vietminh pay dearly in blood and pain for their victory. On May 7, the Vietminh 308th broke through into the center of the French defenses. It was all over. On May 8, the French surrendered. They had lost about 7,500 men killed or wounded. About 10,000 French soldiers were marched off into captivity, over half of whom perished while prisoners-of-war. During the fifty-five-day battle, the Vietminh sustained an estimated 25,000 casualties.[65] But they had won a glorious victory, the most important one of the war. Asians had defeated Europeans in a large-scale pitched battle. They had also broken the spine of French military power in northern Vietnam. The next day the Indochina phase of the Geneva peace conference began.

As the delegates negotiated at Geneva, the war went on in Indochina. Pumped up by his great victory at Dien Bien Phu, the Viet Minh tiger, with teeth bared and looking for the kill, now went after the weary French elephant. The French withdrew to a restricted area around Hanoi and Haiphong. About 80 percent of the country was now under Vietminh control. They held nearly all of Tonkin, most of Annam, and half of Cochin China, including much of the rich Mekong delta. The French army battled for its life while the politicians talked at Geneva.

TO THE BRINK OF WAR

President Eisenhower and his energetic secretary of state, John Foster Dulles, assumed office in January 1953 committed to continuing the Truman-Acheson policies in Indochina. They shared their predecessors' assumptions and goals, believing that the fall of Indochina to the Communists would "cause the loss of all Southeast Asia with disastrous political, economic, and strategic consequences for the United States."[66]

The new administration followed a pattern that would become depressingly familiar throughout the years of the long U.S. involvement in Vietnam. They came to office accepting the necessity and importance of the U.S. stake in that country. They were confident that they could assert the leadership, avoid the mistakes, and develop the new initiatives required to salvage the deteriorating situation in that region. Each new administration soon discovered to its dismay that its options were limited and so was its power to influence the course of political events in Vietnam. Each administration also discovered that increasing commitments of American power and prestige, including a large-scale American war that raged in Vietnam for years, while raising U.S. costs and casualties, never empowered a succession of South Vietnamese governments to solve their serious political, economic, and social problems nor to cope with threats to their security posed by revolutionary insurgencies.

President Eisenhower initially tried to infuse the sagging French war effort in Indochina with new energy, to get the French to fight the Vietminh more aggressively. He tried to persuade them to grant the Bao Dai government greater powers so that it could become a genuine nationalistic alternative to Ho Chi Minh's movement, and Washington increased substantially the amount of military and economic aid going to the French.[67] General Navarre's ill-fated strategy derived from Eisenhower's exerting increased pressure on the French government to make another effort to win the war. He was disappointed to see that despite the increased American aid and his pep talks, the French military situation continued to deteriorate, and their effort to strengthen Bao Dai's regime foundered. The Vietminh retained the military initiative in Indochina and continued to add territory to its domain in Vietnam and eastern Laos.

Weary of a seemingly interminable war that they no longer had any realistic chance of winning despite the increased U.S. aid, the French government sought a compromise solution to the war. Premier Laniel, over American objections, got the Foreign Ministers' Council to place the Indochina War on the agenda of the upcoming Geneva peace conference. The reluctant Eisenhower administration acquiesced in the French decision to seek a political solution to the war. Like the Truman administration that preceded them, Eisenhower and Dulles discovered that they had little leverage with the French who still had not committed their forces to the European Defense Community. Too much pressure from Washington to fight harder in Vietnam and the French might then refuse to join the EDC, undermining European unity and playing into the hands of the Soviet Union. American officials also understood that French manpower commitments to the Indochina War significantly reduced the number of soldiers available for NATO assignments or the hoped for EDC.[68]

As General Giap tightened his grip on the French soldiers trapped at Dien Bien Phu, it become increasingly obvious to both the French and their American sponsors that the French were headed for a major defeat that could spell the end of the war for them. Washington, for the first time, confronted the possibility of direct U.S. military intervention into the Indochina War to try to save the French cause and to prevent the loss of Vietnam to the Communists. The French chief of staff, General Paul Ely, journeyed to Washington to request U.S. military intervention. The administration considered sending naval and air forces to Vietnam. Some U.S. officials even debated the feasibility of air attacks by using tactical nuclear weapons to break the Vietminh siege at Dien Bien Phu. Eisenhower ruled out the use of U.S. ground forces under any circumstances. With the bitter experiences of the stalemated Korean War that had only ended the previous year still fresh in the national memory, Eisenhower was not about to send ground troops to fight in Indochina.[69]

Eisenhower would not consider intervening in Vietnam unilaterally. He insisted that any intervention would have to be an international affair joined by America's European allies, mainly the British. Eisenhower also sought Congressional support for any action America might undertake in Vietnam. On April 3, 1954, Dulles met with the congressional leadership. Both Democrats and Republicans told him that without firm commitments from U.S. allies, especially the British, to join any proposed intervention, they, and by extension the American public, would not go along with it.[70] Since no international support had been forthcoming by this date, Congress, in effect, killed any possibility of a U.S. air attack to save Dien Bien Phu. The next day, Eisenhower rejected the French request.

For the next three weeks, while the battle for Dien Bien Phu went on, and the French approached disaster, the United States tried to enlist allied support for some form of united action in Vietnam. President Eisenhower wrote a long personal letter to his friend Prime Minister Winston Churchill urging him to join an allied coalition to block Communist expansion in Southeast Asia. Eisenhower also held a press conference on April 7 during which he emphasized the crucial geo-political stakes that the United States and the Free World had in the outcome of the Indochina War. He made two major arguments on behalf of Allied interests: First, he stressed that Indochina was a major source of raw materials such as tin and rubber. Second, he stated that if Indochina fell to the Communists, the rest of Southeast Asia would fall very quickly, like a "row of dominoes." Japan would be threatened; American strategic interests would be undermined: "So the possible consequences of the loss are just incalculable to the free world."[71]

Despite the pleas and pressures emanating from Washington, the British Foreign Secretary Anthony Eden, speaking for Churchill, rebuffed the U.S. request to join its crusade to prevent a Communist victory in Vietnam. The British did not share the American faith in the domino theory, and they had no desire to become involved in what they saw as a lost cause. They believed that the French were destined to lose their colonial war, and they had no desire to go down with them. The British also believed that outside military intervention on the eve of the Geneva conference would wreck any prospect for a negotiated settlement of the war and might provoke a Chinese intervention into Indochina.[72]

Even had some agreement for intervention been worked out between the British and the Americans, the terms on which Washington would consider intervening in April 1954 were unacceptable to the French. The United States was willing to try to save the French at Dien Bien Phu only if they would reject a negotiated settlement and agree to continue fighting to win the Indochina War. The French would also have to grant the Americans a greater role in conducting the war and in training Vietnamese forces. Further, the French would have to agree to Vietnamese demands for complete independence. The French rejected all these strings attached to the U.S. aid proposal.[73] They were apparently more willing to risk losing at Dien

Bien Phu and take their chances on obtaining an acceptable negotiated settlement at Geneva than accede to the American demands.

In late April, as the end approached at Dien Bien Phu, the French Foreign Minister Georges Bidault made a desperate eleventh-hour plea for a U.S. air strike to save the French. Unable to count on British or congressional support and unhappy with France's continuing refusal to accept the U.S. conditions for intervention, the administration again refused the French request. The French fate was sealed. On the afternoon of May 7, the Vietminh flag was hoisted over the French command bunker at Dien Bien Phu. The next morning, diplomats from nine nations gathered around a horseshoe-shaped table inside the old League of Nations building in Geneva to open discussions on the "Indochina problem."[74]

THE GENEVA SOLUTION

U.S. officials would have preferred that there be no political solution to the Indochina War; they wanted the French, with U.S. support, to continue fighting and ultimately defeat the DRV forces. Washington also feared that the French, given the war-weariness of the French people and the military and political momentum that the Vietminh had built up in Indochina, would accept a negotiated settlement that would lead to a Communist takeover of Vietnam, Laos, and Cambodia and open the floodgate of Communist expansion in Southeast Asia. The Eisenhower administration gave renewed consideration to a possible U.S. military intervention on the side of the French in the event the conference failed to produce an acceptable diplomatic solution to the war. Adding to American concerns, as the conference dragged on, the DRV armies kept pressure on the French forces and continued to extend their political and military control over the people and territory of Vietnam and Laos.

Nine delegations attended the Geneva conference. There were representatives from Laos, Cambodia, and two delegations from Vietnam, one representing Bao Dai's government and the other representing Ho Chi Minh's. France, of course, attended, as did the Americans, the Soviets, the British, and the Chinese. The Soviet Foreign Minister Vyacheslav Molotov and the British Foreign Secretary Anthony Eden served as co-chairs of the conference. The Americans, in the awkward position of attending a conference that they did not support and whose outcome they feared, played a relatively minor public role in the negotiations. Dulles rarely attended the sessions; the U.S. delegation was headed by Dulles' assistant, undersecretary Walter Bedell Smith. At one point, Chou En Lai, the head of the Chinese delegation, offered his hand to Dulles. Dulles, not wishing to recognize a regime that he loathed, refused to shake Chou's hand and turned away. Dulles' actions humiliated and infuriated the Chinese leader.

Negotiations at Geneva were dominated by the foreign policy concerns of the major powers who negotiated over the heads of the Vietnamese and imposed an agreement on them. Since they were winning the war and controlled most of the land and population of Vietnam, the DRV should have emerged from Geneva with agreements reflecting their strategic superiority. The Vietminh did not achieve political gains at the conference table commensurate with their military triumphs because such a resolution of the Franco-Vietminh war did not conform to the vital interests of the major powers.[75]

While the conference was in session, the United States used the threat of military intervention to strengthen France in relation to the DRV and to lessen Chinese and Soviet support for the Vietminh. Dulles was opposed to any agreement that took away territory from Cambodia, Laos, or Vietnam. He got the British to back the American position and tried to persuade the French to avoid making any settlement that would transfer territory to the Communists. But the French negotiated skillfully at Geneva, and they played the Soviets and the Americans off against each other. On the one hand, French officials threatened Washington with rejection of the proposed EDC, the top U.S. priority in Europe, if the United States insisted on their making unrealistic demands at the bargaining table that might torpedo the conference and prevent a political resolution of the conflict. On the other hand, the French held out to the Soviets the prospect of French rejection of the EDC, which the Soviets desired, if the Soviets could persuade the Vietminh to moderate their demands and to offer the French terms that they could accept. The Soviet leaders, also interested in moderating Cold War tensions and not having major interests in Southeast Asia, played a role in restraining DRV demands. China, fearful of U.S. intervention in the war if it went on much longer and the French position continued to deteriorate, and wanting to keep American military forces out of Indochina, also pressured the Vietminh to reach an agreement acceptable to the French. Gradually, the outlines of a settlement emerged from lengthy negotiating sessions based on the temporary partitioning of Vietnam to allow the regrouping of military forces following a cease fire.

Before an agreement could be fully worked out, Laniel's government fell. His place at Geneva was taken by Pierre Mendes-France, who had assumed office pledged to achieve a settlement by July 21 or resign. Mendes-France came to Geneva committed to disengaging France from the war as quickly and gracefully as possible.[76] There was movement toward a settlement based on partition. With an agreement in sight, the conference recessed for a few days.

At this point, the United States "made the most fundamental decision of its thirty-year involvement" in Vietnam.[77] Washington, seeing that a political resolution to the Franco-Vietminh war was imminent and that the Communists were going to gain control of part of Vietnam, decided to intervene directly. Washington planned to replace the French in Vietnam and to assume responsibility for the defense of Cambodia, Laos, and southern Vietnam in the aftermath of the French defeat. America would pick up the sword that the French were dropping. They would hold the line against further Communist expansion in that region. It was this decision made in the summer of 1954 that made possible the subsequent steps culminating in the American Vietnam War.

The conference resumed, and agreements were reached to end the war on July 19, 1954. A cease-fire was declared, and Vietnam was partitioned at the 17th parallel of north latitude. The agreements specified that the partition line was to be only a provisional military demarcation, "on either side of which the forces of the two parties shall be regrouped after their withdrawal."[78] The DRV forces were to regroup north of the line. Bao Dai's and the French forces were to regroup south of the line. The conferees made clear that they never intended the line to become a permanent political or territorial boundary. The Geneva accords did not create two states; they only created a temporary military division within a single state. To prevent further fighting, both sides were to have 300 days from the date the document was signed to make all force and personnel transfers to either side of the 17th parallel. People were encouraged to move if they wished. There were to be no reprisals against people for the side they had chosen or anything they had done during the war. Both halves of Vietnam were prohibited from entering into any military alliances, bringing in any new military forces, or developing additional military bases. As neither Vietnamese government would tolerate the permanent division of Vietnamese territory, the agreements provided for consultations between representatives of the two zones to begin within a year of the conference. These consultations were to lead to free elections within another year to be supervised by an International Control Commission made up of Poland, India, and Canada. Whichever government won the elections would govern a reunified Vietnam in 1956. The agreements also established cease-fires for Cambodia and Laos and declared these countries to be independent nations under their current governments.[79]

Washington was unhappy with the loss of northern Vietnam to the Communists and refused to be associated with the Geneva agreements. Walter Bedell Smith did not assent to them, observing only that the United States acknowledged their existence and would "refrain from the threat or use of force to disturb them,..."[80] Bao Dai's new premier, Ngo Dinh Diem, denounced the accords and also refused his assent. The war that had ended in defeat for the French was, by extension, also perceived as a serious setback for the United States.

But Eisenhower and Dulles were not entirely displeased with the outcome of the Geneva conference. It could have been much worse. They knew that their power politics, adroit French diplomacy, and Soviet and Chinese pressure had forced Ho to accept half a country at Geneva even though his armies controlled almost the entire country. They also saw that the provisions of the Geneva agreements partitioning Vietnam, permitting a temporary regroupment of forces and people, and calling for nationwide elections within two years to reunify the country amounted to a face-saving formula permitting the defeated French to make a delayed, more or less graceful exit from Indochina. Washington believed that within the two years allotted to them under the Geneva agreements they could work with the people in southern Vietnam and they could turn Bao Dai's government into a nation-state that would provide the people of Vietnam a genuine alternative to Communism. They also believed that they could effect arrangements that would protect the strategic security of Southeast Asia in the aftermath of the partial Communist victory in Vietnam and that would confine the spread of Communism to northern Vietnam.

Even before the Geneva conference had officially ended, the United States was pledging its support to the Bao Dai government and preparing to bend and to break some of the agreements.[81] It turned out that the Geneva accords did not produce a permanent political solution to the Indochina conflict, only a temporary military truce. The "conference was merely an interlude between two wars—or rather, a lull in the same war."[82]

LESSONS UNLEARNED

There is a kind of symmetry between the reactions of the Americans and the Vietminh to the outcome of the Geneva conference. Both came away disappointed, but at the same time both also perceived opportunities to exploit in the settlement and both hoped that the future would go their way. Ho Chi Minh had been willing to settle for only half of Vietnam at Geneva because he feared that the United States would intervene militarily if a reasonable settlement were not arranged. American military forces in Vietnam could impede Ho's planned scenario for Vietnam, so he wanted to keep them out. The Geneva accords kept the Americans out and also prepared the ground for the departure of the French. Only the discredited Bao Dai regime remained as Ho's political competition. He was confident that he could win the upcoming elections, and he looked ahead to governing a reunified Vietnam under Lao Dong control.[83] Neither side was aware of it at the time, but the Americans and the Vietminh had launched themselves on a collision course over who would control southern Vietnam after 1956.

The Communist forces were winning the Franco-Vietminh war at the time of the Geneva conference and had there been no diplomatic solution to the Franco-Vietminh conflict, the DRV forces, barring a major commitment of U.S. forces, would most likely have inflicted a total military defeat on the French within another year. The Eisenhower administration had a simplistic view of the outcome of the war. They thought that the French had lost for two reasons: They had lacked the determination and firepower to defeat the

DRV forces, even with substantial U.S. help. They were also an anachronistic colonial power trying to cling to the remnants of empire in Indochina and could not bring themselves to offer the Vietnamese a genuine nationalistic alternative to the Vietminh. Eisenhower and Dulles both believed that American intervention in southern Vietnam could succeed because the United States was a vastly richer and more powerful nation that was coming to help Bao Dai build a modern nation-state. American technology, know-how, and good intentions would work where the French efforts had failed.

Washington's diagnosis of the French defeat was partially correct. The French were losing in Indochina in part because they had never sent enough troops to give themselves a realistic chance to win the war and because most Vietnamese perceived the Bao Dai government to be only a cover for continuing French domination. But there were other, more important, factors that were determining the outcome of that war. We have to reorient our analysis and our frame of reference in order to understand what was happening to the French in Indochina in 1954. The proper question to ask was not why the French were losing, but why were the Vietminh winning? If we focus on the reasons why the Vietminh were winning the war, we necessarily have to look at the Vietnamese and what they were doing. What the Vietnamese accomplished in their country determined the outcome of the Franco-Vietminh war. The French, backed by the United States, were fighting a war that they could not realistically expect to win in 1954, even had they been willing to send more troops and to offer Bao Dai's government independence. By that late date, Indochina was no longer France's to lose; it had been lost by 1945.

Vietnam, during the years of the Franco-Vietminh war, was still a colonial society with many serious social and economic problems, all of which contributed to popular support for the revolutionaries. Inflation, high taxes, and usurious interest rates all bore heavily on the people of Vietnam, especially the rural poor. Government corruption and incompetence coupled to official indifference to the welfare of the rural population strengthened discontent and played into Vietminh hands.[84]

In addition to the indigenous social and economic conditions, the organizational strength of the revolutionaries played a crucial role in bringing them their ultimate success. The revolutionary political organization of the Vietminh and the extraordinary leadership of Ho Chi Minh were the decisive determinants. Even during the final years of the war, the party apparatus continued its organizing efforts both in the urban areas and in the villages of Vietnam. Most important, the party succeeded in retaining control of the nationalistic aspirations of most of the Vietnamese people regardless of their politics. Ho had a rare combination of talents: He was both a skilled organizer and a charismatic figure, a visionary who gave expression to the nationalistic aspirations of most Vietnamese. He was a combination of Lenin and Ghandi. The revolution's prime strength always was politics, not war.

Ho Chi Minh, Troung Chin, and Vo Nguyen Giap also perceived that in the long run the chief weakness of the French war effort in Vietnam was not that their soldiers could not fight effectively or that they were pursuing a colonial agenda, but that it was undermined by a psycho-political weakness, the declining public support in France for the Indochina war. Lack of popular support proved to be the French Achilles' heel. The loss of popular support for the war undermined the political will of a succession of French governments to conduct it vigorously and eventually forced them to the conference table where they negotiated agreements that provided for their departure from Indochina. Vietminh party leaders grasped the importance of this psycho-political factor and developed a sophisticated military, political, and diplomatic strategy to attack their enemy's will to fight.[85]

Years later, when the North Vietnamese and the National Liberation Front forces fought another war, this time against the American successors to the French and the Vietnamese successors to Bao Dai, they remembered the lessons that they had learned during the war with France: What the Vietnamese do and what happens in Vietnam are crucial to the outcome of the war. Be patient, they learned, and fight a protracted war. Exploit the social and economic conditions created by a series of corrupt, ineffective, and elite-based governments. Rely on party organization and political discipline. Retain the voice of Vietnamese nationalism. Use strategies designed to undermine popular support and to erode the political will of the foreign government to continue the war. These strategies enabled the Communists to defeat the French. They also used the same strategies to defeat the Americans twenty years later.

The American war in Vietnam fought between 1965 and 1973 largely replicated the French war. There were, of course, differences between the two conflicts; there was no American equivalent of Dien Bien Phu. Americans made much greater use of helicopters and employed vastly greater airpower. The Americans also used military force on a much larger scale than the French. But the similarities between the two wars were quite remarkable and significant. Their duration and outcomes were similar. Both began with high hopes and ended in disaster for the Western powers and in victories for the Asian Communists. Both the Americans and the French tried to use their technological superiority, which gave them greater firepower, mobility, and control of the air to win their wars of attrition. They found that these advantages were not sufficient to defeat the complex politico-military strategies employed by their enemies. Neither the French nor the Americans ever succeeded in creating stable governments that offered the Vietnamese people a viable alternative to the Communists. Both never developed pacification strategies that effectively neutralized the efforts of insurgent political cadres to maintain support among the rural population. Neither nation ever developed ARVN forces strong enough to defend themselves against the Communist forces that were receiving support from China and the Soviet Union.

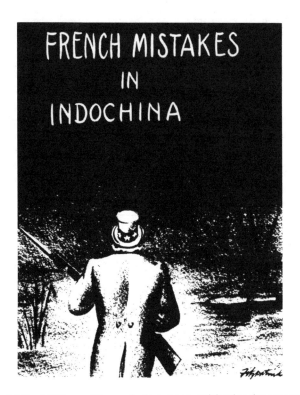

Editorial cartoonist Daniel Fitzgerald's prophetic cartoon anticipating the outcome of the American Vietnam intervention. Uncle Sam marches into the heart of darkness to replicate the French disaster.
Source: St. Louis *Post Dispatch*

Both only used Vietnamese forces extensively after domestic public support for the wars had seriously eroded. "The areas that caused the most problems for the French in South Vietnam were also the worst trouble spots for the Americans."[86]

The French and Americans were eventually defeated and were forced to negotiate agreements that provided for their withdrawal from Vietnam mainly because the long-running wars had become unpopular among their home populations and had eroded the wills of their governments to continue them. During both wars, the Vietnamese revolutionaries, sensing that the loss of popular support was the fatal weakness that would eventually undermine both the French and the American war efforts, patiently and skillfully employed a variety of political, military, and diplomatic strategies that promoted war weariness on the Western home fronts.

Many French and American war veterans felt that they had made sacrifices in vain. They had fought well in a losing war and had returned home to civilian populations who did not understand or appreciate what the soldiers had done: They returned to encounter civilian populations who had lost faith in the war and ignored them, or worse, condemned them. The long, losing wars also had devastating impacts on national morale and national prestige in both countries and drained both countries of significant amounts of their wealth.

Eisenhower and Dulles, and their successors, enmeshed in the ideology of containment and its domino correlatives, responding to the political imperatives of domestic anti-Communism, never understood nor heeded the lessons of the Franco-Vietminh war. American leaders, heedless of history, contemptuously indifferent to the French analogue, would in time duplicate their disaster.

NOTES

1. Kahin, *Intervention*, p. 9.
2. Doyle, Edward; Lipsman, Samuel; and others, *Passing the Torch*, (Boston: Boston Publishing Co., 1981), pp. 16–17; Isaacs, Harold, *No Peace for Asia* (New York: MacMillan, 1947), pp. 152–175. Isaacs was an American journalist in Saigon who wrote a first-hand account of Anglo-French cooperation in the South in 1945–1946 to suppress the Vietnamese nationalist revolution. He also documented the Anglo-French use of Japanese troops against the Vietnamese.
3. Dunn, Peter M., *The First Vietnam War* (New York: St. Martin's, 1985). Dunn has written a history of the complex political and military conflict in Vietnam during the first year after World War II that he states made up a "First Vietnam War." According to Dunn, the French–Vietnamese conflict, 1946–1954, was the "Second Vietnam War," and the war waged between U.S./ARVN forces and the NLF/PAVN forces, 1965–1973, was the "Third Vietnam War."
4. Quoted in Pettit, *The Experts* , p. 11.
5. "Jacques Phillipe Leclerc," second only to De Gaulle himself as a war hero in France, was the assumed name of Jean de Hautecloque. His true identity was known only to a few. The scion of an aristocratic family, de Hautecloque had escaped from France when the Nazis occupied his country. He fled to North Africa where he raised the first Free French Army. His African troops spearheaded the French efforts in the liberation of Paris. De Hautecloque had changed his name to protect his wealthy family from Nazi reprisals.
6. Buttinger, *A Dragon Defiant*, p. 81; O'Ballance, Edgar, *The Indo-China War, War, 1945–1954* (London, Faber and Faber, 1964), pp. 59–60. Ho replaced Giau in early 1946 with Nguyen Binh, who was assigned responsibility for fighting a guerrilla war in southern Vietnam against the French.
7. Hammer, *Struggle*, pp. 135–140; Chen, *Vietnam and China*, pp. 120–129. McAlister, John T., Jr., *Vietnam: The Origins of Revolution* (New York: Knopf, 1969)
8. Doyle, *Passing the Torch*, pp. 18–20; Duiker, *The Communist Road to Power*, pp. 114–118.
9. Kahin, *Intervention*, p. 19.
10. In defense of his strategy of accepting the return of the French for a few years to get the Chinese out of Vietnam, Ho berated a group of VNQDD leaders, who wanted to keep the Chinese in Vietnam in order to keep the French out: "You

fools! Don't you realize what it means if the Chinese stay? Don't you remember your history? The last time the Chinese came, they stayed one thousand years! As for me, I prefer to smell French shit for five years rather than Chinese shit for the rest of my life." Quoted in Doyle, *Passing the Torch*, p. 21.

11. A copy of the Preliminary Franco–Vietnamese Convention of March 6, 1946, is printed in Porter (ed.), *Vietnam Documents*, vol. 1, pp. 95–97, Document 59; Sainteny, Jean, *Histoire d'une Paix Manquee* (Paris: Amoit Dumont, 1953) is an insider's account of French Indochina policy in 1945–46; and Chen, *Vietnam and China*, pp. 146–150; Chen observes that the 1946 period was the most difficult time for Ho. He had to maneuver among the French, Chinese, and domestic opponents with great skill and delicacy of touch to survive. The most comprehensive account of the negotiations leading to the March 6 agreement is found in Devillers, *Histoire du Vietnam*, chaps. 11–13.

12. Between August and October 1945, Ho Chi Minh wrote seven letters to U.S. leaders appealing for support for Vietnamese independence. He used moral, legal, political, and economic arguments to try to persuade President Truman and Secretary of State Byrnes to support his cause. In one letter, Ho even proposed that Vietnam be placed on the same status as the Philippines, that is, he asked that Vietnam be allowed to become an American territory. Because America did not recognize Ho as the head of a legitimate government, all the letters were ignored. Gradually, Ho and the Vietminh lost faith in the U.S. commitment to Asian nationalism and realized that America supported French efforts to reimpose colonialism on Vietnam. Copies of several of Ho's letters are printed in Porter (ed.), *Vietnam Documents*, vol. 1, pp. 83–86, 95.

13. Quoted in Doyle, *Passing the Torch*, p. 23.

14. Hammer, *Struggle*, pp. 159–174.

15. O'Ballance, *The Indo-China War*, p. 75.

16. Kahin, *Intervention*, pp. 23–24; Hammer, *Struggle*, pp. 181–191.

17. Doyle, *Passing the Torch*, p. 26.

18. Duiker, *The Communist Road*, p. 127.

19. *Ibid.*, pp. 128–131; O'Ballance, *The Indo-China War*, pp. 74–85. The Vietminh military treatise was written by Troung Chinh, the leading Vietminh theoretician and ideologist, who, in later years, was closely identified with the pro-Chinese faction within Hanoi's ruling circle. Troung Chinh borrowed much of his doctrine from Mao's book, *On Protracted War*.

20. O'Ballance, *The Indo-China War*, pp. 79–80.

21. Duiker, *The Communist Road*, pp. 131–132.

22. *Ibid.*, p. 133.

23. Vo Nguyen Giap, "Activate Guerrilla Warfare," a directive issued by Giap November 17, 1947, printed in Porter (ed.), *Vietnam Documents*, vol. 1, Document 113, pp. 169–171.

24. Duiker, *The Communist Road*, p. 136.

25. Hammer, *Struggle*, pp. 224–228; Kahin, *Intervention*, pp. 25–26. About the only people supporting Bao Dai's government were some wealthy landowners and businessmen, some Catholics, and some of the religious sectarians. No prominent nationalists of any stripe signed on.

26. Kahin, *Intervention*, pp. 28–33.

27. Duiker, *The Communist Road*, pp. 139–140.

28. Shaplen, Robert, *The Lost Revolution: The U.S. in Vietnam, 1946–1966*, rev. ed., (New York: Harper & Row, 1966), pp. 69–75; see the Platform of the Vietnam Worker's Party, February 19, 1951: "The primordial task of the Vietnam revolution, therefore, is to drive out the imperialist aggressors to gain complete independence and unity for the people,...and root up the vestiges of feudalism and semifeudalism so that there is land for those who till it, to develop the People's Democratic Regime, and to lay the foundations for socialism." A copy of the platform is printed in Porter (ed.), *Vietnam Documents*, vol. 1, Document 212, pp. 337–344.

29. O'Ballance, *The Indo-China War*, pp. 104–105.

30. *Ibid.*, pp. 106–107.

31. *Ibid.*, pp. 114–115.

32. *Ibid.*, pp. 116–117. Of the border campaigns, the worst individual disaster for the French forces occurred following their loss of Dong Khe. They decided to evacuate an outpost on a ridge near Cao Bang. Giap used six infantry battalions to ambush the Cao Bang column, battering 4,000 soldiers and forcing them into headlong retreat. Bodard, Lucien, *The Quicksand War: Prelude to Vietnam* (Boston: Little, Brown, 1967), translated from the French, *La Guerre d'Indochine: L'enlisement* (Paris: Gallimard, 1963) and *La Guerre d'Indochine: L'humiliation* (Paris, Gallimard, 1965) has an account of the battle.

33. Duiker, *The Communist Road*, pp. 144–145.

34. National revolutions were occurring in Burma, Malaya, and Indonesia at the same time the Vietnamese were fighting the French.

35. Telegram from Secretary of State Acheson to the U.S. Consulate in Hanoi, May 20, 1949. A copy is printed in Porter (ed.), *Vietnam Documents*, vol. 1, Document 131, pp. 198–199. Acheson commented on Soviet recognition of the DRV in a State Deparment bulletin issued February 13, 1950, in which he said; "The recognition by the Kremlin of Ho Chi Minh's Communist movement...should remove any illusions as to the 'nationalist' nature of Ho Chi Minh's aims and reveals Ho in his true colors as the mortal enemy of native independence in Indochina." The U.S. Department of State *Bulletin*, 22 (February 13, 1950) is also printed in Porter, Document 156, p. 225.

36. Department of State Policy Statement, September 27, 1948. This is the first full-length statement of U.S. Indochina policy. It is significant for its revelations of American unhappiness with all possible outcomes of the war and American frustration at finding itself with neither any leverage to influence an outcome nor having any practical solution to impose if it could. A copy of this policy statement is found in Porter (ed.), *Vietnam Documents*, vol. 1, pp. 178–181, Document 121.

37. Kahin, *Intervention*, pp. 36–37. Between 1946 and 1949, America provided indirect, covert, and extensive financial and military assistance via metropolitan France for the French colonial war in Indochina. This aid remained hidden to avoid public criticism of both its purpose and cost.

38. *Ibid.*, pp. 37–38. Kahin has found evidence suggesting that of the $525 million in U.S. aid to support the French budget in fiscal 1953, almost half came from ECA counterpart funds released for the use of the French military in Indochina.

39. On March 12, 1947, President Truman appeared before Congress to give his most famous and successful speech that called for enactment of an aid package for Greece and Turkey. The substance of his address has become known as the Truman Doctrine, and it announced the first application of the developing U.S. policy of containment of Communism in southern Europe and the rationale for

such a policy. The speech amounts to a declaration of idelogical warfare against the Soviet Union and is one of the opening salvos of the Cold War.

40. Herring, *America's Longest War*, p. 12.
41. Kahin, *Intervention*, p. 29; Hess, Gary, *The United States' Emergence as a Southeast Asia Power, 1940–1950* (New York: Columbia University Press, 1987).
42. *Ibid.*, pp. 29–30.
43. *Ibid.*, p. 30.
44. Gardner, *Approaching Vietnam*, pp. 80–86.
45. Herring, *America's Longest War*, p. 15.
46. Shaplen, *Lost Revolution*, pp. 57–69. What Bao Dai said was "What they call a Bao Dai solution turned out to be just a French solution. The situation in Indochina is getting worse everyday."
47. Morrocco, John, and the editors of the Boston Publishing Co., *Thunder from Above: Air War, 1941–1968* (Boston: Boston Publishing Co., 1984), a volume in *The Vietnam Experience* series. In the summer of 1950, Congress authorized $164 million for arms, ammunition, planes, ships, trucks, jeeps, and tanks for the French war effort in Indochina. At about the same time, the U.S. economic and technical assistance program for the Bao Dai government committed $50 million over a two-year period. The first U.S. military advisers arrived in Vietnam in August 1950. The first U.S. military aid arrived in September: eight C-47s.
48. *Ibid.*, pp. 21–22.
49. Shaplen, *Lost Revolution*, pp. 87–91.
50. Duiker, *The Communist Road*, p. 146.
51. O'Ballance, *The Indo-China War*, pp. 120–139. The two DRV divisions that fought in the Battle of Vinh Yeh were the 308th and the 324th. Both were infantry divisions equipped with Chinese weapons.
52. Duiker, *The Communist Road*, his note on p. 355.
53. My account of the Battle of Hoa Binh is taken from O'Ballance, *The Indo-China War*, pp. 159–168.
54. Duiker, *The Communist Road*, pp. 152–153.
55. *Ibid.*, p. 154.
56. Duiker, *The Communist Road*, pp. 154–155; Kahin, *Intervention*, p. 39. At the time of the Battle of Dien Bien Phu, total French forces in Indochina numbered about 500,000. Only about 80,000 of them were French, over half of whom were non-commissioned and commissioned officers. The French did not send conscripts to fight in their Indochina colonial war. The rest of the French Indochina Expeditionary Force was made of French Foreign Legion forces, French North African troops, Indochinese, predominantly Vietnamese, troops, and Bao Dai's inchoate Vietnamese National Army (ARVN).
57. "Report by Ho Chi Minh of the Fourth Conference of the Party Central Committee," January 25–30, 1953 (extract). Printed in Porter (ed.), *Vietnam Documents*, vol. 1, Document 251, pp. 422–423.
58. O'Ballance, *The Indo-China War*, pp. 208–209.
59. Porter (ed.), *Vietnam Documents*, vol. 1, Document 292, "Speech by Premier Laniel Before the National Assembly," March 5, 1954, (Extracts), pp. 495–497.
60. *Ibid.*, "Report by Giap to Senior Field Commanders on the Dienbienphu Campaign," January 14, 1954 (Extract), Document 292, pp. 493–494.

61. *Ibid.* "Appeal by Vo Nguyen Giap to All Cadres and Fighters, Units and Services, on Beginning the Dienbienphu Campaign," March 1954, Document 295, pp. 497–498.

62. O'Ballance, *Indo-China War*, pp. 218, 225, and 230; Fall, Bernard, *Hell in a Very Small Place: The Siege of Dien Bien Phu* (New York: Lippincott, 1967), pp. 177–180.

63. O'Ballance, *Indo-China War*, pp, 213–217. Another 4,000 to 5,000 troops parachuted into Dien Bien Phu during the battle to join the defenders.

64. *Ibid.*, p. 224; Giap's porters had hauled in U.S.-made 105-mm. howitzers that the Chinese had given him. These artillery were larger than most of the French guns. The Chinese Communists had captured these American guns from the defeated Chinese Nationalist forces during their civil war in the late-1940s.

65. Duiker, *The Communist Road*, p. 162; there is a fine account of the Battle of Dien Bien Phu in Doyle, *Passing the Torch*, pp. 62–85. Of the 18,000 defenders of Dien Bien Phu, fewer than half were French. The others included Legionnaires, mainly Germans, Africans, and over 6,000 loyal Vietnamese.

66. Herring, *America's Longest War*, p. 25.

67. Kahin, *Intervention*, p. 42. In fiscal 1953, the Eisenhower administration spent $1.3 billion, 61 percent of the total cost of the war for that year. For 1954, America financed 78 percent of the total cost. The total cost to Americans for supporting the French colonial war in Indochina from 1950 to 1954 came to over $2.8 billion. Tuchman, *March of Folly*, p. 257, states that most of the U.S. aid money "trickled away into the pockets of profiteering officials."

68. Herring, *America's Longest War*, p. 29.

69. The most thorough exploration of Eisenhower's decision not to intervene in Vietnam at the time of the Dien Bien Phu crises is George C. Herring and Richard H. Immerman, "Eisenhower, Dulles, and Dienbienphu: 'The Day We Didn't Go to War'" Revisited," *Journal of American History*, vol. 71 (September, 1984), pp. 343–363; see also Kahin, *Intervention*, pp. 45–46. General Matthew Ridgway, Army chief of staff and the man whose leadership stopped the Chinese advance in Korea and saved the UN expeditionary force from possible defeat and expulsion, strongly advised Eisenhower against putting U.S. ground troops into Indochina.

70. Kahin, *Intervention*, p. 48.

71. Herring, *America's Longest War*, pp. 34–35.

72. Porter, (ed.), *Vietnam Documents*, vol. 1, Document 315, "Telegram from Dulles in Geneva to the State Department," April 25, 1954 in, pp. 542–543.

73. Herring, *America's Longest War*, p. 35. It is not true, as has sometimes been written, that the United States offered the beleaguered French the use of two nuclear weapons in the spring of 1954 in order to save Dien Bien Phu.

74. Karnow, Stanley, *Vietnam: A History* (New York: Viking Press, 1983), p. 198.

75. Kahin, *Intervention*, pp. 52–53.

76. Kahin and Lewis, *The United States in Vietnam*, p. 43.

77. Kahin, *Intervention*, p. 66.

78. "Agreement on the Cessation of Hostilities in Vietnam," July 20, 1954, in Porter, (ed.), *Vietnam Documents*, vol. 1, Document 378, p. 642.

79. *Ibid.*, pp. 642–652; also see "The Final Declaration of the Geneva Conference on the Problem of Restoring Peace in Indochina," July 1954, Document 380, pp. 654–655. The Geneva Accords constitute two distinct, related agreements: (1) A bilateral armistice agreement signed on July 20, 1954 by Brigadier General Henri Delteil on behalf of the French forces fighting in Indochina and by Ta Quang

Buu on behalf of the People's Army of Vietnam that partitioned the country into two temporary regroupment zones. (2) A Final Declaration issued on July 21. It was endorsed by oral assent by all but Walter Bedell Smith representing the United States and Bao Dai's representative who both refused to give their approval. Its key provisions include Chapter 6, which states that "the military demarcation line is provisional and should not in any way be interpreted as constituting a political or territorial boundary," and Chapter 7, which spells out the terms for preparing for and holding elections in order to reunify Vietnam in 1956.

80. *Ibid.*, "Declaration by Walter Bedell Smith, Representing the U.S. Delegation to the Geneva Conference," July 21, 1954, Document 381, p. 656.

81. Kahin and Lewis, *The United States in Vietnam*, pp. 59–62.

82. Karnow, *Vietnam*, p. 199.

83. Duiker, *The Communist Road*, pp. 163–164; Kahin and Lewis, *The United States in Vietnam*, p. 47. The Vietminh would never have accepted partition without guarantees of elections within two years to reunify Vietnam being written into the agreements.

84. Duiker, *The Communist Road*, pp. 166–167.

85. *Ibid.*, p. 168.

86. Thayer, Thomas C., *War without Fronts: The American Experience in Vietnam* (Boulder, Colo.: Westview, 1985); also see Dunn, Peter M., "The American Army: The Vietnam War, 1965–1973" in Beckett, Ian F. W., and Pimlott, John, eds., *Armed Forces and Modern Counter-Insurgency* (London: Croom Helm, 1985), pp. 80–81, 85. Dunn faults the Americans for not seeking the advice of the French or to absorb "their bitterly-learned lessons." The U.S. Army "became, in effect, a large French Expeditionary Corps—and met the same frustrations."

AMERICA'S MANDARIN

3

Premier Diem is the Churchill of Asia....History may yet adjudge Diem as one of the great figures of the twentieth century.

Lyndon Johnson

DIEM TAKES CHARGE IN THE SOUTH

During the summer of 1954, the Eisenhower administration firmly committed itself to creating a new nation in the southern half of Vietnam in order to block further Communist expansion in Southeast Asia. The National Security Council (NSC), meeting a month after the Geneva conference that had worked out the political settlement ending the Franco–Vietminh war, interpreted the Geneva agreements as a serious setback for the United States and a major victory for the Communists that gave them a salient for applying pressure to the nations of Southeast Asia. The NSC report called for the United States to negotiate new international agreements in order to provide strategic security for the new country that they were going to create in southern Vietnam, and to protect Laos, Cambodia, Thailand, Burma, and the other nations of Southeast Asia.[1] To fulfill the policy recommendations of the NSC review, Secretary of State Dulles orchestrated the Southeast Asia Treaty Organization (SEATO).

The new security arrangements were embodied in the Pact of Manila signed September 8, 1954. SEATO created a loosely constructed alliance including the United States, Great Britain, France, Australia, New Zealand, and three Southeast Asian nations (the Philippines, Thailand, and Pakistan). Dulles, by attaching a protocol to the SEATO agreement that projected an umbrella of protection over Laos, Cambodia, and southern Vietnam, circumvented the provisions of the Geneva Accords, which had tried to neutralize Indochina.[2] Cambodia promptly repudiated the SEATO protocol, and Laos was later excluded by treaty. But the French and Bao Dai accepted the protection offered by SEATO for the temporary military regroupment zone south of the 17th parallel created at Geneva, which the protocol referred to as "the free territory under the jurisdiction of the State of Vietnam."[3]

Washington viewed SEATO as a defensive alliance erected to block Chinese expansion in Southeast Asia and also to thwart a possible invasion of southern Vietnam across the 17th parallel by the Hanoi regime. But the new treaty organization never proved effective as a collective security arrangement. It lacked military muscle; it only called for its members to consult with one another in the event of an attack on a signatory or one of the Indochina countries covered by the protocol. Unlike NATO, SEATO was never a military alliance requiring a collective military response to aggression. Dulles, aware of SEATO's strategic weakness, hoped that it could nevertheless function as a deterrent to Communist aggression in Southeast Asia. SEATO did help to promote the diplomatic fictions, which the United States was proclaiming, that the southern half of Vietnam had quickly evolved from a temporary administrative zone into a free and independent state and that the 17th parallel had just as quickly metamorphosed from a transient demarcation line into a permanent political boundary. SEATO was also useful in later years because the Indochina protocol furnished a legal justification for American intervention into Vietnam to deter North Vietnamese aggression against South Vietnam.[4]

The man Washington selected in the summer of 1954 to head the new state that they planned to create in southern Vietnam was a staunch Vietnamese nationalist, Ngo Dinh Diem. The new leader was born near the imperial city of Hue on January 3, 1901, one of nine children of Ngo Dinh Kha. Kha was a wealthy man and had risen to be court chamberlain and keeper of the eunuchs to Emperor Thanh Thai. The Ngos were Catholics, and even as a boy Diem stood out for his unusual piety and devotion to religious duties. For a time he considered becoming a priest. He later changed his mind and gave up an opportunity to study in France. He attended Quoc Hoc lycee in Hue, the same school that Ho Chi Minh, another mandarin's son, had attended ten years earlier. Graduating at sixteen, Diem enrolled in the French-run School for Law and Administration in Hanoi where he performed brilliantly, graduating at the top of his class. Following graduation, Diem moved immediately into government service. Within a few years, Diem had reached mandarinic rank and was the provincial chief of a district containing 300 villages.[5]

An ardent Vietnamese patriot, Diem early demonstrated an abiding hatred of the French for their domination of his country and of the Communists whom he regarded as enemies of Vietnamese nationalism. In 1932 the young emperor, Bao Dai, aware of Diem's energy and administrative talents, appointed him Minister of the Interior. Diem eagerly threw himself into his new job. He proposed a long list of reforms to modernize the ministry and to give it real authority. Neither Bao Dai nor his French masters would accept the reforms, and Diem, angry and disillusioned, resigned.[6] He never held another government position until he became premier under American auspices in 1954.

Scholarly and reclusive by nature, Diem lived in his father's village near Hue. He refused all offers from the Japanese, the Vietminh, and Bao Dai to participate in various governments that were formed after World War II. Once he was captured by Vietminh guerrillas who took him to Ho Chi Minh. Ho offered Diem a position in his government, which he declined with the explanation that a Vietminh guerrilla had murdered his older brother. When the French set up Bao Dai's puppet government in 1949, Diem urged the emperor to ask the French for greater autonomy; Diem was disappointed when Bao Dai declined to do so.[7]

In 1951, Diem came to America and lived for two years at a Maryknoll seminary in Lakehurst, New Jersey. From that base, he traveled around the country campaigning for Vietnam's independence. He attracted the support of prominent Americans including Francis Cardinal Spellman, the leading spokesman for American Catholics. Through Cardinal Spellman he met Democratic Senators John Kennedy and Mike Mansfield, and Supreme Court Associate Justice William O. Douglas.[8] In the summer of 1954, when it appeared that France would lose the Indochina War and the Communists might take over Vietnam, Washington decided to intervene to replace the French and to try to save the south. American officials looked around for a leader of southern Vietnam whom they could back. They wanted no part of Bao Dai, the titular head of the French-backed regime in Saigon, who preferred living on the Riviera with his mistress to residing in Saigon. Dulles had become aware of Diem, thanks to the efforts of Diem's lobby of prominent supporters. Diem's administrative experience, his staunch patriotism, and his anti-Communism appealed to the Americans. Bao Dai appointed him premier in June.[9]

Upon arriving in Saigon June 25, 1954, Diem discovered that the government he had inherited from the French rested on an inefficient and corrupt bureaucracy, a demoralized army whose fighting prowess and loyalty to him were both questionable, and a fragmented capital city seething with a bizarre amalgam of fierce political rivalries. Local military and political leaders conspired with the French and Bao Dai to ensure an early demise to Diem's fledgling administration. Compounding his troubles, the Geneva agreements, promulgated on July 21, called for nationwide elections to unify the country within two years. Ho Chi Minh and the Lao Dong were odds-on favorites to win these forthcoming elections and to take over the whole country.

Throughout the fall and winter of 1954 and 1955, Diem was caught in the midst of a bitter conflict between the French and Americans for influence in southern Vietnam. The French and American partnership in Indochina had always been riven with tension, mutual suspicion, and resentment. The French bitterly observed that the United States was trying to supplant them in southern Vietnam. Their charges were confirmed when Eisenhower wrote Diem a letter on October 23, 1954, pledging U.S. economic and military assistance.[10] When the French delayed turning over full powers of governance to Diem until December, American officials suspected that the French were trying to hang on in the South and also build bridges to the Hanoi regime in order to protect extensive French investments in the country. American officials also knew that the French were encouraging Diem's political rivals and were trying to undermine Diem because he was strongly pro-American and anti-French. Franco–American Vietnamese disputes were exacerbated by the French rejection of the American plan for a European Defense Community a month after Geneva.[11]

American backing enabled Diem to eventually overcome all his political foes. Key support came from an American Central Intelligence Agency (CIA) group headed by Air Force Colonel Edward G. Landsdale, a legendary and controversial figure during the long U.S. involvement in Vietnam. Colonel Landsdale quickly became a close friend and trusted adviser to Ngo Dinh Diem. Landsdale and General J. Lawton "Lightning Joe" Collins, Eisenhower's special envoy to Vietnam, foiled a military coup headed by dissident Army Chief of Staff General Nguyen van Hinh, who plotted to overthrow Diem in the fall of 1954. They saved Diem by informing Hinh's backers that if the coup went forward, the United States would cut off all funding for the Vietnamese army.[12]

American support also helped Diem cope with a massive influx of refugees who fled northern Vietnam in the fall of 1954 following the Communist takeover. About 800,000 civilians, 600,000 of them Catholics, moved south of the 17th parallel under the provisions of the Geneva accords permitting free movement between regroupment zones. The Catholic emigrants were mostly peasants who fled their villages in the districts of Phat Diem and Bui Chi in the Red River delta south of Haiphong. Whole parishes under the leadership of parish priests left the North. Diem's officials settled them in villages in southern Vietnam in the vicinity of Saigon and in areas of the central highlands that were regarded as strategically significant.[13]

General Joseph Lawton "Lightning Joe" Collins, President Eisenhower's personal representative to the South Vietnamese government, greets Ngo Dinh Diem in March 1955.
Source: National Archives

Even though many of these Catholic peasants were uncertain and fearful about life under the Communists and voted with their feet, the mass migration south was not an entirely spontaneous folk movement. The Catholic Church, American and French officials, and the Diem administration all promoted the migration. The Catholic migrants were urged to come south, both to form a base of support for the Diem government and to serve as compelling symbols of the Cold War. The mass migration of northern Catholics received extensive media coverage in America. American officials and journalists depicted the migrants as pitiable refugees fleeing Communist tyranny for the freedom and religious tolerance they would find in southern Vietnam. To spur the migration along, Landsdale's CIA agents used propaganda and psychological warfare operations to induce reluctant villagers to flee North Vietnam.[14] The United States played a major role in transporting the people south. U.S. naval ships hauled hundreds of thousands of these northerners, and private American religious and charitable agencies helped the migrants.

The migrants more than doubled the South Vietnamese Catholic population which, augmented by the newcomers, totaled about 10 percent of the southern population by 1955. These northern Catholics became an important part of Diem's political base. In return, they generally enjoyed a privileged status under his rule. Native southern villagers often resented these new-comers from North Vietnam, regarding them in much the same manner as native white southerners had regarded the northern carpetbaggers who had come south after the American Civil War to live and work.[15]

Diem's government nearly fell in the spring of 1955 when he challenged two powerful religious sects and also confronted the Binh Xuyen, the crime lords of Saigon and Cholon. The Cao Dai and the Hoa Hao claimed millions of followers; both had their own private armies and exercised political control over large areas of southern Vietnam. The Cao Dai strongholds were in the Mekong delta, and the Hoa Hao dominated a region northwest of Saigon. Long accustomed to autonomy under the French, they refused to submit to the authority of Diem's new national government. After all parties failed to nego-tiate an acceptable political compromise, the sects, with French support, joined forces with the Binh Xuyen in March 1955. Together they attacked Diem's struggling government.[16] The political demise of Diem appeared to be nigh.

Open war raged in the streets of Saigon. General Collins, who had been skeptical of Diem's abilities for months, flew to Washington to tell Eisen-hower that Diem was finished, that he lacked the requisite qualities of leadership to prevent a Communist takeover of southern Vietnam, and that he had been beaten by a cabal of religious sectarians, gangsters, and French officials. Eisenhower accepted Collins's judgment and prepared to with-draw U.S. backing for Diem. While Collins was en route back to Vietnam to inform Diem that he no longer had American support, Diem, with Landsdale's support, took the actions that saved his government and re-tained U.S. backing. Landsdale bribed the leaders of the Cao Dai to join Diem, and most of their forces were integrated into Diem's army. Landsdale also used bribe money to induce most of the Hoa Hao soldiers to either join Diem or to remain neutral. Diem then ordered his army to attack Binh Xuyen forces that were assaulting the presidential palace. Several American mili-tary advisers supported Diem's troops who routed the gangster-warriors. With Landsdale's help, Diem had overcome his political enemies and out-maneuvered the French.[17] Even though many blocks of the city lay in ruins, Diem was master of Saigon and now controlled his army, which had been augmented by the addition of thousands of sectarian troops. Diem had come back from the edge of disaster to find himself a hero in American eyes. Colonel Landsdale was midwife to the birth of South Vietnam; he was one of the prime creators of the new state.

Eisenhower shelved his plan to replace Diem, and he and Dulles re-em-braced the determined leader as the only man who could create the new U.S.-sponsored state in southern Vietnam. In the aftermath of Diem's crush-ing of his opponents and securing power, the French abandoned whatever remained of their hopes to retain influence in the South and made prepara-tions to leave. By March 1956, the last French soldiers and civilian officials would depart Saigon, ending nearly 100 years of French colonial rule.

Diem, having vanquished his foes and shaken free of lingering French influence, confident of the strong backing of the United States, now moved to eliminate Bao Dai, who was still the nominal head of the emerging South Vietnamese state. While the emperor remained in France, Diem arranged a referendum in which people could vote either for Bao Dai or for Ngo Dinh Diem as head of state. Even though Diem would surely have beaten Bao Dai in a fair election, he took no chances. His henchmen rigged the election to assure an overwhelming mandate for himself. Before the vote was held, Diem mounted a propaganda campaign against Bao Dai through the government-controlled press and radio. The referendum was held on October 23, 1955. Diem's soldiers supervised the polling places, and Diem's officials counted the ballots. Diem was urged by his U.S. advisers to settle for a 60 percent majority. But Diem wanted more, and his enthusiastic election managers obliged him. Some districts tallied more votes for Diem than there were voters. The Saigon-Cholon area, with 450,000 registered voters, cast 605,025 votes for Diem. At the end of the day, Diem announced that he had won, with 98.2 percent of the vote.[18] The political career of Bao Dai, Vietnam's last emperor, was at an end. A vote of the people had made Diem sole head of the South Vietnamese government.

As he consolidated his authority, Diem could rely on the political support of four main groups: (1) the sizeable Catholic population, now more than doubled in size by the addition of the northern exiles; (2) a small but influential class of wealthy planters; (3) the Vietnamese serving in the government bureaucracies, the police, and in the armed forces; and (4) a new urban middle class created by the massive flow of U.S. funds to South Vietnam. For twenty years, U.S. economic assistance maintained Diem's regime and all its successor regimes. It allowed a generation of enterprising southerners to enjoy a life style that could not be supported by the indigenous economy and one that quickly collapsed in 1975 when the great American money spigot was shut off. The members of this new class fully understood that their affluence was absolutely dependent on the American pipeline, which would continue to pump money into South Vietnam only so long as the United States backed whatever government happened to be in power in Saigon. Aware of these political and economic realities, most of the new Vietnamese bourgeoisie unfailingly backed Saigon, regardless of who ruled, and its American connection.[19]

The major component of the American economic aid program to South Vietnam was embodied in the Commodity Import Program (CIP). The CIP began in January 1955. Originally designed to absorb purchasing power to hold down inflation that would have been ignited by the rapid injection of large sums of money into the relatively small Vietnamese economy, the CIP also enabled the United States to fund the cost of Diem's army, police, and civil service. He was relieved of the need to tax the Vietnamese people because, in effect, the American taxpayers were underwriting the costs of his government. The most important part of the CIP was a method of subsidizing imports whereby the United States furnished dollars to Diem's officials who, in turn, sold them to licensed local importers who bought them with piasters at about one-half the official exchange rate. The importers then purchased American imports with their cut-rate dollars. They imported mostly consumer goods, luxury items, and relatively few capital goods. The piasters government officials collected from the sale of the dollars that had been given to them by American CIP officials were put into a fund used for paying South Vietnam's police, soldiers, and officials and for meeting other government expenses. Any additional revenues required by the government were raised by taxing the imports subsidized by the CIP. The commodity-import system generated the consumer goods that the new middle class wanted at prices they could afford. It also kept taxes down, kept inflation rates low, and paid for most of the costs of Diem's and his successors' governments.[20] It also purchased the loyalty of the new urban middle classes to Diem and whomever might come after him in Saigon and also to their American sponsors.

The Commodity Import Program did have some adverse long-run impacts on the economy and on many of the people of South Vietnam. While the CIP greatly expanded the size of the urban middle classes and made some Vietnamese wealthy, it created a narrowly based prosperity that never reached into the countryside or benefited the rural masses who made up 90 percent of the southern Vietnamese population. The villagers could never afford to participate in the new consumer economy that American aid dollars sustained. The gap between city affluence and rural poverty widened. Saigon prospered while mass poverty persisted in the countryside. The CIP, in effect, created an artificial economy that could last only as long as American officials were willing to pump hundreds of millions of dollars of American tax money into South Vietnam each year. The CIP also brought wholesale corruption and graft. Importers eagerly paid huge bribes to government officials to get licenses that practically guaranteed their becoming rich. Sizeable black markets flourished. The CIP, which brought in mostly consumer goods, also retarded South Vietnamese industrial development. There were no incentives for Vietnamese entrepreneurs to import capital goods and to set up factories to produce items that could be imported cheaply from America and sold for windfall profits.

The South Vietnamese economy did not industrialize or move toward self-sufficiency. South Vietnam remained an economic dependency of the U.S. capitalist juggernaut. In the long run, two of the chief reasons for the failure of Diem and his successors to achieve stable and popular governments in South Vietnam were their failures to promote economic development and to establish a popular base of support among the rural masses. The seductive lure of the CIP is partly to blame for both failings.

As the time for holding nationwide elections in Vietnam as called for in the Geneva agreements approached, Diem made it known that he had no intention of permitting them to be held in his half of Vietnam. The United

States backed Diem's actions even though it was inconsistent with America's calls for free elections in other divided countries such as Germany and Korea, and U.S. officials feared that Diem's refusal to hold the elections might provoke a Communist attack across the 17th parallel.[21] Given Ho Chi Minh's country-wide reputation as a nationalist leader and given the fact that northern Vietnam contained 14 million people to only 11 million for Vietnam south of the 17th parallel, the Communists would surely have won the elections had they been held as scheduled in July, 1956.

Diem justified his refusal to hold the elections by stating that his government did not "consider itself bound in any respects by the Geneva Agreements which it did not sign."[22] He also contended that the Vietnamese Communists were responsible for the partition of his country and that only his government stood for the fulfillment of the nationalist aspirations of all Vietnamese people to live within a unified, independent Vietnam. Until the Hanoi government permitted genuine freedom and democracy in its territory there could be no election.[23] Diem failed to mention another reason for not holding the elections. President Eisenhower acknowledged that had elections been held during that summer of 1956 to reunite Vietnam in accordance with the provisions of the Geneva accords, Ho Chi Minh would have gotten 80 percent of the votes.[24]

During the mid-1950s, while the United States was backing Diem's efforts to consolidate his power and his refusal to hold scheduled national elections, the major arena of Cold War conflict between the United States and the Soviet Union was shifting to the Third World, that is, to the emerging nations of Africa and Asia. Among these countries, many of them like Vietnam—newly independent former colonies of European imperial powers—America and the USSR competed for influence. For Washington, this shifting context of the US-USSR Cold War rivalry imparted enhanced importance to the growing American stake in Vietnam. America's commitment to Diem deepened.[25] By mid-1956, American officials had made fundamental commitments to Vietnam. After Eisenhower had settled in with Diem following his refusal to hold the elections called for in the Geneva protocol, none of Ike's successors found themselves able to get out of Vietnam until America had fought its longest war.

REVOLUTION IN THE NORTH

While Diem was taking charge in the South, Ho Chi Minh directed a Communist version of nation-building in the half of Vietnam that lay north of the 17th parallel. Although the Communists did not have to confront the political challenges to their rule in North Vietnam that Diem had to face in South Vietnam, the serious economic challenges facing the Communist leaders were more daunting than those facing Diem. Most of the fighting during the

Franco-Vietminh war had occurred in northern Vietnam; consequently, the damage to the war-torn economy of Tonkin was much greater than any damage done to the southern half of the country. When the French and non-Communist Vietnamese pulled out in the fall of 1954, they "gutted basic services, and sabotaged or dismantled industries as they withdrew from the North."[26] Much of the technical and skilled manpower in northern Vietnam also left with the French. North Vietnam had fewer resources and more people than South Vietnam. Agricultural productivity was low. The separation of the country deprived North Vietnam of its traditional source of rice. Only an emergency loan from the Soviets enabled North Vietnam to import rice from Burma in 1955 and avoid a famine.[27] Although China and the Soviet Union provided economic and technical assistance for Ho Chi Minh's revolutionary reconstruction of that portion of Vietnam under Communist control, that aid amounted to only a fraction of the assistance that the United States lavished on South Vietnam during the same period.

The new government that the revolutionaries established in Hanoi in the fall of 1954 was cast in the Marxist-Leninist mold. All power was concentrated within the executive directorate (Politburo) of the Lao Dong, headed by Ho and his senior colleagues. Opposition parties were forbidden on the grounds that non-Communists could not possibly be Vietnamese patriots. This Communist rationale for repression of all opposition represented an inversion of the logic used by American Cold Warriors, and by Diem as well, which held that Communists could not possibly be national patriots because their primary loyalties lay with an external power. The Vietnamese Communists permitted a national legislature to exist, and regularly scheduled elections were held, but the legislature had no power independent of the Politburo, who ignored its laws whenever it wanted to and routinely presented it with programs to approve. "People's democracy" in practice meant that the people were free to obey the edicts of the party directorate who decided all policy. Correct ideological principles as determined by party functionaries gave Ho's government its legitimacy; popular approval, while desired, was not required.

Political authority at all levels, down through urban neighborhoods, rural villages and hamlets, work places, schools, and occupations, was wielded by party members organized into blocs, called cadres. These cadres also monopolized local government offices. Through the cadres, both party doctrine and government policy, often one and the same, reached to every citizen. When fully articulated, the party apparatus was the mechanism for collectivizing the entire society.[28] The cadres, using a combination of positive incentives and coercion, worked especially hard to impose collectivist discipline on the rural population.

While Diem, with American help, was maneuvering to overcome his many political rivals in Saigon, Ho Chi Minh announced on January 1, 1955, that the time had come to implement his long-held Communist principles of economic and social organization. He launched a two-point program for rebuilding the northern economy and restructuring it along socialist lines:

> We shall endeavor to restore our economy, agriculture, commerce, industry, and transport, gradually to raise our living standards. We shall continue our work of mobilizing the masses for land rent reduction and land reform....[29]

It was through rebuilding and radically restructuring the northern economy that the Communist leaders sought to achieve their major objective: a self-sufficient industrializing economy within five years.

When the government turned to the difficult task of rebuilding the war-shattered economy, its first priority was rebuilding the transportation and communication systems that lay in shambles. One of the first projects that the government undertook was the rebuilding of the railroad that linked Hanoi with Lang Son at the Chinese border. Under relentless pressure from party officials, 80,000 workers rebuilt the lines in six months. The human costs of this forced labor were high: deaths, injuries, illness, malnutrition, and exhaustion.[30] Rebuilding the railroad was crucial to the development of the northern economy because it linked Vietnam not only with China but also with the Soviet Union and with the East European Communist countries. Over North Vietnam's Hanoi-Lang Son railroad would come over $2 billion of industrial and military equipment that "fueled its recovery and later its war against South Vietnam."[31]

China, the traditional overlord of Vietnam, furnished extensive economic assistance to the North Vietnamese. Ho journeyed to Beijing in 1955 where he was met personally at the airport by the august Mao himself.[32] Between 1955 and 1960, Chinese aid to North Vietnam totaled about $225 million and thousands of Chinese technicians worked in various projects all over the country. The Chinese interest in helping Ho modernize his country was to ensure that a friendly regime protected China's southern flank; the Chinese did not want either the United States or the Soviet Union to dominate Indochina. Ho, for his part, was quite willing to accept the Chinese aid on behalf of his desperately poor, war-battered economy; but he also recalled the long history of Chinese domination of his country and took care not to become dependent on China. He was not about to sacrifice his country's hard-won independence or freedom of action.

Ho Chi Minh also traveled to Moscow in 1955 where he was warmly received by the Soviet leaders. Ho had lived and worked in the Soviet Union during the 1920s and 1930s, and he derived his political ideology from Leninist doctrines. His goal was for North Vietnam to industrialize along Soviet lines; the Soviet Union served as his model. The Soviets granted the North Vietnamese a wide array of aid programs. Soon northern Vietnam was swarming with Soviet technicians, engineers, agricultural experts, and managers helping the North Vietnamese to industrialize their predominantly rural and agrarian economy.

But Ho was no more likely to become a Soviet puppet than he would become a dependent of China. He rather skillfully extracted much aid and technical assistance from both countries, retained his freedom of maneuver, played one Communist power off against the other, and moved his country in the direction of economic self-sufficiency. By contrast, the Diem government in southern Vietnam, between 1955 and 1960, became ever more dependent on U.S. economic and military aid to finance its government, to keep its consumer economy going, and to protect its security. Contrary to official U.S. views, Diem's regime was much more a creature of U.S. foreign policy than Ho's ever was the creature of Chinese and Soviet diplomacy.

Agricultural reform played the crucial role in Communist plans for economic development of their country during the late-1950s. Industrialization would be retarded until they could make their rural economy more productive. Party officials also wanted to drive a sizeable part of the rural population, which made up about 85 percent of the total population, off of the land in order to ease population pressures in the countryside and to furnish workers for developing industries. Party planners believed that the ultimate solution to the problem of low farm productivity would be the collectivization of agriculture. Large-scale, mechanized collective farms would raise productivity and eliminate surplus rural populations. But to placate the land-hungry peasantry for whom socialism held no attractions, the Communists "preceded collectivization with a program of land reform."[33] Lands belonging to wealthy landlords were seized and turned over to the poor. Since there were not enough rich landowners to satisfy the massive land hunger of North Vietnam's rural poor, roving political cadres of land reformers classified some of the wealthier peasants as landlords. Their lands were confiscated, they were imprisoned, and sometimes killed.[34]

Land reform accomplished both its political and economic objectives. About 2,000,000 peasants received land. The landlord class was destroyed and a new class of landowners composed of middle peasants strongly supportive of the Hanoi regime took control of the villages. But many abuses and atrocities accompanied the North Vietnamese land reform. Thousands of people were dispossessed, imprisoned, beaten, and murdered. The excessive brutality of the land reformers provoked a rebellion among Catholic farmers in Nghe An province in November 1956. The farmers protested to the International Control Commission that had been created at Geneva to monitor the armistice. Militia forcibly dispersed the peasants who fought back. To halt the spreading violence, Ho Chi Minh sent a division of regular army troops to suppress the rebellion. Thousands of people were killed, injured, or deported.[35] Conditions got so bad that Ho Chi Minh was forced to call a halt to the land reform program, order the release of prisoners, and to apologize publicly for the abuses and mistakes that party cadres had committed. The harsh land reform program and the methods used to implement it left a residue of bitterness and distrust as well as deep divisions in the countryside between the beneficiaries and the victims of land reform.

Although preoccupied with consolidating his rule, rebuilding the northern economy, and implementing socialism, Ho expected the reunification elections to be held in the summer of 1956 as scheduled. He also expected to win the elections and shortly thereafter to assume leadership of a unified, independent Communist-controlled Vietnam, which had been his lifelong goal. Hanoi assumed that the French, who had pledged to hold the elections, would still be in control of affairs in South Vietnam when it came time to hold them. But by the spring of 1956, the American-backed regime of Ngo Dinh ruled South Vietnam. Bao Dai had been deposed, all French troops had been withdrawn, and French influence in Vietnam had ended.

During 1955 and 1956, North Vietnamese officials repeatedly tried to establish communication with Diem and to start consultations in preparation for the elections. Diem ignored them. They also tried to persuade the members of the International Control Commission to get the electoral process underway; its members were not responsive to Hanoi's requests. Neither the Chinese nor the Soviets showed much interest in seeing that the electoral provisions of the Geneva accords were carried out. As 1956 ended, it was evident that none of the members of the International Control Commission and none of the major powers was going to back North Vietnamese efforts to hold the elections.[36]

Although disappointed and angry, the leaders in Hanoi, preoccupied as they were with internal matters and lacking support from the major Communist powers, were not prepared to resort to force to unify their country in 1956. Ho Chi Minh also feared that he might provoke a U.S. military intervention if he sent his troops south of the 17th parallel. Perceiving that no one outside of Hanoi appeared to be concerned about holding the elections and that the North Vietnamese did not intend to force the matter, Washington was confident that it could build a viable non-Communist nation in the southern half of Vietnam in violation of the Geneva agreements. Their optimism proved to be short-lived.

AN EXPERIMENT IN NATION BUILDING

The ambitious American effort to create a non-Communist nation-state in southern Vietnam in the middle and late-1950s took on the aspects of a crusade in Southeast Asia. By 1958, over 1,500 Americans were at work in South Vietnam on various projects. South Vietnam received the largest single share of the American foreign aid budget, and the U.S. mission headquartered in Saigon was the largest in the world. The mission, under the nominal direction of the U.S. ambassador to Saigon, comprised myriad government agencies, each with its own personnel, budget, and programs. In addition to the regular embassy staff, these agencies included the Central Intelligence Agency (CIA), The United States Information Agency (USIA), the United States Operations Mission (USOM), and the Military Assistance-Advisory Group (MAAG). MAAG was undoubtedly the most important of these agencies, because building up the South Vietnamese army (ARVN) was the top U.S. priority; about 80 percent of the total American assistance program for South Vietnam went to building up their military forces.[37] Washington believed that before South Vietnam could have a chance to survive and to develop its economy it had to be able to defend itself.

MAAG had been assigned primary responsibility for training the ARVN. The 342 members of the American advisory group inherited a challenging assignment. They found the South Vietnamese military forces that they were to try to whip into fighting shape to be in a sorry state. ARVN soldiers were poorly trained and poorly equipped. ARVN were short officers, certainly qualified officers. "Diem tended to value political reliability in senior officers far more than military expertise."[38] Consequently, the officer corps, especially at the senior level, was riven with political intrigue. Diem, who functioned as his own minister of defense, frequently bypassed the military chain of command to give orders directly to unit commanders.

MAAG advisers also discovered that the South Vietnamese army lacked patriotism. Commanders lacked any national feeling for their country. Most of its senior officers had fought with the French Expeditionary Force during the Franco-Vietminh war. Most spoke French better than they did Vietnamese, and many were French citizens. None of Diem's senior commanders had ever been associated with the resistance to French colonialism, the supposed foundation of Diemist nationalism and South Vietnamese patriotism. Insubordination was rampant, and seniors were reluctant to discipline subordinates who had political connections. Army Chief of Staff General Le Van Ty bluntly told General Samuel T. Williams, the MAAG commander, that "many of our units would disappear into the countryside at the very start of the reopening of hostilities."[39]

Corruption in the ARVN was rampant. Many South Vietnamese officers saw their military careers as an opportunity to enrich themselves. Senior officers often developed enterprises on the side that included black marketeering, drug operations, and prostitution. Some regional commanders set themselves up as warlords in outlying districts, and their soldiers collected taxes from the villagers.[40]

General Williams and his advisory teams went to work to try to turn a thoroughly politicized, thoroughly corrupt South Vietnamese army that was incapable of fighting into an effective military organization. American-style training schools and methods were implemented. Thousands of Vietnamese officers were sent overseas to attend U.S. military schools. ARVN was trimmed from a bloated 250,000-man force to a leaner, more efficient 150,000 troops. Soldiers were equipped with modern weapons and were taught modern tactics. The "heart of the American advisory effort was the Combat Arms Training Organization (CATO),"[41] an operations staff that controlled all the MAAG field detachments assigned to the various Vietnamese commands from the corps level down to the infantry, artillery, or armored battalions in the field. Advisers played key roles in determining the effectiveness of the training and discipline that ARVN units acquired.

The effectiveness of the American advisers was sometimes hindered by language and cultural barriers. Few Americans could speak Vietnamese (or French), knew anything about Vietnamese culture, and sometimes displayed racist attitudes, calling the Vietnamese "natives." Some American advisers vented anti-Asian stereotypes, viewing their Vietnamese charges as passive, cunning, and incapable of understanding modern technology. For their part, the Vietnamese were slow to learn English, often resented their aggressive, brusque American advisers, did not always train conscientiously, and many of them remained suspicious that the Americans had come to replace the French as their new colonial masters. U.S. advisers had to spend much time reassuring their South Vietnamese counterparts that they had not come as conquerors; they had come to help South Vietnam achieve independence and to be able to defend itself.

By the late-1950s, the American effort to turn ARVN into a modern and disciplined fighting force had been only partially successful. The South Vietnamese army still lacked sufficient qualified officers; Diem still insisted on selecting senior commanders on the basis of their politics rather than their professional competence. Corruption continued to pose problems. But the chief shortcoming of the new model ARVN was that MAAG had trained it for the wrong mission.[42] MAAG advisers, perceiving that Diem appeared to have eliminated all political opposition, concluded that an invasion across the 17th parallel posed the chief threat to the security of South Vietnam. The U.S. advisers were also influenced by their Korean experiences where many of them had helped the South Koreans to build up their defenses against another invasion from the North Koreans. The American advisers therefore created a South Vietnamese army with the capability of fighting a conventional main force war that could defeat an external invader and were dismayed to discover that the ARVN could not cope with the guerrilla insurgencies that arose in South Vietnam to challenge Diem's rule in the late-1950s.[43] By training the ARVN forces for the wrong mission, the Americans also revealed that they had failed to understand the lessons learned at such great expense by the French in the Indochina War.

Along with military assistance, America pumped over $1 billion in foreign aid into the South Vietnamese economy during the late-1950s, most of it into the aforementioned Commodities Import Program (CIP) that sustained the South Vietnamese government and created a new class loyal to Diem and his American sponsors. The United States also provided over $150 million in direct economic and technical aid. U.S. money repaired war-damaged roads and railroads, enhanced agricultural productivity, improved schools, raised public health standards, and a group of advisers from Michigan State University improved the performance of South Vietnamese police and public administrators.[44]

Massive U.S. economic, technical, and military aid enabled Diem's government to take hold in Saigon. By 1957 the American experiment in nation building in southern Vietnam appeared to be a stunning success. From unpromising beginnings in the summer of 1954, Ngo Dinh Diem had risen to preside over a stable government protected by a modern army and sustained by a flourishing consumer economy. To celebrate his success, America's mandarin made a triumphal visit to the United States in May 1957. Washington rolled out the red carpet, and President Eisenhower welcomed him at the airport:

> You have exemplified in your corner of the world patriotism of the highest order. You have brought to your great task of organizing your country the greatest of courage, the greatest of statesmanship."[45]

Diem was praised in the American media and feted at public gatherings as a miracle worker, who, with American help, had done the impossible: The gutsy little leader had overcome the inveterate political fragmentation of Saigon to create a strong, stable government, a showcase of freedom. South Vietnam was offered to the world as a model of enlightened Southeast Asian foreign policy in action. A thriving South Vietnam proved that foreign aid worked. America was helping an Asian people help themselves. The South Vietnamese had established a free society and were holding the line against the further spread of Communism in Indochina. Beijing's and Hanoi's expansionist tendencies were being contained north of the 17th parallel, and the Soviet master plan for Southeast Asia was being thwarted. Diem kept his favorable U.S. media image until his government was engulfed by revolution during the early 1960s.

But beneath the glittering surface of public celebration, however, all was not going well in Vietnam south of the 17th parallel even during 1957, Diem's *annus mirabilis*. Diem did not believe in nor did he implement a democratic political system in South Vietnam. To please his American sponsors, Diem established a constitutional system in 1956 modeled on the United States Constitution with executive, judicial, and legislative branches. Formally his creation, the Republican Government of Vietnam (GVN or RVN) was a constitutional democracy. But Diem was observing the forms, not practicing the substance of democracy. The constitution lodged almost all powers of government in the executive branch. Diem's powers resembled those of the Vietnamese emperors or the French Governors-General, not the limited powers of the American president.[46] The South Vietnamese judiciary never established its independence from the all-powerful executive, and

Diem controlled all judicial appointments. Diem also had considerable legislative authority; the National Assembly could only initiate legislature covering comparatively minor matters.

Diem also moved to assert his authority over all South Vietnam. He extinguished the regional autonomy of Cochin China and southern Annam. He appointed province chiefs for South Vietnam's forty-one provinces, and he appointed all administrators for the nation's 246 districts. Diem also extended his rule to the villages themselves. By decree he abolished elective village councils and then appointed officials to supervise the affairs of the country's 2,500 villages and 16,000 hamlets, the levels of government with which the peasants identified. Diem was motivated to take control of the South Vietnamese government at all levels for two reasons: It accorded with his conceptions of authoritarian governance, and he was concerned that the Vietminh might win many village elections if they were allowed to take place.[47]

As a result of Diem's centralizing thrust, South Vietnam had the most authoritarian governmental system in its history. Neither the imperial Confucian administrators nor the French colonial administrators had ever completely abolished the tradition and practices of village autonomy. There was also a symmetry between what Diem was doing in South Vietnam and the centralization that Ho Chi Minh's government implemented in North Vietnam through the agency of the Lao Dong. One ironic consequence of ridding Vietnam of French colonialism was that Diem and Ho saddled the Vietnamese people with the most ruthlessly authoritarian governments in their history, in the name of "freedom" in South Vietnam and "people's democracy" in North Vietnam.

Diem also filled government positions with a preponderance of northern and central Vietnamese. The highest ranking positions contained the highest proportions of northerners and centralists. Diem and his family were from Hue and were Catholics. Many of the northern Catholics who had migrated south in the fall of 1954 filled civilian and military positions in his government. Southerners resented these outsiders, who enjoyed special privileges, did not speak their dialects, and were not familiar with or much interested in their problems. This regional imbalance caused special problems for the Diem government's relations with many southern peasants and prevented the central government from ever winning their trust or loyalty. Southern Buddhist peasants especially resented having northern Catholics, who looked down on them and were indifferent to their welfare, administering their affairs.[48]

Diem relied heavily on his family to govern South Vietnam. Behind a democratic facade, nearly total power "remained lodged with Diem and his immediate family."[49] The Ngos were the ruling family of South Vietnam. The most powerful members, after Diem, included Diem's brother, Ngo Dinh Nhu, and Nhu's wife, who functioned as South Vietnam's First Lady. (Diem never married.) Diem's brothers, Ngo Dinh Thuc, the Archbishop of Hue and Catholic primate of Vietnam, and Ngo Dinh Can, ruled central Vietnam. Several other relatives and in-laws held important offices, including Madame Nhu's father, who was South Vietnam's ambassador to the United States for many years.

The Can Lao, a secret political party directed by Nhu, was the major instrument of family rule. Cells of the Can Lao reached into every agency of the government, infiltrated the South Vietnamese army, controlled the National Assembly, the police, the militia, the schools and colleges, the media, and entered into every level of the administrative apparatus of the Diem government.[50] The Can Lao cells furnished the sinews that connected all the parts of Diem's authoritarian political system in much the same fashion as the Communist party operated north of the 17th parallel.

Diem's family regime moved to eliminate or suppress all opposition in South Vietnam. Their major targets were Vietminh supporters who had remained in the south following the armistice and who controlled many of the southern villages. Nhu spearheaded a drive to eliminate the Vietminh presence in South Vietnam. During 1955 and 1956, thousands of Vietminh cadres rallied to the Diem government or else were imprisoned. Diem issued ordinances in 1956 and 1959 that gave government officials virtually a free hand to root out any opposition to his regime.[51] Diem's repression fell most heavily on the countryside, on the peasants. In theory, Nhu's campaign aimed only to root out the Communists, but it also included anyone opposed to or suspected of opposing Diem: religious sectarians, intellectuals, journalists, socialists, and liberals. During the middle 1950s and after, the people of Vietnam were victimized by twin tyrannies. There was one in South Vietnam, bankrolled by American taxpayers, and another in North Vietnam, granted extensive economic and technical assistance by China and the Soviet Union. Totalitarian Communism had taken root in North Vietnam; in South Vietnam, a police state apparatus with fascistic overtones, directed by Diem's younger brother Nhu, had been implemented.

In addition to destroying their traditional village autonomy, appointing outsiders to administer their affairs, and mounting oppressive campaigns to root out all opponents, Communist and non-Communist alike, the Diem government's approach to land reform also alienated many peasants. Landlords loyal to Diem were allowed to repossess rice lands that Vietminh cadres had confiscated during the Franco-Vietminh war and given to poor peasants. Special courts established to adjudicate landlord–tenant disputes were dominated by landlords and by officials responsive to landlord interests. Programs designed to hold land rents to no more than 25 percent of the value of the annual crop often were inefficiently administered. A program to settle villagers on abandoned lands in the Mekong delta promised to be popular, but Diem's insistence that the people buy the land from the government angered many peasants. Another program to distribute rice-growing lands to tenants succeeded in providing some tenants with land; but only about 10 percent of the eligible poor peasantry in southern Vietnam were able to get the land, which came from expropriated French estates that Diem's government had purchased from their former owners with funds provided by the United States. Landlords were also allowed to retain sizeable landholdings, up to 250 acres, for their own use, further limiting the extent of Diem's land reform efforts.[52]

Starting in 1957, the Diem government initiated a resettlement program for some of the Catholic refugees from North Vietnam and for peasants from overpopulated coastal enclaves. They were resettled on lands in areas within the sparsely populated central highlands. The new settlers were placed in fortified villages on lands claimed by Montagnard tribes who practiced a form of slash-and-burn agriculture. In addition to taking their lands, Diem also attempted to impose his rule on the Montagnards and to Vietnamize them. Long accustomed to autonomy and allowed to retain their cultural identities under French rule, the Montagnards fiercely resented the intrusive Diemist policies. By 1958, some of the Montagnards were rebelling against the government.[53] Later, the Communists were able to win the support of some of the Montagnard tribes by exploiting their grievances against the GVN.

During the years when U.S. government officials and journalists were extolling Diem's triumphs in the South, many of his policies were alienating the rural masses. In truth, the United States in South Vietnam "devoted little attention to political matters and despite its massive foreign aid program, exerted little influence."[54] Even though Diem's government was absolutely dependent on American aid for its survival, U.S. officials had very little leverage they could use against the strong-willed ruler. Diem was convinced that only he knew what needed to be done and knew how to do it. He sensed, rightly, that the Eisenhower administration was content just to have a functioning "free," that is, anti-Communist, government in the southern half of Vietnam preventing the spread of Communism. Democracy in South Vietnam would be nice, but it could always be implemented later. He also believed that the Americans would be forced to go along with him no matter what he did or did not do so long as the family oligarchy maintained a tough anti-Communist stance in South Vietnam. Again, Diem was correct, because it was not until the early 1960s, when Diem's government was engulfed by revolution, that worried American officials began pressing him to make reforms.

Diem's political ideology, an unwieldy mix of doctrines called "personalism" developed by his brother Nhu to provide an ideological alternative to Communism, blended Confucian, Catholic, and Marxist principles. It added up to a rationale for a species of paternalistic despotism: As the leader-father of his people, Diem knew what was good for his country, and it was his duty to implement the policies that would achieve the Diemist conception of the general good. The people's duties were to respect and obey their leader. Personalistic theory called for a government for the people, but not of the people or by the people. In fact, Diem viewed his people, if by the people one refers to the villagers who constituted 90 percent of the South Vietnamese population, as potential enemies who must be kept under surveillance and tight administrative control. It was inevitable that the Diem family oligarchy, because of their inattention to the needs and their insensitivity to the sensibilities of the people, their promulgation of policies that alienated much of the population, and, most of all, their ruthless attacks on all their opponents, would provoke resistance to their rule. In time, that resistance evolved into an armed rebellion. Hanoi took over and directed that rebellion, which evolved into revolution.

THE ROOTS OF REVOLUTION

According to the provisions of the Geneva agreements that arranged an armistice and proposed a political settlement for the Franco-Vietminh war in 1954, the armed forces and supporters of both sides were allowed 300 days in which to withdraw to one of the two regroupment zones: with the French and their supporters retiring to the zone south of the 17th parallel and the Vietminh and their supporters moving north. During the 300-day interim, about 800,000 people moved south. An estimated "50,000 to 90,000 Vietminh sympathizers went to the North while approximately 10,000 to 15,000 remained in the South."[55] The Vietminh cadres remaining in South Vietnam were under instructions to protect the remaining revolutionary forces in the region, to maintain the party apparatus, and to retain their influence in the villages sympathetic to the Vietminh program. Neither these "stay-behinds" nor their leaders in Hanoi anticipated the rapid decline of French influence in South Vietnam or the emergence of the Diem government backed by a strong U.S. presence. They also did not anticipate that the elections to unify the country would be aborted. These Vietminh stay-behinds formed the nucleus of the armed rebellion that would erupt within a few years in South Vietnam.

During the first few years of Diem's administration, opposition had come mainly from the right of the political spectrum, from the sects and from the Binh Xuyen. During these years the Vietminh stay-behinds, following their instructions, involved themselves mostly in peaceful political activity, preparing for the upcoming unification elections that they expected to win. They were shocked and angry when the promised elections were never held. They were also disappointed that the major powers, including their Communist allies, accepted the cancellation of the elections and that Hanoi was not prepared to force the issue. Some left the Vietminh ranks, but most remained loyal to Hanoi and to its goal of a unified and independent Vietnamese nation under a Communist government.

Nearly all Vietnamese, northerners and southerners, Communists and non-Communists, held to a "concept of a single all-embracing nation." These widely and deeply held nationalistic sentiments were not understood by American officials who had embarked on a crusade to create a new nation south of the 17th parallel. Unaware of or else ignoring the strong sense of national identity held by most Vietnamese citizens, a succession of American administrations advanced the notion that those Vietnamese who happened to live south of the 17th parallel under a free government had developed "their own sense of nationhood and patriotism" that was distinct from the sentiments held by the Vietnamese living north of that line under a Communist regime. But the idea of a permanently divided Vietnam was no more acceptable to Diem, his successors, or their followers than it was to Ho Chi Minh or his followers. Nor was it any more acceptable to that broad spectrum who did not support either the Communists or the Diemists. "Adherence to the principle of a unified Vietnam was common to almost all Vietnamese; where they differed was under what authority it should be reunited."[56] Both Diem and Ho believed that there should be and could be only one Vietnamese nation, as did their fellow citizens. For the Vietnamese there was only one homeland; the conflict was over who should rule at home.

These nationalistic aspirations to live within a unified country, embraced by nearly all Vietnamese, explain why no "South Vietnamese" national consciousness ever evolved. There existed only a region cut off from the rest of Vietnam by an arbitrary line drawn by diplomats who never intended for it to become a permanent political boundary. It never did become permanent except in U.S. foreign policy formulations. What did evolve in the southern part of Vietnam by the late-1950s were three broad political groupings. One was loyal to Diem and his successors and supported their American patrons. A second group supported the Vietminh and looked to national reunification under the leadership of Ho Chi Minh. A third force also evolved, composed of elements who held to a goal of wanting to live in a Vietnamese nation governed neither by Saigon nor Hanoi.[57] The rebellion that became a revolution that became the U.S. war in Vietnam was always a struggle for control of one country. For the Vietnamese, there never were nor could there ever be two Vietnamese nations.

In 1956, the head of the southern branch of the Vietnamese Communist Party, Le Duan, a veteran revolutionary leader and member of the Politburo, recommended rebuilding military forces in South Vietnam and reviving guerrilla activities to protect the political cadres. He was concerned for the survival of the Lao Dong political apparatus in South Vietnam because of defections, attrition, and the depredations of Nhu's campaigns to root out Communist influences in southern Vietnam.[58] Hanoi was not responsive to Duan's request. The Communist leadership in North Vietnam was fully engaged in nation-building enterprises of its own and had no desire to provoke U.S. military intervention in South Vietnam, especially given the lack of support for Vietnam's reunification from the USSR and China. The Soviets, under Khrushchev's leadership, were promoting peaceful coexistence with the Western powers; China, absorbed with its own national development, had no stomach for any more Korean-style military conflicts with the United States. The Soviets even went so far as to propose that the United Nations admit both North and South Vietnam in 1957, apparently acknowledging a permanent partition of the country, a position absolutely contradictory to the desires of Hanoi's leaders.

Hanoi's leaders also told Duan that before there could be military action in South Vietnam, the southern party apparatus would have to be reorganized and rebuilt. Consequently, the political directorate strongly reaffirmed its policy of calling for peaceful political activity in South Vietnam. Duan wrote a pamphlet outlining Hanoi's policies to the southern cadres.[59] While affirming Hanoi's contention that the revolution in South Vietnam would develop peacefully and Diem's government would inevitably fall because of its inherent political weaknesses, Duan also advocated a more militant policy looking to actively promoting reunification and preparing the southern cadres for possible revolutionary activity to come. Some southerners read into Duan's ambiguous tract a call for more militant actions, including armed struggle. Duan's paper served as Hanoi's policy in South Vietnam until 1959 when fast-developing events in that region forced the political directorate to change it.

The southern Communists did have some successes in 1957 and 1958. They exploited popular dissatisfaction with Diem's methods and policies in some districts. But Diem's drive to root out the Lao Dong was effective in many areas. Cadre members were arrested, imprisoned, and killed. In many districts, the party apparatus disappeared or was reduced to a harried rump scrambling to elude Nhu's "hound dogs."[60] Some cadre members resorted to violence in some districts. They murdered Diemist police and village officials. In such scattered fashion, the rebellion in South Vietnam began a death at a time in 1957 when some cadres took violent reprisals against the GVN minions.[61] But Nhu kept the pressure on and continued to eradicate Communist cells in the South. The worst year for the southern Communists and their cause was 1958. They were reduced to pockets of resistance in a few regions, struggling to survive, without any help from Hanoi, and under tremendous pressure applied by Nhu's Can Lao operatives, the police, and ARVN units.

"In desperation, local leaders in many areas began to act on their own initiative."[62] Armed units were formed in response to attacks by Diem's forces, even though these actions violated Hanoi's policy. Guerrilla units were formed in Quang Ngai province, in the U Minh forest, in the Mekong delta, and in War Zone D, a region northwest of Saigon and a longtime Vietminh stronghold. War Zone D would become a key basing area during the revolution because it was near the Cambodian border and also allowed access to the Mekong delta and central highlands, two areas of extensive Communist activity. By the end of 1958, the insurgents "had clearly reopened the deferred war of national liberation."[63]

Hanoi began developing a new policy in March 1959 in response to the growing militancy among their southern cadres and fears that Diem's repression would permanently weaken the revolutionary organization in South Vietnam. The Communist leadership also perceived the growing popular discontent in the South with Diem's policies and methods of governance and wanted to exploit it, but they had also concluded that Diem could not be overthrown by purely political means. His overthrow would require military activity. Among the Communist leaders, debates turned on how high a priority to assign the growing southern rebellion and on what combination of political and military strategies should be used in South Vietnam to overthrow Diem and to reunify the country. They hoped to continue developing the northern economy and to avoid an overt military strategy that would provoke the United States into direct intervention. If that happened, there would be a full-scale, protracted war that would surely engulf them. Such a prospect Hanoi devoutly wished to avoid if at all possible.[64]

A Politburo directive issued in May 1959 authorized the formation of a base in the central highlands for political organizing leading to limited guerrilla warfare.[65] A few months later, the Central Committee widened the scope of permissible politico-military activity to include other regions as opportunities developed and circumstances required. It also instructed the North Vietnamese army to establish a special transportation unit with the capability of moving weapons, ammunition, people, and supplies overland from North Vietnam to South Vietnam along an infiltration route that ran through Laos. This infiltration route would become famous as the Ho Chi Minh trail. In addition, Hanoi began to send southern cadres that had regrouped in North Vietnam following the 1954 armistice down the Ho Chi Minh trail to join the southern insurgency. Many of these "regroupees" had received special training in revolutionary tactics while in North Vietnam, and, once they returned south, they assumed leadership positions in the developing insurgency.

THE INSURGENCY ESCALATES

In 1959 and 1960, the level of conflict between Diem's forces and the revolutionaries intensified all over South Vietnam. Guerrillas raided ARVN outposts and assassinated thousands of Diemist village officials. The Communists staged significant uprisings in two areas that had been long-time insurgent strongholds, Ben Tre Province in the lower Mekong delta and in the Tra Bong District in Quang Ngai province near the northern coast of South Vietnam. In Tra Bong the insurgents were able to fight off Diem's troops and to establish "liberated zones" incorporating dozens of villages and thousands of people.[66] Political agitation continued in many districts and many villages that had formerly been controlled by the GVN now passed into the hands of the insurgents.

Diem struck back hard at his enemies in an effort to contain the rising insurgency. Nhu continued his efforts to break the back of the Communist organizations. ARVN troops raided guerrilla strongholds. Diem, with strong U.S. backing, implemented a program to isolate villages from the guerrilla forces by relocating the people in areas were ARVN forces could protect them. A series of fortified villages, called "agrovilles," were constructed in strategic areas, and the peasants were relocated. The agroville program demonstrated how far out of touch Diem was with the rural population of South Vietnam and raised the level of popular antagonism toward his government. The peasants deeply resented being forcibly removed from their ancestral lands. They were not adequately compensated for their losses, and they were forced to work on community projects without pay. Originally, Diem's officials planned to construct eighty agrovilles. But peasant resistance and insurgent attacks led to the abandonment of the program at the end of 1960 after only twenty-two villages had been built. After the war, it was discovered that the architect of the agroville scheme, Colonel Pham Ngoc Thao, was a Communist agent. He had sold the plan to Diem, then designed it in such a way as to make sure that the peasants were angered and alienated from Diem's government. From the revolutionaries' point of view, Thao's agroville program was a smashing success.[67]

As the southern insurgency escalated, the Third Party Congress of the Lao Dong, meeting in Hanoi in September 1960, formally endorsed the revolution. It adopted a resolution stating that the Vietnamese revolution now had two primary goals: completing the socialist revolution in North Vietnam and liberating South Vietnam in order to complete reunification of the country. The resolution stated that the two goals were of equal importance and integrally related.[68]

In order to achieve its revolutionary goal in South Vietnam, the Party Congress also approved plans to reorganize the developing revolutionary forces in the south and to form a new united front. Following the Congress, the military cadres in the south gathered to form a united military command. On February 15, 1961, the People's Liberation Armed Force (PLAF) was formed. Tran Luong, a southerner, was chosen to head the PLAF command, but soon after his appointment, several generals arrived in South Vietnam from the People's Army of Vietnam (PAVN) to reactivate the southern command that had directed Vietminh forces during the Franco-Vietminh war. It was known as the Central Committee Directorate for the South (Truong Uong Cuc Mien Nam). The Americans referred to the southern command as COSVN (Central Office for South Vietnam). The southern command, which had direct ties to the Lao Dong Politburo, in early 1962, took control of the PLAF with its 17,000 main force troops. In addition to its main force units, the PLAF also included guerrillas who operated at district levels and local, part-time irregulars who were farmers by day, indistinguishable from other villagers, and terrorists by night. It is these PLAF forces that American soldiers called the "Vietcong." No revolutionary organization in South Vietnam ever called itself the Vietcong. Ngo Dinh Diem coined the term Vietcong, a contraction of the phrase, "Viet-nam Cong-san," meaning "Vietnamese who are Communists." Diem had coined the term to disparage all his political opponents, both Communist and non-Communist alike, by calling all of them Vietcong.[69]

While the PLAF was forming, at a meeting held "somewhere in South Vietnam" on December 20, 1960, delegates created the National Liberation Front for the Liberation of South Vietnam (NLF or Mat Tran Dan Toc Giai Phong Mien Nam Viet Nam). The NLF was a reincarnation of the Vietminh Front tactic adapted to southern Vietnamese politics. Its Central Committee included representatives of the sects, Catholic and Buddhist organizations, labor, intellectuals, women, nationalists, socialists, and Montagnards. Below the Central Committee, the NLF had various administrative levels paralleling the various levels of government. Its basic units of organization were the village-level associations.[70] The overall structure of the NLF resembled a pyramid, with the Central Committee forming the apex and the village associations forming the base.

At their founding conference, the NLF organizers adopted a ten-point program, which, like its Vietminh predecessor, stressed nationalistic rather than revolutionary goals.[71] Most of its leadership was not recruited from Communist ranks, although some like Chairman Nguyen Huu Tho had close links with the Vietminh. In fact, at all levels, the number of Communist party members permitted to assume leadership roles within the NLF was strictly limited. The Hanoi leadership had taken care to disguise its relationship with the National Liberation Front, which had the appearance of an autonomous organization composed of a broad spectrum of southern nationalists whose main political goals were expelling the Americans, replacing Diem's government with a democratic coalition government, and seeking peaceful reunification with North Vietnam.[72] The NLF represented itself to be a democratic political alternative to the authoritarian Diem regime. The political composition of the NLF, its program, indeed its very existence, proved to many observers that the rebellion was an indigenous southern uprising. For many critics of American policy in Vietnam, the NLF was a standing contradiction to Washington's oft-proclaimed charge that the southern insurgency was in reality an invasion from North Vietnam.

Was the rebellion in South Vietnam in fact a spontaneous insurgency provoked by Diemist repression? It was true that by 1960 there was throughout South Vietnam a hostility to Diem's government that stretched across a broad political spectrum. This popular antagonism fueled the rising level of insurgency. But it is also evident that Hanoi organized and directed the rebellion in South Vietnam from its inception. Party leaders provided the organizational structure and leadership that gave the southern insurgency the focus and dynamism it needed to mount a serious challenge to the GVN. "The insurgency was a genuine revolt based in the South, but it was organized and directed from the North."[73]

The NLF was not a spontaneous formation of dissident southern nationalists. It was formed in accordance with directives issued by Hanoi. The autonomy granted the NLF that permitted it a measure of organizational and programmatic independence may have been a necessary concession to southern concerns, but it also served to disguise the role Hanoi played in orchestrating the southern revolution.[74] Hanoi hoped that its exercise in political camouflage would enable it to avoid an armed confrontation with the United States.

Even if the NLF was not initially Communist-dominated, it quickly came to be. Hanoi controlled the NLF through the People's Revolutionary Party (PRP) created in January 1962. The PRP formed the inner core pyramid of the NLF. The PRP merged with the southern branch of the Lao Dong, and it was affiliated with COSVN and thus connected to the Hanoi political directorate. PRP cadres operated within all departments and at all levels of the NLF and provided education, administration, coordination, and leadership. The PRP was the hidden government of the NLF.[75] From the Politburo through COSVN and the PRP, the NLF and PLAF were directed by Hanoi, which viewed the developing revolutionary situation in southern Vietnam to be a continuation of the national revolution that had been going on in Vietnam since August of 1945.

It is also evident that Hanoi did not set out to overthrow the Saigon government in 1956 after the scheduled elections that would have given the Communists control of all Vietnam were aborted. It only gradually embraced revolutionary goals. Initially, party leaders hoped to achieve reunification by peaceful political means. By 1959 they understood that Diem's government, while repressive and unpopular, because of its U.S. backing, was too strong to be toppled by political means. By 1960, after years of delay and internal debate, the political directorate in Hanoi, whose hand was forced by the developing revolutionary situation in southern Vietnam and the demands of the militant southern cadres, found itself supporting a revolution in South Vietnam as a necessary means to achieve its long-standing goal of a unified Vietnam under its control. But even at that late date, they still hoped to avoid a protracted war with the U.S. backers of Diem's government. The ever-rising level of conflict between Saigon and the insurgents had forced Hanoi to embrace a revolutionary struggle that they would have preferred to avoid if they could have found an alternative political route to reunification.[76]

While Hanoi directed the formation of the PLAF and the NLF, the insurgency in the southern countryside continued to spread, and the level of violence steadily escalated. The number of districts and villages under rebel control increased rapidly. Compounding the GVN's problems, in November 1960 Diem narrowly averted a military coup. It was led by Colonel Nguyen Chanh Thi, commander of an elite paratroop brigade, and Colonel Doung Van Dong. The coup may have had the backing of some American officials who had lost confidence in Diem and had pledged to support the coup leaders if they were successful. The coup attempt and the fact that it almost succeeded highlighted the growing vulnerability of Diem's government.[77]

U.S. military advisers, now worried about the survival of the GVN, began to shift the emphasis of their military training of ARVN units from conventional warfare to counter-insurgency tactics.[78] The American ambassador to South Vietnam, Elbridge Durbrow, tried to persuade Diem to reform his government and to mobilize public support. He suggested that Diem ought to allow greater civil liberties and freedom of the media, restore village elections, and offer more economic assistance to the peasants.[79] Diem ignored Durbrow's advice and tightened his control of the South Vietnamese government. MAAG officials, concerned to develop an effective military response to the insurgency, strongly opposed Durbrow's efforts to reform Diem. They felt such pressures to push Diem toward democracy at a time when his government was under stress, both from the rebels and from disloyal army elements, could only undermine him and endanger the whole nation-building enterprise. As 1960 ended, even though the American experiment in nation building in South Vietnam was clearly imperiled, Washington did not make any major moves to salvage Diem. Eisenhower was preoccupied with crises elsewhere in the world and was preparing to turn the reins of government over to his successor elected in November, John Fitzgerald Kennedy.[80]

Even as Diem struggled to control his army and to fight the rebels at the end of 1960, Washington was more concerned about developments in Laos than they were in South Vietnam. At the time of the Geneva Accords when Laos had received its independence, the Royal Lao government had a mildly pro-Western tilt. The United States, replacing the French, in the name of anti-Communism, lavished economic and military aid on the small, landlocked, and sparsely populated nation. A Communist-led movement, the Pathet Lao, led by Prince Souphanouvong and backed by the North Vietnamese, had taken control of the eastern two provinces of Laos in 1957. Prince Souvanna Phouma, the leader of the royalist forces, had negotiated an agreement with Prince Souphanouvong, establishing a neutralist Laos under a coalition government.

The Eisenhower administration, angry at this arrangement, using the CIA, installed a right-wing, pro-Western government in Laos under the rule of General Phoumi Nosavan. Prince Souvanna was ousted from office, and Prince Souphanouvong was imprisoned. One day in August 1960, while General Phoumi was out of town, a military coup led by paratroop Captain Kong Le seized power. Captain Le invited Prince Souvanna to form a neutralist government. General Phoumi, reacting to the coup, proclaimed his own government and marched on the capital, Vientiane. Prince Souvanna fled to Cambodia, and Captain Le joined the Pathet Lao forces. The United States continued to back General Phoumi, and the Soviets backed the neutralist-Pathet Lao coalition. As 1960 ended, the crisis in Laos was intensifying: a civil war that could draw both the United States and the Soviets into the Laotian cockpit beckoned. When Eisenhower on his last day in office (January 19, 1961) briefed Kennedy on Southeast Asian problems, he talked mostly about the problems in Laos, and the possibility of American military intervention there, never once mentioning Vietnam to Kennedy.[81]

A FAILED EXPERIMENT

When Washington intervened in Indochina at the time of the Geneva agreements to create a new nation in the southern half of Vietnam and to prevent the further spread of Communism in Southeast Asia in the aftermath of the French military defeat, American officials confidently believed that they could succeed where the French had failed. Ignorant of Vietnamese history and culture, and not understanding the breadth and depth of Vietnamese nationalistic feelings, Eisenhower, Dulles, and their advisers did not fully realize the perils of the situation into which they eagerly rushed.

They did not grasp the fundamental political reality of Vietnam, that there was little basis for erecting a viable nation-state in the southern half of a country whose inhabitants had a strong sense of national identity and a proud tradition of national independence stretching back over 900 years before the coming of the French. The Vietnamese people may have quarreled violently among themselves for years over what kind of government should rule their country, but nearly all Vietnamese agreed that there was only one Vietnam to rule. In addition, conditioned by their history and culture to be wary of outsiders, many Vietnamese resented the American presence, viewing American officials as colonial surrogates for the French. Even had Diem been a philosopher-king and American advisers paragons of tact and efficiency, they would eventually have been challenged by Ho Chi Minh and his followers, who would not tolerate partition of their country, the American presence, or a Diemist government. Ho would have sought and received assistance from the Chinese and Soviets. Vietnam was fated for either reunification or perpetual turmoil. As it turned out, neither Diem nor any of his successors, nor the vast panoply of American aid programs, nor American military power were able to create a durable new nation out of half-a-nation.

Ngo Dinh Diem was a man of considerable ability and courage; he was hard working, conscientious, and patriotic. He could not be corrupted by money. He was the best available man for the Americans to support in 1954, and he was the ablest of a succession of South Vietnamese leaders that the

United States backed during the twenty-year existence of what remained in the eyes of most Vietnamese a political contrivance called South Vietnam. South Vietnam was a figment of American anti-Communist diplomatic imperatives in Southeast Asia and could only be sustained by immense infusions of American economic aid and military power.[82] When American military forces withdrew and U.S. aid declined, South Vietnam was quickly extinguished by PAVN forces. Few Vietnamese on either side of the 17th parallel ever expected any other outcome.

But Diem also had his flaws and shortcomings as a leader. His obsolescent political philosophy and authoritarian methods of governance prevented his ever achieving a broad base of popular support. Diem's favoritism toward his Catholic co-religionists, the shortcomings of his land reform programs, his failure to promote industrialization, his assault on village autonomy, and his repressive attacks on all his critics and opponents had alienated the majority of Vietnamese from his regime by the late 1950s. He was especially unpopular among the rural masses whom he distrusted and disliked. By 1960, Diem faced a powerful and expanding revolutionary opposition that he could not contain. The insurgency was provoked by his political failings and was directed and supported from Hanoi.

Only the caprice of the American electoral calendar saved President Eisenhower from having to face the failure of his nation-building experiment in southern Vietnam and the failure of his policy in Laos as well. It would be the fate of his successor to have to choose between abandoning South Vietnam and Laos to the Communists or significantly raising the American stakes in Indochina. It is a major part of the developing American ordeal that Kennedy felt compelled to raise the American stakes in Vietnam.

NOTES

1. Porter (ed.), NCS 5492/2 "Review of U.S. Policy in the Far East," August 20, 1954, *Vietnam Documents*, vol. 1, Document 386, pp. 666–668.

2. Porter (ed.), South East Asia Collective Defense Treaty, September 8, 1954, *Vietnam Documents*, vol. 1, Document 389, pp. 672–675.

3. *Ibid.*, p. 675.

4. Tuchman, *March of Folly*, pp. 270–272; Herring, *America's Longest War*, p. 45.

5. Bouscaren, Anthony T., *The Last of the Mandarins: Diem of Vietnam* (Pittsburgh: Duquesne University Press, 1965), pp. 11–17; Fitzgerald, Frances, *Fire in the Lake: The Vietnamese and the Americans in Vietnam* (New York, Vintage, 1973), pp. 107–108.

6. Bouscaren, *The Last of the Mandarins*, p. 17; Shaplen, *Lost Revolution*, pp. 107–108.

7. Shaplen, *Lost Revolution*, pp. 111–112.

8. *Ibid.*, pp. 112–113; Scheer, Robert, *How the United States Got Involved in Vietnam* (Santa Barbara, Calif.: Center for the Study of Democratic Institutions, 1965), pp. 13–16.

9. It is not known precisely how or why Bao Dai was persuaded to appoint Diem to be his prime minister. Cooper, Chester L., *The Lost Crusade: America in Vietnam* (Dodd, Mead, 1970), pp. 120–128, believes that Dulles persuaded Bao Dai to appoint him in the hopes that Diem could ease out the French and defeat the Communists. If Diem succeeded in these endeavors, Bao Dai could then return to Vietnam as the ruler of a reunited, independent nation. Also see Karnow, *Vietnam*, pp. 217–218.

10. Porter, (ed.), "Letter from Eisenhower to President Ngo Dinh Diem," Oct. 23, 1954,*Vietnam Documents*, vol. 1, Document 395, pp. 681–682. Eisenhower clearly hedged U.S. aid commitments to Diem. The key sentence reads, "The Government of the United States expects that this aid will be met by performance on the part of the Government of Viet-Nam [sic!] in undertaking needed reforms."

11. Gardner, *Approaching Vietnam*, pp. 327–338; Herring, *America's Longest War*, pp. 49–50.

12. Landsdale, Edward Geary, *In the Midst of Wars: An American's Mission to Southeast Asia* (New York: Harper & Row, 1972), pp. 170–176; Scigliano, Robert, *South Vietnam: Nation Under Stress* (Boston: Houghton Mifflin, 1964), p. 18.

13. Kahin, *Intervention*, pp. 75–77; Scigliano, *South Vietnam*, pp. 52–55. According to Scigliano, in 1960 there were 1,014,000 Catholics in South Vietnam, more than half of whom were recent migrants from northern Vietnam. For that same year, Catholic officials estimated the total Catholic population of Vietnam at 1,807,784, of whom 793,000 resided in the north. In 1960, Catholics represented 9 percent of South Vietnam's population, 6 percent of North Vietnam's population, and about 7 percent of the total population.

14. Landsdale, *In The Midst of Wars*, pp. 165–170; Kahin, *Intervention*, pp. 76–77.

15. Doyle and others, *Passing the Torch*, pp. 141–142.

16. There are several accounts of Diem's struggles to defeat his myriad political opponents and to establish his government in the south. See Doyle and others, *Passing the Torch*, pp. 120–130; Landsdale, *In the Midst of Wars*, pp. 154–227, 244–312; and Shaplen, *Lost Revolution*, pp. 100–128.

17. Landsdale, *In the Midst of Wars*, pp. 260–312.

18. Kahin, *Intervention*, p. 95.

19. *Ibid.*, pp. 84–85.

20. *Ibid.*, pp. 84–88; Scigliano, *South Vietnam*, pp. 125–137. Kahin states that of the $322.4 million dollars in economic aid for South Vietnam spent in 1955, 87 percent of those funds, $280 million, were channeled through the CIP. The flow of CIP funds was large enough to allow Diem to accumulate a dollar reserve of $216.4 million by 1960.

21. Herring, *America's Longest War*, p. 55.

22. Eisenhower, Dwight David, *The White House Years: Mandate for Change, 1953–1956* (New York: Doubleday, 1963), p. 372.

23. Porter, (ed.), Declaration of the Government of Vietnam on Reunification, August 9, 1955, *Vietnam Documents*, vol. 2, Document 1, pp. 1–2.

24. *Ibid.*

25. Herring, *America's Longest War*, p. 56.

26. Turley, William S., *The Second Indochina War: A Short Political and Military History, 1954–1975* (New York: New American Library, 1986), p. 18.

27. Karnow, *Vietnam*, p. 225.

28. Doyle and others, *Passing the Torch*, pp. 102–103.

29. Quoted in Doyle and others, *Passing the Torch*, p. 102.

30. *Ibid.*, pp. 103–104.

31. *Ibid.*, p. 104.

32. Neither the Russian premier Nikita Khrushchev nor the American president Richard Nixon were met personally upon their arrival in Beijing by Mao. When he greeted Ho Chi Minh at the airport, Mao was acknowledging the visit of an Asian revolutionary nationalist of a stature equivalent to his own.

33. Duiker, William, *Vietnam: A Nation in Revolution* (Boulder, Colo.: Westview, 1983), p. 107.

34. Karnow, *Vietnam*, pp. 225–226.

35. Turley, *The Second Indochina War*, p. 19; Karnow, *Vietnam*, pp. 225–226; also see Moise, Edwin E., *Land Reform in China and North Vietnam* (Chapel Hill, N. C.: Univ. of North Carolina Press, 1983), pp. 178–240 and his article, "Land Reform and Land Reform Errors in North Vietnam," *Pacific Affairs*, vol. 49 (Spring, 1976), pp. 70–92. Moise says about 5,000 peasants were executed. Porter, Gareth, *The Myth of the Bloodbath: North Vietnam's Land Reform Reconsidered* (Ithaca, N. Y.: Cornell University Press, 1972). Porter has done a careful study to determine the number of people killed during the Communist land reform programs of 1955 and 1956. He finds that about 2,500 people lost their lives.

36. Note from Pham Van Dong to the Geneva Co-Chairs, April 9, 1956, insisting that the Geneva agreements required both the French and Diem's government to hold elections, in Porter, (ed.), *Vietnam Documents*, vol. 2, Document 8, pp. 15–16; also see Note from the British Embassy in Moscow to the Soviet Foreign Ministry, April 9, 1956, informing the Russians that the British government did not agree that South Vietnam was required to hold the elections, in *Ibid.*, pp. 17–18; see also Message from the Two Co-chairs of the Geneva Conference to the Governments of the Democratic Republic of Vietnam and the Republic of Vietnam, May 8, 1956, in which the Russians essentially conceded that they would not push for reconvening the Geneva Conference or the holding of elections, in *Ibid.*, pp. 19–20; see also Kahin, *Intervention*, pp. 88–92.

37. Herring, *America's Longest War*, p. 57.

38. Spector, Ronald H., *Advice and Support: The Early Years, 1941–1960* (Washington, D. C.: Center of Military History, U.S. Army, 1985), p. 278.

39. *Ibid.*, p. 280.

40. *Ibid.*, p. 281.

41. *Ibid.*, p. 289.

42. *Ibid.*, pp. 268–274; Herring, *America's Longest War*, pp. 58–60.

43. Herring, *America's Longest War*, p. 61.

44. Scigliano, *South Vietnam*, pp. 102–129.

45. The Eisenhower quote is taken from a video clip from "America's Mandarin," part three of the television documentary series "Vietnam: A Television Series," produced by Boston WGBS and the Public Broadcasting System (PBS), first shown in October 1983.

46. Scigliano, *South Vietnam*, pp. 30–31.

47. Shaplen, *The Lost Revolution*, pp. 132–134.

48. Scigliano, *South Vietnam*, pp. 51–55.

49. Kahin, *Intervention*, p. 95.

50. The full name for the Can Lao was Can Lao Nhan Vi Cach Mang Dang (Personalist Labor Revolutionary Party).

51. Kahin, *Intervention*, pp. 96–97. On January 6, 1956, Diem introduced Ordinance No. 6. According to its language, anyone considered a danger "to the defense of the state and public order" could be arrested. Diem later promulgated the notorious Law 10/59, which went into effect on May 6, 1959. Under its terms, anyone who committed or aimed to commit sabotage, or infringed upon the security of the state, or belonged to a subversive organization, would be sentenced to death by special military courts within three days of being charged, and there would be no appeal.

52. Scigliano, *South Vietnam*, pp. 104–105, 120–124. At the time of Diem's ascension to power in the South, about 40 percent of rice lands were owned by 2,500 people, one-quarter of 1 percent of the rural population. Tenant rentals were commonly 50 percent of the crop, and tenants often had to furnish their own equipment, water buffalo, labor, seeds, and anything else needed to produce the crop. There were 1,584 French landowners expropriated and about 111,000 tenants received the lands, about 10 percent of South Vietnam's tenant farmers.

53. Kahin, *Intervention*, p. 99.

54. Herring, *America's Longest War*, p. 63.

55. Duiker, *The Communist Roads*, pp. 172–173.

56. Kahin, *Intervention*, p. 103.

57. Turley, *The Second Indochina War*, pp. 7–9.

58. *Ibid.*, p. 21.

59. Duiker, *The Communist Road*, p. 175.

60. Interview with Dr. Pham Thi Xuan Que on videotape in "America's Mandarin," one of the documentaries in the "Vietnam: A Television History," cited in note 45 above. She said "hound dogs" was the term for Nhu's secret police.

61. Race, Jeffrey, "The Origins of the Second Indochina War," *Asian Survey* (May, 1960), pp. 381 ff.

62. Duiker, *The Communist Road*, p. 184.

63. *Ibid.*, p. 184; quote is from Millett, Allan R., and Maslowski, Peter, *For the Common Defense: A Military History of the United States of America* (New York: The Free Press, 1984), p. 545.

64. *Ibid.*, pp. 186–190.

65. Turley, *The Second Indochina War*, pp. 24–25; Porter (ed.),"Communique of the 15th Plenum of the Lao Dong,"May 13, 1959, *Vietnam Documents*, vol. 2, Document 21, pp. 44–46. This communique reflects the crucial decision made by the Communist leaders to permit armed struggle in the south as part of the insurgent strategies to undermine Diem's GVN.

66. Duiker, *The Communist Road*, pp. 190–193.

67. Doyle and others, *Passing the Torch*, pp. 157–159.

68. Duiker, *The Communist Road*, p. 194.

69. Turley, *The Second Indochina War*, pp. 30–31.

70. Pike, Douglas, *Vietcong: The Organization and Technique of the National Liberation Front of South Vietnam* (Cambridge, Mass.: MIT Press, 1966), pp. 77–84, 109–118; and Duiker, *The Communist Road*, p. 197.

71. Porter (ed.),"Manifesto of the South Viet Nam National Front for Liberation," December, 1960, *Vietnam Documents*, vol. 2, Document 37, pp. 86–89. The moderate nature of its program was to serve as a bridge linking the Communists and non-Communist nationalists in a common cause, the overthrow of the "disguised

colonial regime of the U.S. imperialists" and the American "lackey" "the dictatorial Ngo Dinh Diem administration."

72. Duiker, *The Communist Road*, pp. 196–198.

73. *Ibid.*, p. 198.

74. Turley, *The Second Indochina War*, pp. 31–32.

75. Pike, *Vietcong*, pp. 136–150.

76. Porter (ed.), "Address By Lao Dong Party Secretary Le Duan," April 20, 1960, *Vietnam Documents*, vol. 2, Document 27, pp. 68–70. Duan's speech is the most authoritative public statement of Hanoi's evolving policy toward the South. It stressed that Hanoi wanted above all else to avoid a war that would bring in the Americans and engulf North Vietnam.

77. Rust, William J., *Kennedy and Vietnam: American Vietnam Policy 1960–1963* (New York: Da Capo Press, 1985), pp. 1–20; Spector, *Advice and Support*, pp. 369–371; and Kahin, *Intervention*, pp. 123–126.

78. Spector, *Advice and Support*, pp. 349–361.

79. Porter (ed.), "Memo from Ambassador Elbridge Durbrow to President Ngo Dinh Diem," October 14, 1960, *Vietnam Documents*, vol. 2, Document 31, pp. 75–78. In a tactfully worded, lengthy memo, Ambassador Durbrow, who had cleared the memo with Secretary of State Christian Herter beforehand, suggested many reforms for President Diem to make. Diem, who resented Durbrow's intrusion into such "internal matters," chose to disregard them all.

80. Herring, *America's Longest War*, pp. 70–71.

81. Doyle and others, *Passing the Torch*, pp. 186–187.

82. Gravel, Mike, ed., *The Pentagon Papers: The Defense Department History of U.S. Decisionmaking in Vietnam* (Boston: Beacon Press, 1971), Vol. II, p. 22; Baritz, Loren, *Backfire: Vietnam: The Myths That Made Us Fight, the Illusions That Helped Us Lose, the Legacy That Haunts Us Today* (New York: Ballantine, 1985), p. 16. According to Baritz: "South Vietnam was an American invention,...What was invented was not the place called South Vietnam, obviously, but the idea about the place." The southern military zone never evolved into a nation whose people shared a common culture, purpose, or identity.

RAISING THE STAKES

4

Vietnam represents the cornerstone of the Free World in Southeast Asia, the keystone to the arch, the finger in the dike....Vietnam is crucial to the free world in fields other than military. Her economy is essential to the economy of Southeast Asia; and her political liberty is an inspiration....We must assist the inspiring growth of Vietnamese democracy and economy.

John F. Kennedy

COLD WAR CRISES

When John F. Kennedy took the oath of office on January 20, 1961, the world appeared to be a dangerous place. Everywhere in Asia and Africa, Third World nations were breaking free from colonialism and struggling to establish stable governments. Nikita Khrushchev, seeing possibilities for advancing Soviet interests in the turmoil generated within the emerging nations, vowed his support for anticolonial "wars of national liberation." Khrushchev, emboldened by Soviet breakthroughs in space and missile technology in the late 1950s, crowed that Communism was superior to capitalism and told anxious Americans that their grandchildren would live under Communism. Kennedy, sensing the American Cold War angst during his 1960 presidential campaign, had attacked what he called the "horse and buggy" policies of the Eisenhower administration that he charged had permitted the U.S. economy to stagnate and had allowed the Soviets to gain the initiative in the Cold War. Kennedy vowed to "get the country moving again" and to regain American primacy in world affairs.

In order to rally the nation to face the challenges he saw, Kennedy struck an alarmist note in his inaugural address. He sounded the theme of a nation embattled, facing crises around the world, with the fate of the free world hanging on the outcome of the long twilight struggle between the Soviet Union and the United States. He warned that the time was short, that the perils were grave, and that the news would get worse before it got better. But he also struck a pose of gallant defiance: He welcomed the challenge "of defending freedom in its hour of maximum danger." And he warned the Soviet leaders, "Let every nation know, whether it wishes us well or ill, that we shall pay any price, bear any burden, meet any hardship, support any friend, oppose any foe to assure the survival and success of liberty."[1]

Despite evidence of a growing rift between China and the USSR, Kennedy and his senior advisers embraced the containment ideology held by his predecessors, Eisenhower and Truman. The New Frontiersmen viewed Communists forces as an interlocked threat that must be checked by the United States around the globe. Kennedy and his men also shared a penchant for action. They eagerly picked up the gauntlet that Khrushchev had thrown down and sought arenas in which to challenge Soviet initiatives. The new secretary of defense, Robert McNamara, a Republican and formerly president of Ford Motor Company, called for and got the largest peace-time increase in defense spending in U.S. history. The United States immediately embarked on a crash program to build up both its strategic nuclear arsenal and its conventional military forces.

The Kennedy administration scrapped the Eisenhower doctrine of "massive retaliation" for "flexible response," strategic versatility that permitted a calibrated U.S. response to any Soviet-backed uprising without having to risk a nuclear confrontation. Recognizing that the Third World would be the principal Cold War battleground, the new administration developed its counterinsurgency capabilities. President Kennedy also wanted to eliminate the "conditions in which Communism flourished," placing emphasis on developing programs of economic and technical assistance for Third World nations that "would channel revolutionary forces into peaceful, democratic paths."[2]

Kennedy and his advisers shared many of the assumptions and illusions of the Eisenhower administration concerning Vietnam and Southeast Asia. They viewed Vietnamese Communism as an advance arm of Chinese and Soviet Communism and absolutely dependent on them for its sustenance rather than having a largely autonomous national foundation.[3] To the New Frontiersmen, South Vietnam remained a domino threatened by external aggression whose fall would imperil other Southeast Asian nations and threaten vital U.S. national security interests. Like the members of the Eisenhower administration that preceded them, Kennedy and his advisers believed that they could develop the programs and take the initiatives necessary to control the political destiny of southern Vietnam. As a senator, Kennedy had been a strong backer of Ngo Dinh Diem; he had consistently supported the Eisenhower policy of keeping Vietnam partitioned and maintaining a non-Communist state in its southern half. Kennedy quickly made ensuring the survival of South Vietnam a top foreign policy priority, confident that the new counterinsurgency forces that he planned to deploy to Vietnam would enable Diem to defeat the insurgents and demonstrate that Soviet-sponsored wars of "national liberation" could not succeed in the Third World.

Other factors increased Kennedy's commitment to retaining a non-Communist government in southern Vietnam. His thin margin of victory in the 1960 election made him vulnerable to Republican charges that he was "soft" on Communism. Ironically, he had leveled similar charges at Eisenhower during the recent campaign, and he knew full well that Nixon and other Republican leaders would be quick to retaliate if he should appear irresolute in the pursuit of anti-Communist foreign policy objectives or if the Communists should make advances anywhere in the world. As a Democratic president, he also felt vulnerable to the legacy of McCarthyism and memories of the "loss of China." Further, the Bay of Pigs fiasco, occurring early in his presidency, probably reinforced his inclination to take a tough anti-Communist stance in Southeast Asia.[4]

Kennedy's first Southeast Asian challenge came in Laos rather than in Vietnam. Eisenhower had warned his youthful successor that Laos was the most acute Cold War crisis of the moment and told him that if Laos were lost, the entire Far East would soon follow. The old general advised military intervention if necessary to save that country from a Communist takeover.[5] In Laos, the Eisenhower administration had been backing General Phoumi's right-wing government, which was engaged in a small-scale civil war with neutralist and Communist forces that were backed by DRV forces and aided by the Soviet Union. Phoumi's government verged on collapse as Kennedy took office, and the young president was forced to act quickly to try and salvage it.

Kennedy seriously considered military intervention in Laos in March 1961, then decided against it because the Joint Chiefs of Staff told him that it might take 60,000 troops and possibly nuclear weapons if the Chinese intervened as they had in Korea. Probably Kennedy's failure to intervene in Cuba at the time of the Bay of Pigs disaster killed any possibility of sending troops into Laos. How could Kennedy explain to the American people his willingness to send troops to Laos 9,000 miles away if he was unwilling to send them to Cuba ninety miles away? Renouncing the military option in Laos, Kennedy sought a political resolution of the civil war.

The Soviets and the British agreed to reconvene the Geneva Conference and to try to work out a negotiated settlement among the Pathet Lao, neutralist, and pro-Western factions. Eventually a formula evolved at Geneva, and an agreement was signed July 23, 1962.[6] Laos became a neutral nation governed by a coalition under Prime Minister Prince Souvanna with the pro-Western and Communist factions sharing power. The new coalition government was a fragile creature that favored the Pathet Lao and its North Vietnamese backers, who kept thousands of troops in eastern Laos in violation of the Geneva agreement.[7] The Communists controlled the eastern half of the country including two provinces bordering Vietnam containing major infiltration routes along the developing Ho Chi Minh trail. (Kennedy also violated the Geneva agreement on Laos when he authorized the CIA to conduct military operations in that country that involved arming 9,000 Meo tribesmen in order to strike against the Ho Chi Minh trail.[8])

As he was deciding to seek a political settlement in Laos, Kennedy's concern for South Vietnam was growing because Diem's position continued to deteriorate. Almost as soon as the new president had settled into the Oval Office, he had received a pessimistic report from General Landsdale stating that the southern insurgents were increasing their numbers, were extending their control over more and more terrain and villages, and were getting closer to taking over the shaky Diem government. Landsdale called for an increase in U.S. aid to the GVN, a 20,000-man increase for the ARVN, and he urged that the South Vietnamese armed forces be taught quickly how to confront the revolutionaries with the "tactics and strategy of unconventional warfare."[9]

Despite their rising worries over Diem's survivability, for most of their first year in office Kennedy officials continued Eisenhower's policies in South Vietnam. In May 1961, Kennedy approved a few actions to try to shore up Diem's weakening position. He ordered an increase in the MAAG contingent in South Vietnam by 100 advisers, approved the 20,000-man increase for the ARVN, and sent in 400 Special Forces troops (Green Berets) to train South Vietnamese forces in counterinsurgency tactics. He also dispatched Vice President Lyndon Johnson to South Vietnam to assure Diem of continuing strong U.S. support. In addition, the president authorized covert operations against North Vietnam. South Vietnamese paramilitary units were sent into the DRV on espionage, sabotage, and psychological warfare missions. Finally, Kennedy established a task force headed by Walt Rostow to consider additional measures that the United States might have to take if the Communist threats to Laos and South Vietnam increased: bombing North Vietnam, blockading its ports, and sending U.S. combat forces to South Vietnam.[10] The president's actions in the spring of 1961 represented a minimal response that did not move the U.S. commitment in Vietnam much beyond the levels achieved under Eisenhower. They were intended mainly to buy time, to keep options open, and to enable Kennedy and his advisers to deal with U.S. foreign policy crises elsewhere.

In the fall of 1961, events forced President Kennedy to give even more attention to Vietnam. Hanoi increased the rate of infiltration of regroupees into the South. The insurgents sharply increased the military pressures on Diem's floundering government. NLF forces escalated their military campaigns, threatening to overrun the Mekong delta. Vietcong main force units also launched a major offensive in central South Vietnam. They seized Phuoc Vinh, the capital of Phuoc Long province, sixty miles northwest of Saigon. NLF regular forces attacked other provincial towns in the central highlands. President Diem, frightened by the rising level of military activity, called for additional American military aid. The Joint Chiefs of Staff (JCS) considered sending U.S. combat forces to the embattled country.[11]

Kennedy, not wanting to send American combat forces to Vietnam, sent instead his personal military adviser, General Maxwell Taylor, accompanied by Rostow, on a fact-finding mission. Taylor's findings submitted to the president on November 3 were starkly pessimistic. They confirmed the rot in the GVN: Diem's government was ineffective and unpopular. The ARVN forces refused to take the offensive against the insurgents. Taylor recommended that the United States undertake a "limited partnership" with the GVN by significantly increasing its military support for Diem and by upgrading the performance of GVN paramilitary and local defense forces in order to free the ARVN regulars for combat against the NLF forces. He also recommended sending 8,000 U.S. combat troops.[12]

While administration officials were absorbing Taylor's report, Kennedy received another recommendation, this one written by Undersecretary of State Chester Bowles and by Averell Harriman, the chief American negotiator at Geneva. Bowles and Harriman frankly doubted Diem's ability to survive, opposed increasing the U.S. commitment to the GVN, and proposed instead that Kennedy seek a negotiated settlement in Vietnam. They called for an expanded agenda at Geneva, currently dealing with Laos, to work out a negotiated solution for Vietnam based on the 1954 Geneva Accords.[13]

Kennedy's advisers had given him clear choices for Vietnam. He could either expand the U.S. commitment in an effort to seek a military solution or he could try for a negotiated settlement. He quickly ruled out a negotiated settlement for Vietnam. Having already opted for negotiations on Laos, having suffered the Bay of Pigs fiasco, and having accepted the Berlin Wall, Kennedy feared that a decision to seek a political settlement in Vietnam would send the wrong signal to Khrushchev and other Soviet leaders who already believed that Kennedy was not tough enough to stand up to Soviet pressure tactics. Further, Kennedy feared domestic political reprisals from his anti-Communist flank if he opted for negotiations on Vietnam as well as Laos.

On the other hand, the president refused to send U.S. combat troops, which would significantly raise the American commitment in South Vietnam. He feared that the introduction of American combat forces would jeopardize the Laotian negotiations at Geneva. Kennedy was skeptical that

U. S. Army Special Forces on a clear and search mission with Montagnard troopers. President Kennedy believed that these "Green Berets," trained to perform counterinsurgency missions, would enable the South Vietnamese government to win the hearts and minds of the people and defeat the Vietcong insurgency.
Source: USMI Photo Archives.

U.S. combat forces could solve Diem's problems, believing that the South Vietnamese would have to defeat the insurgents. Kennedy also feared that once American soldiers engaged in combat and took casualties, the pressures to send more troops would be intense. Once he started sending troops, where would it end? Diem himself did not welcome combat troops. He wanted increased U.S. financial support and equipment to strengthen his own forces, not U.S. armies fighting in his country.[14]

Kennedy tried to solve the Vietnam dilemma by choosing the middle ground. Influenced by a memo from Secretary of State Dean Rusk and Secretary of Defense Robert McNamara, the president rejected Taylor's proposal to send combatants. But Kennedy approved Taylor's proposals to increase significantly the number of U.S. military advisory and combat support personnel and equipment, including helicopters, transport, and reconnaissance aircraft. He approved funding to increase the ARVN force levels and to upgrade their training and equipment. In addition, efforts were made to improve district forces and local security forces. Kennedy hoped that these actions would arrest the steady political and military erosion occurring in South Vietnam. He also knew that the large increases in the number of U.S. advisory and support personnel would violate the Geneva Accords of 1954. Accordingly, in December 1961, the State Department issued a White Paper that claimed renewed aggression by Hanoi in violation of the Geneva agreements justified the U.S. escalatory actions in South Vietnam.[15] Kennedy's decisions in November 1961 formed the basis of the U.S. Vietnam policy for the remainder of his presidency.

Because many Kennedy administration officials believed that the inept and repressive South Vietnamese government itself was a major cause of the insurgency and an obstacle to defeating it, all their aid increases were approved with the proviso that Diem would take actions to reform his government and to broaden his base of support. But Diem stubbornly resisted American pressures to get him to reform his administration and his army. He made it clear to U.S. Ambassador Frederick Nolting that South Vietnam's governance was an internal matter beyond the province of American officials. He told Nolting bluntly that the GVN "did not want to be an American protectorate."[16] The United States quickly yielded to Diem. But by refusing to confront Diem or to make increased U.S. assistance contingent upon his reforming his government, American officials encouraged the South Vietnamese leader to continue traveling down a self-destructive path that would ultimately destroy the limited U.S.–Diem partnership, Diem's government, and Diem himself.

The persistent refusal of Diem and his successors to make reforms that would have made their governments more liberal, more democratic, and more responsive to the needs and welfare of the peasants was a major cause of the ultimate Communist victory and American defeat in South Vietnam. In Diem's case it was much more than stubbornness, pride, and arrogance. He and Nhu believed that they knew how to run their government better than their U.S. advisers, and they resented and rebuffed American efforts to intervene in what they regarded as an internal matter. They also perceived that America had committed itself to their cause and would continue to provide them with support even if they did not make the requested reforms. They understood that the Americans preferred stability and continuity above all else. Further, they knew that the Americans would not pressure them severely to make changes while they were under the stress of insurgent assaults because U.S. officials feared undermining their fragile regime and aiding the rebels.

But there were other, more important, reasons why Diem and subsequent leaders of South Vietnam, mostly army generals, could never make the necessary reforms that might have strengthened their governments and improved their chances for long-term survival. These factors also shed light on the underlying South Vietnamese political limits that continually frustrated U.S. efforts in Vietnam and ensured the eventual U.S. defeat and the demise of South Vietnam. Diem and all his successors did not respond to U.S. requests for reform because they could not, at least not without grave risk to their survival.

In the first place, they would lose legitimacy, the perceived right to govern, in the eyes of their own people if they appeared to be neo-colonial puppets, doing what their American masters dictated. That was a charge consistently made against them by Hanoi and NLF propagandists. Second, the South Vietnamese governments, whether headed by a civilian or a general, were essentially military dictatorships. Their power, their ability to govern, depended mainly on the support of powerful senior military officers whose loyalty had to be purchased, often corruptly. Any effort to move beyond the coterie of generals and reach out to other classes by making reforms that threatened or appeared to threaten the interests of generals, such as land reform, a wider suffrage, or village autonomy, risked provoking a coup d'etat and loss of power.[17]

There was another restraint, another dilemma, that American officials concerned to reform South Vietnamese governments could never overcome. Genuine reform that might have broadened a regime's popular base also would have risked bringing to power a leader who might have sought a ceasefire, opted for negotiations with NLF officials, formed a neutralist coalition government, and asked the Americans to leave. U.S. officials regarded such possibilities as tantamount to an American defeat because they believed that such a government would soon be dominated by NLF leaders who would eventually seek a reunion with Hanoi. In short, a succession of South Vietnamese governments dared not reform and American officials dared not push them too hard toward reform. These unresolved political dilemmas constituted an integral part of the American ordeal in Vietnam.

A LIMITED PARTNERSHIP

Kennedy's November 1961 decisions to violate the military provisions of the 1954 Geneva agreements and to increase drastically American military support levels for the GVN were intended to keep Diem in power at the same time keeping the American commitment in South Vietnam limited, preserving the administration's freedom of action, and maintaining U.S. control of events in Vietnam. Kennedy was not trying to win in Vietnam; he was doing only enough not to lose. By opting for the limited partnership, he revealed that he was not prepared to make a tough decision to either try to negotiate a settlement and withdraw or to send large numbers of American combat forces and try to win the war in South Vietnam.

Instead of biting the bullet, Kennedy only took a few nibbles at it, hoping that they would be sufficient but knowing that if the increased support levels proved inadequate, he would again have to confront the crisis. Kennedy had inherited a commitment in South Vietnam from Eisenhower. He would not abandon it, fearing the loss of American prestige and power vis-a-vis the Soviet Union and political damage to his administration at home if he did. The costs of pulling out appeared to him greater than the costs of getting in deeper.[18] Without fully realizing it, Kennedy had "maintained the momentum of American involvement,"[19] a momentum that, tragically, neither he nor his successor could arrest before the United States plunged into a large and lengthy war that it eventually lost.

To implement the newly formed limited partnership with the GVN, the United States rapidly expanded its military presence in southern Vietnam. A reorganized and expanded military mission, the Military Assistance Command, Vietnam (MACV), commanded by General Paul Harkins, replaced MAAG. Thousands of American advisers poured into South Vietnam during 1962. Hundreds of U.S. helicopters, reconnaissance, and transport aircraft arrived, with American pilots and maintenance personnel on board. Special Forces units moved into the central highlands to train Montagnards in various kinds of counterinsurgency operations. American advisers accompanied ARVN forces into combat zones, and American helicopter pilots flew ARVN troops into battle. Although American forces were officially limited to advisory and support roles, Americans on the ground and in the air increasingly found themselves in combat situations as the war escalated. By the summer of 1962, American soldiers were fighting and dying alongside their ARVN counterparts in South Vietnam.[20]

During the first half of 1962, bolstered by the large increases in U.S. advisers, support personnel, and equipment, the South Vietnamese army took the offensive against the Vietcong insurgents. Using helicopters flown by American pilots, ARVN commanders moved into Vietcong strongholds northwest of Saigon and the U Minh forest along the Gulf of Thailand. South Vietnamese Air Force (VNAF) pilots incinerated villages with napalm and made use of defoliation techniques to deny the guerrillas use of crops and livestock. The ARVN 7th Division attacked a guerrilla stronghold in the Plain of Reeds, eighty miles southwest of Saigon, killing scores of Vietcong in three days of fighting. In July, ARVN forces launched a major offensive in Kien Hoa Province. A month later, ARVN forces, supported by U.S. helicopters, invaded the Ca Mau peninsula.[21]

The ARVN mounted larger offensives against Vietcong strongholds later in the year. In November, a force of more than 2,000 troops, transported by over fifty U.S. helicopters, launched a full-scale attack in War Zone D northwest of Saigon. It was the advent of the helicopter more than any other contribution the Americans made to the GVN war effort during the 1962 buildup that enhanced the fighting abilities of the ARVN forces. Helicopters, which began arriving in Vietnam in December 1961, transformed the face of the war. They were flown on combat assault missions, provided transport and ferry services, and supplied Special Forces camps deep in the central highlands. Other important helicopter missions would evolve with experience, including gunships and medevac units.

As the conflict expanded in 1962, U.S. advisers discovered that there was not just one war in South Vietnam, but several, each with its own terrain, methods of warfare, and strategic importance. The Mekong Delta, a watery world of flat expanses, of rice paddies, and of irrigation canals, dominated by the many tributaries of the Mekong river, constituted one war region. Travel in the delta regions was mostly by boats and sampans. In 1962, the Vietcong had about 10,000 regular troops and at least that many guerrilla irregulars in the delta. Operating out of bases located in remote, impenetrable swamps, the insurgents were almost immune from attack and enjoyed uncontested mobility in this strategic region containing 60 percent of the South Vietnamese population and producing about 75 percent of its annual rice crop.[22]

Beginning about fifty miles north of Saigon and running north for almost 200 miles, varying in elevation from 500 to over 3,000 feet, lay the mountain plateaus of the central highlands. Here, another kind of war raged. Dominating central Vietnam, the highlands were sparsely inhabited by Montagnard tribes. The Vietcong often recruited the Montagnards, historically hostile to the Vietnamese, who regarded them as primitives. Since troops could not operate effectively in the highlands without Montagnard support, both the Americans and the GVN tried to wean the Montagnards away from the insurgents. By the spring 1962, several ARVN divisions were deployed in the central highlands to try to contain the Communists because the forces that could control this region held the key to the strategic security of the populated coastal enclaves.[23]

North of the central highlands lay the jagged peaks of the Truong Son Mountains, a rugged wilderness of rain forests, steep ridges, roaring rivers, and foul weather. In this region, South Vietnam narrowed to a width of thirty to sixty miles. Lying just below the Demilitarized Zone (DMZ) and bordering Laos to the west, the Truong Son Mountains were a major infiltration route for the Vietcong. The rugged peaks rising to 8,000 feet were almost impenetrable to ARVN forces. The guerrillas dominated the region, frequently overrunning ARVN units and ambushing their reconnaissance patrols.[24]

At the same time that its armies, with enhanced U.S. support, went after the Vietcong, the GVN implemented a "strategic hamlet" (ap chien luoc) program. Strategic hamlets were designed by Eugene Staley and promoted by a British advisory mission headed by Sir Robert Thompson, who had used strategic hamlets to defeat a Communist insurgency in Malaya during the mid-1950s. Through the strategic hamlets, Thompson planned to complement the ARVN military effort by offering the Vietnamese villagers physical security and economic development. Peasants would be removed from areas of Vietcong activity to secure villages defended by ARVN forces initially and then later by specially trained local militia. Civic action teams would restore village self-government and implement social and economic programs that would benefit the villagers.

American counterinsurgency enthusiasts supported the strategic hamlet program. They understood that the threat the revolutionaries posed to the GVN was more political than military. To defeat the Vietcong insurgency, it would be necessary to cut it off from its popular base in the rural villages. Winning the war in the villages, winning the villagers' hearts and minds, required more than weapons. It required furnishing the peasants with positive economic and social incentives for supporting the South Vietnamese government. Before these programs could be implemented, the GVN would have to guarantee the physical security of the villagers, both to insulate them from insurgent attacks and to deny the guerrillas access to provisions and recruits. Kennedy administration officials believed that the strategic hamlet program promised to separate the Vietcong from the villagers and thereby kill the rebellion.[25]

Diem embraced the idea of isolating the Vietcong from the rural population. Under the rubric of Operation Sunrise, the first fortified villages were under construction in March 1962 in Binh Doung province, a heavily forested Vietcong stronghold forty miles northwest of Saigon. ARVN forces dispersed the insurgents. By summer, several strategic hamlets had been carved out of the jungle, accommodating over 3,000 people. The new villages were equipped with schools, medical clinics, markets, and a defense force.[26]

Diem hailed the strategic hamlet program as the ultimate solution to the problems of rural pacification and reconstruction. Diem's brother, Nhu, was particularly enthusiastic and became the driving force behind the program. He saw the strategic hamlets not only as a means of isolating the people from the Vietcong and regaining loyalty to the GVN via social and economic development but also as vehicles for social control, political indoctrination, and ideological transformation. With the villagers under the control of the GVN, Nhu planned to convert them all to his philosophy of Personalism. During the summer of 1962, Operation Sunrise was expanded to other provinces, and by the end of the year Diem and Nhu had made it a national program. They declared 1962 to be the year of the strategic hamlet.

SOCIAL REVOLUTION IN THE SOUTH

The initiative seized by the ARVN forces during 1962 proved to be temporary. Despite using helicopters and having U.S. advisers integrated into the command and staff structure of the South Vietnamese forces at every level, the ARVN forces were prone to operational failures. It proved difficult for the South Vietnamese military to locate and trap the elusive Vietcong guerrillas amidst the swamps and paddy lands of the delta. Peasants sympathetic to the insurgents would provide intelligence to and warn the guerrillas of ARVN or provincial force movements, giving them ample time to escape. The large-scale ARVN sweeps through Vietcong-infested regions usually netted few casualties, prisoners, or captured weapons and stores. As soon as the South Vietnamese forces withdrew, the Vietcong returned to reestablish their networks.

During the latter half of 1962, the insurgents built up their forces and continued to make political gains in the northern Mekong delta region. The delta was split into northern and southern halves by the Bassac River, one of the many tributaries of the Mekong. Historically, the southern delta region had been a Communist stronghold since the days of the Vietminh. During 1962, the Vietcong and GVN forces fought for control of the people and resources of the northern half. The VC gradually gained the ascendancy despite the improved efforts of the ARVN, who were bolstered by U.S. equipment and field advisers.

During this time, the number of main force units the Vietcong could field expanded. The size of their maneuver battalions increased, and their training, discipline, and tactical capabilities improved. Their recruits came mainly from the ranks of the southern peasantry, although their forces were significantly enhanced by about 5,800 infiltrators coming into the south via the Ho Chi Minh trail during 1962.[27] Most of these infiltrators were regroupees, southerners who had gone north in 1954 and 1955, and they constituted highly motivated, thoroughly indoctrinated, specially trained cadres who moved into leadership positions within the Vietcong ranks. Insurgent firepower also increased, coming mostly from captured American weapons acquired when the rebels overran ARVN outposts or ambushed small units. The insurgents also obtained some modern Chinese weapons, automatic rifles and mortars, that had been brought down the Ho Chi Minh trail. Vietcong planners devised tactics to counter the heliborne assaults of the ARVN forces. As their strength, confidence, and tactical sophistication improved, the guerrillas proved more willing to stand and fight the South Vietnamese forces, who still enjoyed tremendous advantages in firepower and numbers.[28]

The escalating conflict in the vital northern delta region came to a head early in 1963 during the Battle of Ap Bac, the most important battle of the developing war in southern Vietnam.[29] In late December, ARVN forces learned of the presence of a heavy concentration of enemy troops near the hamlet of Ap Bac located in Dinh Tuong province forty-five miles southwest of Saigon. Here was a golden opportunity for the ARVN 7th Division, led by Colonel Bui Dinh Dam and considered to be one of the finest units in the South Vietnamese army, to attack and destroy a major Vietcong force. Instead, the battle that occurred on January 2, 1963, turned out to be a stunning rebel victory and an ARVN fiasco. It revealed all the shortcomings of the South Vietnamese armed forces and served as an ominous sign of the future.[30] It also thrust into prominence the senior U.S. military adviser to the ARVN 7th Division, Lieutenant Colonel John Paul Vann, one of the authentic American heroes of the Vietnam era.[31]

The ARVN battle plan called for South Vietnamese forces to launch a three-pronged attack on rebel troops. The Eleventh Regiment Battalion from the 7th Division, helilifted to the battle site, was to attack from the north. Two companies of Civil Guard troops, provincial forces under the command of the province chief, Major Tho, also a Diem favorite, attacked from the south. In addition, a company of the 7th Division, transported in Armored Personnel Carriers (M-113s), commanded by Captain Ba, another Diemist protege, would assault from the west. These attacks were to be supported by artillery fire and tactical bombers, with reserve forces standing by to be helicoptered in if required. Circling overhead in his Army L-19 spotter plane, Colonel Vann, advising Colonel Dam, would coordinate the attacks.

The planned assault resembled an open claw and inside the claw, dug into the Ap Bac treeline, was the Vietcong 514th Battalion, a crack main force outfit of approximately 320 soldiers, reinforced by local guerrillas. Against the 3,000 ARVN and provincial troops, supported by armor, artillery, helicopters, and bombers, the 514th had only automatic rifles, two 30-caliber machine guns, grenades, and a few light mortars. They also had limited stores of ammunition, only about enough for one day's fighting.[32] As the battle began, it appeared that the heavily outnumbered and outgunned rebels, having no exit, would be quickly overwhelmed and destroyed.

The ARVN Eleventh Regiment battalion made their helicopter landings to the north uncontested. Vietcong forces, probing south, encountered the provincial troops. A fierce firefight ensued before the VC retreated to their tree line. Major Tho then ordered his Civil Guards, who had been roughed up by the rebels, to halt their advance. Colonels Dam and Vann then brought in the reserve force to land west of the Ap Bac tree line. The Vietcong riflemen opened fire on the approaching helicopters, ten slow, heavy-bodied H-21s carrying the troops, and five sleek new HU-1 gunships (nicknamed Hueys) flying escort. The VC hit fourteen of the fifteen ships, shooting down five helicopters with rifle fire. The reserve forces that landed sustained heavy casualties, and the survivors were immediately pinned down in the paddy fields by fire coming from the tree line. The company of M-113s, commanded by Captain Ba, were delayed for hours by Captain Ba's caution. When they finally arrived, they were ineffective against the entrenched Vietcong forces.[33] Guerrillas armed only with small arms fire were able to neutralize ten-ton armored behemoths because the ARVN soldiers lacked leadership, nerve, discipline, and tactical competence.

Colonel Vann, observing from the air, incredulous and outraged by the unwillingness of the Saigon forces to attack the VC positions, exhorted Colonel Dam to order both Major Tho and Captain Ba to move their troops forward in order to assault the tree line. They both refused to obey Dam's orders. Vann then requested an airborne unit from Saigon to be brought in to try to salvage the battle. But the order for the paratroopers had to go through Major General Huynh Van Cao, formerly 7th Division commander and now the commander of IV Corps with control over military operations in the northern delta. Cao, whose rank owed more to his political connections than to his professional competence, delayed calling in the airborne forces for several hours, then landed them at a site that permitted the Vietcong forces to withdraw from the field during the night. Cao, under secret orders from Diem to keep ARVN casualties low, chose defeat at Ap Bac in order to protect his career rather than seek the victory that could have been his.[34] ARVN politics had snatched defeat from the jaws of victory to the immense frustration of Vann, the other American advisers, and a few ARVN officers who were prepared to fight. VC casualties were light, eighteen killed and thirty-nine wounded. About eighty Saigon troops were killed as were three Americans. Over a hundred Saigon soldiers were wounded.

What could have been a major ARVN victory turned instead into a significant victory for the NLF and its forces. It was much more than a tactical military success for the Vietcong, who had stood and fought against superior forces. It was a smashing psychological victory that NLF propagandists used to recruit more troops and to win the allegiance of more hamlets to their cause. Ap Bac also signaled that the momentum of the expanding war was again in NLF hands. By summer 1963, many of the villages of the strategic northern delta either supported the NLF or took a neutral stance. The GVN mainly controlled only the towns and cities scattered over the region. As the NLF regulars developed larger force units, greater firepower, and tactical sophistication, the ARVN forces grew increasingly reluctant to encounter them.[35]

For the ARVN forces and Diem's government, "Ap Bac epitomized all the deficiencies of the system."[36] The battle served as a paradigm for military failure. For Diem, the political loyalty of General Cao and Colonel Dam represented above all else coup insurance. He wanted the 7th Division available to rush to Saigon if necessary to repel possible challenges to his regime by dissident ARVN generals. Diem was determined to keep ARVN battle casualties low because he and his brother Nhu believed that both the November 1960 coup attempt and another attack on Diem's life that occurred in February 1962, when two disgruntled Vietnamese Air Force pilots bombed his palace, had been provoked by casualties sustained by ARVN forces fighting the rebels. Diem preferred political survival to waging an aggressive war against the Vietcong in the countryside. General Cao and Colonel Dam preferred losing a battle to risking Diem's displeasure and dismissal from their commands. It was a matter of priorities, and Diem considered rebellious ARVN generals more dangerous foes then the NLF insurgents supported by Hanoi. For Diem and his family, the key to remaining in power lay in retaining a favorable balance of loyal ARVN forces and keeping U.S. economic and military support.

Ap Bac revealed the long-present shortcomings of an army whose leaders were more expert at political intrigue than at fighting battles. Further, the officer class of Diem's army came mostly from urban middle and upper class families, often Catholic and French speaking. They held their enlisted troopers, who were mostly peasant conscripts or mercenaries, in contempt. It dismayed Colonel Vann to discover that ARVN officers were indifferent to the welfare of the troops entrusted to their commands, never associated with them, and did not want to lead the troops in battle. One ARVN officer told Vann that the reason he became an officer was so that he did not have to go out in the field with the troops.[37] Further, Ap Bac demonstrated the pitfalls of going to war with troops who were afflicted with low morale and whose performance suffered from a lack of training. Many ARVN soldiers openly admitted that they were afraid of the guerrillas, considered themselves inferior to them, and did not want to engage them in a firefight.[38] The ARVN troopers also lacked positive incentives for fighting and their leaders failed to provide them with any. They were serving time in the South Vietnamese army, not a cause.

By contrast, at Ap Bac the NLF forces had stood their ground against fearsome weapons and troops that outnumbered them ten-to-one, and they had fought with great skill, tenacity, and courage for a cause in which they believed, a cause for which they were willing to die. American wealth, military technology, and advisory leadership could not compensate for the deficiencies of an army that did not want to fight and whose leaders were under orders not to incur many casualties. Vann, who angrily condemned the ARVN performance at Ap Bac, generously praised his enemies for their valor and discipline shown that day along the tree line near Ap Bac.[39]

While the Saigon armed forces were losing ground to the insurgents in the northern delta, the much-vaunted strategic hamlet program was coming unraveled in the same region. Most delta peasants had been forcibly relocated, many to hamlets whose security could not be guaranteed. Many of these insecure hamlets were overrun or infiltrated by the VC. Even in the secure hamlets, many of the programs that were supposed to bind the people to Saigon were never implemented. Since promised land reforms were not implemented, many relocated peasants ended up losing ancestral lands that they had been forced to abandon and they got none in return from GVN officials. Even though the United States provided ample funds for strategic hamlet services, most were never implemented because of official corruption, incompetence, or both.

In regions where the strategic hamlets were more successful, Vietcong terrorists often attacked the villages, intimidated the people, and kidnapped or murdered Diemist officials. The fundamental problem with this major initial U.S.–South Vietnamese effort at counterinsurgency, the main reason that the strategic hamlets failed, was that Diem and Nhu viewed them primarily as a means of extending their political control over the rural population rather than as furnishing an opportunity to provide the peasants with positive incentives for supporting the GVN. Rural Vietnamese could find little in the strategic hamlet program that worked for their benefit. Although South Vietnamese officials generated much ballyhoo and rigged statistics that vastly exaggerated the number of strategic hamlets constructed and their resident populations, the GVN continued to lose popular support at the rice roots level throughout the latter half of 1962 and into 1963.[40]

The decline in ARVN's military effectiveness and the failures of the strategic hamlet program reflected the political deterioration occurring in South Vietnam from mid-1962 to mid-1963 despite the escalations of the Kennedy administration.[41] The NLF guerrillas continued to grow in numbers and enhance their military capabilities. More important, the Vietcong political cadres continued to gain the support of increasing numbers of villagers in the countryside. Very often, the military actions of the guerrillas supported and advanced the political goals of the insurgency.

There were many reasons why increasing numbers of South Vietnamese peasants chose governance by Hanoi-backed NLF officials over that provided by American-backed GVN officials in 1962 and 1963. In part, the peasants reacted to the political shortcomings of many Diemist officials: their repressiveness, their corruption, and their ineptitude, as well as their lack of genuine interest in the peasants' needs and problems. The GVN simply never gave many villagers any reason to support it and often provided reasons to reject it. In part, the villagers reacted to ARVN and provincial troops who failed to provide them with physical security and who sometimes abused the peasants, stole their food, rice crop, tools, and animals. Often, indiscriminate ARVN use of artillery and bombers injured, maimed, and killed civilians and destroyed their homes. The abuses and failures of the strategic hamlet program angered and alienated many peasants. In part, the villagers were coerced, intimidated into at least passive support for the rebels. The NLF use of terror, which included kidnappings and selective assassinations of Diemist officials, landlords, collaborators, informers, and spies, often carried out with great brutality, could be very effective. NLF propagandists also played on the xenophobia of the peasants, invoking bitter memories of French colonialism and linking the Diem government and its American patrons to the hated colonial past.[42]

But skilled and dedicated NFL organizers also developed many positive incentives with which to win over the villagers whose support was absolutely crucial to their cause. Highly disciplined party cadres often practiced the "three withs": They lived with the villagers, they ate with the villagers, and they worked with them in the rice fields. These cadres were trained to treat the villagers with courtesy, to listen to them, and to respond to their needs. NLF cadres often brought land reform that gave land confiscated from Diemist landlords to poor, landless peasants. They restored traditional village autonomy. They organized farmers, women, and young people into village associations under local leadership. They appealed to traditional Vietnamese values of family, communalism, and the strong nationalist feelings of the peasants. In propaganda terms, the VC cadres offered themselves as liberators. They were liberating the people from Diemist

taxation, repression, corruption, and subservience to the American imperialists.[43] In 1962 and 1963, a revolution directed by the Hanoi Politburo was
taking hold in many parts of the southern Vietnamese countryside. It been
underway in Vietnam since 1945 and had verged on completion in 1954 only
to be thwarted by the partition of the country, the subsequent American
intervention, and the establishment of the Diem government. It had revived
as the 1950s ended and was gaining momentum in the early 1960s.

Even though the situation in southern Vietnam was deteriorating,
Washington saw no reason for reappraising its policy. In Saigon, both
Ambassador Nolting and MACV Commander Paul Harkins proclaimed that
progress was being made. At a December 12, 1962, press conference, President Kennedy spoke optimistically about the war.[44] Premier Diem pronounced the counterinsurgency program a success and insisted that the GVN
military forces were containing the insurgents in the countryside. Diemist
officials prepared elaborate color-coded phony maps and fabricated body
counts that misled gullible U.S. officials in Saigon and Washington who were
strongly inclined to believe in them.

The wall of U.S. and GVN official optimism was breached by some
younger members of the American press corps assigned to cover the Vietnam
war. Because these journalists accompanied the ARVN forces into the field and
interviewed advisers like Colonel Vann who talked frankly with them about the
outcome of Ap Bac and other engagements, they discovered that Saigon was
losing the war in the delta. The ablest of these young journalists were David
Halberstam of the New York *Times* and Neil Sheehan, a reporter for United
Press. Their articles denounced the Diem regime, calling it both inept and
corrupt, and they held Diem primarily to blame for the failing GVN effort. They
called the strategic hamlet program a sham. They challenged official statistics
that inflated both the numbers of strategic hamlets constructed and the numbers
of Vietcong killed.[45] Halberstam filed stories describing the military and political gains that the rebels were making in the northern Mekong delta.[46]

Angry American officials denied the journalists' accounts and accused
them of hurting the American-South Vietnamese war effort. General Harkins,
who insisted that Ap Bac had been an ARVN victory, accused Halberstam of
being unfair to Diem and of writing lies to make him look bad.[47] President
Kennedy, angered by Halberstam's columns, tried to get *Times'* publisher
Arthur O. Sulzberger to recall him. Sulzberger rebuffed the president, and
Halberstam stayed in Vietnam.[48] The reporters responded to these attacks and
pressures by accusing U.S. officials of deceiving the American people about the
growing American involvement in battles that were being lost.[49]

Ironically, there were no fundamental conflicts between the reporters
and the American officials in Saigon; they sought the same goals. The
journalists were patriotic supporters of America's Vietnam policies, not
adversaries. Like Colonel Vann who befriended them, they were Cold
Warriors, ideological anti-Communists who believed in the U.S. cause in

Vietnam and who wanted the GVN to defeat the NLF insurgents and their North Vietnamese backers. But the journalists could see that the war was being lost. They saw through the lies of Saigon officials and the fatuous American official optimism based on deceptions. What the reporters were trying to do was warn Washington and the American people that the war was failing. Unless Diem and Nhu were replaced or radically altered their approach to governance and war, the war would surely be lost and the Communists would win.[50]

Behind the declarations of official optimism, internal reports told a more realistic story of growing tension between Diem and U.S. officials and of a failing war. The relation between the GVN and Washington, always more *Gesellschaft* than *Gemeinschaft*, deteriorated in 1963. Both Diem and Nhu were alarmed by the rapid buildup of the American advisory apparatus. They resented the assertiveness of many Americans, which they often interpreted, correctly, as arrogance and a desire to take over conduct of the war against the rebels. CIA reports confirmed the political deterioration occurring in the delta region and elsewhere.[51] Colonel F. P. Serong, an Australian counterinsurgency expert, sent a secret report to General Harkins describing the failure of the ARVN forces to provide security for or to win the support of the rural population.[52] American officials continued to press Diem to make democratic reforms, which he feared would undermine his regime, provoking Nhu to public criticism of the Americans. During 1963 the U.S.–GVN partnership became increasingly strained; it appeared more and more to be a marriage of inconvenience.

Senator Mike Mansfield, an Asian scholar and longtime supporter of Diem, at President Kennedy's behest, led a fact-finding trip of several Senators to Vietnam in December 1962. On his return he warned Kennedy that the war in Vietnam was becoming an American war that could not be justified by current American security interests in Southeast Asia. He reported that the U.S. escalations had made the Diem regime more unstable and ARVN forces less able to contain the growing NLF insurgency. Further escalation would be a prescription for disaster. Additional efforts necessary for the survival of the GVN would have to come from Saigon, not Washington, and if they were not forthcoming, America should either reduce its commitments to South Vietnam or get out.[53] Kennedy had no intention of walking through the door that Mansfield opened for him. He continued the American military buildup during the first half of 1963. He also continued to support Diem's government despite the growing rift.[54]

THE DECLINE AND FALL OF NGO DINH DIEM

Suddenly, the Buddhist crisis exploded in Hue, which proved to be the beginning of the end of Ngo family rule. The crisis erupted May 8, 1963, when government troops fired into a crowd protesting orders forbidding the

The Buddhist revolt against The Diem family's rule intensified when Thich Quang Duc, an elderly monk, immolated himself by fire on a busy downtown Saigon street June 11, 1963. Dramatic photographs of the gruesome event made the front pages and television news highlights around the world.
Source: USMI Photo Archives.

flying of flags celebrating the 2,507th anniversary of the Buddha's birth. Nine demonstrators were killed. Buddhist leaders accused Diem of religious persecution and demanded religious freedom. Diem refused their demands and denied that his soldiers were involved, blaming the shootings on the Vietcong. Diem's rigid and deceptive response provoked additional demonstrations.

The Buddhist revolt reached new dimensions on June 11 when an elderly Buddhist monk, Thich Quang Duc, immolated himself in front of large crowds on a busy street in downtown Saigon. American news photographers and reporters, alerted beforehand by Buddhist leaders, were at the scene, and soon horrific pictures and accounts of the burning monk made the front pages and television news highlights in America and around the world.[55] World opinion, shocked by the dramatic photograph, criticized Americans for supporting a government that persecuted religious worshippers. American advisers brought intense pressure on Diem to rescind the ban and to conciliate the Buddhists. But Ngo Dinh Nhu, Diem's *eminence grise*, continued to denounce and to red-bait the Buddhists. Nhu and his wife also advised Diem to ignore the American demands and to suppress the Buddhist revolt.[56]

The Buddhist rebellion, which was more a political than religious uprising, had long been in the making. Its roots lay in the mass emigration from the North following the Geneva agreements of July 1954, when nearly a million Catholics streamed south to form a popular base of support for

Diem's emerging government. Under Diem's family rule, Catholics received favored treatment and enjoyed special privileges and opportunities. Priests enjoyed political influence; most district and province chiefs were Catholics. South Vietnam's 1.6 million Catholics constituted a favored minority in a country in which about 11 of its 14 million people were Buddhists.[57]

The Buddhist uprising in Hue reflected not only the passions of the moment, but accumulated resentments deriving from years of discrimination and social repression. The rebellion also reflected a growing militancy on the part of younger, more political monks, who were determined to challenge Diemist proscriptions and to seek a greater role in public life. Thousands of high school and college students, traditionally apolitical, took to the streets in Saigon and Hue to support the Buddhists. Many ARVN soldiers, themselves Buddhists, sympathized with the protesters. American efforts to reconcile the two warring factions failed. The Buddhists failed to present a coherent list of demands and Diem refused all but token concessions.[58] Madame Nhu inflamed the crisis with her shrill denunciations of the Buddhists and ghastly humor when she called Quang Duc's flaming sacrifice "a barbecue"[59] and offered to furnish the gasoline and matches for more immolations. By midsummer the war against the Vietcong had virtually halted, and South Vietnamese society appeared on the verge of disintegrating. The demonstrations and fiery sacrifices continued. Washington officials were deeply troubled and divided over what to do.

On the night of August 21, Diem and Nhu perpetrated a series of wanton acts that sealed their fate in American eyes. Nhu's American-trained praetorian guards, assisted by local police forces, raided pagodas in several cities. Temples were desecrated, 1,420 monks were arrested, and dozens more were killed or injured in these brutal assaults of religious sanctuaries.[60] President Kennedy was stunned and outraged at these latest actions of deranged rulers who appeared bent on committing political suicide. Alarmed ARVN generals began to plot the overthrow of the Ngos before chaos engulfed everyone.

There were several coup plots occurring more or less simultaneously. Some of them had been underway prior to the pagoda raids. The earliest dated from the end of June and had been started by Tran Kim Tuyen, Diem's diminutive national intelligence chief. Tuyen was helped by Colonel Do Mau, director of Military Security Services. Other junior officers joined the plot. American agents encouraged the coup plotters. Nhu's assaults on the pagodas were driving the army officers, many of whom were Buddhists, and the Americans together.[61]

Nhu, who inhabited a Graustarkian world, learning of the existence of the plots and sensing the danger to the regime posed by the developing alliance between American officials and the dissident army officers, embarked on a bizarre scheme to preserve his family's power. He sought a rapprochement with the NLF and with Hanoi. He tried to reach the NLF leaders through intermediaries. He succeeded in making contact with

Hanoi. Nhu apparently was making serious moves toward an accommoda-tion with the enemy and to oust the Americans whom he detested. His actions only increased the growing resolve of some American officials to get rid of him and his outspoken wife, and maybe Diem too, if he insisted on retaining his brother and sister-in-law.[62]

The chief planner of the coup that eventually toppled Diem was Major General Tran Van Don, the commander of ARVN. He worked closely with Lieutenant General Duong Van "Big" Minh, who would head the new government if the coup succeeded. Don made contact with American offi-cials through an old friend, CIA agent Lucien Conein, who became the principal liaison between the generals and American officials as the coup plot developed. On August 24, a group of anti-Diem officials within the State Department sent a cable to the newly appointed American ambassador to Saigon, Henry Cabot Lodge. Lodge was instructed to give Diem a chance to get rid of Nhu, but, if Diem refused, the message indicated that Diem himself might have to go. Lodge was also instructed to inform the generals that the United States was prepared to abandon Diem if he continued to prove uncooperative and that Washington would support a replacement govern-ment. Kennedy approved sending the cable to Lodge.[63]

Ambassador Lodge supported the coup plotters. He sized up Diem as rigid and unreformable; Lodge also perceived that the South Vietnamese president would never separate himself from his brother. Working through Conein, Lodge assured the generals planning Diem's overthrow that they would have U.S. support if the coup d'etat succeeded.[64] But the generals, unable to gain the support of key officers commanding troops in the vicinity of Saigon, and fearful of Nhu's machinations, aborted the coup in late August, placing it on indefinite hold.

Meanwhile, South Vietnam continued to disintegrate. Diem could not conciliate the Buddhists and their supporters, the Nhus remained in power, and the Kennedy administration remained deeply divided over how to handle a deepening crisis that threatened to lose the war and to collapse South Vietnam. As was his wont when faced with tough policy decisions, President Kennedy dispatched another fact-finding mission to South Viet-nam, this one headed by Marine General Victor Krulak from the Defense Department and Joseph Mendenhall of the State Department.

Their reports only added to Kennedy's confusion: General Krulak's report exuded optimism. He reported that the coup had failed, that the ARVN forces were winning the war, and that the United States should continue its support of Diem. Mendenhall's report was starkly pessimistic. He reported that South Vietnam verged on breakdown, that a religious war between Catholics and Buddhists threatened, and that the war against the Vietcong was being lost. Only the removal of Nhu and maybe the replacement of Diem could possibly salvage a nearly hopeless situation. Kennedy, obviously exasperated, asked them, "You two did visit the same country, didn't you?"[65]

As the political crisis in South Vietnam escalated during the fall 1963, President Kennedy conferred with his two leading advisers, special military representative General Maxwell Taylor and secretary of defense Robert McNamara, both just returned from a fact-finding trip to Saigon. *Source*: National Archives

Kennedy, frustrated by the inability of American officials to manage the chaotic political life of South Vietnam, nevertheless was not prepared to consider seeking a negotiated settlement or extricating the United States from what appeared increasingly to be a no-win situation. Nor did he want to bomb North Vietnam, send American combat forces, or take over the political life of the country. He and his advisers were so preoccupied with day-to-day crisis managing in South Vietnam that they had lost the capacity to think in terms of long-range U.S. interests in Southeast Asia or to confront fundamental issues. Kennedy was not prepared to consider any plan of action that might involve the abandonment of a long-standing American commitment in southern Vietnam or Americanizing the war. "The administration drifted along, divided against itself, with no clear idea where it was going."[66]

Kennedy, following weeks of indecision, in early October sent still another fact-finding team, which was headed by Robert McNamara and General Maxwell Taylor, to appraise the general political and military situation in South Vietnam. Their report "badly misjudged the actual conditions in South Vietnam."[67] They reported that the war effort had made great progress since 1962, which simply was not true. The NLF controlled much more territory and population in the fall of 1963 in the Mekong delta region than it had 18 months earlier. McNamara and Taylor reported that prospects for a coup against Diem were slim, even though the coup planners were again busily at work with American support on the plot that would topple Diem in a few weeks. The report also exaggerated the effectiveness of applying selective pressures to Diem in order to get him to stop persecuting the Buddhists and to rebuild his base of support among the urban elites. Ambassador Lodge understood that Diem appeared to be unreformable and would never separate himself from Nhu.[68]

Despite its flaws, Kennedy embraced the recommendations of the McNamara-Taylor report, adopting a policy of applying selective pressures against Diem. He made cuts in some of the programs of economic and military aid to South Vietnam. Kennedy also recalled the CIA station chief in Saigon, John Richardson, who was known to be friendly with Ngo Dinh Nhu. These measures, perhaps intended as such by Kennedy, were taken as signals by General Don and the other coup planners to accelerate their plotting and to seek greater support from the Americans. Lodge, through Conein, assured the conspirators that the United States would do nothing to hinder the coup and would extend military and economic support to any new regime that broadened its base of popular support, effectively prosecuted the war, and cooperated with U.S. officials.[69]

The Kennedy administration remained hopelessly divided over whether to support Diem or the coup planners. Many influential advisers in the CIA, Defense Department, and MACV continued to support Diem. State Department officials believed that Nhu and Diem had to go. "Kennedy himself vacillated, adhering to the policy of not overtly supporting a coup, but not discouraging one either."[70] He relied on Lodge, who was on the scene and who backed the coup plot. As the coup became imminent, Kennedy's chief concerns appear to have been that it might fail or that the United States would be implicated.[71]

As October 1963 came to an end, Saigon seethed with rumors, plots, and counterplots. General Don and his co-conspirators had planned their coup scrupulously. They had secured the support of key generals commanding troops in the vicinity of Saigon, they neutralized the forces of generals remaining loyal to the Ngos, and they established a precise timetable of operations. Nhu, knowing that a coup attempt was nigh, but not knowing precisely which generals and troop units were involved, schemed furiously to flush out the conspirators, even going so far as to concoct an elaborate fake coup that involved one of the generals who, unbeknownst to Nhu, was part of the real coup.

The coup d'etat that destroyed Diem and Nhu began on November 1 at 1:30 (P.M.) Saigon time. The coup leaders moved their forces into place, seizing control of key military and communication facilities. Once certain that a coup against them was underway, Diem and Nhu, from a command post inside the presidential palace, tried frantically to contact ARVN units that they thought still remained loyal to them. They quickly discovered that all had either joined the coup, had been jailed or killed, or could not get their forces to Saigon. Generals Don, Minh, and the others had planned well. The Ngo brothers refused the generals' repeated demands to surrender. They tried unsuccessfully to lure the coup leaders to the palace for consultations, a stalling device that had worked to thwart the November 1960 coup attempt.

At 4:30 P.M., Ngo Dinh Diem phoned Ambassador Lodge at the American embassy. The following conversation ensued:

DIEM:	Some units have made a rebellion and I want to know what is the attitude of the U.S.?
LODGE:	I do not feel well enough informed to be able to tell you. I have heard the shooting, but am not acquainted with all the facts. Also, it is 4:30 A.M. in Washington and the U.S. Government cannot possibly have a view.
DIEM:	But you must have some general ideas. After all, I am Chief of State. I have tried to do my duty. I want to do now what duty and good sense require. I believe in duty above all.
LODGE:	You have certainly done your duty. As I told you only this morning, I admire your courage and your great contribution to your country. No one can take away from you the credit for all you have done. Now I am worried about your physical safety. I have a report that those in charge of the current activity offer you and your brother safe conduct out of the country if you resign. Had you heard this?
DIEM:	No. (pause) You have my phone number.
LODGE:	Yes. If I can do anything for your physical safety, please call me.
DIEM:	I am trying to re-establish order. (hangs up)[72]

Lodge, the American point man in Saigon for the coup, responded disingenuously to Diem's call for help. Diem, who was not obtuse, no doubt inferred the American position from Lodge's offer of asylum: The Americans would do nothing to interfere with the coup, that the United States was, in effect, selling out an ally whom it had helped to install in power and whom it had supported for nearly a decade. Diem's response, eloquent in its own way, was to hang up on the American ambassador.

At about 7:00 P.M., Diem and his brother exited the palace through a secret underground passageway and fled to the home of a friend, a wealthy Chinese merchant residing in the Cholon district. Hours later, ARVN troops overwhelmed the guards and occupied the presidential palace. The next morning Diem and Nhu phoned General Don's headquarters. They offered to surrender in exchange for pledges of safe conduct. Don accepted their offer. They were taken prisoner in front of a small chapel near the house of their friend. While riding in the back of an armored car that had been sent to fetch them, they were murdered, apparently on orders of the coup leaders who feared that the Ngo brothers might find a way to return to power if they remained alive. They were buried in unmarked graves somewhere in Saigon.[73]

In Saigon, news of the successful coup d'etat brought a joyous response. People poured into the streets to celebrate the overthrow of a despised and feared tyrant whose power base, at the time of his downfall, had shrunk to a handful of family members, a few government bureaucrats, and some military retainers. In Saigon, citizens cheered the ARVN soldiers who had taken part in the coup and, assuming that U.S. officials had ordered the coup, praised all Americans they encountered on the streets.

American official spokesmen in Saigon and Washington claimed to have known nothing about the coup and insisted that they had had no part in it. They said that it was an internal political matter involving only quarreling factions of Vietnamese politicians. In fact, the Americans were deeply implicated in the coup. They were aware of it from its inception, and they had encouraged it. Lucien Conein met often with the plotters and functioned as a conduit among the generals, Lodge, and Washington. Conein was with General Don the day that the coup was implemented and Diem overthrown.[74] Without American financial support, promises of noninterference, and most of all, pledges to continue to provide economic and military aid to any replacement government that would emerge from a successful coup, the coup would not have occurred. Certainly, President Kennedy and the other Americans had not ordered Diem's or Nhu's deaths. Kennedy was shocked and deeply troubled at the news of their murders, perhaps feeling responsible for them. But no one had taken any steps to ensure their survival other than making contingency plans for granting them asylum preparatory to removing them from the country. No one told Don and Minh that the Americans wanted Diem and Nhu alive.

The response in Hanoi to the coup was mixed. On the one hand, the Communists were pleased. The coup had rid South Vietnam of an uncompromising anti-Communist zealot who had also staunchly opposed the French. Diem had been a leader with some claim to rival Ho as a symbol of Vietnamese nationalist aspirations. The successful coup also confirmed Hanoi's claims that the Diem regime was a corrupt, unpopular regime that had lost all right to rule. On the other hand, the Communists had to be concerned because the new government, a military junta led by General Minh, had a potential for achieving a broader base of support. Minh was a southerner and a Buddhist who had been one of the leaders of a coup that had overthrown a tyrant. Ominously, the new government had the strong backing of the Americans, and General Minh pledged to prosecute vigorously the war against the NLF. Initially, Hanoi sent out peace feelers to the new South Vietnamese government, but when Ho perceived that Minh was determined to fight on, he ordered the NLF forces to continue their struggle.[75]

THE COUP AND THE QUAGMIRE

Ironically, American support for the coup that had made it possible weakened rather than strengthened the security of southern Vietnam. It ushered in a protracted period of political instability in South Vietnam that hindered counterinsurgency efforts and was one of the causes of large-scale American military intervention in 1965. None of a succession of South Vietnamese governments was as effective as Diem's had been, for all its flaws, either in governing southern Vietnam or fighting the insurgents. American officials who had supported the coup were so enmeshed in the process that they had given little thought to what kind of leaders might come to power after Diem's downfall. They were so convinced that Diem and Nhu had to be removed from power that they just assumed that whoever replaced them would be an improvement.

Having decided to get rid of Diem and to keep the coup plot from him, American officials did not inform Diem that they were no longer willing to tolerate his rejecting their advice and his repressive methods after Americans had been tolerating them for nearly a decade. Ambassador Nolting said of the coup: "I don't think it was fair, just, or honorable to our ally of nine years standing to do this behind his back."[76] General Harkins condemned U.S. support of the coup while not informing Diem.[77] Madame Nhu, traveling in the United States at the time, attributed American support of the coup that killed her husband and brother-in-law to American "arrogance" and "contempt for the Vietnamese people."[78] Lodge's friendly meeting with Diem on the morning of the coup and his evasive answers to Diem's urgent questions while the coup was underway epitomized the hypocrisy of some American officials in Vietnam toward a patriot who had fought for his country's independence for over twenty years.

American complicity in the coup strengthened the American commitment to South Vietnam and "tied the United States to all succeeding regimes."[79] President Johnson, who had supported Diem and argued against the coup, believed that Kennedy's involvement in the coup was the worst error made by the United States during its long involvement in Vietnam. It made the United States responsible for the fate of successive governments. Morally, it locked America deeper into the South Vietnamese quagmire. It also set in motion a train of events that "eventually forced President Johnson in 1965 to choose between accepting defeat or introducing American combat forces."[80]

Three weeks after the coup, Kennedy's assassination overshadowed the murders in Saigon. At the time of his death, Kennedy's Vietnam policy was in disarray. His apologists are on record suggesting that had he lived he was planning to extricate the United States from South Vietnam and that there would have been no American war in that country.[81] The historical record suggests otherwise. In a televised interview with Walter Cronkite broadcast on September 2, 1963, Kennedy told the American people:

> Those people who say that we ought to withdraw from Vietnam are wholly wrong, because if we withdraw from Vietnam, the Communists would control Vietnam. Pretty soon Thailand, Cambodia, Laos, Malaya would go and all of Southeast Asia would be under the control of the Communists and under the domination of the Chinese.[82]

Kennedy retained a strong commitment to the American effort in Vietnam to the end. Had he lived, he and his advisers, most of whom helped forge Johnson's Vietnam policy, would probably have reacted much as Johnson did in 1964 and 1965 and would have done what he did. Had he lived, President Kennedy probably could not have avoided an American war in Vietnam.

What Kennedy might have done can never be known. What can be known is the Vietnam policy of his abbreviated presidency. Kennedy and his advisers accepted the major assumptions and axioms of the containment ideology and its domino correlative. They were conventional Cold Warriors who believed unquestioningly that retaining a non-Communist South Vietnam was vital to the strategic security of the United States. The main consequence of their words and deeds was to increase sharply the American stake in Vietnam from 1961 to 1963.

Vietnam represented President Kennedy's "great failure in foreign policy."[83] "It has been his most enduring legacy."[84] Often preoccupied with other foreign policy crises, he never gave Southeast Asia enough attention. He never asked the hard questions. Only his brother, Robert, could do that. Robert Kennedy once asked at a National Security Council meeting: What if no South Vietnamese government could resist a Communist takeover? If it could not, he stated that America should extricate itself from the region.[85] The president never confronted that potentiality; his administration reacted to Southeast Asian crises and improvised policy on an ad hoc basis.[86] The president preferred to take cautious middle courses. His middle courses of action managed to stave off disaster and to increase the American Vietnam commitment. During Kennedy's presidency, the levels of economic and military aid to the GVN increased significantly. At the time of the coup, South Vietnam was costing the United States $1.5 million per day, and there were 16,500 military advisers in the country, including counterinsurgency forces. Some of these advisory forces engaged sporadically in combat.

Kennedy "bequeathed to his successor a problem eminently more dangerous than the one that he had inherited from Eisenhower."[87] Johnson soon discovered the quagmire in which Eisenhower and Kennedy had enmeshed America. When Johnson confronted the stark choices of either accepting defeat or going to war, he chose war by using the flexible response military forces handed down by Kennedy.

NOTES

1. Excerpts from Kennedy's inaugural address are taken from a copy of the speech printed in Sorensen, Theodore C., *Kennedy* (New York: Harper & Row, 1965), pp. 275–278. Sorensen was special counsel to the president, his chief domestic adviser and speech writer. Sorensen is also the principal author of *Profiles in Courage*, Kennedy's Pulitzer Prize-winning account of courageous senators. Sorensen was Kennedy's closest adviser for much of his political career. Sorensen's account is the most informed that we will ever have of the Kennedy presidency, the memoir that Kennedy himself might have written.

2. Herring, *America's Longest War*, pp. 74–75.

3. Kahin, *Intervention*, p. 126.

4. *Ibid.*, p. 127.

5. Porter (ed.), *Vietnam Documents*, vol. 2, Document 38, pp. 90–92, is a memo of the July 19 meeting between Eisenhower and Kennedy; Clifford, Clark, "A Vietnam Reappraisal," *Foreign Affairs*, vol. 47 (July 1969), pp. 604–605; Parmet, Herbert, *JFK: The Presidency of John F. Kennedy* (New York: Penguin, 1983), p. 81.

6. Protocol to the Declaration of the Neutrality of Laos, July 23, 1962, in Porter (ed.) *Vietnam Documents*, vol. 2, Document 77, pp. 156–160. The nations attending the Geneva conference signing the protocol included Burma, Cambodia, Canada, the People's Republic of China, The Democratic Republic of Vietnam (North Vietnam), France, India, the Kingdom of Laos, Poland, the Republic of Vietnam (South Vietnam), Thailand, the Soviet Union, Great Britain, and the United States. The protocol reads that all foreign troops and paramilitary forces were to be removed within 30 days. 750 U.S. MAAG forces departed as did a few Russians who were mostly pilots. The 10,000 plus PAVN troops remained in Laos in violation of the protocol.

7. O'Ballance, Edgar, *The Wars in Vietnam: 1954–1980* (New York: Hippocrene, 1981), pp. 28–31.

8. Herring, *America's Longest War*, p. 78.

9. Doyle and others, *Passing the Torch*, p. 181. Kennedy, who had a special interest in counterinsurgency, believing it to be the most effective instrument available for checking Third World guerrilla forces, moved to beef up U.S. Special Forces training programs that had begun under the Eisenhower administration in the late 1950s. At the president's direction, special warfare training centers began preparing U.S. soldiers to challenge guerrillas in the jungles and mountains of Laos and Vietnam. Kennedy also read the works of revolutionary theorists including Mao Zedong, Vo Nguyen Giap, and an Argentinian terrorist who had helped Castro come to power in Cuba, Ernesto "Che" Guevara, and he made these tracts must reading for his advisers.

10. Sheehan, Neil, Smith, Hedrick, Kenworthy, E. W., and Butterfield, Fox, *The Pentagon Papers: The Secret History of the Vietnam War* (New York: Bantam, 1971), "National Security Action Memorandum 52," pp. 126–127.

11. Doyle and others, *Passing the Torch*, pp. 191–193; O'Ballance, *Vietnam Wars*, pp. 42–43.

12. Cablegram from General Taylor to Kennedy, Nov. 1, 1961, printed in Porter (ed.), *Vietnam Documents*, vol. 2, Document 70, pp. 140–142. Taylor recommended sending an 8,000-man military force to repair the extensive damage caused by recent floods, forces that could also perform combat missions. Kennedy rejected his suggestion. See also Sheehan et al., *The Pentagon Papers*, Documents 26, 27, 28, and 29, pp. 141–150.

13. Karnow, *Vietnam*, p. 248.

14. Kahin, *Intervention*, p. 134.

15. Herring, *America's Longest War*, p. 84; Berman, Larry, *Planning a Tragedy: The Americanization of the War in Vietnam* (New York, W. W. Norton, 1982), pp. 16–23; Pelz, Stephen, "John F. Kennedy's 1961 Vietnam War Decisions," *Journal of Strategic Studies*, vol. 4, (December 1981), 356–385; Department of State, *A Threat to Peace* (Washington, D.C.: U.S. Government Printing Office, 1961), the State Department White Paper documenting Hanoi's violations of the Geneva Accords exaggerates the amount of Hanoi's support for the NLF and it contradicts CIA intelligence findings. The Rusk-McNamara memo dated November 11, 1961, appears in Sheehan and others, *The Pentagon Papers*, pp. 150–153.

16. Quoted in Herring, *America's Longest War*, p. 84.

17. Blaufarb, Douglas, *The Counterinsurgency Era* (New York: The Free Press, 1977), pp. 85–88.

18. Gelb, Leslie H., with Betts, Richard K., *The Irony of Vietnam: The System Worked* (Washington, D.C.: The Brookings Institution, 1979), pp. 75–79; Pelz, Stephen, "John F. Kennedy's 1961 Vietnam War Decisions," pp. 356–385.

19. Doyle and others, *Passing the Torch*, p. 197.

20. Tuchman, *March of Folly*, p. 299. The Eisenhower administration observed the 1954 Geneva Accords limits on foreign military personnel in South Vietnam. There were about 650 American advisers in South Vietnam in January 1961. By the end of the year there were over 3,000 advisers and support personnel, 9,000 by the end of 1962. At the time of Kennedy's death, there were 16,500. America's limited war in Vietnam began in early 1962.

21. O'Ballance, *The Vietnam Wars*, pp. 43–44; Miroff, Bruce, *Pragmatic Illusions: The Presidential Politics of John F. Kennedy* (New York: David McKay, 1976; Maitland, Terrence; Weiss, Stephen; and the editors, *Raising the Stakes* (Boston: Boston Publishing Co., 1982), pp. 19–21.

22. Blaufarb, *Counterinsurgency Era*, pp. 113–115.

23. Maitland and others, *Raising the Stakes*, p. 23.

24. *Ibid.*

25. Kahin, *Intervention*, pp. 140–141; Herring, *America's Longest War*, pp. 85–86; and Duiker, *The Communist Road*, pp. 201–203; Miroff, *Pragmatic Illusions*, pp. 158–160.

26. Maitland and others, *Raising the Stakes*, pp. 14–15, 18–19.

27. O'Ballance, *The Vietnam Wars*, p. 43.

28. Sheehan, Neil, "Annals of War: An American Soldier in Vietnam, Part 2, A Set-Piece Battle," *New Yorker*, vol. 64, No.19 (July 1988), pp. 35–36; Halberstam, David, *The Making of a Quagmire: America and Vietnam During the Kennedy Era*, rev. ed. (New York: Knopf, 1988), pp. 56–66.

29. The Vietnamese word for hamlet is ap. The main action during the Battle of Ap Bac took place in the tree line near the village of Bac.

30. Halberstam, *Quagmire*, pp. 72–73.

31. John Paul Vann arrived in South Vietnam in March 1962, soon becoming the senior adviser to the ARVN 7th Division. He quickly established himself as one of the best officers in the U.S. Army. He returned to the states after his year's tour as adviser and retired from the Army. Deeply committed to the American cause in Vietnam, Vann returned in 1965 as a civilian official. Until his death in June 1972, Vann was the most effective American adviser involved in counterinsurgency and pacification activities. He corresponded with and briefed American leaders including President Nixon and MACV commanders, generals Creighton Abrams and Frederick Weyand.

32. For accounts of the Battle of Ap Bac, see Sheehan, Neil, *A Bright Shining Lie: John Paul Vann and America in Vietnam* (New York: Random House, 1988), pp. 203–265; Palmer, Dave Richard, *Summons of the Trumpet*, (New York: Ballantine, 1978), pp. 37–51; and Halberstam, *Quagmire*, pp. 67–81;

33. Sheehan, "Annals of War, Part 2," pp. 58–60.

34. *Ibid.*, pp. 60–63; Halberstam, *Quagmire*, pp. 76–81.

35. O'Ballance, *The Vietnam Wars*, pp. 43–47; Duiker, *The Communist Road*, pp. 214–215.

36. Halberstam, *Quagmire*, p. 79.

37. Sheehan, "Annals of War, Part 2," pp. 57–58; Halberstam, *Quagmire*, pp. 52–55.

38. Sheehan, "Annals of War, Part 2," pp. 53–54.

39. *Ibid.*, p. 62

40. Hilsman, Roger, *To Move a Nation* (New York: Delta, 1967), pp. 87–88. Hilsman, a State Department official and counterinsurgency expert, was initially a strong supporter of the strategic hamlet enterprise; Blaufarb, *Counterinsurgency Era*, pp. 116–127; Pike, *Vietcong*, pp. 61–73. According to Pike, p. 102, NLF cadres kidnapped 9,000 officials and murdered 1,700 in 1962 and kidnapped 7,200 and murdered 2,000 in 1963.

41. Porter (ed.), "Short-term Prospects in South Vietnam," extract from a memo by Roger Hilsman, Dec. 3, 1962, *Vietnam Documents*, vol. 2, Document 87, pp. 169–174. Hilsman noted the deterioration of internal security in South Vietnam occurring in 1962.

42. Maitland and others, *Raising the Stakes*, pp. 37–41.

43. *Ibid.*, pp. 42–47.

44. From a videotape, "America's Mandarin," in the television series, "Vietnam: A Television History."

45. Herring, *America's Longest War*, p. 92.

46. See article entitled "Vietnamese Reds Gain in Key Area," that appeared under Halberstam's byline on the front page of the August 15, 1963, New York *Times*; Rust, *Kennedy in Vietnam*, pp. 81–84; Sheehan, Neil, "In Vietnam, the Birth of the Credibility Gap," New York *Times*, Oct. 1, 1988, p. A15.

47. U.S. Army Military History Research Collection, Senior Officers Debriefing Program, Conversations between General Paul D. Harkins and Major Jacob B. Cough, Jr., recorded at Carlisle Barracks, Penn., p. 53.

48. Karnow, *Vietnam*, pp. 296–297.

49. Halberstam, *Quagmire*, chap. 11, pp. 148–155, gives his account of the press controversy; Miroff, *Pragmatic Illusions*, pp. 157–158.

50. Sheehan, "In Vietnam, the Birth of the Credibility Gap," p. 15; Knightley, Phillipp, *The First Casualty* (New York: Harcourt, Brace, Jovanovich, 1975), pp. 376–383.

51. Kahin, *Intervention*, pp. 143–145.

52. Maitland, *Raising the Stakes*, p. 56.

53. Extract of Report to the President on Southeast Asia-Vietnam, by Senator Mike Mansfield, Dec. 18, 1962, in Porter (ed.), *Vietnam Documents*, vol. 2, Document 88, pp. 174–176.

54. Kahin, *Intervention*, pp. 146–147.

55. David Halberstam witnessed Quang Duc's self-immolation. He called it a "scene of medieval horror," *Quagmire*, p. 113.

56. "Thich" means reverend, or the reverend. Madame Nhu's given name was Le Tran Xuan, meaning "beautiful spring." This beautiful, charming, powerful, energetic, bold, and arrogant woman was a fanatical supporter of the Diem government, a religious bigot, and puritanical moralist.

57. Shaplen, *Lost Revolution*, pp. 191–192.

58. *Ibid.*

59. Videotape, "America's Mandarin," from the television series, "Vietnam: A Television History."

60. Kahin, *Intervention*, p. 152.

61. Shaplen, *Lost Revolution*, pp. 197–201.

62. Kahin, *Intervention*, pp. 153–156.

63. Sheehan and others, "Cablegram from the State Department to Ambassador Henry Cabot Lodge in Saigon, August 24, 1963, Document 35, *Pentagon Papers*, pp. 194–195. Its key passages: "U.S. government cannot tolerate situation in which power lies in Nhu's hands. Diem must be given chance to rid himself of Nhu and his coterie....If in spite of all your efforts, Diem remains obdurate and refuses, then we must face the possibility that Diem himself cannot be preserved."

64. Kahin, *Intervention*, pp. 159–160.

65. Hilsman, *To Move a Nation*, pp. 501–505.

66. Herring, *America's Longest War*, p. 102.

67. *Ibid.*, p. 103.

68. Porter (ed.), Extract from "Report of the McNamara-Taylor Mission to South Vietnam," October 2, 1963, *Vietnam Documents*, vol. 2, Document 109, pp. 201–203.

69. Kahin, *Intervention*, p. 171.

70. Herring, *America's Longest War*, p. 104.

71. Sheehan and others, *Pentagon Papers*. There is extensive cable traffic among U.S. officials in Washington and Saigon, both favoring and opposing the coup during the month preceding it. See Documents 48–58, pp. 213–231.

72. *Ibid.*, "Lodge's Last Talk with Diem," Document 59, p. 232.

73. Shaplen, *Lost Revolution*, pp. 208–211. Shaplen says about $600,000 was funnelled through the U.S. embassy to the coup leaders who used it to bribe key generals stationed near Saigon into supporting the coup. Lucien Conein says that only $42,000 was spent, and this money was not used for bribes.

74. Interview with Lucien Conein recorded on videotape, "America's Mandarin," from the television series, "Vietnam: A Television History."

75. Duiker, *The Communist Road*, pp. 219–221.

76. Nolting is quoted on videotape, "America's Mandarin," from the television series, "Vietnam: A Television History."

77. U.S. Army Military History Research Collection, Senior Officers Debriefing Program. Conversations between General Harkins and Major Cough recorded at Carlisle Barracks, Penn., p. 54.

78. Interview with Madame Nhu recorded on videotape, "America's Mandarin," from the television series, "Vietnam: A Television History."

79. Berman, Larry, *Planning*, p. 28.

80. *Ibid.*

81. O'Donnell, Kenneth P., and Powers, David F., with Joe McCarthy, *Johnny, We Hardly Knew Ye: Memories of John Fitzgerald Kennedy* (Boston: Little, Brown, 1972), pp. 15–17. O'Donnell overheard Kennedy say that after being reelected he planned to extricate the United States from Vietnam; Hilsman, *To Move a Nation*, chap. 34: "If Kennedy Had Lived?" pp. 524–537. Hilsman asserts that Kennedy believed in counterinsurgency and was skeptical about using U.S. military power in Vietnam. Hillman says that had he lived Kennedy would probably have opted for a negotiated settlement before he would have Americanized the war.

82. Quoted on videotape, "Lyndon Johnson Goes to War, 1964–1965," from the television series, "Vietnam: A Television History."

83. Schlesinger, Arthur M., Jr., *A Thousand Days* (Greenich, Conn.: Fawcett, 1965), pp. 909–910.

84. Walton, Richard J., *Cold War and Counter-Revolution: The Foreign Policy of John F. Kennedy* (Baltimore: Penguin, 1972), p. 201.

85. Hilsman, *To Move a Nation*, p. 501; Schlesinger, Arthur Meier, Jr., *Robert Kennedy and His Times*, (Boston: Houghton Mifflin, 1978) Vol. 2, pp. 746–747.

86. Rust, *Kennedy in Vietnam*, p. x.

87. Herring, *America's Longest War*, p. 107.

AMERICA GOES
TO WAR

5

If we ran out on Southeast Asia, I could see trouble ahead in every part of the globe—not just in Asia but in the Middle East and in Europe, in Africa and Latin America. I was convinced that our retreat from this challenge would open the path to World War III....I knew our people well enough to realize that if we walked away from Vietnam and let Southeast Asia fall, there would follow a divisive and destructive debate within our country....A divisive debate over who lost Vietnam....

Lyndon B. Johnson

THE SAME ONLY MORE

As Lyndon Johnson and his foreign policy advisers turned their attention to Vietnam in late November 1963, they operated within a world diplomatic environment they perceived to be changing. The Sino-Soviet split appeared to be irrevocable; Some U.S. officials believed that the two major Communist powers might have a war one day. The Sino-Soviet split also bore directly upon the expanding war in southern Vietnam. Hanoi supported China in its conflicts with the Soviets and "Soviet influence in Vietnam was negligible."[1] America no longer faced an international Communist monolith bent on world domination; the Soviet-Chinese conspiracy had fragmented into quarreling moieties.

Relations between the United States and the Soviet Union had improved markedly since their confrontation in Cuba in October 1962 over Soviet efforts to install intermediate range missiles on Cuba. Negotiating a nuclear test ban treaty and grain deals with the Soviets in mid-1963 encouraged some U.S. officials to hope for a lasting detente with the USSR. But America continued its policy of non-recognition of China, trying to isolate the PRC from international life. U.S. officials saw China as an expansionist state seeking to assert leadership of revolutionary forces in Southeast Asia and elsewhere among other Third World nations.

To American officials, Southeast Asia appeared especially vulnerable to Chinese intrusions in late 1963. South Vietnam was descending into political chaos in the aftermath of Diem's death. Both leftist and rightist forces challenged the fragile neutralist government of Laos. In Cambodia, Prince Sihanouk had cast off both U.S. aid and offers of protection. In Indonesia, Sukarno was seeking Chinese support for his war against a pro-Western government in Malaysia, a country in which China had supported an insurgency during the early 1950s. Washington feared that China might try to exploit the political turmoil in countries along its southern periphery and that the food-short Chinese might be tempted to overrun the rich rice baskets of Southeast Asia.

The winds of change blowing in other regions of the world heralded the dawning of a more polycentric world order in late 1963. In Western Europe, De Gaulle was challenging the U.S. dominance of the NATO alliance and was trying to reassert French influence in Vietnam. Rioting, revolution, and rising anti-Americanism in Latin America fueled U.S. fears of a spreading Castroism within a region long dominated by the Yanqui colossus. Birthing pains among African nations emerging from colonialism posed threats to world stability. A superpower confrontation in the Congo had been averted in 1961 by a United Nations intervention. American officials feared that the Communist powers might become involved in some of these Third World trouble spots and that such interventions could bring, *inter alia*, confrontations with the United States and the threat of nuclear war. It is within this context of a more fluid, more unstable, and more polycentric world order in which the chief threat to American strategic interests appeared to emanate from Chinese expansionism in Southeast Asia, that Johnson and his men forged their Vietnam policies.

President Johnson inherited from his late predecessor both a commitment to South Vietnam and a group of advisers who had orchestrated that commitment. A brilliantly successful domestic politician, Johnson was initially neither very knowledgeable about nor confident of his grasp of foreign affairs. The methods that had worked for him at home—a subtle amalgam of strong-arm politics, favors, flattery, and compromise to form coalitions based on a consensus of all interested parties—could not be applied to the international realm. In contrast to his mastery of domestic political processes, Johnson found himself often beyond his depth when conducting U.S. foreign policy. Compounding his difficulties in Southeast Asia, in addition to the frustrating limits on American power to influence events in that troubled region, was Johnson's profound ignorance of the history and culture of the Vietnamese people. He never grasped the dynamics of the Vietnamese revolutionary war strategy that the United States was trying to counter nor did he ever comprehend the ideologies or the psychologies of its leaders.

To a much greater degree than Kennedy, Johnson relied on the knowledge and judgment of his senior foreign policy advisers. From late-1964 to mid-1965, during which Johnson transformed "a limited commitment to assist the South Vietnamese government into an open-ended commitment to preserve an independent, non-Communist South Vietnam,"[2] and took his nation to war, the men who most influenced the shaping of Southeast Asian policy were a coterie of Kennedy holdovers: Secretary of Defense Robert S. McNamara, National Security Adviser McGeorge Bundy, Secretary of State Dean Rusk, and Ambassador to South Vietnam Maxwell Taylor. Of these men, McNamara, through his *ex officio* clout, forceful personality, and a keen analytic mind that absorbed enormous amounts of factual data, exerted the greatest formative influence on Johnson's Vietnam policy.[3]

Vietnam did not dominate Johnson's presidency during his first year as it would later; he had entered the White House committed to fighting another kind of war than the one raging in southern Vietnam. Early in his presidency, he had declared "unconditional war on poverty in America."[4] Johnson intended the fight against poverty to be an integral part of what he labeled a "Great Society," a broad range of welfare, social reform, and civil rights legislation that he would soon propose to Congress.[5] In Johnson's expansive view, his Great Society would fulfill the social vision of the New Deal by eradicating residual poverty and racial injustice. The new president would use the powers of the federal government to bring the 40 million Americans still denied equal access to the American dream into the socioeconomic mainstream. Creating his Great Society would also ensure Johnson, a man of vaulting ambitions and possessor of an outsized ego, an honored place in the national memory.

It is one of the many ironic dimensions of the American Vietnam ordeal that Lyndon Johnson, the man whose highest goal had been to expand the American system in order to incorporate all its citizens, felt compelled to Americanize the war in Southeast Asia, a foreign war that soon curtailed his domestic war on poverty, slowed the march of civil rights, destroyed the consensus that he had forged to create his "New Jerusalem," and strangled his beloved Great Society before it could be fully realized. The war in Southeast Asia that President Johnson and his advisers set in motion eventually claimed the lives of over 58,000 of their fellow citizens, many of whom had come from the ranks of the disadvantaged classes whom Johnson had committed himself to helping. From the ranks of the strongest supporters of Johnson's ill-fated Great Society reform program would come some of the most cogent critics of his Vietnam war policies.

Johnson and his advisers quickly embraced the U.S. commitment in Vietnam, considering it to be an integral part of the Kennedy agenda that the new president, in his first speech to the American people, had pledged to continue.[6] Johnson's immediate goal was to deter aggression in Southeast Asia and to give South Vietnam and the other nations on the periphery of Asian Communism the help they needed to maintain their stability and sovereignty. Like Truman, Eisenhower, and Kennedy before him, Johnson considered Southeast Asia to be a vital strategic interest of the United States. He brusquely dismissed any suggestions that the region might be of only marginal importance or that the United States might consider withdrawing from South Vietnam. Two days after becoming president, he asserted: "I am not going to lose Vietnam. I am not going to be the president who saw Southeast Asia go the way China went."[7]

Although Johnson embraced immediately the U.S. commitment in South Vietnam, he shared Kennedy's reluctance to invest large amounts of American military power in the region. He did not want to fight another land war in Asia nor did he want to bomb the North. He feared that large-scale American military intervention would undermine the ability of the South Vietnamese forces to fight their enemies aggressively. The new president also feared that the injection of American combat forces into the Vietnam war would provoke adverse reactions throughout the world and trigger uprisings of domestic opposition that could stifle his domestic reform program and cost him the 1964 presidential election. He rejected initial proposals from the Joint Chiefs of Staff to "undertake major air and ground operations against North Vietnam."[8]

Within 48 hours of Kennedy's death, Johnson held a full-scale briefing on Vietnam which was attended by all his senior foreign policy advisers. He was informed that the new military government of South Vietnam was struggling. It was not broadening its base of support, and the war was going badly for ARVN forces in many provinces. At this meeting Johnson opted for a continuation of Kennedy's policy of sending U.S. military advisers to South Vietnam along with substantial amounts of economic and military aid, and, additionally, he approved the conduct of covert operations against eastern Laos and North Vietnam. The conferees drafted a National Security Action Memorandum (NSAM 273) stressing the continuity of policy between his and his predecessor's administrations: "It remains the Central Objective of the United States in South Vietnam to assist the people and government of that country to win their contest against the externally directed and supported Communist conspiracy."[9]

NSAM 273, along with subsequent increases in the number of advisers and the amount of aid going to South Vietnam, and a step-up of covert operations against the DRV, constituted Johnson's Vietnam policy for the first year of his presidency. It represented a policy of doing the same that Kennedy had done, only doing more of it in the hopes of achieving U.S. policy goals.

COUP SEASON

As Johnson reaffirmed the U.S. commitment to Saigon, General Minh, the leader of the Military Revolutionary Council (MRC), the new ruling junta in South Vietnam, rid his country of the last vestiges of Ngo family rule. General Minh unshackled the press, emptied Ngo Dinh Nhu's political prisons, and restored Saigon's vibrant cafe and night life. Saigon once again became a cheerful and noisy cosmopolitan city. Once again the city's fragmented political life erupted. Religious sectarians, socialists, and especially the Buddhists and Catholics, quarreled heatedly over the political future of their fragile state.

In the South Vietnamese countryside, the NLF continued to enhance its control of people and territory.[10] In December 1963, meeting in Hanoi in special session, the Central Committee of the Lao Dong, after much debate and disagreement among the delegates, made a series of crucial decisions that decisively influenced the course the insurgency in South Vietnam would take over the next 18 months and that would eventually provoke U.S. full-scale entry into the war. The Committee issued a directive calling for an escalation of the southern insurgency and for increased support for the revolution from the DRV. The Communist leaders knew that they were running out of regroupees to send south and that they could not win the war without a major commitment of their own military forces. Preparations were made to improve the Ho Chi Minh trail complex and to infiltrate PAVN units into southern Vietnam. The Communist leadership decided that the time had come to move toward the final stage of the revolutionary struggle, a general counteroffensive paralleled by popular risings in the cities, that would topple the fledgling South Vietnamese government. They realized that their escalations ran the risk of a war with the United States, but they hoped that their efforts would bring about the rapid collapse of the South Vietnamese government and the forced withdrawal of their American patrons without a fight. Fatalistically, Hanoi officials, in their pursuit of a strategy designed to bring them victory in the South, accepted the risk of a war with Americans while hoping to avoid it.[11]

The new Saigon government alarmed U.S. officials when it proved to be politically inept and demonstrated that it was more interested in seeking a negotiated settlement of the conflict than in fighting the PLAF forces. Hoping to move the conflict in South Vietnam from the military to the political plane, the MRC sought the support of rural elements, Buddhists, and even factions within the NLF. The Saigon generals opposed any proposals by Americans to increase the U.S. advisory role in the conduct of ARVN operations or to expand the war against the NLF. Most members of the

Military Council, including generals Minh and Don, had formerly served in the French colonial forces, and they were responsive to French President Charles De Gaulle's offers to help the Vietnamese achieve a peaceful reunion of their country free of external influences, including American influence.

Johnson administration officials, both in Saigon and Washington, were angry at the prospect of French intrusion into Vietnamese politics, of a ceasefire, of negotiations with NLF elements, and of the formation of a neutralist coalition government that might ask the Americans to leave. Such possibilities risked the collapse of the American rationale for intervention in southern Vietnam that had prevailed for a decade.[12]

From the American perspective, the political and strategic situation in southern Vietnam deteriorated after Diem's demise. The Buddhists and Catholics, the most powerful political factions in Saigon, waged bitter internecine warfare. In the rural areas, provincial government verged on collapse. The remaining strategic hamlets were being dismantled, often by their peasant occupants who viewed them more as internment camps than havens.[13] The NLF continued to expand its influence in the South. The MRC proved unable to govern the fractious politicians of South Vietnam and unwilling to fight the Vietcong.

The coup that had destroyed Diem had also deepened the divisions among American officials concerned with the conduct of Vietnam policy. General Harkins, who had opposed the coup, in turn opposed the new government because of its unwillingness to fight the NLF aggressively. Ambassador Lodge, who had spearheaded the American support of the coup that destroyed Diem, backed Minh and the other MRC leaders and tried to isolate Harkins from policy affairs.

Among ARVN leaders, tensions and rivalries persisted. One of these leaders, Major General Nguyen Khanh, who had supported the coup but was not a member of the ruling Council, began plotting his own coup to overthrow the Minh-Don group. Khanh was motivated by his fears that the current leaders could not manage the war against the PLAF. He was supported by General Harkins and some members of Harkins' military advisory group, particularly Colonel Jasper Wilson. Wilson helped shift the balance of power among ARVN commanders toward Khanh and kept Harkins informed of the plot's progress. Khanh's coup also enjoyed the tacit support of Taylor and McNamara who wanted to be rid of leaders whom they perceived to be inept, pro-French neutralists unable to either fight or govern.[14] The bloodless coup that brought Khanh to power occurred January 30, 1964. President Johnson, himself having opposed the overthrow of Diem, was pleased with the advent of Khanh who appeared eager to cooperate with American officials and to get on with the war.

Khanh's ploy opened the coup season in southern Vietnam. There would be five more coups during the next year and South Vietnam would have seven governments in 1964 alone. As the succession of coups and rickety governments made a travesty of South Vietnamese political processes and poisoned political life, American officials pleaded with their charges to maintain at least a semblance of political stability. Without a stable government in Saigon, the war against the Vietcong would surely be lost.

Hoping that he was the man to rally his people and to turn the war around, American officials strongly backed General Khanh. McNamara and Taylor accompanied Khanh on a barnstorming tour of South Vietnam, a public relations effort designed to sell the little-known new leader to his own people. The trio appeared at rallies in several cities, with Khanh standing in the middle, flanked by Taylor and McNamara, both raising Khanh's arms in a triumphant display of Allied unity. At these rallies, McNamara liked to shout "Vietnam Muon Nam" (Vietnam a thousand years), but he failed to achieve the proper pitch and pronunciation so crucial to speaking Vietnamese correctly. To many Vietnamese in the audience, McNamara seemed to be saying, "Southern duck wants to lie down."[15] These rallies may very well have had the opposite effect from that intended by the Americans. They made Khanh, a short, squat man standing between two tall American officials, appear inconsequential, even undignified. Khanh appeared to be a mere puppet serving U.S. policy.

Back from his dubious efforts at promoting General Khanh, McNamara submitted a pessimistic report to Johnson on March 16, 1964. In his report, he noted the deterioration of the strategic situation in the South occurring since Diem's downfall. He estimated that the Vietcong now controlled about half the population and half the territory of South Vietnam. He also noted that in many areas administered by Saigon, much of the population had no interest in supporting the ARVN cause. ARVN desertion rates and draft dodging were high while the Vietcong were energetically recruiting new forces in many provinces. Displacing Minh with Khanh had not arrested the growing antiwar and neutralist sentiment among people residing in Saigon-controlled areas, especially among the Buddhists. To revive the sagging war effort, McNamara recommended increasing the size of ARVN forces, augmenting U.S. economic and military aid, and beginning planning for possible bombing raids on North Vietnam.[16]

The next day Johnson met with the National Security Council to consider McNamara's recommendations. After a brief debate, Johnson decided to implement many of McNamara's proposals, a decision that amounted to continuing the U.S. advisory role in South Vietnam on an expanded scale. National Security Action Memorandum 288 (NSAM 288) issued March 17 restated the American goal: to preserve an independent, non-Communist South Vietnam, which was necessary to prevent all Southeast Asia from turning Communist and to prove to the rest of the world that Communist wars of national liberation could be curtailed. NSAM 288 called for a national mobilization plan to put South Vietnam on a war footing and for major increases in the number of ARVN forces. The memorandum also approved increases in various U.S. aid programs and in the number of American military advisers serving in South Vietnam.[17]

Johnson hoped that these measures would be enough to check the mounting insurgency in southern Vietnam, but he also understood that if it could not be curtailed, he would have to take other measures including attacks on North Vietnam. Understanding that a lack of progress in South Vietnam might require various kinds of punitive responses against North Vietnam, the Joint Chiefs, in late May, proposed a sequence of carefully graduated military operations against North Vietnam. These operations were not designed to destroy that country, rather they were intended to persuade Hanoi to stop supporting the insurrection in southern Vietnam by threatening the northerners with ever greater punishment if they did not desist.[18] These proposals also revealed a growing tendency among U.S. officials to look to North Vietnam for a solution that continued to elude them in South Vietnam.[19]

In addition to these contingency plans, Johnson, who believed that Harry Truman had made a serious mistake when he failed to seek congressional approval for the Korean intervention in 1950, planned to seek a Congressional authorization if and when he decided to take the war to North Vietnam. In order to be ready for that possibility, Johnson ordered the preparation of a draft congressional resolution that would give the president the authority to take whatever actions he thought necessary to defend South Vietnam.[20]

The new measures authorized by NSAM 288 proved to be ineffective. Khanh quickly showed himself to be an ineffective war manager. The insurgents continued to maintain the initiative, and their military forces became more aggressive. The Vietcong, as they continued their assaults on ARVN forces, also launched terrorist attacks against U.S. advisers. Saigon's numerous political factions continued their quarrels with each other and with General Khanh.

In June 1964, President Johnson, increasingly frustrated by the inability of the Khanh government to stem the Vietcong tide and convinced that the revolution taking place in South Vietnam amounted to aggression from North Vietnam, sent a warning to Hanoi via Blair Seaborn, the Canadian representative on the International Control Commission (ICC). Seaborn was instructed to tell the North Vietnamese leadership to stop supporting the Vietcong effort in South Vietnam or else the United States would attack North Vietnam with devastating results. DRV Premier Pham Van Dong, meeting with Seaborn, defiantly told him to tell the American leaders that the DRV would continue to support the NLF until it prevailed. He also told Seaborn emphatically that the American choices in Vietnam amounted to either continuing indefinitely a war they could not win or else accepting a neutral south Vietnam and withdrawing.[21]

IN DUBIOUS BATTLES

During the first few days of August 1964, a series of controversial incidents took place in the Gulf of Tonkin involving U.S. and North Vietnamese naval forces. These incidents brought about the implementation of many of the proposed military actions against North Vietnam including the first U.S. bombings of North Vietnamese targets. They also brought about the enactment of a congressional resolution that granted President Johnson a blank check to wage war in Vietnam.

On Sunday morning August 2, three North Vietnamese patrol boats suddenly attacked the destroyer USS *Maddox*, which was engaged in an electronic surveillance mission, code named DESOTO patrol, off the coast of North Vietnam. Two nights earlier, South Vietnamese patrol boats had attacked North Vietnamese military and radar installations on the offshore islands of Hon Me and Hon Nieu in the vicinity where the *Maddox* was patrolling when it was attacked. The South Vietnamese raids were part of a series of covert operations called Operations Plan 34-Alpha (OPLAN 34-A) periodically conducted against North Vietnam. The CIA and military-intelligence groups carried out raids and other clandestine operations in order to harass and to confuse the North Vietnamese. The North Vietnamese naval command, apparently linking the DESOTO patrol with the earlier night's OPLAN 34-A assaults, ordered its boats to attack the *Maddox* whose patrol route brought it at times to within eight miles of North Vietnam's mainland coast and within four miles of its offshore islands.[22]

In a brief and intense encounter, *Maddox* opened fire with its three-inch and five-inch guns, badly damaging one of the attacking boats. Naval aircraft operating from the nearby carrier USS *Ticonderoga* strafed the patrol boats, inflicting damage as the crafts sped back toward their bases. The *Maddox* sustained very minor damage (one enemy 12.7 mm. machine-gun bullet pierced one its aft electronic gunfire directors.)[23]

In Washington, 10,000 miles away, President Johnson reacted angrily but with restraint to the news of an attack on an American warship. Some of his advisers called for retaliatory air strikes against North Vietnamese targets. One of those officials who favored this course of action was the newly appointed U.S. Ambassador to South Vietnam, General Maxwell Taylor. South Vietnam's ruler, General Khanh, also called for air strikes against North Vietnam.[24]

Resisting pressures to bomb North Vietnam, Johnson instead directed the Navy to order the *Maddox* to resume its patrols, this time joined by another destroyer, the USS *Turner Joy*. The president took these actions to assert traditional U.S. claims to freedom of the seas and to demonstrate to the North Vietnamese officials that the United States was not intimidated by the patrol boat assaults. Johnson had been notified that additional OPLAN-34-A raids were scheduled for the same general area the night of August 3. His advisers had also informed him that they believed that the North Vietnamese patrol boats had attacked the *Maddox* because their leaders apparently connected the DESOTO patrol with the OPLAN-34-A attack, so Johnson knew that ordering the destroyers to resume their patrols risked additional attacks on the U.S. warships. He thought it necessary to run risks in order to send North Vietnam's leaders a message.[25]

At 7:15 P.M., on the evening of August 4, Captain John J. Herrick, on board the *Maddox*, the commander of the DESOTO operation, received a warning from the National Security Agency (NSA) that three North Vietnamese boats operating in the vicinity of Hon Me island were preparing to attack the two destroyers. At 8:35 P.M., the *Maddox* picked up three radar contacts traveling at high speeds about thirty-five miles to the north. Shipboard analysts evaluated the blips on their radar screens as North Vietnamese patrol boats attempting to set an ambush for the destroyers near the island where the U.S. warships had been steaming the previous night. The two ships wheeled about and headed southeast in the direction of the *Ticonderoga*, about two hundred miles away. About thirty minutes later, both destroyers, spotting three more radar contacts, went to general quarters and called for air support. Four jets soon arrived overhead from *Ticonderoga*, having been dispatched fifty minutes earlier, and searched the area but could find no enemy boats. At 9:40 P.M. the confusion began. Both destroyers, now sixty miles from the North Vietnamese coast and 180 miles north of the DMZ, began shooting at radar targets. Herrick also began sending messages stating that his ships were under attack. The sonar operator on board *Maddox* reported many torpedoes in the water. Crewmen on board both ships reported that they saw torpedo wakes in the water.[26]

The weather was bad that night in the gulf. There were clouds, rain storms, heavy surface fog, and it was a moonless night. Twenty-knot winds churned the sea. Surface visibility was near zero. Herrick's attack reports were based on evaluations of radar and sonar contacts. Neither ship suffered any damage. Naval aircraft flying cover over the two destroyers at low altitude and searching for the alleged attacking boats could never find the boats nor did the pilots ever see any torpedo wakes, even though they could easily spot the wakes of the destroyers.[27]

For two hours the two destroyers zigged and zagged furiously around an area of the Gulf in efforts to avoid what their officers thought were torpedo attacks. They fired hundreds of rounds of three and five-inch shells at their invisible targets, laid depth charges at shallow depths, and even tried to ram their unseen attackers. The Navy pilots, on orders from the destroyers, fired missiles into the ocean at ghost targets. Herrick, trying to evaluate the confusing situation, dispatched a later message expressing his doubts that either of the U.S. warships had been attacked the night of August 4. He did state that he believed that enemy patrol boats had attempted an ambush earlier in the evening, but that it never occurred because Herrick had maneuvered his ships away from the ambush area. He urged a complete evaluation of the night's events before any further action was taken. He attributed the radar and sonar contacts to weather effects, and to his crew's inexperience and anxiety.[28]

While the two destroyers raced around firing at unseen targets, in Washington, Johnson, informed that a second attack in as many days had been made on U.S. ships on the high seas, angrily ordered retaliatory air strikes against North Vietnamese targets. Johnson also decided that it was a propitious moment to have his long-awaited congressional resolution enacted. McNamara, the chief architect of Johnson's evolving war policy, and being eager to strike at the North Vietnamese, took charge of preparing the reprisal attacks. While the Joint Chiefs of Staff readied a strike execute order, McNamara sought confirmation that the second attack had occurred. He discounted Captain Herrick's cautionary message. He asked Admiral U.S. Grant Sharp, Commander of the Pacific Fleet (CINCPACFLT), about the latest reports from the destroyers. Admiral Sharp, who had not read Herrick's cautionary message at the time McNamara called him, told McNamara that there was little doubt that a second attack had occurred. The evidence which convinced McNamara that there had been a second attack came from NSA radio intercepts of North Vietnamese naval communications which had been made during the battle.[29]

Three years after America had gone to war in Vietnam, the Senate Foreign Relations Committee conducted a full-scale investigation of the Gulf of Tonkin incidents. Several of its members challenged the validity of the August 4 attack. McNamara, testifying before the committee, insisted that the NSA intercepts proved that the attack in question had taken place. But electronic intelligence experts have refuted his contention. Ray S. Cline, formerly CIA deputy director of intelligence, who carefully analyzed the contents of the NSA intercepts, concluded that the messages, received at the time of the second attack, were in reality a belated summary of the previous encounter occurring August 2.[30] Louis Tordella, a former deputy director of the NSA, after a careful analysis of the same intercepts, reached the same conclusion.[31]

Years later, James B. Stockdale further undermined McNamara's credibility concerning the Tonkin Gulf incidents. On August 2, 1964, Commander Stockdale was the flight leader of the aircraft that had driven off the patrol boats attacking the *Maddox*. On August 4, when the second attack was supposed to have occurred, Stockdale also led the flight that provided supporting cover for the two destroyers that dark and stormy night out in the Gulf of Tonkin. Stockdale was later shot down over North Vietnam and consequently spent eight years in a Communist prison camp. He endured brutal tortures with extraordinary courage and strength. He finally returned home to a hero's welcome and later rose to the rank of vice admiral. Admiral Stockdale has written a revealing account of the events of that controversial night in the Gulf of Tonkin:

> I had the best seat in the house from which to detect boats—if there were any. I didn't have to look through surface haze and spray like the destroyers did and yet I could see the destroyers' every move vividly. Time and time again I flew over the *Maddox* and the *Joy*, throttled back, lights out, like a near-silent stalking owl, conserving fuel at a 250-knot loiter speed....When the destroyers were convinced that they had some battle action going, I zigged and zagged and fired where they fired....The edges of the black hole I was flying in were still periodically lit by flashes of lightning—but no wakes or dark shapes other than those of the destroyers were ever visible to me.[32]

Ironically, on August 5, 1964, Stockdale led one of the raids against North Vietnam retaliating for an attack that he believed never occurred. He remembered thinking at the time that Washington officials had acted hastily and irrationally. Five days later, Stockdale was visited by two of McNamara's assistants who asked him if there had been any boats attacking the destroyers the night of August 4. President Johnson voiced his doubts that a second attack had occurred a few days after ordering the retaliatory raids when he told an adviser, "Hell, those dumb, stupid sailors were just shooting at flying fish." Johnson did, however, order the DESOTO patrols to continue, but he also separated them from OPLAN 34-A raids. On the night of September 18 there occurred a replay of the August 4 incident complete with radar and sonar contacts, reports of torpedoes in the water, ships firing at unseen targets, aircraft flying overhead unable to spot any enemy boats, and advisers calling for more retaliatory raids. LBJ, cautious this time, refused to order more sorties against North Vietnamese targets.[33]

But McNamara, in the crisis atmosphere prevailing in Washington on August 4, 1964, preferred quick action to thoughtful analysis. At a short National Security Council Meeting, McNamara confirmed the second attack for the president, and plans for the retaliatory raids were finalized. President Johnson wanted the reprisal raids timed so that they would be occurring at the same moment that he would be explaining to the American people why he had ordered the bombing of North Vietnamese targets.[34]

But the air raids, code-named PIERCE ARROW, were delayed and did not occur until several hours after the president's speech. Naval aircraft from the *Ticonderoga* and USS *Constellation* flew sixty-four sorties against four North Vietnamese patrol boat bases and a supporting oil-supply facility. The raiders destroyed or damaged twenty-five patrol boats and about 90 percent of the oil storage complex. During the strikes, two U.S. aircraft were shot down. One pilot, Lt. (j.g.) Everett Alvarez, was captured. He was the first of 826 American pilots and air crewmen known to have been captured by the North Vietnamese, and he spent eight and one-half years as a prisoner of war.[35]

On August 6, the Senate committees on Foreign Relations and Armed Services met in joint session to consider the administration's resolution. Senator William J. Fulbright, chairman of the Foreign Relations Committee, presided over the hearings. Fulbright was Johnson's close friend and political ally; Johnson urged Fulbright to get the resolution through quickly so that it would have the maximum impact. At the committee hearings, McNamara presented the administration's version of events. McNamara portrayed the complex and ambiguous incidents occurring in the Gulf of Tonkin as clear and simple acts of aggression: They were unprovoked attacks against U.S. ships engaged in routine patrols in international waters. He made no mention of the OPLAN-34-A raids, and he did not tell the senators that the destroyers were on spy missions. Although he was aware that the North Vietnamese had presumed a linkage between the OPLAN-34-A raids and the DESOTO patrols, McNamara told the senators that he could give no rational explanation for the attacks. He portrayed them as mindless and suicidal acts of aggression.[36]

All but one of the senators on the two committees accepted McNamara's duplicitous version of the Gulf of Tonkin incidents. The lone challenge came from Oregon's Wayne Morse. An anonymous Pentagon leaker had informed Morse of the OPLAN-34A raids, and Morse tried to link the clandestine raids with the attacks on the ships. McNamara categorically denied that there could be any connection and reiterated that the *Maddox* was on routine patrol in international waters both times it was attacked.[37] No other senators were interested in pursuing Morse's line of questioning or challenging McNamara's testimony. The committees voted thirty-one to one to send the resolution to the full Senate; Morse cast the lone dissenting vote.

The next day Fulbright, who would turn against the war within a year and become the Senate's most prominent dovish critic, guided the resolution rapidly through the full Senate, allowing only perfunctory debate. Long accustomed to routinely approving presidential foreign policy initiatives and apparently unconcerned about the possible uses a president might make of the proposed resolution, nearly all the senators approved it unquestioningly. Maryland Senator Daniel Brewster asked Fulbright if the resolution would approve sending armies to fight in Vietnam. Fulbright told him that it would. Wisconsin Senator Gaylord Nelson proposed an amendment making it clear that Congress, by passing the resolution, was not authorizing a change in the U.S. advisory role in Vietnam nor approving an expansion of the U.S. commitment in South Vietnam. Fulbright, who agreed in principle with Nelson, talked him out of adding the amendment by telling him that it would only cause confusion and delay. Kentucky's John Sherman Cooper asked Fulbright if the resolution would grant the president the power to take the country to war. Fulbright, who would come to repudiate the error that he made in rushing the Gulf of Tonkin resolution through the Senate, replied that it would.[38] Senator Morse continued to oppose the resolution. He was joined by 83-year-old Alaska Senator Ernest Gruening, who opposed the broad grant of power to the president conveyed by the resolution, calling it "a predated declaration of war." Morse, knowing that the resolution would soon clear the senate overwhelmingly, presciently told his colleagues: "We are in effect giving the president...war-making powers in the absence of a declaration of war. I believe that to be a historic mistake."[39]

With only Morse and Gruening dissenting, the Senate approved the resolution eighty-eight to two. The House passed it unanimously, 416-0, after a forty-minute discussion. The news media accepted official versions of the events and editorialized in support of the retaliatory raids. A public opinion poll released August 10, the same day Johnson signed the resolution, showed 85 percent of the public supported the air strikes. Johnson's approval ratings in the polls shot up from 42 percent to 72 percent immediately following the retaliatory attacks.[40]

The resolution that Johnson would later use as a congressional authorization for war had an Orwellian official title: The Joint Resolution to Promote the Maintenance of International Peace and Security in Southeast Asia. It soon became known as the Gulf of Tonkin resolution. The key language in the 300-word document that granted Johnson the constitutional authority he later used to wage a war in Vietnam follows:

> The Congress approves and supports the determination of the President, as Commander-in-Chief, to take all necessary measures to repel any armed attacks against the forces of the United States and to prevent further aggression....The United States is therefore prepared, as the President determines, to take all necessary steps, including the use of armed force, to assist any member or protocol state of the Southeast Asia Collective Defense Treaty requesting assistance in defense of its freedom.[41]

Johnson intended that the reprisal raids and prompt congressional passage of the resolution serve several political purposes. Washington sent Hanoi and its allies a message that Americans were united in their determination to stand firm in Vietnam. The Administration also sent General Khanh and his South Vietnamese critics a message that America was determined to back his shaky government. At home, by demonstrating that the president could defend U.S. interests in Vietnam without expanding the war, Johnson silenced Republican presidential challenger Arizona Senator Barry Goldwater, who had previously urged the escalation of the war. Goldwater had no choice but to support the air strikes and to vote for the resolution. By neutralizing Goldwater, Johnson effectively removed the war issue from the upcoming election campaign. The first congressional debate on Vietnam had brought "a near-unanimous endorsement of the president's policies and provided him an apparently solid foundation upon which to construct future policy."[42]

In rallying support for the reprisal raids, however, Johnson and his leading advisers had misled both the Congress and the public. Later, when Senator Fulbright and other congressional leaders realized that they had been deceived by the administration, they turned angrily against a war that they now believed Johnson and McNamara had tricked them into approving. Fulbright was especially bitter, believing that Johnson had deliberately misled him by indicating, at the time that the president asked him to run the Gulf of Tonkin resolution through the Senate, that his administration had no intentions of subsequently taking America to war.

The president had also expanded the U.S. commitment in Vietnam to include not only defending South Vietnam "but also to responding to North Vietnamese provocations."[43] The long-standing barrier against taking the war north of the DMZ had been breached. PIERCE ARROW represented both a culmination and a prologue: It was the capstone of the U.S. policy that limited American involvement in Vietnam to an advisory role that had been in place for a decade; it also foreshadowed the abandonment of that advisory role and the escalations that led to direct intervention in Vietnam.[44] The American response to the Gulf of Tonkin incidents, characterized by official confusion, faulty judgment, and duplicity, was a crucial link in the chain of events that eventually plunged the United States into full-scale war in Vietnam.

Johnson did not, as many Americans later suspected, seek the congressional resolution as a blank check for bringing the United States into a war to which he had already committed himself after his reelection. In August 1964, Johnson still hoped that the United States could sustain a non-Communist government in southern Vietnam without having to fight an American war in that region. He rejected his advisers' periodic suggestions that he should order more bombings of North Vietnam. He clung to that hope throughout his fall campaign for reelection. Johnson did not want to be a war president. Following his election, he intended to concentrate on implementing that wide range of modern social legislation that he had earlier labeled the Great Society. He feared that a war would divide Americans and undermine his reform program.

Vietnam was not a prominent issue in the campaign, in part because of Johnson's politically adroit reaction to the Gulf of Tonkin incidents, but also because public interest in Vietnam was still relatively slight. The news media rarely gave the events of Vietnam extensive coverage in the fall of 1964. The conflict to date had been characterized by relatively small-scale, low intensity warfare. The American role was limited; costs and casualties were light. Most Americans were relatively uninformed and unconcerned about *la guerre sale* occurring in a small, poor country located in a remote corner of the globe.[45] The 1964 presidential election campaign focused on domestic issues and on the question of which candidate would make the better leader.

The president made few campaign appearances until late September, and when he made speeches, he made only a few references to Vietnam. Johnson hoped that these scanty remarks about Vietnam would persuade the American public that he did not intend to expand the U.S. role in Southeast Asia, that he did not seek a wider war. He appeared to commit himself to not sending American combat troops to fight a land war in Asia. At Eufaula, Oklahoma, on September 25, he said "We don't want our American boys to do the fighting for Asian boys. We don't want to get involved in a nation with 700 million people and get tied down in a land war in Asia."[46] At Akron, Ohio, on October 21, he said "But we are not about to send American boys nine or ten thousand miles away from home to do what Asian boys ought to be doing for themselves."[47]

These remarks, taken out of context, would appear to be explicit promises by Johnson not to Americanize the Vietnam war. In the years that followed, after America was enmeshed in a controversial war and Johnson had become a controversial leader, these remarks, made during the heat of the 1964 campaign, would provoke bitter accusations that the president had lied to the American people about his intentions in Vietnam in order to achieve his reelection.

But if we read these and other speeches closely, we can discern that Johnson injected qualifiers and other ambiguous remarks into his texts. In his campaign speeches, Johnson also stated that America would not abandon its commitments in Vietnam. He hinted that he might change his mind later about bombing North Vietnam and that he might even send U.S. combat troops.[48] These rhetorical escape hatches represented the efforts of a canny politician who knew that he had obtained the necessary authority from Congress to commit America to war in Vietnam if he determined that he must. Johnson also knew that if the situation in South Vietnam deteriorated further, he might decide that he had to bomb North Vietnam and even to send U.S. combat troops. Hence the escape hatches carefully allowed for those contingencies. At the same time, to assure his reelection by a landslide margin, Johnson gave his audiences false assurances that he would never take the nation to war in Indochina when he knew that he might have to in the near future. While he did not talk about this possibility during the reelection campaign, he knew that the situation in South Vietnam was deteriorating. He also knew of the contingency planning by his advisers for bombing North Vietnam and for sending U.S. combat troops to South Vietnam.

Johnson's rhetorical subterfuges worked. He obtained his landslide victory in November, crushing the conservative crusade of Barry Goldwater. The Democrats rolled up their largest congressional majorities since the glory days of the New Deal and prepared to implement Johnson's Great Society program. But the master manipulator from the banks of the Pedernales would later pay a high price for the methods that he used to gain his easy political victories in the summer and fall of 1964: Many Americans would later turn against the war in part because they no longer trusted the man in the White House.

ROLLING THUNDER

During the months between the Gulf of Tonkin incidents and Johnson's landslide victory on November 3, 1964, political turmoil prevailed in South Vietnam. The NLF forces continued to take control of more and more of the country. On August 16, General Khanh, taking advantage of a period of euphoria generated in Saigon by the U.S. retaliatory attacks on North Vietnam, tried to acquire dictatorial powers. Buddhists and students took to the streets to protest this power grab, and forced Khanh to back down. In September, Lam Van Phat, an ARVN general who formerly had been a waiter in a Paris restaurant, attempted to overthrow Khanh. Ambassador Taylor intervened in the chaotic South Vietnamese political process to deflect Phat's bid for power. With Taylor's blessing, a countercoup, led by a group of younger officers, called the "Young Turks," which included Nguyen Cao Ky, Nguyen Van Thieu, and Nguyen Chanh Thi, restored Khanh to power. In October the generals selected a civilian, Harvard-educated Tran Van Huong, formerly mayor of Saigon, to be prime minister. General Khanh stepped down to become commander-in-chief of the South Vietnamese armed forces in return for his promise to stay out of politics. Despite his pledge, Khanh and the Young Turks remained the powers behind the new civilian leadership. Huong, when asked at a press conference who was the man best able to lead South Vietnam effectively, paused, smiled, and said "you got me there."[49] Huong's frank response was eloquently expressive of the political confusion prevailing in Saigon and other South Vietnamese cities.

While the political turnstiles were spinning in Saigon during the fall of 1964, the PLAF was escalating the war. On October 11, three Vietcong battalions attacked ARVN forces in Tay Ninh province northeast of the capital city and they inflicted heavy casualties. On November 1, Vietcong guerrillas attacked Bien Hoa airport on the outskirts of the capital city. Mortar shells rained down on the airfield, killing four and wounding seventy-two Americans. The VC also destroyed five B-57 bombers, and damaged eight other U.S. aircraft. It was the first Vietcong attack on a major U.S. military installation. Later in the month, the NLF forces mounted their largest offensive of the war to date. In two weeks two Vietcong regiments occupied most of Binh Dinh, a key populous coastal province.[50] As November 1964 ended, President Johnson and his advisers had to confront a major crisis in Vietnam: the failure of the policy of the same only more that he had inherited from Kennedy.

As 1964 approached its end, the Communists were close to victory in Vietnam for the third time in twenty years. They had been there in August 1945 when the Japanese occupation came to an end only to have the French return. They got close again in June 1954 following Dien Bien Phu only to be denied victory by major power diplomacy and American intervention in southern Vietnam. They would be denied victory once again by the U.S. decision to Americanize the war during the first half of 1965. Direct American intervention forced Hanoi "to resort to a higher level of revolutionary war, but it did not substantially resolve the underlying political problems in the GVN or arrest the seemingly inexorable slide of the South toward Communism."[51] Another decade would pass before the Communists would again approach victory. In 1975, there would no longer be anyone able and willing to deny them their long-sought goal.

As the political coherence and military capability of the South Vietnamese government rapidly eroded in late 1964, it was evident to Johnson's advisers that the policies that they had been shaping since they had come to office with Kennedy in 1961 had failed. But since their reputations were so closely tied to these policies, it was extremely difficult for them to detach themselves from them and to conceive of other policy tracks such as distancing the United States from the Saigon regime, reducing the American commitment, seeking a negotiated settlement, or even withdrawing and permitting the collapse of South Vietnam. Even if these advisers could have imagined such alternatives, and even if such policies might have served the national interest, such proposals would have shown their previous counsels to have been incorrect and it might have cost some of them their jobs. In addition, by the end of Johnson's first year in office, many of the skeptics who might have tried to warn the president about the futility and dangers of military escalation were no longer in government service. Since Kennedy's death, they had either resigned or Johnson had dismissed them from office. Thus, LBJ heard fewer dissenting voices and was exposed to a narrower range of options than was his predecessor.[52]

As South Vietnam's political crisis deepened, the erroneous assumptions and misperceptions upon which the U.S. advisory policy was based were never seriously questioned nor reexamined. Most of Johnson's advisers concluded that the way to rescue a failed policy was by doing more not less. They called for military escalation, specifically for bombing North Vietnam. They could not be sure that bombing would succeed, but they hoped that it might. They preferred escalation to negotiations, withdrawal, or to continuing the present policy. Johnson's advisers perceived escalation to be the only way to protect the U.S. commitment in which they all had a personal stake.[53]

By the end of November, Johnson's advisers had formed a consensus to bomb North Vietnam. According to its various advocates, bombing the DRV could achieve a variety of benefits. In their judgment, it would interdict the infiltration of Communist men and material into South Vietnam, it would boost morale in Saigon, and it would induce Hanoi to abandon the insurgency in the South by punishing North Vietnam so severely that its leaders would soon understand that they could not hope to support the PLAF except by incurring unacceptable losses.[54]

There was also a schism among Johnson's advisers about the kind of bombing campaign being proposed for North Vietnam. This division pitted the president's civilian advisers against his military advisers. The civilians, led by McNamara and the Assistant Secretary of Defense for International Security Affairs John T. McNaughton, called for a limited air war, of gradually applying air power to North Vietnam. Starting with a few carefully selected minor targets, this kind of air war was devised to send Hanoi a signal that it must either stop supporting the NLF or face the gradually increasing destruction of its country. The controlling assumption among the gradualists was that at some point the increasing pain inflicted upon the North Vietnamese by the bombing would induce Hanoi to abandon its support of the revolution in South Vietnam rather than see its military facilities, transportation systems, and industrial sectors destroyed. Gradualist bombing was designed to give Johnson maximum flexibility; he could increase or decrease the pressure in response to Hanoi's behavior. Because this type of bombing was gradual and limited, it's advocates believed that it would not provoke Chinese or Soviet entry into the conflict.[55] It would be a "slow squeeze," designed to save South Vietnam from North Vietnam.

Military advocates of bombing, led by Air Force chief of staff General John P. McConnell and Admiral Sharp, urged Johnson to launch a "fast squeeze" from the beginning. They wanted full-scale air attacks on North Vietnam's military bases, transportation systems, and industrial infrastructures. They argued that only a massive and intense bombing campaign could force Hanoi to the bargaining table on American terms. They believed that only fear of national extinction would force Hanoi to abandon the revolution in South Vietnam.[56]

As Johnson's civilian and military advisers quarreled among themselves about how best to escalate the war, one adviser strongly opposed bombing North Vietnam. George Ball, Undersecretary of State, the number-two man in the State Department, had previously studied the effects of strategic bombing on Germany during World War II and knew its limitations. Ball did not believe that bombing would either weaken North Vietnam's war-making ability or demoralize its population. He had also served in the French embassy during the Franco-Vietminh war and he understood the nature of the political-military struggle going on in Vietnam. He doubted that bombing North Vietnam was the proper counter to Hanoi-supported revolution in South Vietnam. He also doubted that bombing North Vietnam could raise morale in South Vietnam.

Ball raised some challenging questions: Suppose, he asked, that Hanoi stopped supporting the NLF. Could the ARVN forces, given the current disarray in Saigon, defeat them even if the Vietcong had to go it alone? He pointed to the risks entailed by bombing: Suppose, in retaliation for the bombing, the North Vietnamese invaded South Vietnam in force? The United States would either have to send its armies or accept a Communist victory. No matter how it was done, gradually or all-out from the start, he warned Johnson that bombing could bring the Chinese and the Soviets into the war; it could also heal the rift between the two Communist powers. Most important, Ball warned Johnson that once he started down the escalatory road, the United States would not be able to control events. Ball told Johnson that as wars expand they tend to outpace the ability of leaders to control them. He suggested that negotiations, with all their risks, including their leading to a neutral government in the South and an American departure, better served the national interest than any scenario likely to come from bombing.[57]

Ball made no headway either with Johnson or with his other advisers. While conceding that bombing might not work, Johnson and his advisers discounted all Ball's arguments and warnings. Rejecting withdrawal or negotiations, they insisted that bombing was necessary to avert a complete collapse in Saigon; "the administration turned to air power as the only acceptable solution to an urgent problem."[58] Johnson's civilian advisers also prevailed over the military proponents of all-out bombing. On November 27, 1964, a Working Group headed by William Bundy developed a gradualist bombing campaign to be implemented in two stages. Phase one, which would last for 30 days, called for air strikes along the major infiltration routes in eastern Laos and for reprisal strikes against North Vietnam in response to NLF attacks on U.S. installations or personnel. While phase one bombings were being carried out, Ambassador Taylor would try to get South Vietnam's squabbling politicians to resolve their differences. Once Saigon's politics were stabilized, phase two would kick in: a systematic aerial war of rising intensity carried out against North Vietnamese military targets which would last for several months.[59]

Johnson delayed implementing phase one bombing mainly because of the persisting political instability in South Vietnam. He told his advisers that he would not order any bombing of North Vietnam until the South Vietnamese politicians had put their political house in order and were able to carry on the war against the insurgents. Ambassador Taylor conveyed Johnson's concerns to the top echelons of Saigon's military and civilian leadership: There would be no bombing of North Vietnamese targets until South Vietnam had a stable government. Some of the generals apparently did not receive or understand Taylor's message because in mid-December, Air Marshal Nguyen Cao Ky and General Nguyen Chanh Thi made a bid for power that amounted to another coup attempt. President Johnson, informed that yet other coup was underway in Saigon, angrily exclaimed: "I don't want to hear anything more about this coup shit! I've had enough of it, and we've got to find a way to stabilize those people out there!"[60]

Taylor, furious at Ky's and Thi's blatant display of political irresponsibility in the face of imminent danger, gave the South Vietnamese generals a traditional Army-style chewing out:

> I made it clear that all the military plans which I know you would like to carry out are dependent on government stability. Now you have made a real mess. We cannot carry you forever if you do things like this.... You people have broken a lot of dishes and now we have to see how we can straighten out this mess.[61]

The South Vietnamese generals were embarrassed and angered by Taylor's tactless and condescending reproach, although he did persuade them to support Huong's government. Meanwhile, the Buddhists, sensing the war weariness and desires for a negotiated settlement among many segments of the population, launched a new wave of protests including more immolations by fire. The Buddhists also called for Ambassador Taylor to resign. In Hue, riotous students attacked the U.S. Information Service library.[62] The protests had taken on a distinctly anti-American as well as an anti-government cast. U.S. officials began to fear that a government which would be willing to negotiate with the NLF and favor the expulsion of Americans might arise from the chaos that had become the political norm in Saigon. General Khanh fed these fears by making overtures to some of the Buddhist factions and parroting some of their anti-American sentiments.

While confusion reigned in the streets of Saigon, Vietcong forces inflicted a series of defeats on ARVN troops. The worst of these defeats occurred as the new year began at Binh Gia, about forty miles southeast of Saigon. Two of ARVN's elite units, a Ranger battalion and a Marine battalion, supported by armor, artillery, and U.S. helicopters, were chewed up by forces of the Vietcong 9th Division, the first PLAF main force unit to reach divisional size.[63] At Binh Gia, there were 445 South Vietnamese and 16 American casualties against only 32 confirmed VC casualties.[64] On January 6, 1965, Ambassador Taylor sent an extremely pessimistic assessment of the situation in South Vietnam to President Johnson. Taylor feared that a political collapse was imminent and that a neutralist government reflecting a Khanh-Buddhist alliance could come to power in Saigon unless a bombing campaign were implemented.[65]

Johnson's advisers, including Taylor, in a classic inversion of logic, now argued that the reason for delaying the bombing, Saigon's chronic political instability, had become the main reason for implementing it immediately. Bombing might not win the war but it could fend off political collapse in southern Vietnam. George Ball has commented on his colleagues' reasoning processes:

The establishment dove...George Ball, shown here being sworn in by Chief Justice Earl Warren, to be the U. S. ambassador to the UN, had been Johnson's only senior adviser who opposed Americanizing the Vietnam war.
Source: National Archives

I was not surprised when my colleagues interpreted the crumbling of the South Vietnamese government, the Vietcong's increasing success, and a series of defeats of South Vietnamese units not as proving that we should cut our losses and get out, but rather that we must promptly begin bombing to stiffen the resolve of the corrupt South Vietnamese government. It was classical bureaucratic casuistry. A faulty rationalization was improvised to obscure the painful reality that America could arrest the galloping deterioration of its position only by the surgery of extrication.

We must, they argued, commit our power and prestige ever more intensely to stop the South Vietnamese government from falling completely apart, negotiating covertly with the Liberation Front or Hanoi, and ultimately asking us to leave. It was Catch-22 and the quintessence of black humor.[66]

Despite the pressure being applied by both his civilian and military advisers, Johnson continued to delay implementing the bombing campaign against North Vietnam. He was not convinced that it should be undertaken as long as the South Vietnamese political situation remained so unsettled. However, Pleiku would change Johnson's mind. Early on the morning of February 7, 1965, the Vietcong attacked a U.S. airfield at Pleiku and a nearby helicopter base at Camp Holloway in the central highlands. The VC inflicted heavy casualties. They killed nine and wounded 137 Americans.[67] Twenty-two helicopters and fixed-wing aircraft were destroyed or damaged during the insurgent assault. Within a matter of hours, Johnson had ordered the JCS to implement FLAMING DART, a series of reprisal air strikes against pre-selected North Vietnamese targets. For two days naval and South Vietnamese Air Force (VNAF) aircraft flew retaliatory strikes against North Vietnamese sites located just north of the DMZ.

Still undeterred, the Vietcong struck again on February 10. They attacked a hotel which housed members of the 140th Maintenance Detachment, an Army aircraft repair unit, at Qui Nhon, a coastal city eighty-five miles east of Pleiku. After the assaults, rescuers pulled twenty-three bodies and twenty-one wounded soldiers from the rubble.[68] Again Johnson retaliated, this time with heavier air strikes against military targets in North Vietnam. This time Washington did not characterize the air strikes as tit-for-tat reprisals, but called them generalized responses to a continuing pattern of aggressive acts. "The administration had moved from reprisals to a continuing, graduated program of air attacks against North Vietnam."[69] McGeorge Bundy, who was visiting Vietnam at the time of the Pleiku attack, wrote Johnson a long memo calling for the implementation of sustained bombing. On February 13 Johnson authorized ROLLING THUNDER, a systematic, gradually expanding bombing campaign using both American and VNAF aircraft to strike at North Vietnamese targets. It began March 2.[70]

However, Pleiku served more as a pretext than a cause. Ultimately, Johnson's change of heart occurred because his advisers finally convinced him that if the bombing campaign were not undertaken, the GVN would simply collapse. Johnson conceded that taking the war north could provide the Saigon government with a reprieve and give it a chance to stabilize itself. Beginning with sporadic strikes against minor targets just north of the DMZ, Johnson gradually expanded the air war against North Vietnam until it became a systematic, large-scale effort that struck major targets located all over the country. ROLLING THUNDER, the U.S. and VNAF air war against North Vietnam, had begun. It would continue, with occasional bombing halts, for over three years.

As Washington made its decisions to initiate an air war against North Vietnam, the political sands in Saigon shifted once again. On February 14, General Khanh appointed Phan Huy Quat, a physician, to be prime minister. Quat quickly selected a new cabinet that included four other doctors. Americans soon dubbed Quat's government the "medicine cabinet." A few days after the medicine cabinet took office, a coup attempt erupted. It was led by Colonel Pham Ngoc Thao and General Lam Van Phat, who had been the instigator of the failed coup attempt back in September 1964. They intended to oust General Khanh from his position as commander of the ARVN. But Air Marshal Ky used his control of the Air Force to disperse the coup forces. Both Thao and Phat quickly disappeared from public view.

But Marshal Ky and General Thieu, the leaders of the "Young Turks," hitherto aligned with Khanh, then convened a meeting of the Armed Forces Council. The council voted to remove Khanh from his position as commander-in-chief of ARVN and to affirm its support for Quat and his medicine cabinet. Khanh tried to rally ARVN generals to his support but he failed. Colonel Wilson, who had helped Khanh come to power thirteen months earlier and whom Khanh trusted, persuaded him to resign and to leave the country. The Young Turks, after trying to get rid of Khanh because of his growing alliance with the Buddhists and his efforts to establish contacts with NLF elements, finally ended Khanh's year in power. Taylor, who had backed the Young Turks, had also wanted to be rid of Khanh because he was skeptical that a Khanh-controlled government could be relied on to support the air war against North Vietnam. Ambassador Taylor feared that Khanh might seek a neutralist alternative to continuing the war.[71] General Westmoreland believed that Ky and Thieu had staged a mock coup in order to depose Khanh: a farce in order to humiliate Khanh and to show the other generals that he no longer had control of the South Vietnamese army.[72] Khanh's departure cleared the way for the Young Turks who, with American blessings, would soon become the military rulers of the GVN.

DAHLIAS AND GLADIOLI

The gradualist strategy of the air war quickly proved to be ineffective. Its failure rebutted the predictions of Johnson's senior advisers that a gradualist bombing campaign against North Vietnam would save the GVN from impending military defeat and political collapse and bring Hanoi to the bargaining table. Supplies from North Vietnam for the PLAF continued to pour into many parts of South Vietnam. A State Department Intelligence Note on the effects of bombing found that the air strikes had not diminished the morale of the North Vietnamese people. In fact, State Department analysts found that the U.S. bombing had increased North Vietnamese resolve and enabled the North Vietnamese leaders to tighten their control over the populace.[73] Bombing North Vietnam also failed to bolster morale in South Vietnam, failed to halt the entropic tendencies of Saigon politics, and failed to grant a reprieve to the GVN from the steadily increasing NLF military and political offensives. "The military and political fabric of the southern regime continued to unravel even more rapidly than before."[74]

President Johnson had hoped that bombing North Vietnam would obviate the sending of American combat forces into South Vietnam, but the restrained manner in which he implemented the air war against North Vietnam ensured that it could not. Gradually taking the war to North Vietnam increased rather than decreased the pressures on Washington to send troops into South Vietnam. Soon after the bombing campaign had begun, Johnson's advisers pressed him to move to the second escalatory stage, sending in the combat forces. The troops were needed to protect U.S. air bases in South Vietnam from NLF attacks. More ominously, bombing had also provoked the introduction of PAVN forces into South Vietnam. Previously, Hanoi had been careful to infiltrate only supplies and southern regroupees into South Vietnam. They had been restrained from sending their own combat forces south out of fear of provoking U.S. military intervention.

With the launching of the air war against them, Hanoi's leadership believed that they had little to lose and once U.S. combat forces began to arrive in strength they felt that they had even less to lose by bringing their own military forces into the war in the South. Six weeks after the first American combat forces arrived in Vietnam, U.S. intelligence agencies were reporting that they had detected PAVN units operating in southern territory.[75] "ROLLING THUNDER was a fateful U.S. decision in Vietnam primarily because it brought about what its opponents feared, massive ground retaliation by the North Vietnamese, without bringing about what its proponents sought, the DRV to the conference table on terms then acceptable by the U.S."[76]

There is a direct linkage between the gradually expanding bombing campaign against North Vietnam and Washington's decision to send the first American combat troops to South Vietnam. General Westmoreland, fearing PLAF attacks against the large American air base at Danang which was essential for conducting the air war, requested two battalions of Marines to provide ground security for that facility.[77] The MACV commander had no faith in ARVN forces that had been assigned to protect the air field.

Ambassador Taylor initially opposed Westmoreland's request for troops on several grounds. Citing the French experience, Taylor questioned whether American troops could fight a guerrilla war successfully in Southeast Asian jungles. He also believed that the introduction of U.S. combatants would tempt the ARVN commanders to unload more of the burden of the fighting onto the Americans. He could foresee American combatants taking full responsibility for the war "amid a population grown as hostile to [the] American presence as it had been to the French."[78] Most of all Taylor worried that the introduction of even a small contingent of U.S. combat forces with a specific and limited mission would remove an important limit on U.S. involvement in South Vietnam, a limit that U.S. officials had observed since the beginning of the Indochina wars. It would be a foot in the door to an ever-widening commitment, and once that first step was taken, it would be very difficult to hold the line.[79] Washington ignored Taylor's prophetic objections; Johnson promptly approved General Westmoreland's request for security forces that had previously been endorsed by Admiral Sharp, the man in charge of the air war and Westmoreland's immediate superior in the chain of command. Johnson's crucial decision was made without much deliberation, planning, or thought about its possible consequences.

The landing of American troops that transformed the Vietnam war and the U.S. role in it occurred on the morning of March 8, 1965, at a beach south of Danang. At 9:03 A.M., Marine Corporal Garry Powers leaped from his amphibian landing craft, waded through ankle-deep water, and jogged up the wet sand. He was the first of the more than 2.7 million young men and women who would serve in South Vietnam over the next seven years. As wave after wave of Marines streamed ashore in full battle gear that spring morning, they encountered throngs of pretty Vietnamese girls who placed leis of yellow dahlias and red gladioli around their necks. The mayor of Danang made a welcoming speech celebrating the festive occasion. Overhead, helicopter gunships searched for Vietcong snipers in the nearby jungle-covered hills.[80]

Just as Taylor had prophesied, a few weeks after the Danang landings, repercussions were already coming to a head. Westmoreland, fearing security threats to other U.S. military installations and disturbed by intelligence reports that the NLF planned "to seize a large sector of the central highlands, there to establish a government to challenge Saigon's, and drive eastward to the coast to cut South Vietnam in two," asked Washington for two Army divisions, one to deploy in the highlands, the other to send to the Saigon area.[81] Admiral Sharp, Army Chief of Staff Harold Johnson, along with the other members of the JCS, impatient with what they viewed to be Johnson's too-cautious approach to the war, all aggressively endorsed General Westmoreland's request.

President Johnson had come face to face with the dilemma that his predecessors who had previously involved the United States in Vietnam—Truman, Eisenhower, and Kennedy—had all managed to evade: either accept the collapse of the South Vietnamese government or send U.S. combat forces into that country. He had reached the crunch point. Johnson and his advisers had trapped themselves. They had ruled out the options of withdrawal, of negotiations, or of an all-out air war against North Vietnam. Knowing that the limited air war was not producing the desired results nor was it likely to any time soon, Johnson and his advisers knew that if they did not send combat forces soon, the GVN would probably go under before year's end. And having convinced themselves that defeat for the South Vietnamese regime would result in unacceptable diplomatic disasters for America and would activate a vicious right-wing political assault on their liberal Democratic administration at home, Johnson and his men could only accept the ineluctable logic of their policy formulations and agree to send more combat forces, albeit fewer than the military leadership wanted.

On March 29, a gray Renault sedan stalled on Saigon's Vo Di Nguy, a street running alongside the American embassy. Within minutes, 300 pounds of plastic explosives packed in the trunk of the car erupted into a giant fireball. The powerful blast extensively damaged the embassy. It killed twenty and injured over a hundred people who were either working in the embassy, were passersby, or were dining in restaurants across the street from the American headquarters. As dazed and bleeding embassy staff members stumbled out of the wrecked building only to encounter the litter of bodies in the street, Saigon police shot and killed the Vietcong terrorist who had stalled the explosives-laden car near the embassy.[82]

Two days later, President Johnson met with members of the National Security Council to review U.S. Vietnam policies. On April 2, he made a series of decisions that moved America closer to war: 20,000 additional troops would be sent to Vietnam; the air war would be expanded; South Korea, Australia, and New Zealand would be asked to send troops to Vietnam; most important, additional Marine combat units would be deployed in the vicinity of Danang and their mission would be expanded to include offensive operations against Vietcong forces within a fifty-mile radius of the Marine bases.

On April 6, 1965, with Taylor's reluctant approval, McGeorge Bundy issued NSAM 328 implementing Johnson's decisions.[83] On that date there were about 27,000 American troops in South Vietnam, most of them noncombatants. Within a few weeks, thousands of combat troops would be pouring "in country." Confronted with a choice, as he put it in his own words, "of running in or running out of Vietnam," Johnson chose to run in. While he expanded the American military presence and changed its mission from advice and static defense to limited offensive operations against the NLF forces, Johnson chose not to inform the American people of those important moves. At a press conference he stated that "I know of no far-reaching strategy that is being suggested or promulgated."[84]

As the air war against North Vietnam expanded and the first ground combat troops were being sent into South Vietnam, public opinion polls showed that a large majority of Americans supported the continuing U.S. efforts in Vietnam.[85] But it was also during the spring of 1965 that vocal critics of Johnson's war policies surfaced: not only those who criticized him for doing too much, but those who attacked him for not doing enough. The words "hawk" and "dove" entered the growing public discourse on the war.[86] The words were not precise descriptive terms, but they identified the two emerging strands of public opinion critical of the administration's war policies. Hawks favored a stronger military effort, an all-out air war and sending more U.S. combat forces. Doves called for an end to the bombing of North Vietnam and opposed sending American combat forces to South Vietnam. Many doves also wanted a negotiated settlement of the conflict followed by a U.S. withdrawal. The first vocal opposition to the war appeared on university campuses. Professors at the University of Michigan, Harvard, and the University of California at Berkeley staged "teach-ins" featuring speakers who condemned Washington's war policies. On April 12, about 15,000 students gathered in the nation's capital to stage the first antiwar protest march.

Aware of the developing hawkish and dovish criticisms of his Vietnam policies, President Johnson, on the evening of April 7, delivered a major speech at Johns Hopkins University in which he reaffirmed the American commitment to South Vietnam. Johnson attempted to silence his critics on both the Left and the Right. He tried to appear tough enough to satisfy the hawks, but soft enough to give the doves hope. He told the American people "we are there because we have promises to keep...," "we are also there to strengthen world order...," and "we are there because there are great stakes in the balance...." He forcibly stated that the United States would remain in Vietnam as long as was necessary to protect South Vietnam, and that he would use whatever force was necessary to repel aggression. But he also stated that the United States remained ready for "unconditional discussions" if they would lead to a peaceful settlement. Johnson added that when the war was over and South Vietnam could live in peace without fear of aggression from North Vietnam, America would sponsor a billion-dollar developmental program for the Mekong river valley, a kind of TVA for Southeast Asia that would include North Vietnam.[87] In his speech, Johnson was trying not only to persuade Americans to support his Vietnam policies, but to find the right mix of sticks and carrots that would persuade Ho Chi Minh to settle on U.S. terms. Concerning Johnson's offer of developmental funds to the North Vietnamese, presidential aide William Moyers later said, "if Ho Chi Minh had been George Meany, Lyndon Johnson would have had a deal."[88]

The public responded favorably to the president's Johns Hopkins speech. Reactions in Congress were mostly supportive. Media editorializing was generally enthusiastic. The thousands of letters and telegrams sent to the White House ran five-to-one in favor of the president. But his words failed to satisfy or silence most hawks or doves. Soon after the speech, the term "credibility gap" appeared in the media to describe the skepticism voiced by some journalists and politicians over whether or not the Johnson administration was being entirely candid about its present Vietnam policies.[89]

On April 8, responding to Johnson's offer of unconditional discussions put forth in the Johns Hopkins speech, North Vietnam's premier, Pham Van Dong, offered Hanoi's basis for negotiations. It consisted of four points: (1) The United States would have to stop its bombing and withdraw from Vietnam, (2) The 1954 Geneva accords must be reinstituted, (3) The internal affairs of South Vietnam must be settled in accordance with the program of the NLF, and (4) the peaceful reunification of Vietnam.[90]

Washington regarded Hanoi's terms as unacceptable. Johnson and his advisers were especially concerned about point 3, which they understood to be calling for a NLF takeover of the GVN. Notwithstanding their rejection of specific DRV proposals, it is doubtful that the Johnson administration was seriously interested in a negotiated settlement of the conflict in April 1965. Washington feared that the South Vietnamese government was too weak militarily and politically to risk a negotiated settlement, although for political reasons they knew that they had to appear to want a settlement. Johnson understood that if two-thirds of the American population supported his Vietnam policies in the spring 1965, two-thirds also favored a negotiated settlement of the war. But at that time Johnson intended to apply more military power in the hopes of strengthening the position of the GVN to a point at which future negotiations could promise a settlement on terms acceptable to Washington. A short bombing pause in May did not elicit any reduction in PLAF activity, although it defused domestic critics who accused Washington of not wanting negotiations, which may have been its main purpose.

Hanoi was probably not serious about negotiations either in April 1965. The North Vietnamese leaders were proposing terms more to improve relations with the Soviet Union who had endorsed the four-point peace program and whose economic and military assistance would be crucial in a protracted war with the United States than to settle the conflict in Vietnam. Washington and Hanoi had reached a diplomatic impasse; both sides, regardless of what they said for political and public relations purposes, made non-negotiable demands that each knew were unacceptable to the other: The United States would not compromise on its insistence that an independent non-Communist South Vietnamese state be allowed to exist in the southern part of Vietnam. Hanoi would not compromise its goal of a NLF-dominated coalition government taking over in South Vietnam, which they believed would lead inevitably to the peaceful reunification of Vietnam under Communist control. By summer, both sides had abandoned their diplomatic sparring and were going after each other on the battlefield.[91]

On April 20, McNamara, Taylor, the Joint Chiefs, and other high-ranking American officials met in Honolulu to chart the next phase of the American military buildup. Since Washington had agreed to send some combat forces to South Vietnam, Taylor had opposed increasing their numbers and had been trying to confine those troops "in country" to security patrols in the immediate vicinity of coastal air bases. General Westmoreland's staff challenged Taylor's enclave concept. They asserted that his enclave strategy represented "an inglorious static use of U.S. forces in overpopulated areas with little chance of direct or immediate impact on the outcome of events."[92]

At Honolulu, Westmoreland, backed by the Joint Chiefs, requested seventeen additional Army maneuver battalions, specifically, the 173rd Airborne Brigade, and all necessary support forces; he also wanted authorization to deploy them in unrestricted offensive operations. With McNamara leading the way, the conferees worked out a compromise. Taylor abandoned his opposition to further combat deployments. Westmoreland got his infantry battalions plus an additional 40,000 troops, including 7,000 "Third Country" forces from South Korea and Australia. But the MACV commander accepted Taylor's proposal that the troops would be assigned to four enclaves which would be established at Chu Lai, Qui Nhon, Quang Ngai, and Bien Hoa.[93] The Honolulu decisions, although they did not meet all the military's operational demands, significantly increased the number of U.S. combat troops in South Vietnam and "marked a major step toward a large-scale involvement in the ground war." The new strategy also represented a growing shift of emphasis from the air war against North Vietnam to the ground war in South Vietnam.[94]

As the Johnson administration made the decisions which brought America closer to war in the spring of 1965, Washington responded to a crisis in the Dominican Republic, a small and poor Caribbean nation with a long history of U.S. domination. In late April, Johnson, told that pro-Castro elements had infiltrated a revolutionary movement making a bid for power in the Dominican Republic, sent U.S. Marines and Army infantrymen to suppress the revolt. American forces blocked the rebellion and succeeded in stabilizing the politics of the country. Elections were held in 1966, and a moderate government came to power that protected U.S. strategic and economic interests in that country.

No independent observer has ever found convincing evidence that Cubans had infiltrated the ill-fated insurgency. But polls showed public opinion strongly supported the U.S. military incursion, although liberals and foreign critics attacked the intervention which violated the charter of the Organization of American States (OAS) and abrogated the long-standing U.S. pledge to refrain from military intervention in Latin America. The Dominican campaign was limited in duration, and few American lives were lost. Success in the Dominican operation encouraged Johnson to try more of the same in Vietnam, and he assumed that similar success there would ultimately silence any domestic or foreign detractors who might protest his policies. He ignored the implications of the liberal protests, refusing to see them as possible harbingers of opposition to his escalatory Vietnam policies.[95]

On May 4, Johnson asked Congress for $700 million to support the American military operations in Vietnam. Johnson made it clear to the lawmakers that he would regard a vote for the money as an endorsement of his Vietnam policies. Even though Johnson's evasive and ambiguous rhetoric made it difficult for many legislators to understand just what Johnson's Vietnam policies were at this time or what his future intentions might be, they could not very well vote against funding for American boys already in the field. Both houses approved the appropriation quickly, without debate. Johnson would later insist that this vote and the Gulf of Tonkin resolution refuted dovish critics who claimed that he never gave Congress a chance to pass judgment on his Vietnam policies.[96]

In South Vietnam, despite the bombing, increased U.S. aid, and the introduction of some U.S. combat forces, ARVN forces verged on disintegration. Desertion and draft avoidance rates were high. The politicized ARVN officer corps had virtually given fighting the war over to the Americans and were doing what they did best, engaging in constant political intrigue and using their military positions to enrich themselves. The PLAF forces, strengthened by the addition of PAVN regulars now fighting in South Vietnam, went on the offensive. In Phuoc Long Province northwest of Saigon, VC regiments attacked a Special Forces camp at Dong Xoai and also attacked Song Be, the provincial capital. At Ba Gia, in the coastal province of Quang Ngai, another VC regiment destroyed two ARVN battalions. In the central highlands, NLF forces overran several district towns and besieged a Special Forces camp at Duc Co, a remote site in Pleiku province. With ARVN losses running high and its military organization nearing collapse, General Westmoreland concluded that only the rapid, large-scale introduction of U.S. combat forces could avert defeat.[97]

If the South Vietnamese military situation was bad, its political situation was disastrous. The fifth Saigon government within a year came to power when the Young Turks overthrew the "medicine cabinet" of Phan Huy Quat in early June. Taylor and Westmoreland were glad to see Quat go. His supporters included a faction of Buddhist monks who wanted to end the war. Quat also opposed the introduction of large-scale U.S. combat forces into his country. The new government was headed by a Military Directorate of ten senior ARVN officers led by a triumvirate: Air Marshal Ky, General Thieu, and General Nguyen Chanh Thi. All were pro-American and they all favored Americanizing the war. Ky became prime minister and Thieu became head of the military forces.

The Ky government represented the *reductio ad absurdum* of the South Vietnamese political process. The regime was hardly a government at all; it was a committee of generals who did not represent any South Vietnamese groups in the political sense. Having no political base and with much of its armed forces incapable of fighting, the new government could survive only with massive American economic, diplomatic, and military support. In the name of self-determination and to ensure the continuation of the war against the NLF and the PAVN forces in South Vietnam, Washington supported a political facade in Saigon that was devoid of any meaningful popular support and, in order to survive in power, was forced to surrender control of its war to the U.S. combat forces.

DECISIONS FOR WAR

In early June, Westmoreland and the JCS requested an additional 150,000 troops. They also called for abandoning the modified enclave strategy and supplanting it with an offensive strategy. They warned that anything less than a rapid, large-scale commitment of U.S. forces with the freedom to fight aggressively risked imminent defeat in South Vietnam.[98] Among Johnson's senior civilian advisers, only George Ball opposed a major commitment of U.S. ground combat forces to Vietnam. Ball continued to press for disengagement, but he was outnumbered and outranked. In mid-July, Robert McNamara, after another of his many trips to Saigon, confirmed the military leaders' warnings that failure to act decisively would probably have meant defeat for the GVN within a few months. He also told Johnson that vigorous U.S. involvement in the war could avoid defeat in the short run and produce victory in the long run. McNamara recommended sending an additional forty-four battalions, which would bring the total U.S. force level in Vietnam to 179,000 by year's end.[99]

McNamara's recommendations triggered a week of intensive discussions among the President and his advisers stretching from July 21–28 during which "Johnson made his fateful decisions, setting the United States on a course from which it would not deviate for nearly three years and opening the way for seven years of bloody warfare in Vietnam."[100]

Although he made the momentous decisions that Americanized the Vietnam war, that transformed both the character of the conflict and the U.S. role in it, Johnson did reject the military's call for an all-out air war, mainly because he feared that it would provoke Chinese military intervention as it had happened in Korea. He committed 175,000 (later raised to 220,000) combat troops to South Vietnam. Johnson also granted Westmoreland the authority to commit American troops to combat in any situation where the MACV commander deemed their use necessary to strengthen the GVN forces. An important threshold had been crossed. A new course had been set, the end of which was not in sight. The decision to build up and to use American combat forces amounted to an open-ended commitment to defend South Vietnam. The amount of force required to defeat the enemy would depend on Hanoi's response to the U.S. buildup and the Communists' willingness to raise their own stake in the war's outcome. Johnson, probably without fully realizing it, had walked into a war of indeterminate size and duration.[101]

These presidential decisions, most strongly influenced by McNamara's memos and McNamara's oral arguments made in the sequence of discussions held over several days in late July, are among the most important decisions ever made during the long history of U.S. involvement in Southeast Asia. During the last week of July 1965, the president decided that American boys would henceforth have to do what Johnson, during his presidential campaign in 1964, had suggested to his fellow citizens that he believed only Asian boys should do for themselves, that is, fight a land war in Southeast Asia.

Chairman of the Joint Chiefs Earle Wheeler urged President Johnson to put the nation on a war footing by calling the Reserves and National Guard to active duty. The president refused to mobilize the Reserves and the National Guard because he feared that such an act might precipitate a divisive congressional debate which would undermine the coalitions he was forming to enact Great Society legislation. McNamara, the *primus inter pares* among Johnson's advisers, urged him to declare a state of national emergency, to seek a tax raise, and to place the July decisions squarely before the American people. Johnson refused to take any of these actions because he did not want to alarm the major Communist powers, did not want to threaten his domestic reform agenda, nor did he wish to stir the passions of the American people.[102]

In retrospect, Johnson's failure to seek a declaration of war from Congress, to tell the American people plainly that the United States was going to war against both North Vietnam and the National Liberation Front that it controlled, and his failure to mobilize the Reserves and National Guard were major political and strategic blunders that limited the American war effort and hastened the rise of opposition to the conflict among the public and within the halls of Congress.[103]

On the morning of July 28, Johnson met with congressional leaders. Later in the day he held a televised press conference. He continued to mislead Congress, the press, and the American people about his Vietnam decisions. The president insisted that he had not authorized any change of policy when in fact he had committed the nation to war. While acknowledging that he was sending 50,000 more troops, he downplayed his intention to send more soldiers later and his agreement to give the military what they wanted, thereby understating significantly the costs and casualties that he knew lay ahead.

President Johnson quietly took the nation to war in late July 1965. At the time, many Americans probably did not realize that their nation was headed for war. Most of those who understood that America was entering a war probably did not give it much thought, assuming that now that the United States was in it, it would be a relatively short, small-scale affair with the powerful, well-equipped, and well-trained U.S. combat forces gaining an inevitable victory over the Communists.

CONSENSUS AND CONFUSION

"Displaying the consummate skill that had become his trademark, Johnson in the last week of July [1965] shaped a consensus for his Vietnam policy in his administration, in Congress, and in the country."[104] The President saw himself as rejecting both the extremes of withdrawal and rapid escalation. Instead, he believed that he was taking the middle course of measured escalation. What Johnson did not understand was that his support, while widespread, was thin. Beneath the consensual surface, relatively few Americans understood or strongly supported his Vietnam war policies. There were probably many people who supported the war at the time simply because President Johnson appeared to be a capable and strong leader; they trusted his leadership. When war costs and casualties vastly exceeded anticipated levels and the conflict endured far longer than expected, Johnson's carefully crafted consensus collapsed into quarreling factions of hawks and doves.

Johnson and his advisers forged a Vietnam war policy that rested upon a number of myths and misperceptions, some of which they had inherited from previous administrations. Some of Johnson's advisers knew that international relations were more complex and dynamic in 1965 than they had been in the 1950s. They understood the implications of the Sino-Soviet split, and they sensed that emerging polycentrism heralded a breakup of the bipolar world dominated by the United States and the USSR. But the president and his advisers remained thralls of the containment ideology and its domino correlative just as the Truman, Eisenhower, and Kennedy administrations before them. Most of Johnson's aides perceived Ho Chi Minh to be an agent of Chinese expansionism. They believed that the line against Communism had to be drawn and held in southern Vietnam, lest all Southeast Asia become vassal to the Asian colossus and American strategic interests in that crucial region be undermined. They believed that America would be humiliated if it withdrew from Vietnam. The United States would be exposed as a "paper tiger." They feared that China and the USSR, emboldened by an American debacle, would support Third World insurgencies wherever they appeared. America would lose credibility in the world; its allies would be demoralized and they would no longer trust the United States to honor its commitments.

Johnson and his advisers also embraced the McCarthyite myth that had haunted liberal Democrats since the Chinese revolution of 1949. To Johnson and his aides, it was axiomatic that the loss of any additional territory in Southeast Asia to Communism spelled political disaster for them and their party at home. The loss of southern Vietnam to the Communists would galvanize a Rightist political backlash that could destroy Johnson's beloved Great Society and cost him the upcoming election. Johnson was determined not to replicate the fate that had befallen Truman.

Johnson's ignorance of Vietnamese history and culture, shared by his senior advisers, coupled to his habit of thinking in terms of Cold War cliches, caused him to misread the nature of Vietnamese nationalism and to misunderstand the nature of the revolutionary insurgency in southern Vietnam. Johnson apparently never understood that Ho Chi Minh and his revolutionary Communist movement more nearly embodied Vietnamese nationalism than did the succession of corrupt military dictatorships that the United States backed, nor could he understand that the Hanoi-backed insurgency in southern Vietnam enjoyed widespread popular appeal in part because it expressed Vietnamese nationalistic aspirations to be free of foreign influences. All the president could see was Communist aggression from North Vietnam that he felt compelled to stop.

Johnson and his aides also made a series of faulty judgments as they took the nation to war. They badly underrated their enemy. They underestimated Hanoi's determination, political discipline, fighting ability, and diplomatic skill. They could never bring themselves to admit that a small, poor Asian nation, even with substantial assistance from China and the Soviet Union, might withstand a large-scale application of U.S. military power for years. Likewise they overestimated the strategic capabilities of the American military forces, both in air and ground operations. Without accurately accessing the capabilities of their enemies or the particular limitations and obstacles U.S. military forces would encounter in Vietnam, Johnson and his advisers assumed that the mere application of sizeable amounts of U.S. military force would be sufficient to bring victory. In addition, having drastically underestimated the future size, cost, and duration of the war that they began in July 1965, the administration had also overestimated the willingness of the American people to go on year after year paying in lives and dollars for a military stalemate.[105]

Johnson understood his Vietnam war strategy to be a holding action which was essentially defensive in nature. He was not trying to defeat North Vietnam nor to destroy the NLF. But he would punish the North Vietnamese from the air, and the American combat forces in South Vietnam would prevent the Communists from winning the revolution. He believed that, in time, Hanoi would grow weary of punishment and persistent failure and agree to let South Vietnam live in peace. Washington had chosen to wage a limited defensive war against a determined foe waging an unlimited strategic offensive.

Johnson's short-term centrist leadership was brilliantly successful in forging a consensus among his advisers, Congress, the media, and the American people in support of Americanizing the Vietnam war in July 1965. At the same time he also succeeded in pushing landmark Great Society measures through Congress, among them Medicare, the Voting Rights Act, and federal aid to education. Johnson gambled that a measured escalation of the bombing of North Vietnam and a limited commitment of ground combat forces to South Vietnam would enable him to achieve his goals in Southeast Asia soon enough to allow him to fulfill his commitment to social justice at home. He believed that America could afford to fight a limited war in Vietnam at the same time that it completed the New Deal at home. He refused to choose between the Great Society and the war in Vietnam. LBJ's frontier faith in American omnicompetence led him to believe that the United States could afford both "guns and butter." But in the long run, the price paid for seeking this middle-of-the-road consensus was military stalemate in Vietnam and political stasis at home, "a middle road of contradictions and no priorities for action."[106] Johnson, who went to war in Vietnam to preserve his Great Society later had to sacrifice Great Society to pay for the Vietnam War.

In the summer of 1965, Washington began sending its armies off to fight a major war in Vietnam. The American ordeal had arrived.

NOTES

1. Herring, *America's Longest War*, p. 113.
2. *Ibid.*, p. 108.
3. Halberstam, David, *The Best and the Brightest* (Greenwich, Conn.: Fawcett, 1969, 1971, 1972), pp. 424–427. Halberstam affixed his ironic label, the best and the brightest, to the men who crafted America's disastrous Vietnam policy. His best and brightest included Rusk, McGeorge Bundy, McNamara, Taylor, and Westmoreland, as well as Kennedy and Johnson.
4. Gelb and Betts, *The Irony of Vietnam*, p. 97. The Johnson quote is from the videotape, "Lyndon Johnson Goes to War, 1964–1965," from the television series, "Vietnam: A Television History."
5. Leuchtenburg, William, *A Troubled Feast: American Society Since 1945* (Boston: Little Brown, 1983), p. 138. Speaking at Ann Arbor, Michigan, on the University of Michigan campus, Johnson announced his Great Society reform program. He stated that the Great Society rested upon liberty and abundance for all, and it demanded an immediate end to poverty and racial injustice.
6. Moss, George, *America in the Twentieth Century* (Englewood Cliffs, N.J.: Prentice Hall, 1989), p. 340. Johnson spoke to Congress and to the American people for the first time as president five days after Kennedy's assassination. It was probably the most important speech of his presidency, and the words that counted the most that evening were his pledges that he and his advisers would continue Kennedy's domestic and foreign policies.
7. Halberstam, *Best and Brightest*, p. 364.
8. *Ibid.*, p. 116.
9. Sheehan and others, *Pentagon Papers*, "Excerpts from National Security Action Memorandum 273," Nov. 26, 1963, Document 60, pp. 232–233; Bornet, Vaughn Davis, *The Presidency of Lyndon B. Johnson* (Lawrence, Kansas: University of Kansas Press, 1983), pp. 66–68.
10. Maitland and others, *Raising the Stakes*, PP. 94–96.
11. Turley, *The Second Indochina War*, pp. 57–60; Duiker, *The Communist Road*, pp. 221–223; and Doyle, Edward; Lipsman, Samuel; Maitland, Terrence; and the editors, *The North* (Boston: Boston Publishing Co., 1986), pp. 40–43.
12. Kahin, *Intervention*, pp. 183–191.
13. Herring, *America's Longest War*, pp. 110–111.
14. Kahin, *Intervention*, pp. 194–207.
15. Maitland and others, *Raising the Stakes*, pp. 100–101.
16. Sheehan and others, "McNamara Report on Steps to Change the Trend of the War," March 16, 1964, *Pentagon Papers*, Document 63, pp. 277–283. In the report McNamara identifies the greatest weakness in the present situation to be "the uncertain viability of the Khanh government."
17. *Ibid.*, "Excerpts from National Security Action Memorandum 288 'U.S. Objectives in South Vietnam,'" March 17, 1964, Document 64, pp. 283–285. By the end of 1964, there were 23,300 U.S. advisers in South Vietnam, an increase of about 7,000 for the year.

18. *U.S.News and World Report*, July 23, 1984, "The 'Phantom Battle' that Led to War," p. 58.

19. Herring, *America's Longest War*, p. 119.

20. Porter (ed.), "Draft Resolution on Southeast Asia," June 11, 1964, *Vietnam Documents*, vol. 2, Document 151, pp. 283–285. The resolution was written by William Bundy, assistant secretary of state for Far Eastern Affairs.

21. Porter (ed.), "Notes by Canadian ICC Representative Blair Seaborn on Meeting with Pham Van Dong," June 18, 1964, *Vietnam Documents*, vol. 2, Document 155, pp. 291–292. Blair noted that Dong told him that the choices in Vietnam were either a *guerre a outrance* which the United States could not win in any event or neutrality; Herring, George (ed.), *The Secret Diplomacy of the Vietnam War: The Negotiating Volumes of the Pentagon Papers* (Austin, Texas: University of Texas Press, 1983), pp. 8–9; and Goodman, Allen E., *The Lost Peace* (Palo Alto, Calif.: Hoover Institution Press, 1978), pp. 19–20.

22. The main primary source for the Tonkin Gulf incidents occurring between August 1 and August 5, 1964, is the U.S. Congress, Senate, Committee on Foreign Relations, "Hearings on the Gulf of Tonkin, the 1964 Incidents," 90th Congress, 2nd Session, February 1968 (Washington, D.C.: GPO). The most authoritative secondary account is Marolda, Edward J., and Fitzgerald, Oscar P., *The U.S. Navy and the Vietnam Conflict*, vol. 2: From *Military Assistance to Combat, 1959–1965*. Washington, D.C.: U.S. Government Printing Office, 1986, Chaps. 14 and 15, pp. 393–462.

23. *U.S. News and World Report*, "The Phantom Battle," July 23, 1984, pp. 59–60.

24. Kahin, *Intervention*, pp. 214–215.

25. Porter (ed.), "Telegram from Rusk to Taylor," August 3, 1964, *Vietnam Documents*, vol. 2, Document 163, pp. 301–302. Rusk told Taylor, "We believe that present OPLAN 34A activities are beginning to rattle Hanoi, and the *Maddox* incident is directly related to their effort to resist these activities.

26. *Ibid.*, "Chronology of Events Relating to the Gulf of Tonkin Incidents By Joint Reconnaissance Center, U.S. Navy," August 10, 1964 (Extract), Document 170, pp. 313–315; "The Phantom Battle," pp. 61–62; Davidson, Phillip B., *Vietnam at War: The History, 1946–1975* (Novato, Calif.: Presidio, 1988), pp. 317–320.

27. *U.S. News and World Report*, "The Phantom Battle," pp. 62–63.

28. *Ibid.*, p. 63; Maitland and others, *Raising the Stakes*, p. 159. In his cautionary message, Herrick reported: "Review of action makes many reported contacts and torpedoes fired appear doubtful. Freak weather effects and overeager sonarman may have accounted for many reports. No actual visual sightings by *Maddox*. Suggest complete evaluation before further action."

29. Kahin, *Intervention*, p. 222.

30. Interview recorded on videotape, "Lyndon Johnson Goes to War, 1964–1965," from the television series, "Vietnam: A Television History."

31. *U.S. News and World Report*, "The Phantom Battle," p. 64.

32. Stockdale, James B., and Stockdale, Sybil, *In Love and War* (New York: Harper and Row, 1984), pp. 3–36. Stockdale is quoted in Kahin, *Intervention*, p. 223.

33. *U.S. News and World Report*, "The Phantom Battle," p. 66. The North Vietnamese have always denied that there was a second attack; they insist that it was fabricated by the U.S. National Security Agency. However, they celebrate August 5 as a naval holiday, commemorating it as the day that their naval forces chased the *Maddox* away from their shores, their first naval victory over the U.S. forces.

34. Kahin, *Intervention*, pp. 223–225.

35. *U.S. News and World Report*, "The Phantom Battle," p. 65.

36. Maitland and others, *Raising the Stakes*, pp. 160–161.

37. *U.S. News and World Report*, "The Phantom Battle," pp. 65–66.

38. Gelb and Betts, *Irony of Vietnam*, pp. 103–104; Hoopes, Townsend, *The Limits of Intervention: How Vietnam Policy was Made—and Reversed—During the Johnson Administration* (New York: W. W. Norton, 1987), p. 26.

39. Quoted in Maitland and others, *Raising the Stakes*, p. 161.

40. Polls cited in *Ibid.*, p. 39, and Herring, *America's Longest War*, p. 123; O'Keefe, Kevin J., in an unpublished paper on print media coverage of the Gulf of Tonkin incidents, found that most newspaper and newsmagazine accounts of those events were uncritically accepting of official versions and were nearly unanimous in their editorial support of President Johnson's actions.

41. Porter (ed.), "The Gulf of Tonkin Resolution," August 7, 1964, *Vietnam Documents*, vol. 2, Document 167, p. 307; seven years later, when the long American war in Vietnam was winding down, Congress repealed the Tonkin Gulf resolution.

42. Herring, *America's Longest War*, p. 123.

43. *Ibid.*

44. Gelb and Betts, *Irony of Vietnam*, p. 101.

45. Davidson, *Vietnam at War*, p. 322.

46. Quoted in Goldman, Eric, *The Tragedy of Lyndon Johnson* (New York: Dell, 1968), p. 279.

47. Quoted in *Ibid.*, p. 281.

48. Goldman calls Johnson's rhetorical insertions "escape hatches."

49. Maitland and others, *Raising the Stakes*, pp. 162–163; Huong's quote is recorded on videotape, "Lyndon Johnson Goes to War, 1964–1965," from the television series, "Vietnam: A Television History."

50. Davidson, *Vietnam at War*, p. 323.

51. Duiker, *The Communist Road*, p. 233.

52. Kahin, *Intervention*, pp. 245–246; Thomson, James B., "How Could Vietnam Happen? An Autopsy," *Atlantic*, vol. 221 (April 1968), pp. 50–52. Officials who resigned or were dismissed included Paul Kattenburg and Roger Hilsman. Thomson, an East Asia specialist, left the government for Harvard in 1966.

53. Thomson, "How Could Vietnam Happen?", p. 52; Gallucci, Robert, *Neither Peace nor Honor: The Politics of American Military Policy in Viet-Nam* (Baltimore: The Johns Hopkins University Press, 1975), pp. 35–58.

54. Herring, *America's Longest War*, p. 124; Duiker, *The Communist Road*, p. 236.

55. Davidson, *Vietnam at War*, pp. 336–339.

56. *Ibid.*, pp. 339–340; Millett and Masloski, *For the Common Defense*, p. 549.

57. Ball, George W., "A Light that Failed—Top Secret: The Prophecy the President Rejected," *Atlantic*, vol. 230 (July 1972), pp. 33–49. The substance of the article is a memo Ball wrote October 5, 1964, which Johnson later read carefully and took quite seriously. Ball hoped to get Johnson and his advisers to examine the erroneous assumptions underlying U.S. Vietnam policies and to realize that there were other options available besides escalation. Ball failed and left office in 1966.

58. Herring, *America's Longest War*, p. 126.

59. Sheehan and others, "Final Draft Position Paper Produced by Working Group," *Pentagon Papers*, Document 88, pp. 373–378.

60. Remarks attributed to Johnson by Jack Valenti in interview recorded on video-tape, "Lyndon Johnson Goes to War, 1964–1965," from the television series, "Vietnam: A Television History."

61. Sheehan and others, "Account of Taylor's Meeting with Saigon Generals on Unrest," December 24, 1964, *Pentagon Papers*, Document 89, pp. 379–381.

62. Herring, *America's Longest War*, p. 129.

63. Davidson, *Vietnam at War*, pp. 333–334.

64. Kahin, *Intervention*, p. 262.

65. *Ibid.*, pp. 263–265.

66. Ball, George W., *The Past Has Another Pattern* (New York: W. W. Norton, 1982), pp. 389–390; Ball is quoted in Kahin, *Intervention*, p. 275; Berman, *Planning a Tragedy*, pp. 45–52.

67. Davidson, *Vietnam at War*, pp. 335–336.

68. Maitland and others, *Raising the Stakes*, pp. 170–171.

69. Herring, *America's Longest War*, p. 129.

70. Sheehan and others, "McGeorge Bundy Memo to Johnson on 'Sustained reprisal' policy," February 7, 1965, *Pentagon Papers*, Document 92, pp. 423–427. The tone of Bundy's memo is grim. Even as he advocates bombing he concedes that it might fail to improve the situation in South Vietnam, adding that even if it fails it will be worth it because it will show that we did all we could.

71. Kahin, *Intervention*, pp. 294–305.

72. Westmoreland, William C., *A Soldier Reports* (New York: Dell, 1976), pp. 123–124.

73. The State Department note is cited in Berman, *Planning a Tragedy*, p. 51.

74. Quote is from Kahin, *Intervention*, p. 306; Sheehan and others, *Pentagon Papers*, "McCone Memo to Top Officials on Effectiveness of Air War," Document 97, pp. 440–441.

75. *Ibid.*, p. 307. Other sources have reported the presence of PAVN forces in South Vietnam earlier than April 1965. Westmoreland, *A Soldier Reports*, p. 161, places PAVN units in South Vietnam by December 1964. Davidson, *Vietnam at War*, pp. 324–325, relies on Westmoreland.

76. Kattenburg, Paul, *The Vietnam Trauma in American Foreign Policy, 1945–1975* (New Brunswick, N.J.: Transaction, 1980), pp. 131–132. Kattenburg is quoted in Berman, *Planning a Tragedy*, pp. 51–52.

77. Westmoreland, *A Soldier Reports*, p. 157.

78. *Ibid.*, pp. 157–158.

79. Porter (ed.), "Telegram from Taylor to Rusk," March 18, 1965, *Vietnam Documents*, vol. 2, Document 195, pp. 364–365. As Westmoreland requested more troops, Taylor continued to voice his objections and to doubt their efficacy.

80. Maitland and others, *Raising the Stakes*, pp. 174–175.

81. Westmoreland, *A Soldier Reports*, p. 161.

82. Maitland and others, *Raising the Stakes*, PP. 183–184.

83. Sheehan and others, "Order Increasing Ground Forces and Shifting Mission," April 6, 1965, *Pentagon Papers*, Document 98, pp. 442–443. According to Item 11: "The actions themselves should be taken as rapidly as practicable, but in ways that should minimize any appearances of sudden changes in policy,...The President's desire is that these movements and changes should be understood as being gradual and wholly consistent with existing policy."

84. Quoted in Maitland and others, *Raising the Stakes*, P. 184.

85. Poll cited in Turner, *Dual War*, p. 116.

86. Goldman, *Tragedy of Lyndon Johnson*, pp. 476–477.

87. Johnson's statements are cited in Turner, *Dual War*, pp. 128–129.

88. Moyers' quote is from an interview recorded on videotape, "Lyndon Johnson Goes to War, 1964–1965," from the television series, "Vietnam: A Television History." Johnson and Moyers apparently did not know that the Mekong river did not run through North Vietnam.

89. Turner, *Dual War*, pp. 131–132.

90. Hanoi's Four Points are reprinted in Gettleman, Marvin E.; Franklin, Jane; Young, Marilyn; and Franklin, Bruce, (eds.), *Vietnam and America: A Documented History* (New York: Grove, 1985), pp. 274–275.

91. Kattenburg, *Vietnam Trauma*, pp. 130–133; Duiker, *The Communist Road*, pp. 241–242.

92. Quoted in Westmoreland, *A Soldier Reports*, p. 166.

93. Porter (ed.), "Memorandum for the President by McNamara," April 21, 1965, *Vietnam Documents*, vol. 2, Document 198, pp. 370–371; Doyle, Edward; Lipsman, Samuel, and the editors, *America Takes Over* (Boston: Boston Publishing Company, 1982), pp. 10–11, from the series, "The Vietnam Experience." Chu Lai, one of the sites chosen for a Marine air field near the coast fifty-five miles south of Danang, is not a Vietnamese place name. When General Victor Krulak chose the site, it had no name. He suggested that it be called "Chu Lai," the Mandarin Chinese characters for his name.

94. Herring, *America's Longest War*, p. 132.

95. Moss, *America in the Twentieth Century*, pp. 348–349.

96. Herring, *America's Longest War*, p. 135.

97. Morrocco, John, and the editors of the Boston Publishing Co., *Thunder from Above: Air War, 1941–1968* (Boston: Boston Publishing Co., 1984), pp. 81–83, a volume in the series, *The Vietnam Experience*; Westmoreland, *A Soldier Reports*, pp. 173–177.

98. Westmoreland, *A Soldier Reports*, pp. 179–182.

99. Sheehan and others, "McNamara's Memo on July 20, 1965, on Increasing Allied Ground Force," *Pentagon Papers*, Document 105, pp. 456–458. The memo was drafted on July 1 and revised July 20.

100. Herring, *America's Longest War*, pp. 138–139.

101. There are detailed accounts in Kahin, *Intervention*, pp. 366–401, and in Berman, *Planning a Tragedy*, pp. 105–153, that anatomize the decision making process of July 21 to July 28, 1965, that plunged America into a land war in Asia. Clark Clifford, a friend of Johnson's, and Senator Mike Mansfield joined with George Ball to try to warn the president of the perils of getting involved in a major war in Southeast Asia. He rejected their advice. See also Schandler, Herbert Y., *The Unmaking of a President: Lyndon Johnson and Vietnam* (Princeton, N.J.: Princeton University Press, 1977), pp. 30–31.

102. Herring, *America's Longest War*, pp. 139–140.

103. Summers, Harry G., Jr., *On Strategy: A Critical Analysis of the Vietnam War* (New York: Dell, 1982), pp. 49–50.

104. *Ibid.*, p. 142.

105. *Ibid.*, pp. 142–143.

106. Gelb, Leslie, "Vietnam: The System Worked," *Foreign Policy*, vol. 3 (Summer 1971), p. 164.

THE CHAIN
OF THUNDERS

6

Front line combat in Vietnam was remarkably similar to the battles fought by those soldiers on the point who charged the Bloody Angle at Spotsylvania, who stormed the Nazi fortifications along the Siegfried Line, who broke through the Japanese defenses before Manila, and who assaulted the Chinese and North Korean entrenchments on Pork Chop Hill. The casualty figures tell the story.

Harry G. Summers, Jr.

THE STRATEGY OF LIMITED WAR

Americans went to war during the summer of 1965 confident that the Vietnamese insurgents could not withstand for long the application of U.S. military might. They assumed that the United States, the world's richest and most powerful nation, needed to do little more than flex its high-tech military muscles and it would triumph in Southeast Asia. President Johnson had gambled on a relatively quick and cheap U.S. victory in order to save South Vietnam, to implement his Great Society, and to preserve his broad-based consensus supporting containment of Communism abroad and social reform at home.

Two and a half years later the nation found itself mired in a frustrating and costly war. As 1967 drew to a close, America had committed 486,000 troops to Vietnam and was spending over $2 billion per month on the conflict. Despite these large investments of their nation's manpower and wealth, far in excess of what anyone had anticipated when the war began, many Americans feared that the United States was not winning the war in Vietnam. To them the conflict appeared to be stalemated; they faced the dismaying prospect of a protracted war with ever mounting costs and casualties. Many citizens had concluded that it had been a mistake for the United States to have become involved in the Vietnam War.

During most of 1967, support for the conflict and for Johnson's leadership was declining among Congress, the media, and the public. A debate between hawks and doves over Johnson's war policy was building in Congress and echoing in the streets. Within the White House, presidential advisers were dividing into hawkish and dovish factions. Facing rising war costs, Congress was abandoning Johnson's Great Society reform program. Widening social fissures heralded the breakdown of consensus. In Newark, Detroit, and elsewhere, angry black rioters put entire blocks of cities to the torch. Violence in Vietnam bred violence at home.

The prime cause of America's entanglement in a stalemated war of increasing magnitude was the failure of America's leaders to develop effective strategies for achieving national political objectives in a limited war milieu of the kind that the United States had gotten itself into in Vietnam.[1] Traditionally, U.S. military leaders have not devoted themselves to the development of national strategy, or grand strategy as it is also called, specifically with the development of the military means required to achieve particular national goals. "The Americans had won every war since (and including) the Civil War by an overwhelming combination of superior manpower and weight of materiel, a superiority which minimized the importance of strategy."[2]

As the rivalry between America and the Soviet Union intensified in the aftermath of World War II, both sides built up potent thermonuclear arsenals. Strategists in both nations spawned new strategic theories as they struggled to control these extraordinarily powerful weapons. Within America, given the absence of military theorists, strategic analysts for the nuclear age were recruited from civilian ranks, many from academia. At institutes and "think tanks," theorists such as Herman Kahn fashioned strategic concepts for the nuclear era. For the most part, military professionals ignored the theories propounded by civilian strategists, considering them arcane intellectual exercises irrelevant to solving the practical problems of war fighting in the atomic age.

One of the theories developed for the nuclear age by civilian strategists was the concept of limited war. It rested on two beliefs: first, that a nuclear war with the Soviet Union (later expanded to include China) had to be avoided at all cost, for it could never be won given the immense destructive power of the nuclear weaponry possessed by both sides; and, second, that the United States must contain Communism, which was spreading in the Third World via local, small-scale wars. One theory of limited warfare assumed the gradual application of economic and military assistance, diplomatic pressure, covert operations, and military force at the site of Communist or Communist-inspired insurrections. Limited-war doctrine called for the employment of these instrumentalities with restraint and skill. A deft touch was required to use just enough and the right mix of persuasion, money, aid, and force necessary to defeat a rebellion and to contain the spread of Communism, without provoking a response from the USSR or China that could cause a nuclear confrontation.

The theory of limited war received its first application during the Korean conflict. That war had started when North Korea, seeking to bring the entire country under Communist control, invaded South Korea June 25, 1950. President Truman, assuming that the North Korean invasion was supported, perhaps directed, by the Soviet Union to further Soviet expansionist ambitions in Asia, quickly made the decision to intervene militarily. American objectives were not only to defend South Korea against Communist aggression but to contain the spread of Communism without provoking a confrontation with the Soviets that could lead to World War III.

Reacting to the Chinese intervention into the Korean war five months later which caught him by surprise, UN Commander General Douglas MacArthur, wanted to undertake military initiatives against China. He ran up against the civilian proponents of limited war who insisted on confining the UN forces to the Korean battlefield.[3] MacArthur and his supporters chafed at the limitations placed on UN forces while their Chinese adversaries freely used their homeland for logistics support, for basing aircraft, and for sanctuaries.

A dispute over the objectives for which the Korean war was being fought lay at the core of the conflict between MacArthur and Truman. MacArthur wanted to inflict a major defeat on China and to liberate all of Korea from Communism. Truman sought the limited political objective of restoring the status quo, of ensuring the survival of a non-Communist South Korea below the 38th parallel. Truman's overriding concern was the avoidance of a confrontation with the Soviets then aligned with China. Truman removed MacArthur from his command when MacArthur publicly criticized the Truman administration's limited war strategies and political objectives. This dispute between civilian and military leaders, which erupted during the Korean war over strategies and objectives, foreshadowed similar conflicts occurring during the Vietnam war.

Following the end of the Korean war, a decade would pass before America would again resort to limited war in order to contain the spread of Communism in Asia. But, in Vietnam, U.S. limited war strategists came up against a sophisticated and complex revolutionary war strategy employed by the North Vietnamese and the NLF, whereas in the Korean war American forces had only engaged in conventional war against the North Korean and Chinese armies. During 1962 and 1963, President Kennedy cautiously pursued a small-scale limited war policy in Vietnam based on furnishing the

South Vietnamese government diplomatic, economic, and military assistance, accompanied by the use of covert operations, counterinsurgency tactics, and the deployment of thousands of U.S. military advisers. Following Kennedy's assassination, Lyndon Johnson immediately embraced the limited U.S. commitment in Vietnam and gradually expanded it.

During the first half of 1965, in order to stave off the imminent collapse of the South Vietnamese government, Johnson escalated the conflict, first by bombing North Vietnam, and when that strategy proved ineffective, by sending American combat forces to fight the Vietcong and PAVN forces in southern Vietnam. Johnson chose to expand drastically the limited war, which he had inherited, rather than to accept the Kennedy administration's failure to develop an effective strategy that would have enabled the South Vietnamese government to survive. From Johnson's vantage point, the fall of Saigon would have meant intolerable disaster: the failure of the U.S. strategy of limited war to contain Communism in Indochina, a failure that threatened to crumble the entire U.S. Cold War foreign policy edifice that had been constructed since 1945.

At the time that he made these escalatory decisions, Johnson could not know that he had committed U.S. forces to a long, costly, and ultimately losing war. One of the causes of that eventual disaster would be defects inherent in the U.S. concept of limited war as well as in its application to Indochina. U.S. efforts to fight a limited war in Vietnam were also complicated by disputes among Johnson's civilian and military advisers over how best to implement military strategy, disputes that added ambiguities to Washington's conduct of the war. The architects of America's limited war in that region never improvised a grand strategy that could counter the sophisticated strategy used by their determined foes.

The major U.S. objectives in Vietnam included enabling the GVN to extend its control over all of that country lying south of the 17th parallel, defeating the PLAF and the NVA forces fighting in South Vietnam, forcing Hanoi to withdraw its forces from the south and to renounce its support of the southern insurrection, and deterring Chinese expansion into Vietnam, Indochina, or anywhere in Southeast Asia. Achieving these goals amounted to a virtually unlimited strategic agenda.

American policy makers never generated the strategies to accomplish most of these objectives. One reason for their failure was their unwillingness to order a total mobilization of American human and economic resources. Vietnam would be a limited war for limited ends using limited assets.[4] Another cause of failure lay in the fact that U.S. military strategies in Vietnam were incompatible. On the one hand, Johnson limited the American military effort in Vietnam in order not to provoke Chinese or Soviet military intervention. On the other hand, he counted on a comparatively quick and easy victory over the NLF and Hanoi. Having limited the use of American military power to avoid war with China and a possible nuclear confrontation with the Soviet Union, and having seriously underestimated their enemy's capacity to resist American power, Washington "did not confront the crucial question of what would be required to achieve its goals until it was bogged down in a bloody stalemate."[5]   Bound by their doctrine of limited war to contain Communism in southern Vietnam while avoiding confrontations with China and the USSR, and concerned to limit the war for domestic political reasons, American officials never developed the means to defeat their enemies and to save their allies before popular support for the war collapsed.

When the United States eventually was forced to curtail the air war and to withdraw its ground combat forces from Vietnam because public opinion would no longer support a war that involved sustaining massive U.S. casualties and costs, the GVN remained dependent on U.S. military aid, military advisers, and air and logistics support for its survival.   After the U.S. aid programs were reduced and military support were withdrawn, PAVN forces overwhelmed the demoralized GVN army and South Vietnam was extinguished.

Having surrendered the formulation of limited war strategy to civilian analysts and having failed to conceive of any alternative, Johnson's military advisers had no choice but to go along with it.   But his military advisers resented the restrictions that civilian officials imposed on the air war against North Vietnam, restrictions that they believed prevented them from inflicting enough damage to force Hanoi to stop supporting the southern insurgency. They continually pressured Johnson to intensify the air war against North Vietnam.   But the military's call for full-scale bombing attacks risked Chinese military intervention, a risk Johnson, with vivid memories of Korea, refused to run.   In 1967, Johnson eased his controls and permitted an expanded air war.

Although they exercised tight control over the selection of targets for the air war against North Vietnam, civilian leaders in Washington, other than confining the ground war to the territory of South Vietnam, left the framing of strategies for its conduct to the Joint Chiefs and to General Westmoreland.[6] Initially, Johnson's military advisers accepted these geographic limits imposed on the ground war because Westmoreland did not have enough combat forces or a sufficiently developed logistics support system for conducting campaigns within South Vietnam and simultaneously undertaking cross-border operations into Laos, Cambodia, and southern North Vietnam. In time, military leaders would also challenge civilian restrictions clamped on the ground war, which they viewed as needlessly delaying the achievement of U.S. objectives in Southeast Asia.

WAR OF ATTRITION

General William Childs "Westy" Westmoreland was the "key American military actor in the Vietnamese drama."[7]   As commander of the Military Assistance Command—Vietnam (COMUSMACV), Westmoreland held tac-

The inevitable general...William C. Westmoreland, the American field commander in Vietnam from 1965-1968. Here, COMUSMACV addresses some of the U.S. troops on October 31, 1966. *Source*: National Archives

tical command over the American war that began in the summer of 1965. He and his staff devised the strategy of attrition that was in place from July 1965 until President Nixon supplanted it with Vietnamization in August 1969. During his tenure of duty in Vietnam, General Westmoreland won the most important campaign of the war, the Tet Offensive, fought during the early part of 1968, a series of battles in which RVNAF and U.S. forces destroyed the PLAF. Westmoreland was also the principal adversary of the commander-in-chief of the North Vietnamese Army, General Vo Nguyen Giap, who, after defeating the French, ultimately defeated American efforts to control the political destiny of South Vietnam.

Westmoreland has been called the "inevitable general."[8] From the outset of his military career he appeared destined for distinction. Westmoreland compiled a superb World War II record serving as an artillery officer with the 9th Infantry Division, which saw extensive action in North Africa, Normandy, and Germany. He also fought in Korea, where he reached the rank of brigadier general at the relatively youthful age of 38. After Korea, he continued to advance his career with choice assignments including a tour as superintendent of the Military Academy. Westmoreland assumed command of U.S. forces in Vietnam in June 1965. The Vietnam war proved to be a difficult and frustrating experience for the inevitable general. He became a controversial figure, often the target of criticism, most often from doves, but also from hawkish critics who believed that his strategy of attrition could never produce victory in Vietnam.[9]

Westmoreland quickly decided to use an attrition strategy. It was the traditional American way of war that had produced victories in all major U.S. wars since the American Civil War. Attrition played to the American strengths—firepower and mobility—and it minimized U.S. casualties. Attrition warfare also appeared to promise an opportunity for winning the war more quickly than protracted counterinsurgency operations. Denied by the exigencies of the American limited-war policy of an opportunity to wage a war of annihilation by invading North Vietnam, Westmoreland believed that attrition campaigns in South Vietnam were the next best strategy available. Westmoreland also felt that he had no choice but to use an attrition strategy because North Vietnam was committing its main force units to the war in South Vietnam.[10]

At the time no one proposed any alternative. Westmoreland's attrition strategy was quickly endorsed by Army Chief of Staff Harold Johnson, by the Joint Chiefs, and by civilian leaders including Secretary of Defense McNamara and President Johnson. If Westmoreland were the inevitable general, attrition was the inevitable U.S. war strategy in Vietnam. But "the Army applied the doctrine and force structure it had developed for conventional contingencies in Europe and Korea against insurgent forces practicing a form of revolutionary warfare."[11] A major reason for the failure of the Americans to gain more than a military stalemate in the Vietnam war after years of large-scale warfare was their reliance on a conventional strategy against adversaries who employed unconventional revolutionary war strategies that enabled them to avoid defeat at the hands of a much more powerful army.

As he and his staff planned it, Westmoreland's strategy of attrition was to unfold through three phases, anticipating a U.S. victory by the end of 1967. During phase one, U.S. troops would be used to protect the developing American logistics system, that is, military bases, air fields, and lines of communication. Westmoreland also believed that American combat forces would have to be committed to battle during this first phase because enemy main force units operating in the vicinity of Saigon and the central highlands continually attacked GVN forces. Westmoreland viewed the military situation in the summer of 1965 as precarious. The Vietcong controlled half the territory and population of South Vietnam. VC offensives launched in May were destroying ARVN units at the rate of a battalion per week, and the insurgents were overrunning many district headquarters. PAVN offensives in the central highlands sought to take control of that vital region and to threaten the coastal cities. Typically, political chaos reigned in Saigon. A South Vietnamese political collapse and a Vietcong victory before the end of the year both appeared possible. Westmoreland's objectives during phase one were to protect the populated areas, to thwart enemy operations, and to halt the downward slide of the war.[12]

Assuming that the military situation could be stabilized by the end of 1965 and that the South Vietnamese would have stopped losing by then, Westmoreland's planners called for phase two to begin in 1966. American forces would take the initiative and, wherever possible, eliminate the enemy's base camps and sanctuaries. These large-unit sweeps into enemy basing areas were to be the tactical operations that came to be known as "search and destroy" missions. Westmoreland assumed that by attacking key enemy basing areas, he could force the Vietcong main units to fight, giving the U.S. forces an opportunity to use their superior firepower to "find, fix, and finish the enemy." General Westmoreland anticipated phase two lasting a year. It was assumed that the back of the insurgency would have been broken by the end of phase two. Phase three would begin in 1967; it would be essentially a mopping up exercise. Remaining insurgent forces would be destroyed or pushed back to remote areas where they would pose no threat to village security or to GVN forces.[13]

U.S. planners assumed that the tasks of pacification and of building up the GVN military forces would be pursued during all three phases. They expected that by the time the U.S. war of attrition would be completed, most of the people of South Vietnam would be living in villages free of Vietcong pressure. They also assumed that the GVN military forces would be strong enough to handle any lingering security threats to South Vietnam. With the VC forces neutralized and PAVN units forced back into North Vietnam, Hanoi would have to negotiate on U.S. terms. American combat forces would be withdrawn.[14] As the American war in Vietnam unfolded, Westmoreland's strategic plan would prove easier to draft than to implement; in fact, it proved impossible to implement fully for many reasons.

As Westmoreland began deploying U.S. combat units during the summer of 1965, his operations were hampered seriously by inadequate logistics support systems. President Johnson's failure to mobilize the Reserves and National Guard and to rely completely on increased draft calls and enlistments to meet the expanding manpower needs of the rapidly escalating war created serious problems for Westmoreland. The regular Army had few engineering, logistics, and service units on active duty. Military planners had assumed that in the event of war, Reserve and National Guard units would be mobilized to provide these crucial support services. When Johnson, ignoring the advice of the Joint Chiefs, refused to call the Reserves to active duty for political reasons, Westmoreland faced a crisis in supplying and supporting the combat units that were pouring into the war zone.[15] Many units found their ammunition in short supply. Other combat units arrived understrength and without all their equipment or supplies.

At the time that the American war in Vietnam began, South Vietnam possessed only one deep-water port, the commercial docks located fifty miles inland at Saigon. Since warehouse and storage areas were not equipped to handle the massive influx of war materiel, military supplies piled up on the Saigon docks. Vietcong sappers destroyed huge quantities of the arriving U.S. supplies. South Vietnamese workers stole equally large quantities of material for their use or for sale on the black markets. For the rest of 1965, Westmoreland had to delay the tactical deployment of maneuver units because of weak logistics support.[16]

Working furiously under adverse conditions, the Seabees, the Army Corps of Engineers, and civilian contractors constructed additional deep-water ports, warehouses, jet-capable air fields, roads, and bridges. The world's most productive economy was soon sending a cornucopia of equipment and supplies over 9,000 miles to its warriors fighting in Vietnam; 1st Logistical Command developed a superb supply system that not only kept American soldiers supplied with ammunition, guns, tanks, and planes, but also with toilet paper, shaving lather, socks, beer, soft drinks, and ice cream.[17] Within a year, Westmoreland had accomplished "what has properly been called a logistics miracle. The Americans who fought in Vietnam were the best fed, best clothed, best equipped army the nation had ever sent to war."[18]

There were also serious problems inherent in the magnificent logistics success story. American troops were so well supplied with luxuries that many of them quickly lost enthusiasm for the hardships of extended field operations. The supply system was also colossally expensive and wasteful. Sometimes soldiers expended enormous amounts of ammunition to kill one enemy soldier. The promiscuous use of firepower was also responsible for many accidental deaths. A large number of U.S. troops were killed by "friendly fire" from American aircraft, artillery, mortars, and machine guns. Many other U.S. troops were also killed in the numerous accidents involving the handling, the transporting, the storing, and the guarding of ammunition. Bombs and bullets intended for use against their enemies all too often accidentally killed Americans. Most of all, the effort necessary to make the U.S. Army the best supplied in our history tied up large numbers of military personnel in noncombat activity. The U.S. force in Vietnam was also the least efficient army in U.S. military history. Ironically, the fact that America's army in Vietnam was the best supplied force in U.S. history itself contributed to its decline and eventual defeat.[19]

Although Westmoreland had few combat units and U.S. logistics were still in the chaotic stage, he felt that he had to attack Vietcong units operating in some areas in order to take the pressure off beleaguered ARVN forces. On June 28, troops of the 173rd Airborne Brigade, the first Army unit to see combat in Vietnam, climbed aboard helicopters at Bien Hoa air base on the

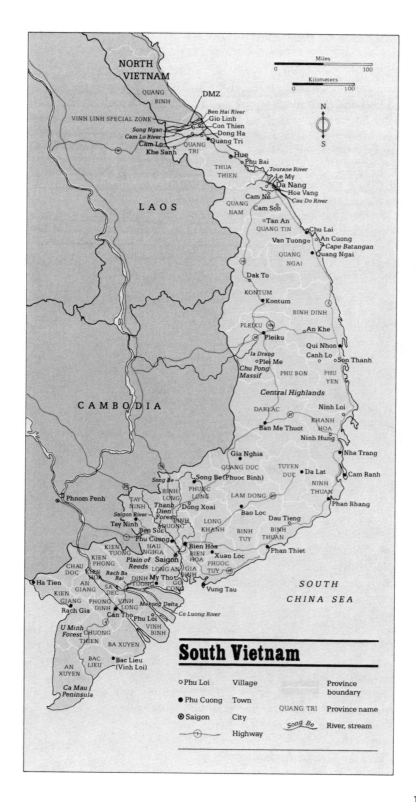

South Vietnam

outskirts of Saigon. They were accompanied by a battalion of Australian soldiers and several battalions of ARVN infantry. Westmoreland was sending the 173rd and their allies on the war's first "search and destroy" mission. They were flown into War Zone D, a jungle-infested area thirty-five miles northwest of Saigon that had long been a Vietcong stronghold. The VC chose not to engage the green U.S. sky troopers or their allies on that operation. After two days of inconclusive skirmishing, the troops returned to Bien Hoa. One American had been killed and eight wounded. "This American foray 27 June locked the United States into a ground war in Asia."[20]

The 173rd Airborne Brigade made several more incursions into War Zone D during the ensuing months, each of them ending much like the first: withdrawal after a few days of skirmishing with an elusive enemy not much interested in fighting. In early November the troops of the 173rd once more helicoptered into War Zone D. One of the soldiers gave the operation the sarcastic name of HUMP. ("Hump," "humping," and "humping the boonies" were the soldiers' terms for long and exhausting marches over rugged jungle-covered terrain in hot, humid weather under the heavy weight of rucksacks crammed with extra rations and ammunition.) But Operation HUMP turned out to be a fierce and brutal campaign. In a remote region of War Zone D, several Airborne platoons ran into a large force of Vietcong hiding in thick jungle. This time the VC wanted a fight. The combat was intense, some of it savage hand-to-hand fighting. The noise level from rocket, machine gun, and automatic rifle fire was so high that officers and noncoms had to convey orders to their men by hand signals. Both forces sustained heavy casualties in a day-long battle that ended when the VC broke contact and disappeared into the jungle.[21]

The first big battle of the developing American war occurred in I ("Eye") Corps, the northernmost combat sector controlled by the 3rd Marine Amphibious Force under the command of General Lewis Walt.[22] On August 15, 1965, Marine intelligence learned from a VC deserter the exact location of the 1st Vietcong Regiment. It was holed up in hamlets on the Batangan peninsula fifteen miles south of the new Marine base at Chu Lai. General Walt concluded that the regiment posed a threat to Chu Lai and he ordered the Marines to attack it.[23]

Quickly, the Marines organized a large-scale amphibious assault, code-named Operation STARLITE,[24] on the Vietcong positions. An assault battalion of the 3rd Marines landed on the sandy peninsula in order to pin the enemy against the sea. Another battalion came ashore in the enemy's rear. The two Marine battalions slowly worked their way forward over several days, squeezing the black pajama-clad Vietcong between them. As the Marines advanced, tactical aircraft strafed and naval gunfire bombarded the VC positions. The Vietcong regiment was destroyed; about 700 enemy troops were killed. The Marines lost 50 dead and 150 wounded. Operation STARLITE was a major American victory.[25]

Operations STARLITE and HUMP served as preliminaries for the most important battle of phase one. It occurred in a remote region of the central highlands between October 18 and November 24, 1965. Westmoreland's chief worry during the summer of 1965 was that a PAVN offensive would conquer the central highlands, drive to the coast, and sever Saigon from the northern provinces. He planned to counter the NVA drive with the 1st Air Cavalry Division (air mobile) based at An Khe. Westmoreland wanted the Air Cavalry to beat back the PAVN thrust and to keep open Route 19, the main highway running from Pleiku to Qui Nhon.

The 1st Cavalry brought a new concept to warfare; it combined infantry, artillery, and aviation functions into one unit possessing 435 helicopters. The Air Cavalry went to war in the air. Because rugged terrain and remote locations posed no obstacles for the Air Cavalry, they appeared to be the best force to use to blunt the PAVN offensive. The stage was set for the first battle pitting North Vietnamese regulars against an elite American combat force. Both sides were sending in their first strings for a campaign that was to have a decisive impact on the American conduct of the entire war.[26]

By early October, General Giap had committed three NVA regiments to the campaign, the 32nd and 33rd, with the 66th held in reserve in Laos. These units were joined by some crack Vietcong forces. On October 19, the 32nd and 33rd struck a U.S. Special Forces camp at Plei Me on the Cambodian border twenty-five miles southwest of Pleiku and ambushed an ARVN relief column sent to help the embattled defenders. The NVA regiments then lay siege to the special forces camp. Their objective was to destroy Plei Me, perhaps other camps in the area, and to capture Pleiku. The North Vietnamese would then be positioned to strike east toward the coast. Westmoreland countered with the Air Cavalry, which supported the ARVN relief force with air and artillery attacks. U.S. firepower inflicted heavy casualties on the enemy and broke the siege of Plei Me.[27]

With their opening gambit checked, the PAVN forces retreated to the west. Westmoreland ordered the 1st Air Cavalry to search out and to destroy the NVA forces. He was taking a gamble. The air mobile concept had never been tested in combat. The 1st Cavalry was understrength. Many of its soldiers were weakened from bouts with malaria, and many of their helicopters were not operational. The Air Cavalry would have to operate in unfamiliar and rugged terrain dominated by jungle-shrouded mountains. Even the open spaces between the jagged peaks were covered with shrubs and elephant grass as high as a man's head. The search area, the Ia Drang valley, covered about 1,500 square miles of desolate country inhabited only by a Montagnard tribe, the Jarai.[28] To add increased danger, the inexperienced 1st Cavalry was also going after the regiments of one of the finest light infantry in the world.

The first phase of the Battle of the Ia Drang lasted for two weeks, from late October to November 14. It consisted of searches punctuated by brief and violent clashes whenever the Americans located NVA units. The largest of these battles occurred on November 6 when two Air Cavalry companies ran into an NVA ambush. Both sides were bloodied in a brief but brutal firefight.[29] Another week of sporadic clashes preceded the major battles of the Ia Drang campaign.

By November 10 the PAVN forces had eluded their pursuers and had made their way to the sheltering crevices of the Chu Pong massif, a mountain range at the southern end of the Ia Drang valley near the Cambodian border. There they planned to rest and to regroup for another assault on the camp at Plei Me. As the NVA forces took refuge in the Chu Pong mountains, Major General Harry W. O. Kinnard, the Air Cavalry commander, ordered air searches of the area around the massif. After aerial reconnaissance, Kinnard ordered the 1st Battalion, 7th Cavalry, to attack the largest landing site in the valley at the foot of the mountains, named "Landing Zone X-ray."[30] The 1st Battalion helicoptered in on November 14. Inadvertently, the 1st Cavalry had launched its attack right in the midst of a NVA staging area. The PAVN tactical commander, General Chu Huy Man, instantly ordered the 66th and 33rd NVA regiments to counterattack. The climactic phase of the Battle of the Ia Drang was joined.

Within a few hours, 1st Battalion was engulfed "in fighting as fierce as any ever experienced by American troops."[31] Lieutenant Colonel Harold G. Moore, Jr., commanding the embattled battalion, brought in air strikes and artillery support, and also urgently requested reinforcements. The NVA rained rocket and mortar fire on Landing Zone X-ray in an effort to deny 1st Battalion its reinforcements. Despite heavy fire, another battalion landed at Landing Zone X-ray to join the fight. For three days, fighting raged in the vicinity of Landing Zone X-ray, an area about the size of an American football field. The two U.S. battalions beat back repeated attacks by one of the NVA regiments that was trying to overrun their perimeter. The combat was intense, "resulting in savage, close quarter fighting, sometimes in hand-to-hand combat. One U.S. soldier was found dead, his hand clutching the throat of a dead enemy infantryman."[32]

Air Cavalry pilots flew in and out of the landing zone under heavy fire, bringing in ammunition and supplies and hauling out wounded and dead soldiers. Air Force tactical bombers bombed and strafed enemy positions. Artillery, hauled to nearby firebases by powerful CH 47 Chinook cargo helicopters, rained thousands of rounds on the North Vietnamese. B-52 strategic bombers flying out of Guam, each carrying a 36,000-pound payload, used for the first time in support of ground operations, pounded the NVA positions.[33]

The battle for Landing Zone X-ray ended on November 16. Having failed to break through the U.S. perimeter and having sustained huge losses from American artillery and bombs, the North Vietnamese withdrew from the battle site and retreated into Cambodia. Over the next few days there were occasional firefights between the air cavalrymen and straggling NVA units, the last occurring on November 24. The Battle of the Ia Drang was over. Soon afterward, the Americans also withdrew from the river valley and were flown back to their base at An Khe. U.S. officials estimated that the North Vietnamese may have lost as many as 3,000 soldiers killed and more than 1,000 wounded of the 6,000 that they had committed to battle. The three enemy regiments were decimated. They did not return to action for more than six months. The PAVN threat to the central highlands had been eliminated. About 300 American soldiers had been killed during the five weeks of fighting around Plei Me and in the Ia Drang valley.[34]

U.S. forces won a significant victory at Ia Drang. Westmoreland, strongly committed to an attrition strategy, found confirmation for his views in the favorable ratio of U.S. to enemy losses. He was convinced that search and destroy missions would eventually defeat both the Vietcong and the PAVN forces fighting in South Vietnam. The Battle of the Ia Drang locked the attrition strategy in place for nearly four years.[35] The campaign also vindicated the air mobile concept; henceforth, helicopter assaults would be the mainstay of U.S. tactics in Vietnam.[36] Westmoreland was also impressed by the performance of the green U.S. sky troopers fighting a tough foe under egregious conditions.

But thoughtful military analysts concerned themselves with some of the implications of the Battle of the Ia Drang. They wondered about the accuracy of the estimates of enemy casualties that, according to some skeptical soldiers on the scene, were merely WEGs (wild-eyed guesses) that probably drastically inflated the numbers.[37] They also wondered why the 1st Cavalry so quickly abandoned the Ia Drang valley after the weeks of hard fighting, leaving the region vulnerable to future PAVN infiltrations. They were not reassured by the Army's explanation that the valley had no strategic significance and that the chief purpose of the operation had been to kill as many Communists as possible.

The Ia Drang campaign signaled that the Vietnam war was entering a new phase; it had evolved into two parallel wars. The long-standing conflict between the GVN forces and the Vietcong for control of the countryside continued. "Superimposed on the older war was the more recent and more conventional struggle between the NVA and the Allied forces."[38] In the future there would be fewer small-scale, low intensity campaigns between South Vietnamese forces and Vietcong guerrillas and more large-scale conventional warfare between invading NVA main force units and American troops. Future battles would require more U.S. forces and would portend higher U.S. casualties.

The Battle of the Ia Drang also indicated that the Air Cavalry had a serious tactical limitation. Once out of their helicopters and on the ground, American combat units were immobilized. The lightly armored NVA troopers used their foot mobility to outmaneuver the Americans. Only if the NVA attacked could the Americans engage them in battle. Only then could the

Americans, using their far greater firepower, inflict more casualties than they took. But if the enemy chose to elude American assault units, as the Vietcong troops did repeatedly in War Zone D earlier in the year, and as the retreating NVA troops did for two weeks in the Drang river valley, the Air Cavalry troops could not force a fight because they were not willing to leave their landing zones to go plunging off into the jungle in pursuit of their more mobile enemy.

Throughout the Ia Drang campaign, the NVA had retained the initiative. If the PAVN forces wished to evade the U.S. forces or to engage in brief, small-scale firefights, they had the maneuverability to do so. Having learned the hard way what U.S. firepower could do to their regiments if they chose to go to battle with the Americans, PAVN forces could be expected to adjust their tactics to reduce combat losses in future campaigns. How would U.S. search and destroy missions attrite a mobile enemy that could control the terms of engagement?[39]

But as 1965 ended, Westmoreland had achieved the objectives of phase one of his strategic plan. The military situation had stabilized. He had 184,000 U.S. troops in South Vietnam and more were on their way. The Vietcong found that they could not sustain the momentum that they had built up earlier in the year. The PAVN offensive in the central highlands had been blunted. The ARVN forces had stopped losing the war. Since the advent of American combat forces during the summer of 1965, most war news had been favorable to the U.S. side. Within the United States, the war continued to enjoy widespread popular support. *Time* magazine named General Westmoreland its "Man of the Year" for 1965.

If it were true that the Allies had stopped losing by year's end, it was also true that they were far from winning the war. Even as security in South Vietnam had been strengthened in many areas, enemy infiltration had increased. There were about 20,000 NVA troops fighting in South Vietnam, constituting one-third of the enemy's combat effectives. U.S. intelligence officials put the total enemy strength at year's end at 221,000, far more troops than ever before. The Vietcong/PAVN forces were matching the U.S. escalations. Intervention had saved the GVN from imminent collapse; it also transformed a revolutionary conflict into a prolonged and lethal international war.[40]

There were few major battles in South Vietnam during 1966, although there were many small-scale firefights all over the country. In the northern sector, U.S. Marines engaged frequently in combat operations against Vietcong forces and also defended the region just below the DMZ from NVA attacks. Westmoreland could not implement phase two of his attrition strategy according to schedule in 1966 primarily because manpower shortages delayed his buildup of combat forces. His policy of limiting soldiers to a one-year tour in the combat zone also delayed the U.S. buildup and was a continuous source of manpower instability throughout the war. Further, most of the arriving troopers and their officers had never seen a moment's

An M-48 tank returning to base after a search and destroy mission against the enemy in the fall of 1966.
Source: U.S. Army Photo

combat. Their training in the states before arriving "in country" had not prepared them for the rigors of warfare. Westmoreland spent most of the year acclimating, training, and building up the U.S. combat force levels. He was preparing his troops for the large-scale operations that would characterize the fighting during 1967.

American troops also had to adapt to the unique conditions of the Vietnam battlefield. Unlike World War II or Korea, the Vietnam conflict was a frontless war. There were no territorial objectives to be taken. There was no vital center of enemy resistance to be destroyed; all of South Vietnam was a fluid battlefield. Military operations had to be highly mobile, multilinear, and nondirectional.[41] Battles occurred over the entire country. They could occur wherever and whenever the VC or PAVN forces picked a fight. They could occur in remote, sparsely populated highlands or borderlands, or they could occur amid the populous delta and coastal regions. The American objective in these sporadic encounters was to attrite as many of the enemy as possible while using their superior air mobility and firepower to minimize their own casualties.

Westmoreland never had enough combat effectives to occupy an area after a battle, so, inevitably, the American forces would be withdrawn after a campaign had ended. Enemy forces often returned to these areas soon after the American pullout. In such a formless war, the only measures of progress, of "winning," came to be statistics: the number of enemy soldiers killed, captured, or persuaded to surrender, of enemy weapons captured, and of enemy supplies and food stores destroyed. It was not an orderly war with territorial goals but a ragged war of numbers, numbers that never added up to a U.S. victory before American public support for the war weakened and time ran out.

In the fall of 1966 the United States mounted the largest search and destroy mission to date, Operation ATTLEBORO, that prefigured the big-unit war of 1967. In late October General Westmoreland sent a large Allied force consisting of the 1st Infantry Division, units from two other U.S. infantry divisions, the 173rd Airborne Brigade, and a large contingent of ARVN troops into War Zone C, long a Vietcong stronghold, an area north-west of Saigon in Tay Ninh Province that bordered Cambodia. The Vietcong 9th Division, accompanied by a NVA regiment, had attacked a special forces outpost in that region and then overran a relief column sent to assist it.[42] In a series of battles spread over a month, the 22,000-man allied force, supported with B-52 strikes and artillery, killed over 1,100 enemy soldiers and captured tons of supplies before driving their adversaries across the border into Cambodia.[43]

As 1967 dawned, Westmoreland was more convinced than ever that large-scale search and destroy missions such as Operation ATTLEBORO provided the means for the destruction of North Vietnamese regular forces and Vietcong main force units. He believed that subsequent ATTLEBORO-type operations would be the keys to eventual Allied victory. He "forged jumbo operational plans as the dominant pattern of strategy for the upcoming year."[44] Even though there would continue to be hundreds of small-scale operations all over South Vietnam during the year, 1967 would be the year in which Westmoreland got his big-unit war.

He had at his disposal 390,000 U.S. soldiers, including seven divisions, two airborne and two light infantry brigades, an armored regiment, and a Special Forces group. They were supplemented by "third country" forces from South Korea, Australia, and New Zealand. In addition, ARVN, which had expanded rapidly in 1966, could field eleven divisions. Total RVNAF (Republic of South Vietnam Forces), in addition to the ARVN units, included territorial forces, security forces, local troops, and irregulars. Westmoreland's Combined Campaign Plan for 1967 assigned RVNAF the tasks of securing and pacifying areas under their control while the U.S. forces carried the brunt of the fighting against the Communists. His goals included securing South Vietnam's borders and beating back NVA attacks across the DMZ, neutralizing the VC forces in War Zones C and D, eradicating Vietcong sanctuaries in the vicinity of Saigon, defending the strategic central highlands against PAVN incursions, driving the VC and PAVN forces back from the populated regions, and providing security for the populated regions of South Vietnam.[45]

The first of the 1967 big unit campaigns occurred in a region about forty miles north of Saigon in a strategic area sandwiched between War Zones C and D, called the Iron Triangle, which served as a staging area for VC attacks against GVN installations in the vicinity of Saigon. The Iron Triangle, bounded on two sides by rivers and on a third by jungle, incorporated about forty square miles of nearly impenetrable territory covered by trees, vines, bushes, and shrubs. Underneath the dense forest and jungle growth lay miles of tunnels, caverns, and chambers, some of which dated from the Vietminh campaigns against the Japanese during World War II. Thousands of insurgents could inhabit this subterranean labyrinth, an inviolable sanctuary, seemingly immune from counterattacks or efforts at destruction. On the fringe of the region, nestled in a loop of the Saigon River, lay the village of Ben Suc, many of whose estimated 3,500 residents had been supporting the Vietcong for years.[46]

Wanting to eliminate once and for all the threat to the Saigon regime posed by the Vietcong redoubt buried within the recesses of the Iron Triangle, General Westmoreland in early January 1967 launched a massive operation, code-named CEDAR FALLS, lasting three weeks and involving 30,000 U.S. and ARVN forces.[47] The first phase of the operation was to dispose of the threat posed by the villagers of Ben Suc. If, according to Vietcong doctrine, itself derived from Maoist theory, the people are the "sea" in which the guerrilla "fish" must swim, MACV strategists concluded that permanently eliminating the threat posed by the Vietcong forces marshalled in the Iron Triangle necessarily involved "draining the sea" by removing the villagers and razing the village.

On January 8, 1967, an armada of U.S. transport helicopters suddenly descended upon Ben Suc. Instantly, a force of hundreds of American and ARVN soldiers surrounded the village. They met with little resistance from the sullen villagers. Although the arrival of the helicopters caught them by surprise, most of the hardcore Vietcong fighters and their supporters in the village at the time escaped. All the villagers were rounded up and transferred to a refugee camp at Phu Loi near Phu Cuong, fifteen miles downriver. Specially trained destruction teams then moved in. Giant tractors, called Rome plows, fitted with wide bulldozer blades, cleared huge swatches of jungle, exposing the tunnel complexes. Demolition teams destroyed the houses above the ground and the tunnel complexes below. Within a few days "the village of Ben Suc no longer existed."[48]

While Ben Suc was being demolished, U.S. combat forces ranged across the Iron Triangle searching for Vietcong units. Because the Vietcong commander chose not to engage the American forces, most of the VC scattered and fled. Despite the corps-sized operation, the superior American mobility, and the vastly greater U.S. firepower, the tactical initiative remained with the Vietcong commander. He could choose to fight or not to fight; he could therefore control both the scale of the fighting and his casualty rate.

Soldiers of the 173rd Airborne Brigade walking a road in the Iron Triangle during Operation CEDAR FALLS.
Source: U.S. Army Photo

During the three weeks of CEDAR FALLS operations, about 700 Vietcong were killed and another 700 were either captured or turned themselves in under the "chieu hoi" (open arms) program, run by the GVN that granted amnesty to Vietcong defectors. American forces also destroyed enemy structures, equipment, and food supplies. Volunteers from the 1st Infantry Division's special chemical unit, nicknamed the "tunnel rats," combed the nearly twelve miles of tunnels that were exposed at various locations in the Iron Triangle. Among their discoveries the tunnel rats found a power station, a fully equipped field hospital, a weapons factory, and a regional PLAF headquarters.[49]

The entire region was then bombed, shelled, strafed, and burned to destroy any remaining structures or tunnels that could be of use to the Vietcong. In an effort to deter Vietcong reentry into the Iron Triangle, the area was declared to be a "free fire zone," which meant that artillery and air strikes could be made in the region without prior approval of GVN officials and without warning to its inhabitants. As the Allies departed the Iron Triangle, they were convinced that they had dealt the Vietcong a serious setback. They had rendered one of their enemy's long-time bastions and staging areas unusable and had severed the Vietcong military and political connections with the people inhabiting its vicinity. They had permanently removed a serious security threat to the GVN. They soon discovered that "they were wrong."[50]

The VC quickly returned to the Iron Triangle. They rebuilt and resupplied their base and once again threatened the region around Saigon. The razing of Ben Suc and the forced relocation of all its residents amounted to an admission that the ARVN forces were failing to pacify the peasants. Some villagers were killed and others brutally treated by ARVN soldiers in the process of relocating them. Most of the villagers of Ben Suc were angry about their forced move. They lost their homes, their ancestral lands, and all their possessions except for what they could carry with them. They found conditions in the refugee camp at Phu Loi to be miserable; initially, each family was allotted only ten square feet of living space in hastily constructed shelters. About all CEDAR FALLS brought the Saigon government "was a devastated forest and a horde of hostile refugees."[51]

Using the same forces and more, the United States mounted a larger operation called JUNCTION CITY against War Zone C about a month after CEDAR FALLS. The American soldiers made special efforts during JUNCTION CITY to trap Vietcong combat units and to force a fight with them, thus avoiding a repetition of CEDAR FALLS, when most of the VC slipped through their grasp. But mostly the Vietcong avoided combat during JUNCTION CITY, and the bulk of their forces fled across the Cambodian border. Even so, over a three-month period, American officials reported about 3,000 enemy soldiers killed.[52] But War Zone C was not neutralized, the Vietcong 9th Division was not put out of the war, and no efforts were made at pacification of the villagers living in the region. War Zone C continued to be used as a VC basing area after the Allied withdrawal.

One dimension of the ground war that limited the effectiveness of JUNCTION CITY were the rules of engagement civilian leaders imposed on

Soldiers prepare to destroy one of the many Vietcong tunnels that were exposed during the campaigns in the Thanh Dien Forest region of the Iron Triangle during Operation CEDAR FALLS January 1967.
Source: U.S. Army Photo

Riflemen moving down a jungle trail in War Zone C during Operation JUNCTION CITY March 1967.
Source: U.S. Army Photo

American forces fighting in South Vietnam. Even though both the VC and the NVA forces repeatedly violated Cambodian neutrality, U.S. forces were never allowed to pursue their enemies into Cambodia or to attack any Cambodian populated areas. The Vietcong 9th Division commander, aware that U.S. mobility and firepower had eliminated the inviolability of VC basing areas inside South Vietnam, and wishing to evade the mounting American pressure on his forces, took his troops into adjacent Cambodian sanctuaries where they joined PAVN combat units.

But Westmoreland's powerful forces had to stop at the Cambodian border. The rules of engagement in effect confined them to defensive efforts aimed at attriting a resourceful, highly maneuverable enemy who could escape beyond the fixed boundaries of the ground war in southern Vietnam in order to rest, resupply, regroup, replenish ranks, and then renew attacks on GVN targets in South Vietnam. U.S. military commanders vainly sought to get these rules of engagement modified in order to permit U.S. troops to pursue opposing forces to their destruction even if that would mean some fighting on Cambodian soil and inflicting damage and casualties on that neutral nation.[53]

While Operations CEDAR FALLS and JUNCTION CITY were being conducted in III Corps Tactical Zone in the vicinity of Saigon; to the north in II Corps Tactical Zone, battles for control of the central highlands raged. Units of the 4th Infantry Division under the command of Major General William R. Peers, operating out of their base camp at Pleiku City, battled forces from the 1st and 10th NVA divisions. Small units from both sides engaged in fierce firefights of short duration amid "some of the most difficult tropical terrain in the world"[54] in Kontum province. There, among huge trees, as tall as 250–300 feet, where little sunlight filtered through a tropical rain forest and triple-canopied jungle even at midday, PAVN regulars chose where and when to attack U.S. forces. The Americans counterattacked, trying to kill as many of the enemy as they could, often sustaining heavy losses themselves. Both sides lost many soldiers in vicious jungle-mountain warfare.

In other action in the central highlands, General Peers deployed units of his 4th Division along the South Vietnamese border in western Pleiku. His objective was to deny invading PAVN forces access to South Vietnam's

Soldier with an M-60 machine gun. The M-60 was a powerful, versatile, and reliable weapon. It could either be fired from the hip or from the prone position using a tripod.
Source: USMI Photo Archives

strategic heartlands. From April to October, U.S. and NVA troops fought a series of battles in the rolling tropical plains of western Pleiku near the Cambodian border. The hard-fighting U.S. forces succeeded in beating back numerous NVA thrusts. By October, General Peers discerned that the major Communist push would be an invasion of Kontum province directly north of Pleiku.[55] There, a month later, occurred the Battle of Dak To, the decisive battle that determined the outcome of the campaigns waged for control of the central highlands during 1967.

Dak To was the site of a U.S. Army Special Forces camp set amid towering mountains in central Kontum province. The camp lay in a valley ringed by 6,000-foot peaks and ridges. Fighting had begun during the summer when NVA forces had entrenched themselves in bunker complexes along the hilltops and ridgelines above the camp. For months gruelling battles took place in the vicinity of Dak To between PAVN forces from the 24th NVA Division and Allied forces that included the 3rd Brigade of the 1st Cavalry Division and some elite ARVN ranger units. In early November a battalion of the 173rd Airborne and a brigade from the 4th Infantry Division were flown in to join the battle. The Allies prepared to find and to assault the NVA positions.

During the first two weeks of November, U.S. patrols made contact with NVA units, enabling the American troops to call in artillery barrages, tactical aircraft, and high-flying B-52s to pound the enemy positions. On November 17, the fighting around Dak To intensified when a patrol from the 173rd Airborne Brigade came upon the 174th NVA Regiment entrenched in bunker complexes running along the eastern slope and the summit of a peak known on American maps as Hill 875. Hill 875 lay twelve miles west of the Special Forces camp, about two miles from the point where the borders of South Vietnam, Cambodia, and Laos merge.[56] "The fight for Hill 875 would ultimately climax the Battle for Dak To, as well as the 1967 campaign for the highlands."[57]

The 2nd Battalion, 503rd Infantry, of the 173rd Airborne was ordered to move in and to clear the enemy from Hill 875. It took five days of hard fighting to secure the mountain. During the battle, the paratroopers of 2nd Battalion lost so many men that another airborne battalion and units of the 4th Infantry Division had to be brought in. On November 23, the Americans reached the summit of Hill 875 only to discover that the defenders had abandoned their positions during the night. The 174th had accomplished its mission, which had been to cover the withdrawal of the NVA forces retreating into Cambodia and Laos.[58]

The taking of Hill 875 ended the Battle of Dak To. U.S. officials estimated that during the campaign the North Vietnamese lost about 1,400 KIA (killed in action) compared to 289 American and 49 ARVN dead.[59] The Battle of Dak To was also the last of the border campaigns in the central highlands for the year. The Allied forces had repulsed the NVA invaders, and the strategic central highlands remained under South Vietnamese control.

As the border battles raged in Pleiku and Kontum provinces for control of the central highlands, to the north in I Corps Tactical Zone the Marines held the line against efforts by NVA units to infiltrate across the DMZ into northern South Vietnam.   Along Route 9, a dirt road that ran east-west across the country's northernmost province of Quang Tri, from the sandy coastal plains to the mountainous border with Laos, the Marines had constructed a series of fire support and patrol bases: at Dong Ha, Cam Lo, Khe Sanh, and Lang Vei. The facility at Khe Sanh already served as a Special Forces camp.   Teams of Montagnards, involved in the secret war in Laos that aimed at interdicting enemy supplies coming down the Ho Chi Minh Trail, operated out of Khe Sanh. Route 9 roughly paralleled the DMZ, and most of the Marine firebases lay ten to fifteen miles south of the DMZ. Forward of these fire bases, perched on a hill three miles south of the DMZ near Con Thien (Hill of Angels), the Marines had constructed their most important fire base.[60]

Artillery batteries from the NVA 325th C Division shelled the northern fire bases sporadically. In April 1967 a regiment from the 325th occupied several hills in the vicinity of Khe Sanh in preparation for an attack on the camp. The Marines, in a series of vicious hill fights, drove the PAVN forces from the heights and ended that threat to Khe Sanh.[61] In September, NVA forces besieged Con Thien. PAVN artillery and rocket barrages on Con Thien and a nearby base at Gio Linh were followed by infantry assaults that tried to overrun the Marine perimeters.

U.S. forces eventually broke the sieges of Con Thien and Gio Linh with a combination of massed firepower and aggressive ground tactics. A combination of artillery and naval gunfire, tactical aircraft strikes, and B-52 bombings hit the enemy positions along the DMZ. Marine troopers, using claymore mines, machine guns, and automatic rifles, beat back the PAVN charges, inflicting severe casualties. The hellish Battle of Con Thien ended October 20. American estimates of NVA losses for that battle were 2,000 KIA. Over 200 Marines died in the conflict.[62] At year's end, the Marines still retained all their forward bases. They had withstood sieges, repelled infantry assaults, and blocked all NVA efforts to infiltrate units across the DMZ. Within a few months the Americans would discover that the bloody campaigns initiated by the NVA forces at Con Thien and Dak To in the fall of 1967 were part of a strategic plan designed to lure American forces into remote border regions in northern and central South Vietnam in preparation for the surprise Vietcong/PAVN assaults on the country's cities and towns during the Tet campaign of early 1968.

Westmoreland's attrition strategy during 1967 had accomplished major objectives. American troopers had pushed many of the VC main force units and guerrillas away from populated areas, forcing them to flee to remote regions of the country or else to seek refuge in Cambodian sanctuaries in order to avoid destruction. Vietcong-controlled areas in South Vietnam had been significantly reduced. The Vietcong found that they no longer had any

The Vietnam War

Major battles
U.S. bases
Areas of guerilla activity

Communist countries
Allied with U.S.
Neutral countries

safe havens inside South Vietnam; nowhere were they safe from the reach of American firepower. NVA forces were driven out of the central and northern border provinces of South Vietnam, often with heavy casualties. As 1967 ended, American officials estimated that 180,000 enemy soldiers had been killed since 1965. Assuming a sizeable official inflation of body counts, it is clear that American forces had inflicted severe losses on the enemy. The number of PLAF volunteers declined, forcing the NLF to rely on conscription, which many villagers resented. U.S. combat forces and Westmoreland's aggressive tactics prevented a GVN collapse and a Vietcong victory, both of which probably would have occurred before 1965 ended, if not for the massive American intervention.

But the U.S. attrition strategy also had limits, and it was grounded on some dubious assumptions. Westmoreland assumed that American forces would be able to use their superior firepower and mobility to destroy enemy forces at a greater rate than they could be replaced, at the same time they would keep U.S. casualties low and within politically acceptable limits. But the VC and NVA units retained the tactical initiative in most firefights. They avoided pitched battles when the odds were not in their favor and deftly sidestepped major U.S. sweeps. If the odds favored them, they launched attacks at times and places of their choosing. They determined where and when they wanted to fight and for how long; thus they controlled the tempo of their losses. If their casualties reached unacceptable levels, they broke off battles and melted into the jungle. "The pace of fighting was dictated by the North Vietnamese and by the Vietcong, not by the United States."[63]

They also exploited the restrictions placed on U.S. forces. They knew that American troops could not pursue them and that U.S. aircraft could not strike them whenever they sought the safety of their cross-border sanctuaries in Cambodia and Laos. They also took advantage of the weather, when heavy rains, thunderstorms, and thick fog hampered American air operations. When retreat was impossible, both the Vietcong and PAVN troops found that they could nullify the U.S. firepower advantage by swiftly closing with the American troops and fighting at close quarters.[64]

MACV planners did not anticipate the remarkable ability of the Communists to absorb huge manpower losses and to continue the war. Despite suffering proportionately far greater casualties than the armies of most nations that have lost wars in the twentieth century, the Vietcong/PAVN forces carried on the fight year after year. MACV planners also could not foresee that their pursuit of victory via attrition amounted to an open-ended U.S. military commitment that might eventually require more forces than President Johnson would find politically acceptable to send. Finally, they failed to anticipate that rising U.S. casualties, although proportionally and absolutely far lower than the losses of either the Vietcong or of the PAVN forces, would become a major cause of the Vietnam war's growing unpopularity in the United States.[65]

Although the Americans frequently inflicted serious damage on the enemy forces, they had not defeated the Communists as 1967 ended. Because Westmoreland never had enough U.S. combat-effectives to occupy an area following a large-unit search-and-destroy sweep and the ARVN forces were usually unable to secure or pacify these areas, the Vietcong returned and re-established their bases following Allied withdrawals. In addition, Westmoreland never had enough forces both to fight the enemy main force units and to secure all the rural areas where most of the villagers lived.

A column of U.S. Army riflemen moving across a rice paddy in Quang Ngai Province. Young Vietnamese accompany some of the soldiers and carry their gear.
Source: USMI Photo Archives

Many Vietcong guerrillas retained their capability of operating within the populated regions. The NLF's political infrastructure remained intact. Many of the NLF political cadres retained their ties to the villagers. In South Vietnam, as 1967 ended, thousands of insurgent "fish" continued to swim in the South Vietnamese "sea." The United States had won all the major battles since the Battle of the Ia Drang, but it had not won the war. Back in the summer of 1965, General Westmoreland had estimated that the war could be won by the end of 1967. By the end of 1967, he had nearly 500,000 soldiers fighting what appeared to many as a stalemated war.

Attrition warfare also had adverse consequences that hindered the U.S. effort at nation building. The massive use of firepower disrupted the South Vietnamese economy, inadvertently killed civilians, and generated millions of refugees. The refugees were herded into squalid camps or else fled to the cities where they survived as an uprooted fringe population representing potential Vietcong fifth columns.[66] The U.S. war thus weakened the social fabric of a fragmented nation and further alienated people from a fragile government that had never enjoyed the support of much of the rural population. The U.S. takeover of the war represented an explicit expression of the Americans' lack of confidence in the South Vietnamese military forces and further undermined the resolve of troops all too willing to let the Americans do the fighting.[67]

THUNDER FROM THE AIR

ROLLING THUNDER, the strategic air war waged by the U.S. Air Force, the air attack arm of the U.S. Navy, and the VNAF against North Vietnam, paralleled the ground war raging in South Vietnam. The air war against North Vietnam evolved in phases. "During each phase, a different emphasis was placed upon targets, and the scope and intensity of the attacks varied as well."[68] Washington implemented the first phase during the spring and summer of 1965. Allied planes attacked infiltration routes in North Vietnam just above the DMZ to try to destroy the ability of the North Vietnamese to infiltrate men and supplies into South Vietnam in support of the insurgency.

Within a few months, it was evident to the planners of ROLLING THUNDER that the gradualist bombing campaign of limited scope had failed to reduce appreciably North Vietnam's ability to infiltrate men and supplies into South Vietnam. Hanoi also gave no indication that they were ready to negotiate an end to the war on anything like American terms. Conceding the air war's ineffectiveness, General Earle Wheeler, chairman of the Joint Chiefs, advised Johnson to intensify the aerial campaign, to order more sorties, and to strike at key North Vietnamese military and industrial targets. After a brief debate in July 1965 among senior administration officials in which George Ball, the hawks' nemesis, was the only adviser to oppose escalating the air war, Johnson ordered major increases in the number of air strikes. He also expanded the target list. For the rest of 1965, Johnson and McNamara gradually expanded the air war against North Vietnam, although they refused to order an all-out air assault to destroy the war-making ability of North Vietnam, as called for by the Joint Chiefs and Admiral U.S. Grant Sharp, the commander of ROLLING THUNDER.[69]

As 1965 ended, the air war had failed to accomplish its strategic goals, even though it had expanded into a large-scale operation involving thousands of sorties monthly. The target list had expanded to include military bases, transportation systems, and supply depots as well as intensified bombing of the major infiltration routes out of North Vietnam. Hanoi was infiltrating more men and supplies into the south than ever before, and North Vietnam continued its strong backing of the southern insurgency. Further, American intelligence sources showed that the bombing, far from hurting the morale of the North Vietnamese people, had unified them behind their government.[70]

Johnson's military advisers blamed the continuing failure of the air war on the self-imposed restrictions of civilian leaders. But McNamara remained confident that at some point the gradually escalating bombing campaign would cross a threshold, would reach a point where Hanoi would stop supporting the southern insurgency rather than continue to absorb punishment and to risk losing their painstakingly constructed industrial infrastructure.[71]

After Johnson ordered a bombing pause from December 24, 1965, to February 1, 1966, in a futile effort to get negotiations going, both the air war and the debate over it resumed.[72] Once again the Joint Chiefs pressured McNamara to escalate the bombing, but they changed their plan from an all-out attack to bombing North Vietnam's POL (petroleum products, i.e., gasoline, oil, and lubricants) facilities located near the cities of Hanoi and Haiphong. General Wheeler insisted that the destruction of these facilities would cripple Hanoi's ability to move men and supplies south. Pentagon analysts thoroughly studied the POL proposal for months. Since the sites were located near cities, there was a high risk of civilian casualties. The oil storage areas were also heavily defended by anti-aircraft batteries, by surface-to-air missiles (SAMs), and by North Vietnamese air force fighters. Johnson also worried that such a major escalation of the war might provoke Hanoi to expand the war in South Vietnam or worse, it might bring the Chinese and the Soviets into the conflict. After months of discussion, Johnson finally approved the POL raids, although he retained powerful misgivings about them. On the day that the first attacks were carried out, a distraught president, fearful that they might somehow go wrong, told his daughter, Luci, "Your daddy may go down in history as having started World War III....You may not wake up tomorrow."[73]

On June 29, 1966, Navy fighter-bombers from USS Ranger on YANKEE STATION in the Gulf of Tonkin and Air Force fighter-bombers flying out of bases in Thailand, struck three POL sites located "in the heart of North Vietnam."[74] The attacks were highly successful. They were the first air strikes near Hanoi and Haiphong, and they caught the enemy by surprise. Facilities near the two cities accounting for about 60 percent of North Vietnam's POL storage capacity were destroyed with the loss of only one American plane. The USSR and China both condemned the air strikes and promised increased aid to North Vietnam but made no gestures toward intervention.

Delighted with these results, relieved that U.S. losses were slight and that the Chinese and Soviets reacted moderately, Johnson ordered additional POL strikes. During July and August 1966, Navy and Air Force planes attacked oil storage facilities in the North Vietnamese heartland. By the time the POL campaign ended September 4, 75 percent of Hanoi's oil storage capacity had been destroyed. Soviet-bloc tankers that hauled in Hanoi's POL supplies could no longer offload their cargoes in Haiphong because U.S. bombers had destroyed the port's pumping equipment.[75] But North Vietnamese air defenders made the Americans pay a high price for the July and August POL campaigns. Anti-aircraft batteries and SAMs downed over seventy U.S. aircraft during those two months. Hoa Lo prison in Hanoi, given the ironic nickname of "the Hanoi Hilton" by the Americans flyers, became the residence for years for dozens of American pilots and crewmen shot down over North Vietnam while flying POL missions.

U.S. officials monitoring the POL operations concluded that the attacks constituted a strategic failure. Having anticipated the raids long before President Johnson finally ordered them, the North Vietnamese had decentralized their POL supply systems. Stored in fifty gallon drums in small camouflaged sites near major transportation arteries, dispersed POL supplies proved hard to find and extremely costly to destroy. Although the air strikes knocked out a high percentage of Hanoi's oil storage capacity, they destroyed only a small amount of their POL stores. POL imports via rail from China quickly replaced the losses.

At the conclusion of the U.S. POL campaign, a joint CIA-DIA (Defense Intelligence Agency) report found that Hanoi retained "the capability to continue support of activities in South Vietnam at even increased combat levels."[76] McNamara also commissioned a study of the second phase of ROLLING THUNDER by the Institute for Defense Analysis (IDA), an independent agency from outside the government composed of distinguished American scientists, none of whom was an opponent of the Vietnam war. The IDA report was bluntly critical of strategic bombing. Whatever damage ROLLING THUNDER had done to North Vietnam's facilities and equipment had been more than offset by the increased flow of economic and military aid from the Soviet Union and from China. The scientists not only found the POL campaign to have failed, they doubted that any amount of strategic bombing could either reduce appreciably North Vietnam's infiltration of men and supplies to the southern war theater or induce Hanoi's leaders to call off their strong support of the revolutionary war in South Vietnam:

> It must be concluded, therefore, that there is currently no adequate basis for predicting the levels of U.S. military activity that would be required to achieve the stated objectives—indeed, there is no firm basis for determining if there is *any* [emphasis theirs] feasible level of effort that would achieve these objectives.[77]

The failure of the POL raids disillusioned Robert McNamara, one of the principal architects of the American air war in Vietnam, and ended his advocacy of increased bombing. He began to identify with the small but growing number of Washington officials who were becoming disenchanted with the American war policy in Vietnam. In time these doves came to outnumber the hawks among Johnson's advisers. Following the Tet offensive, Johnson would abandon his failed policy of gradual escalation in pursuit of military victory in Vietnam. Just as the architects of ROLLING THUNDER had predicted, the bombing campaign did eventually find a breaking point, but that breaking point turned out to be Washington's willingness to continue a costly air war for marginal gains, and not Hanoi's willingness to back the southern insurgency.

To substitute for the bombing campaign that they perceived to be a failure, the scientists who drafted the IDA report proposed building an electronic barrier across the DMZ and the segment of the Ho Chi Minh trail complex that wound through the Laotian panhandle as the most effective way of reducing infiltration into South Vietnam.[78] McNamara became a powerful advocate of the electronic barrier, which was later partially built, as an alternative to the bombing of North Vietnam.

McNamara's move toward dovishness set off another debate within Washington over the effectiveness of the bombing campaign against North Vietnam. The Joint Chiefs, wedded to the belief that if enough bombing were done against enough targets soon enough it would be effective, continued to call for escalating the air war against North Vietnam. McNamara assumed the leadership of the advocates of scaling back the bombing campaign. Johnson was caught in the middle of his advisers' intramural dispute. By the spring of 1967, after the failure of another bombing pause to start the negotiations process, Johnson, siding with his military advisers, escalated the air war. ROLLING THUNDER entered the third phase, its most intensive and important phase, which included air strikes against hitherto exempted major industrial targets: electrical production plants and North Vietnam's only steel factory. U.S. aircraft mined North Vietnamese harbors and estuaries and bombed previously off-limits targets near the Chinese border. "ROLLING THUNDER grew fangs."[79]

By the fall of 1967, ROLLING THUNDER had spared few North Vietnamese targets of any economic or military consequence. The air war raged at peak intensity as measured by the scope of permissible targets, numbers of sorties flown, and bomb tonnage dropped. Johnson had granted the Joint Chiefs and Admiral Sharp the air war that they had been demanding for years. The third phase would last until April 1, 1968, when, in the throes of a political crisis created by the Tet campaigns, President Johnson de-escalated the air war.

The Tet offensive mounted by the Vietcong and PAVN forces proved dramatically that the bombing campaign "to interdict the flow of men and supplies to the South had been a signal failure."[80] Most of the resources necessary for the enemy to mount and to sustain a large-scale campaign had flowed down the Ho Chi Minh trail despite the intensive bombing of North Vietnam. Tet also converted Johnson to the cause of de-escalating the bombing. But most military advisers retained their faith in the efficacy of strategic bombing even after Tet had demonstrated its manifest failure.

Why did ROLLING THUNDER fail? The Joint Chiefs and Admiral Sharp insisted that political restrictions imposed by civilians caused it to be ineffective.[81] But during the third phase of the air war, virtually every target in North Vietnam that the Joint Chiefs claimed to be of strategic significance was either destroyed or damaged before Tet occurred. ROLLING THUNDER, even when waged at its maximum intensity for months, neither stopped the flow of goods to South Vietnam nor broke Hanoi's will.

Johnson's military advisers have also insisted that had the bombing campaign been intense from the outset, North Vietnam would not have had time to develop its air defenses, to disperse its industries and POL stores, or to prepare its people to withstand the air war. Hanoi would have been forced to abandon its support of the southern revolution or else risk national extinction. Such conjectures are dubious. When ROLLING THUNDER began, Hanoi's leaders expected that U.S. aircraft would soon attack industrial targets and bomb population centers. They quickly mobilized all their resources to defend against an unrestricted air war. They also prepared for an American invasion of North Vietnam and for a protracted war. They prepared for far worse than they ever got or that the Joint Chiefs ever proposed delivering, and never did they indicate that they were prepared to end their support of the southern rebels. Further, an all-out air assault on North Vietnam could have provoked Chinese intervention, a peril that no responsible policy maker in Washington dared ignore: "There is no basis to saying with any certainty that air power unfettered by political considerations would have 'won' the air war in Vietnam. Various outcomes of a more rapid escalation [were] possible, not all of them favorable to victory."[82]

Between 1965 and 1968, ROLLING THUNDER inflicted about $600 million worth of damage on North Vietnam. It crippled the country's nascent industrial sector and disrupted its agriculture. Several cities were leveled, and others sustained severe damage. The government diverted thousands of people from agricultural work to air defense activities and to the repairing of roads and bridges. Food supplies diminished, and only extensive aid from the USSR and China enabled millions of North Vietnamese to maintain even a subsistence level diet. The quality of education and health care available in North Vietnam declined. Although Washington never adopted a policy of directly targeting civilians, the bombing campaign nevertheless claimed thousands of North Vietnamese civilian lives.[83]

ROLLING THUNDER eventually proved to be exceedingly costly. Before Johnson ordered the bombing of North Vietnam halted October 31, 1968, America lost 950 planes costing about $6 billion. A Pentagon study found that every dollar's worth of damage inflicted on North Vietnam cost the American taxpayers $10.00. Whatever can be claimed for the air war against the North, it was not cost effective.[84] There were other costs: Captured U.S. pilots and air crewmen provided Hanoi's leaders with a bargaining chip that they later used in negotiating with American officials. ROLLING THUNDER also gave the Communists a propaganda advantage that they exploited to influence world and American public opinion. Robert McNamara wrote in a memo to President Johnson: "The picture of the world's greatest superpower killing or seriously injuring 1,000 noncombatants a week, while trying to pound a tiny, backward nation into submission,...is not a pretty one."[85]

Domestic opponents of the war seized on ROLLING THUNDER, denouncing it as expensive, futile, and wrong. Both the civilian and military advocates of ROLLING THUNDER had assumed that the destruction or the threat of destruction of North Vietnam's industrial sector would cripple Hanoi's ability to supply the insurgents fighting in South Vietnam and persuade it to negotiate an agreement permitting South Vietnam to survive. That assumption proved to be one of the many grave errors in judgment made by those who led the nation to war.

While ROLLING THUNDER unfolded against the North Vietnam, America waged a large-scale air war in South Vietnam against the Vietcong. Air operations in South Vietnam were an integral part of the U.S. attrition strategy. Although the American media gave the ground war in South Vietnam far more coverage, to the war leaders in Washington the air war was at least as important. The southern air war reflected the same logic that underlay the aerial campaign against North Vietnam: that America would use air power extensively to force Hanoi to stop its aggression in South Vietnam. The air war in South Vietnam also suffered from the same misjudgments: underestimating the enemy's determination and his ability to counter U.S. air power.[86] The air war in South Vietnam was also much larger, lasted far longer, and was much more diversified than the bombing campaign against North Vietnam.

Strikes against guerrilla bases and supply routes constituted two-thirds of the U.S. air operations undertaken in southern Vietnam. These pre-planned attacks, based on aerial reconnaissance and intelligence reports, attempted to deny the Vietcong "safe havens where they could train and rest troops, store ammunition and food, and plan offensive operations."[87]   Giant B-52 Stratofortresses from the Strategic Air Command (SAC) often participated in these air strikes undertaken against guerrilla strongholds and supply lines. Code-named ARC LIGHT, the flights of B-52s, initially flying from Andersen Air Force Base on the U.S. island territory of Guam 2,800 miles away, approached their targets at altitudes from 30,000 to 36,000 feet. They were both invisible and inaudible; they combined the element of surprise with devastating power. A flight of six B-52s, each plane capable of carrying from eighteen to twenty-seven tons of bombs, using a carpet bombing technique in which all the bombs were released according to a predetermined pattern, could saturate a target area in a matter of seconds. "Carpet bombing could change the face of the earth."[88] ARC LIGHT strikes often caused enormous destruction and heavy casualties. B-52s constituted the most frightening weapon in the U.S. arsenal deployed in the Vietnam war. After surviving a B-52 assault, a terrified Vietcong guerrilla called carpet bombing "the chain of thunders."[89]

If U.S. air strikes were scheduled for populated areas or for sites near populated areas, clearance had to be granted by South Vietnamese officials, either by the province chief or by the military commander responsible for the area. Friendly populations were supposed to have advance warning that the area in which they resided had been designated a target area. Although American officials denied it, air attacks in or near populated areas claimed civilian casualties, as proven by examinations of hospital admissions records. Advance

Giant B-52 strategic bombers were the most feared weapon in the American arsenal. Here, a cell of Stratofortresses release their bombs over a suspected Vietcong stronghold.
Source: U.S. Air Force Photo.

warning was not always provided and not always understood when furnished.[90] Subject to approval by South Vietnamese officials, areas known to be controlled by the Vietcong and not inhabited by friendly villagers were designated "free fire zones." These areas could be bombed without clearance from local officials or without warning to any inhabitants who might be in the area.[91]

After the pre-planned strikes against guerrilla sanctuaries and supply lines, the most frequent kind of missions flown in South Vietnam were close air support operations carried out by Air Force, Marine, and Army pilots who usually flew from air fields located in South Vietnam. These strikes provided crucial added fire power for ground combat forces locked in battle with Vietcong units.[92] These missions also helped keep down U.S. casualties. These close-in attacks were called in by ground commanders or by forward air controllers (FACs) flying over the combat area. The FACs would mark the location of enemy forces with smoke flares to guide the pilots as they roared in to fire rockets, 20 mm. cannons, air-to-ground missiles, or to drop iron bombs, phosphorous bombs, or napalm canisters on their targets. B-52s also flew support missions in South Vietnam, often with devastating results.

Along with its pre-planned strikes and close support missions, the Air Force also conducted an extensive campaign of aerial defoliation, code-named Operation RANCH HAND, in South Vietnam to deprive the guerrillas of their forest cover and to destroy Vietcong food crops. Defoliation was

An Air Force C-123 on a defoliation mission over jungle terrain in South Vietnam during Operation RANCH HAND.
Source: U.S. Air Force Photo

a civilian counterinsurgency program initiated by President Kennedy on a small scale in 1962 over the objections of his senior military advisers who feared that the United States might be accused of resorting to chemical or biological warfare.[93] As the war escalated, Operation RANCH HAND expanded rapidly. Air Force C-123s, specially fitted with 1,000-gallon tanks and with bars of spray nozzles attached to the underside of their wings, flew hundreds of sorties during the years 1965 to 1967. Over the door of the RANCH HAND briefing room at Tan Son Nhut air base, hung a plaque with the sardonic inscription, "Only You Can Prevent Forests."[94]

Crews aboard the RANCH HAND C-123s used a variety of color-coded herbicides on their missions. The most effective herbicide proved to be Agent Orange. It contained an extremely toxic chemical agent, 2,4,5-T (Dioxin). One C-123 could haul 11,000 pounds of Agent Orange that it dispensed over a 300-acre target area in about four minutes. Within a few weeks, all the plants, shrubs, and trees in the sprayed area had withered, turned brown, and died. Lush, green forests turned quickly into barren, brown moonscapes following a RANCH HAND spraying. During 1967, the peak year of Operation RANCH HAND, Air Force crews sprayed about 1.5 million acres, 40 percent of which were croplands. Before the defoliation campaign ended, more than 100 million pounds of chemicals were sprayed over millions of acres of South Vietnamese forests and crops. Operation RANCH HAND destroyed an estimated one-half of South Vietnam's timberlands and left behind unknown human costs.[95]

Operation RANCH HAND in time became controversial. On June 26, 1969, a report appeared in a South Vietnamese newspaper alleging that a toxic ingredient found in Agent Orange caused birth defects in children born to women who had been exposed to the herbicide. Later that year a study by the National Institute of Health presented evidence that Dioxin caused malformed babies. A study done under the auspices of the American Association for the Advancement of Science to investigate the effects of spraying in Vietnam found that some of the forested areas that had been sprayed with Agent Orange had not regenerated. On April 15, 1970, the Defense Department suspended the use of Agent Orange. The last RANCH HAND mission, using other herbicides, flew from Tan Son Nhut air field on January 7, 1971.[96]

Years after the Vietnam War had ended, scientific researchers were still trying to determine the specific effects exposure to Dioxin could have on people. Veterans, exposed to Agent Orange during the war, have reported recurring health problems, including skin rashes, breathing dysfunctions, various kinds of cancers, and birth defects in their children, which they believe have come from their exposure to Dioxin. A class action suit against the Veterans' Administration brought by veterans who were exposed to Agent Orange while serving in Vietnam was settled out of court in 1985.[97]

Another facet of the U.S. air war in Indochina entailed air operations within neutral Laos. At the beginning of 1965, the southern panhandle of Laos, which shared a 450-mile-long border with Vietnam, had been turned into a supply corridor supporting Vietcong military operations in South Vietnam. The heart of that supply corridor was the Ho Chi Minh trail.[98] A few months before ROLLING THUNDER began against North Vietnam, President Johnson ordered American aircraft to interdict traffic coming south along the Ho Chi Minh trail running through the Laotian corridor. The bombing campaign in Laos gradually expanded until it reached a volume of 3,000 sorties per month during the fall of 1967.

The air war waged in Laos from 1965 through 1967, like its counterpart waged against North Vietnam, also failed strategically. Bad flying weather and rugged jungle-covered mountainous terrain continually hampered U.S. air operations. Because the Ho Chi Minh trail through Laos consisted of a vast web of small roads and trails, most of which were invisible from the air, U.S. pilots could only interdict a portion of the weapons, military supplies, and soldiers coming into South Vietnam. Enemy countermeasures and self-imposed restrictions on the bombings further reduced the effectiveness of the air war in Laos. At the height of the U.S. campaign against the Ho Chi Minh trail along the Laotian corridor, enemy forces were infiltrating more supplies into South Vietnam than ever before.[99]

THE OTHER WAR

While drastically escalating the Vietnam War and transforming America's failed advisory role into a full-scale military effort to suppress the Vietcong

President Johnson confers with the leaders of the Republic of South Vietnam at Honolulu, February 6, 1966. The man in the middle is Prime Minister Nguyen Cao Ky. Next to him is President Nguyen Van Thieu.
Source: National Archives

insurgents and to discourage their North Vietnamese backers, American officials supported the Ky regime's efforts to build a new nation in southern Vietnam. Ky's performance as prime minister pleasantly surprised Washington. He managed to survive in office and the chronic instability that had plagued South Vietnamese politics since the anti-Diemist coup of November 1963 ebbed. In fact, the June 1965 coup that brought Ky to power would prove to be South Vietnam's last. In February 1966, to evade growing opposition to the Vietnam war among liberal senators led by William Fulbright, who was holding hearings before his Senate Foreign Relations committee on all aspects of administration war policy, Johnson traveled to Honolulu with his senior advisers in order to meet with Ky and other high South Vietnamese officials.

On February 6, in Honolulu, Johnson publicly embraced Ky and urged him to emphasize the other war in Vietnam, which was to build a South Vietnamese nation, to develop the South Vietnamese economy, to improve the lives of the Vietnamese, and to win their allegiance.[100] Ky, who had been briefed by U.S. officials before coming to Hawaii, made a speech replete with ambitious plans for implementing a social revolution throughout South

Vietnam that would revitalize its economy and would ensure a prosperous and free South Vietnamese nation for the future. Johnson, delighted by Ky's speech, put his arm around the South Vietnamese leader and told him, "Boy, you speak just like an American!"[101] At the conclusion of the conference, through a joint communique, Johnson and Ky pledged to work for the welfare of the ordinary people and to bring about the end of poverty, disease, and ignorance in South Vietnam. The communique read like a South Vietnamese version of the Great Society. It gave pacification a high priority and a momentum that lasted for the duration of the American war in Vietnam.[102]

Ky, emboldened by Johnson's public show of support at Honolulu, returned to Vietnam determined to strengthen his grip on the South Vietnamese government. Backed by U.S. officials, Ky persuaded the Military Directorate to dismiss a powerful rival, one of the triumvirs, General Nguyen Chanh Thi, the I Corps commander. The I Corps area included Danang and Hue, South Vietnam's second and third largest cities. Ky's firing of Thi provoked a major political crisis in South Vietnam, resulting in a brief civil war that occurred inside the war already raging in South Vietnam.

The Buddhists, quiescent for nearly a year, under the leadership of Trich Tri Quang, suddenly erupted. They took to the streets of Hue to protest Thi's dismissal. Their revolt quickly spread to Danang, Saigon, and other South Vietnamese cities. The Buddhists also revived their demands for free elections and for a restoration of civilian rule. Other disaffected groups joined their movement, including students, trade unionists, some religious sectarians, and even some dissident army and police elements. Several Buddhist monks and a nun committed self-immolation by fire in support of the movement. Although they were careful not to make their ultimate political goals explicit, the Buddhists hoped that the elections would bring a coalition government to power in South Vietnam that would end the war, negotiate a settlement with the NLF, and expel the Americans. Above all, the Buddhists wanted the political destiny of South Vietnam to be determined by Vietnamese.[103]

Henry Cabot Lodge, having replaced Maxwell Taylor and back in South Vietnam for another stint as the U.S. ambassador, fearful that free elections could bring a neutralist government to power that would proceed to negotiate an end to the war and throw the Americans out, endorsed Ky's efforts to suppress the Buddhists and their supporters. So did General Westmoreland and President Johnson, both of whom were alarmed by the outbreak of civil unrest in the midst of an expanding war.

When the Buddhists had risen against the Diem regime three years earlier, the American officials had supported them, mainly because the Kennedy administration perceived Diem and his brother Nhu to be uncooperative. The Ngo brothers had rejected American advice and had been unwilling either to reform their government or to prosecute vigorously the war against the PLAF. But in the spring of 1966, with the U.S. stake in the Vietnam war far greater than it had been in the Diem era, Ky cooperated with

American officials, sought and followed their advice, and strongly supported the expanded U.S. war effort against the NLF and the North Vietnamese.

Assisted by General Westmoreland, Ky moved against the Buddhists. On the morning of April 5, U.S. C-130 transports flew 2,000 ARVN troops into the Danang air field. Ky, personally leading two battalions of ARVN Marines, announced that he had come to "liberate Danang." Ky's show of force, designed to overawe his opponents, only provoked them. The local ARVN commander, General Nguyen Van Chuan, who sided with the rebels, used his troops to confine Ky's forces to the Danang air base. He also warned Ky that if he tried to move his troops out of the air base there would be fighting. Ky, embarrassed, was forced to back down. He announced that he would withdraw his troops from Danang and seek a rapprochement with the Buddhists. After meeting with Buddhist leaders, General Thieu, Ky's chief of state, announced that elections for a constituent assembly would be held within a few months and civilian government would soon be restored. Reacting to these concessions from the military government, Tri Quang and the other Buddhist leaders called off their protests.[104]

By canceling their protests, the Buddhists played into the hands of the wily Ky and Thieu who never intended to keep their promises. Confident of U.S. support, they were stalling for time until they could mount a larger effort against the rebels. On May 15, 1966, Ky launched another assault on Danang. With U.S. aircraft again providing logistic support, Ky sent in larger forces armed with tanks, artillery, and other heavy weapons. There followed two days of bitter and intense fighting in the streets of Danang during which hundreds of soldiers and protesters were killed. Ky's heavily armed forces crushed the revolt.[105] His forces also suppressed the dissident movement in Saigon, but Hue, the center of the Buddhist resistance, remained in dissident hands.

Supporters of the Buddhist movement in Hue, angered by the U.S. backing of Ky as well as by his betrayal, burned the U.S. consulate and the USIS (United States Information Service) library there. They also unfurled banners demanding the ouster from Vietnam of all foreign influences. Soon thereafter, Ky's forces assaulted the dissident positions in the former imperial capital. By June 19, Hue was once again under government control. Tri Quang was arrested along with hundreds of bonzes, students, and other protesters. The Buddhist political movement was crushed. Ky and Thieu, rescinding their promises to hold elections within a few months, announced that the military junta would remain in power until elections took place sometime in 1967.

While the civil war between Ky's forces and the Buddhists was taking place, most South Vietnamese military operations against the Vietcong ground to a halt. American soldiers were both baffled and angered by the internecine struggle occurring at a time when the U.S. military effort in Vietnam was rapidly expanding, American troops were doing most of the fighting, and American casualties were growing. One U.S. soldier angrily asked: "What are we doing here? We're fighting to save these people, and they're fighting each other!"[106]

The suppression of the Buddhist uprising during the spring of 1966 signaled the end of the Buddhists as a major factor in the South Vietnamese political calculus. Their movement lost its political coherence. The ARVN generals had defeated their last major political rivals; the possibility of a civilian alternative to military rule in South Vietnam no longer existed. After nearly three years of political conflict that had begun with the coup that brought down the Diem regime, during which none of a succession of governments could provide even the rudiments of political leadership, a measure of stability was returning to South Vietnam's civic life. Following the suppression of the Buddhists, the Vietnamese people living under the control of the GVN perceived that the rule of the generals could not be challenged as long as the Americans maintained such a powerful presence in their country and stood solidly behind the military rulers. "The middle ground that the Buddhists had been building up between the Saigon military and the NLF was cut away and prospects destroyed for anything resembling a viable 'third force.'"[107] Politics in South Vietnam had been polarized. The people's practical choices were reduced to either rule by the ARVN generals or by the NLF-Hanoi forces.

U.S. officials, in addition to committing more troops to the expanding war against the PLAF and NVA forces, had to inject American power into the areas of South Vietnam under the GVN's administrative control. Given the absence of indigenous support for the GVN, it was necessary for American forces to provide guarantees that the governmental apparatus would remain in the hands of Vietnamese willing to support American policies and goals. U.S. officials often staffed GVN agencies and programs at the provincial and district levels. The GVN took on more of the attributes of a neo-colonial American dependency.

Following the suppression of the Buddhists, both American and Vietnamese officials tried to implement effective pacification programs among the rural populations of South Vietnam. At the Honolulu conference in early February 1966, President Johnson had made pacification a top priority. Johnson personally identified with the people of South Vietnam and what he assumed to be their desires to live in a free, peaceful, and prosperous society. He also believed that military action alone could never defeat the Vietcong. The Saigon government would have to win the allegiance of the villagers, and Johnson thought that the best way to win them over was to help improve their lives.

Responding to the American pressure, with funding and expert advice provided by American officials, the Ky government implemented a Revolutionary Development program (RD). Consciously imitative of the NLF cadres, fifty-nine-person revolutionary development teams were sent into South Vietnamese villages. Team personnel were trained to provide physical security for the villagers, to assist in government reorganization and political development, to establish schools and literacy programs, and to assist in social and economic development.[108] They lived among the people and "carried out hundreds of tasks to build popular support for the government and to undermine the Vietcong."[109]

As was the fate of earlier pacification efforts, Revolutionary Development failed. The inept and corrupt GVN never developed an adequate program. Cadres were hastily trained, and there were never enough teams available to service all of South Vietnam's hamlets and villages. District officials sometimes undercut the revolutionary developmental teams' efforts; sometimes ARVN troops extorted money from the villagers and stole their pigs and chickens. Wary villagers, knowing from experience that GVN promises often exceeded its ability to implement them, were slow to cooperate with the RD teams. The absence of physical security posed more serious problems for the South Vietnamese pacification programs. Since U.S. troops were preoccupied with the war against the Vietcong main force units, providing village security devolved upon the ARVN forces. But they were incapable of supplying adequate security in many areas. In some locales, ARVN troops were the security problem. In insecure areas, the Vietcong often terrorized the revolutionary development teams. VC terrorists kidnapped and murdered thousands of RD cadres in 1966 and 1967.[110]

The failure of Revolutionary Development also raised three fundamental questions about the GVN's approach to pacification: (1) Pacification could not succeed as long as corrupt officials and rogue ARVN units continued to prey upon the villagers. There was no evidence that Ky's regime seriously intended to reform itself and to eliminate these abuses. (2) Given the peasant preoccupation with land owning, land reform would have to form the heart of any long-range pacification program that hoped to win the allegiance of the peasantry. Ky's lack of commitment to land reform and his responsiveness to the interests of large local landowners ensured the continuing failure of Revolutionary Development. (3) To overcome the fragmentation of South Vietnamese society and the alienation of the rural masses from the ruling urban elites, villagers would need to have been given a sense of participation, an active involvement in the government for pacification to work. The peasants would have had to see people from their villages rising to positions of authority within the government system to identify with the GVN, to connect its operations to their interests and welfare. Ky's government never tried to breach the profound divisions existing within the South Vietnamese social structure by recruiting district or provincial officials from the villages.

Johnson, in March 1967, to promote pacification, folded it into Westmoreland's command. All civilian and military personnel involved with aspects of pacification were put into a hybrid agency called Civil Operations and Revolutionary Development Support (CORDS). The MACV deputy placed in charge of CORDS was Robert Komer, an energetic civilian bureaucrat. CORDS in time generated successful pacification programs in many regions of the South.[111]

While it pursued the will-o'-the-wisp of pacification following the suppression of the Buddhists, the South Vietnamese military regime also implemented democratic political reforms, but in carefully limited fashion to ensure that the generals retained control of the government. Pressure for drafting a constitution and holding elections came mainly from the Johnson administration. Washington wanted to legitimate the South Vietnamese government in American eyes and thereby gain increased domestic support for the expanding war. In early 1967, South Vietnamese voters elected a constituent assembly. The newly elected assembly, assisted by U.S. constitutional scholars, proceeded to draft a new constitution modeled on the U.S. Constitution. It created a bicameral legislature, but it granted the executive branch most of the powers of government and permitted the president to assume dictatorial powers in the event of an emergency that could be declared at his discretion. Further, the president needed only to obtain a plurality of the votes to be elected. This provision prevented opposition candidates from joining together in a runoff to defeat the government's candidates.[112]

Elections under the new constitution were held in September 1967. The most serious political conflict that occurred during the campaign pitted the supporters of Ky against the supporters of Thieu to see which man would head the government ticket. Ky eventually gave way, and Thieu ran for president with Ky as his vice presidential running mate. They were challenged by ten civilian candidates. Since Communists and neutralists were barred from seeking office, Buddhists were boycotting the election, and the opposition consisted of obscure men with small local followings, Thieu and Ky were running under conditions that made their defeat extremely unlikely. Even so, the Thieu-Ky ticket received only 35 percent of the vote. They were also embarrassed by the electoral performance of an political unknown, Truong Dinh Dzu, an obscure civilian candidate running on a platform calling for negotiations with the National Liberation Front, who came in second with 17 percent of the votes.[113]

Within a political culture where the right to govern traditionally derived from the mandate of heaven and where people felt a moral obligation to obey their rulers, their slender electoral victory did not give the Thieu-Ky regime greater legitimacy, a broader political base, or increased political power. Two-thirds of South Vietnam's carefully circumscribed electorate preferred alternatives to Thieu and Ky. If all the South Vietnamese people had been permitted to vote in a genuinely free election, they might have registered a preference for a government that would have sought to negotiate an end to the war. Thieu and Ky survived in power not because their government was popular or intrinsically powerful but because it had the backing of the Americans.

Some American officials convinced themselves that the election showed that democratic government had come to South Vietnam and that the Thieu-Ky regime had achieved a popular base of support. Most South

Vietnamese voters held a different view. They understood that they had participated in a carefully arranged, essentially meaningless political ritual mainly to please their American patrons. "Many Vietnamese regarded the entire process as 'an American-directed performance with a Vietnamese cast.'"[114] But the Thieu-Ky victory, however dubious it might be within a Vietnamese political context, meant that the military junta would remain in power, Americans would remain in South Vietnam, and the war would go on.

During the period from mid-1965 to the end of 1967, while the Americans escalated both the air war in North Vietnam and the ground war in South Vietnam, albeit only achieving a stalemate with their enemies, the South Vietnamese government failed to eliminate its underlying political weaknesses. Pacification floundered, and the Thieu-Ky regime remained a narrowly based military directorate dependent on continuing American support in order to survive. In the long run, the large-scale U.S. military effort could not compensate for the continuing failure of the South Vietnamese to erect a viable nation. The American war proved either irrelevant to nation building or else exacerbated its problems. The continuing political failures of the Saigon regime were a major cause of the eventual U.S. failure in Vietnam; they proved to be the Achilles' heel of the U.S. war effort.

The impact of the U.S. war with its half million troops, thousands of civilians, and billions of dollars strained and disrupted the South Vietnamese economy.[115] Saigon became a boom town whose prosperity was based on war. The former "Paris of the Orient" became a crowded, noisy metropolis, its streets clogged with traffic and its restaurants, bars, nightclubs, and hotels teeming with American soldiers, civilian advisers, and journalists. Many Saigonese found work providing services to the Americans and to their fellow Vietnamese who profited from the war economy. Crime and corruption flourished on a grand scale. The black market became a big business trafficking in stolen American consumer goods, weapons, and illegal currency exchanges.[116]

As the American presence in South Vietnam expanded, tensions between the Americans and Vietnamese increased. Because of their profound cultural differences, the Americans and Vietnamese had to struggle to understand each other across a vast chasm of mutual ignorance and misperceptions. The exigencies of fighting a war and building a nation exacerbated the already tense relations between the two allies. Because the Vietcong had infiltrated every echelon of both the government's civilian agencies and its armed forces, security leaks posed chronic problems. U.S. commanders were forced to keep all Vietnamese off their major bases and to withhold details of major military operations from their ARVN counterparts.

"The paradox arose of the Americans fighting on behalf of an army (and a government) that they treated with disdain, even contempt." Many U.S. troops were fighting to save people that they did not regard as worth saving from Communism. American soldiers often spoke openly and contemptuously of their South Vietnamese allies. They wondered why the enemy's soldiers always seemed braver and fought harder than the ARVN forces. A stark contradiction evolved between the official political objectives for which Americans were fighting in Southeast Asia—the freedom and independence of the South Vietnamese people—and the reality of a war in which Americans often bypassed both the GVN and its military forces as they designed and carried out U.S. campaigns aimed at defeating the Vietcong and the NVA.[117]

The apparent indifference of many Vietnamese to the welfare of U.S. soldiers who were dying in battle trying to protect them infuriated American troopers. The uncanny ability of the villagers to avoid mines and booby traps that killed and maimed U.S. soldiers led many troopers to assume that these people cooperated with the enemy or that they were the enemy. American soldiers, on entering a village after taking fire from it or its vicinity, unable to tell which of its inhabitants were "friendlies" and which of them were Vietcong sympathizers, tended to assume that all the villagers were either real or potential enemies. Such attitudes, when held by frightened and angry young soldiers armed with automatic rifles, machine guns, and grenade launchers, could have tragic consequences.[118]

DIPLOMATIC CHARADES

As the Vietnam war expanded, pressures for a negotiated settlement of the conflict also escalated. From mid-1965 until the end of 1967, White House officials estimated that as many as 2,000 individual efforts were made to get peace talks started between Washington and Hanoi. President Johnson claimed in his memoirs that he personally followed seventy-two negotiation initiatives.[119] Neither side dared ignore the many diplomatic efforts initiated by third parties concerned to bring American and North Vietnamese negotiators together to halt the war, but they consistently refused to make the concessions necessary to initiate serious peace talks. The more both sides invested in the conflict, the less willing they were to consider negotiating. The escalating military stalemate bred a diplomatic impasse.

Hanoi repeatedly denounced U.S. involvement in Vietnam as a violation of the 1954 Geneva Accords. North Vietnamese leaders insisted that the United States would have to cease all acts of war against Vietnam, dismantle its bases, and remove all its military forces before any talks could begin. They further insisted that the political destiny of South Vietnam would be determined in accordance with the program of the National Liberation Front. The Saigon regime would be replaced by a coalition government dominated by the NLF. Hanoi's leaders clearly

indicated that they considered the question of Vietnam's unity to be fundamental and nonnegotiable: "The unity of our country is no more a matter for
negotiations than our independence."[120]

According to the view from Hanoi, there was no role for the United
States to play in determining the political destiny of South Vietnam. America
would have to withdraw all its troops from that country, after which the GVN
would doubtless collapse or be overthrown, and Hanoi would proceed to
unify Vietnam under its control. Ho Chi Minh believed that great power
diplomatic interests and the U.S. intervention in Vietnam after Geneva had
deprived the Vietminh of the political dividends that should have accrued
from their military victory over the French, which was control of an independent and unified Vietnam.

The Communists were determined never to entrust their political future
to others again. This time they and they alone would determine the political
outcome of the latest Vietnam war, that is, the current phase of a war that
had been going intermittently since 1946. Hence, they made American
withdrawal from Vietnam a precondition for negotiations and declared the
unity of Vietnam to be a non-negotiable item. Given the battlefield realities
existing during the 1965-to-1967 period, Hanoi's hardline diplomatic stance
did not represent the negotiating position of a nation seriously concerned
with a diplomatic resolution of the Vietnam war; they reflected the diplomatic posture of leaders who were determined to win the war and confident
that in time they would.

Washington promulgated its negotiating position at the beginning of
1966. Johnson, planning to escalate the air war against North Vietnam, halted
the bombing during the Christmas holiday. He combined the bombing halt
with a diplomatic offensive, sending administration officials around the
world and across America to explain that the United States was ready to
negotiate with Hanoi without insisting that they meet any preconditions. But
the United States offered to halt the bombing of North Vietnam only after
Hanoi had stopped infiltrating men and supplies into South Vietnam. America would withdraw all its troops from South Vietnam only after an "acceptable political settlement" had been reached. While agreeing that the political
destiny of South Vietnam would have to be worked out by the South
Vietnamese themselves, Washington refused to allow the NLF to join any
South Vietnamese government. They would allow for their views to be
represented, but only after Hanoi stopped all "acts of aggression." "Beneath
these ambiguous words rested a firm determination to maintain an independent, non-Communist South Vietnam."[121] Johnson's insistence that he favored unconditional negotiations masked a U.S. diplomatic stance that was
no more acceptable to Hanoi than its stands were to Johnson. McNamara
also acknowledged that part of Johnson's motivation for halting the bombing
was to prepare American and world public opinion for more escalations.[122]
Johnson did not expect Hanoi to accept his overtures.

Hanoi promptly denounced the U.S. bombing pause as a sham and rejected Johnson's terms for negotiations. The North Vietnamese, regarding Vietnam as one country and dismissing as a species of political fiction the American claim that a sovereign nation with a legitimate government existed in the southern half of Vietnam, sharply differentiated between what they regarded as illegitimate American interventions into the affairs of their country and their own legitimate involvement in Vietnam's internal affairs. Hanoi refused to consider performing any reciprocal acts to get the Americans to halt the bombing and insisted that only their negotiating positions offered bases for a correct political settlement of the war.[123] Johnson, anticipating the rebuff, resumed the air war against North Vietnam on January 31, 1966.

In 1966 and 1967, even though both sides remained far apart and neither country appeared willing to make the kinds of concessions that might have brought them closer to negotiations, various third parties tried to bring Hanoi and Washington to the bargaining table. One of these initiatives involved a Polish diplomat, Januscz Lewandowski. He persuaded U.S. officials to offer North Vietnam a proposal that he claimed would circumvent Hanoi's refusal to consider reciprocal actions in return for a bombing halt: In exchange for the United States halting the bombing, Hanoi would have only to give private assurances that they would stop their infiltration into South Vietnam within a reasonable time. When American officials could verify that the infiltration had in fact stopped, Washington would freeze its combat forces at current levels, and negotiations between the two sides could begin.[124]

Lewandowski's initiative, code-named MARIGOLD, never had a chance. A few days before the Polish envoy was scheduled to meet for talks with Communist leaders in Hanoi, Johnson ordered U.S. aircraft to bomb rail yards near the center of the capital. Some of the planes inadvertently bombed nearby residential neighborhoods and caused civilian casualties. Hanoi, assuming that Johnson was combining a new negotiating proposal with an expanded bombing effort, refused to meet with Lewandowski. It is unlikely that Hanoi was prepared to accept the Polish diplomat's formula had the air attacks not occurred; however, the bombing killed whatever prospects MARIGOLD may have had because the North Vietnamese refused to be pressured into negotiations, or to give the appearance of being pressured into negotiations. Lewandowski had to abandon his efforts, and "the Polish initiative ended in fiasco."[125] In 1967, a peace initiative developed by British Prime Minister Harold Wilson that attempted to employ the good offices of Soviet President Alexei Kosygin met a similar fate.

During the period when both sides were expanding their war effort, all third party initiatives, however well intentioned or balanced, were predestined for failure. Getting negotiations started between Washington and Hanoi depended mainly on the willingness of the belligerents to compromise. Neither was prepared to do so because each side remained confident that it was going to win the war and that it would then be in a position to force the other side to make concessions that would be tantamount to accepting political defeat. Leaders in Washington and Hanoi both strove to appear responsive to all serious peace proposals. They also tried to exploit those proposals for propaganda purposes to make it appear that their adversary was the one pressing the war, was not interested in genuine negotiations, and was the aggressor.

In 1967, as both international and domestic pressures for a negotiated settlement intensified, each side became slightly more flexible. Hanoi suggested that reunification might occur over a long period. Johnson, in a speech in San Antonio, Texas, on September 29, indicated that he would stop the bombing if it would lead to productive peace talks. But both sides remained far apart.[126] Johnson remained committed to maintaining a pro-Western government in power in South Vietnam. Hanoi remained committed to unifying all of Vietnam under its control. Negotiations could not bridge that gulf.

Both countries continued to try to win the war to control the political destiny of South Vietnam. There is no reason to assume that any of the peace initiatives could have succeeded no matter how adroitly they were handled, given the unwillingness of the belligerents to make concessions. Because both sides indulged in diplomatic charades, "the search for negotiations with Hanoi between 1965 and 1968 is one of the most fruitless chapters in U.S. diplomacy."[127] Johnson's judgment was essentially sound when he concluded that Hanoi was not willing to negotiate an end to the war on terms that he could accept, and therefore the many diplomatic initiatives undertaken in 1966 and 1967 were destined for failure. But the president failed to understand that the American goal of an independent South Vietnam under the control of the GVN could never be achieved either by fighting a limited war or by negotiations.[128] Johnson could fight, he could fight and negotiate, or he could negotiate. Ultimately, it did not matter.

THE WAR AT HOME

By the spring of 1967, any illusions Americans had about achieving a quick and easy victory in Vietnam had long vanished. America found itself mired in an escalating military stalemate in Indochina. Nor could the United States get an acceptable political solution to the conflict given the battlefield realities, the grave political weaknesses of the GVN, and the negotiating stance taken by Hanoi. U.S. casualties announced on March 10, 1967—232 killed in action and another 1,381 wounded, over 1,600 casualties in all—were the highest yet for any week of the war. A few days later, Congress passed a $20 billion supplemental appropriations bill to pay for the rising costs of the war.[129]

As the costs and casualties of the war soared far above anticipated levels, Johnson found himself caught in the midst of a rising debate within his administration between hawkish military advisers who wanted to expand the war and dovish civilian advisers led by McNamara, who sought to stabilize American ground force levels, curtail the bombing of North Vietnam, and seek a negotiated settlement. A rising public debate over the increasingly controversial war paralleled the inner debate among Johnson's senior advisers.

Hawks, a mix of conservative Republicans, southern Democrats, and Cold War liberals, devout believers in the containment ideology, viewed the conflict in Vietnam as a crucial component of the global struggle with Communism for control of the planet's political future. They felt strongly that America must hold the line against Communist aggression lest an important ally in Southeast Asia succumb to the red tide. Hawks believed that if South Vietnam fell to the Communists, the Soviets and Chinese would press their advantage elsewhere in that strategically important region. Additional allies and neutral nations would fall to Communism, and the security of America itself would be undermined. Hawks, convinced that America possessed the military power to demolish the Vietcong and North Vietnamese forces if the wraps were removed, were frustrated by the restraints that civilians had clamped on the U.S. forces. They demanded that President Johnson "do whatever was necessary to attain victory."[130]

Doves, a more diverse assemblage than the hawks, opposed the Vietnam war. During 1966 and 1967, their numbers were increasing, and their opposition was intensifying. Most doves were recruited from one of three main groupings inhabiting the Left of the American political spectrum: old-line pacifists, who had opposed U.S. participation in previous wars; young radicals on college campuses who belonged to the Student Non-Violent Coordinating Committee (SNCC) and the Students for a Democratic Society (SDS), the principal organizations of the New Left; and antiwar liberals, the largest of the dovish groups.[131]

The antiwar liberal indictment of the Vietnam conflict was wrapped in the fabric of moral revulsion. Perceiving no threat to American security, liberals repudiated the domino theory, the principal ideological justification for the American war in Vietnam. They viewed the Vietnam war as essentially a civil war, an internal struggle between contending factions of Vietnamese for political control of their country. They understood the war to be a regional conflict largely outside the Cold War context, irrelevant to the ongoing conflicts of interest between the United States and the Soviet Union. Vietnam, Laos, and Cambodia were countries of marginal strategic significance. Liberals could see no vital U.S. interest at issue in the Vietnam war. They also believed that the American backing of a succession of corrupt, repressive, and inept South Vietnamese military rulers represented a lamentable betrayal of American democratic ideals. The spectacle of American soldiers killing Vietnamese soldiers and being killed by them in the name of a morally bankrupt and strategically dubious cause was a needless horror.

Many liberals added pragmatic criticisms to their moral indictment of the U.S. war in Vietnam. The conflict was dividing Americans, sowing divisions that increasingly strained the social fabric and exacerbated other tensions and antagonisms within the U.S. body politic. American preoccupation with Vietnam was also undermining the commitment to civil rights and to social reform at home. The Great Society programs including the war on poverty were being starved for the sake of an unnecessary war. The war also represented a drain of wealth and resources that could be better spent improving public schools and cleaning up the environment.

To call the various organizations and activities constituting the opposition to the expanding war in Vietnam a "movement" is misleading, for the term "movement" implies a coherency of organizational structures and a congruency of tactics, strategies, goals, and ideologies that never existed among left-wing antiwar groups. A schism evolved between liberal and radical antiwar activists. Liberals wanted to stop an unnecessary, futile, and unjust war, not to remake U.S. society. Radicals saw the war as symptomatic of a fundamentally unjust capitalist-imperialist system that exploited people both at home and abroad, a system that they felt compelled to radically restructure along socialist lines. Stopping the war was only a way station en route to achieving a radical reformation of the U.S. political economy and culture.

Liberals focused on peaceful and legal means of protesting what they regarded to be an unjust and unnecessary war. Radicals often moved beyond protest to various forms of civil disobedience: to resistance and direct confrontation, sometimes leading to violent encounters with police and the National Guard. At the extreme fringe of radical antiwar activity, revolutionary bands committed themselves to the violent overthrow of the "Amerikan" system. The major political weakness of the antiwar organizations, which seriously hampered their effectiveness, was their inability to unite on such matters as rhetoric, methods, and goals. Intragroup tensions and factional conflicts often impaired their various antiwar activities as well.[132]

Opposition to the war took various forms. Senator Fulbright held televised hearings on all aspects of the administration's war policy before his Foreign Relations committee. He and his dovish colleagues grilled administration defenders, such as Secretary of State Dean Rusk, and provided George Kennan, General James Gavin, and other prominent critics of the war a national forum for venting their dissenting views. Millions of viewers watched the hearings. Fulbright's investigations gave antiwar sentiment a legitimacy that it had previously lacked and strengthened the ranks of critics of U.S. war policy.[133]

Antiwar rallies, marches, and demonstrations increased in size, occurred more frequently, and developed more militant tactics during 1967, the first year of significant nationwide protest against the Vietnam war. Protesters marched daily in front of the White House chanting, "Hey, hey, LBJ, how many kids have you killed today?" and "Ho, Ho, Ho Chi Minh, [the] NLF is going to win."[134] In California, several antiwar organizations planned a Stop

By 1966, opposition to the escalating American war in Vietnam was increasing. In February, Senate Foreign Relations Committee chairman, William Fulbright, (pictured here on the right), held hearings on the war. Fulbright and his dovish colleagues subjected administrative leaders like secretary of state Dean Rusk (seen here on the left), to hours of grilling about all aspects of the war.
Source: National Archives

the Draft Week for mid-October 1967. On Monday, October 13, as newly drafted young men arrived in buses for their physical examinations and induction into the Army, a peaceful sit-in was held at the entrance to the Oakland (California) Induction Center at 5:00 a. m. After the group refused orders to leave, the police moved in and arrested over a hundred demonstrators. The next day, by 6:00 a. m., thousands of militants, many affiliated with SDS, surrounded the entrance to the induction center. After refusing police orders to disperse, they were attacked by police. The entrance to the induction center was cleared within a few hours. Scores of demonstrators were injured. On Friday, perhaps 10,000 militants showed up and blocked the entrance to the induction center for hours. Some of the demonstrators also blocked streets, fought with police, and disrupted traffic. Many demonstrators and police were injured during the day-long melee.[135]

A week after the demonstrations at the Oakland induction center, the largest antiwar demonstration of 1967 occurred. On October 21, the National Mobilization Committee and other antiwar organizations staged a rally in front of the Lincoln Memorial in Washington, D.C., attended by an estimated 100,000 people. About 35,000 of the demonstrators also marched across the Memorial Bridge to an entrance of the Pentagon where they held another rally. A group of perhaps four thousand militant protesters attempted unsuccessfully to blockade the Pentagon, the nerve center of the U.S. war effort.[136]

Prominent individuals who made well-publicized symbolic gestures of defiance constituted another dimension of the growing opposition to the war. Heavyweight boxing champion Muhammad Ali, a member of the Black muslim sect, refused induction into the Army on religious grounds. Government attorneys argued successfully that Muslims were not eligible for conscientious objector status because they did not oppose all wars, only particular wars. Ali's draft board pronounced his religious views "insincere" and refused his request for a deferment. Ali replied

> It would be no trouble for me to accept on the basis that I'll go into the armed services boxing exhibitions in Vietnam, or traveling the country at the expense of the government, if it wasn't against my conscience to do it. I wouldn't give up the millions that I gave up and my image with the American public,…If I wasn't sincere.[137]

Ali was convicted of draft evasion in June 1967, stripped of his heavyweight title, and sentenced to five years in prison. He stayed out of prison on bond until the Supreme Court overturned his conviction on a technicality. Ali lost five of his prime years as a professional athlete for refusing to be drafted. He became one of the controversial personalities of the Vietnam war era, venerated by opponents of the war and despised by its supporters.

The draft had become a generational obsession by 1967. A large majority of young men who came of draft age during the Vietnam war era avoided military service.[138] A large majority of these evaders found legal means of avoiding the draft and the war. They obtained deferments or exemptions by exercising their legitimate rights under the prevailing conscription system. Others manipulated the system to achieve their deferments or exemptions. Motivated primarily by a desire to avoid the Vietnam-era draft, they went to college, got married and fathered children, or obtained jobs in "critical" (exempted) occupations. Medically fit young men, aided by draft counselors and sympathetic doctors, found ways to obtain deferments, often on psychological grounds.

The successes of millions of young, mostly middle and upper-middle class men, in evading the conscription system either legitimately or illegitimately, shifted the burden of fighting the war to youths from working class, minority, and poor backgrounds. The vast majority of U.S. conscripts who fought in the Vietnam war were plucked off of the lower rungs of the American socioeconomic ladder. They were the young men who were either too poor, too uneducated, too unskilled vocationally, too lacking in political influence, or too patriotic to avoid the war. The draftees who had to fight the

U.S. Vietnam war were a cross section, not of the entire society, but of its relatively disadvantaged classes. Going to Vietnam was the price paid by young men who lacked the means to avoid conscription.[139]

Other draft-eligible young men chose drastic methods of avoiding the draft and the war. Thousands of young men refused to register for the draft upon turning eighteen. Hundreds of thousands refused induction when called. About 40,000 fled the country, mostly to Canada, to avoid military service. Some, in desperation, maimed and mutilated their bodies in order to disqualify themselves from military service. A handful of young men, adopting the protest method of South Vietnam's Buddhist monks and nuns, publicly immolated themselves.[140]

Many draft-age young men joined the Reserves or the National Guard to avoid active duty and a possible tour in Vietnam. But during the peak years of the war, when monthly draft calls ranged between 30,000 and 50,000 selectees, nearly all Reserve and National Guard units had filled up and most had long waiting lists. Applicants usually needed political clout to get into one of those draft sanctuaries. It was always possible that the Reservists and the National Guard could be called to active duty and be shipped off to Vietnam at any time. But Johnson, rejecting the advice of his senior military advisers and Secretary of Defense McNamara, refused to activate most of these forces. His refusal accorded with his desire to fight a limited war that would have a limited domestic impact. The Reserves and the National Guard remained havens for affluent draft evaders for the duration of the war. A high percentage of draft-eligible college graduates and professional athletes could be found in the ranks of the Reserves and the Guard during the war.[141] A future vice president, J. Danforth Quayle, was one of the many affluent young men who obtained a coveted National Guard assignment and side-stepped a possible tour of duty in Vietnam.

What impact did the antiwar demonstrations have on the war? Many of those who participated in antiwar activities believe that the demonstrations helped bring an earlier end to the war than would have been the case had there been no organized antiwar activity. Some of these same people have also been troubled by the charge that they encouraged the nation's enemies and hindered a U.S. war in which 58,000 of their fellow Americans perished. Many former hawkish military and civilian leaders, and many citizens who strongly supported the U.S. war in Vietnam, are convinced that antiwar activists aided the enemy and hurt the national war effort. They believe much of the antiwar activity was disloyal, even treasonous, and they angrily accuse the antiwar activists of having prevented victory in a war that the nation could have won.

It is difficult to determine precisely what impact, if any, antiwar activity had on the American conduct of the war because the evidence is skimpy. It is undoubtedly true that U.S. domestic opponents of the Vietnam war encouraged Hanoi. They gave the Communist leaders confidence that they would eventually prevail. But it does not follow that the Communists would not have persisted as they did or that they would have been more willing to comprise with the Americans had there been no antiwar activity in this country. From the beginning of the war, the Communists were implacable and unyielding.[142] They were prepared to fight for decades and to make great sacrifices to ensure the ultimate triumph of their cause. They did not require a U.S. antiwar movement to continue their efforts.

Antiwar protests had no visible impact on administration war policy. Demonstrations neither inhibited Johnson from escalating the war when he thought he must nor did they incline him to scale back the U.S. war effort and make greater efforts to seek a negotiated settlement sooner than he thought he had to. Johnson adhered to his policy of graduated escalation and apparently remained confident, until the Communists staged the Tet Offensive in early 1968, that the limited war strategy would succeed, that American forces would eventually prevail. The growing doubts about the war among some of Johnson's civilian advisers do not appear to have been engendered primarily by the growing antiwar activities. Those doubts were implanted by rising costs and casualties incurred in the pursuit of war strategies that were not bringing victory, that appeared to be capable of achieving only an escalating stalemate.

Did antiwar protest activity turn public opinion against the war or accelerate the rise of popular opposition to the war? The loss of public support for the Vietnam war eventually forced the United States to withdraw its combat forces from Southeast Asia. American withdrawal made possible a subsequent Communist victory. Former hawks are both bitter and vehement on this point. They are convinced that the antiwar movement, in tandem with what they believe to have been biased media coverage of the conflict, particularly television news coverage, turned the American people against the Vietnam war, thereby depriving the nation of a victory in a major war that it could have and should have won.[143] For these embittered conservatives, a Communist-controlled Vietnam serves as a constant reminder of the power of left-wing antiwar protests and media distortions that, in their view, exaggerated the wrongs and shortcomings of both the U.S. war effort and America's South Vietnamese clients while turning a blind eye toward the atrocities and repressions of the enemy. They believe that these antiwar efforts eventually demoralized the public, caused a loss of faith in the U.S. effort, and forced the American withdrawal from Vietnam, which, tragically, paved the war for a Communist triumph.

The evidence, furnished by the many public opinion polls taken during the Vietnam war era, refutes these charges. It was not the antiwar protesters who turned the American public against the war. The vocal left-wing antiwar "movement" never constituted more than a small minority whose political base was confined largely to college students and faculty members recruited from some of the nation's most prestigious private and public universities, such as Harvard, Columbia, the University of Michigan, and the Berkeley campus of the University of California, the vital center of antiwar activities during the Vietnam era. In fact, contrary to popular impressions, many young (age 20–29), college-educated men supported the war. According to the polls, they were the most hawkish group in the nation. The typical dove during the Vietnam war era was much more likely to be a kindly grandmother than a young college-educated man.[144]

Divisions within and among antiwar organizations, a lack of leader-ship, and unsuccessful or counter-productive tactics all marred the effectiveness of antiwar activities. But the main reason that the antiwar movement failed to turn public opinion against the war was because it could not. That was because there was a clear disjuncture among opponents of the war. There were, in reality, two distinct antiwar currents flowing in America by 1967. One constituted the small, vocal left-wing antiwar activity previously described. What gave these antiwar activists such unity as they possessed was the shared conviction that the U.S. war in Vietnam was wrong. They were also convinced that America must cease all acts of war and withdraw from Indochina. South Vietnam's fate did not matter to most of these vociferous opponents of war. The more radical among them cheered on the NLF and the NVA, and hoped to remake American society and culture.[145]

The other, vastly larger, antiwar current represented a rough cross section of Americans and eventually included a majority of the population. These folks were not organized, never vocal, and not given to public demonstrations of their views. Their opposition to the war was passive, not active; pragmatic not principled. It was largely confined to the private realms of life, diffuse, and inarticulate, although it registered in the public opinion polls and showed in votes for antiwar candidates and ballot measures. Their opposition to the war was rooted in the belief that the nation was paying too high a price in lives, dollars, inflation, higher taxes, social disorder, and political polarization to go on supporting a war that had already grown far larger than anyone had ever anticipated and appeared to be an endless, escalating stalemate. The most important of the many causes of pragmatic opposition was the spreading perception that the war was not being won.[146] These practical opponents of the war viewed the feeding of more and more U.S. soldiers and dollars into a conflict that America did not appear to be winning as a colossal waste of human and material resources. But these pragmatic opponents of the Vietnam war also despised the left-wing antiwar activists. In fact, many of them hated college-based antiwar protesters worse than they hated the stalemated war in Vietnam.[147]

A conflation of the two antiwar currents never occurred nor could it occur. The doves could never bridge the ideological divide separating them. They could never make common cause to protest a war that they both opposed. Their only shared emotion was mutual disdain. They retained fundamental differences: The vocal activists focused on what the war was doing to Vietnam. The pragmatic opponents of the war focused on what the war was doing to America. The vocals perceived the war to be wrong; the pragmatics viewed it as pointless.[148]

It was the rising pragmatic opposition to the Vietnam war that was registering most of the numbers in the 1967 public opinion surveys that showed a growing opposition to the war because these quiet foes of war were about ten times more numerous than the vocal opponents.[149] It would be the widespread opposition of the pragmatic opponents of the war, mostly patriotic, law-abiding, and God-fearing mainstream Americans, that would eventually force U.S. withdrawal from Vietnam and would ensure America's defeat in Southeast Asia, not the noisy protests of the comparatively few left-wing dissenters.

Most pragmatic enemies of the Vietnam war were not influenced by the vocal antiwar groups whose ideology, style, tone, rhetoric, and tactics they repudiated. The growing legions of quiet Americans coming to oppose the war linked the left-wing opponents of the war to radicalism, violence, disloyalty, countercultural life styles, postures of intellectual superiority, and shrill self-righteousness, all of which they loathed.[150] Most Americans who came to oppose the war did so despite the leftwing anti-war opposition, not because of it. Some analysts have advanced the thesis that the left-wing antiwar movement actually prolonged the war.[151]

Most Americans in the summer of 1967 were neither hawks nor doves. "If any bird symbolized the growing public disenchantment with Vietnam,...it was the albatross." A housewife expressed the contradictory attitudes generated by the war: "I want to get out but I don't want to give up."[152] Polls taken in August showed that a majority of respondents believed that the U.S. intervention in the Vietnam war had been a mistake; they also strongly disapproved of Johnson's war policies. Press editorials and Congressional leaders increasingly voiced criticisms of U.S. Vietnam policy. Polls registered a widening "credibility gap" as a pervasive mistrust of government spread through the body politic. Some Americans saw the Vietnam war as only the most dramatic symbol of a spreading malaise infecting American society, a society increasingly marked by race riots, street demonstrations, and violent crime. As the American consensus fractured and civility disappeared from public life, people feared that the Great Society had become a sick society.[153]

A GOVERNMENT DIVIDED

The growing public controversy over the war reflected deepening divisions within Johnson's administration over his war policy. The Joint Chiefs and General Westmoreland joined forces in the spring of 1967 in an effort to enlarge the war. Westmoreland, confident that his war of attrition would eventually produce victory, requested 200,000 additional troops to expand the ground war against the VC/NVA forces. The Joint Chiefs strongly endorsed his troop request. At the same time, they called for additional escalations of the war. They called for a mobilization of reserve forces. They also sought authorization for cross-border operations into Cambodia and Laos to clean out the VC/NVA sanctuaries in these neutral nations. They further proposed an invasion across the DMZ. In addition, they asked for an expanded air campaign against North Vietnam and for permission to mine North Vietnam's major ports. Only such measures, they argued, could defeat the rebels and force Hanoi to abandon its support of the southern insurgency.[154]

These escalatory requests by the military collided with moves by some of Johnson's civilian advisers led by McNamara to curtail the bombing of North Vietnam, to hold the line on ground troops, and to seek a negotiated settlement of the conflict that would allow the United States to extricate itself gracefully from the Vietnam quagmire. McNamara and other civilian officials in the Defense and State departments had been disillusioned by the failure of both the air war against North Vietnam and the ground war against South Vietnam to defeat the Vietcong, to discourage Hanoi, or to strengthen the Saigon regime.

By the summer of 1967, Johnson found himself caught amidst the divisions among his senior advisers. He instinctively sought a middle course between the hawks and the doves. He refused most of the requests of the Joint Chiefs except for enlarging the air war against North Vietnam, but he agreed to send Westmoreland 55,000 additional troops. He rejected McNamara's suggestion to scale back the U.S. war effort, having lost confidence in his Secretary of Defense's judgment.[155] Johnson's decisions were based on domestic political considerations not strategic criteria. His decisions amounted to a continuation of his policy of graduated escalation. He perpetuated the military stalemate without confronting the flaws within the U.S. strategy of limited war.

In the fall of 1967, Johnson, alarmed by growing opposition to the war, launched an attack on antiwar activists. He believed, mistakenly, that vocal left-wing antiwar groups were turning mainstream Americans against the war. He also believed, again mistakenly, that Hanoi was directing the antiwar movement. He ordered the CIA, in violation of its charter, to investigate antiwar groups to find evidence of their ties to foreign Communists. Although CIA agents found no evidence that either foreign or domestic Communists controlled the antiwar movement, Johnson falsely claimed that they had.[156] The FBI infiltrated many antiwar organizations. The FBI also used *agents provocateurs* to provoke violent confrontations with police and to take other violent actions that would discredit antiwar organizations in public eyes.[157]

At the same time that Johnson ordered the CIA and the FBI to go after the peace movement, he mounted a public relations campaign designed to bolster popular support for his war policy. Johnson believed that American forces were winning the war. The reports that he received from MACV headquarters constantly reported news of progress: of large numbers of the enemy killed, of supplies captured, and of villages pacified. Johnson discounted the critics of the war among the Congress, the media, and the public. He regarded them as uninformed, lacking in nerve, and, in some cases, disloyal. Johnson tended to personalize criticisms of his war policy and he deeply resented them. He believed the criticisms to be unfounded and unfair. Johnson felt that if his critics only understood what he was trying to do, they would support him enthusiastically.[158]

Presidential aides formed a citizens committee headed by former presidents Truman and Eisenhower to rally public opinion behind the war. Johnson met with an informal advisory group composed of elder statesmen. These former top officials, dubbed the "wise men," endorsed Johnson's war policy, although they voiced concern about spreading public disenchantment with the war. Johnson also brought General Westmoreland home to make upbeat speeches about Vietnam. Westmoreland, good soldier that he was, never uttered a discouraging word. He told a National Press Club audience, "we have reached an important point when the end begins to come into view." In answer to a question following his speech, Westmoreland said he believed that America could begin phasing down the level of U.S. forces and turn more of the fighting over to ARVN.[159] Soon after Westmoreland's speech, Johnson held a press conference. He passionately defended his war policy, insisted that America must honor its commitments, and stated that U.S. forces were making progress.[160] Westmoreland, back in Vietnam, announced that the enemy had suffered such severe losses that he could no longer mount an assault anywhere in Vietnam. Johnson's public relations campaign succeeded. Polls showed a 6 percent increase in public support for his war policy at year's end.[161]

But even as Johnson mounted his "success offensive," vowed to stay the course, and insisted that U.S. forces were winning their war of attrition, he quietly began considering a change of strategy. The "wise men" had suggested that he turn over greater responsibility for fighting the war to the ARVN forces. Retiring Secretary of Defense McNamara's final memo to Johnson proposed what would be later called Vietnamization. McNamara proposed a new strategy "aimed at reducing U.S. casualties and giving the South Vietnamese greater responsibilities for their own security."[162]

Although he might be thinking about a change of strategy, Johnson still held to his main goal of preserving a non-Communist nation in southern Vietnam. As 1967 ended, Johnson remained determined to prevail in Vietnam and confident that he would. He did not know that for six months the Communists had been planning a major offensive designed to "liberate" South Vietnam and to force the Americans out of that country. As 1967 ended, they readied their forces to launch it. The Tet-68 Offensive would be the most important campaign of the American war in Vietnam, and it would provoke a major crisis in Washington.

NOTES

1. Thompson, James Clay, *Rolling Thunder: Understanding Policy and Program Failure* (Chapel Hill, N.C., University of North Carolina Press, 1980), pp. 10–11; Summers, *On Strategy*, p. 18.

2. Davidson, *Vietnam at War*, p. 337.

3. *Ibid.*, p. 338.

4. Thompson, *Rolling Thunder*, p. 11.

5. Herring, *America's Longest War*, p. 145.

6. Krepinevich, Andrew F., Jr., *The Army and Vietnam* (Baltimore, Md.: The Johns Hopkins University Press, 1986), p. 165; Palmer, Bruce, Jr., *The 25-Year War: America's Military Role in Vietnam* (New York: Simon and Schuster, 1985), pp. 174–177; Johnson is reported to have boasted, "I won't let those air force generals bomb the smallest outhouse…without checking with me."

7. Davidson, *Vietnam at War*, p. 369.

8. Furguson, Ernest B., *Westmoreland: The Inevitable General* (Boston: Little, Brown, 1968).

9. *Ibid.*; Davidson, *Vietnam at War*, pp. 369–386; essay in Summers, Harry G., Jr., *Vietnam War Almanac* (New York: Facts on File, 1985), pp. 357–359.

10. Westmoreland, *A Soldier Reports*, pp. 186–193.

11. Krepinevich, *Army and Vietnam*, p. 164.

12. Westmoreland, *A Soldier Reports*, pp. 187–188.

13. *Ibid.*

14. *Ibid.*

15. Stanton, Shelby L., *The Rise and Fall of an American Army: U.S. Ground Forces in Vietnam, 1965–1973* (New York: Dell, 1985), p. 21.

16. *Ibid.*, p. 23.

17. Palmer, Dave Richard, *Summons of the Trumpet* (New York: Ballantine, 1978), pp. 111–113.

18. Herring, *America's Longest War*, p. 151.

19. Stanton, *Rise and Fall*, p. 23; Palmer, *Summons of the Trumpet*, pp. 169–170. The ratio of noncombat to combat effectives within the American force structure in Vietnam was six to one. In early 1969, American troop levels in Vietnam peaked at 543,000. At the time, only about 75,000 of these troops directly engaged in combat; 470,000 were serving in various support functions.

20. Davidson, *Vietnam at War*, pp. 349–350. Doyle and others, *America Takes Over*, p. 40; Stanton, *Rise and Fall*, p. 44.

21. Stanton, *Rise and Fall*, pp. 45–46.

22. General Walt in turn was under COMUSMACV's (Westmoreland's) ultimate command authority. South Vietnam was divided into four combat sectors: I (Eye) Corps, II Corps (the central highlands), III Corps (Saigon and vicinity), and IV Corps (the Mekong delta). MACV directly controlled U.S. combat operations in Corps II, III, and IV. The South Vietnamese army also had a corps commander in each zone and the U.S. Army and ARVN generals and their staffs

coordinated operations in each corps zone. MACV and ARVN commanders shared a joint command structure. In the IV Corps region, there were few American and PAVN forces.

23. Stanton, *Rise and Fall*, pp. 34–35.

24. Operation STARLITE was originally named SATELLITE. The name was changed by mistake when a Marine clerk, typing by candlelight after the electrical generators went down, misread the order.

25. Boettcher, Thomas D., *Vietnam: The Valor and the Sorrow* (Boston: Little, Brown, 1985), pp. 317–319; Stanton, *Rise and Fall*, pp. 34–39.

26. Summers, Harry G., Jr., "The Bitter Triumph of Ia Drang," *American Heritage Magazine* (Jan.-Feb. 1984), pp. 56–58.

27. Palmer, *Summons of the Trumpet*, pp. 119–120.

28. Herring, George C., "The 1st Cavalry and the Ia Drang Valley, 18 October–24 November 1965," in Heller, Charles E., and Stofft, William A., *America's First Battles* (Lawrence, Kansas: University Press of Kansas, 1986), pp. 313–314. "Ia" was the Jarai word for river.

29. *Ibid.*, p. 315.

30. Summers, "The Bitter Triumph of the Ia Drang," p. 53.

31. Westmoreland, *A Soldier Reports*, p. 204.

32. Herring, "The 1st Cavalry and the Ia Drang Valley," p. 318; Westmoreland, *A Soldier Reports*, pp. 204–205; and Davidson, *Vietnam at War*, pp. 360–362.

33. Morrocco, *Thunder from Above*, pp. 88–93; Palmer, *Summons of the Trumpet*, pp. 128–130.

34. Herring, "The 1st Cavalry and the Ia Drang Valley," p. 319; Westmoreland, *A Soldier Reports*, p. 204.

35. Harry G. Summers, Jr., "The Bitter Triumph of Ia Drang," p. 58, suggests that, ironically, the victories at Ia Drang contributed to the eventual U.S. defeat in Vietnam. It gave American soldiers a sense of invincibility; after Ia Drang, they believed that all they had to do was to keep fighting battles and they would inevitably win the war. They failed to see that the war was changing, failed to focus on the major enemy, and failed to see the connection between the Ia Drang campaign and defeating the NVA. They lost sight of the major objective of the war and eventually lost it.

36. Krepinevich, *The Army and Vietnam*, pp. 168–169; Stanton, *Rise and Fall*, pp. 57–58; Morrocco, *Thunder from Above*, p. 171.

37. Herring, "The 1st Cavalry and the Ia Drang Valley," p. 323.

38. Palmer, *Summons of the Trumpet*, p. 140.

39. Thompson, W. Scott, and Frizzel, Donaldson D. (eds.), *The Lessons of Vietnam* (New York: Crane, Russak, 1977), pp. 73–74; Palmer, *The Summons of the Trumpet*, p. 323. Palmer says the "Americans had almost as little foot mobility as their foe had helicopter mobility."

40. Duiker, *The Communist Road*, p. 239; Turley, *The Second Indochina War*, p. 66.

41. Stanton, *Rise and Fall*, pp. 76–77.

42. Westmoreland, *A Soldier Reports*, p. 234; Krepinevich, *The Army and Vietnam*, pp. 190–191.

43. Rogers, Bernard W., *Cedar Falls–Junction City: A Turning Point* (Washington, D.C.: U.S. Government Printing Office, 1974), pp. 73–74; Stanton, *Rise and Fall*, pp. 101–102.

44. Stanton, *Rise and Fall*, p. 125.

45. *Ibid.*, p. 126. MACV officials estimated total enemy combat strength at 285,000 at the end of 1966.

46. Schell, Jonathan, *The Real War* (New York: Pantheon, 1987), pp. 59–74; Morrocco, *Thunder from Above*, p. 172; Palmer, *Summons of the Trumpet*, pp. 168–171.

47. Westmoreland, *A Soldier Reports*, pp. 268–269; the U.S. units involved in Operation CEDAR FALLS included the 1st and 25th Infantry Divisions, the 173rd Airborne Brigade, and the 11th Armored Cavalry Regiment.

48. Schell, *Real War*, pp. 86–121; Doyle and others, *America Takes Over*, p. 105.

49. *Ibid.*, pp. 107–108.

50. Palmer, *Summons of the Trumpet*, p. 176.

51. Schell, *Real War*, pp. 133–188; quote is from Doyle and others, *America Takes Over*, p. 108.

52. Rogers, *Cedar Falls–Junction City*, pp. 154–157; Westmoreland, *A Soldier Reports*, p. 269.

53. Stanton, *Rise and Fall*, pp. 127–129. The U.S. military was confined to a ground war within the geographic boundaries of South Vietnam until President Nixon, in April 1970, authorized an incursion of limited scope and duration into particular regions of Cambodia bordering South Vietnam.

54. O'Ballance, *Wars in Vietnam*, p. 108; Stanton, *Rise and Fall*, p. 150.

55. Stanton, *Rise and Fall*, p. 161.

56. Westmoreland, *A Soldier Reports*, p. 313; hills on U.S. Army maps are designated according to their height in meters. Hill 875 was 875 meters high.

57. Stanton, *Rise and Fall*, p. 164.

58. *Ibid.*, pp. 165–168; Doyle and others, *America Takes Over*, p. 182.

59. Westmoreland, *A Soldier Reports*, pp. 312–313; Davidson, *Vietnam at War*, p. 469.

60. Stanton, *Rise and Fall*, pp. 170–171.

61. Westmoreland, *A Soldier Reports*, pp. 263–264.

62. *Ibid.*, pp. 265–266; Doyle and others, *America Takes Over*, pp. 160–161; O'Ballance, *Wars in Vietnam*, p. 107. Elements of the PAVN 324-B Division were also involved in the fighting at Con Thien; Morrocco, *Thunder from Above*, pp. 174–175.

63. Thompson, Robert, *No Exit from Vietnam*, (New York: David McKay, 1969) p. 135.

64. Krepinevich, *The Army and Vietnam*, p. 167. Krepinevich believes that the fatal flaw of Westmoreland's attrition strategy was that it could not force the enemy to engage in big unit fights. The U.S. could never win as long as the enemy avoided major battles; Morrocco and others, *Thunder from Above*, p. 94.

65. Mueller, John E., "The Search for a 'Breaking Point' in Vietnam: The Statistics of a Deadly Quarrel," *International Studies Quarterly*, vol. 4, (December 1980), pp. 497–519. General Giap has estimated PAVN manpower losses for the war at 600,000 soldiers killed. If his guess was accurate, North Vietnam lost about 3 percent of its prewar population. For America to have sustained an equivalent loss, its battle deaths would have had to reach about 7,000,000.

66. Herring, *America's Longest War*, pp. 155–156.

67. Schandler, *The Unmaking of a President*, pp. 31–32; Herring, *America's Longest War*, p. 155.

68. Thompson, *Rolling Thunder*, p. 35.

69. Morrocco and others, *Thunder from Above*, pp. 64–65.

70. Palmer, *Summons of the Trumpet*, pp. 156–157.

71. Thompson, *Rolling Thunder*, pp. 45–48.

72. President Johnson played politics with bombing pauses in 1965, 1966, and 1967. He did not expect Hanoi to offer to negotiate on terms he could accept. He used pauses to show world and U.S. opinion that Hanoi was the aggressor.

73. Quoted in Morrocco and others, *Thunder from Above*, P. 127.

74. *Ibid.*, p. 128; Mersky, Peter B., and Polmar, Norman, *The Naval Air War in Viet-Nam* (New York: Kensington, 1981), pp. 118–121.

75. Morrocco and others, *Thunder from Above*, pp. 130–131.

76. Porter, (ed.), "Intelligence Memoranda By the Directorate of Intelligence, CIA," May 12 and May 23, 1967, *Vietnam Documents*, vol. 2, Documents 261 and 262, pp. 466–470. Gallucci, *Neither Peace nor Honor*, pp. 64–70; Thompson, *Rolling Thunder*, pp. 51–53.

77. Sheehan and others, "Vietnam Bombing Evaluation By Institute for Defense Analysis," *Pentagon Papers*, Document 117, pp. 506–507.

78. Turley, *The Second Indochina War*, p. 97; Stanton, *Rise and Fall*, pp. 174–175.

79. Palmer, *Summons of the Trumpet*, p. 162; Porter, (ed.), "Memorandum for McNamara By the Joint Chiefs of Staff," JCSM-30767, June 2, 1967,*Vietnam Documents*, vol. 2, Document 263, pp. 470–472.

80. Thompson, *Rolling Thunder*, p. 64.

81. Sharp, Ulysses S. G., *Strategy for Defeat: Vietnam in Retrospect* (San Rafael, Calif.: The Presidio Press, 1978). Admiral Sharp argued that an intensive bombing campaign could have won the war. But in 1965, the rate of infiltration into South Vietnam had been 1500 men per month; in 1966, 4500 men per month; in 1967, as the air war intensified, the rate of infiltration increased to 6000 men per month. In January, 1968, on the eve of the Tet Offensive, 20,000 men infiltrated into South Vietnam.

82. Littauer, Raphael, and Uphoff, Norman (eds.), *The Air War in Indochina*, rev. ed. (Boston: Beacon, 1972), p. 36. The passage is also quoted in Thompson, *Rolling Thunder*, p. 64; Lewy, *America in Vietnam*, pp. 389–396. By 1967 China was undergoing its Cultural Revolution; it was less able to intervene in North Vietnam, but Johnson would never rule out that possibility.

83. Turley, *The Second Indochina War*, pp. 95–96.

84. Enthoven, Allen C.; and Smith, K. Wayne, *How Much is Enough? Shaping the Defense Program, 1961–1968* (New York: Harper and Row, 1971).

85. Sheehan and others, "Secretary McNamara's Position of May 19 on Bombing and Troops," *Pentagon Papers*, Document 129, p. 580.

86. Thayer, *War Without Fronts*, pp. 79–86; Morrocco, *Thunder from Above*, p. 74.

87. Morrocco and others, *Thunder from Above*, p. 84.

88. *Ibid.*, pp. 88–89.

89. *Ibid.*

90. Thayer, *War Without Fronts*, pp. 129–132.

91. *Ibid.*

92. *Ibid.*, pp. 83–84.

93. Morrocco and others, *Thunder from Above*, p. 85.

94. Buckingham, William A., Jr., *Operation Ranch Hand: The Air Force and Herbicides in Southeast Asia, 1961–1971* (Washington, D.C.: GPO, 1982).

95. Herring, *America's Longest War*, p. 151.

96. Boettcher, *Vietnam: The Valor and the Sorrow*, pp. 258–259; Morrocco and others, *Thunder from Above*, p. 180.

97. Jacobs, James B., and McNamara, Dennis, "Vietnam Veterans and Agent Orange," *Armed Forces and Society*, vol. 13 (Fall 1986), pp. 57–79. Veterans who brought suit against the Veterans Administration had great difficulty proving scientifically and legally that their and their children's health problems had been caused by their exposure to Dioxin while serving in Vietnam.

98. Morrocco, *Thunder from Above*, p. 180.

99. *Ibid.*

100. Sheehan and others, "Johnson's Remarks to Officials of U.S. and Saigon at Honolulu," *Pentagon Papers*, Document 111, pp. 495–496.

101. Quoted in Karnow, *Vietnam*, p. 444.

102. Blaufarb, *Counterinsurgency Era*, pp. 232–233.

103. Kahin, *Intervention*, pp. 413–414.

104. *Ibid.*, pp. 423–425.

105. Doyle and others, *America Takes Over*, pp. 78–79.

106. From interviews with soldiers on videotape, "America Takes Charge, 1965–1967," from the television series, "Vietnam: A Television History."

107. Kahin, *Intervention*, p. 432.

108. Blaufarb, *The Counterinsurgency Era*, pp. 225–229.

109. Herring, *America's Longest War*, p. 158.

110. *Ibid.*, pp. 158–159; 3,015 RD personnel were kidnapped or murdered during a seven-month period in 1966.

111. Blaufarb, *The Counterinsurgency Era*, pp. 229–231; Herring, *America's Longest War*, p. 159; Davidson, *Vietnam at War*, pp. 431–432.

112. Herring, *America's Longest War*, pp. 159–160.

113. Karnow, *Vietnam*, pp. 451–452.

114. Shaplen, Robert, *The Road from War: Vietnam, 1965–1971* (New York: Harper & Row, 1971), p. 151; also quoted in Herring, *America's Longest War*, p. 160.

115. Herring, *America's Longest War*, p. 161.

116. *Ibid.*, p. 162. In 1954, Saigon had a population of 550,000; in 1961, 1,000,000. In December 1967, U.S. officials estimated that 2,200,000 people lived within the city and another 1,000,000 in the suburbs of Gia Dinh province. By then, one-fifth of the country's population resided in or near the city.

117. Schandler, *The Unmaking of a President*, pp. 31–32. Quote is from Schandler, p. 32; Interviews with soldiers recorded on videotape, "America Takes Charge, 1965–1967," from the television series, "Vietnam: A Television History."

118. *Ibid.*

119. Goodman, *The Lost Peace*. pp. 23–26.

120. Quoted in Gareth Porter (ed.), *A Peace Denied: The United States, Vietnam, and the Paris Agreement* (Bloomington, Ind.: Indiana University Press, 1975), p. 29; also quoted in Herring, *America's Longest War*, p. 165.

121. Herring, *America's Longest War*, p. 166.

122. Goodman, *The Lost Peace*, p. 28.

123. *Ibid.*, p. 35–36.

124. Karnow, *Vietnam*, pp. 493–494; Goodman, *The Lost Peace*, pp. 39–42.

125. Herring, *America's Longest War*, p. 167.

126. Turner, *Lyndon Johnson's Dual War*, pp. 191–198; Doyle and others, *America Takes Over*, pp. 136–137.

127. Goodman, *The Lost Peace*, p. 24.

128. *Ibid.*

129. Schandler, *The Unmaking of a President*, p. 49

130. Herring, *America's Longest War*, p. 170.

131. Debennedetti, Charles, *The Peace Reform in American History* (Bloomington, Ind.: Indiana University Press, 1984), pp. 175–177.

132. Moss, George, "News or Nemesis: Did Television Lose the Vietnam War," unpublished essay, 1988, p. 88.

133. Doyle and others, *America Takes Over*, pp. 141–152.

134. Quoted in Herring, *America's Longest War*, p. 173.

135. Powers, Thomas, *Vietnam: The War at Home* (Boston: G. K. Hall, 1973), pp. 236–238.

136. *Ibid.*, pp. 238–240; Norman Mailer, *The Armies of the Night: History as a Novel, the Novel as History* (Cleveland: World Publications, 1968) is a novelistic account of the march on the Pentagon written by a participant who is also one of America's foremost writers.

137. Moss, George, "The Vietnam Generation, 1964–1973," unpublished essay, 1984, p. 13; Baskir, Lawrence M., and Strauss, William A., *Chance and Circumstance: The Draft, the War and the Vietnam Generation* (New York: Random House, 1978), pp. 63, 79, 97.

138. Moss, "The Vietnam Generation," pp. 3–7. Between August 10, 1964, when President Johnson signed the Gulf of Tonkin Resolution formally making the Vietnam conflict an American war, and March 28, 1973, when the last American soldier exited Vietnam, about 27 million young men reached draft age; 16 million of them avoided military service. Of these 16 million, 9 million obtained deferments or exemptions, 4 million drew high lottery numbers during the two years that the lottery draft operated, and the other 3 million young men avoided military service because of the inefficiencies of the conscription system that lost, misfiled, or otherwise mishandled their files.

139. *Ibid.*, pp. 5–6; Baskir and Strauss, pp. 8–10.

140. Baskir and Strauss, *Chance and Circumstance*, pp. 62–90.

141. Moss, "The Vietnam Generation," p. 9.

142. Kimball, Jeffrey P., "The Stab-in-the-Back Legend and the Vietnam War," *Armed Forces and Society*, vol. 14 (Spring 1988), p. 449.

143. Moss, "News or Nemesis," pp. 86–92, 101–103.

144. Mueller, John E., *War, Presidents, and Public Opinion* (New York: John Wiley, 1973), pp. 136–140.

145. Moss, "News or Nemesis," p. 93.

146. Davidson, *Vietnam at War*, p. 451; Moss, "News or Nemesis," pp. 93–94.

147. Schuman, Howard, "Two Sources of Antiwar Sentiment in America," *American Journal of Sociology*, vol. 78 (Nov. 1972), pp. 519–535. The most frequent reasons pragmatic opponents of the war gave for their opposition were (1) the U.S. was not winning, (2) American soldiers were being killed, (3) U.S. resources were being wasted, and (4) the war was a Vietnamese responsibility. Few of these practical opponents of war raised any moral considerations about any aspect of the war or showed any concern about what the war might be doing to Vietnam

and its people. Schuman was also aware of the disjunctive relationship between the two antiwar currents: "extreme dislike of war protesters was shown by many people who...indicated their opposition to the war."

148. *Ibid.*, pp. 520–523, 528–532.

149. Converse, Philip E., and Schuman, Howard, "'Silent Majorities' and the Vietnam War," *Scientific American*, vol. 222 (June 1970), p. 24. The authors characterize the two antiwar cultures in these terms: "One current is made up of a tiny fraction of the population, but one that is highly educated, articulate, and visible. The other group tends to be less educated than the national average, and is much less politically visible, although it is far larger than the set of vocal critics—perhaps by a factor of 10 or more."

150. Schuman, "Two Sources of Antiwar Sentiment in America," p. 534–535. Schuman writes: "Public disillusionment with the war has grown despite the campus demonstrations, not because of them."

151. Mandelbaum, Michael, "Vietnam—The Television War," *Daedalus*, 111:4 (Fall, 1982), p. 165. The author cites the argument "that the antiwar movement had the *opposite* [emphasis his] effect from the one it intended, that it helped *prolong* [emphasis his] the American military presence in Vietnam."

152. Both quotes are from Herring, *America's Longest War*, p. 174.

153. Oberdorfer, Don, *Tet! The Turning Point in the Vietnam War* (New York: The Da Capo Press, 1971), pp. 79–81; Herring, *America's Longest War*, pp. 174–175; Mueller, *War, Presidents, and Public Opinion*, pp. 112–113. Three times during 1967 the Gallup poll asked people: "Do you think the Johnson administration is or is not telling the public all it should know about the Vietnam war?" Each time only 21 to 24 percent answered "yes," 65 to 70 percent answered "no."

154. Sheehan and others, "Westmoreland Cable to Joint Chiefs on Troop Needs," March 28, 1967, *Pentagon Papers*, Document 123, pp. 560–565. Had Westmoreland received his 200,000 troops, there would have been about 680,000 U.S. troops in Vietnam eventually; "Joint Chiefs Report to McNamara on Troops Needs," April 20, 1967, Document 124, pp. 565–567; and "Notes on Johnson's Discussion with Wheeler and Westmoreland," April 27, 1967, Document 125, pp. 567–569.

155. Karnow, *Vietnam*, pp. 507–508.

156. DeBenedetti, Charles, "A CIA Analysis of the Antiwar Movement: October 1967," *Peace and Change*, vol.9 (Spring 1983), pp. 31–41. According to the CIA report to Johnson on the peace activists, "Many have close Communist associations but they do not appear to be under Communist direction." Despite the report, Johnson met with a bipartisan congressional group including House minority leader Gerald Ford on October 24 and told them that he had a "secret" report that documented Communist control of the October 21 march on Washington.

157. Gitlin, Todd, *The Whole World Is Watching: Mass Media in the Making and Unmaking of the New Left* (Berkeley, Calif.: University of California Press, 1980), pp. 186–189.

158. Oberdorfer, *Tet!*, pp. 98–99.

159. Quoted in Karnow, *Vietnam*, p. 514; Schlandler, *The Unmaking of a President*, p. 62. Neither Westmoreland nor Johnson ever used the phrase, "we can see the light at the end of the tunnel." That cliché phrase was coined by Henry Cabot Lodge.

160. Quoted in Turner, *Lyndon Johnson's Dual War*, p. 205.

161. Dougan, Clark; Weiss, Stephen; and the editors of Boston Publishing Company, *Nineteen Sixty-Eight* (Boston: Boston Publishing Co., 1983), a volume in the series, *The Vietnam Experience*.

162. Schandler, *The Unmaking of a President*, p. 57; Small, Melvin, "The Impact of the Antiwar Movement on Lyndon Johnson, 1965–1968: A Preliminary Report, *Peace and Change*, vol. 10 (Spring 1984), pp. 1–22. Small suggests that the social conflict and disorder generated by the antiwar movement took its toll on Johnson. It was the prospect of political polarization that drove the alarmed and weary president to consider a change in strategy.

THE YEAR
OF THE MONKEY

7

For twenty years first the French and then Americans have been predict-ing victory in Vietnam. But for twenty years we have been wrong. The history of conflict among nations does not record another such lengthy and consistent chronicle of error. It is time to discard so proven a fallacy and face the reality that a military victory is not in sight, and that it probably will never come.

Robert Kennedy

SURPRISE ATTACK!

Taking advantage of the cease-fire called to celebrate Tet, the beginning of the lunar new year and Vietnam's most important holiday, 84,000 enemy soldiers launched simultaneous attacks on South Vietnam's major towns and cities during the early morning hours of January 30, 1968.[1] They attacked the national capital, 36 of 44 provincial capitals, and 64 of 242 district capitals. Within South Vietnam's beleaguered towns and cities, ARVN forces, their ranks depleted by the absence of many soldiers who went home for the holidays, fought to defend governmental and military installations, the major targets of the enemy assaults. Neither the South Vietnamese nor the American military commands had anticipated the timing, the intensity, the scale, or the level of coordination achieved by the PLAF/NVA Tet-68 Offensive.[2]

Although caught by surprise, GVN and U.S. troops quickly recovered and counterattacked effectively. Nearly everywhere they repulsed the attackers quickly, usually inflicting severe losses. General Westmoreland quickly judged the Communist offensive to be a complete military failure.[3] Tet-68, the largest and most important campaign of the American Vietnam war, amounted to a major tactical defeat for the Vietcong and NVA forces.

But news of the Tet *coup de main* broke like a thunderclap across America. The fact that the enemy could mount a major military effort all over South Vietnam and catch the allies by surprise shattered all illusions of impending American victory in the war. Tet suggested that all the years of bombing, of attrition warfare, of pacification, of body counts, and of official claims that America was winning the war had not meant a thing. In the wake of Tet, many shocked, angry, and confused Americans realized that the United States had involved itself in a stalemated war in Southeast Asia. Although suffering major tactical reverses, Hanoi scored a decisive psychological and thus a political victory over the United States and its GVN allies.[4] Tet constituted a major turning point in the Vietnam war. After Tet-68, President Johnson felt compelled to scale down the bombing of North Vietnam and to put a ceiling on the number of U.S. troops committed to South Vietnam. After Tet, America could not win the Vietnam war on any politically acceptable terms.

Hanoi had been planning the Tet campaign since the spring of 1967. Tet-68 was a belated response to the Americanization of the war that had occurred in the summer of 1965. Washington's decisions in July 1965 to escalate the conflict in South Vietnam posed a severe challenge to the Vietnamese revolution. Given American firepower, the Communist leaders understood that any effort on their part to match Westmoreland's strategy of attrition would cost them heavy casualties and would also run the risk of extending the war to North Vietnam. But if they did not respond vigorously to the American threat, the Communist leaders feared that the southern insurgency could be discouraged or even defeated, postponing the achievement of Hanoi's goals of revolution and reunification of the country.[5]

The decision to respond to the U.S. military buildup was made in December 1965 at the Twelfth Plenum of the Central Committee of the Lao Dong meeting in Hanoi. Knowing that they probably could not defeat the Americans militarily, Hanoi's leadership opted for a strategy of protracted struggle. Eschewing the possibility of military victory in the near future, they discerned two enemy political weaknesses that they believed they could exploit: the inherent instability of the Saigon regime and the potential softness of public support for the Vietnam war within the United States.[6] Hanoi's leaders knew that the introduction of American combat forces had not eliminated the underlying political weaknesses of the GVN, and they expected that their propaganda efforts would fan the flames of antiwar sentiment within the United States that had surfaced at the time Johnson took America to war.

To exploit these perceived weaknesses, the directive issued at the close of the Twelfth Plenum called for the Lao Dong to mobilize the armed forces and the people to

> foil the war of aggression of the U.S. imperialists…, so as to defend the North, liberate the South, complete the national people's democratic revolution in the whole country, advancing toward the peaceful reunification of the country.[7]

Senior NVA military commanders, including General Giap, publicly endorsed the Politburo's strategy of protracted warfare, which amounted to countering Westmoreland's strategy of attrition with an attrition strategy of their own. They aimed at keeping the tactical initiative, keeping pressure on both the American and GVN forces, and inflicting a high level of costs and casualties on both. The implementation of Communist-style attrition warfare in the South was the prime responsibility of one of its chief advocates, General Nguyen Thi Thanh, the aggressive commander of the PLAF forces.[8]

Throughout 1966 and into 1967, General Thanh vigorously pursued Hanoi's protracted warfare strategy. It proved to be a disappointment. The Communists incurred severe losses while attaining few desirable strategic or political results. U.S. forces won all major battles. American troop levels continued to increase, and Westmoreland aggressively pursued his big-unit style of attrition warfare. The U.S. antiwar movement had no discernible impact on Johnson's determination to bomb North Vietnam or on his decision to fight a gradually escalating ground war. Thanh's strategy also failed to induce Washington to seek a negotiated solution. The GVN, with all of its deficiencies, appeared to be more stable in the spring of 1967 than when Hanoi had implemented the protracted war strategy. Many Vietcong units and some NVA units fighting in South Vietnam had been decimated. Others had been driven out of South Vietnam or forced to take refuge in sparsely populated peripheral areas in the central highlands. The NLF infrastructure controlled fewer villages and less territory in South Vietnam than it had at the time when the Twelfth Plenum had decided to fight attrition with attrition.[9]

Disappointed with the results of the protracted war strategy and convinced that victory could come only from a combined general offensive and popular rising of the South Vietnamese, Hanoi's leaders, in the spring of 1967, decided that a major offensive should be launched the following year. General Thanh took charge of the planning until his death, which might have resulted from U.S. bombing, on July 6, 1967. Planning for the new strategy continued under his successor, General Pham Hung. Final approval of the general offensive/general uprising was given at the Lao Dong's Fourteenth Plenum held in November.[10]

Hanoi's leadership persuaded itself that the political situation in South Vietnam had evolved to a point where a revolutionary uprising could occur in response to a successful Communist offensive. They viewed the Buddhist revolt that had taken place in Danang and Hue during the spring of 1966 as an indicator that the GVN was ripe for overthrowing. The Communist leaders expected the military victories achieved during the intended offensive to trigger an uprising which would be led in the towns and cities by Vietcong organizers.[11] If the general uprising succeeded, the GVN would be overthrown. It would be replaced by a coalition government dominated by the NLF. There would be a cease-fire, and the Americans would be forced to withdraw from South Vietnam. The country could then proceed toward reunification and the completion of its national revolution that the Vietminh had begun in 1945.

Lao Dong leaders believed that the offensive strategy had a reasonable chance of success. Even if it fell short of total victory, they expected it to discourage the United States and to shake the foundations of the GVN by undermining the faith of the South Vietnamese in the ability of their own government to protect them, "thus increasing the likelihood of a negotiated settlement favorable to the revolutionary cause."[12] Neither desperate nor overconfident, the Communist leaders saw their strategy of the General Offensive-General Uprising (Tong Cong Kich-Tong Khoi Nghia, or TCK-TKN) as a calculated gamble. It would replace the strategy of protracted warfare that had shown little promise of achieving desired goals after more than two years of bloody efforts. Most of North Vietnam's aging revolutionary leaders viewed the new strategy as a risk worth taking.

The Communists launched phase one of TCK-TKN in October 1967 with a series of assaults along the periphery of South Vietnam. They struck at Song Be and Loc Ninh near the Cambodian border, at Dak To in the central highlands, and at Con Thien, just south of the DMZ. Their goals were to inflict casualties and to draw the U.S. forces away from populated areas to these sparsely populated border regions, which would leave the urban populations of South Vietnam unprotected from the Tet assaults planned for phase two. These peripheral attacks were powerful, fighting was fierce, and casualties were heavy on both sides. In every area, the Communists were beaten and forced to retreat to their cross-border sanctuaries. Communist losses, though substantial, achieved their strategic purpose; they induced Westmoreland to move U.S. and ARVN forces away from populated areas.[13]

By late fall 1967, the U.S. military command in Saigon, noting that the rate of infiltration down the Ho Chi Minh trail had increased sharply, suspected that the Communists were preparing for a major offensive early in 1968. Captured enemy documents and interrogations of VC and NVA defectors confirmed these suspicions. Westmoreland concluded that the main enemy offensive would occur in I Corps, just south of the DMZ. He believed that the Communists would try to capture the two northernmost provinces of South Vietnam, Quang Tri and Thua Thien, that were separated from the rest of South Vietnam by mountains reaching to the sea. Westmoreland strengthened the U.S. forces at Khe Sanh and other forward bases near the DMZ. He did not consider Saigon or the other cities of South Vietnam to

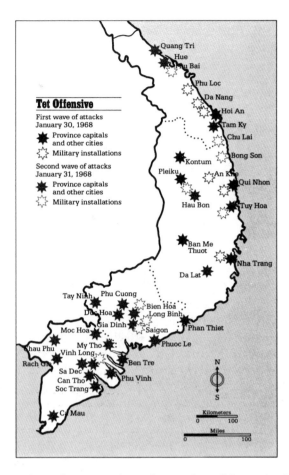

Tet Offensive

First wave of attacks
January 30, 1968
★ Province capitals and other cities
☆ Military installations

Second wave of attacks
January 31, 1968
★ Province capitals and other cities
☆ Military installations

be facing any serious dangers. As a show of confidence in the improving South Vietnamese forces, MACV had entrusted the defense of Saigon and other urban areas to ARVN.[14]

On January 10, Lieutenant General Frederick Weyand, commander of III Corps, warned Westmoreland that intelligence data indicated that the enemy was shifting his forces from the border regions to Saigon and to other cities in South Vietnam. Weyand's views were confirmed by General Philip Davidson, the head of MACV's intelligence division. In response to these warnings, Westmoreland moved some U.S. forces to the vicinity of Saigon and placed others in the corridors running from the border toward the capital. He also persuaded General Thieu to keep half his ARVN forces on duty during the Tet holidays. These precautionary moves possibly saved Saigon from an enemy takeover during Tet. But Westmoreland remained convinced that the major enemy push would come in the north and that it would occur before the Tet holidays.[15]

The hole in the wall of the U.S. embassy compound in downtown Saigon blasted by a suicide squad of Vietcong sappers at the start of the Tet-68 offensive. Americans, led to believe that the enemy was verging on defeat, were shocked by this violent assault on the American citadel. *Source*: U.S. Army Photo

Phase two of TCK-TKN, which Americans knew as the Tet-68 Offensive, began on the morning of January 30 when PLAF/NVA forces launched a nationwide assault on South Vietnam's cities and towns. At 2:45 a. m., a team of Vietcong commandos blasted a hole in the wall surrounding the U.S. Embassy compound in downtown Saigon and entered the courtyard. They battled a detachment of American military police for the next six and one-half hours in the courtyard before all the VC were killed or captured. Although it was of no tactical consequence and it resulted in a quick defeat for the Vietcong as did most of the Tet battles, the firefight inside embassy walls had a dramatic impact within the United States. Americans were shocked to learn that an enemy who was supposedly on his last legs could bring the war to the symbolic heart of American power within South Vietnam's capital.[16]

Within hours of the embassy assault, other Vietcong forces attacked targets in or near Saigon, including the presidential palace, the headquarters of both MACV and the South Vietnamese joint general staff, and the GVN's radio station. In every instance the attackers were driven off and suffered heavy losses. Some ARVN units, under severe pressure, fought effectively. They were reinforced by U.S. troops, who used their superior firepower to inflict severe casualties on the outgunned Vietcong. Nothing remotely resembling a popular rising occurred.[17]

But the Vietcong's Tet attacks left Saigon's inhabitants shocked and dazed. Their sense of security, their feeling that they were safe from a remote conflict that only engulfed the countryside, had been shattered as they experienced the contagion of war firsthand. The fighting within the city, particularly the use of American firepower, did extensive damage to sections of Saigon. Thousands of families were left homeless in the wake of the fighting that had saved them from a possible Communist takeover.

Everywhere in South Vietnam, from the DMZ in the north to the Ca Mau Peninsula in the south, local Vietcong units attacked urban centers in force. In Nha Trang, a coastal city of 120,000 located about 180 miles north of Saigon, enemy soldiers attacked a naval training center. VC forces struck targets in Kontum and Pleiku, two central highlands cities. At Danang, ARVN and U.S. forces, alerted by a VC defector that an attack was imminent, met the enemy on the outskirts of the city. In none of these assaults did the attackers accomplish their missions. They were driven back everywhere with heavy losses.[18]

In the Mekong delta, that vast, flat, green, and watery expanse that constituted South Vietnam's rice bowl, the Vietcong attacked thirteen of sixteen provincial capitals and many of the district capitals. ARVN forces generally performed ineffectively in the delta region, and American forces had to be rushed to many towns and cities to drive out the attackers. An estimated 5,000 VC were killed and hundreds captured during the fighting in the delta. Most of the local guerrillas and political cadres were wiped out during phase two.[19]

The ferocity of the fighting during Tet climaxed at Hue. In a battle lasting a month, two NVA regiments and two VC elite battalions battled eight American and thirteen ARVN battalions in one of the most savage battles of this or any other war. "The furor of the Tet-68 Offensive would become symbolized by the catastrophic destruction incurred in this grim city struggle."[20]

Located near the coast midway between Danang and the DMZ, Hue had an official population of 100,000, which was swollen by the influx of thousands of war refugees, at the time of the Tet-68 Offensive. The Perfume River runs through the city, with two-thirds of the population living north of the river, mostly within the walls of the Citadel (Old City), and one-third residing south of the river in the westernized New City. Until Tet, Hue had remained free of war. Both sides had treated it with respect, and Hue was considered an open city.[21] There was a sizeable U.S. presence in Hue, and many other foreigners lived and worked there. It was the most beautiful of Vietnam's cities, with its unique blend of traditional and cosmopolitan cultures.

On the morning of January 31, the NVA/VC forces, achieving complete tactical surprise, overwhelmed the ARVN defenders and took control of the Citadel and much of the New City within a few hours. Two U.S. Marine companies from Phu Bai, a few miles to the south of Hue, joined with ARVN forces to counterattack the next day. The counterattack stalled in the face of determined NVA/VC resistance. Over the next few days, both the Americans and South Vietnamese augmented their forces in Hue. Starting February 5, naval gunfire from ships of the Seventh Fleet, which was positioned offshore, pounded targets inside the Citadel from a range of fifteen miles.

A Marine emerges through a blown wall during hand-to-hand fighting in the streets of Hue, February 6, 1968.
Source: U.S. Marine Corps Photo

Both VNAF and U.S. aircraft napalmed and strafed targets within the Old City. On the ground, Marine rifle companies advanced grimly from house to house in savage fighting.[22]

By February 9 the Marines had reclaimed the sectors of the city lying south of the river. ARVN units had reclaimed much of the Citadel. But in the southeastern sector of the Citadel, including the Imperial Palace, the NVA/VC forces held a series of strong points. The Communists inflicted heavy casualties on the attacking South Vietnamese. The hard-pressed ARVN troops were joined by elements of the 1st Battalion, 5th Regiment, U.S. Marines, on February 12. For days the carnage of close combat took a deadly toll on both the ARVN forces and the Marines of the 1st/5. On February 24, elements of the 3rd ARVN Regiment raised the RVN flag over the Citadel and the battered remains of the Palace of Perfect Peace. It took the Allies another week of scattered fighting to crush isolated pockets of resistance and to round up NVA/VC stragglers. The Battle of Hue ended March 2, 1968. Over 8,000 soldiers on both sides died in the month-long battle. Seventy-five percent of the city's population was rendered homeless. The stench of death hovered over the littered landscape. The exhausted survivors gazed in horror at the remains of Hue, the once-proud and lovely imperial city, that "had been blasted into corpse-strewn rubble."[23] Hue had been saved, but destroyed.

Concurrent with the Battle of Hue, the Communists had occupied Gia Hoi, a sector of the city lying north of the Perfume River and east of the walled Citadel. Within Gia Hoi the Communists established a provisional government of sorts and set about implementing their revolution. Cadres held rallies, made speeches, and organized groups of students, workers, and teachers into administrative units. The Communists also applied terror. They purged Gia Hoi of all "reactionary elements" by liquidating anyone who had an affiliation with the Saigon regime. They executed about 2800 people, often in brutal fashion, or they buried them alive. They sent a stark message: No one associated with the GVN was safe from insurgent reprisals anywhere in South Vietnam.[24]

The victims of Communist "hit squads" included officials of the national government, city officials, civil servants, community leaders, military personnel, police, priests, and teachers. Foreign victims included many Americans, Germans, Filipinos, Koreans, and nationals of other countries. In November 1969, President Nixon cited the Communist mass murders committed during their Tet-68 occupation of Hue as a justification for his policy of gradually withdrawing American troops from South Vietnam. He asserted that if the U.S. withdrew its forces precipitously, as many Americans were demanding, that the massacre at Hue would become a prelude for a nightmare, a bloodbath of massive proportions.[25]

Before the Battle of Hue ran its course, the Communists had launched phase three of TCK-TKN in a remote corner of Quang Tri province, sixty miles northwest of the battered former imperial city. Two elite PAVN

A group of U.S. Marine 106 mmm. recoilless riflemen take cover from heavy Vietcong fire during an intense moment of the fighting in Hue.
Source: U.S. Marine Corps Photo

Khe Sahn,...A panoramic view of the sand-bagged perimeter bunkers. U.S. Marine defenders held on to the remote outpost lying below the DMZ during a 77-day siege by North Vietnamese regulars.
Source: U.S. Air Force Photo

divisions, the 304th and 325-C, lay siege to the Marine base at Khe Sanh. The base, perched on a plateau near the corner formed by the DMZ and the Laotian border, blocked enemy infiltration along Route 9. It could also be used to stage an invasion of Laos to cut the Ho Chi Minh trail at a key choke point near Tchepone if America chose to expand the war. Four Marine battalions of the 26th Marines under the command of Colonel David E. Lownds, reinforced by one battalion of ARVN Rangers, 6,000 men total, defended the main base and surrounding hill strong points at Khe Sanh. They faced an estimated 30,000–40,000 crack PAVN troopers.

General Giap had planned phase three to be the capstone of TCK-TKN. If the phase two attacks on the cities succeeded in bringing about popular uprisings and the collapse of the Saigon regime, Giap's divisions would try to drive the U.S. Marines out of Khe Sanh. If the NVA forces succeeded, they could end the Second Indochina War with a stunning military victory.[26]

The Battle of Khe Sanh received extensive media coverage within the United States. Americans feared for the lives of the Marines, who were crowded into their isolated outpost, subjected to intensive artillery and mortar bombardments, and seemingly in danger of being overrun. Journalists noted uneasily that Khe Sanh resembled Dien Bien Phu, the French fortress that the Vietminh had isolated and overrun in May 1954. The fall of Dien Bien Phu had been a catastrophic defeat for the French. It had destroyed their will to continue the Franco-Vietminh war. Would history repeat itself at Khe Sanh? Would the United States suffer its first major defeat of the Second Indochina War? If such a military disaster occurred, would it be the end of the American Vietnam war? President Johnson fretted that Khe Sanh might be lost to the Communists. Asserting that he did not want "any damn Dinbinfoo" on his watch, Johnson anxiously raised the possibility of using tactical nuclear weapons at Khe Sanh if the enemy verged on overrunning it.[27]

The fears of the journalists and President Johnson were exaggerated. Khe Sanh bore only a superficial resemblance to Dien Bien Phu, and there was never any serious danger of the NVA forces overrunning the base or of driving out the Marines. General Giap had been able to defeat the French at Dien Bien Phu in 1954 for two major reasons: He had had superior firepower, and he had been able to cut the aerial lifeline to the fortress. But, at Khe Sanh, the combination of American air power and artillery fire gave the Americans a vast superiority over the NVA forces, and Giap's forces could not interdict Westmoreland's air supply system to the base. In fact, one of the reasons Westmoreland had installed the Marines at Khe Sanh was because he hoped to lure Giap into a set-piece battle. Confident that the Marines, supported by artillery and bombers, could hold the base against whatever forces the NVA committed to battle, Westmoreland viewed Khe Sanh as the ideal place to call the awesome American firepower into play. If Giap's forces took the bait and tried to overrun Khe Sanh, Westmoreland believed that they would be obliterated by artillery fire and bombing.[28]

The siege of Khe Sanh began on the morning of January 20 when NVA forces hit the base and its hilly outposts with barrages of artillery, rocket, and mortar fire. The Battle of Khe Sanh developed as a full-scale conventional campaign fought between two national armies in an important arena of the war. The I Corps Tactical Zone, consisting of the five northernmost provinces of South Vietnam (Quang Nam, Quang Tin, and Quang Ngai, in addition to Quang Tri and Thua Thien) was the largest and most complex combat area in South Vietnam. Within that region the enemy mounted a potent mix of insurgent and conventional tactics that often put severe pressures on the allied forces. During 1967 the fighting in I Corps accounted for half the enemy KIAs and the Marines suffered half of the U.S. KIAs.[29]

Westmoreland reacted to Giap's siege of Khe Sanh by executing Operation NIAGARA, which had been prepared for use against the NVA in the event they attacked the base. NIAGARA represented a mighty concentration of firepower composed of B-52s, tactical aircraft, and artillery directed at the enemy positions.[30] As the Battle of Khe Sanh unfolded, artillery duels between PAVN and Marine gunners, around-the-clock air raids on the NVA positions, and periodic vicious firefights whenever enemy units attacked one of the surrounding strong points were daily occurrences. On February 7 a

Special Forces camp at Lang Vei, south of Khe Sanh, was destroyed by NVA forces using Soviet PT-76 light tanks. It was during the Khe Sanh campaign that the enemy first used armor in South Vietnam. The loss of Lang Vei enabled the NVA to put more pressure on the Marines defending Khe Sanh. Three weeks later the key battle of the Khe Sanh campaign took place. From February 29 to March 1, following the heaviest enemy artillery barrage of the campaign, a regiment of the NVA 304th attacked Khe Sanh from the east. But U.S. artillery and bombers cut the regiment to pieces before any of its units reached the base perimeter.[31]

The destruction of the 304th regiment marked the turning point in the battle. Although there were harassing attacks made by the enemy over the next several days, the NVA mounted no more major assaults. The PAVN forces began withdrawing by March 11. Giap apparently decided to pull his forces back from Khe Sanh because of the failure of the phase two campaigns and because he had concluded that the U.S. forces could not be beaten at Khe Sanh. Scattered fighting occurred in the vicinity of the base until the end of the month. A relief force of Marines and Air Cavalry troops reached Khe Sanh on April 8, allowing Colonel Lownds and his Marines to leave the base. Their ordeal had ended. The siege of Khe Sanh had lasted seventy-seven days; it had claimed the lives of more than 200 Marines. Estimated NVA losses totaled 1,602 KIA.[32]

In addition to their losses at Khe Sanh, the countrywide assaults during the Tet-68 Offensive cost the attackers horrendous casualties. From January 29 through March 31, 1968, combined Vietcong and PAVN losses were estimated at 58,000. The Vietcong, who had staged most of the attacks, "were largely destroyed as an effective military menace to the South Vietnamese government."[33] After Tet, the VC were generally limited to minor skirmishes. The PLAF main force units had to be reconstituted by using NVA regulars infiltrated south down the Ho Chi Minh trail.

In many provinces, many of those in the Vietcong political infrastructure, which had been painstakingly erected over the years, were also killed or captured during the Tet-68 battles. The VC cadres had come out into the open to organize and to lead the uprisings that were expected to follow the assaults on the towns and cities. The expected uprisings never materialized, and the VC cadres were eliminated. Nowhere in South Vietnam did risings occur. Nowhere in South Vietnam were the Vietcong welcomed by the South Vietnamese people, nor did any defections from GVN political or military ranks occur. In fact, the ARVN forces fought well despite being caught by surprise.[34] After Tet there was no chance that the Saigon regime would be overthrown by a revolution from within South Vietnam. After the spring of 1968, the Vietnam war became, for the most part, a conventional war between the main forces units of the allies and the PLAF/NVA.

U.S. military leaders in Washington and Saigon considered Tet-68 to be the greatest tactical victory of the war for the U.S. and ARVN forces. In the wake of his greatest success, having taken advantage of an opportunity to hurt the enemy badly, General Westmoreland was eager to mount a major counteroffensive and to win the war.[35] But Tet-68 proved to be the great paradox of the American Vietnam war. Tet brought Americans defeat encased within victory. Tet turned out to be a short-term U.S. victory that prepared the way for the long-run defeat of the American cause in Southeast Asia.

POLITICAL CRISIS

The scope, scale, and intensity of the Vietcong Tet offensive shocked most Americans. Nightly, television news beamed the sights and sounds of fierce battles in the streets of Saigon and Hue into American living rooms. Viewers watched Vietcong commandos fighting inside the American embassy compound; they witnessed the summary execution of a Vietcong terrorist by General Nguyen Ngoc Loan, chief of South Vietnam's National Police, on a cobblestone street in Saigon. Daily press reports filed from cities all over South Vietnam highlighted the surprise attacks and the extensive destruction that they caused. Initial wire stories, later corrected, exaggerated the Communist successes, and contributed to a widely shared sense that Tet had been an allied disaster.[36]

A quotation from an Associated Press report had tremendous impact. On February 7, Air Force Major, Chester I. Brown, conducted a press tour through the shattered Mekong delta town of Ben Tre. The town had been occupied by the VC. U.S. troops were called in to reclaim the town. In order to eject the VC, the Americans used heavy artillery and helicopter gunships that leveled most of the town's buildings and killed many of its inhabitants. Surveying the remains of Ben Tre, Brown matter-of-factly told AP reporter Peter Arnett, "It became necessary to destroy the town to save it."[37]

Major Brown's phrase encapsulated a basic contradiction of the U.S. war effort in South Vietnam. Americans were fighting in Vietnam to protect the freedom of the South Vietnamese people and to enable them to build a nation. But U.S. weaponry was destroying the South Vietnamese society in the process of trying to liberate it. The military means overwhelmed the political ends. For the people of Ben Tre, the existential alternative to rule by the Vietcong was death and destruction at the hands of their saviors. If America had to destroy its friends in order to save them, of what use was the war to us, or, *a fortiori*, to our friends? The anonymous major's remark gained wide currency in the United States and became one of the staples of antiwar discourse for years.

While the media stressed the surprising power of the enemy offensive, official cables to Johnson and other leaders in Washington presented a more realistic account of Tet-68. From his reading of the secret cable traffic, Johnson knew that the Vietcong had suffered heavy casualties, that the

ARVN troops were fighting effectively, that the people were not rallying to the NLF banner, and that the enemy attacks were failing almost everywhere. Johnson, knowing that Tet was an allied tactical victory, tried to counter the sensational media coverage and to reassure the American people.[38] He held a press conference on February 2 to convince the public that the Tet Offensive had failed. Administrative officials appeared on public affairs programs and made speeches around the country to convey the message that Tet was a great allied victory and a disastrous Communist defeat.

The Johnson administration's public relations efforts to salvage popular support for the U.S. Vietnam war policy in the aftermath of the Tet assaults failed. Much of the press and the public continued to regard Tet as a disaster. What administration spokesmen did not understand was that it was not that journalists or the American people thought that the Communists were winning the Tet battles. That was not the problem. The public was shocked by the fact that the Tet offensive had occurred, that it could occur. The very fact that it had occurred made Tet a psychological disaster in this country, that the enemy could mount and execute a surprise offensive of massive proportions all over the country under the noses of U.S. and South Vietnamese officials. Tet-68 exploded all the official reassurances that the U.S. was winning the war, that the Vietcong were on their way out, and that the war would end soon. To most Americans, Tet confirmed what many of them already suspected, that the Johnson administration had not been telling the truth, that America had become involved in an endless war that was consuming ever-rising numbers of lives and dollars.

Despite their outward show of confidence, Johnson and his senior advisers had been shaken by the scale, scope, and intensity of the Communist Tet-68 Offensive. They were also alarmed by the prospect of further offensives in South Vietnam and by Communist initiatives in other parts of the world. On January 23, just before Tet, the North Koreans had suddenly seized an intelligence-gathering ship, USS *Pueblo*, operating near their coast, after having tolerated such espionage operations for years. About the same time, South Korean police discovered an assassination plot against South Korean president Chung Hee Park that was masterminded in North Korea. CIA operatives warned that the Soviets might provoke another crisis over Berlin, a perennial Cold War flash point. Washington also received reports of increased unrest in the Middle East.[39] Johnson may have thought that the Tet-68 attacks, including the siege at Khe Sanh, constituted parts of a worldwide Communist effort to score Cold War victories over America and its allies.

Johnson's military advisers responded to Tet by proposing to widen the war. The Joint Chiefs wanted to expand the bombing campaign against North Vietnam. Johnson, concerned above all with holding Khe Sanh, refused to take any additional military actions against North Vietnam. He asked General Westmoreland if he needed any additional troops to prevent a defeat at Khe Sanh. Westmoreland, confident that he could hold the fort with what he had, replied that he did not need any more combat troops. But he was concerned about his logistic ability to support the forces that he had committed to I Corps, and he requested some additional airlift and helicopter support.[40]

In early February 1968, General Wheeler, the chairman of the Joint Chiefs, was thinking about much more than Vietnam. In Johnson's willingness to send Westmoreland whatever additional forces he might need to avoid a politically damaging defeat at Khe Sanh, Wheeler saw an opportunity to rebuild the American strategic reserve and to replenish U.S. military forces stationed elsewhere in the world. The deployments to Vietnam had not been based on the military demands of the situation, but on the forces available without calling up the strategic reserve in the United States, the Reserves and the National Guard. NATO forces assigned to Germany and the forces committed to South Korea had been depleted.[41] These forces had all been skeletonized, stripped of their best officers and non-coms, in order to send more troops to the Vietnam War.

Faced with Communist threats in North Korea and Berlin, and maybe elsewhere, the Joint Chiefs had concluded that U.S. strategic assets had been stretched too thin. General Wheeler, believing that Tet would force Johnson's hand, thought that he could persuade Johnson to take the politically risky step of mobilizing the reserves and of putting the country on a full war footing. Wheeler maneuvered Westmoreland, who had initially declined Johnson's offer of more combat troops, into requesting additional forces. Then the Joint Chiefs put pressure on Johnson to provide the forces not only for Vietnam but to restock the stateside strategic reserve so that the military would be better positioned to meet Communist threats to U.S. interests elsewhere.[42] They were disappointed when Johnson deferred their request to mobilize the reserves and agreed to send General Westmoreland a force of only 10,500 troops, which could be provided without calling up the Reserve.

Wheeler pursued his goal of a reserve mobilization, which he believed to be necessary to enable the United States to meet the military demands of the Vietnam War and to fulfill its other strategic commitments in a dangerous world. He obtained Johnson's approval to travel to Vietnam to assess General Westmoreland's immediate and future manpower needs. After conferring, Westmoreland and Wheeler came up with a planned troop request designed to meet both MACV's Vietnam needs and to defend other American interests in the world. The troop request was composed of three force packages: The first increment of 108,000 men would be sent to Vietnam by May 1, 1968. Additional increments of 42,000 and 56,000 men would be sent by September 1 and December 1, respectively, 206,000 men total. But only the first increment would be sent to Vietnam for sure. The other two increments would constitute the strategic reserve in the United States, which was not to be deployed in Vietnam unless the North Vietnamese mounted a successful offensive.[43]

Wheeler presented the troop request to Johnson and his advisers on February 28, 1968. Wheeler accompanied his report with a pessimistic appraisal of the military situation in Vietnam that contradicted General Westmoreland's previous optimistic appraisals. Wheeler told Johnson that the initial Tet attacks nearly succeeded in a dozen places, that the ARVN forces had been thrown on the defensive, and that pacification had suffered setbacks. "In short it was a very near thing."[44] Wheeler also told Johnson and his advisers that Westmoreland would need to augment his forces significantly if he was to respond effectively to the challenges posed by Tet-68: to counter the enemy offensive, to eject the NVA forces fighting in I Corps, to restore security to the towns and cities, to restore security in the populated regions of the countryside, and to regain the initiative with a counteroffensive of his own. To accomplish all these objectives, Wheeler insisted that Westmoreland would require large numbers of additional troops.[45] By accentuating the negative aspects of the military situation in Vietnam, Wheeler tried to frighten Johnson and other senior officials into supporting a call-up of the reserves, part of which would be used to replenish depleted U.S. force levels elsewhere, which was the Joint Chiefs' major objective.

The magnitude of the troop request stunned Johnson and his civilian advisers, and Wheeler's pessimistic assessment of Tet alarmed them. The departing secretary of defense, Robert McNamara, the *bete noire* of the military hawks to the end, "in his valedictory meeting as a member of the cabinet," strongly opposed sending more U.S. troops to Vietnam. McNamara said that feeding another 200,000 soldiers into combat would merely be doing more of the same. They would make no difference. The North Vietnamese, as they had previously, would simply match the American escalation with one of their own. They certainly had the capability of doing so. McNamara pointed out that bombing had consistently failed to impair the Communists' ability to infiltrate whatever men and supplies they required. He believed that the key to improving the situation in South Vietnam was not to send more U.S. troops but to increase the resources and responsibilities of the South Vietnamese army.[46]

At the February 28 meeting, General Wheeler confronted the president with two bitterly unattractive choices. If Johnson met the Army's request for an additional 206,000 troops, it would mean transcending the parameters of limited war. The Reserves would have to be mobilized to provide the manpower, and the economy would have to be put on a war footing to meet the vastly increased expenditures. That would mean tax increases and probably economic controls. Worse, Johnson would have to take these politically unpalatable actions in an election year, and at a time of rising domestic opposition and disillusionment with the war and his leadership. But if he refused the Wheeler–Westmoreland request to increase troops levels in Vietnam by 40 percent, he would be sending a clear signal to friends and foes alike that the upper limits of the American military commitment in South

Vietnam had been reached. He would be acknowledging that American strategic goals had either been abandoned or pushed far into the future.[47] Further, with U.S. military forces stationed around the world having already been stretched dangerously thin to provide the 536,000 troops currently in Vietnam, failure to meet the Army's request for 206,000 additional soldiers might render the U.S. government incapable of responding effectively to threats to its strategic interests elsewhere.

Johnson, shocked by General Wheeler's report, refused to make such a critical decision on the spot. He asked his new secretary of defense, Clark M. Clifford, who was attending the meeting, to head a study group to examine all facets of the troop request. Johnson solemnly told Clifford to study the matter thoroughly and carefully, then to give him "the lesser of evils."[48]

Johnson's directive to Clifford inaugurated the most important debate over what action to take in Vietnam ever undertaken within any administration during the long history of U.S. involvement in Southeast Asia. For the first time there would be an agonizing reappraisal of all aspects of the U.S. Vietnam war policy. During the reassessment process, hawks and doves waged a bureaucratic war for the heart and mind of Lyndon Johnson. At stake was nothing less than the future course of the Vietnam war and its eventual outcome. Everyone at the meeting that day sensed that a decisive moment in the war had arrived. They also knew that Clark Clifford was the man who was going to determine on which side of the historic divide President Johnson would choose to walk.

Clifford, although a newcomer to Johnson's inner circle, was a seasoned Democratic party insider and elder statesmen. He had managed Harry Truman's 1948 campaign when the feisty president had scored his famous upset over the consensus favorite, Thomas Dewey. Clifford had also been a valued adviser of President John F. Kennedy. Prior to appointing him to replace McNamara, Johnson had often sought Clifford's advice on a whole range of issues.[49] Clifford was an establishment centrist who had embraced the Cold War ideology characteristic of his generation of political leaders. He had supported Johnson's Vietnam war policy since its inception. Johnson brought Clifford on board as McNamara's replacement primarily because he had assumed that his new defense secretary would continue to back his war policy.

Unknown to Johnson, Clifford had already begun to have doubts about the validity of the domino theory, which was the chief ideological prop for the American war effort in Vietnam. In September 1967, Johnson had sent Clifford to accompany Maxwell Taylor on a trip to Asia to persuade several of the American allies in that region to increase their troop commitments in Vietnam. Clifford was surprised to learn that the leaders of Thailand, the Philippines, South Korea, New Zealand, and Australia neither wished to send more troops to Vietnam nor felt particularly threatened by the fact that North Vietnam had over 100,000 troops in South Vietnam. Clifford asked himself, If these Asian and Pacific island nations proximate to the Vietnam war felt no fear of Communist expansion, could it be that U.S. officials had exaggerated the potential threat to the stability of these countries posed by the Communist revolution in Vietnam?[50] The man whom Johnson thought to be a hawk was questioning the ideological rationale for the Vietnam war at the time he replaced McNamara. When Clifford had completed his reappraisal of the Vietnam war policy, he was convinced that it must be changed. Clifford, the putative hawk, had been transformed into a dove.

To complete the task Johnson had given him, Clifford quickly formed a task force, which included several of the president's senior civilian and military advisers, Dean Rusk, Secretary of the Treasury Henry H. Fowler, Undersecretary of Defense Paul Nitze, the Director of the CIA Richard Helms, National Security Adviser Walt Whitman Rostow, General Wheeler and General Taylor. The Clifford Task Force turned immediately to examining the Army's request for 206,000 additional troops as well as the means by which it could be met. The problem was that all previous troop requests had been fulfilled without mobilizing reserve forces. But it was precisely this political barrier which would have to be broken to meet the military's latest demands. Such a large troop increase would also have an adverse impact on the economy and would require large cuts in governmental spending elsewhere. Sizeable cuts would have to be made in Great Society programs. Foreign aid would be gutted.[51] To meet the military's latest request for more guns, Clifford was shocked to discover that Johnson would have to surrender a lot of butter.

As the task force members studied the troop request problem, Clifford began to ask fundamental questions about the American Vietnam policy, many of which were questions that Johnson had never raised, and questions that were exceedingly difficult to answer. By raising these basic issues, Clifford broadened the task force's focus. Although the task force had been formed to study the military's request for more troops, it began to reappraise the entire American Vietnam war effort. For Clifford, the real question was not how to send 206,000 more troops to Vietnam, rather it was should America continue on its present course in Vietnam? Clifford raised other fundamental questions about the American war policy and found that senior civilian and military officials either could not provide answers or else furnished him with dismaying answers:[52]

1. Will 200,000 more troops win the war? No one could be sure.
2. If not, how many more will be needed to win and when? No one knew.
3. Can the enemy respond with a buildup of their own? They could and they probably would.
4. What would be involved in committing 200,000 more men to Vietnam? A reserve call-up of up to 280,000 men, increased draft calls, and an extension of tours of service for most men on active duty.
6. How much would it cost to meet the latest troop request? An estimated $2 billion per month.

The man who turned the Vietnam war around...In March 1968, Clark Clifford, the new secretary of defense, helped persuade Lyndon Johnson to abandon his bankrupt policy of graduated escalation and replace it with an early version of Vietnamization.
Source: National Archives

7. What would be the impact on the economy? Credit restrictions, tax increases, and probably wage and price controls. It would also worsen the balance of payments and lower the value of the dollar.
8. Can the bombing stop the war? No, not by itself.
9. Would stepping up the bombing decrease U.S. casualties? Very little, if at all.
10. How long must we keep sending U.S. troops and carrying the main burden of combat? Nobody knew. The South Vietnamese forces are far from ready to replace the U.S. forces.

During his review, Clifford asked General Wheeler for a presentation of the military plan for attaining victory in Vietnam. General Wheeler told him that there was no military plan for victory. Astonished, Clifford asked him why. Wheeler told him that there was no plan because U.S. forces operated under three major political restrictions: They could not invade North Vietnam because such action would possibly bring the Chinese into the war. They could not mine Haiphong, North Vietnam's principal port, because Soviet ships might be sunk. They could not pursue the enemy into Laos and Cambodia because such initiatives would widen the war both politically and geographically. Clifford then asked, given these restrictions, how could America hope to win the Vietnam war? Wheeler replied, without enthusiasm, that eventually the enemy would reach a point when he would decide that he could not continue the war because he could no longer tolerate the damage that the strategy of attrition was inflicting. Clifford then asked General Wheeler how long he thought it would take for the current attrition strategy that was in place to induce Hanoi to abandon the insurgency in South Vietnam? Wheeler could not make an estimate.[53]

Following days of fundamental analysis of the American war policy, Clifford concluded with a series of observations that starkly revealed the bankruptcy of the American strategy of limited war in Southeast Asia:

> I could not find out when the war was going to end; I could not find out the manner in which it was going to end. I could not find out whether the new requests for men and equipment were going to be enough, or whether it would take more and, if more, how much; I could not find out how soon the South Vietnamese forces would be ready to take over. All I had was the statement, given with too little self-assurance to be comforting, that if we persisted for an indeterminate length of time, the enemy would choose not to go on.
> And so I asked, "Does anyone see any diminution in the will of the enemy after four years of our having been there, after enormous casualties, and after massive destruction from our bombing?
> The answer was that there appeared to be no diminution in the will of the enemy.[54]

Clifford believed that the most probable outcome of sending 206,000 more troops to Vietnam would be to raise the level of combat and casualties. "I was convinced that the military course we were pursuing was not only endless, but hopeless."[55] Sending more troops would only raise the level of devastation, further Americanize the war, and leave the United States farther than ever from its goal of achieving an independent South Vietnam. Clifford therefore concluded that the United States should send no more troops to South Vietnam. Instead, the American goal "should be to level off our involvement and work toward gradual disengagement."[56] Having made his decision, Clifford set out to implement it, to convince Johnson that the time had come to alter course in Vietnam. Clifford knew that Johnson would have to abandon his policy of gradual escalation because it was not working, nor had it showed promise of ever working. Further, it was harming the national interest and dividing the American people.

JOHNSON AGONISTES

Johnson received the Clifford task force's report on March 4. It contained General Wheeler's belief that the troop request should be met. But to achieve the goal of 206,000 additional troops in Vietnam during 1968, the report made clear to Johnson that he would have to call 262,000 reservists to active duty, increase draft calls, and extend the tours of most men currently serving on active duty.

More significantly, the task force's report also called for a reassessment of the U.S. Vietnam policy, especially in relation to U.S. global strategic interests. It hinted that American would have to establish a limit for its involvement in Vietnam and abide by it. The report also asserted that no amount of additional U.S. troops in Vietnam could achieve American objectives there unless the South Vietnamese government achieved a broader popular base and fought more effectively.[57] Clifford hoped that the report would cause Johnson to focus on the fundamental questions of U.S. Vietnam policy raised by the Wheeler-Westmoreland troop request issue. He also hoped to sow seeds of doubt in Johnson's mind about the wisdom of continuing to escalate the war.

The president read carefully and pondered over the report for several days. He discussed what he should do in Vietnam with several advisers, including members of the task force. Rostow urged him to go all out and make a maximum effort to win the war. Johnson's initial instinctive reaction to the Communist Tet Offensive had been to do just that. He was angry, and he wanted to strike back. Johnson also believed that an aggressive post-Tet counteroffensive coupled to an intense bombing campaign could break Hanoi's will. He felt ready to mobilize the reserves, not only for Vietnam but to strengthen the overall American strategic posture in the world.

What partially deterred him from striking back hard was the Clifford task force's report. Johnson was persuaded to make any further commitment of American forces to Vietnam contingent upon on the South Vietnamese government improving its capabilities for governing and fighting. He also knew that Westmoreland was already taking the offensive against the enemy with the U.S. forces he had on hand.[58] MACV did not appear in any immediate need of additional forces to take the fight to the Communists and to hold Khe Sanh. Johnson discounted Wheeler's previous pessimistic assessment. Johnson also responded positively to a proposal from Rusk to consider curtailing the bombing of North Vietnam. Rusk persuaded Johnson that a partial bombing halt might offset some of the domestic opposition to the war, and it could even elicit a favorable response from the North Vietnamese that would move both sides closer to negotiations.[59] By March 7, Johnson was moving toward two new positions: setting a troop ceiling for Vietnam and a partial bombing halt. In the "Battle for Lyndon Johnson," Rostow, Wheeler, and the other hawks appeared to be losing ground to the growing number of doves among them.

Whatever possibility remained of Johnson sending large numbers of additional troops to Vietnam diminished when New York *Times* reporters Hedrick Smith and Neil Sheehan broke the story on March 10 that Johnson was considering a troop increase of 206,000 troops.[60] The impact of the *Times'* scoop, which penetrated the veil of secrecy Johnson had draped over the top-secret deliberations, was dramatic. White House spokesmen denied, unconvincingly, that the president was considering such a large troop request from General Westmoreland. Johnson's credibility gap widened. A storm of public criticism erupted. If Tet were such a great allied victory, people demanded to know, why did General Westmoreland need 200,000 more troops? Other influential print and electronic media voices editorialized against the proposed troop increase and called for changes in the Vietnam war policy. On Capitol Hill, Tet had convinced many wavering congressmen and senators that the United States was not winning the war, that it had locked itself into a stalemated conflict in Vietnam. Many of them opposed the proposed troop increase.

Dramatic evidence of flagging congressional support for the Vietnam War surfaced shortly after the *Times* story broke. Clark Clifford and General Wheeler conferred with hawkish leaders on the House and Senate Armed Services Committee. These people, mostly conservatives, all Cold Warriors and staunch supporters of the war effort to date, told Clifford and Wheeler that they could not support a reserve call-up or a large increase in the number of U.S. troops fighting in Vietnam. Senator Richard Russell, a close friend and mentor of Johnson, one of the most powerful and conservative senators on Capitol Hill, made a profound impression on Clifford when he told him and General Wheeler that he believed that the United States had made a serious mistake by involving itself in Vietnam in the first place. Clifford wondered, If Senator Russell and his fellow hawks did not support a troop increase, then who would?[61]

Powerful political currents were swirling across the nation by March 1968. "The Tet Offensive,...legitimatized the Vietnam war as a political issue." It "liberated politicians, journalists, and commentators from their previous commitments to the war."[62] The search for alternative war policies became a legitimate, even obsessive political preoccupation. Because 1968 was a presidential election year, the war became an integral part of the national electoral process. The search for alternatives, for a way out of a war that had become unpopular and seemingly unwinnable, unpopular mainly because it appeared unwinnable, had become the leading issue of the embryonic presidential race. Presidential candidates from both parties began to criticize Johnson, his war policy, and the proposed troop increase.

The first of these candidates to challenge the president was an obscure Democratic senator from Minnesota, Eugene McCarthy. McCarthy had no money, no organization, apparently no serious ambition to be president, and he did not like making campaign speeches; but he felt compelled to offer his presidential candidacy to opponents of the Vietnam war as a conduit through which their opposition to that war could flow into the developing presidential election. When the Minnesota senator entered the New Hampshire presidential primary scheduled for March 12, the pundits wrote off his quixotic challenge. They expected the upstart maverick to be crushed by the master politician in the White House who, despite his credibility gap and the albatross of war, retained the powers of presidential incumbency and the skill to use them.[63]

McCarthy, running on a single issue, opposition to the Vietnam war, surprised everyone with a strong showing in New Hampshire. Aided by hundreds of young volunteers who went door-to-door on his behalf, McCarthy came within 500 votes of defeating President Johnson in a state where the electorate had hawkish inclinations. McCarthy's surprising showing came as a political revelation. Analysts read the New Hampshire results as evidencing far greater public dissatisfaction with the war and with Johnson's leadership than anyone had realized. McCarthy's strong showing exposed Johnson's political vulnerability at the outset of the presidential campaign. If a seeming political lightweight like McCarthy could almost beat President Johnson in a hawkish state, what might a more formidable antiwar candidacy do nationwide? The Democratic primary election results "buoyed the hopes of the president's critics in both parties."[64]

At the time, everyone interpreted McCarthy's strong showing in New Hampshire to be a peace vote, a vote for disengaging from Vietnam. But post-election studies have explained the mystery of how an unknown dovish candidate could have done so well in a hawkish state against the president. Among McCarthy voters in the 1968 New Hampshire primary, a three-to-two majority favored taking a harder line against the Communists in Vietnam; they favored escalating the American war effort and winning. In November, more New Hampshire voters who had cast their votes for McCarthy in the Democratic primary the previous March voted for the hawkish third-party candidate George Wallace, who was running on a platform calling for a U.S. victory in Vietnam, than voted for either Richard Nixon or Hubert Humphrey. The hawks of New Hampshire voted for the dovish McCarthy either because he was the only protest candidate running and they did not care about his ideology or else because they misunderstood McCarthy's position and thought that he was a hawkish critic of Johnson's policy.[65]

McCarthy's strong showing in New Hampshire lured a more powerful dovish presidential candidate into the political arena four days later, New York Senator Robert F. Kennedy, the younger brother of the late president and heir to the Camelot mystique. McCarthy did not have a

The antiwar candidate...Senator Eugene McCarthy of Minnesota entered the Democratic presidential race in early 1968. His surprisingly strong showing in the New Hampshire primary in March 1968 set shock waves through the American body politic.
Source: National Archives

realistic chance of unseating Johnson, but Kennedy could mount a formidable challenge: He had plenty of money, name recognition, and a vast personal following among the American electorate. With Kennedy's entry into the 1968 Democratic presidential race, Johnson faced a long and divisive battle for his party's nomination. Even if he managed to beat back Kennedy's challenge and to win renomination, Johnson would be taking a divided Democratic party into the general election against Richard Nixon, the probable Republican nominee, who could be expected to make Johnson's increasingly unpopular war the leading issue.

After New Hampshire came the Wisconsin primary, set for March 19. Johnson's political advisers informed him that recent polls taken in that midwestern state showed both McCarthy and Kennedy positioning themselves to beat him. The Wisconsin voters, more dovish than New Hampshire's electorate, viewed McCarthy and Kennedy as peace candidates and saw Johnson as a war candidate. If the president wanted to retrieve his candidacy, he was told that he would have to make a dramatic gesture toward peace in Vietnam.

On top of the disturbing political news in New Hampshire and Wisconsin, Johnson also heard some disconcerting economic and financial news. The American inflation rate was rising because of increased spending on the war. The consumer price index in 1967 rose more than it had in any year since the Korean War. The last quarter of 1967 also showed a deficit in America's international balance of payments. That deficit caused uncertainty about the value of the dollar in international money markets. Many currency speculators sold their dollars, causing a run in the gold markets. During the first half of March 1968, the central banks of various countries had to supply almost $500 million in gold to help stabilize the dollar's value to which all other currencies were pegged. American banks alone had sold over $300 million worth of gold by March 14.

A financial crisis was averted only by an emergency effort by the treasurers and central bankers of several countries who created a system of monetary exchanges that temporarily curtailed gold selling on the free market.[66] The jittery international money market sent a signal to Johnson and to Treasury Secretary Henry Fowler that if the United States were to send 206,000 additional troops to Vietnam as requested, then the large increase in government spending required to pay for such an escalation of the war would in turn necessitate either sharp increases in taxes or sharp reductions in spending for Great Society and foreign aid programs, or both. If the troops were sent to Vietnam and Congress did not take the painful political medicine of tax increases and spending cuts in an election year, the United States would be risking the collapse of the dollar and a serious international financial crisis. International trade would be disrupted; the U.S. economy and those of its major trading partners could suffer serious damage.[67]

By mid-March a combination of strategic, political, and economic considerations convinced Johnson that he could not approve the deployment of 206,000 additional troops to Vietnam, or anything approaching those numbers. At the time, Allied forces appeared to be holding their own. The NVA assault on Khe Sanh was ending, Hue had been reclaimed, and intelligence data indicated that there was little likelihood of further PLAF/NVA assaults against South Vietnamese cities. Public opinion polls, media editorials, and congressional leaders had convinced the president that domestic opposition to any large increase in U.S. forces in Vietnam was both widespread and deeply entrenched, even among many hawks.

From mid-March, Johnson was inclined to move in two new directions: to send only token American troop increases to Vietnam, which could be raised without necessitating a major reserve call-up, and to take actions to build up the military forces of South Vietnam. For the first time, Johnson had to put a cap on the number of American forces that he would commit to Vietnam. Powerful historical forces had required the president to close the open-ended commitment that he had made in July 1965. On March 24, Johnson approved sending Westmoreland a mere 13,500 additional troops. They would turn out to be "the last increment of American military manpower committed to the Vietnam war."[68]

On March 15, Clifford, convinced that America could never win the Vietnam war because of the powerful political and economic factors that were imposing limits on U.S. military activity, told Johnson that America could not win the war, that he had to change the direction of U.S. policy, and that he would also have to make a sincere and realistic proposal for starting negotiations with Hanoi. Clifford suggested that a cutback in the bombing of North Vietnam would be a first step that could lead to negotiations. Clifford, whom the president had brought in to support his war policy, in effect told the president that his basic policy was wrong, that he and his advisers had been misguided, that he had lost control of the situation, and that if he continued to press forward, he would call forth a national disaster.[69] Johnson was astonished, angered, and disturbed by Clifford's comments.

Over the next several days Clifford repeatedly pressed his views on the harried president. Although annoyed, and occasionally rebuffing Clifford, Johnson continued to listen to his secretary of defense. He also continued to consult with other advisers, such as Rostow and Rusk, who supported his war policy. On March 17 and March 18, Johnson made two aggressive speeches in which he defended his war policy and criticized both his hawkish and dovish critics. The speeches failed to elicit any noticeable popular support. Johnson's political advisers told him that the two speeches had damaged his reelection prospects and that he must make some conciliatory gestures toward peace. Johnson and his speech writers were also at work on a major speech to be delivered to the American people on March 31 in which he would announce both his decision on the troop request and he would inform the nation of his policy for the post-Tet phase of the Vietnam war. Clifford was acutely aware of the fact that the president had given no indication that he had accepted any of his recommendations or what he intended to say in his speech.

Clifford, fearful that Johnson would reject his recommendations and decide to continue a policy that could lead only to national disaster, advised the president to meet again with the "wise men," the distinguished group of elder statesmen who had supported him at their meeting on November 2. Johnson agreed. The meeting was set for March 24. In calling for Johnson to hold another meeting with the "wise men," Clifford was gambling that the

Tet Offensive and its consequences had caused the elder statesmen to reconsider their support of the president's policy. Clifford hoped that they would inform the president that they believed a change of course in Vietnam was necessary. He was also gambling that Johnson, who admired and trusted the "wise men," would heed their advice.[70]

Johnson had already talked with the most influential member of the "wise men," the former secretary of state, Dean Acheson. Acheson, who had previously held extensive discussions on the Vietnam war with Clifford and some of Johnson's other influential advisers, told Johnson that neither the time nor the assets were available to accomplish U.S. military objectives in Vietnam. The force of 500,000-plus Americans currently in South Vietnam could neither expel the NVA nor subdue the Vietcong. Acheson also told the president that public opinion would never support an expanded war effort, nor would it support the present level of military activity indefinitely. Acheson further stated his judgments that the ineffective ground war had to be changed, that the bombing of North Vietnam had to be halted, and that the war must be ended as soon as possible without sacrificing the American commitment to South Vietnam.[71] Acheson's frank remarks doubtless made an impression on Johnson.

The "wise men" gathered at the White House on March 25. Those present included Acheson, many former advisers of Kennedy and Johnson such as George Ball, McGeorge Bundy, Cyrus Vance, General Maxwell Taylor, Henry Cabot Lodge, and others.[72] They met with many of Johnson's current advisers and received briefings on the current political and military situation in Vietnam. The next day they assembled for lunch at the White House to present their views to President Johnson. Present with Johnson were General Westmoreland and the man who would soon succeed him as MACV commander, his deputy, General Creighton W. Abrams. The two generals brought the "wise men" up to date on the tactical situation in Vietnam. However, "the Wise Men were not focusing on Vietnam, but on the political situation in America."[73] The Communist offensive had spawned a political crisis in the United States, and the "wise men" wanted to be sure that the president grasped its full implications for his war policy.

With Acheson, the *primus inter pares*, leading the way, each of them told the president what he thought. Most, like Acheson, had changed their views about the U.S. war policy since November 2. While a few still firmly supported the current policy, the consensus among them was that "some action had to be taken to begin to reduce the American involvement in Vietnam and to find a way out."[74] All agreed that a troop increase would be folly and that the South Vietnamese must shoulder a greater burden of the fighting.

Johnson was shaken by what he heard at lunch that day. The "wise men," all of whom had previously supported his policy as recently as last November, had mostly spoken against it. The Tet Offensive and its consequences had dramatically transformed their views. The "wise men" told

Johnson to abandon what they viewed as a hopeless strategy. They advised him to cut his losses and to prepare to exit Vietnam. The GVN would have to learn to defend itself. Several of the "wise men," who, as former advisers within his administration, had helped Johnson forge his Vietnam policy of graduated escalation, now told him that it had failed and that he would have to abandon it.

Johnson's meeting with the "wise men" yielded the result that Clifford had hoped it would. Johnson at last clearly understood what his new secretary of defense had been telling him for weeks: The Tet Offensive had significantly increased and intensified opposition to the war in America among elite groupings, including emboldened clergy, prominent laymen, influential media editorial writers, and members of Congress. Further escalation of the war was politically impossible. The time had come to stop expanding the war in the pursuit of unattainable goals. Johnson would either have to scale down the war or else court political disaster.[75]

Following the March 25 meeting, Johnson worked on his speech, which was scheduled to be delivered to the nation March 31. Clifford was involved in the speech-writing process, working with Harry McPherson, Johnson's principal speech writer. During the final days before it was to be given, Clifford played a key role in determining both the content and the tone of the most important speech about the Vietnam war that Johnson ever delivered.[76]

Johnson delivered his speech Sunday evening March 31 from the Oval Office. He appeared haggard; he spoke more slowly and more softly than usual. His voice sounded like that of a man who had been carrying a heavy load for a long time. That night, the weary president announced four major decisions that changed the course of the Vietnam war and had a decisive impact on American political life.

1. He repeated the offer of negotiations that he had made the previous September at San Antonio. Johnson would halt all bombing of North Vietnam whenever that action would lead to productive negotiations. As a conciliatory gesture and as a first step to de-escalate the Vietnam war, he announced an unconditional partial bombing halt. All bombing north of the 20th parallel would be stopped immediately.

2. He told the American people of his decision to send only 13,500 additional support troops to Westmoreland over the next five months. He was rejecting Westmoreland's request for a major troop increase. There would be no further escalation of the ground war in South Vietnam.

3. He stated that the U.S. effort in Vietnam would henceforth focus on expanding and improving the military capabilities of South Vietnam's armed forces and that they would gradually assume a greater responsibility for defending themselves.

4. As he approached the end of his forty-seven–minute speech, Johnson acknowledged that there was disunity in the country. He warned Americans of the perils of disunity and then concluded his speech with a stunning pronouncement that he said he hoped would restore unity:

With America's sons in the fields far away, with America's future under challenge right here at home, with our hopes and the world's hopes for peace in the balance every day, I do not believe that I should devote an hour or a day of my time to any personal partisan causes or to any duties other than the awesome duties of this office....Accordingly, I shall not seek, and I will not accept, the nomination of my party for another term as your president.[77]

Almost no one, foreign observers, political commentators, hawks, doves, Clifford, nor most of Johnson's other advisers had anticipated his resignation. Everyone had assumed the inevitability of his candidacy for reelection. Johnson had caught the nation and the world by surprise.

On April 3 Hanoi declared its readiness to have its delegates make contact with U.S. representatives so that they could both decide how and when to end all bombing and other acts of war against the DRV. The United States responded positively to Hanoi's gesture. Talks between Washington and Hanoi opened in Paris on May 13. These negotiations began a diplomatic process that would, years later, bring the U.S. war in Vietnam to a close.[78] On April 4 the Pentagon formally denied Westmoreland's request for 206,000 more troops and placed a ceiling of 549,500 on U.S. troop deployments to South Vietnam. There would be no more requests for American troops from MACV commanders in South Vietnam.[79] The open-ended military commitment had been officially closed.

The Tet Offensive, although it left the Communists with devastating tactical defeats and horrendous casualties, also brought them a tremendous psychological and political victory within the United States which forced President Johnson to abandon his strategy of graduated escalation. He replaced it with an early version of what would become Vietnamization under his successor Richard Nixon. It was a major turning point of the war. Johnson's dramatic change of direction had been brought about by domestic political developments, by economic and financial considerations, and, most of all, by the efforts of Clark Clifford and the "wise men" who persuaded him to change course during their discussions held with the president in the latter half of March. "March 31, 1968, marked an inglorious end to the policy of gradual escalation."[80]

But Tet amounted to a serendipitous historical transition, at least within Johnson's frame of reference. The president never intended nor could he foresee that his March 31 decisions would alter the course of the war or determine its outcome. He did not see himself as abandoning U.S. goals nor initiating any fundamental policy changes. He remained powerfully committed to stopping North Vietnamese aggression and to achieving an independent non-Communist state in Southern Vietnam. He viewed the partial bombing halt, the leveling off of the American military role in South Vietnam, and the building up of the South Vietnamese armed forces as being steps toward the achievement of U.S. goals in South Vietnam while at the same time placating public opinion at home. Johnson viewed his actions as political accommodations which were needed to buy time for his policies to work. He was shifting tactics to save a strategy that had come under concerted attack and had lost popular support. Johnson attempted to reposition himself politically to persevere in a righteous cause that he believed protected vital security interests of the United States in Southeast Asia. Clark Clifford, in tandem with the "wise men," persuaded Johnson to alter his war policy on March 31, but they failed to shake his commitment to an American military victory in South Vietnam or to undermine his belief that his strategy of limited war would one day prevail.

Johnson did not understand that his March 31 decisions set in motion a process that eventually "unravelled our Vietnam commitments."[81] Tet was a watershed. After Tet, a U.S. military solution was no longer possible in South Vietnam primarily because the American people no longer had the patience or the willingness to continue furnishing the vast resources still required to attain it. Whether Johnson realized it or not, after Tet, only a political solution to the Vietnam war was possible.[82] Johnson's partial bombing halt began a diplomatic process that would one day bring a end to the American war in Vietnam, a *denouement* that would open the door to a Communist victory. In the short run, Tet was a major U.S. tactical victory and a severe Communist defeat. But in the long run, Tet turned out to be a crucial strategic Communist victory and a fatal U.S. defeat.

At the time that Johnson made his fateful decisions, the United States had over 1,000,000 troops stationed abroad in more than forty countries. Since 1945, America had enmeshed itself in a global network of treaties and military alliances. By March 1968, the military forces required to defend U.S. strategic interests around the world had been stretched dangerously thin to send 536,000 troops to Vietnam. The powerful U.S. economy that sustained both American global commitments and the war in Vietnam was showing symptoms of decline. The hard practical limits to the total military assets that the world's mightiest nation–state could afford to commit to its limited war for limited goals in Southeast Asia had been reached by the spring of 1968.

The United States, a nation whose per capita gross national product (GNP) was at least 100 times larger than Vietnam's, whose thermonuclear arsenal had the capability of obliterating Vietnam, could not apply enough of its awesome military power to achieve the strategic goals that it had set for itself. In addition to competing global strategic commitments, economic strains, and rising domestic political opposition, the refusal of America's SEATO allies to commit more troops to the Vietnam cockpit during the fall of 1967 limited the allied Vietnam war effort.

The inefficient and class-biased conscription system strained to furnish 40,000–50,000 young men a month for military service because of the exemptions and deferments factored into Selective Service and because of wholesale draft avoidance and resistance. The numbers of soldiers provided by the draft were insufficient to meet the replacement needs of the U.S. military around the world during 1968 much less to continue a large-scale military buildup in Vietnam had one been ordered.[83] The insufficiencies of the draft combined with Johnson's refusal to mobilize the Reserves deprived the U.S. military of the manpower it required to meet its domestic and global strategic commitments and to fight an enlarged war in Vietnam.

America could not use nuclear weapons in the Vietnam war to supplement its conventional firepower because U.S. leaders feared both the domestic and world reaction to using atomic bombs on a nation of poor Asian peasants who posed no direct threat to U.S. vital interests. American public opinion polls showed consistent and overwhelming popular opposition to using nuclear weapons in Vietnam. In addition, U.S. strategic planners in Washington did not want to use nuclear bombs in Vietnam because of the absence of suitable targets and because they did not want to alarm or anger the Soviets and Chinese who might feel compelled to intervene militarily in Vietnam, or, worse, to respond in kind.

In March 1968 a confluence of powerful historical forces caused Johnson to abandon his policy of graduated escalation. Given the hard practical limits imposed on the size of the war effort America could mount in Vietnam in the spring of 1968 and after, and given the determined war waged by a resourceful enemy supported by China and the USSR, it is evident in retrospect that military victory in Vietnam was beyond available American strength. Under such circumstances, a U.S. military victory was probably never a realistic strategic possibility in Southeast Asia. It was that reality that American leaders might have foreseen had they had greater knowledge of Vietnamese history and culture, had they understood the reasons for the French strategic failure in 1954, and had they had a realistic understanding of the limits that would impinge upon American power that could be committed to fighting a limited war in a region that was never vital to U.S. strategic interests. A more cautious and wiser leadership, able to escape the confines of containment ideology and domestic anticommunist imperatives, might have avoided the ordeal of fighting a long, losing war in Vietnam.

THE TELEVISED WAR

Television coverage of some of the fierce Tet battles highlighted the fact that Vietnam was America's first televised war, the first war to be shown night after night in American living rooms. For years, color video brought Americans the sights and sounds of men at war. The Vietnam war was also the first major war that the United States ever lost. Many Americans believe that television was a major cause of the American defeat in Southeast Asia. That is, they believe that America lost history's first televised war precisely because it was televised.

General Westmoreland and others, including journalist Robert Elegant, have insisted that America lost a war in Vietnam that it could have won.[84] They have blamed the defeat on the mass media, particularly the television networks, for turning American public opinion against the war and eventually forcing a U.S. withdrawal from Vietnam, which allowed the Communists to overwhelm the South Vietnamese defenders and to take over the entire country in the spring of 1975.

Westmoreland has stated that the news media, especially television, snatched defeat from the jaws of victory in the aftermath of Tet-68, just when the allies had a battered enemy on the ropes and ready for the kill. He has asserted that a golden opportunity to mobilize U.S. military resources for a maximum effort to win the Vietnam war in a year or two was lost because television news coverage of the Tet campaigns turned the public against the war in early 1968 and prevented Johnson from escalating the conflict.[85] Westmoreland's stab-in-the-back thesis, that powerful and hostile media, particularly television news coverage, were primarily responsible for the American strategic defeat in Vietnam, is embraced by many Americans who hold that the U.S. military intervention in Southeast Asia was a noble cause that could and should have been successful.[86]

The thesis that the media, particularly television, were responsible for losing the Vietnam war, or were a major cause of the American defeat in Vietnam, is groundless and untenable, for many reasons. Most historians of the Vietnam war and most analysts of mass media dismiss it as without merit.[87] Television news coverage of the Vietnam war up to the time of Tet was overwhelmingly favorable; television journalists consistently represented American soldiers as fighting aggressively and winning every major battle en route to inevitable victory in the war.[88] During the first few years of television coverage of the war, the networks rarely showed American soldiers getting killed or wounded. Remarkably little American blood got spilled on television prime-time news. Typical video sequences of combat action showed U.S. troops moving across rice paddies or an air strike from a distance. Sometimes one heard the muted sounds of rifle fire or the rhythmic whir of helicopter rotors.[89]

The only public opinion poll that ever asked people how watching television news coverage of the Vietnam war influenced their attitudes toward the war found that 83 percent of the respondents said they felt more hawkish after watching the news.[90] At the time this poll was taken—July 1967—other polls showed that 50 percent of Americans believed that U.S. entry into the war had been a mistake.[91] These polls showed that opposition to the Vietnam war and to Johnson's war policy was massive despite, not because of, television news coverage, which was highly favorable at the time. Many Americans had turned against the war and had distrusted Johnson's leadership long before Tet.

Television news coverage of the war became more critical during the Tet battles, and, for the first time, television provided viewers with a steady diet of live-action coverage of the carnage. Viewers witnessed the destructiveness and brutality of war, of American soldiers fighting and dying in the streets of Saigon and Hue. But evidence from public opinion polls taken soon after the Tet attacks have undermined Westmoreland's thesis. At a time when the media exaggerated the tactical gains made by the enemy, portrayed Tet as a great shock and disaster for America, and showed American soldiers being killed in combat, public opinion polls registered temporary rises in popular support.[92]

Proponents of the stab-in-the-back thesis often cite Peter Braestrup's writings to substantiate their charges. Braestrup, a former Marine officer, Vietnam journalist, and media scholar, produced a massive study of the media coverage of Tet. He found that during the first few days of the Tet Offensive the public was misled into thinking that the Vietcong were winning when in fact they were losing, and losing badly, almost everywhere. He has criticized journalists for their inaccurate and misleading stories. To Westmoreland, Braestrup's critique proved that distorted media coverage misled Americans and turned them against the war; biased reportage turned a tactical victory into a major defeat that eventually cost America a war.[93]

But a careful reading of Braestrup's study has shown that he furnishes the proponents of the stab-in-the-back thesis neither aid nor comfort. Braestrup himself did not embrace the thesis and has challenged those who did.[94] Braestrup took pains to make clear that he did not charge either print or television journalists with biased coverage during Tet. He has never said that Tet-68 coverage by either the print or television journalists, however deficient in the early stages, turned public opinion against the Vietnam war. In fact, he believed that such claims were impossible to substantiate: "No empirical data exist to link news coverage with changes in public opinion."[95]

Braestrup contended that skewed media coverage of the Tet campaigns exacerbated a growing political crisis in Washington that would have occurred even if those journalistic accounts had been clinically accurate. He believed that it was Johnson's indecisive leadership in the weeks following Tet that caused the falloff of popular support for the war that occurred in March. For Braestrup, changes occurring in public opinion of the Vietnam war in the weeks following Tet were caused by failures of political leadership and not by television news or by the other media coverage of the battles.[96] Ironically, the administration's propaganda efforts in the fall of 1967, which were aimed at convincing Americans that the United States was winning the war and that it would end soon, magnified the public shock and disillusionment that occurred during the Tet campaigns and widened the credibility gap.

When trends in public opinion on the Vietnam war have been matched with trends in television news coverage of the conflict, it has been shown that a majority of the American people turned against the Vietnam war before television news coverage of the conflict became predominantly negative. Despite more negative emphasis in their television coverage of the war during and after Tet, on the whole, the network television news coverages continued to be more positive than negative until the fall of 1969. A majority of Americans had developed dovish views on the Vietnam war long before then.[97] Television coverage of the war normally lagged behind public opinion.

The increasingly critical television coverage of the war that occurred at the time of Tet and after represented a response by media journalists to public opinion, not an effort to shape it. The stab-in-the-back theorists, in their confusion and their haste to make the media into a scapegoat, have inverted the relationship between television news coverage of the Vietnam war and public opinion concerning the war and presidential leadership. Westmoreland, Elegant, and many others failed to understand that it was public opinion that influenced television coverage of the war much more than it was television coverage that influenced public opinion on the war.

As public support for the war dropped, television news coverage became more critical. The news networks were merely catching up to what their viewers were already thinking about the war and the U.S. leadership; they were not telling them what to think. When Walter Cronkite, the most popular and influential television anchor during the Vietnam war era, declared at the end of his newscast on the evening of February 27, 1968, that the war was a stalemate, the erstwhile hawk was aligning his views with those of his Middle American constituents. Numerous public opinion polls show that Cronkite told Americans nothing that most of them did not already believe.

The stab-in-the-back theorists also faced another difficulty. Westmoreland's insistence that victory was within the U.S. grasp following Tet, if Johnson had only sent the requested troops and taken the other escalatory steps called for at the time, was dubious. At the time, Clark Clifford and most Pentagon analysts had concluded that Hanoi had both the political will and the military assets to match any and all U.S. post-Tet escalations. Hanoi could also count on the Chinese, who would probably have intervened militarily if the North Vietnamese ever faced national extinction. Had Johnson escalated the war after Tet, he most likely would not have achieved strategic victory within a year or two. Most likely Johnson would have attained only continuing military stalemate at a far higher level of costs and casualties. Such a continuing costly stalemate in Vietnam would have brought intensified opposition, political polarization, and violent conflict within the United States that could have undermined American political stability.

The basic problem with the stab-in-the-back thesis is that it represents a lamentable failure of historical understanding. Powerful economic, political, and strategic forces determined the outcome of the Vietnam war and caused the eventual American strategic defeat. The role of the media, including television news coverage, in determining that outcome was peripheral, minor, trivial, in fact, so inconsequential it is unmeasurable. It was the course taken by the Vietnam war—the United States had locked itself into a stalemated conflict of rising casualties and costs—coupled to a loss of confidence in the integrity and competence of the government, all of which were highlighted and intensified by the Tet Offensive, that turned public opinion against the Vietnam war.

Public opinion turned the media, particularly television news, against the war. Had the cathode ray tube never been invented, and had censorship been imposed on Vietnam war news or had all the journalists covering the war in Southeast Asia been cheerleaders for the allied side, public opinion would have turned against the Vietnam war just as it did against the Korean War. The Korean war was popular when the UN forces appeared to be rolling toward an easy victory over the North Koreans in the fall of 1950. Following the surprise Chinese intervention in late November 1950, and the subsequent stalemated warfare that went on for years, public opinion polls consistently showed that a majority of Americans did not support the Korean war. Yet television news was in its infancy, most U.S. households did not have television sets, war news from Korea was heavily censored, and U.S. war correspondents were all supportive of the UN effort.[98] Those who blame the television networks for the American defeat in Vietnam promulgate a myth that may serve hidden political and ideological agenda, but they do not explain why the United States lost the war.

TALKING AND FIGHTING

The talks between American and North Vietnamese representatives that began in Paris on May 13 deadlocked instantly. President Johnson, doubting that the talks could be productive and wary of Communist propaganda, demanded concessions from Hanoi in exchange for a complete bombing halt. The American delegation, led by Averell Harriman, refused to accept any cease-fire terms that would require the withdrawal of American forces from South Vietnam while allowing the Ho Chi Minh trail to remain open and allowing PAVN forces to remain in South Vietnam. The Americans also refused to consider any political settlement of the conflict that did not guarantee the continued survival of a free, non-Communist government in South Vietnam. The North Vietnamese delegation, headed by Xuan Thuy, quickly rejected the American demand for a reciprocal deescalation to get the bombing completely stopped. Hanoi also rejected any ceasefire proposals that would limit their ability to support the war in South Vietnam and refused to consider any political solution that allowed the Thieu–Ky regime to survive.

Given the fact that the military initiative in South Vietnam had passed to the Allies in the months following the Tet Offensive, the North Vietnamese probably were not interested in conducting substantive negotiations at that time. They preferred to wait until the political and military balance shifted toward their side. Hanoi's approach to the Paris talks was to use them as part of a larger strategy of talking while fighting. They intended to use the negotiations underway in Paris to get a complete bombing halt, to highlight differences between the Americans and South Vietnamese in an effort to drive the allies apart, and perhaps to exploit the antiwar sentiment within the United States that was growing rapidly in the wake of Tet.[99] Hanoi coordinated its diplomacy with its war effort. For the Communists, negotiations were not a means for ending the war, they were part of an integrated military-political-diplomatic strategy designed to achieve their major objectives: the withdrawal of the Americans, the overthrow of Thieu, and the creation of a coalition government in South Vietnam; that is, to win the war. They had agreed to the Paris talks to try to achieve objectives via negotiations that they could not achieve by fighting, particularly getting a complete bombing halt.

Since both sides refused to make the necessary compromises required to move the negotiations forward, the Paris talks proved sterile for months. Meanwhile, America pressed its war in South Vietnam: 1968 was the bloodiest year of the American Vietnam war. More U.S. combatants fought in more battles that year than in any other. During 1968 more than 14,000 American soldiers were killed, the highest total for any year of the war. Shortly after Tet, Westmoreland mounted the largest search-and-destroy operation of the war: forty-two American and thirty-seven ARVN armored and infantry battalions scoured the countryside around Saigon trying to locate and eliminate the VC/NVA units that had survived Tet. Westmoreland also wanted to prevent further attacks on the capital city. Eventually, the 110,000 allied troops involved in the gigantic operation formed a ring of steel around Saigon.[100]

During the latter half of 1968, the American Vietnam war was characterized by hundreds of battalion-sized operations and thousands of actions involving companies and platoons. In countless small unit operations, American forces attempted to find, fix, and destroy the enemy forces all over South Vietnam. While these land battles raged, specially trained Army and Navy units waged riverine warfare against Vietcong guerrillas amid the watery wastes of the Mekong delta.[101]

Although the air war against North Vietnam had been curtailed, aerial warfare in South Vietnam reached new intensity during 1968. The number of air strikes flown against guerrilla sanctuaries and supply lines increased as Air Force and Navy bombers that had been committed previously to raiding North Vietnam's military and industrial sites joined the air war in South Vietnam. After Tet, carpet bombing raids on enemy positions by cells of giant B-52s trebled. American planes also stepped up their bombing of the Ho Chi Minh trail running through the Laotian corridor.[102]

U.S. military action included assaults into the border regions adjacent to many of the South Vietnamese cities that the Vietcong and PAVN forces had attacked during Tet. One of the most spectacular operations occurred in the I Corps Tactical Zone following the vicious fighting to reclaim Hue. U.S. forces struck NVA staging areas located in the A Shau valley, which lay in the southwestern corner of Thua Thien province adjacent to the Laotian border. Remote and rugged, the A Shau valley had been a Communist stronghold for years. It was from that region that NVA forces had attacked the northern provinces as well as the city of Hue. MACV officials feared that the enemy might use the A Shau to launch additional attacks, so they mounted an operation to destroy the PAVN bases in the valley. Two battalions of the U.S. 7th Cavalry, the 1st and the 5th, helilifting in to attack the NVA, ran into the fiercest air defenses encountered in South Vietnam. Ten assault helicopters were shot down and another thirteen were severely damaged by deadly fire coming from antiaircraft batteries lodged in the hills and mountains that ringed the valley.[103] In addition to the air defenders of the A Shau, helicopter and tactical aircraft pilots had to contend with some of the most hazardous flying weather of the entire war. Dense fogs, thick clouds, and driving rainstorms generated by the summer monsoons often reduced visibility in the target areas to near zero.

Sweeps by the 7th Cavalry troops who survived the antiaircraft fire and dangerous flying weather failed to find many NVA forces. The NVA had chosen not to fight and had slipped into cross-border sanctuaries located in nearby Laos. But the Americans captured sizeable amounts of food and stores that the departing enemy had left behind. After the 7th Cavalry was pulled out, elements from Major General Melvin Zais's elite 101st Airborne, the famed "Screaming Eagles," air-assaulted into the A Shau valley in an effort to catch the NVA returning to their bases. The 101st also failed to find many PAVN soldiers who wanted to stand and fight.[104] By the end of August 1968, the Americans had withdrawn from the A Shau, and the North Vietnamese had returned. Elements of the 101st would return to the valley the next year, and they would encounter some NVA units who would stand and fight.

In addition to action in the A Shau valley, U.S. troops also fought along the northern border in the vicinity of the DMZ. The Marines' main objective in this region, following their successful defense at Khe Sanh, remained sealing the border against enemy infiltration. Marine units patrolled along Route 9, attacking and counterattacking any North Vietnamese forces trying to infiltrate the northern provinces or to attack their positions. One of the fiercest of many battles occurring in this area took place near Con Thien on October 25. In a seven-hour fight, an armored company completely destroyed a North Vietnamese bunker complex.[105] The NVA suffered many losses during the latter half of 1968 in the vicinity of the DMZ, but they managed nevertheless to achieve a stalemate. NVA units continued to infiltrate the region and continued to battle the Marines and other American forces. The stalemate in the north would be broken only years later when the U.S. forces were pulled out of their positions during a phase of President Nixon's Vietnamization program.

Extensive fighting also occurred in the southern part of I Corps, in Quang Ngai province. One of the most gruesome tragedies of the Vietnam war occurred in this region when American soldiers, using automatic rifles, grenade launchers, and machine guns, massacred an estimated 300 to 400 civilians at two hamlets, My Lai and My Khe, on the morning of March 16, 1968. Both hamlets comprised part of Son My village located near the coast in the Son Tinh district of Quang Ngai province. The soldiers who massacred the women, children, and old men of My Lai belonged to the 1st and 2nd Platoons of Charlie Company, 1st Battalion, the 11th Infantry Brigade, which was attached to the Americal Division under the command of Major General Samuel Koster.[106]

> The Americal Division suffered from grave command and control problems, stemming from poor training and a lack of leadership, from division down to platoon level, which permitted civilian mistreatment. Some elements of its 11th Infantry Brigade were little better than organized bands of thugs, with the officers eager participants in the body count game.[107]

After the perpetration of the atrocities, members of the brigade and divisional staffs succeeded in covering it up for a time. The American people were not to learn of the hideous incident until a year later and then from independent media sources who exposed the Army's attempted cover-up.[108] An official Army board then conducted a thorough sixteen-months-long investigation of the incident and its cover-up. Fourteen officers were found to be complicit in covering up war crimes. Additionally, thirteen soldiers, four officers and nine enlisted men, were charged with committing war crimes and crimes against humanity. Subsequently, all thirteen of the soldiers accused of war crimes either had the charges against them dropped or else they were acquitted. All, that is, except Lieutenant William Calley, whose 1st Platoon was estimated to have killed over 200 of the villagers that lethal morning in My Lai. A court martial convicted Calley of mass murder.[109]

The mass murders at My Lai and My Khe were a grotesque consequence of many factors: a formless war of attrition in which military success was measured statistically by counting corpses; small-unit actions fought in populated regions against an enemy who relied on village support to sustain his insurgency; the frustrations of fighting a war that appeared to be both unpopular and unwinnable; race prejudice, which encouraged many U.S. soldiers to regard Vietnamese peasants as "mere gooks," as less than fully human; the fear, rage, and hatred arising from fighting an enemy who set deadly mines and booby traps that maimed and killed GIs and who then melted into the jungle or merged into the rural population; paranoia arising from the inability of U.S. soldiers to tell friendly villagers from enemies and therefore to assume that they all were real or potential foes; the lowered quality of conscripted troopers and junior officers who increasingly constituted fighting units in Vietnam after Tet; and the poor leadership, the inadequate training, the lack of discipline, and the thuggery that character-ized the Americal Division and especially the 11th Infantry Brigade, also known as the "Butcher Brigade."

After learning of the massacre, some Americans worried about how many other My Lais might have gone undetected. They feared that perhaps the only unique feature of the My Lai massacre was its discovery. Some also wondered if the American military might have had a policy of targeting civilians suspected of aiding the enemy. In various forums, hundreds of Vietnam veterans claimed that they had participated in, witnessed, or heard of atrocities committed against civilians in South Vietnam. Some people found cold comfort in the fact that the Vietcong and NVA forces were guilty of systematic atrocities and the cold-blooded murders of thousands of civil-ians. There was also a troubling inconsistency in finding one young junior officer guilty of mass murder in a war where long-range artillery fire and aerial bombing had killed thousands of civilians since the Americanization of the war. In the eyes of many Americans, William Calley was more a victim and a scapegoat than a war criminal.

"The extent of American atrocities in Vietnam cannot be established with any precision."[110]   According to available evidence and testimony, American soldiers frequently committed atrocities against Vietnamese civil-ians, and they became more frequent in the years after Tet. However, MACV never had an official policy of targeting civilians nor even of informally sanctioning attacks under certain circumstances. Killing, attacking, or using unnecessary force against civilians in situations where they posed no danger to U.S. military personnel was illegal, and always in violation of extant rules of engagement. Even the thugs of the Americal Division knew that what had occurred at My Lai and My Khe was both illegal and wrong. That is why they covered it up with falsified reports and sham inquiries. Most U.S. soldiers serving in Vietnam did not commit atrocities against civilians, nor is there hard evidence that there were any other large-scale My Lai-type massacres where American troopers deliberately murdered hundreds of old men, women, and children.[111]

Six weeks after the massacres, the Vietcong launched another wave of attacks against Saigon and other South Vietnamese cities. The fighting in and near Saigon was vicious and lasted for weeks. It was not until early June that ARVN and U.S. forces crushed all remaining enemy resistance. Like its vastly larger predecessor, the Vietcong mini-Tet Offensive also failed tacti-cally. There was a third, even weaker, round of Vietcong urban assaults in August, a mini-mini-Tet, that Allied intelligence anticipated and an Ameri-can preemptive strike easily crushed.[112]

These subsequent enemy offensives showed that the Vietcong were feeling the effects of their terrible losses sustained in February. They fought in smaller units, avoided direct attacks on American installations, and were

The U.S. Army 45th MUST (Mobile Unit, Self-Contained, Transportable) Surgical Hospital Staff serving in Tay Ninh Province, 1968. Thousands of women served in the American Vietnam war, many as Army nurses. 1968 was the heaviest year of fighting for Americans—14,592 KIA and about 150,000 were wounded. The extraordinary efforts of hospital units like the 45th MUST saved the lives of many severely wounded soldiers. American soldiers received the best medical support ever available to men in war.
Source: USMI Photo Archives

forced to use younger and less-experienced fighters. More and more NVA troopers had to be fed into the depleted Vietcong main force units. In the aftermath of their defeats at Tet, the North Vietnamese Politburo had to refashion its military strategy. It abandoned offensive operations and reverted to defensive tactics. The Communists resumed a version of protracted warfare. During the latter half of 1968, enemy actions were largely confined to sporadic standoff rocket and mortar attacks on Allied positions.[113]

In the fall of 1968, General Abrams abandoned the strategy of attrition warfare that had been in place since 1966 in South Vietnam. He shifted the American focus from small-scale combat operations to pacification and Vietnamization. With negotiations underway in Paris, American and South Vietnamese officials launched an accelerated pacification program to bring as many of South Vietnam's villages as possible under the control of the Saigon government. American combat forces found themselves forming security shields to prevent Vietcong forces from entering populated areas. Allied officials focused their efforts in the areas where the Vietcong had suffered their worst losses and could not thwart the accelerated allied pacification efforts. CORDS and South Vietnamese officials also stepped up the Chieu Hoi program that offered amnesty to Vietcong defectors, and, with assistance from CIA officers, they implemented the PHOENIX program, an intelligence-gathering operation aimed at exposing and neutralizing the Vietcong infrastructure.[114] Pacification made little progress for the rest of 1968. Saigon controlled only a few more villages at year's end than it had before the Tet Offensive erupted, and no one could be sure that all the people living in "friendly" villages truly supported the GVN and the U.S. military effort.

Simultaneously with its enhanced pacification efforts, the United States pressed forward with Vietnamization. Efforts were made to expand and to modernize the South Vietnamese armed forces. Authorized force levels were increased from 685,000 to 850,000, and the South Vietnamese soldiers were provided with more modern weapons. There was noticeable improvement in the performance of the Saigon forces by the end of the year, but fundamental deficiencies persisted. Draft evasion and desertion remained both chronic and massive. There was also no discernible enthusiasm for Vietnamization on the part of the South Vietnamese leaders. Having become quite comfortable with American soldiers doing most of the fighting and dying for them, Thieu and Ky appeared to be in no hurry to alter the situation.[115]

Part of the problem with implementing Vietnamization derived from the fact that South Vietnam's leaders had not been consulted before Johnson decided that Vietnamization would be the new focus of the post-Tet American effort.[116] Neither South Vietnamese political desires nor RVNAF military capabilities had anything to do with the U.S. decision to begin the process of Vietnamization. Johnson had been forced to turn to Vietnamization because of American domestic political exigencies.[117]

The surprisingly effective performance of some of the ARVN units during Tet battles had given U.S. leaders in Washington and Saigon some grounds for hoping that Vietnamization might work, that the South Vietnamese government would, in time, develop the capacity to defend itself. But there was never any realistic basis for believing that the GVN could ever carry out Vietnamization successfully. The main reason that American soldiers were fighting in Vietnam was because Washington did not believe that the South Vietnamese could defend themselves against the insurgency directed from Hanoi. Nothing had really changed since Tet. Most of the ARVN troops who had fought hard during the Tet battles did so because they were fighting for survival, not because they had suddenly become patriots or brave, aggressive warriors. They displayed the "back-to-the-wall courage of the cornered."[118]

The fundamental reality that foreclosed any possibility of a successful Vietnamization program lay in the fact that General Thieu's and Marshall

Ky's power depended on maintaining the loyalty of a coterie of ARVN generals who held their commands because of their political reliability, not because they were competent, honest, or patriotic warriors. The price that the leaders of the GVN would have had to pay for eliminating incompetence and corruption within their civilian and military bureaucracies would have been a fall from power. Insistence on reform would have amounted to committing political suicide. Because the South Vietnamese government and army remained rotten at their core, and because American leaders neither had the leverage nor the will to impose radical reforms on South Vietnam's leadership, no amount of U.S. economic and military support could ever make Vietnamization work well enough to defeat their powerful and resourceful enemies.[119]

Despite the stepped-up Allied military activity, the accelerated pacification program, and the beginnings of Vietnamization, the military and political balance in South Vietnam had changed little as 1968 ended. The Vietcong forces had suffered losses, were weaker, and controlled fewer villages and a smaller portion of the South Vietnamese population than they had before the Tet Offensive; but much of the Vietcong infrastructure remained intact. American military operations after Tet inflicted heavy losses on the enemy, destroyed staging areas, and disrupted supply lines; but the VC/NVA main force units remained intact. They remained a formidable foe at year's end.[120]

The Saigon government improved somewhat during 1968. It was stronger and more stable after Tet than it had ever been. Many of the South Vietnamese people, angry at the Communists for violating the Tet truce and for attacking their cities, turned to the Thieu government. Many city residents, hitherto smug in their sense of safety from the ravages of war and apathetic toward the government, now felt vulnerable and understood that their security depended on the ARVN forces. Thieu's government actively involved citizens in repairing the extensive damage incurred by South Vietnam's cities during Tet. His government also launched new programs to combat corruption and to curb rampant inflation.

By mid-summer 1968, Thieu, with U.S. support, had gained the upper hand over his arch-rival, General Ky. Thieu's anti-corruption program was one-sided; it aimed chiefly at the corruption of Ky and Ky's supporters and ignored the corrupt practices of Thieu loyalists. Thieu gradually replaced cabinet members and province chiefs loyal to Ky with military men loyal to him. The political savants, who frequented the sidewalk cafes of Tu Do street, began calling Thieu "the little dictator."[121] He would survive in power until the eve of South Vietnam's extinction.

But chronic political weaknesses persisted in South Vietnam. Tet generated nearly a million new refugees to add to the millions already inhabiting the slums, back alley labyrinths, and suburban hovels of Saigon and other cities. The massive needs of the war refugees went largely unattended.

Land reform in South Vietnam stalled because Thieu favored landowners. Corruption at all levels of the Saigon government and military persisted. The Buddhists, the sects, and other non-Communist political groupings refused to support the GVN, perhaps hoping that it would fail and that they could then pick up the pieces. The Saigon regime, despite a few cosmetic gestures toward civilian rule, remained, in essence, a narrowly based military dictatorship. Another of the Tu Do street savants commented on the status of the GVN after Tet: "The dung heap is the same. Only the flies are different."[122] There were other problems stemming from the fact that Vietnamization and the U.S. negotiations with Hanoi exacerbated tensions between U.S. and GVN officials. The South Vietnamese feared and resented what appeared to them as American efforts to impose a settlement on them and then to get out, leaving the GVN at the mercy of the Vietcong and the NVA forces fighting in South Vietnam.[123]

The tensions in South Vietnam paralleled the political turmoil in the United States during that turbulent year. The presidential election evolved amidst a backdrop of the worst violence, social conflict, and political polarization seen in America since the Civil War. The Vietnam war had combined with domestic insurgencies to create profound schisms, between white and black, between affluent and poor, between young and old, between "hippies" and "straights," between hawks and doves, and between the practitioners of the so-called new politics and the political establishment. Robert Kennedy, seeking the Democratic nomination as an antiwar candidate, and Richard Nixon, who was seeking the Republican nomination, both feared that the institutional framework of the world's oldest democracy might not be able to contain the powerful centrifugal forces threatening to spin out of control.[124]

On the evening of April 4, Martin Luther King, Jr., was assassinated as he stood on a balcony outside a Memphis motel room. That night the ghettos of America exploded in fury. There were riots in 130 cities. Thirty-nine people, mostly blacks shot by police and the National Guard, were killed, and thousands of people were injured; 75,000 National Guard and federal troops were mobilized nationwide to quell the erupting violence.[125] In the nation's capital, site of some of the worst rioting, looting, and burning, barbed-wire barriers and machine gun emplacements surrounded government buildings to protect them from any attacks.

Many demonstrations convulsed college campuses during the spring of 1968, most of them protesting the Vietnam war. The most violent uprising occurred in April at Columbia, one of the most distinguished universities in the country. On this prestigious Ivy League campus, black militants combined with antiwar radicals to protest both the university's complicity with the Vietnam war and its plans to construct a new gymnasium in an area that would require the relocation of blacks living in apartments on the building site. During the demonstration, students occupied campus buildings and refused orders to vacate them. University officials called in the New York

A martyr for freedom...Senator Robert Kennedy during his final campaign against the Vietnam war abroad and for social justice at home. His murder in Los Angeles the night of June 5, 1968, destroyed any chance of the antiwar forces winning control of the Democratic convention. *Source*: National Archives

City police, who forcibly removed the students. In the process, hundreds of students were arrested, and about 150 were injured.[126] Following the police action, student protesters called a strike that forced the university to curtail its spring 1968 semester.

From April to early June, Eugene McCarthy and Robert Kennedy waged a spirited primary campaign for the Democratic presidential nomination in the aftermath of Johnson's withdrawal speech. A third candidate for the Democratic nomination, Vice President Hubert Humphrey, knowing he had no chance against McCarthy and Kennedy in many of the primaries because of his support of Johnson's Vietnam war policy, quietly lined up delegates from the states that did not hold primaries. Johnson, who hated Kennedy and did not believe McCarthy had the qualifications to be president, supported Humphrey's candidacy.

Kennedy beat McCarthy in most of the primaries because of his remarkable ability to appeal to black voters, Hispanics, and the poor and the disadvantaged generally, as well as to white working class voters and to affluent middle class liberals. McCarthy beat Kennedy once, in the Oregon primary on May 25, the first electoral defeat ever suffered by a Kennedy. Next up was the important California primary. After a hard fight, Kennedy won a narrow victory on June 5. He appeared to have a fighting chance to win the Democratic presidential nomination. But shortly after delivering a victory speech to his supporters in the ballroom of the Biltmore Hotel in Los Angeles the night of June 5, he was assassinated by Sirhan Sirhan, a Arab nationalist who said he was angry at Kennedy's strong support of Israel.[127] Senseless violence once again intensified widely shared fears that anarchy and civil conflict would overwhelm the political process. With Kennedy's murder, the antiwar forces within the Democratic party lost any chance to capture their party's presidential nomination. It would go to Humphrey, who, with Johnson's help, would have the votes of a large majority of the convention delegates.

Political violence in America during the tormented year of 1968 climaxed in Chicago at the time of the Democratic convention. The National Mobilization to End the War in Vietnam (MOBE) and the Youth International Party (Yippies) planned a series of demonstrations in Chicago to protest the Vietnam war. The demonstrations were timed to coincide with the holding of the Democratic convention during the last week of August. Chicago's mayor, Richard Daley, the host of the Democratic convention, vowed that antiwar demonstrators would not disrupt his city or its convention. The stage was set for the most violent confrontation between antiwar protesters and police of the Vietnam war era.

In the days preceding the convention, thousands of youthful antiwar activists filtered into Chicago, gathering mainly in Grant and Lincoln parks, far from the convention site, which was the International Amphitheater, near the stockyards. To meet the anticipated threat to law and order, Mayor Daley mobilized his entire 12,000-man police force. In addition, the governor of Illinois assigned 5,649 of the National Guard to round-the-clock duty in Chicago, and President Johnson ordered 5,000 federal troops flown to Chicago to be available if needed. The assembled police, National Guard, and federal troops outnumbered the protesters whose numbers never exceeded 10,000–12,000.[128]

Tension built during the days of the Democratic convention, which convened at the Amphitheater Saturday, August 24. There were skirmishes in the parks between protesters and police. For several days the police and National Guard succeeded in keeping the demonstrations far from the convention site and nearby hotels where the delegates were staying and where various candidates for the presidential nomination had set up their headquarters.

The Democratic convention was controlled by Humphrey's supporters. They easily defeated efforts by antiwar delegates to adopt a peace plank for the party platform. Humphrey's nomination was scheduled for Wednesday evening, August 28. That night about 3,000 protesters managed to elude the police, and set out for the convention site. Phalanxes of police blocked their way at the intersection of Michigan Avenue and Balbo, miles from the Amphitheater. The police ordered the marchers, who did not have a parade permit, to disperse. The protesters refused and began chanting, "Fuck you LBJ! Fuck you LBJ!" Within minutes hundreds of police attacked the demonstrators, clubbing at random. They also used tear gas to disperse the protesters. Nearby, television cameras recorded the violence in all its gory detail. Seeing the television cameras, demonstrators began chanting, "The whole world is watching! The whole world is watching!"[129]

While violence reigned in the streets of Chicago, the Democratic convention gave Hubert Humphrey a first ballot nomination. The major antiwar candidate, Eugene McCarthy, finished a distant second. By the time the convention closed, nearly 700 people had been jailed, more than 800 citizens and 150 police injured, and one demonstrator had been killed. Many who witnessed the violence on television were everlastingly horrified and fearful that American fascism might be wearing the blue uniform of the Chicago police. A far larger number of viewers endorsed the police attacks on demonstrators, whose radical politics and countercultural life styles they perceived as intolerable threats to the good order and public morality of American civilization. But whether one sided with the police or protesters, or refused to take sides in an increasingly polarized society, the violence surrounding the Democratic convention dramatized the ominous fact that there could be no peace in America until peace came to Vietnam.[130]

The violent events in Chicago played into the hands of the Republican presidential candidate, Richard Nixon, who had been nominated at an orderly convention in Miami three weeks before the Democrats' tumultuous gathering. In his acceptance speech, a poised and confident Nixon had sounded the themes that would dominate his fall campaign: the need for national unity, the demand for "law and order," and the urgent need for peace in Vietnam, although not peace at any price.[131] These themes would have strong appeal to millions of voters yearning for the return of social peace and for an end to a hated war. A third party candidate, Governor George Wallace of Alabama, the American Independence Party leader, also sought the presidency in 1968. Wallace took a hawkish stand on the war, calling for an American victory in Vietnam. When the general campaign began in September, polls gave Nixon a 15 percent lead over Humphrey and also showed that Wallace commanded considerable popular support.

Humphrey, whose candidacy had emerged from the political ruins of Chicago, appeared to have no chance. He headed the ticket of a party profoundly divided over the Vietnam war. He had little money and no national campaign organization. For weeks his campaign floundered along. But as the 1968 election entered its final month, Humphrey's campaign suddenly sprang to life. Eugene McCarthy endorsed Humphrey, and many antiwar Democrats returned to the party fold; they preferred a flawed liberal to their nemesis Nixon. As Humphrey's campaign gained momentum, Nixon's hitherto smooth-running campaign appeared to stall. Wallace's popular support in the north declined as trade union leaders campaigned vigorously for Humphrey. Polls taken throughout October showed Humphrey steadily closing the gap with Nixon and Wallace fading. Humphrey appeared to have a chance to win.

Johnson, who despised Nixon and wanted to help Humphrey beat him, and knowing that a dramatic peace gesture could put the Democratic candidate over the top, spoke to the American people on Thursday evening, October 31. Johnson announced a complete halt of all bombing of North Vietnam effective midnight October 31, five days before the election, and stated that a peace settlement was coming soon. Johnson was persuaded to halt all bombing of North Vietnam by Harriman, who had told Johnson that a bombing halt would clear the way for the start of substantive negotiations with Hanoi. The Communists had indicated informally that they were prepared to begin serious peace discussions within a few days of a complete bombing halt and that they would also accept the Saigon government's presence at the Paris talks. (The United States, had, in return, agreed to accept a representation from the NLF.) General Abrams assured Johnson that a bombing halt would pose no threat to Allied forces in South Vietnam, especially since Johnson had promised Abrams that he would shift the aircraft engaged in bombing North Vietnam to the aerial war against the Ho Chi Minh trail in Laos.[132]

Johnson's election-eve speech propelled Humphrey forward. Public opinion polls taken over the weekend showed Nixon's lead had evaporated. The pundits pronounced the election "too close to call." A Harris poll released Monday, November 4, the day before the election, showed Humphrey ahead of Nixon 43 percent to 40 percent.[133] Humphrey appeared poised to pull off the biggest political upset since Truman had defeated Dewey twenty years earlier.

But the Vietnam war, which appeared to have eliminated Humphrey early, then brought him back to the verge of victory, now intruded at the last moment to deprive him, narrowly, of the presidency. General Thieu, aware that the unilateral U.S. bombing halt had not required any reciprocal deescalations by Hanoi, announced that South Vietnam would not attend the Paris talks. Thieu's rubber-stamp National Assembly condemned President Johnson's "betrayal of an ally." Americans realized that the killing would go on in Vietnam despite the bombing halt, and that Johnson's peace initiative was not going to halt the war any time soon. Another Harris poll taken Monday showed Nixon had regained the lead. The eleventh-hour South Vietnamese demurral apparently gave Nixon his narrow victory. Out of 73 million votes cast, his winning margin was a scant 500,000, less than seven-tenths of 1 percent.[134]

Following two weeks of U.S. pressure and promises of continuing support, Thieu reluctantly agreed to send a delegation to the Paris talks. There followed a debate that went on for weeks over the shape of the negotiating table and the positioning of the four delegations at the table. By the time negotiations involving the four concerned parties began, Johnson's administration was in its final days. Although it probably cost Humphrey his chance to win the 1968 presidential election, "it seems highly doubtful that South Vietnamese intransigence sabotaged an opportunity for a peace settlement."[135] Hanoi's new flexibility coming toward the end of 1968 did not extend beyond getting the bombing halted, which they managed without having to make any concessions in return. On the substantive issues, Hanoi would have probably accepted nothing less than a U.S. withdrawal and the end of the Thieu regime, both of which were unacceptable to Johnson. In the fall of 1968, neither Washington nor Hanoi was prepared to make the compromises that could have led to peace in Vietnam. The Tet Offensive and its aftermath had only hardened the diplomatic impasse.

As the year ended, Americans yearned for an end to the stalemated war, but they would be bitterly disappointed to discover that their Vietnam ordeal was destined to endure another four years.

NOTES

1. Tet is a celebration of the beginning of the lunar new year. It is the most important Vietnamese holiday. There is no American equivalent. It is a combination Fourth of July, Thanksgiving, Christmas, and New Year's Eve. Families plan months in advance for Tet, and the celebrations begin on the eve of the new year. During the Vietnam War it was customary for both sides to observe a 36-hour cease-fire during Tet, and 1968, the year of the Monkey, was supposed to be no exception.

2. Stanton, *Rise and Fall*, p. 220. Palmer, Bruce, Jr., *The 25-Five War: America's Role in Vietnam* (New York: Simon and Schuster, 1985), pp. 78–79. One of the reasons MACV was surprised by the size of the enemy forces involved in the Tet-68 attacks was because their intelligence reports had underestimated both enemy strength and the rate of infiltration into South Vietnam. Adams, Samuel, "Vietnam Coverup: Playing with Numbers," *Harper's Magazine* (May 1975), p. 41, accuses Westmoreland of deliberately undercounting the Vietcong in order to deceive civilian leaders in Washington into thinking the United States was winning the Vietnam war. A CBS video documentary, "The Uncounted Enemy: A Vietnam Deception," broadcast January 23, 1972, leveled the same charge. General Westmoreland's libel suit against CBS was settled out of court.

3. Oberdorfer, *Tet!*, p. 34.

4. Brodie, Bernard, "The Tet Offensive," Frankland, Noble, and Dowling, Christopher (eds.), *Decisive Battles of the Twentieth Century* (London: 1976), pp. 319–321.

5. Duiker, *The Communist Road*, p. 240.

6. Porter (ed.), "Letter from Le Duan to Nguyen Chi Thanh, Commander-in-Chief of the PLAF," March, 1966, *Vietnam Documents*, vol. 2, Document 222, p. 416; Duiker, *Communist Road*, p. 242.

7. Quoted in Duiker, *Communist Road*, pp. 242–243.

8. Doyle, Edward; Lipsman Samuel; Maitland, Terrence; and the editors of Boston Publishing Company, *The North* (Boston: Boston Publishing Co., 1986), a volume in the series, *Vietnam Experience*, pp. 52–56; Duiker, *The Communist Road*, p. 248.

9. Davidson, *Vietnam at War*, pp. 434–441.

10. Duiker, *The Communist Road*, pp. 263–264; Oberdofer, *Tet!*, pp. 42–43.

11. Porter (ed.), "Directive from Province Party Standing Committee to District and Local Party Organs on Forthcoming Offensive and Uprisings," Nov. 1, 1967, *Vietnam Documents*, vol. 2, Document 268, pp. 477–480. This document shows that the Communists were not depending on spontaneous risings of the people in the towns and cities at the time of the TET-68 general offensive. The directive reveals detailed plans for coordinating military attacks on GVN offices with organized political activity by cadre leaders.

12. Duiker, *The Communist Road*, pp. 264–265.

13. Krepinevich, *The Army and Vietnam*, pp. 237–238; Duiker, *The Communist Road*, pp. 265–266.

14. Westmoreland, *A Soldier Reports*, pp. 411–416.

15. *Ibid.*, pp. 410–421.

16. Oberdorfer, *Tet!*, pp. 2–40, has a detailed account of the dramatic battle inside the U.S. embassy compound.

17. Stanton, *Rise and Fall*, pp. 208–216.

18. *Ibid.*, pp. 228–233; Oberdorfer, *Tet!*, pp. 122–131.

19. Stanton, *Rise and Fall*, pp. 231–233.

20. Quote is from *Ibid.*, p. 221.

21. Summers, Harry G., Jr., *Vietnam Encyclopedia*, pp. 199–200.

22. Stanton, *Rise and Fall*, p. 228.

23. *Ibid.*

24. Krepinevich, *The Army and Vietnam*, p. 250; Oberdorfer, *Tet!*, p. 232.

25. President Nixon made his remarks during a speech delivered to the American people on the evening of November 3, 1969. He said: "We saw a prelude of what would happen in South Vietnam when the Communists entered the city of Hue last year. During their brief rule there, there was a bloody reign of terror in which some 3,000 civilians were clubbed and shot to death. With the sudden collapse of our support, these atrocities of Hue would become the nightmare of the entire nation...."

26. Palmer, *Summons of the Trumpet*, pp. 215–216; Davidson, *Vietnam at War*, pp. 551–554.

27. Johnson is quoted in Pisor, Robert, *The End of the Line; The Siege of Khe Sanh* (New York: Ballantine, 1982), p. 100; Westmoreland, *A Soldier Reports*, pp. 444–445; Davidson, *Vietnam at War*, pp. 564–566; and Pisor, *The End of the Line*, pp. 121–122, discuss the possible use of nuclear weapons at Khe Sanh. After Johnson raised the matter with General Wheeler, Wheeler asked Westmoreland. Believing that he might have to use atomic weapons at Khe Sanh, Westmoreland convened a secret planning group to study the matter. When articles appeared in newspapers accusing Westmoreland of wanting to use nuclear weapons at Khe Sanh, Johnson ordered Westmoreland to halt all nuclear planning.

28. Davidson, *Vietnam at War*, pp. 552–553.

29. Stanton, *Rise and Fall*, pp. 235–238; Davidson, *Vietnam at War*, pp. 552–553.

30. Davidson, *Vietnam at War*, pp. 558–559.

31. Stanton, *Rise and Fall*, pp. 238–242.

32. Davidson, *Vietnam at War*, pp. 559–561; Pisor, *End of the Line*, pp. 233–238.

33. Stanton, *Decline and Fall*, p. 233.

34. Pike, Douglas, *War, Peace, and the Vietcong* (Cambridge, Mass.: The M.I.T. Press, 1969), pp. 125–127; Schandler, *The Unmaking of a President*, p. 77–78.

35. According to Oberdorfer, *Tet!*, who cites official U.S. and South Vietnamese figures, 58,373 PLAF and PAVN soldiers died between January 29 and March 31, 1968. During that time, 4,954 RVNAF soldiers, and 3,895 Americans from all branches of the Armed Forces, were killed.

36. Oberdorfer, *Tet!*, pp. 158–171; Schandler, *The Unmaking of a President*, pp. 80–81.

37. Quoted in Oberdorfer, *Tet!*, p. 184. Arnett was the only journalist to hear the major's remark, and it was Arnett's wire service account that put the famous quote into circulation. Kendrick, Alexander, *The Wound Within: America in the Vietnam Years, 1945-1974* (Boston: Little Brown, 1974), p. 251.

38. Schandler, *The Unmaking of a President*, p. 83.

39. Johnson, Lyndon, *The Vantage Point*, pp. 382–386.

40. Schandler, *The Unmaking of a President*, pp. 92–97.

41. Davidson, *Vietnam at War*, pp. 492–496.

42. *Ibid.*, pp. 497–498.

43. Schandler, *The Unmaking of a President*, pp. 105–111; Davidson, *Vietnam at War*, pp. 497–505.

44. Porter (ed.), "Report of the Chairman, Joint Chiefs of Staff, General Earle G. Wheeler, on the Situation in Vietnam," February 27, 1968, *Vietnam Documents*, vol. 2, Document 279, pp. 501–504.

45. *Ibid.*

46. Schandler, *The Unmaking of a President*, p.116.

47. *Ibid.*, pp. 118–119. The quoted material is on p. 119.

48. Johnson, *The Vantage Point*, p. 392.

49. *Ibid.*, pp. 235–236.

50. Clifford, Clark M., "A Viet Nam Reappraisal: The Personal History of One Man's View and How It Evolved," *Foreign Affairs*, vol. 47 (July 1969), pp. 606–607. A fascinating account by the man mainly responsible for inducing Lyndon Johnson to change the course of U.S. Vietnam policy in the aftermath of Tet-68.

51. Schandler, *The Unmaking of a President*, pp. 138–140.

52. Questions and answers are taken from Clifford, "A Vietnam Reappraisal," pp. 610–611.

53. *Ibid*, p. 611.

54. *Ibid.*, pp. 611–612.

55. *Ibid.*, p. 613.

56. *Ibid.*, p. 613.

57. Porter (ed.), "Memorandum for the President from the 'Clifford Group,'" (Extract), *Vietnam Documents*, vol. 2, Document 230, p. 505. Schandler, *The Unmaking of the President*, contains a detailed description of the draft memo for the president, pp. 167–176. The draft was written by William Bundy and Paul Warnke.

58. Johnson, *The Vantage Point*, pp. 396–398.

59. *Ibid.*, pp. 398–401.

60. Sheehan, Neil; and Smith, Hedrick, "Westmoreland Requests 206,000 More Men, Stirring Debate in Administration," New York *Times*, Sunday, March 10, 1968, p. 1. Sheehan's and Smith's scoop did not come from leaks as Johnson suspected, but from perceptive, resourceful, and shrewd reportage. They pieced the story together from many sources.

61. Schandler, *The Unmaking of a President*, p. 211.

62. Both quotes come from *ibid.*, p. 220.

63. McCarthy, Eugene J., *The Year of the People* (New York: Doubleday, 1969), pp. 67–72; White, Theodore H., *The Making of a President, 1968* (New York: Atheneum, 1969), pp. 83–85.

64. Schandler, *The Unmaking of a President*, p. 223.

65. Converse, Philip E.; Miller, Warren E.; Rusk, Jerold G.; and Wolfe, Arthur C., "Continuity and Change in American Politics: Parties and Issues in the 1968 election," *American Political Science Review*, vol. 63 (December 1969), pp. 1,083–1,092; Moss, *News or Nemesis*, pp. 95–96; Jan Vermeer has called to my attention the fact that many New Hampshire hawks misread McCarthy's candidacy, perceiving the dove to be a hawk.

66. Johnson, *The Vantage Point*, pp. 314–318.

67. *Ibid.*, pp. 318–321.

68. Schandler, *The Unmaking of a President*, p. 236. This token increment brought the total authorized U.S. forces in Vietnam to 549,000. On April 30, 1969, U.S. troop deployment in Vietnam peaked at 543,400.

69. Clifford, "A Vietnam Reappraisal," pp. 613–614; Schandler, *The Unmaking of a President*, pp. 243–246, 251.

70. Johnson, *The Vantage Point*, pp. 409–413.

71. Oberdorfer, *Tet!*, pp. 294–295.

72. The "wise men" present at the March 25 White House meeting included Dean Acheson, George Ball, McGeorge Bundy, Douglas Dillon, Cyrus Vance, Arthur Dean, John J. McCloy, General Omar Bradley, General Matthew Ridgway, General Maxwell Taylor, Robert Murphy, Henry Cabot Lodge, Abe Fortas, and Arthur Goldberg.

73. Quoted in Schandler, *The Unmaking of a President*, p. 262. The remark was made by Walt Rostow. General Westmoreland became the Army chief of Staff.

74. *Ibid.*, p. 263.

75. Johnson, *The Vantage Point*, pp. 417–418; Sheehan, *A Bright Shining Lie*, pp. 721–722.

76. *Ibid.*, pp. 420–421.

77. Johnson's March 31 speech is printed in *Public Papers of the President of the United States, Lyndon B. Johnson, 1968–1969*, vol. 1 (Washington, D.C.: U.S. Government Printing Office, 1971), pp. 469–476; key passages, with analysis, are in Schandler, *The Unmaking of a President*, pp. 282–287. Johnson resigned mainly because if he had not stepped down then, neither the American people nor Hanoi would have believed that his proposals were anything more than election year ploys to placate domestic public opinion.

78. Goodman, *The Lost Peace*, pp. 65–67. Both sides quarreled for a month over the site of the preliminary talks before Paris was chosen. Peace talks began May 13, but they were unproductive for months.

79. Schandler, *The Unmaking of a President*, pp. 288–289.

80. Herring, *America's Longest War*, p. 207.

81. Schandler, *The Unmaking of the President*, p. 319.

82. Kissinger, Henry, "The Vietnam Negotiations," *Foreign Affairs*, vol. 47 (January 1969), pp. 214–216.

83. Moss, "The Vietnam Generation," pp. 6–8, 10–12.

84. Westmoreland, *A Soldier Reports*, pp. 427–428, 438–439, 471–472, 554–557; Elegant, Robert, "How to Lose a War: Reflections of a Foreign Correspondent," *Encounter* (August 1981), pp. 73–74.

85. Westmoreland, *A Soldier Reports*, pp. 427–428, 438–439.

86. Kimball, Jeffrey P., "The Stab-in-the-Back Legend and the Vietnam War," *Armed Forces and Society*, vol. 14 (Spring 1988), pp. 438–439.

87. Historians include George C. Herring, *America's Longest War*; Stanley Karnow, *Vietnam: A History*; and Bruce Palmer, Jr., *The 25-Year War*. Daniel C. Hallin, *The Uncensored War: The Media and Vietnam*; George Moss, *News or Nemesis: Did Television Lose the Vietnam War?* Hammond, William, *The U.S. Army in Vietnam: The Military and the Media, 1962-1968* (Washington, D.C.: The U.S. Army Center of Military History, 1988) are the most thorough analyses of television news coverage of the Vietnam war and its effects.

88. Hallin, Daniel C., *The Uncensored War: The Media and Vietnam* (New York: Oxford University Press, 1986), p. 110. Hallin states, "In the early years of the war, roughly up to the Tet offensive,…television coverage was lopsidedly favorable to American policy in Vietnam,…"

89. Patterson, Oscar, III, "An Analysis of Television Coverage of the Vietnam War, *Journal of Broadcasting*, vol. 28 (Fall 1984), pp. 401–402.

90. The poll appeared in *Newsweek*, vol. 70 (July 10, 1967), pp. 20–24.

91. Mueller, *Wars, Presidents, and Public Opinion*, pp. 88–89.

92. See Table 4.6 showing policy preferences in Vietnam appearing in Mueller, *Wars, Presidents, and Public Opinion*, p. 107. Public opinion polls taken in early February, immediately after the Tet attacks, showed that the number of people calling themselves hawks rose from 56 percent to 61 percent and the number calling themselves doves dropped from 28 percent to 23 percent.

93. See Braestrup, Peter, *Big Story: How the American Press and Television Reported and Interpreted the Crisis of Tet 1968 in Vietnam and Washington*, 2 vols. (Boulder, Colo. Westview, 1977). A one-volume abridged edition was published by Yale University Press in 1983.

94. Braestrup, Peter, "The Press and the Vietnam War," *Encounter* (April 1983), p. 92.

95. Braestrup, Peter, "The Tet Offensive—Another Press Controversy: 2," in Harrison Salisbury (ed.), *Vietnam Reconsidered: Lessons from a War* (New York: Harper & Row, 1984), pp. 167–168.

96. *Ibid.*, p. 171.

97. Mueller, *War, Presidents, and Public Opinion*, p. 91, cites a poll taken in September 1968 showing 48 percent of Americans favoring a dovish position, and 43 percent favoring a hawkish position. This is the first time doves outnumbered hawks. The upsurge in popular support for the war immediately following the Tet Offensive was a short-lived rally-around-the-flag reflex. Popular support dropped sharply, both for the war and for Johnson's war policy, reflecting the public's perception that Johnson's leadership was indecisive in a time of crisis. Johnson was more unpopular than the war.

98. *Ibid.*, pp. 23–114; Moss, *News or Nemesis*, pp. 35–43.

99. Goodman, *The Lost Peace*, pp. 65–68; Karnow, *Vietnam*, p. 566.

100. Stanton, *Rise and Fall*, pp. 259–260.

101. *Ibid.*, pp. 255, 259, 262–263.

102. Morrocco, *Thunder from Above*, pp. 184–186.

103. Doughan, Clark; Weiss, Stephen; and the editors of Boston Publishing Company, *Nineteen Sixty-Eight* (Boston: Boston Publishing Co., 1983), pp. 142–144, a volume in the series, *Vietnam Experience*; Stanton, *Rise and Fall*, pp. 248–249; Palmer, *Summons of the Trumpet*, pp. 263–264. The 7th Cavalry had served in many of

America's previous wars. The 7th Cavalry was also George Armstrong Custer's outfit at the time he was killed at the Battle of the Little Big Horn in 1876.

104. Stanton, *Rise and Fall*, 249–250.

105. *Ibid.*, pp. 251–254.

106. Lewy, *America in Vietnam*, pp. 324–25; Dougan, *Nineteen Sixty-Eight*, p. 79.

107. Stanton, *Rise and Fall*, p. 258.

108. An independent journalist, Seymour M. Hersh, exposed the Army's cover-up of the My Lai massacre. See his book, *Cover-Up: The Army's Secret Investigation of the Massacre at My Lai 4* (New York: Random House, 1972).

109. "Conversations between Lt. General William R. Peers and Lt. Colonel Jim Breen and Lt. Colonel Charlie Moore," in Oral History collection of U.S. Army Military History Institute, Carlisle Barracks, Penn., pp. 33–44, 56–58; Peers, William R., *The My Lai Inquiry* (New York: W. W. Norton, 1979), *passim*; Palmer, Bruce, *25-Year War*, pp. 85–86, 170–171; Stanton, *Rise and Fall*, p. 258. Calley was initially sentenced to life imprisonment at hard labor. Following lengthy reviews of his case in both military and civilian courts, his sentence was reduced to ten years. After serving twenty-six months, he was paroled in 1974.

110. Lewy, *America in Vietnam*, p. 311.

111. *Ibid.*, pp. 324–331. Lewy has studied the issue of American war crimes and atrocities committed during the Vietnam war. See his chapter 9, "Atrocities: Fiction and Fact," pp. 307–342, and chapter 10, "The Punishment of Atrocities and War Crimes," pp. 343–373; also see Westmoreland's views, *A Soldier Reports*, pp. 494–501.

112. Porter (ed.), "COSVN Directive," June 10, 1968, *Vietnam Documents*, vol. 2, Document 285, pp. 512–516; Palmer, *Summons of the Trumpet*, pp. 264–265; Stanton, *Rise and Fall*, pp. 259–263.

113. Duiker, *The Communist Road*, pp. 276–278; Davidson, *Vietnam at War*, pp. 540–544. During the first six months of 1968, Hanoi lost an estimated 100,000 PLAF and NVA troops, about half of their entire strength at the beginning of the year.

114. Blaufarb, *Counterinsurgency Era*, pp. 266–274; Herring, *America's Longest War*, p. 212.

115. Clifford, "A Vietnam Reappraisal," p. 614; Herring, *America's Longest War*, pp. 212–213

116. Davidson, *Vietnam at War*, p. 531.

117. Herring, *America's Longest War*, p. 208.

118. Davidson, *Vietnam at War*, p. 531.

119. *Ibid.*, p. 532; Bluefarb, *Counterinsurgency Era*, pp. 302–305.

120. Herring, *America's Longest War*, p. 213.

121. Quoted in Dougan and others, *Nineteen Sixty-Eight*, p. 126; Davidson, *Vietnam at War*, pp. 544–547; Lipsman, Samuel, Doyle, Edward, and the editors of Boston Publishing Co., *Fighting for Time* (Boston: Boston Publishing Co., 1983), pp. 88–90.

122. The unidentified Saigonese is quoted in Dougan and others, *Nineteen Sixty-Eight*, p. 123.

123. Herring, *America's Longest War*, pp. 214–215.

124. Schlesinger, Arthur M., Jr., *Robert Kennedy and His Times*, vol. 2 (Boston: Houghton Mifflin, 1978), pp. 930–931.

125. Moss, *America in the Twentieth Century*, p. 370.

126. O'Neill, William L., *Coming Apart: An Informal History of America in the 1960s* (New York: Quadrangle, 1971), pp. 289–291.

127. Schlesinger, *Robert Kennedy*, pp. 955–956.

128. Moss, *News or Nemesis*, pp. 96–99.

129. Hodgson, Godfrey, *America in our Time: From World War II to Nixon: What Happened and Why* (New York: Vintage, 1976), pp. 370–372. Immediately after they broadcast images of the violence taking place in the streets of Chicago, the three television networks were deluged by letters, telegrams, and phone calls by irate viewers. By an eight-to-one margin, the viewers condemned the demonstrators and what they perceived as biased television reportage favoring the protesters. During the ensuing two weeks, Mayor Daley received 75,000 letters from all over the country; 90 percent of them praised his police. Public opinion polls confirmed that a large majority of Americans were angered by the demonstrators and supportive of the Chicago police.

130. Dougan and others, *Nineteen Sixty-Eight*, p. 175.

131. *Ibid.*, p. 176.

132. Johnson, *The Vantage Point*, pp. 513–529; Goodman, *The Lost Peace*, pp. 69–73.

133. Dougan and others, *Nineteen Sixty-Eight*, p. 180.

134. *Ibid.*, pp. 180–182; Nixon haters are fond of telling a story that Nixon, to ensure his election, contacted Thieu through an intermediary, Anna Chinnault, to have her tell him to refuse to attend the peace conference and to promise him that he could get a better deal from Nixon after he won the election. They accuse Nixon of sabotaging the peace talks to win an election. There are at least three things wrong with the story. (1) There was no peace settlement to sabotage. (2) Thieu did not need Nixon to tell him to boycott the peace talks. (3) Thieu had already concluded that he could probably get better terms later.

135. Herring, *America's Longest War*, p. 219

THE WAR TO END
A WAR

8

We designed a war we were going to lose, and we managed to lose it the way we designed it.

Newton Gingrich

NIXON'S WAR

On January 20, 1969, Richard M. Nixon became the 37th president of the United States, and "Johnson's war" in Vietnam became "Nixon's war." The new president owed his narrow electoral victory primarily to American frustrations with the stalemated war, that is, to Johnson's inability either to win it or to end it. Nixon, since 1954, had been known as a hawk on the Indochina wars. As vice president, Nixon had called for U.S. military intervention in May 1954 to save the French at Dien Bien Phu. In 1955 he had stated that expansionist China posed the greatest threat to U.S. strategic interests in Southeast Asia and that it might become necessary to use nuclear weapons to halt Chinese aggression. Nixon strongly backed the Johnson administration when it committed America to war in Vietnam during the summer of 1965. In 1966 and again in 1967, Nixon opposed calls for negotiations with Hanoi. He believed that such calls only encouraged the Communists to fight on. Nixon insisted that negotiations should occur only after all NVA forces had been driven from South Vietnam.[1]

During the 1968 presidential campaign, Nixon had frequently criticized Johnson's gradualist use of military force in Vietnam because it had produced neither military victory nor a negotiated settlement of the war. Conceding that a military victory was no longer possible, Nixon suggested that the road to a negotiated settlement of the Vietnam war ran through Moscow and not through Hanoi. Because North Vietnam could not continue its war in South Vietnam without Soviet backing, Americans should work for "a broad political accommodation with the Soviet Union—for detente—"[2] to reduce or to end Soviet aid to North Vietnam. He stated that if the Soviets wanted Hanoi to end its war in South Vietnam, the North Vietnamese would have no choice but to negotiate its conclusion. Asserting that ending the Vietnam war was necessarily the top national priority, Nixon stressed the importance of ending the war honorably and in such fashion that the U.S. withdrawal from Vietnam would never be or even appear to be an American defeat. For him, the maintenance of an independent non-Communist South Vietnamese government was crucial. Ensuring a free South Vietnam was a major American commitment and a vital national interest. Preserving South Vietnam was also necessary for the United States to maintain its credibility as a great power with both friends and foes. How America ended its war in Vietnam would determine if there would soon be another war or if the world would enjoy a lasting peace.

As his campaign for the presidency developed, Nixon fleshed out his ideas for ending the Vietnam war. He suggested that if he were elected, he would move on a variety of non-military fronts, that he had a plan, which he did not disclose in detail, for ending the war.[3] But Nixon did not have a plan, secret or otherwise, for ending the Vietnam war; he brought to the White House only a few general principles pertaining to a settlement that he had formulated over the years. He gradually improvised a Vietnam strategy during his first year in office.

Some of Nixon's ideas concerning the Vietnam war were similar to the views of Henry A. Kissinger, who would become Nixon's National Security adviser. Kissinger, a former Harvard professor who had written extensively on foreign policy and national security issues during the 1950s and 1960s, shared Nixon's view that the first order of foreign policy business must be the phasing out of the American Vietnam war and that it had to be done in honorable fashion. But Kissinger had never been an enthusiastic supporter of the U.S. military intervention in Vietnam. He probably believed that Johnson and his advisers had made a serious error in geopolitical judgment when they decided to send American combat forces to Vietnam in 1965, when they tried to find a military solution for what was essentially a problem of politics. However, Kissinger argued in 1969, how or why America got into the war no longer mattered because "ending the war honorably is essential for the peace of the world."[4]

Both Nixon and Kissinger, who quickly became Nixon's chief foreign policy adviser and envoy, shared the conviction that they must extract the

U.S. sea power had a major role in the American Vietnam war. Here, the battleship USS *New Jersey* lying offshore in Gulf of Tonkin waters, fires a salvo from one of its 16-inch guns, the largest guns in the world.
Source: U.S. Navy Photo

United States from what had become a major liability.[5] They also believed that to accomplish their major foreign policy goals they would have to concentrate the power to conduct American foreign policy into their hands. Achieving such power required bypassing the advisory agencies and the bureaucracies in the Defense Department, the State Department, and the CIA. They believed that an energetic and decisive foreign policy could come only from the new partnership forming in the White House, from Nixon and from Kissinger, in consultation with a few senior advisers. Early in his presidency, Nixon told Kissinger, "you and I will end the war."[6]

Nixon and Kissinger felt that Johnson's *modus operandi*, decision making by consensus, had been a slow and cumbrous process. Further, consensus required a variety of lowest common denominator decisions, which often reflected the bureaucratic interests of senior officials. Consensus decisions were expressions of the power balance within Johnson's administration among members of the Joint Chiefs, the State Department, the Defense

Department, the CIA, and the National Security Council, whether or not such decisions made strategic or diplomatic sense. Nixon and Kissinger believed that Johnson had used the consensus process because he had lacked confidence in his abilities to conduct foreign and strategic policy. Nixon and Kissinger both were certain that they possessed the requisite expertise to rise above the miasma of bureaucratic consensus politics. They believed that they could make the bold, decisive moves ending the American war in Vietnam, reorienting American relations with the major Communist powers, and achieving a stable and peaceful world order that accorded with U.S. interests.

Nixon and Kissinger came to power sharing the illusions held by their predecessors in the three previous administrations. They believed that they were unique, that they brought to office the requisite knowledge, boldness, and imagination required to achieve a satisfactory outcome to the long American Vietnam involvement. They would devise strategies for making Hanoi accept terms that the North Vietnamese had consistently rejected for years; they would use Soviet leverage to get a settlement. Consequently, Nixon and Kissinger were doomed to replicate the experience of their predecessors. Once in power, they discovered that they had inherited intractable problems in Vietnam. They also found that their power and options were limited and that many of their assumptions and ideas did not work. They discovered, to their dismay and immense frustration, that they had limited freedom of maneuver, even less than their predecessors, because of several factors: the stalemated war, Hanoi's protracted war strategy, Soviet unwillingness to prod Hanoi to end the war, General Thieu's fears that any settlement that America might make with Hanoi threatened his country's prospects for survival, and powerful domestic political constraints.

Nixon's narrow electoral victory carried with it no mandate whatsoever. Because of the presence of a strong third-party candidate, George Wallace, Nixon won the presidency by only a plurality (with 43 percent of the popular vote). In November 1968, 57 percent of the voters preferred a candidate other than Richard Nixon for president. Congress remained firmly in the control of large Democratic majorities. Many liberal Democratic congressman and senators were now freed from the inhibitions of having to support Johnson's war.[7]

Public opinion polls taken in early 1969 showed that large majorities of Americans wanted a quick end to the U.S. war and favored an early withdrawal of all American forces. But most Americans did not want to see the United States defeated in Vietnam, and they believed that it was important to stop the spread of Communism in Southeast Asia. The same people who wanted a quick end to a war that they neither wanted to lose nor see escalated while also stopping the spread of Communism in Southeast Asia, exhibited little concern for the welfare of the South Vietnamese people or for the survival of their government.[8] Such views may have defied logic, but they set limits to what Nixon and Kissinger could do as the two forged an American strategy for Vietnam.

The new president and his chief adviser confronted a contradiction as they improvised a U.S. Vietnam policy and strategies to make it work: Any terms acceptable to Hanoi for ending the war were unacceptable to them, to their allies in South Vietnam, to the U.S. congressional majority, and to a majority of Americans. Further, Nixon and Kissinger faced a double dilemma: Powerful domestic and international political constraints foreclosed their using options that might break the military stalemate and permit a negotiated settlement that could resolve the impasse. Domestic criticism of the costs of the war encouraged the president to withdraw American troops, but unilateral American force withdrawals also encouraged Hanoi to refuse to make any concessions to achieve a settlement.

Johnson had passed on to his successors a war that could neither be won nor ended except on terms that amounted to a major American defeat. The Nixon administration and the American people would endure four more years of war in Indochina before they could accept what had been inevitable since Tet-68, perhaps inevitable since the U.S. intervention in southern Vietnam back in 1954, that is, strategic defeat, and they finally accepted it in January 1973 only by disguising that defeat within the rhetoric of "peace with honor." "Peace with honor" glossed over the ineffable strategic reality of the war: "American withdrawal from the war and the survival of the South Vietnamese government...had always been contradictory objectives."[9]

VIETNAMIZATION

As Nixon set out to end the war, he ruled out the two extreme solutions, immediate withdrawal or massive escalation. Nixon understood from the beginning of his presidency that his only feasible option was an American withdrawal.[10] For Nixon, the only significant question concerned the way America withdrew. Would it be precipitous, an ignominious American defeat, or would it be measured and honorable, assuring the survival of South Vietnam? There is no evidence that Nixon ever deluded himself with fantasies of winning a military victory over North Vietnam or that he delayed ending the war because he was trying to win it, as radical and liberal antiwar critics have charged. The long delay in ending the war arose from Nixon's preoccupation with how the war was to be terminated and with what consequences, domestic and international. Although Nixon never tried to win the war, he fought ferociously for years not to lose it, or at least to appear not to lose it. Nixon waged a long, slow, costly, and bitter American retreat from Indochina.[11]

Nixon sent a letter to the North Vietnamese leaders expressing his desire for peace. He proposed as a first step the mutual withdrawal of "external forces" (American and NVA) from South Vietnam and the restoration of the DMZ as a boundary between the two countries of North Vietnam and South Vietnam. He also proposed, at Kissinger's suggestion, that the Paris negotiations follow a two-tiered approach, with Washington and Hanoi concentrating on mutual troop withdrawals while Saigon's representatives and the NLF negotiated a political settlement of the civil war. At the same time that Nixon sent his letter to Hanoi he sent Kissinger to tell the Soviet ambassador to the United States, Anatoly Dobrynin, that a peace settlement in Vietnam must precede any accommodation between the United States and the Soviet Union. That is, the American Vietnam war must end before detente could occur. To signal to both Hanoi and Moscow that his administration would not be bound by the old limits, Nixon accompanied these diplomatic initiatives with bombings of VC/NVA sanctuaries in the eastern provinces of Cambodia bordering southern Vietnam.[12]

The bombing also represented a response to Communist attacks carried out in many districts and provinces of South Vietnam on February 22, 1969, and they also fulfilled a long-standing request of the Joint Chiefs to strike at VC/NVA bases in Cambodia that lay beyond the reach of allied troops. Johnson had always rejected the Joint Chiefs' request out of his fear of widening the war. The bombing operation, code-named MENU, began March 18. B-52s bombed the VC/NVA Cambodian sanctuaries in several locales. MENU began with a BREAKFAST phase. As the war went on and the bombing of Cambodia continued, BREAKFAST was followed by LUNCH, LUNCH by SNACK, SNACK by DINNER, DINNER by DESSERT, and DESSERT by SUPPER. Nixon ordered intermittent bombing raids on Cambodia through August 1969. After August, the bombing continued on a regular basis until May 1970, when air strikes in Cambodia began openly in support of allied ground operations against North Vietnamese bases.[13]

Because the bombings occurred in a neutral country and represented a widening of the war both geographically and politically, the Nixon administration tried to keep them secret from the American people. But accounts of the secret bombing of Cambodia, based on news leaks from White House officials, soon appeared in the New York *Times*, the Washington *Post*, and other papers. Nixon, angered by the leaks, tried to stop them. He ordered FBI director J. Edgar Hoover to wiretap the phones of eleven officials and four newsmen suspected of leaking information about the bombing to the media.[14]

In May 1970, at the time of the American incursion into Cambodia, Nixon ordered the bombing of target sites in North Vietnam and tried to keep this action secret. After another press leak, the New York *Times* ran a story about the renewed bombing of North Vietnam. Once again Nixon ordered wiretaps put on the phones of suspect officials and journalists. In July 1971, the New York *Times* began publishing the *Pentagon Papers*, a secret Defense Department history of the long U.S. involvement in Vietnam, leaked to them by a former Defense Department official, Daniel Ellsberg, and Anthony Russo. To stop further press leaks and to discredit Ellsberg, White House officials formed a special unit, the plumbers. President Nixon, increasingly frustrated by his inability to end the Vietnam war and convinced that his policies, even his ability to govern, were under attack from his "enemies" in the federal bureaucracies, in Congress, in the media, and in the universities, ordered the plumbers to take whatever actions were necessary to stop press leaks. Wire tapping had led to the forming of the plumbers. It was a natural progression from the actions of the plumbers to the "dirty tricks" of the 1972 presidential election, one of which was the Watergate burglary and its attempted cover-up.[15] The genesis of the Watergate scandals that eventually destroyed the Nixon presidency lay in Nixon's siege mentality arising from his inability to forge a rapid end to the Vietnam war, which led him to countenance ruthless measures intended to squelch his political opponents.

None of Nixon's and Kissinger's initial efforts to end the Vietnam war produced any noticeable results. Neither the VC/NVA February offensive nor the U.S. bombing of Cambodia changed the military balance in Vietnam. The stalemate on the battlefield was matched by a continuing diplomatic standoff in Paris. The Soviets made no effort to persuade North Vietnam to end the war. Both the North Vietnamese and South Vietnamese governments rejected the U.S. proposal for a mutual withdrawal of American and PAVN forces from South Vietnam. The Saigon government refused to recognize or to negotiate with representatives of the NLF. The double deadlock continued.[16]

Perceiving that his initial efforts to end the war had failed, Nixon used a televised speech on May 14 to propose a comprehensive eight-point Vietnam peace plan that he hoped would break the diplomatic logjam. Most of the eight points referred to the proposed troop withdrawal and other military matters. The president also tried to resuscitate the two-tier formula separating the military and political dimensions of the struggle, by stating that "the political settlement is an internal matter that ought to be decided by the South Vietnamese themselves...."[17]

Nixon followed his speech with a trip to Midway Island in early June where he met with General Thieu. After conferring with Thieu, Nixon announced on June 8 that he was recalling immediately 25,000 American troops from Vietnam. U.S. disengagement had begun. Lest Hanoi or the Soviets read the wrong message into the troop pull-out, Nixon followed his Midway pronouncements with several speeches attacking antiwar critics and affirming that his administration would keep America's commitments abroad.[18]

These additional diplomatic and military moves also failed to extract the slightest concession from Hanoi. The Communists could neither be pressured nor lured into altering their basic negotiating stance. They reiterated the peace terms that they had maintained since talks had begun in May 1968: the total and unconditional withdrawal of all U.S. forces from Vietnam

President Nixon and General Thieu met for the first time on Midway Island June 8, 1969. After conferring with the South Vietnamese leader, Nixon announced that he was immediately recalling 25,000 U.S. troops from Vietnam. Vietnamization had become U.S. policy. Henry Kissinger, National Security Adviser, appears in background.
Source: National Archives, Nixon Collection

and the replacement of the Thieu government with a provisional govern-ment.[19] On the battlefield the VC/NVA continued its protracted war strat-egy. The war went on, although the scale and intensity of fighting declined during the year, casualties dropped, and Hanoi pulled some of its forces back across the DMZ. The North Vietnamese were prepared to wait out the Nixon administration, confident that declining domestic support for the war would eventually force Washington to withdraw the American forces just as the loss of support at home had forced the French to withdraw their forces from Indochina during the previous war.[20] Hanoi's leaders understood that if the U.S. forces did not win in time they would lose; the North Vietnamese had only not to lose and in time they would win. They confidently embraced General Tran Hung Dao's dictum, which he expressed in 1284 as his forces outlasted the invading armies of the reigning superpower of that era, "Time is always in our favor."[21]

By the summer of 1969, it was evident that the concepts and strategies that Nixon and Kissinger had brought to Washington to end the American Vietnam war had failed to deliver the promised result. Congressional criti-cism of the continuing war was on the rise, and the peace movement, quiescent since the violence in Chicago, announced plans for fall demonstrations. Fearful that domestic discontent would undermine his efforts to get Hanoi to negotiate an acceptable agreement, Nixon turned to what he called his "go for broke" strategy, an all-out effort to end the war, either by a diplomatic agreement or by the use of military force. The president sent a letter to Ho Chi Minh urging a settlement, but with the added warning, amounting to an ultimatum, that if no progress were made by November 1, Nixon would have no choice but to resort to "measures of great consequence and force."[22] Nixon sent Kissinger to see Dobrynin again to warn him that there remained little time for a peaceful solution to the impasse at Paris.

Nixon also ordered Kissinger to form a select National Security Council group to develop plans for a "savage, punishing" blow aimed at North Vietnam.[23] Nixon and Kissinger were seeking that one powerful and decisive stroke that would destroy the will of the North Vietnamese to continue the war in South Vietnam. Kissinger told the select group at their first meeting in early September, "I can't believe that a fourth-rate power like North Vietnam doesn't have a breaking point."[24] By the end of the month, the group had developed a thick loose-leaf notebook of attack plans, code-named DUCK HOOK. DUCK HOOK included mining Haiphong, North Vietnam's major port, implementing a naval blockade of the North Vietnamese coast, and mounting air strikes on both military targets and population centers. In addition, the planners considered the options of bombing the Red River dikes to flood the major rice-growing region of North Vietnam, and they proposed closing down the rail supply lines to China. DUCK HOOK planners also analyzed possible uses of tactical nuclear devices in North Vietnam.[25] Not averse to using press leaks himself if they could advance his policies, Nixon let journalists know that he was considering a range of military options. He probably intended the leaks as warning signals to Moscow and Hanoi that the time left for diplomacy had grown short and that his patience had worn thin. Nixon also vowed to a group from Congress that he would not be the first president ever to lose a war.[26]

Nixon's "go for broke" strategy fizzled. Hanoi could not be intimidated, although the Communists did agree to hold secret talks with the Americans outside the framework of the Paris negotiations. On August 4, 1969, Kissinger met privately with Xuan Thuy for the first of what proved to be a long series of secret talks between Kissinger and DRV envoys lasting until the Paris Agreement was negotiated in January 1973. At that first meeting, Thuy rejected all of Kissinger's proposals, dismissed Nixon's epistolary ultimatum to Ho Chi Minh, and repeated Hanoi's litany that there could be no agreement until the United States had removed all its troops from Vietnam and had sacrificed the Thieu government.[27] On August 15, Ho Chi Minh formally replied to Nixon's letter. The North Vietnamese leader ignored the ultimatum, rejected Nixon's overtures, and restated Hanoi's basic

President Nixon visited South Vietnam July 30, 1969. Here he chats with soldiers of the 1st Infantry Division at Dian, near Saigon. The 1st, "The Big Red One," served in South Vietnam from October 1965 to April 1970 and fought in most of the major battles occurring in III Corps Tactical Zone.
Source: USMI Photo Archives

position, insisting that it was the only correct formula for peace. Hanoi radio added to Nixon's chagrin by wishing the American peace movement splendid success with its upcoming demonstrations.[28]

By fall 1969, Nixon, infuriated by Hanoi's intransigence and by dovish antiwar critics whom he believed encouraged North Vietnam's resistance to his diplomatic overtures, faced stark choices: He could undertake a major military escalation of the war, or he could beat a humiliating diplomatic retreat. His gut reaction was to strike back at his enemies. He wanted to hurl U.S. air power at the North Vietnamese and to blockade their ports. But he was advised by Secretary of State William Rogers and Secretary of Defense Melvin Laird not to escalate the war because such action would doubtless arouse the doves in Congress, in the press, in the academies, and in the streets. More important, Kissinger's select group of military planners concluded that air strikes and a blockade would probably not wring any concessions from Hanoi nor diminish its ability to support the war in South Vietnam. A strong American military operation directed against North Vietnamese targets would also suggest that Nixon was trying for a military victory in a war that he had promised to phase out. Nixon's hoped-for "savage, punishing" blow could not be found; it was, in reality, a phantasm. Discovering that military escalation would not be effective, unwilling to make concessions that would mean compromising his notion of peace with honor, facing rising domestic opposition and impending peace demonstrations, Nixon found himself bereft of a Vietnam policy.[29]

Caught in a bind largely of his own making, Nixon could only fall back on Vietnamization, the policy that he had inherited from Johnson. Having discovered that his and Kissinger's strategies could not end the war, Nixon convinced himself that Vietnamization could. The United States would withdraw its military forces from South Vietnam while continuing to provide substantial military and economic assistance to the GVN to build it up to a point where it could deflect the VC/NVA attacks and survive on its own. Nixon believed that if he could rally the American people behind him, accelerate the buildup in South Vietnam, and persuade Hanoi that the America would never abandon Thieu, he might be able to convince North Vietnam's leaders that it would be to their advantage to negotiate an acceptable settlement with the United States in the short run rather than have to deal with a strong South Vietnamese government in the long run. Vietnamization would be Nixon's fall-back route to an honorable peace. The results of Vietnamization would be three more years of war for Americans, thousands of additional U.S. battle deaths, multi-billion dollar expenditures, continuing domestic turmoil and anguish, and, in the end, the collapse of Saigon and total victory for the North Vietnamese. En route to that tragic outcome, Nixon's presidency would be destroyed, the second administration to fall victim to the ordeal of Vietnam.

While Nixon groped for a Vietnam war policy, the Vietnam Moratorium Committee (VMC) organized the largest peace demonstrations in American history. Its leadership was liberal; many of its organizers had worked for Eugene McCarthy or for Robert Kennedy during the 1968 Democratic presidential campaign. VMC leaders like Sam Brown wanted to reach beyond the college campuses and into the cities and towns of America, where they hoped to involve millions of ordinary people in the antiwar effort. On M-Day, October 15, 1969, demonstrations were staged all over the country. Between 500,000 and 1,000,000 people participated. In a large parade in Manhattan, Wall Street financiers walked alongside housewives, civil rights leaders, hippies, and disillusioned Vietnam veterans. Most significant of all, groups of U.S. soldiers stationed at various sites in South Vietnam wore black armbands to show their support for Moratorium day. The antiwar movement had joined the war.[30] Pleased with the initial moratorium, organizers announced they were scheduling another one to be held November 13–15, highlighted by a march on Washington.

In between moratoriums, the Nixon administration launched its counteroffensive against its critics. The president unleashed Vice President Spiro T. Agnew. Agnew, an energetic and articulate polemicist, went on the oratorical warpath. In a series of speeches he stridently attacked administration foes. He labeled the antiwar protesters "an effete corps of impudent snobs who characterize themselves as intellectuals."[31] Agnew also lambasted what he termed the "liberal establishment press," accusing the media of biased coverage of the Nixon administration and its Vietnam war policy.

Nixon followed Agnew with a major televised address to the nation the evening of November 3. It was the longest and most important speech of his presidency to date. He timed the speech so that it fell midway between the two moratoriums. His chief goals were to declare war on the antiwar movement and to rally the American people in support of his Vietnam war policies.

The president vigorously attacked his antiwar critics. He called them an irrational minority trying to thwart the will of the large majority of Americans. He defended U.S. intervention in Vietnam, and he defended the American Vietnam war. He cited the commitments to Vietnam made by three previous administrations, and he vowed to stay in Vietnam until he achieved an honorable and lasting peace. Nixon used the speech to spell out his Vietnamization policy. He insisted that it would produce an honorable peace by enabling the South Vietnamese to save themselves while he withdrew U.S. forces and reduced American casualties. Citing the Communist mass murders at Hue during the Tet-68 campaign and the thousands of deaths in North Vietnam that had accompanied land reform during the mid-1950s as precedents, the president invoked the chilling specter of a bloodbath facing the South Vietnamese, especially the 1.5 million Catholics among them, if the U.S. precipitously pulled out its forces and left the South Vietnamese people at the mercy of the Communists. He appealed powerfully to the American people's patriotism, to their sense of honor, and to the ideal of American greatness. He concluded his speech with a stirring call for support for Vietnamization by the mass of the American people whom he called "the great silent majority," ending with "North Vietnam cannot humiliate the United States. Only Americans can do that."[32]

Nixon's Vietnamization speech proved to be shrewd and successful. He put his critics in the Congress, the press, and the peace movement on the defensive. Even though the second Moratorium was larger and more successful than the first, especially the march in Washington, it had no discernible impact on the war. Nixon had sold the American people a policy that he claimed would produce an honorable peace and save American lives. By calling attention to and labeling the "silent majority," Nixon broadened his base of support and gave millions of Americans a new political identity. Pro-Nixon rallies appeared in a number of cities. Polls taken after the speech showed that 70 percent of the American people supported Vietnamization. Following the fall moratoriums, the peace movement went into decline for a time. Congressional and media criticism of the war waned. The country quieted. Most Americans appeared willing to give Nixon's policies a chance to succeed. He had bought time for Vietnamization. Nixon, delighted with his success, boasted that he "had floored those liberal sons of bitches with the TV speech," and "we've got those liberal bastards on the run now; we've got them on the run and we're going to keep them on the run."[33]

It was much easier for Nixon to manipulate American public opinion by claiming that Vietnamization would produce peace with honor than it was for American and South Vietnamese officials to turn it into an effective policy. There was some improvement in RVNAF forces in 1969 and 1970. Force levels were increased, and they were equipped with modern weapons. Some ARVN units, when properly led, and even some district and local forces, fought effectively. The South Vietnamese air force and navy were both enhanced. Pay and conditions of service were improved for all branches of the South Vietnamese armed forces.

But RVNAF still faced many serious problems. Systematic corruption and mass desertion persisted. Paper force levels looked impressive, but they were inflated by 15–20 percent because ARVN commanders padded unit rosters with the names of nonexistent soldiers. In addition, Vietnamization required a modern South Vietnamese army. A modern army required large numbers of competent officers, experienced non-commissioned officers, and skilled people to perform a wide variety of tasks and missions. Furnishing RVNAF with all the officers and skilled manpower demanded by the Vietnamization process required an elaborate network of training installations, skilled instructors, and equipment. Neither the skilled personnel nor good training facilities were available in sufficient numbers to give Vietnamization a chance to succeed.[34]

Another fundamental problem plagued Vietnamization. The backbone of ARVN was supposed to be its infantry divisions, but these divisions lacked mobility. Each division served in its home area, and most of its personnel were recruited from its home area. Often, family and dependents accompanied the soldiers into the field, with the result that hovels and tent cities grew up alongside division cantonments. ARVN infantry divisions were essentially static territorial units, unavailable for offensive operations or counterattacks. With soldiers' families clustered around the camps, an enemy attack guaranteed disaster, mass desertions and incredible confusion as soldiers fled their units in order to help their wives and relatives to safety.[35]

Although Nixon did not realize it, Vietnamization rested on a fantasy, that these motley home guards masquerading as maneuver units could be molded into a modern strike force that would be able to hold its own against the disciplined battle-tested units of the NVA. Possibly, with enough time, at least some of the RVNAF deficiencies—its lack of capable officers and noncoms, its lack of skilled manpower, its lack of training facilities, and its lack of maneuverability—could have been corrected. However, irresistible political pressures on Nixon to end American involvement in the war guaranteed that Vietnamization could never have nearly enough time to succeed. "Vietnamization can be seen in its true light—an American self-serving illusion."[36]

During 1969 and into 1970, one aspect of nation building was working, the accelerated pacification program under the direction of William Colby, who had replaced Robert Komer as head of CORDS. General Abrams strongly backed pacification and he deployed American units to help provide village security. General Thieu also enthusiastically supported many pacification programs. Additional villages and hamlets were reclaimed from the Vietcong. By the end of 1969, an estimated 80 percent of the rural population lived in secure or relatively secure areas. In many areas of South Vietnam, the threat posed by the insurgency receded. The number of Vietcong defectors, both soldiers and cadres, rose significantly. Project PHOENIX neutralized the VC infrastructure in some areas. Members of the clandestine apparatus were identified, imprisoned, often tortured during interrogations, and in many cases killed. Both the number and quality of the VC/NVA forces appeared to decline. Many villages developed their own local governments and self-defense forces. Roads were opened, bridges were repaired, schools were established, and hospitals were built. Thieu instituted a land reform program. New strains of livestock were introduced. Peasants received tractors, steel plows, and other modern farm equipment. The rural economy improved; rice production increased in 1969 in South Vietnam for the first time in years.[37]

On the battlefield, the scale and intensity of fighting declined during 1969. Because Hanoi continued its defensive protracted war strategy and deliberately avoided large-scale combat, General Abrams assigned more of his forces to the tasks of pacification, and to the support, training, and advisory missions involved in preparing the RVNAF forces to take over responsibility for defending themselves. The MACV commander also dismantled his divisions, breaking them down into small platoon and company-sized task forces to assign them patrol, reconnaissance, and territorial security missions. He ordered small-scale offensives mounted against enemy basing areas near the DMZ and along the Laotian and Cambodian borders. These offensives attacked NVA supply depots and supply lines; their objective was to attrite the enemy's logistics system and thereby keep them off balance and on the defensive.

Abrams united the disparate dimensions of the U.S. war effort in Vietnam. He fused the war of attrition, previously a big-unit war aimed at destroying enemy bases and personnel, with Vietnamization and nation building. For the first time since the American war began, U.S. forces implemented an integrated strategy. They were fighting one war instead of two.[38]

One of the most notorious battles of the American Vietnam war occurred in late spring 1969. It has passed into history as the Battle of Hamburger Hill, a name apparently provided by the soldiers who had to fight it. In March, MACV intelligence officers had noted that NVA forces were again building up their logistics systems in the forbidding A Shau valley, ostensibly preparing for offensive actions in I Corps. General Zais's "Screaming Ea-

A U.S. Army rifle squad moves through defense forest cover. Much of the fighting in Vietnam involved small unit warfare-intense firefights that suddenly erupted when enemy squads made contact.
Source: USMI Photo Archives

gles," the 101st Airborne (Air Mobile), were ordered back into the area to destroy them. During April and early May, soldiers from units of the 101st that had been helilifted into the A Shau valley found several new supply caches and other evidence of a PAVN logistical build-up taking place in the area.[39]

On May 10, a combined force of U.S. Marines, an ARVN regiment, and the 101st Airborne's 3rd Brigade, 187th Infantry, air assaulted into a rugged area of thickly-jungled mountains along the west side of the A Shau valley near the Laotian border. The next day, soldiers in B Company of the 187th Infantry discovered that NVA forces had fortified a series of ridges cloaked in thick jungle. These ridges appeared on American maps as Hill 937. Hill 937 was known to the Vietnamese as Dong Ap Bia (Mount Ap Bia). As B Company troops advanced up the slopes of Dong Ap Bia, they were hit by concentrated machine-gun fire coming from enemy bunkers dug into the crests of the montane ridges. B Company was forced to withdraw; artillery and air strikes were called in to hammer the NVA positions. Thus began a fierce ten-day battle for Dong Ap Bia, which the world would soon know as Hamburger Hill.[40]

On May 13, two companies of the 187th's 1st Battalion tried to take the hill only to be driven back by rocket and machine-gun fire from the bunker occupants, two battalions of the 29th NVA Regiment. The men of the 187th were reinforced, and they attacked again, only to be driven back once more. There was a pause in the fighting while the enemy bunkers were subjected

Air assault troopers of the elite 101st Airborne "Screaming Eagles" debarking their helicopter at a landing zone in the A Shau Valley in May 1969.
Source: USMI Photo Archives

to intensive artillery fire and air strikes for thirty-six hours. On May 18, two battalions made another assault of the hill, one going up the southern slope and the other the northern slope. The weather halted this attack. Heavy rains had turned the hillside, denuded of foliage by the artillery fire and air attacks, into mud; the soldiers, as they tried to advance up the mountain, kept slipping and sliding back down the slopes. Finally, on May 20, following another sustained artillery and air bombardment of the enemy positions, a four-battalion force reached the crest of Dong Ap Bia only to find that the NVA troops had abandoned the bunkers during the night. A few days after the hill had been taken, orders came down to abandon it because it had no tactical or strategic significance.

The Battle of Hamburger Hill received extensive press coverage and quickly ignited public controversy. The men of the 101st had fought hard and taken heavy casualties for an objective that was soon abandoned. Many troopers bitterly criticized the command decision that had required the seemingly pointless sacrifice of many men. Journalists aired the soldiers' complaints. Senator Edward Kennedy, one of the prominent war critics, called the battle "senseless and irresponsible."[41] General Zais defended the action; he stated that the 101st Airborne's mission had been to seek out the enemy and to destroy them wherever they found them. Zais pointed out that the enemy had lost an estimated 650 KIA during the ten-day fight, whereas U.S. battle deaths at Dong Ap Bia totalled 56, a kill ratio of better than ten to one.[42]

Hamburger Hill turned out to be the last campaign of the now abandoned attrition strategy, and it was also the last battle of the Vietnam war in which victory was determined by a body count. In reaction to the controversy aroused by the battle, President Nixon ordered the Joint Chiefs to tell General Abrams to hold down American casualties in future battles. At the heart of the controversy over Hamburger Hill were not so much questions of tactics or casualties, but of what kind of war Americans were now waging in Vietnam and for what goals. The conflict was no longer a war of search and destroy, of attrition. It had become a war based on a new strategy of small-unit warfare aimed at destroying enemy logistics systems, which was also being integrated with pacification and nation-building efforts. The Battle of Hamburger Hill had occurred during the transitional period. Shortly after the controversial battle, the president announced the first U.S. troop withdrawals from the Vietnam war.

"Not only were American troops leaving South Vietnam, but the offensive spirit was leaving the American army."[43] The bitterness expressed by some of the soldiers of the 101st Airborne over the fighting at Dong Ap Bia was a sign that America was beginning to reap a pernicious harvest from its lengthy and inconclusive war in Southeast Asia, the progressive demoralization of the American ground forces serving in Vietnam. Until 1968 the U.S. armed forces in Vietnam had fought well. The Army that America sent to fight the Vietnam War was the best the nation had ever had. The troops were the strongest and healthiest, the best-educated, and the best-trained in U.S. military history. They were equipped with powerful and effective weapons, and they were supported by a remarkable logistics system that made them the best-fed and best-supplied soldiers in the history of warfare. Wounded soldiers received better medical treatment quicker than any soldiers who had ever fought in war. They were led by competent professionals at all levels from sergeants to generals. Troops fought aggressively, with great courage and tenacity, in pursuit of their objectives. Their morale was high and their discipline taut. They believed in the cause for which they fought, and they remained confident of victory. They won every major battle they fought, and they nearly always inflicted far heavier casualties on their enemies than they sustained.

The decline of the American Army that began in 1968 and got progressively worse in 1969, 1970, and 1971, was caused by a multiplicity of factors and circumstances.[44] Nixon's Vietnamization policy was a major cause of the breakdown in morale and discipline. The president emphasized his commitment to seeking a negotiated peace, of not trying to win a military victory. U.S. troop withdrawals reinforced the notion that America was pursuing a no-win policy in a war that would probably end soon for the United States.

Soldiers asked themselves, Why fight? Why get wounded or killed in a war that we are not trying to win? A sardonic rhetorical question gained wide currency after 1969: Who wants to be the last soldier to die in Vietnam? As American troops were being pulled out of Vietnam, many soldiers cared only about surviving their year in "'Nam" and returning to the "real world" (the United States) alive. "Short-timer's fever," especially among soldiers with a few weeks to go on their year's tour, became widespread by 1969. Its symptoms included an acute fear of being killed or seriously wounded, a reluctance to engage in combat, a generally poor performance of all duties, a rebellious attitude toward military authority, and withdrawal from social activities with buddies. Short-timers cared little about their units, about accomplishing their mission, or about the fate of the South Vietnamese people.

By 1969, the class-biased Selective Service had delivered a army of conscripts to Vietnam who were plucked mainly from working class and disadvantaged backgrounds. The fact that most middle class youths were avoiding the war was itself a source of resentment and declining morale among the troops in the field. The soldiers manning rifle companies in Vietnam understood that the price they were paying for being poor, for being poorly educated, for being without employable skills, and for possessing no influence or political clout was having to fight a war that many of their more affluent countrymen were avoiding, that the nation no longer believed in, and that their government no longer was trying to win.[45]

By 1969 the quality of both the officer corps and the non-commissioned officer corps had declined significantly. In 1965, the officer corps had been made up mainly of career professionals and Reserve Officer Training Corps (ROTC) graduates. The unpopularity of the Vietnam war caused a severe reduction in ROTC enrollments, and, by 1969, dozens of ROTC programs had been expelled from college campuses. To make up the shortages, the Army was forced to turn to Officer Candidate School (OCS) products who, generally, possessed lower educational attainments and ability levels.

The non-commissioned officer corps had severe shortages of experienced sergeants by 1969. Promising young privates were hurried through twenty weeks of stateside advanced training and given sergeants' stripes. These young, inexperienced buck and staff sergeants, called "Instant NCOs" or "shake n' bakes" by sarcastic soldiers, were then rushed to Vietnam and thrown into combat. Platoons of "grunts" (the most frequently used nickname that Army and Marine combat infantrymen gave themselves), could find themselves going into combat led by twenty-two-year-old second lieutenants just out of OCS and inexperienced twenty-year-old "shake n' bake" sergeants just arrived from stateside.[46]

Army personnel practices during the Vietnam war era exacerbated the morale and discipline problems created by assigning young and inexperienced officers and noncoms to combat units, and undermined unit cohesion. The Army wanted to build up a large pool of officers with combat experience;

majors and lieutenant colonels were given six-month tours as battalion commanders. Many of these officers were concerned only about advancing their careers, about "getting their tickets punched." Some of these officers did not care about the welfare of the men they were assigned to lead. When ordering the men under their commands to fight, they hovered over the battlefield in command helicopters, safely above the fray. Soldiers sometimes refused to put their lives on the line for such uncaring and unprofessional officers whose principal military goal appeared to be compiling a good dossier.[47]

The growing unpopularity of the war and the activities of antiwar protesters also undermined the morale of soldiers serving in Vietnam. Grunts loathed college antiwar protesters, viewing them as a privileged class of cowards and traitors. But the knowledge that millions of Americans no longer believed in the war or supported it with any enthusiasm caused resentment and confusion among many troops, who came to doubt the purpose of the war and to doubt whether the sacrifices they were making were worthwhile or were even appreciated. They felt abandoned by a nation that was abandoning the war that they still had to fight. By 1969, some soldiers serving in Vietnam had turned against the war and wore the symbols of the stateside antiwar protesters, love beads and peace medallions, on their uniforms. Some soldiers grew their hair long and sprouted full beards, in violation of military dress and appearance codes that increasingly went unenforced in the field. Soldiers sometimes saluted one another with the two-fingered peace sign.[48]

The Army's switch from aggressive big-unit search and destroy missions to small-scale holding actions in support of Vietnamization and pacification in 1969 also sapped the soldiers' motivation and undermined their morale and discipline. They grew reluctant to expose themselves to danger on operations that they knew were only intended to buy time until the South Vietnamese took over and the Americans went home. The war became not just unfinished business, but unfinishable business, and therefore to be avoided whenever possible. "Search and evade" operations were added to the tactical repertoires of many squads and platoons. Soldiers sent out on patrols were careful to search only areas where they knew the enemy would not be found. Sometimes they did not patrol at all, and they filed a faked report of a search that never took place. Combat refusals increased in 1969 and became more frequent in 1970 and 1971.[49] The cumbersome and overloaded military justice system could not handle the increasing incidence of combat refusals in Vietnam. Often, punishment for refusing a lawful order to fight was left to field commanders, who in many cases meted out light punishments or ignored the incidents.

From 1969 on, the U.S. Army appeared to be at war with itself. As morale and discipline ebbed, as search and avoid tactics and combat refusals increased in frequency, both officers and noncoms who took an aggressive approach to combat or who enforced rules and regulations strictly risked assassination at the hands of demoralized or rebellious troops. Such assassinations had occurred in previous wars but never so frequently. A new term came into use, "fragging" (the term came from fragmentation grenade, a weapon that was readily available, easy to use, and left no fingerprints or other incriminating evidence when used to kill an unpopular officer or noncom). The Army reported ninety-six fragging incidents in 1969 and 209 in 1970. In those two years, seventy-five officers and noncoms lost their lives to assassins. Court martials were held in fewer than 10 percent of fragging cases because of the lack of evidence and witnesses. Most soldiers who committed fraggings in Vietnam literally got away with murder.[50]

In addition to fragging, racial violence occasionally racked military installations in Vietnam starting in 1969. Army life in Vietnam had become a racial pressure cooker. Many black soldiers, angry over the discrimination and prejudice that they had encountered in civilian society and in the Army, often denounced white attitudes and sometimes denounced whites as well. Whites frequently replied in kind. Some black soldiers, influenced by black nationalist doctrines, developed an Afro-American style of appearance and behavior that white officers, often southerners with traditional racial attitudes, found threatening. Racial animosity was generally suppressed in combat situations, but in rear basing areas racial enmities sometimes exploded. Race riots, even racially motivated firefights, occurred.[51] Black-white racial conflict was a social pathology that the Army inherited from the American society it served. Racial tensions in Vietnam were exacerbated after 1968 by the pressures generated within an army that was trying to fight a war that it was not winning and was afflicted with serious internal problems.

Desertion was another indicator of declining morale and discipline. Thousands of Vietnam-era soldiers deserted in 1969, 1970, and 1971. Desertions were comparatively rare in combat areas, and very few American soldiers defected to the enemy. Neither the Vietcong nor the NVA forces encouraged Americans to desert, nor did either usually offer deserters sanctuary.[52] The Communists wanted the Americans to go home, not to join them.

But for every soldier who deserted, many more troops tried to escape through psychological withdrawal, by using drugs. By 1969, drug abuse had become a serious problem for the Army in Vietnam. A Defense Department survey conducted in 1969 found that about 25 percent of U.S. soldiers serving in Vietnam were using marijuana on either an occasional or regular basis.[53] Far worse, U.S. troops began using hard drugs in late 1969 and early 1970, particularly heroin. The heroin came from the mountainous region stretching across northern Laos, northern Thailand, and northeastern Burma known as the Golden Triangle.[54] High-grade heroin, 80–90 percent pure, flowed into South Vietnam via illicit conduits controlled by high officials in the South Vietnamese government. These officials garnered huge profits from selling the severely addictive drug to American GIs. American officials tacitly accepted the South Vietnamese officials' involvement in drug operations, refusing to investigate them or to make any effort to get them to curtail the drug trade. South Vietnamese pushers aggressively sold the nearly pure heroin to soldiers for $2.00 to $3.00 a vial, a fraction of the price that diluted heroin sold for on the streets in American cities. By 1970, an estimated 7 percent of U.S. soldiers in Vietnam used heroin regularly; by 1971, between 10 and 15 percent. The Army discovered to its dismay in 1971 that it had a heroin plague on its hands, with an estimated 25,000 to 37,000 addicted users.[55]

The gleaming American sword, honed to a keen edge, that had been thrust into South Vietnam in 1965, had become dull and corroded by 1971. The confusions inherent in Nixon's Vietnamization policy, the unfair conscription system, the decline in the quality of officers and non-commissioned officers, dubious Army personnel policies, the antiwar movement and declining domestic public support for the war, racial tensions, and the contagion of drug use had combined to undermine morale, erode discipline, and sap the Army's fighting spirit. One of the reasons why Nixon accelerated the recall of U.S. forces from Vietnam in 1970 and 1971, over the protests of General Abrams and General Thieu, was his awareness that the fighting machine in South Vietnam was disintegrating. It became necessary to remove the Army in order to save it.

WIDENING THE WAR

During the spring of 1970, Nixon had to confront the contradictions inherent in his Vietnam war strategies. At home he faced declining popular support for his policies, rising Congressional opposition, and more peace demonstrations. Negotiations in Paris remained sterile. Vietnamization proceeded slowly. To appease domestic dissent, Nixon announced a phased withdrawal of 150,000 troops from Vietnam over the next twelve months. Both General Abrams and General Thieu strongly protested the size of Nixon's proposed troop withdrawal. They insisted that it would leave the GVN vulnerable to VC/NVA attacks and that it would retard both Vietnamization and nation building.[56] Both Nixon and Kissinger also knew that accelerated American troop withdrawals could only stiffen Hanoi's resolve to make no concessions at Paris and to wait until all the Americans had been forced to leave South Vietnam. On the battlefield, the NVA continued their patient defensive strategy of protracted warfare. Only when most Americans had departed would General Giap shift to the offensive and move in to destroy the South Vietnamese forces.

But an event occurred that caught both Washington and Hanoi by surprise and changed the shape of the Vietnam war. The neutralist leader of Cambodia, Prince Norodom Sihanouk, was overthrown by his pro-Western prime minister, General Lon Nol, on March 18, 1970. For years Sihanouk had attempted to keep Cambodia at peace by playing off the

Chinese Communists and the North Vietnamese against the Americans and the South Vietnamese. He had allowed the NVA to establish bases in Cambodian provinces bordering South Vietnam, and he had also granted Hanoi the use of the port of Sihanoukville from which they supplied their forces fighting in the southern half of South Vietnam. Sihanouk had also tolerated the secret U.S. bombing of the NVA bases and sanctuaries in Cambodia.[57]

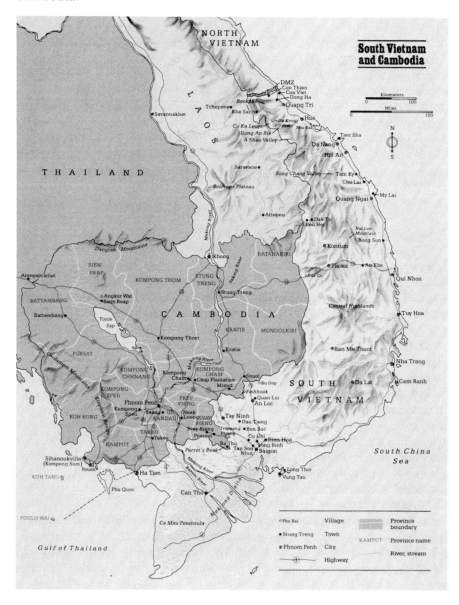

Although caught by surprise, Washington quickly recognized the Lon Nol government and extended American military and economic assistance to Cambodia. Lon Nol barred Hanoi from further access to the port at Sihanoukville, and he ordered the Communists to vacate their bases on Cambodian soil and to get out of his country. Determined to stay in regions that were crucial to the conduct of its war in South Vietnam, Hanoi promptly sent the NVA forces in Cambodia on a drive to the west in the direction of Phnom Penh, the Cambodian capital, to overthrow the Lon Nol government. A CIA report to President Nixon warned that the Communist forces could overthrow the new Cambodian regime; without strong American action a domino might fall in Southeast Asia. With Cambodia in Communist hands, the port at Sihanoukville would be reopened and the entire country would become an enemy basing area outflanking the Allied forces in South Vietnam. "The United States had to intervene in Cambodia decisively or see the war change dramatically for the worse."[58]

The now deposed Sihanouk quickly cast his lot with the Communists. From Peking he announced the formation of a resistance movement. He called for the overthrow of Lon Nol's "illegal" regime, for a Pathet Lao victory in Laos, and for a VC/NVA victory in South Vietnam. China backed Sihanouk's new movement. In Paris, Kissinger met privately with Le Duc Tho, a member of the North Vietnamese Politburo who had replaced Xuan Thuy as Hanoi's chief negotiator. In conversations with Kissinger, Le Duc Tho made it clear that Hanoi had linked the overthrow of Lon Nol's government with the on-going revolutionary war in South Vietnam. Within Cambodia, to enhance their campaign to overthrow the Lon Nol government, China and Hanoi backed the Khmer Rouge, an indigenous Maoist revolutionary movement formed during the early 1960s. The Khmer Rouge, armed and trained by the North Vietnamese, would overthrow Lon Nol's government in the spring of 1975. Once in power, the Khmer Rouge proceeded to impose a murderous regime on the hapless Cambodian people, a government that was responsible for the deaths of at least a million people.[59]

Reacting to the widening war, Nixon believed that the time had come to make a decisive move in Indochina. For years MACV, backed by the Joint Chiefs, had called for ground invasions of Cambodia to destroy the VC/NVA border sanctuaries. Nixon decided that now was time to hit them. Two areas were targeted for attack: the Parrot's Beak, a section of Cambodian land that jutted into South Vietnam to a point only thirty miles west of Saigon, and the Fishhook, a point of land lying fifty-five miles northeast of Saigon. The president approved General Abrams' proposal that American forces attack the Fishhook area while ARVN forces, supported by U.S. air strikes, would attack the sanctuaries in the Parrot's Beak.[60]

Nixon's decision to send U.S. forces into Cambodia was one of the most important and most controversial actions of his presidency. He sent the troops in to serve a variety of tactical, political, and diplomatic purposes.

They would shore up Lon Nol's regime and help keep Cambodia out of Communist hands. They would buy more time for Vietnamization to work in South Vietnam. Nixon decided that the strategic advantages to be gained from the Cambodian incursion outweighed its political liabilities, particularly the domestic controversy that he knew would be aroused by the action. He also hoped that the invasion would put pressure on Hanoi to consider negotiations as an alternative to facing a wider war. Nixon also put the Cambodian crisis in a larger context. He saw it as one of those decisive moments in the Cold War, when the will and character of the American people and its leaders were being tested by events and by their enemies. Nixon vowed to meet the challenge; he would show his mettle in the ongoing struggle between the Communist world and the free world. He would yield neither to domestic critics nor foreign adversaries. Nixon was determined to maintain American credibility with both U.S. friends and foes.[61]

Nixon announced his decision to invade Cambodia, and he explained the reasons for the incursion in a televised speech given the evening of April 30. Nixon claimed that the invasion was necessary to save a friendly government from Communist aggression and that it was necessary to protect American forces still remaining in South Vietnam after the scheduled withdrawal of another 150,000 troops. He also told Americans that one of the major reasons for the invasion was to capture COSVN, the PLAF command center for South Vietnam, located in the Fishhook area. Nixon's tone throughout the speech was belligerent. He defied his critics in the press and congress: "I would rather be a one-term president than be a two-term president at the cost of seeing America...accept the first defeat in its sound 190-years' history." He concluded his speech with some vintage Cold War hyperbole:

> "If, when the chips are down, the world's most powerful nation acts like a pitiful, helpless giant, the forces of totalitarianism and anarchy will threaten free nations and free institutions throughout the world."[62]

As MACV planned the Cambodian campaigns to destroy the enemy bases in the areas of the Fishhook and Parrot's Beak, and any enemy troops that might try to defend them, they knew that many American combat units had already redeployed to the United States or were scheduled to be redeployed soon. The Cambodian incursion would probably be the last opportunity for the Allies to mount a large-scale combat operation involving American assets. It would also put the ARVN units to the ultimate test of combat against enemy forces on a foreign battlefield. The Cambodian invasion would therefore furnish an excellent opportunity to measure the progress that Vietnamization had achieved to date.[63]

On April 29, ARVN forces, with American air and artillery support, penetrated the Parrot's Beak area. They captured some enemy supplies, but the enemy forces in the region eluded the invaders. They did not engage the enemy in much intensive combat. On May 1, following artillery barrages and

Members of Battery B, 21st Artillery, of the 1st cavalry Division (Air Mobile) firing a 105 mm. howitzer from Landing Zone Bronco in Cambodia on June 23, 1970. The Cambodian incursion was the last major campaign of the Indochina war in which U.S. ground combat troops fought. *Source*: U.S. Army Photo

heavy bombing by B-52s, a task force of 15,000 U.S. and ARVN armored and infantry battalions entered the Fishhook region accompanied by helicopter gunships and fighter-bomber strike aircraft. The operation was code-named TOAN THANG 43. It was the largest tactical operation involving U.S. forces in a over a year. The fighting was not intensive because the VC/NVA forces chose to abandon their bases and supply depots in the region rather than stand and fight against overwhelming forces. Further, the American forces operated in Cambodia under tight ground rules. They had orders to travel no farther than nineteen miles beyond the Vietnamese border, and U.S. commanders had been told to keep U.S. casualties down. The Americans also had to be out of Cambodia by June 30.[64]

All American forces had withdrawn from Cambodia by June 29. Operation TOAN THANG 43 had been a partial tactical success. Large quantities of enemy ammunition, weapons, and rice had either been captured or destroyed. All enemy installations and basing facilities had been destroyed. COSVN operations had been disrupted. But most of the main enemy units had avoided battle. They had retreated to the interior and survived intact.

The pressure on Lon Nol's forces had been eased, and the Cambodian army had time to build up its strength. An endangered domino was saved for a time, but the temporary U.S. incursion could not remove the long-run threat to Lon Nol's survival posed by the Khmer Rouge. The VC/NVA losses of men, facilities, weapons, and supplies, plus the closing of the port at

Sihanoukville, probably set back their offensive timetable twelve to fifteen months. It also put increased pressures on the Ho Chi Minh trail because it was the sole remaining source of supply for the VC/NVA forces fighting in southern South Vietnam. The Cambodian invasions also eased the danger to the remaining American forces in Vietnam.[65]

But the tactical gains the Americans made from TOAN THANG 43 were largely offset by the liabilities of a wider war in Southeast Asia. Even though Nixon had committed himself to winding down the American war in Vietnam, he had expanded the theater of military operations to include another country. Further, the United States had acquired another fragile client in Indochina, Lon Nol's fledgling government. Nixon committed U.S. economic and military resources to help Cambodia defend itself against VC/NVA and Khmer Rouge attacks at the same time that he was pulling U.S. forces out of South Vietnam. The American Vietnam war had become the Second Indochina war.

Although American aviators and armored units involved in the Cambodian incursion had fought aggressively when they had the opportunity, some American infantry companies indulged in search and evade tactics to avoid combat during TOAN THANG 43. Most ARVN units involved in the Cambodian incursions performed poorly. They failed to fight aggressively. Their armored units developed severe maintenance problems because they lacked competent maintenance personnel and sufficient spare parts. They had persistent command and control problems. For example, they failed to coordinate artillery fire with their mobile operations and had to rely on American artillery. Further, any improved ARVN performance was premised on having strong U.S. air support, support that they were not always going to have. Insofar as the Cambodia operation had been a test of Vietnamization, ARVN flunked the test. That failure had ominous implications for the future survival of South Vietnam after the Americans had all departed and the GVN would have to face its foes alone.[66]

At home, dozens of college campuses erupted in protest over the sudden widening of a war that the president had promised to end. "At Kent State and Jackson State College, six students were killed in angry confrontations with National Guardsmen and police."[67] The killings provoked a massive demonstration in the nation's capital. Twenty-four ROTC buildings on various campuses were either bombed or put to the torch. Students went on strike at many colleges, and some schools were forced to shut down to avoid violence on campus. Summer vacation came a few weeks early in 1970 for thousands.[68]

Although many college campuses exploded in protest, they did not represent the broad spectrum of American public opinion. Polls showed that a majority of Americans supported the Cambodian invasion. Polls also revealed that a strong backlash against student antiwar protest had built up among Middle Americans. Nearly two-thirds of Americans blamed the students for the tragedy at Kent State.[69] State legislatures slashed funds from the budgets of the University of Wisconsin and the University of California

Tragedy struck at Kent State University on May 4, 1970. Troops of the Ohio National Guard fired into a crowd of student protesters, killing four. In this photo, students attend one of their fallen classmates.
Source: National Archives

because of campus antiwar protests.   On May 20, an estimated 100,000 construction workers staged a march through Manhattan in support of President Nixon and his war policy. The "hard hats" waved American flags and sang "God Bless America" as they walked along the streets of New York. Nixon's "silent majority" was no longer silent.

The Cambodian invasion also provoked an outburst of congressional criticism, and the first signs that Congress might challenge Nixon's power to wage war in Indochina.   Content since the rise of the Cold War to let presidents control foreign and strategic policy, the Senate, the more dovish branch of Congress, voted to repeal the Gulf of Tonkin Resolution which had been enacted back in August 1964. Many senators believed that the resolution had served as a retroactive declaration of war. The Senate's gesture was purely symbolic, however. President Nixon claimed that he possessed the authority to wage war based on the war powers clause of the Constitution, and no one challenged him. The Senate also enacted the Church–Cooper amendment, which cut off all funding for military operations in Cambodia effective June 30, 1970.[70] The House of Representatives failed to enact the Church-Cooper amendment; hence, it never became law.   None of these congressional actions impeded the president's power to wage war, but as harbingers of rising congressional opposition, these actions increased the

Thousands gathered in Washington to protest President Nixon's decision to invade Cambodia and the Ohio National Guard's killing of four students on the Kent State (Ohio) campus on May 4, 1970. Among the participants were famed baby doctor Benjamin Spock (speaking into mike) and Bella Abzug, member of Congress. (Next to Doctor Spock and wearing one of her trademark hats)
Source: National Archives, Nixon Collection

pressure on Nixon and Kissinger to find a way to phase out the U.S. war in Indochina or risk having a rebellious legislature end it for them.

Nixon was neither inclined toward nor capable of reconciling his critics. Instead he attacked them, hard. He called the student protesters "bums who were blowing up college campuses." He accused his congressional critics of prolonging the war and told them that if they restricted his war-making powers, they would be responsible for an American defeat in Indochina. Nixon empowered the FBI, the CIA, and military intelligence agencies to use illegal surveillance techniques against radical antiwar groups.[71] By the summer of 1970, the Nixon White House was exhibiting the attributes of a beleaguered fortress. The president and the president's men increasingly held the intensely partisan view that it was them against all the administration's enemies in the press, the Congress, and the antiwar movement who were trying to undermine Nixon's policies and to restrict the president's power to govern. The siege mentality that led to Watergate and the eventual self-destruction of the Nixon presidency had taken root in the White House.

As the embattled president confronted the firestorm of protest provoked by the Cambodian incursion, any hope that he may have held out for breaking the diplomatic deadlock at Paris was dashed. If the Cambodian operation had been intended to pressure the North Vietnamese into making concessions, then it had the precisely opposite effect of hardening Hanoi's position. The North Vietnamese and NLF delegates walked out of the Paris talks in protest over the American invasion of Cambodia and refused to return until after all U.S. troops were pulled out of Cambodia. Nixon's announced withdrawal of 150,000 more American forces in April coupled to the uproar provoked in the United States by the Cambodian incursion could only strengthen Hanoi's determination to continue stalling the negotiations until domestic political pressures forced Nixon to withdraw all American forces from Indochina. Kissinger did offer another peace proposal at Paris, a cease-fire in place, to try to move the talks forward, but Hanoi promptly rejected it.[72] The talks remained deadlocked.

During the 1970 midterm elections, Nixon campaigned energetically against his Democratic congressional critics and denounced the antiwar protesters wherever he campaigned. Vice President Agnew also took to the hustings to campaign against the Nixon administration's political opponents. Both Nixon and Agnew aimed to defeat congressional doves and to replace them with candidates who would support the Nixon administration's war policy. Their efforts mostly failed. A few doves were defeated, but new ones were elected. The Republicans managed a gain of

Bob Hope and troupe entertaining soldiers of the 101st Airborne January 8, 1971. Hope and company made Christmas tours to South Vietnam every year from 1964 through 1972. *Source*: USMI Photo Archives

two senators, but they lost nine House seats. Both houses of the new Congress remained overwhelmingly Democratic, and the new Congress would also be more dovish than its predecessor.

After two years in office, after two years of fighting and diplomatic maneuvering, the man elected president on a promise to bring an end to the Vietnam war discovered to his dismay that the American position had deteriorated. Nixon's freedom of maneuver, never very great, had diminished. He could see no way to end the war any time soon on terms that accorded with his conception of peace with honor. The Paris negotiations remained tightly deadlocked. Hanoi had not budged from its positions staked out when negotiations had begun in May 1968. The United States lacked the power to drive the North Vietnamese troops out of South Vietnam, and Kissinger had found no formula that would persuade Hanoi to withdraw them. The war had also been widened. The United States was now supporting a struggling government in Cambodia that was trying to survive a mounting insurgency backed by North Vietnam and China. In South Vietnam, the RVNAF buildup was faltering. The American troop withdrawal was accelerating. Popular support for Nixon's war policy was ebbing, congressional opposition was growing stronger, and antiwar protest had been revitalized by the Cambodian incursion. As 1970 ended, it was evident that Nixon's improvised policy of Vietnamization was riddled with unresolvable contradictions. It was not working nor showing any promise of ever working.

Although it had been a manifest failure, Nixon, perhaps as much for lack of an alternative as any other reason, adhered to his policy of Vietnamization. Early in 1971, hoping to calm his domestic critics, he announced another speedup in the timetable of U.S. troop withdrawals. Nixon's announcement drew protests from both General Thieu, who knew that Vietnamization was not working and feared its consequences, and General Abrams, who was concerned for the security of the remaining U.S. forces. In response to stepped up NVA infiltration, Nixon also expanded the air war against the Ho Chi Minh trail complex and resumed bombing selected targets in North Vietnam, staging areas north of the DMZ and military targets in the Hanoi-Haiphong area. He also prepared to expand the ground war once again.

MACV and RVNAF intelligence analysts had detected a heavy stockpiling of enemy military supplies at two sites. One site was located about thirty miles west of Khe Sanh, near the Laotian town of Tchepone, and the other was located along the South Vietnam-Laotian border near the northern end of the A Shau valley. From these two bases, NVA units could attack the two northern provinces of South Vietnam, Quang Tri and Thua Thien, and threaten the city of Hue. It was a venerable strategy that the North Vietnamese had tried many times in the past, only to be blocked each time by U.S. troops. Some of these battles had involved the most intense and deadliest combat of the entire war. But now, in early 1971, the Americans were leaving Military Region I (MRI-Corps Tactical Zones were renamed Military Regions in July 1970). How would the South Vietnamese high command respond to this developing threat? Rather than wait for the NVA to attack the northern provinces of their country, General Thieu and his chief of staff, General Cao Van Vien, proposed a campaign to destroy the two supply sites to relieve the enemy pressure building in the north. MACV Commander General Abrams approved the proposed ARVN operation and so did President Nixon. Nixon had approved another expansion of the Indochina War, a ground operation into Laos.

Laos, like Cambodia, was a neutral country, its neutrality formally guaranteed by the 1962 Paris Agreement. But neither side had observed that neutrality from the day it was established and Laos's weak coalition neutralist government, headed by Prince Souvanna Phouma, could not ensure the nation's territorial integrity. The CIA had been waging a secret war in Laos since 1963 involving Meo tribesmen. U.S. aircraft had been bombing targets along the Ho Chi Minh trail in the Laotian corridor since 1965. The North Vietnamese had been occupying part of Laos since the Franco–Vietminh war. By 1971, the NVA controlled all Laotian territory adjoining their own country, and they occupied the entire Laotian corridor, from which they had expelled the native Laotians, as one huge logistics system to support their war in South Vietnam.

General Thieu's and General Vien's main objective for the operation, code-named LAM SON 719,[73] was the destruction of enemy logistics installations and supplies at Tchepone and at a basing area located near the northern end of the A Shau valley. The operational plan also called for holding these facilities for ninety days and for interdicting the flow of supplies down the Ho Chi Minh trail, then withdrawing from Laos before the rainy season began. A successful spoiling operation in Laos coupled to the destruction wrought in the Cambodian sanctuaries the previous year would keep South Vietnam free of any enemy offensives for a year and would buy additional time for Vietnamization.[74]

Two factors made LAM SON 719 unique. It was the first major tactical operation since the American war began in 1965 in which ARVN forces would have to fight without American advisers or U.S. combat units accompanying them in battle. U.S. helicopters and strike aircraft would cover the air above Laos, but on the ground, the South Vietnamese would be on their own. LAM SON 719 would be another test of Vietnamization. South Vietnamese and U.S. officials would find out if the ARVN forces were ready to be weaned from their American dependency. Could they mount a successful invasion into Laos on their own?

The second factor involved the NVA. With the closing of the port at Sihanoukville, the Ho Chi Minh trail had become the jugular of Hanoi's war in South Vietnam; it was vitally important to the NVA war effort to maintain the flow of men and materiel down the trail network. Anticipating an attack at Tchepone, the hub of the Ho Chi Minh trail complex running through the Laotian corridor, Giap had brought in an additional 20,000 well-equipped troops and bolstered their air defense, armor, and heavy artillery capabilities. Unlike the Cambodian incursion, where the VC/NVA forces fled into the interior to avoid battle with the invaders, the PAVN forces in the vicinity of Tchepone were ready and waiting to fight the South Vietnamese invaders.[75]

On February 8, 1971, after preliminary actions, units of the ARVN 1st Airborne Division and 1st Armored Brigade under the command of General Hoang Xuan Lam pushed into Laos along Route 9 west of Khe Sanh. The operation encountered trouble from the outset. North Vietnamese agents placed at high levels within the RVNAF command structure had furnished complete details of the operation to the enemy forces in advance. The element of tactical surprise was completely lacking for LAM SON 719. Then the weather turned bad, and the American aircraft could not fly their air support missions for several days.

ARVN politics also intruded to undermine LAM SON 719's chances for success. General Thieu ordered General Lam to proceed cautiously and to not take heavy casualties. Thieu gave this order because the ARVN 1st Airborne was his palace guard; they were his coup insurance. Their destruction would leave him vulnerable to overthrow by his ARVN rivals. General Lam, a poor soldier but an astute politician, obediently stopped his columns a short distance into Laos. After the ARVN offensive ground to a halt, the powerful NVA forces attacked. Over the next two weeks, the NVA augmented its forces and inflicted mounting casualties on the ARVN forces. Worried about the fate of his palace guard, General Thieu ordered General Lam to remove the 1st Airborne from battle altogether and to replace it with an inexperienced Marine division. Thieu's removal of the 1st Airborne further weakened LAM SON 719. The South Vietnamese president, who had originally proposed the Laotian incursion, in effect, had subverted it for reasons of state. In General Thieu's hierarchy of priorities, political self-preservation ranked well ahead of any spoiling operation into Laos against the PAVN forces.[76] Because of Thieu's meddling, LAM SON 719 achieved only a fraction of its goals. The ARVN forces destroyed some enemy supply depots and disrupted NVA logistics along the Ho Chi Minh trail for perhaps a few weeks.

The difficult part of the operation involved the withdrawal of the ARVN forces. The GVN forces were under intense pressure from NVA infantry and tank assaults, and heavy artillery, through rugged, jungle-cloaked terrain. Between 30,000 and 40,000 NVA troops pursued 8,000 demoralized ARVN soldiers. ARVN's tactical retreat quickly became disorderly and then turned into a rout. In some units, discipline and order collapsed as panic-stricken troops abandoned their equipment and weapons, and fled on foot in the direction of the border. Only intense use of U.S. air power and heroic efforts by American helicopter pilots that together inflicted heavy casualties on the attacking NVA forces, suppressed NVA artillery fire, knocked out enemy tanks, hauled in ammunition, and hauled out ARVN troops, kept the headlong retreat from becoming a debacle. Altogether, during operation LAM SON 719, 108 American helicopters were lost and another 618 were damaged. Eighty-nine American pilots and air crewmen were either killed or reported missing in action, and another 178 were wounded.[77]

LAM SON 719 proved to be a dismal and dispiriting failure for the ARVN soldiers. The South Vietnamese knew that they had been defeated. The American media generally portrayed the Laotian incursion as a disaster. Television cameras showed American viewers images of demoralized ARVN soldiers straggling back to South Vietnam territory. Reacting to yet another widening of the Indochina War, several liberal Senators introduced resolutions aimed at limiting presidential power to conduct military operations in Indochina and cutting off funds for operations in Cambodia and Laos. None of them passed. "The operation revealed the inherent and incurable flaws of the RVNAF, which doomed any realistic hopes of successful Vietnamization."[78]

These flaws included (1) the hopeless incompetence of ARVN's politicized leadership, starting at the top with General Thieu; (2) the continuing inability of the static home-guard infantry divisions to meet the demands of mobile warfare; (3) the lack of professionalism, accentuated by the lack of U.S. advisers who usually coordinated helicopter flights, artillery fire, tank-infantry operations, and air strikes for the ARVN forces; (4) serious problems with communications and maintenance; (5) basic deficiencies in training and discipline; (6) the perennial lack of a fighting spirit when facing NVA troops in intensive combat; and (7) the ARVN's continuing dependence on the American forces. All these failures again exposed Vietnamization for the illusion that it was.[79] ARVN had flunked another test. In a speech delivered the evening of April 7, 1971, President Nixon said that LAM SON 719 proved that Vietnamization had succeeded. The operation had, of course, proven exactly the opposite: Vietnamization had not succeeded and probably would not succeed.

Shortly after the surviving South Vietnamese forces had come reeling back from their ill-fated Laotian incursion, Nixon instructed Henry Kissinger to offer Hanoi some new proposals in Paris that the president hoped would get the stalled peace talks moving. Nixon was probably motivated to make his new offers by three considerations. He understood that military operations like the Cambodian and Laotian incursions were not likely to force Hanoi to negotiate. Recent talks with the Soviets had been productive. The outlines of a major arms control agreement with the Soviets had emerged. Work on the opening to China was promising. A foundation for detente was being structured. Nixon felt, therefore, that he could afford to be more flexible with Hanoi. Nixon also believed that his prospects for reelection in 1972 depended mainly on his ability to end the Vietnam war. But he also knew that he had to avoid the appearance of rushing to make an election year settlement of the war, so his diplomatic initiative in the spring of 1971 was well-timed.

Kissinger, meeting secretly with Xuan Thuy and Le Duc Tho in Paris, offered a new seven-point peace plan. The plan contained two important concessions. Kissinger offered to set a date, December 31, 1971, for the complete withdrawal of all U.S. combat forces from South Vietnam; he also indicated that America was willing to withdraw its troops without requiring a simultaneous withdrawal of North Vietnamese forces. Since the United States had been unilaterally withdrawing its troops for two years, irrespective of Hanoi's troop deployments, Kissinger's latter proposal was not so much a concession as it was simply an aligning of the U.S. negotiating position with military reality. More important, the proposal separated the military issues from the political issues.[80] It would be possible for Washington and Hanoi to negotiate a cease-fire and to defer settlement of the major political question, what kind of government South Vietnam would have, to the postwar period.

Kissinger's new proposals kindled the first serious negotiations between Washington and Hanoi since the talks had begun. Intense secret meetings between Kissinger and Le Duc Tho took place over the next three months. Tho, responding to Kissinger's concessions, offered a nine-point plan of his own. It was the first peace plan that the North Vietnamese had ever offered, and it too contained some concessions. Hanoi agreed to release the American POWs by the end of 1971, simultaneously with the departure of all U.S. troops from Vietnam. Also for the first time, Hanoi did not ask for the removal of Thieu as a precondition for negotiations, only that the United States must stop backing the South Vietnamese leader. In subsequent meetings, Thieu's status proved to be the sticking point between Kissinger and Le Duc Tho. Hanoi insisted that Washington disavow Thieu. Nixon refused to abandon Thieu, fearing anarchy in South Vietnam if Thieu were ousted. This latest round of secret talks broke off in September when it became obvious that the impasse could not be resolved.[81] While the new proposals made by both sides had been promising indicators, neither side was yet prepared to make the sort of concessions that would be necessary to secure an end to America's involvement in the Second Indochina War.

As the latest round of secret talks ended in failure, South Vietnam was preparing to hold its presidential election as called for under the 1967 constitution. General Thieu, acutely aware that he had won the previous election with a plurality of only 35 percent, wanted to win resoundingly this time around. He was also determined to use his considerable powers of incumbency to ensure a landslide victory. Thieu understood the first principle of South Vietnamese politics: Irrespective of constitutional principles and democratic forms, the man who controls the government always wins elections.

When the 1971 electoral campaign began, General Thieu faced serious challenges from two strong rivals, General Nguyen Cao Ky and General Doung Van "Big" Minh. Both men had considerable followings, and either might have been able to defeat Thieu in a fair election. General Minh had a mixed following among Buddhists, southern Catholics, non-Communist intellectuals, and civilian politicians. Minh had also obtained the support of the National Liberation Front mainly because he had called for the creation of a coalition government that would include representatives of the Provisional Revolutionary Government (PRG), which had been created by the NLF in June 1969.[82] The mercurial Air Marshal Ky, hitherto famed for his fanatical anti-Communism, staged a remarkable *volte-face*. He called for recognition of the PRG and supported negotiating an end to the war with the Communist leaders in Hanoi.

It did not matter what Ky and Minh stood for or who supported them; Thieu used his control of the machinery of government to eliminate them from the race. The United States took a public stance of neutrality during the election. Behind the scenes, U.S. officials worked to ensure Thieu's landslide reelection. The Nixon administration was not about to risk losing Thieu, whose reelection it saw as imperative to the U.S. national interest. The election took place October 3, 1971. In a rigged election in which General Thieu was the only candidate, featuring a ballot providing a space only for voting yes for Thieu, in which the polling was supervised by Thieu's soldiers, and the votes counted by Thieu's officials; President Thieu was reelected to another four-year term as South Vietnam's president with 94.3 percent of the vote.[83] From their cafes along Tu Do street, the savants observed that the man they called "The Little Dictator" had gotten his mandate. But mandate for what?

By 1971, most Americans, regardless of their politics, had become thoroughly sick of the Indochina war and wished only that it would go away. Yet the war and its domestic consequences continued to plague the increasingly war-weary population. A group of disillusioned veterans, all claiming to have committed war crimes during their service in Vietnam, staged a poignant demonstration in the nation's capital in April. The veterans, some on crutches and others in wheelchairs, came forward one-by-one, and each angrily threw Vietnam war ribbons and medals onto the steps of the capitol building.[84]

During the spring and summer of 1971, two events brought Americans more anguish and anger connected to the seemingly interminable war. On March 31, a military court convicted Lieutenant William Calley of mass murder for his role in the My Lai massacre of March 16, 1968, and sentenced him to life imprisonment at hard labor. For once, both hawks and doves agreed on something, that Lieutenant Calley had been given a raw deal: Hawks, because they believed that no soldier should be convicted in war time for doing his duty; doves, because they believed that Calley had been a sacrificial figure to cover up the fact that many other war criminals went free. On June 13, the New York *Times* began publishing the *Pentagon Papers*, leaked to them by Daniel Ellsberg and Anthony Russo. The papers caused a furor as people discovered what many dovish critics had suspected all along. Readers found that President Kennedy, President Johnson, and other high officials had consistently misled the American people about their actions and intentions concerning the war. Readers also learned that it had often been the United States that had escalated the war and spurned negotiating initiatives. They discovered that President Kennedy had supported the coup that overthrew Ngo Dinh Diem. Publication of the *Pentagon Papers* widened the credibility gap. Polls showed popular support for the war at an all-time low.[85]

Nixon had tried to prevent publication of the *Pentagon Papers*. The attorney general had secured a court injunction on the grounds that their publication represented a clear and present danger to national security. But Judge Gerhardt Gesell quashed the injunction and the Supreme Court sustained him. A majority on the Supreme Court could not see how publishing the papers compromised national security; they found that publication of the *Pentagon Papers* represented a clear and present danger only to the reputations of former public officials. Nixon, thwarted in his efforts to stop publication of the *Pentagon Papers* through the courts, unleashed the notorious plumbers to plug government leaks and discredit Ellsberg.

PEACE WITHOUT HONOR

As 1972 began, both the battlefields of Vietnam and the American home front were calm. Only about 140,000 American troops remained in Vietnam, of whom no more than 20,000 constituted combat forces, and more would be leaving soon. American battle deaths for 1971 had totaled 1,380, much the lowest for any year since the American war had begun in 1965. The Paris peace talks, both public and private, remained on hold. President Nixon, pleased with the progress of his diplomacy viz-a-viz the major Communist powers, looked forward to summit conferences in February in China and in May in Moscow. He planned to use these conferences to link subsequent progress toward detente to Moscow's and Peking's willingness to pressure Hanoi into negotiating an end to the war.

But the war was about to resume, larger than ever. General Giap was in the final stages of planning what was going to be the largest offensive operation of the war, a spring invasion of South Vietnam. Hanoi viewed a successful offensive as leading either to a collapse or to a serious weakening of the Saigon regime and to forcing America to accept a negotiated withdrawal. Neither Nixon's diplomatic initiatives nor Hanoi's offensive would accomplish their Indochina goals in 1972, "but they did bring the war into a final, devastating phase which would ultimately lead to a compromise peace."[86]

Hanoi's decision to try once again to break the military stalemate had been reached at the 19th Plenum meeting in January 1971. But during the long interval before the offensive would be ready for launching, the Communists decided to continue their small-scale protracted war strategy, the small-unit struggle for control of villages in South Vietnam. Politburo leaders conceded that the GVN pacification programs, especially land reform, had reduced the areas controlled by the PRG and that PLAF force levels were down. But the Politburo leadership also knew that in the long run it was the fighting ability of the GVN forces that mattered more than their pacification programs. Once the Americans had departed, Thieu would be forced to rely on his own forces, and Lao Dong leaders were confident that their 1972 offensive would overwhelm the ARVN. General Giap's main justification for the offensive was that it would break the military stalemate and force the Nixon administration to conclude a settlement that would bring about a complete U.S. withdrawal from Vietnam.[87]

The Twentieth Plenum, meeting in February 1972, approved Giap's final plans for the spring offensive, scheduled to begin in late March, at which time the total American forces remaining in South Vietnam would be drawn down to 100,000, of whom only about 15,000 would be combatants. Although the Communists still considered political action important, they no longer planned for a combination general offensive/general uprising a la Tet-68. Giap hoped that the VC cadres could organize rural areas where he had a greater expectation of achieving military victory, but he did not expect there to be any urban risings unless PAVN main units were in the cities in force to support them.[88]

Giap launched the spring attacks, called the Nguyen Hue Offensive, in three successive stages. Beginning March 30, the first wave poured across the DMZ to strike at ARVN positions in the two northern provinces of Quang Tri and Thua Thien. Three PAVN divisions, totaling about 30,000 men, equipped with an arsenal of modern Soviet-made weaponry that included rockets, missiles, tanks, and heavy artillery, joined in the massive assaults into the northern provinces.[89]

Although Allied intelligence officers had been expecting the big NVA offensive, they had not learned exactly when and where the attacks would come. They also had not anticipated their size nor their power. The ARVN defenses had been placed in the hands of the 1st and 3rd Divisions; they bore the brunt of the NVA assaults. Within a few weeks, the situation had become critical. The PAVN forces had overrun ARVN defensive positions and had wiped out several of their firebases. Compounding the ARVN problems, the incompetent MRI commander, the notorious General Lam of LAM SON 719 shame, ordered the 3rd Division, probably the weakest division in the RVNAF order of battle, to counterattack in the face of superior NVA forces and under terribly unfavorable tactical circumstances. On May 1, the demoralized ARVN troops, accompanied by thousands of frightened family members and panic-stricken civilians, fled in headlong fashion toward the south. NVA gunners, firing into the fleeing masses, inflicted thousands of casualties. On May 1, the provincial capital, Quang Tri City, fell. The entire province lay in NVA hands.[90] The city of Hue, forty miles south of Quang Tri City, was threatened. American officials in Saigon and Washington feared that the GVN might collapse from the pressures generated by the all-out North Vietnamese spring offensive.

Alarmed by the success of the PAVN forces and fearing the fall of Hue and even Danang, General Thieu replaced Lam with General Ngo Quang Truong, probably the finest general in the GVN armed forces. Apolitical, thoroughly professional, and battle seasoned, Truong was a superb leader who could have commanded troops in any army. He organized a defense for Hue and saved the city, and perhaps South Vietnam as well. Truong built up his forces and in late June launched a counterattack. With crucial support provided by U.S. Naval gunfire, tactical air strikes, and B-52 bombing runs, Truong's forces fought effectively through the summer. On September 16, ARVN troops retook Quang Tri City.[91] The northern provinces had been reclaimed by the GVN.

The second wave of the Nguyen Hue Offensive, the NVA attacks on the central front, began in early April. Two NVA divisions penetrated the central highlands at Dak To and Tan Canh. Within a few weeks they had beaten the ARVN defenders and had begun a series of attacks on Kontum City. At the same time that the NVA forces attacked Kontum, another NVA division, assisted by local VC forces, occupied most of the coastal province of Binh Dinh, a long-time Communist stronghold.[92] Once again, the perennial NVA goal, the bisection of South Vietnam, threatened. If the city of Kontum fell, the NVA forces would link up with the VC/NVA forces in Binh Dinh, and Thieu's country would be knifed in two.

The defense of Kontum City was organized and directed by the legendary John Paul Vann.[93] Vann had returned to Vietnam as a minor civilian official following his retirement from the Army in 1964. By dint of his energy, his experience, his intelligence, his forceful personality, and his total dedication to the cause, Vann had worked his way up the bureaucratic ranks to become the leading U.S. adviser in MRII by 1972. Although a civilian, Vann held the equivalent military rank of a major general. When the GVN MRII commander, General Ngo Dzu, an accused drug trafficker, collapsed under the stress of the NVA attacks, Vann took charge of defending Kontum City.

The Battle of Kontum raged for nearly three weeks. The NVA forces launched a series of frontal assaults on the ARVN defenders. Led by a Vann protege, Colonel Ly Tong Ba, who proved a competent professional soldier under fire, the ARVN defenders beat back the NVA attacks. While Colonel Ba's forces were holding them off, Vann called in an air armada of U.S. helicopter gunships, tactical air strikes, and B-52 bombings that decimated the attacking forces. The critical moment in the Battle of Kontum came during the night of May 28, 1972. NVA forces penetrated the ARVN defenses and poured into the city. Only round-the-clock bombing by cells of B-52s finally broke the NVA assault, enabling Ba's battered 23rd Division to clear the city.[94] American air power, especially the intensive B-52 attacks, had saved Kontum City. The last NVA soldier inside Kontum was rousted from his hiding place and killed on June 7.

Two days after achieving his greatest victory, John Paul Vann died in a fiery helicopter crash a few miles south of Kontum City. Vann had given ten years and finally his life trying to save South Vietnam. His body was recovered and flown back to the United States. John Paul Vann was given a state funeral and buried with full honors in a moving ceremony at Arlington National Cemetery. President Nixon, who had been briefed by Vann on several occasions, praised him and posthumously awarded him the Medal of Freedom, the highest award a civilian can receive, for his heroic service in Vietnam.

The third wave of the Nguyen Hue Offensive struck Tay Ninh and Binh Long provinces northwest of Saigon in MR3. Three Vietcong divisions, the 5th, the 7th, and the 9th, manned mostly by NVA troops and commanded by North Vietnamese officers, poured into South Vietnam from their basing areas in Cambodia. The 5th VC Division took Loc Ninh, a town lying about eighty miles north of Saigon on Route 13, a highway leading straight to the South Vietnamese capital. The ARVN forces fell back to An Loc, a town nine miles south of Loc Ninh on Route 13. Failing to take An Loc by frontal assault, the NVA forces besieged the town. The Battle of An Loc raged for weeks.[95] General Thieu, determined to stop the NVA thrust at An Loc, threw in most of his strategic reserves and his elite airborne forces to bolster the defenses of the besieged town.

The crucial battle for An Loc occurred on the morning of May 11. Units of all three enemy divisions launched attacks on the ARVN defenders. The NVA were hit immediately, first by waves of U.S. and VNAF fighter-bombers and then by B-52 strikes. Thirty B-52 strikes struck the NVA forces within twenty-four hours. Entire PAVN units, caught in the open by the big bombers, just vanished in clouds of dust and debris. Although there was fighting in the vicinity of An Loc for a few more days, the battle was over. The ARVN forces had held. The key to victory at An Loc had been Allied air power, especially the mighty B-52s.[96]

Nixon had reacted quickly and decisively to the North Vietnamese invasion. He and Kissinger both knew that the United States had to move quickly to support the South Vietnamese or else the Saigon regime might very well collapse under pressure. They understood that it was essential to defeat the North Vietnamese thrusts militarily. If the NVA offensive succeeded, Nixon could not expect the upcoming summit with the Soviets to be productive nor could he hope to achieve a negotiated end to the war on acceptable terms. He believed that a North Vietnamese victory would be a major strategic and diplomatic disaster for the United States.[97]

On April 4, Nixon decided to mount an all-out air war against the NVA invasion. He did not consider either sending U.S. combat forces back to South Vietnam or using the few remaining maneuver battalions still in

Vietnam. In fact, the American forces scheduled for redeployment continued to leave South Vietnam while the battles forced by the Nguyen Hue offensive raged. On April 6, Nixon told the new commander of the 7th Air Force, General John W. Vogt, "I want you to get down there and use whatever air you need to turn this thing around...."[98] That same day, U.S. fighter-bombers struck targets north of the DMZ. Nixon had revived the air war against the North that had been on hold since October 31, 1968. From around the world, American aircraft carriers and Air Force squadrons raced toward the Indochina war. They were part of President Nixon's rapid, large-scale strategic buildup in Southeast Asia.

On April 10, B-52s struck supply storage centers near the city of Vinh, about 150 miles north of the DMZ. On April 13, B-52s bombed oil storage sites near Hanoi and Haiphong. On April 16, U.S. bombers accidentally hit four Soviet merchant ships lying at anchor in Haiphong Harbor, killing some Soviet seamen. The Soviets protested the bombing of their ships and the deaths of their sailors, but they did not make a big issue of these events, suggesting to Nixon that the Soviets were not going to let the fighting in Vietnam interfere with their upcoming summit meeting with the Americans.

The air campaign against North Vietnam, code-named LINEBACKER, had four primary goals: (1) to send the North Vietnamese, and perhaps the Soviets and Chinese as well, a warning that if Hanoi persisted with its offensive in an effort to win the war or to severely weaken the South Vietnamese government, the North Vietnamese could expect to get hit with the most punishing aerial offensive of the war; (2) to cut off North Vietnam from foreign sources of supply by destroying all its railroads and harbors; (3) to destroy enemy stockpiles of food, ammunition, weapons, and equipment; and (4) to interdict the supplies and equipment moving south toward the battlefields in South Vietnam.[99] In addition to reviving the air war against North Vietnam, Nixon also ordered the most intense air attacks of the war against the invading North Vietnamese forces along their northern, central, and southern fronts in South Vietnam. Within ten days of the launching of the invasions, Allied aircraft were inflicting heavy losses on units of Hanoi's mobilized army on all three of the fronts.

American efforts to separate the North Vietnamese from their Chinese and Soviet sources of supply represented the riskiest move that Nixon made during the Vietnam war. Nixon believed that he had to take the risk to save South Vietnam from military collapse and therefore preserve detente and the chance of an acceptable settlement of the war.[100] At Nixon's request, Kissinger revived the DUCK HOOK plan, which had been drawn up during the summer of 1969 but never used. One of its proposed operations called for the mining of North Vietnam's harbors to stop all ship traffic into Haiphong and other North Vietnamese ports. But before Nixon ordered the ports mined, he wanted to use diplomatic channels to forewarn the Chinese and Soviet leaders of his intentions. The president took these steps to preserve detente, to avoid possible reprisals by the major Communist powers, and to try to reopen secret negotiations with the North Vietnamese emissary, Le Duc Tho.[101]

While applying military pressure to Hanoi, Nixon also applied diplomatic pressure to the Soviets, whom he and Kissinger held responsible for the NVA offensive in South Vietnam. Hanoi could never have mounted the operation without the military hardware furnished by the Soviet Union. Kissinger met secretly with Soviet leader Leonid Brezhnev in Moscow on April 20. Before he would consent to talk to Brezhnev about any of the issues of the impending summit, Kissinger insisted that the Soviet leader agree to put pressure on Hanoi to negotiate an end to the war. Brezhnev agreed; he wanted nothing to subvert the upcoming summit. However, he protested to Kissinger that he did not have the kind of influence with the Hanoi leadership that the Americans appeared to think that he did. Kissinger also persuaded the Soviet leader to arrange another secret meeting in Paris between Kissinger and Le Duc Tho scheduled for May 2, three weeks before the convening of the Moscow summit.[102] Kissinger's trip to Moscow had turned out successfully. He had preserved the upcoming summit conference, and he had convinced the Soviet leaders that they should try to help bring an end to the war.

Kissinger and Le Duc Tho met secretly in Paris on May 2. At the time of their meeting, the North Vietnamese offensive was going well. Quang Tri had fallen, and Kontum and An Loc were under intense attack. Le Duc Tho was confident that the South Vietnamese government verged on collapse, and he believed that American air power could not save the GVN. Le Duc Tho was not interested in negotiations that day; confident of military victory, he rejected all of Kissinger's proposals. Their meeting accomplished nothing.[103]

Disappointed and angered by Tho's response, President Nixon decided to strike hard against the North Vietnamese. He gambled that the Chinese and Soviets both placed greater importance on improving their relations with the United States than they did on retaliating on behalf of their allies. The president growled to his aides, "The bastards have never been bombed like they're going to be bombed this time."[104] On May 8, in a dramatic televised speech, Nixon announced to a startled nation that he had ordered his most drastic escalations of the war: the mining of Haiphong harbor, a naval blockade of North Vietnam, and a massive air war against that country.[105]

As Nixon spoke, Navy jets were dropping mines in the narrow twelve-mile-long channel connecting the port of Haiphong with the Gulf of Tonkin. Twenty-seven freighters, mostly Soviet, were bottled up at Haiphong. For the next three days, Navy aircraft mined the approaches to North Vietnam's other ports and also several inland waterways. The blockade proved to be effective; it quickly cut off the sources of about 85 percent of North Vietnam's war materiel and disrupted all North Vietnamese naval activity.[106] To the immense frustration of the North Vietnamese, Moscow and Beijing reacted coolly to the mining and the renewed bombing of North Vietnam. Nixon and

Kissinger had gambled, and they had won. They had succeeded in isolating Hanoi from its major allies. Neither the USSR nor China did more than issue *pro forma* criticisms of the U.S. actions, and both privately put pressure on Hanoi to end the war. The two major Communist powers wanted the war to end lest it jeopardize the fruits of detente and the major realignment of power then taking place in the world. The Moscow summit occurred on schedule. Meetings were cordial and productive. Nixon and Brezhnev signed several important agreements, including SALT 1, new trade agreements, and a new Berlin treaty.

The domestic reaction to Nixon's dramatic war escalations was mild. There was a flurry of protest demonstrations, but they did not attract large or militant followings. Doves introduced another round of end-the-war resolutions in the Senate, but none of them passed. The fact that Nixon had responded so forcefully, yet exempted the use of American ground forces and kept U.S. casualties low, allowed more people to support his actions. Many Americans regarded Nixon's actions as a justifiable reaction to naked aggression, a military invasion of South Vietnam by North Vietnam. Nixon's bold response also attracted much popular support. The success of the Moscow summit demonstrated that military escalations did not automatically endanger detente. Polls showed strong public support for Nixon's actions. His public approval rating climbed dramatically. In an election year, Nixon's political position had grown much stronger by June than it had been before the North Vietnamese invasion occurred. Nixon's bold actions had paid domestic political dividends.

The NVA offensive ended in September when the ARVN forces expelled the last NVA remnants from Quang Tri City. Nixon's decisive response had prevented a South Vietnamese defeat. Hanoi had committed almost 200,000 troops to the largest military offensive undertaken since the Chinese invaded northern Korea in December 1950. But their efforts to use massed forces to overwhelm the ARVN units had met with disaster; U.S. air power exacted a ghastly toll. The NVA lost an estimated 100,000 troops, most of their tanks, and their artillery in three months. PAVN inexperience and inadequacies made them vulnerable to such catastrophic destruction. Unaccustomed to mobile, mechanized warfare, they often failed to coordinate their infantry and armor attacks. Their primitive logistics system could not provide the huge amounts of ammunition, gasoline, and spare parts required to support their offensive. Giap also appeared not to comprehend the terrible vulnerability of his mechanized forces in a tactical situation where the Allied air forces enjoyed absolute control of the air.

The South Vietnamese also suffered heavy casualties, an estimated 25,000 soldiers killed during three months of fighting. Some ARVN commanders, particularly General Truong and Colonel Ba, demonstrated professional competence under fire. Some ARVN units, particularly the airborne troops, fought courageously under fire. VNAF pilots gave a good account of themselves in many battles. But the PAVN offensive also demonstrated the continuing fundamental shortcomings of the RVNAF forces. Their helicopter and other air transport units were inadequate. Artillery was poorly coordinated and often inaccurate. Communications and intelligence services remained poor. Their logistics system could never function without U.S. assistance. The U.S. advisers directed most of the ARVN combat operations; they were the reinforcing steel rods that held the ARVN military structures together. Many ARVN soldiers continued to perform poorly in combat situations; their morale and nerve would desert them and they fled in panic. Their officer corps remained infested with corrupt and incompetent officers. Worse yet, South Vietnam was running out of men. The pool of draft-age men was running dry. Reserve units were depleted, and many regular units could not replace their losses. Shortages of competent officers and noncoms were more acute than ever following the NVA spring offensive.[107] "The final inescapable truth to emerge from the offensive was that ARVN soldiers...could neither stop the enemy without significant American air support nor could their counteroffensive have succeeded without it."[108]

Once again Vietnamization had flunked a test. On August 22, 1972, the 1st Battalion of the U.S. 7th Cavalry boarded a plane for Texas. The last U.S. ground combat forces had departed. Few American officials in Vietnam, including the man in charge of the Vietnamization process, General Creighton Abrams, held any illusions about the ultimate outcome of the Indochina war.

Washington and Hanoi, having failed to break the diplomatic stalemate by military means during the summer of 1972, moved during the fall to break the military stalemate by diplomacy.[109] Although confident of impending victory over George McGovern, the Democratic challenger, Nixon wanted to fulfill the promise he had made four years ago and to achieve a peaceful settlement of the Indochina war before the November election took place. The North Vietnamese, for the first time in the long war, genuinely desired a peaceful settlement, if it did not contravene their long-range goals of subverting the Thieu regime, implementing a coalition government controlled by the PRG, and achieving national reunification. North Vietnam had been severely damaged by the recent bombing, and its army had been decimated. Hanoi's leaders knew that it would be at least two, perhaps three, years before North Vietnam would have the assets to mount another major offensive. They understood that the Soviets and the Chinese wanted the war to end; their allies were no longer willing to risk detente with America for the sake of Hanoi's war in South Vietnam. Although knowing that the dovish McGovern had no chance to defeat Nixon, the Communist leadership in Hanoi sensed that they might get better terms from Nixon before the election than after his anticipated landslide victory.[110]

Starting in September 1972, Kissinger and Le Duc Tho began a series of meetings in Paris. Within six weeks the outlines of a settlement emerged. By mid-October they had worked out an agreement based on the U.S. concept of a two-tracked agreement that separated the military and political aspects of the conflict. Hanoi agreed to allow General Thieu to remain in power temporarily in exchange for a grant of a political status in South Vietnam to the Provisional Revolutionary Government. Within sixty days of a cease-fire, Hanoi agreed to return all the American POWs and the United States agreed to withdraw all its remaining troops from South Vietnam. Washington's greatest concession was that all NVA troops currently in South Vietnam would be permitted to remain. A tripartite commission made up of delegates from the GVN, the PRG, and "third force" political elements would be created to supervise elections and to administer the agreement. All decisions of the tripartite commission would have to be unanimous, which meant that both the Thieu regime and the PRG representatives would retain a veto over the commission's actions.[111] The agreement deferred the key issue, who would rule in South Vietnam, to an unspecified time in the future. That matter would be resolved by the tripartite commission after the Indochina war had ended.

With most outstanding issues settled between Hanoi and Washington, Kissinger flew to Saigon to get General Thieu's approval of the mid-October agreement, only to discover that the South Vietnamese leader refused to accept it. General Thieu raised several fundamental objections to it and endeavored to prevent ratification of the agreement. He worried especially about the continued presence of large numbers of North Vietnamese forces in southern Vietnam after the Americans had withdrawn all their combat forces.[112] General Thieu preferred that the war in his country continue rather than accept an agreement that he believed endangered the GVN's chances of survival.

Kissinger, concerned primarily with extricating the United States from the war and skeptical of the GVN's prospects for longterm survival, probably hoped "to secure nothing more than a 'decent interval' between an American withdrawal and the resolution of the conflict in Vietnam."[113] Kissinger was angered by Thieu's opposition to the agreement, and he advised Nixon to sign it without Thieu's approval. Kissinger attempted to generate momentum for a pre-election settlement by announcing publicly on October 31 that, "peace is at hand."[114]

But Nixon shared some of Thieu's objections to the mid-October agreement. He also found that former MACV commander William Westmoreland and other military leaders opposed the settlement. Westmoreland urged Nixon to hold out for better terms. Consequently, Nixon backed the South Vietnamese leader's refusal to sign the agreement. Confident of winning an overwhelming victory in the upcoming election, Nixon decided to wait until after his reelection to try to forge an agreement with the North Vietnamese that would improve South Vietnam's prospects for longterm survival.[115] The president's support of General Thieu's intransigence guaranteed that the agreement that Kissinger and Le Duc Tho had forged by the middle of October would fail.

Following Nixon's landslide victory over McGovern on November 7, Kissinger and Le Duc Tho resumed their discussions in Paris. When Kissinger, responding to Nixon's and General Thieu's concerns, introduced many matters for reconsideration that the North Vietnamese assumed had been resolved, and when he also proposed changes that would adversely affect the status of the Vietcong and the North Vietnamese forces in South Vietnam, Le Duc Tho and his colleagues, concluding that they had been tricked, angrily rejected his proposals. When Kissinger warned Tho that Nixon, having just won reelection by an overwhelming margin, was prepared to take whatever action that he felt to be necessary to protect American interests in South Vietnam, the North Vietnamese envoy responded by hardening his position. The North Vietnamese even returned to their old stance of insisting that Thieu would have to be ousted as a precondition for any settlement. After weeks of futile negotiation, convinced that Hanoi did not want an agreement to come out of the sessions, Nixon and Kissinger broke off the talks on December 13.[116] President Nixon had decided to gamble again, to try to resolve the Paris impasse by force.

In a last-ditch effort to force Hanoi to conclude a peace agreement before his new term began, Nixon ordered another air assault against the North Vietnamese. He told the chairman of the Joint Chiefs, Admiral Thomas Moorer,

> I don't want any more of this crap about the fact that we couldn't hit this target or that one. This is your chance to use military power to win this war, and if you don't, I'll consider it your responsibility.[117]

Starting December 18, the sky over Hanoi and Haiphong was filled by the largest American air armada of the war. The bombing operation, code-named LINEBACKER II, which the press quickly dubbed the "Christmas Bombing," provoked furious criticism within the United States. Press editorialists and congressional opponents accused Nixon of terror bombing and of waging war against the civilian population of North Vietnam. European press and government leaders also denounced the U.S. bombing campaign and made similar charges. Swedish Prime Minister Olaf Palme compared the bombing to Nazi atrocities.[118] Congressional critics, on recess for the Christmas holidays, made it clear that when they returned to Washington in January that they would cut off all funds to deprive the president of the ability to wage war in Indochina. Polls showed that the bombing caused a sharp drop in Nixon's approval rating.

Some of the media criticisms of the Christmas Bombing were exaggerated. Only military targets and targets that were not located in densely populated areas were deliberately attacked. U.S. airmen went to great lengths and took grave risks to avoid hitting civilians and civilian structures. Considering the scale and intensity of the attacks, the civilian toll of about 1,500 casualties was remarkably small. Some of the civilian deaths were no doubt caused by NVA SAMS (surface-to-air-missiles), which missed their targets, fell within Hanoi and Haiphong, and exploded. American journalists who visited Hanoi following the bombing were surprised to discover that civilian deaths and civilian property destruction were minor compared to the devastation of targeted areas.[119]

Nixon had signaled to Hanoi that if the North Vietnamese agreed to resume the peace talks that the United States would stop the bombing. On December 28, Hanoi consented; the bombing ceased December 29, 1972. Negotiations between Kissinger and Tho resumed on January 8, 1973. Kissinger perceived that North Vietnam wanted an agreement, and it was hammered out in six days. Both sides compromised in order to reach an accord. Washington again allowed the Communists to maintain an active political and military presence in South Vietnam. Hanoi accepted the existence of the Thieu regime and allowed continuing American aid to the GVN.[120] But the Christmas Bombing had not produced a settlement that differed in any significant measure from the agreement that had been previously worked out by Kissinger and Tho back in mid-October, only to be subverted by Thieu's objections, that had been backed by Nixon.

But this time, Nixon, who sensed that he had just about expended the last of his political capital with the bombing campaign, that he had no more military cards left to play in Indochina, was determined to end the war. He took the best settlement that he could get and then he imposed the settlement on Thieu. To make the agreement more acceptable to General Thieu, Nixon vastly increased the level of military aid going to the GVN. He also gave the South Vietnamese leader a written promise that the United States would continue to support his government. He also promised in writing that the United States would respond in full force if North Vietnam ever launched another offensive in violation of the peace treaty. But Nixon also made it clear to Thieu that if he did not sign the agreement, America would cut off all further assistance to South Vietnam and that he would sign the treaty alone.[121]

Thieu, correctly viewing the agreement as not significantly different from the mid-October understanding that he had rejected, strongly opposed it. After trying unsuccessfully to get changes put in, he had no choice but to accept it. Nixon imposed the agreement on both camps. He had used air power to force Hanoi into negotiating an agreement; he then forced that agreement on Thieu. Nixon finally ended the American war in Indochina, almost four years to the day after he had assumed the presidency committed to ending that conflict within a year or so. America's ordeal was ending. The American Vietnam war was over.

Representatives of all four delegations at the Paris talks, the United States, North Vietnam, South Vietnam, and the PRG, signed the Agreement

President Nixon greets Henry Kissinger upon his return from Paris, where the envoy had just negotiated the Paris Accords ending the American Vietnam war.
Source: National Archives

on Ending the War and Restoring Peace in Vietnam, the Paris Accords, on January 27, 1973. According to the main military provisions of the accords (1) a ceasefire throughout South Vietnam went into effect immediately; (2) at the same time, America ceased all acts of war against North Vietnam and agreed to remove, deactivate, or destroy immediately all the mines that had been laid in North Vietnamese ports, harbors, and waterways; (3) the United States agreed to remove all its remaining forces, including advisory personnel, from South Vietnam and to dismantle all its bases in that country within sixty days; (4) Hanoi agreed to return all American prisoners-of-war within sixty days; (5) the 150,000 NVA troops currently inside South Vietnam were allowed to remain; (6) neither the United States nor the North Vietnamese could send more troops to South Vietnam; and (7) it created two commissions, the Joint Military Commission, made up off representatives from the ARVN and from the VC/NVA forces, and the International Commission on Control, made up of delegates from Hungary, Poland, Indonesia, and Canada, to enforce the cease-fire provisions of the agreement.[122]

According to the major political provisions of the Paris Accords (1) the Thieu government and the PRG were accorded a political status within South Vietnam; (2) both entities would establish a National Council of National Reconciliation and Concord, representing equally the GVN, the PRG, and "third force" elements in South Vietnam (the council would implement the political aspects of the peace accords, including holding elections to determine the future government of South Vietnam); (3) South Vietnam was declared to be a free and independent nation; and (4) all signatories guaranteed that the reunification of Vietnam would be gradual, peaceful, and without coercion.[123] Few of the many provisions of the Paris agreements were ever carried out.

In a speech, Richard Nixon announced that America had achieved "peace with honor in Vietnam."[124] If he truly believed his statement, he was deluding himself and his fellow Americans. The agreement that had taken so long to consummate served primarily as a vehicle that permitted the United States to extricate itself from a war that it could no longer hope to win and which most of its citizens no longer supported or believed in.

The signing of the Paris treaty occasioned no celebrations nor outpourings of joy among the people of South Vietnam or within the Thieu government. The treaty permitted some 150,000 North Vietnamese troops to remain in South Vietnam. The agreement also granted the Provisional Revolutionary Government, the political dimension of the PLAF insurgency, a political status in South Vietnam. The people and areas of South Vietnam under the control of the Vietcong had been granted legitimacy. Having deferred the major question for which the Vietnam war had been fought, who should govern in South Vietnam, which would determine whether an independent South Vietnam would survive, the language of the agreement presumed that the question would be resolved by political means sometime in an unspecified future. But the political mechanisms created to resolve the political issues could not work; they were inherently unworkable.[125] Therefore, and all informed observers on both sides understood this reality at the time, the question of who would govern in South Vietnam would be resolved by force. The Paris Accords did not bring a cease-fire; they only ensured that the Vietnam war would go on without the Americans.

Having concluded at last that they could not force the Americans out of South Vietnam by military means, Hanoi opted to remove U.S. forces by diplomacy, which required accepting the continued existence of the GVN for a few years. But the North Vietnamese had no intentions of renouncing their long-held goals, nor of abiding by the terms of the Paris Accords that interfered with the attainment of their goals. Hanoi's decision to accept the Paris settlement was based on the assumption that once the Americans had left, the VC/NVA forces could defeat Thieu's regime within a few years. The North Vietnamese also understood that the mechanisms for policing the cease-fire, like the mechanisms for resolving the political issues, were unworkable. The South Vietnamese armed forces would never be able to withstand another major NVA offensive on their own; years of Vietnamization had not eliminated RVNAF's basic flaws. Political and military reality in South Vietnam would allow the GVN to survive only as long as it would take Hanoi to rebuild its forces and to mount another offensive, perhaps two or three years.[126]

Only the credible threat of U.S. military retaliation could enforce the Paris Accords and keep South Vietnam alive. But the domestic political reaction to the Christmas Bombing suggested that it had been Richard Nixon's last hurrah. Neither Congress nor the American people would likely support reentry of American naval and air power into combat anywhere in Indochina, much less advisers or ground combat forces. The Communist leaders concluded that Nixon dared not, "risk the political damage that would result from an effort to reimpose U.S. power in South Vietnam."[127] If North Vietnam could not be restrained from military action, if South Vietnam could not defend itself, and if America could not intervene militarily to save the GVN, the demise of South Vietnam was inevitable. Nixon's peace with honor in reality meant ignominious American strategic defeat delayed by an interval of a few years.

The 1973 Paris Accords, which resembled the 1954 Geneva accords in many ways, were essentially a deal between Hanoi and Washington. The United States got its POWs back and its remaining troops out of Vietnam. Hanoi got the bombing of its country halted and the American soldiers out of Vietnam. The Thieu government got nothing, neither peace nor the realistic prospect of a political settlement that could ensure the survival of his country.

The American people paid a high price for the illusory peace that Nixon achieved after four more years of war. It had meant more than 15,000 additional battle deaths and continuing inflation that weakened the U.S. economy and undermined the living standards of millions of American families. The war also perpetuated domestic pathologies, dividing Americans, polarizing politics, and poisoning the political atmosphere. If the main reason that Nixon held out so long for the peace terms that he finally got was to maintain America's primacy in world affairs, he failed. The United States emerged from the wreckage of its lengthy involvement in Southeast Asia with its world power and prestige considerably tarnished.[128] By the time America withdrew from Vietnam, the morale, discipline, and fighting spirit of its Army had seriously eroded.

The Soviet Union had used the years that the United States had entangled itself in a major war in Southeast Asia to achieve strategic parity with its Cold War rival. By 1973, many Americans, achingly weary of war and, for that matter, of all international involvements, increasingly embraced a neo-isolationist outlook. Nixon himself also paid dearly for his prolongation of the Vietnam war. The Watergate scandals, which forced his resignation from the presidency in disgrace and deprived him of an honored place in the national memory, grew out of his inability to end the war quickly. Richard Nixon joined Lyndon Johnson as one of the two most prominent victims of the American crusade to contain the expansion of Communism in Southeast Asia.

A bizarre follow up to the Paris agreements occurred in October 1973 when a Nobel prize committee jointly awarded Henry Kissinger and Le Duc Tho the 1973 Nobel Peace Prize for their efforts to bring an end to the Vietnam war. Kissinger was uneasy about the award, and Le Duc Tho refused to accept it. Kissinger later refused to attend the awards ceremony at the University of Oslo and then donated the $65,000 cash prize that he received to a scholarship fund established to help the children of American soldiers killed or missing in Vietnam. The Nobel Committee had awarded its most prestigious prize to two diplomats who had negotiated a fictitious peace. Former Undersecretary of State George Ball observed: "The Norwegians must have a sense of humor." A New York *Times* editorial writer called the award, "The Nobel War Prize."[129]

NOTES

1. Ambrose, Stephen E., "Nixon and Vietnam: Vietnam and Electoral Politics," lecture given at Kansas State University, October 24, 1988; Goodman, *The Lost Peace*, pp. 78–79.

2. Goodman, *The Lost Peace*, pp. 79–80.

3. According to Ambrose, Richard Nixon's foremost biographer, Nixon never said "I have a secret plan to end the war" during the 1968 campaign. The phrase was a journalistic invention. See Nixon, Richard, "Asia after Vietnam," *Foreign Affairs*, vol. 46 (October 1967), pp. 111–125 and the excerpts from an undelivered radio speech scheduled for March 31, 1968, in Goodman, *The Lost Peace*, pp. 80–81.

4. Kissinger, Henry, "The Vietnam Negotiations," *Foreign Affairs*, vol. 47 (January 1969), p. 234; Kissinger, Henry, *The White House Years* (Boston: Little, Brown, 1979), pp. 228–232.

5. Goodman, *The Lost Peace*, p. 81.

6. Nixon quote is found in Morris, Roger, *Uncertain Greatness: Henry Kissinger and American Foreign Policy* (New York: Harper and Row, 1977), p. 156. Lipsman, Samuel, Doyle, Edward, and the editors of Boston Publishing Company, *Fighting for Time* (Boston: Boston Publishing Co., 1983), pp. 8, 27–28, a volume in the series, *The Vietnam Experience*. See Porter (ed.), "National Security Study Memorandum No. 1," January 21, 1969 (Extracts), *Vietnam Documents*, vol. 2, Document 289, pp. 522–529. Kissinger had his staff draw up a questionnaire (NSSM 1) to be answered by the government agencies involved in the war. He cited the diversity of answers he received to justify concentrating foreign policy decision making in Nixon's and his hands.

7. Moss, *America in the Twentieth Century*, pp. 371–373.

8. Polls cited in Mueller, *Wars, Presidents, and Public Opinion*, pp. 92–93.

9. Schandler, *Unmaking of a President*, p. 321

10. Brandon, Henry, *The Retreat of American Power* (New York: Delta, 1972), pp. 58–59; Goodman, *The Lost Peace*, p. 85.

11. Herring, George C., "The Nixon Strategy in Vietnam," in Peter Braestrup (ed.), *Vietnam as History: Ten Years after the Paris Peace Accords*, (Washington, D.C.: University Press of America, 1984), pp. 51–52.

12. Lipsman and others, *Fighting For Time*, pp. 30–31; Herring, *America's Longest War*, p. 225. The provinces of eastern Cambodia that were bombed during MENU included, from north to south, Kratie, Kompong Cham, Prey Vieng, Svay Rieng, Kandal, Takeo, and Kampot.

13. Kissinger, *White House Years*, pp. 242–249; Davidson, *Vietnam at War*, pp. 589–594.

14. Kissinger, *White House Years*, pp. 252–253; Morris, *Uncertain Greatness*, pp. 158–162. According to Morris, Kissinger approved of the wiretaps and gave the names of some officials and journalists whom he wanted wiretapped to FBI officers. Among those whose phones were tapped: NSC staffers Morton Halperin, Daniel Davidson, and Helmut Sonnenfeldt; Department of Defense assistant Col. Robert E. Pursley; and journalists Hedrick Smith and Henry Brandon, both of the New York *Times*.

15. Morris, *Uncertain Greatness*, pp. 156–159.

16. Lipsman and others, *Fighting for Time*, pp. 31–32.

17. Quoted in *ibid.*, p. 32; Porter (ed.), "Address on Television By President Richard M. Nixon," May 14, 1969 (Extract), *Vietnam Documents*, vol. 2, Document 291, p. 531.

18. Kissinger, *White House Years*, pp. 271–274; Herring, *America's Longest War*, p. 226.

19. Goodman, *The Lost Peace*, pp. 87–88.

20. Duiker, *The Communist Road*, pp. 278–283.

21. See epigraph, chapter 1.

22. Copies of Nixon's July 15, 1969, letter to Ho Chi Minh, and the North Vietnamese leader's response, dated August 15, can be found in Szulc, Tad, *The Illusion of Peace: Foreign Policy in the Nixon Years* (New York: Viking, 1978), pp. 137, 139. Replying to Nixon's letters was one of the last official acts of Ho Chi Minh, who died September 2, 1969.

23. Quoted in Lipsman and others, *Fighting for Time*, p. 36.

24. Quoted in Morris, *Uncertain Greatness*, p. 164.

25. Hersh, Seymour M., *The Price of Power: Kissinger in the Nixon White House* (New York: Summit, 1983), pp. 124–130; Morris, *Uncertain Greatness*, pp. 163–164; Szulc, *Illusion of Peace*, pp. 150–156. Kissinger told the group that it was not the policy of the Nixon administration to use nuclear weapons, but they were not to rule out using a nuclear device to block a passage to China, for example, if that is the only way it can be done.

26. Herring, *America's Longest War*, p. 228.

27. Kissinger, *White House Years*, pp. 278–283. Henry Cabot Lodge, the head of the U.S. team at the Paris talks, had met privately many times with Xuan Thuy prior to Kissinger's August 4 meeting. These talks had all been unproductive.

28. Szulc, Tad, *Illusion of Peace*, pp. 148–149. Nixon, like Johnson, tended to equate criticism of his war policy with subversion. He secretly ordered the FBI, the CIA, and other intelligence agencies to look for connections between the antiwar movement and the enemy.

29. Herring, *America's Longest War*, p. 228.

30. DeBenedetti, Charles, *The Peace Reform in American History* (Bloomington, Ind.: Indiana University Press, 1984), pp. 180–185; Lipsman and others, *Fighting for Time*, pp. 36–37.

31. Quoted in Lipsman and others, *Fighting for Time*, p. 37.

32. Transcript of Nixon's speech delivered November 3, 1969; The speech also appears in Nixon, Richard M., *Public Papers, Richard M. Nixon, 1969* (Washington, D.C.: U.S. Government Printing Office, 1971), pp. 901–909. Although the policy itself had been in place for a year and a half, the term "Vietnamization" was coined by Nixon's secretary of defense, Melvin Laird, in a speech he gave to an AFL-CIO convention in October, 1969. Thereafter, Vietnamization was always

identified as Nixon's Vietnam war policy, although the policy was a creation of his predecessor, Lyndon Johnson.

33. Quoted in Szulc, *Illusion of Peace*, p. 158.

34. Davidson, *Vietnam at War*, pp. 603–606.

35. *Ibid.*, pp. 606–607.

36. *Ibid.*, p. 607.

37. Blaufarb, *Counterinsurgency Era*, pp. 264–278; Sheehan, *Bright Shining Lie*, pp. 731–736; Herring, *America's Longest War*, pp. 231–233; and Davidson, *Vietnam at War*, pp. 609–612.

38. Stanton, *Rise and Fall*, pp. 269–270; Davidson, *Vietnam at War*, pp. 612–613.

39. Stanton, *Rise and Fall*, p. 284.

40. Stanton, *Rise and Fall*, pp. 283–288; Lipsman and others, *Fighting for Time*, pp. 17–23; and Davidson, *Vietnam at War*, pp. 614–615.

41. Quoted in Lipsman and others, *Fighting for Time*, p. 22.

42. Transcript of interview with Melvin Zais, General, US Army (Ret.), 1977, Vol III, pp. 575–588, US Army Military History Institute archives, Carlisle Barracks, Penn. General Zais had a son fighting in the battle of Dong Ap Bia. General Zais believed that the name, "Hamburger Hill," was suggested by a young wire service reporter interviewing a hysterical soldier who had participated in the battle.

43. Davidson, *Vietnam at War*, p. 615.

44. Davidson, *Vietnam At War*, pp. 615–619; Stanton, *Rise and Fall*, pp. 278–280; Lipsman and others, *Fighting For Time*, pp. 92–115; Lewy, *America in Vietnam*, pp. 153–161; Cincinnatus, *Self-Destruction: The Disintegration and Decay of the United States Army during the Vietnam Era* (New York: W. W. Norton, 1981). "Cincinnatus" is the pseudonym used by Cecil B. Currey.

45. Baskir and Strauss, *Chance and Circumstance*, pp. 3–61; Moss, "The Vietnam Generation," pp. 4–9.

46. Stanton, *Decline and Fall*, pp. 279–280.

47. Savage, Paul L., and Gabriel, Richard A., "Cohesion and Disintegration in the American Army," *Armed Forces and Society*, vol. 2 (Spring 1976), pp.362–371; Baritz, *Backfire*, pp. 294–309; Davidson, *Vietnam at War*, pp. 617-619.

48. Lipsman and others, *Fighting for Time*, pp. 92–96.

49. *Ibid.*, pp. 97–100. A CBS News television documentary portrayed a combat refusal that occurred in April 1970 in War Zone C near the Cambodian border during Operation TOAN THANG 43. The soldiers refused an order from their company commander to move down a road, which they assumed was surrounded by enemy soldiers, to a landing zone. The crisis was solved when new orders came down for them to take an alternative, presumably safer, route to the landing zone.

50. Lewy, *America in Vietnam*, pp. 153–158; Cincinnatus, *Self-Destruction*, passim.

51. Lewy, *America in Vietnam*, pp. 154–155; Fiman, Bryan G., and others, "Black-White and American-Vietnamese Relations Among Soldiers in Vietnam," *Journal of Social Issues*, vol. 31 (Fall 1975), pp. 43–6; Lipsman, *Fighting for Time*, p. 102

52. Moss, "Vietnam Generation," p. 14.

53. Cited in Lipsman, *Fighting for Time*, p. 103.

54. McCoy, *The Politics of Heroin in Southeast Asia* (New York: Harper & Row, 1972), p. 9.

55. *Ibid.*, pp. 181–185, pp. 217–222. McCoy accused several high-ranking military officials in the Thieu-Ky government of drug trafficking; McCoy named General Nguyen Ngoc Loan, General Tran Thien Khiem, and General Ngo Dzu. McCoy also charged that American embassy officials refused to investigate these charges and denied that any South Vietnamese officials were involved in drug smuggling. If McCoy was right, U.S. officials, in effect, tolerated high officials in the South Vietnamese government making huge profits from sales of heroin to U.S. soldiers in 1970 and 1971.

56. Porter (ed.), "Nixon Speech," April 20, (Extract),*Vietnam Documents*, vol. 2, Document 295), pp. 539–541; Herring, *America's Longest War*, pp. 233–234.

57. Kissinger, *White House Years*, pp. 458–461; Lipsman, *Fighting for Time*, pp. 127–130, 138–142.

58. Davidson, *Vietnam at War*, p. 625; Herring, "The Nixon Strategy in Vietnam," pp. 55–56; Lipsman, *Fighting for Time*, pp. 146–147.

59. Kissinger, *White House Years*, pp. 468–470. William Shawcross, *Sideshow: Kissinger, Nixon and the Destruction of Cambodia* (New York: Simon and Schuster, 1979), chap. 8, "The Coup," pp. 112–127 has suggested U.S. complicity in the coup that overthrew Sihanouk. He has been vigorously rebutted by Henry Kissinger, *White House Years*, pp. 517–521, notes, pp. 1484–1485. No evidence has surfaced connecting the United States to the anti-Sihanouk coup.

60. Davidson, *Vietnam at War*, pp. 625–627; Palmer, *Summons of the Trumpet*, pp. 294–296.

61. Szulc, *Illusion of Peace*, pp. 252–260; Lipsman, *Fighting for Time*, pp. 152–153; Herring, *America's Longest War*, pp. 235–236.

62. Transcript of Nixon's speech, April 30, 1970; a copy of the speech is printed in Nixon, Richard M., *Public Papers, Richard Nixon, 1970* (Washington, D.C.: U.S. Government Printing Office, 1971), pp. 405–410.

63. Stanton, *Decline and Fall*, pp. 319–321.

64. *Ibid.*, pp. 322–325; Palmer, *Summons of the Trumpet*, pp. 297–301. The U.S. Army units participating in the last big American battle of the war included elements from three divisions: the 11th Armored Cavalry and 3rd Brigade, 1st Air Cavalry; 2nd Battalion, 34th Armor, 25th Infantry; 2nd Battalion, 47th Infantry, 9th Infantry.

65. Palmer, *Summons of the Trumpet*, pp. 299–301; Stanton, *Decline and Fall*, pp. 324–325; Davidson, *Vietnam at War*, pp. 627–629. During Toan Than 43, the VC/NVA lost about 11,000 KIAs, the Allies 976, including 338 Americans. The Allies captured 16,700,000 rounds of small arms ammunition, 23,000 individual weapons, 200,000 rounds of antiaircraft ammunition, and 14 million pounds of rice.

66. Palmer, *The 25-Year War*, pp. 103–104; Stanton, *Decline and Fall*, pp. 324–325.

67. Herring, *America's Longest War*, p. 237.

68. Lipsman, *Fighting for Time*, pp. 181–182.

69. Polls are cited in *ibid.*, pp. 182–183.

70. Morris, *Uncertain Greatness*, pp. 199–201.

71. Brandon, *Retreat of American Power*, pp. 146–149; Herring, *America's Longest War*, p. 238.

72. Morris, *Uncertain Greatness*, pp. 174–175; Kissinger, *White House Years*, pp. 968–972; Goodman, *The Lost Peace*, pp. 105–107.

73. Palmer, *Summons of the Trumpet*, pp. 302–303; Stanton, *Decline and Fall*, pp. 333–334; and Davidson, *Vietnam at War*, pp. 637–641. Thieu named the

proposed incursion into Laos after Lam Son, the birth place of Le Loi, who was a great Vietnamese national hero who had defeated an invading Chinese army in 1427.

74. Davidson, *Vietnam at War*, pp. 637–642.

75. Palmer, *Summons of the Trumpet*, pp. 304–305.

76. Davidson, *Vietnam at War*, pp. 645–649.

77. Fulghum, David, Maitland, Terrence, and the editors of Boston Publishing Company, *South Vietnam on Trial: Mid-1970 to 1972*, (Boston: Boston Publishing Co., 1984), pp. 88–89; Stanton, *Decline and Fall*, pp. 336–337.

78. Davidson, *Vietnam at War*, pp. 651–652.

79. *Ibid.*, pp. 652–654; Stanton, *Rise and Fall*, p. 336–337.

80. Kissinger, *White House Years*, pp. 1016–1023.

81. Porter (ed.), "DRV Nine-Point Plan," June 26, 1971, *Vietnam Documents*, vol. 2, Document 300, pp. 555–556; Goodman, *The Lost Peace*, pp. 111–115; Kissinger, *The White House Years*, pp. 1023–1031.

82. Fulghum, *South Vietnam on Trial*, pp. 102–104.

83. *Ibid.*, pp. 104–108; Herring, *America's Longest War*, p. 245.

84. Herring, *America's Longest War*, p. 242.

85. Poll cited in *ibid.*, p. 243.

86. *Ibid.*, p. 246.

87. Duiker, *The Communist Road*, pp. 288–292.

88. *Ibid.*, pp. 292–293.

89. The three PAVN divisions included the 304th, the 308th, and the 324B.

90. Davidson, *Vietnam at War*, pp. 680–684; Stanton, *Rise and Fall*, p. 343; and Palmer, *Summons of the Trumpet*, pp. 315–319.

91. Fulghum, *South Vietnam on Trial*, pp. 136–142, 145–156; Davidson, *Vietnam at War*, pp. 684–688.

92. Stanton, *Rise and Fall*, pp. 343–344; Duiker, *The Communist Road*, p. 293.

93. Reference 32, chap. 4, this book; Sheehan, *A Bright Shining Lie*, pp. 754–785. Sheehan's critically acclaimed best seller is a superb biography of an extraordinary man who spent more time in South Vietnam than any other American official. It has been said that if the United States had had ten men like John Paul Vann, it might have won the Vietnam war.

94. Davidson, *Vietnam at War*, pp. 688–693; Fulghum, *South Vietnam on Trial*, pp. 184–189.

95. Stanton, *Rise and Fall*, pp. 343–344; Davidson, *Vietnam at War*, pp. 693–697.

96. Davidson, *Vietnam at War*, pp. 706–13; Fulghum, *South Vietnam on Trial*, pp. 150–154, 160–167.

97. Nixon, Richard, *RN: The Memoirs of Richard Nixon* (New York: Grosset and Dunlap, 1978), p. 587.

98. Quoted in Fulghum, *South Vietnam on Trial*, p. 142.

99. Nixon, *Memoirs*, pp. 590–591; Kissinger, *White House Years*, pp. 1119–1121; Fulghum, *South Vietnam on Trial*, pp. 142–143.

100. Nixon, *Memoirs*, pp. 588–589; Kissinger, *White House Years*, pp. 1113–1114.

101. Fulghum, *South Vietnam on Trial*, pp. 144–145.

102. Goodman, *The Lost Peace*, pp. 118–119; Kissinger, *White House Years*, pp. 1135–1137, 1144–1148.

103. Ibid., 1169–1170.

104. Quoted in Herring, America's Longest War, p. 247.

105. Porter (ed.),"Address to the Nation by Nixon," May 8, 1972 (Extracts), Vietnam Documents, vol. 2, Document 305, pp. 566–567; Nixon, Memoirs, p. 605.

106. Fulghum, South Vietnam on Trial, pp. 169–171.

107. Davidson, Vietnam at War, pp. 706–712; Stanton, Rise and Fall, pp. 344–345; Fulghum, South Vietnam on Trial, pp. 183–184.

108. Fulghum, South Vietnam on Trial, p. 184.

109. Herring, America's Longest War, pp. 249–250.

110. Duiker, The Communist Road, pp. 295–296; Goodman, The Lost Peace, pp. 120–121;

111. Goodman, The Lost Peace, pp. 126–129; Lipsman, Samuel, Weiss, Stephen, and the editors of the Boston Publishing Co., The False Peace; 1972-1974, (Boston: Boston Publishing Co., 1985), pp. 9–13, in the series, The Vietnam Experience; Kissinger, The White House Years, pp. 1331–1359. Kissinger denies that all Washington sought was an agreement that would allow the United States to extricate itself from the Indochina War and permit the Thieu government to survive for a "decent interval" before being overthrown by Hanoi. He insists that the settlement achieved in January 1973 would have allowed the Saigon regime to survive indefinitely had not the Watergate scandal subsequently destroyed the Nixon presidency and nullified the settlement.

112. Kissinger, White House Years, pp. 1366–1392; Nixon, Memoirs, pp. 702–703.

113. The quote is from Herring, America's Longest War, p. 252.

114. Kissinger, White House Years, p. 1395. Kissinger may have also been hoping to influence the outcome of the election with his remark.

115. Porter (ed.), "Letter from Richard Nixon to RVN President Nguyen Van Thieu," Nov. 14, 1972, Vietnam Documents, vol. 2, Document 315, pp. 581–583; Nixon, Memoirs, pp. 704–707; Ambrose, "Nixon and Vietnam."

116. Kissinger, White House Years, pp. 1415–1446; Nixon, Memoirs, pp. 732–733; Goodman, The Lost Peace, pp. 151–160; Porter, (ed.), "Press Conference Statement by Kissinger," Dec. 16, 1972, (Extract), Vietnam Documents, vol. 2, Document 318 pp. 587–590. Xuan Thuy, presenting the North Vietnamese view of the negotiations, blamed the delays and breakdown on the fact that the Americans had proposed many substantive changes to the mid-October agreement and had rejected many previously agreed upon issues.

117. Quoted in Herring, America's Longest War, pp. 253–254.

118. Isaacs, Arnold, Without Honor: Defeat in Vietnam and Cambodia, (Baltimore: The Johns Hopkins University Press, 1983), pp. 54–57; Kissinger, White House Years, p. 1453. Kissinger, a German-Jewish immigrant to America, who, as a schoolboy, had to flee his native Bavaria with his family to escape Nazi tyranny, could not resist responding to the Swedish government's charges that the Nixon administration's bombing of Hanoi and Haiphong in December 1972 made them the new Nazis. He reminds his readers that the Swedish government enjoyed a neutral relationship with Nazi Germany during World War II.

119. Lewy, America in Vietnam, pp. 403–404. The North Vietnamese, with long experience of U.S. bombing, also took steps to keep civilian casualties low. They had evacuated much of the population and most who remained in Hanoi and Haiphong found refuge in effective bomb shelters.

120. Duiker, The Communist Road, pp. 296–297; Goodman, The Lost Peace, pp. 160–164; Kissinger, White House Years, pp. 1461–1468.

121. Porter, (ed.), "Letter from Nixon to Thieu," January 5, 1973, *Vietnam Documents*, vol. 2, Document 320, p. 592; Nixon, *Memoirs*, pp. 737–751. Nixon wrote two letters to Thieu pledging U.S. support. One dated November 14, 1972, says, "You have my absolute assurance that if Hanoi fails to abide by the terms of this agreement it is my intent to take swift and severe retaliatory action." The second letter dated January 5, 1973, says, "We will respond with full force should the settlement be violated by North Vietnam."

122. Copies of the Agreement on Ending the War and Restoring Peace in Vietnam, January 27, 1973, are reprinted in Goodman, *The Lost Peace*, pp. 188–199. See also Porter, (ed.), "Letter from Nixon to Pham Van Dong," February 1, 1973, *Vietnam Documents*, vol. 2, Document 324, pp. 599–600. The United States also agreed to create a joint commission to provide postwar economic aid to North Vietnam. When Kissinger visited Hanoi in February, he was prepared to offer North Vietnam $3.25 billion in aid over five years.

123. *Ibid.*; Isaacs, *Without Honor*, pp. 64–68 discusses the major provisions of the treaty, mainly to show that few provisions were ever carried out.

124. Quoted in Isaacs, *Without Honor*, p. 61.

125. *Ibid.*, pp. 62–63; Herring, *America's Longest War*, p. 256.

126. Duiker, *The Communist Road*, p. 299; Davidson, *Vietnam at War*, pp. 730–731.

127. Duiker, *The Communist Road*, p. 299.

128. Herring, *America's Longest War*, p. 256.

129. Quoted in Lipsman and others, *The False Peace*, p. 119.

THE END
OF THE TUNNEL

9

History may...judge that going into Vietnam was one of our country's greatest mistakes.

William Westmoreland

The...lesson [of Vietnam] is that America must never commit its power and authority in defense of a country of only marginal strategic interests when that country lacks a broadly based government or the will to create one.

George Ball

INDECENT INTERVAL

The war in South Vietnam went on despite the signing of the Paris Accords, only it now continued without direct American participation. The Vietnamese people were free for the first time in nearly a century to fight among themselves without interference from foreign intruders. Neither side observed the cease-fire and both ignored or deliberately violated many of the other agreements. Neither side made a serious effort to seek a political settlement. The Lao Dong leaders in Hanoi continued to seek the overthrow of the Thieu regime by both political and military means and to reunify

Vietnam under their control. South Vietnam, dependent on U.S. economic and military assistance since birth, struggled to survive after the Americans had departed. President Nixon, engulfed by the Watergate scandal from March 1973 until his forced resignation of the presidency in August 1974, could not keep the promises of support and protection that he had made to General Thieu.

Congress restricted the president's power to intervene militarily in the Indochina war. Congress also curtailed sharply the amount of American economic and military assistance going to South Vietnam, which undermined both the ability and the will of the RVNAF forces to defend themselves. By the end of 1974, the United States had, in effect, abandoned its long-time client in southern Vietnam. The South Vietnamese economy deteriorated, its people were demoralized, and the military balance of power shifted in favor of the VC/NVA forces. During the spring of 1975, when Hanoi, confident that the United States would not intervene militarily in order to save the Thieu government, mounted another major offensive, the GVN defenses quickly collapsed, and the Thieu government found itself paralyzed and helpless. Neither Kissinger nor Nixon's successor, Gerald Ford, could convince Congress that it should vote additional aid funds for the dying nation. Saigon fell to the Communists on April 30, 1975, and the republic of South Vietnam ceased to exist. The long American involvement in Indochina came to a miserable pass.

A cease-fire in Laos followed the January 1973 Paris agreements. The Communist Pathet Lao and the Laotian government agreed to a cease-fire on February 21, 1973. The arrangement did not bring instant peace to that country, but then the fighting in Laos had not generated the hatred or the destructiveness that it had in Vietnam and Cambodia. As John Kenneth Galbraith once observed, the people of Laos "have not learned to kill each other like the civilized nations."[1] The Laotian Communist leader, Prince Souphanouvong, and the head of the government, Prince Souvanna Phoung, were half-brothers who treated each other with respect. Following the cease-fire agreement, the fighting in Laos continued sporadically. American B-52s ceased bombing in Laos on February 22. The fighting gradually tapered off, and by April 1973 the long civil war in Laos had ended. On September 12, negotiators signed a protocol that cleared the way for establishing a new coalition government, a government that would be increasingly dominated by the Pathet Lao.[2] When Cambodia and South Vietnam fell to the Communists in the spring of 1975, the Pathet Lao took control in Laos.

In neighboring Cambodia, the Khmer Rouge and Lon Nol's forces waged a furious struggle. Lon Nol had offered the rebels a cease-fire soon after the Paris Accords had been signed, but the Khmer Rouge leaders, determined to overthrow the Cambodian government, had rejected it. In February 1973, the insurgents appeared to have victory within their grasp. They had isolated the capital Phnom Penh, and their forces had reached the suburbs of the city, a scant five kilometers away. However, an American airlift supplied the city, and, during six months of intensive bombing, U.S. B-52s annihilated the Khmer Rouge forces attacking Phnom Penh. Having taken about 20,000 casualties, the rebels withdrew the remnants of their forces in August and the Cambodian army mounted a counteroffensive. U.S. air power had saved Lon Nol's rickety regime.

Congress cut off all funds for the U.S. air war in Cambodia, and the bombing stopped on August 15. The B-52s had brought Phnom Penh only a reprieve. The rebels regrouped and resumed their attacks four months later. By early 1974, the Khmer Rouge once again threatened Phnom Penh. Lon Nol's forces had to defend the capital city without American air power. The U.S. ambassador, John Gunther Dean, concluded that the government's cause was hopeless and that its military forces would be defeated. He hoped to find some way to halt the fighting to allow the Americans to leave.[3]

The return of the 653 U.S. prisoners-of-war in February and March 1973 represented the only positive American accomplishment to come out of any postwar negotiations held in accordance with the terms of the Paris agreements. The arrangements worked out called for the POWs to be released in four increments fifteen days apart. The remaining 24,000 U.S. troops on active duty in South Vietnam would depart simultaneously, in four equal-sized increments spaced fifteen days apart. If any snags occurred that delayed the return of the POWs, the remaining U.S. troops would delay their departure from Vietnam.[4]

The first contingent of 115 prisoners-of-war left Hanoi's Gia Lam airport on February 12 and flew to Clark Air Force base in the Philippines. At Clark, the men were given medical examinations and brought up to date on family news and on their current military statuses. Many aviators got to enjoy their first American-style meal in years, steaks and banana splits. They then flew to the United States where they had to endure a media blitz as they were reunited with their families. The other returning prisoners followed in fifteen-day intervals until the last men had been repatriated on March 29. Hundreds of small towns and cities across the United States staged hero's welcomes for individual returnees, usually featuring parades down their main streets followed by official ceremonies in public halls or high school auditoria.

On March 30, the last contingent of 5,200 U.S. soldiers remaining in South Vietnam assembled at Tan Son Nhut air base on the outskirts of Saigon, in readiness for their flights back to the United States. By April 1, 1973, the only American military personnel remaining in South Vietnam were 159 Marines serving as embassy guards and another fifty people serving in the Defense Attache Office as permitted by the provisions of the Paris agreement.

The status of prisoner-of-war is neither intrinsically dishonorable nor heroic. If an aviator was captured by the enemy, it represented an occurrence that the flyer could neither avoid nor prevent. It was an accident perhaps combined with bad luck. But the Vietnam POWs had survived the longest captivity of any prisoners in American military history. As prisoners, they also had often been forced to endure deprivation, harassment, and cruel tortures inflicted by their hateful and inhumane captors. Most of the prisoners endured their agonies heroically, maintaining their military professionalism under extreme duress in accordance with the U.S. Code of Military Conduct.

Colonel Fred V. Cherry, the senior black POW, set an outstanding example. He was tortured for ninety-two consecutive days after his captors failed to break him by appealing to his "blackness." Colonel Cherry's courageous patriotism earned him a lot of pain, a broken rib and a punctured lung.[5] Another reason for celebrating the returning POWs as heroes reflected the reality that, for most Americans, the homecoming of the POWs was the only positive experience to come out of the long American ordeal in Vietnam. It was the only result of the Vietnam war that most Americans could feel any enthusiasm about.

The celebrity status accorded the POWs contrasted starkly with the treatment often given returning ground combat veterans, particularly veterans who returned after 1967. They rarely received parades or official welcomes home. Few Americans appeared to appreciate their sacrifice or thanked them for a job well done. They were often ignored by a society that had carelessly sent them off to fight a war that most Americans were ambivalent about or had lost faith in completely. Returning Vietnam combat veterans found themselves to be embarrassing reminders of a war that no one wanted to think about or talk about. Worse, some people, opposed to the war, took out their animus toward that conflict by insulting or condemning the returning uniformed veterans.

The large majority of returning Vietnam veterans were neither war criminals nor victims. They did not suffer from drug or alcohol addiction nor have acute psychological or physical disabilities. But most veterans had to struggle to come to terms with their war experiences, readjust to civilian routines, and to reintegrate into American society. They often had trouble completing their educations, finding steady work, and maintaining stable marriages and families. They often found that they could not discuss their war experiences, or their thoughts and feelings about the war, with their families or close friends. Many veterans retained bitter feelings that their efforts and sacrifices had been meaningless, that they had fought in the service of a losing cause that had been repudiated or forgotten by most Americans. The experience of fighting the Vietnam war, especially after 1967, brought some soldiers to oppose it, to believe that it was both futile and wrong.[6]

Recent surveys have shown that thousands of combat veterans continue to be plagued by Post-Traumatic Stress Disorder (PTSD) long after the Vietnam war. Veterans afflicted with PTSD suffer a variety of psychological dysfunctions induced by their traumatic wartime experiences. Symptoms can include (1) drug and alcohol abuse; (2) recurring nightmares, often reliving horrible war experiences; (3) chronic depression; (4) psychic numbing, the inability to feel any strong emotion; (5) guilt feelings about their war actions or for having survived when buddies were killed; (6) the inability to experience intimacy; and (7) unpredictable outbursts of aggressive behavior.[7]

There was also a poignant dimension to the joyous homecoming of the POWs. The return of the 653 prisoners doomed the hopes of most of the families of some 2,500 men who had been reported missing in action. Most of these MIAs had been flyers whose planes had gone down over water or over North Vietnam or Laos during the war and whose fate was yet unknown. Under the terms of the Paris agreements, the responsibility for resolving the question of the MIAs devolved upon the Four-Party Joint Military Team (JMT) made up of members from the United States, South Vietnam, North Vietnam, and the PRG.

The Americans on the Joint Military Team quickly discovered that the Communists were in no hurry to resolve the MIA issue. Hanoi preferred to use the information that its officials had on the fate of some of the men missing in action as bargaining chips. The Communists linked providing information on the fate of MIAs to progress on unrelated issues. Little progress had been made and the fate of only a few of the MIAs had been resolved when the Communist delegates started boycotting the JMT meetings in June 1974.[8]

The emotionally charged MIA issue has lingered long after the Vietnam war has ended even though all but one of the MIAs has been declared legally dead. American government officials have repeatedly stated that they have no evidence that any American servicemen are alive or are being held against their will anywhere in Indochina. The National League of Families of American Prisoners and Missing in Southeast Asia continues to demand an accounting from Hanoi and from the American government for the 2,393 people that they still regard as missing. There have been many raids, searches, and expeditions over the years into Indochina to try to find or to account for some of the missing men. Many have insisted that they have seen or heard of live American POWs being held in Laos or Vietnam. Some relatives of MIAs have charged the U.S. government with covering up evidence that it has of Americans still being held in Indochina prisons.[9] Until relations between the United States and Vietnam are normalized, the question of the MIAs can never be closed.

"The 'postwar war' began the instant that peace was proclaimed."[10] Even before the cease-fire had been declared, Vietcong forces had embarked on a series of land-grabbing campaigns in various sectors of South Vietnam. General Thieu responded with offensive operations designed to reclaim these lands and to enhance the total amount of territory and population under the control of the GVN. In February 1973, as the postwar war began,

A Navy commander kneeling before a section of the Vietnam Veterans Memorial. He is accompanying members of the National League of Families of Americans missing in Southeast Asia. All but one of the MIAs have been declared legally dead and their names are among the 58,156 inscribed on the memorial.
Source: U.S. Air Force Photo

the military situation in South Vietnam favored Thieu's forces. U.S. aid had built up the RVNAF forces until they were one of the largest and best-equipped armies in the world.

As a consequence of successful pacification efforts in 1970–1972 coupled to the smashing of the Communist Nguyen Hue offensive during the summer of 1972, the GVN controlled about 75 percent of the territory and perhaps 80 percent of the 19 million inhabitants of South Vietnam. Communist holdings were confined mostly to the thinly populated western periphery of the country and to scattered enclaves in the Mekong delta and the central highlands. Both the surviving Vietcong forces and the approximately 150,000 North Vietnamese forces in southern Vietnam, still battered and short of supplies from the 1972 campaigns, were initially no match for Thieu's forces. During the first year following the Paris agreements, the GVN added both land and people to its holdings. The South Vietnamese forces not only reclaimed most of the lands and villages grabbed by the Vietcong in the fall of 1972, but they also acquired control of some areas that had been in VC hands for years. Thieu was determined to use his military advantage while he had it to try to establish his control over all the land and people of South Vietnam.[11]

Thieu remained convinced that if the Communists rebuilt their forces and launched attacks in South Vietnam that his forces could not contain, Nixon would make good on his pledge to rescue the GVN. Even though all American combat forces had been withdrawn from South Vietnam, Washington continued to provide strong military support for the Thieu government. Thousands of former American military advisers continued to work with ARVN forces, but they had civilian statuses to circumvent treaty provisions. Powerful U.S. naval and air forces remained nearby: in the Gulf of Tonkin, in Thailand, and on the island of Guam. Nixon attempted to maintain a credible threat of U.S. reentry into the war to deter Hanoi from treaty violations and aggressive military actions. Thieu, confident that he could count on U.S. forces to bail him out if he got into trouble, took a hard line toward the Communists. He pursued a policy of the "four no's": (1) no abandonment of territory in South Vietnam, (2) no coalition government with the PRG or neutralists, (3) no negotiations with the Communists, and (4) no Communist or neutralist political activities in South Vietnam.[12]

Hanoi, needing a respite from war to rebuild its shattered military forces, confined its activities in South Vietnam largely to politics during most of 1973. The Communists maintained a low level of resistance to Thieu's forces. They also modernized their logistics capability in South Vietnam. They constructed a macadamized highway and an eight-inch oil pipeline running along the border with Laos and Cambodia from the DMZ to Loc Ninh, about sixty-five miles northwest of Saigon. Hanoi also infiltrated more troops into South Vietnam. During the final months of 1973, about 170,000 PAVN forces and 60,000 Vietcong could be found in South Vietnam. The Communists also decided to resume the war in the south on a limited basis. They attacked ARVN forces in the Mekong delta, the Iron Triangle, and in the central highlands, inflicting heavy casualties and reclaiming some territory and villages.[13]

Within the United States, the burgeoning Watergate scandals had seriously eroded Nixon's popularity, his power to govern, and his ability to influence events in Indochina. During 1973, for the first time in the long war, Congress took decisive actions to end all lingering American military activity in Indochina. In June, Congress passed legislation requiring an immediate end to the bombing of Cambodia and Laos and all other U.S. military operations in Indochina. Nixon vetoed the measure and the House sustained his veto. Congress subsequently forced a reluctant president to accept a compromise proposal that halted the bombing on August 15.[14]

In November, Congress enacted the War Powers Act over another presidential veto. The War Powers Act required that the president inform Congress within forty-eight hours of any decision to deploy U.S. forces overseas, and the new law further mandated that the president must remove these forces within sixty days unless Congress specifically endorsed their deployment. The War Powers Act, in tandem with the Cambodian bombing cut-off, virtually precluded Nixon's committing America to any further military operations in Indochina.[15]

By the end of 1973, Nixon was practically powerless to influence events in Indochina. All the power and popularity that had accrued from his landslide victory over George McGovern and from achieving the Paris Accords had vanished; they had gone up in the smoke of the Watergate scandal and in the face of congressional assertiveness. With his popular approval ratings reduced to historic lows, Nixon fought grimly for his political survival against a rising tide of forces determined to destroy him if evidence implicating him in the Watergate coverup could be found. He could only watch passively as the postwar war escalated and the political settlement that he had tried so hard so long to forge for South Vietnam became a dead letter.[16]

During 1974 the military balance in South Vietnam turned steadily against the ARVN forces even though paper force levels continued to favor the South Vietnamese heavily over their enemies.[17] The Communists systematically exploited strategic weaknesses of the RVNAF forces. Because of Thieu's efforts to gain control over his whole country, many of his divisions were tied down in static defensive positions. ARVN troops had also stretched themselves thin and were vulnerable to attacks wherever the VC/PAVN forces chose to strike. Meanwhile, South Vietnam's economy began to collapse from a combination of declining American support and internal disorders.

Corruption, a chronic problem of the GVN since its inception, scaled new heights during Thieu's final years. Corruption involved most senior officials in the GVN military and civilian bureaucracies and many lower echelon personnel as well. Official efforts to eliminate or to slow the rate of corruption "ranged from the ineffectual to the pathetic."[18] General Thieu tolerated his regime's staggering corruption. Even had he been willing to try to reform his government, he would have failed. The cancer of South Vietnamese corruption had metastasized until it suffused the entire corpus of the Saigon bureaucracy. Had Thieu tried to remove the corruption from all his government's civilian and military agencies, the radical surgery required would have killed the patient.

Except for dismissing a few corrupt officials for cosmetic purposes, Thieu chose to cover up his regime's systemic corruption. U.S. officials, led by the last American ambassador to South Vietnam, Graham Martin, went along with the coverup. Ambassador Martin and other U.S. officials either denied that corruption was a serious problem in South Vietnam or else insisted that it was being eliminated. If U.S. officials were complacent about corruption, most South Vietnamese, victimized in countless ways by fraud, bribery, extortion, and graft, were not. Their anger over government corruption was fueled by economic decline, and they complained bitterly about their predicament.

By mid-1974, Thieu's regime administered a collapsing economy. The rate of inflation had skyrocketed. The cost of living in Saigon had risen 27 percent during the first six months of the year. The price rise for essential commodities was even sharper: rice rose 100 percent, sugar 107 percent, and cooking oil 139 percent. At the same time that retail prices were shooting up, unemployment was rising rapidly. In 1974, an estimated 1 million people, about a fifth of the work force, were without jobs. The piaster was devalued repeatedly against the U.S. dollar; a huge trade deficit evolved that quickly wiped out the GVN's slim foreign reserves. In 1973, a poor rice harvest and an Arab oil boycott had exacerbated South Vietnam's mounting economic miseries. Rice and other food commodities had to be imported, many consumer goods were in short supply, and industries dependent on imported materials slashed their production schedules or, more likely, closed down.[19] The South Vietnamese people suffered from an economic double whammy composed of hyperinflation and deep depression.

The sick South Vietnamese economy was undermined further by the effects of the American pullout. The pullout eliminated about 300,000 jobs as well as a large annual inflow of dollars. In 1970 U.S. soldiers had spent over $500 million, and in 1971, they had spent over $400 million in South Vietnam. In 1974 they spent less than $100 million.[20] Government efforts to arrest the galloping economic deterioration proved ineffectual. By 1974 economic and social conditions were the worst that they had ever been during the nation's twenty year existence. As corruption and economic decay destroyed the morale and cohesion of South Vietnamese society, the RVNAF, its military shield, also began to give way.

One of the major causes of the RVNAF's decline in 1974 was Congress's sharp reductions in the amount of U.S. military assistance going to South Vietnam. The United States spent $2.3 billion in fiscal 1973, but cut spending to only $1.1 billion for 1974.[21] Aid cuts severely hampered the performance of the South Vietnamese armed forces. Helicopter and air force operations had to be curtailed because of gasoline shortages and the lack of spare parts. Artillery rounds and small arms ammunition were in short supply. Unable to maneuver or to fight in the manner that they had been trained because of equipment and ammunition shortages, the morale and confidence of the RVNAF forces, never too high under the best of circumstances, plummeted.

The congressional aid cuts no doubt sapped the strength and morale of the RVNAF forces, but they were not the most important causes of the GVN's growing military weakness. Vietnamization had never worked. Most of the RVNAF's many shortcomings that had always vitiated its fighting abilities had never been corrected. The economic deterioration of 1974 further undermined RVNAF capabilities. Desertions probably exceeded inductions in 1974, and the officer corps grew more corrupt and more politicized than ever.

But the fundamental weakness of the South Vietnamese military forces could be found in the realm of politics. Thieu's government remained what it had always been, a narrowly based oligarchy dependent for its survival on the political loyalty of senior military commanders. It did not and never had embodied Vietnamese nationalism. It could never win the hearts and minds of most South Vietnamese civilians, nor the loyalty and devotion of most of the men serving in its military forces. Thieu's American connection and his skill at political maneuver had kept him in power for years, but neither he nor his government represented a cause or a purpose, a positive reason for which most soldiers would want to fight. South Vietnam had always been a nation made up of political unbelievers, most of whom viewed military service as either an unavoidable disaster or as an opportunity for graft. Mostly, Thieu's soldiers fought when they had to, to survive. As 1974 approached its end, many ARVN soldiers had lost the will to do even that.

During August 1974 Congress slashed U.S. military aid to South Vietnam still further and Nixon, his role in the attempted cover-up of the Watergate burglary established, was forced to resign in disgrace to avoid impeachment, conviction, and removal from office. It was evident that Thieu was running out of American friends, and Americans were running out of reasons for continuing to support his cause. Thieu soon faced the most serious challenge to his rule since taking office. On September 8, a group of Catholics led by Father Tran Huu Thanh publicly protested the extensive corruption that riddled Thieu's government. Thanh's charges set off a torrent of protest against Thieu and his corrupt regime. Thieu made a few efforts to respond to his critics, then he cracked down on the protesters. Thieu's police violently suppressed the protests.[22] Many citizens were bludgeoned into silence; popular support for the GVN was at a low ebb.

The Communist leadership in Hanoi observed the general deterioration of South Vietnamese society and the continuing cuts in American support for Thieu's failing regime during 1974. The hawks in the Politburo believed that the time had come for another all-out war in South Vietnam. The doves took a more cautious stance. They wanted to wait and see if the new American president, Gerald Ford, could persuade Congress to restore military aid funds to Thieu's regime and to see if Ford would be willing to make good on Nixon's promise to recommit U.S. air power in South Vietnam to try to save the GVN in the event of another invasion from North Vietnam.

By fall the hawks had won the debate. What clinched the argument favoring another North Vietnamese attack on South Vietnam was the outbreak of popular unrest in Saigon and Hanoi's perception that U.S. domestic public opinion and congressional opposition would likely prevent Ford from ordering any further American military interventions into South Vietnam. At a key meeting held in October 1974, the Politburo approved a proposal by

General Van Tien Dung, Giap's successor as chief of staff, for a new military offensive scheduled to be launched in South Vietnam in 1975. General Dung had concluded that the war in South Vietnam had reached its final stage. PAVN forces now enjoyed a clear advantage on the battlefield. Dung's strategic plan called for a two-year campaign that would culminate in the overthrow of the Thieu regime and the creation of a coalition government in 1976.[23]

What Hanoi's leaders had seen in Washington in the fall 1974 was what Maoists in Beijing liked to call a "paper tiger."[24] They saw a nation led by an inexperienced president and a dovish congress that was increasingly preoccupied with the deteriorating American economy. Serious internal problems generated by energy shortages and "stagflation" had a far greater urgency for most Americans than the lingering war in Indochina that no longer directly involved American troops. Washington viewed such issues as relations with the major Communist powers, efforts to break the dismal cycle of periodic warfare between Arabs and Israelis, and the quarrels with NATO allies as taking priority over an anachronistic conflict in Southeast Asia that had already gone on much too long and had cost far more in lives and dollars than anyone had ever anticipated. Hanoi's directorate understood that the United States still possessed formidable military power and that these forces were positioned to intervene in Indochina, but they made a judgment that Washington had lost the political will to reenter the war. The Communists were confident that the United States would not jump back into the war to save Thieu's government.

ENDGAME

In mid-December, concluding that the time had come to initiate the final phase of the postwar war, General Dung ordered two divisions of Vietcong and PAVN forces under the command of General Tran Van Tra to attack Phuoc Long, an isolated and poorly defended province near the Cambodian border northwest of Saigon. Dung would use the assault on Phuoc Long as a test, to find out whether Saigon and Washington would respond to a direct attack on South Vietnamese territory that obviously violated the Paris agreements. Within three weeks the Communist forces had overrun the province and captured the provincial capital, Phuoc Binh. RVNAF forces could do little to prevent the disaster. VNAF pilots lacked both the skill and the nerve to fly close air support missions. ARVN helicopter squadrons lacked the airlift capability to fly in reinforcements. ARVN defenders took heavy casualties during the three weeks of fighting in Phuoc Long. The Phuoc Long debacle demonstrated that Thieu's government lacked both the means and the will to defend its territory against a determined enemy. More important, it soon became evident that the Ford administration would not intervene militarily in South Vietnam regardless of the provocation or threat.

When Hanoi's directorate perceived that Saigon could not defend Phuoc Long and that the Ford administration would not intervene, they ordered a second phase of the offensive to begin, a series of attacks to be launched in the central highlands.[25] The North Vietnamese army that General Dung prepared to unleash in the highlands was much improved over that of 1968 or 1972. With considerable assistance from the Soviets, the NVA had modernized its logistics capability, had refined its tactics, and had significantly enhanced its air defense capabilities. The army that was poised to slam into the central highlands was a powerful and mobile strike force capable of defeating the RVNAF forces and overthrowing the GVN. South Vietnam's final agony was about to begin.

On March 10, five PAVN main force divisions, joined by regiments of tanks, artillery, antiaircraft, and engineers, attacked the strategic city of Ban Me Thuot, the capital of Darlac Province. Dung concentrated his forces to mount an overwhelming attack on the city. It fell to the Communists within a week. The fall of Ban Me Thuot represented a strategic disaster for the GVN. With the takeover of that city, the NVA had positioned itself to achieve its long-standing strategic goal, the bisection of South Vietnam.[26] After the fall of Ban Me Thuot, no powerful ARVN forces blocked the PAVN's march to the sea. There were only some isolated ARVN defenders in Pleiku and Kontum City. South Vietnam was about to be cut in two.

While the battle for Ban Me Thuot was being fought, General Thieu made a fateful decision that hastened the destruction of his country. Convinced that the outnumbered and outgunned defenders of Pleiku and Kontum could not hold off the Communist attackers, he ordered his commanders to withdraw their forces. Thieu wanted to redeploy them to try to hold all of South Vietnam south of a line running from Tuy Hoa on the coast to the Cambodian border.[27] Most of South Vietnam's resources and population lay south of this line. General Thieu decided to trade territory for time and for a chance to consolidate his defenses farther to the south. He would accept the loss of the northern half of his nation, the truncation of his country, in exchange for an opportunity to preserve the southern half. Pleiku and Kontum fell within a few days.

Thieu's military commanders in the central highlands had made no plans for a tactical retreat, and they could not execute his withdrawal orders effectively. ARVN military discipline broke down, and the retreat quickly turned into a rout. Hundreds of thousands of terrified civilians joined the demoralized and panicked soldiers, as all fled the highlands toward the coastal city of Tuy Hoa. The two-week trek of soldiers and civilians streaming for the coast turned into a Convoy of Tears. During that hideous fortnight, two-thirds of the 60,000 RVNAF soldiers were killed or captured, and many civilians perished as well. Most of the civilian casualties came from NVA fire as the Communists continually

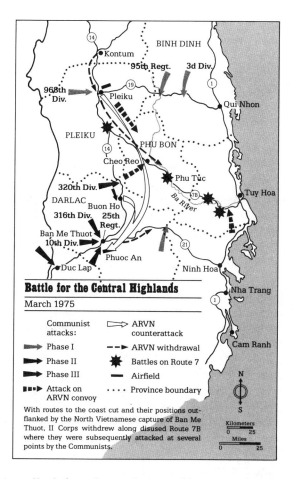

Battle for the Central Highlands

March 1975

Communist attacks: ⇨ ARVN counterattack

▰▰➤ Phase I   --➤ ARVN withdrawal

▰➤ Phase II   ✦ Battles on Route 7

▰➤ Phase III   — Airfield

▰▰➤ Attack on   ···· Province boundary
ARVN convoy

With routes to the coast cut and their positions out-
flanked by the North Vietnamese capture of Ban Me
Thuot, II Corps withdrew along disused Route 7B
where they were subsequently attacked at several
points by the Communists.

attacked the virtually defenseless columns of intermingled soldiers, dependents, and refugees.   Only about 20,000 South Vietnamese soldiers and
perhaps 60,000 civilians reached their destination.[28]

Tuy Hoa provided only temporary respite for the refugees because
it too soon had to be abandoned to the advancing Communists. General
Thieu's decision to abandon the central highlands was a psychological,
strategic, and political disaster that cost his country six provinces, perhaps
200,000 civilian casualties, and more than two divisions of troops. It also
cost him the remaining faith and confidence of the South Vietnamese
people in his abilities to protect them from the invaders. Loss of the
highlands "opened the way for even greater catastrophe in the coastal
cities of South Vietnam."[29] The DRV leaders, perceiving that they could
probably conquer all of South Vietnam before the rainy season struck,
ordered General Dung to move up his timetable for victory one year, from
1976 to the spring of 1975.

As the GVN forces abandoned the central highlands, an even greater South Vietnamese catastrophe occurred in the north. General Dung sent five NVA main force divisions along with artillery, tank, and antiaircraft regiments to attack key sites in the five northern provinces of South Vietnam that constituted Military Region I. The Communist forces quickly overpowered the outnumbered ARVN defenders. Refugees by the thousands poured into Hue and Danang, the two largest cities in the region. As the PAVN forces approached these cities, the South Vietnamese defenses simply melted away. ARVN soldiers and the militia abandoned their weapons and many of them joined the mass air, sea, and land exodus from the doomed cities for Saigon. Chaos engulfed both cities. "The evacuation of Danang capped a disaster of far greater magnitude than the flight from the central highlands."[30] Only about 16,000 South Vietnamese troops were evacuated from Danang. Four infantry divisions, additional main force units, and territorial forces were either dispersed, detained, or destroyed. Of the two million people packed into Danang at the end, perhaps 50,000 got out before the Communist conquerors arrived.

The last flight out of Danang on March 29, 1975, was a World Airways 727 for Saigon. It was commandeered by a mob of 320 uniformed soldiers from the ARVN 1st Division who shoved aside women and children, often trampling members of their own families, in their panic-driven haste to get on board the plane. As pilot Ken Healy began to taxi the big plane toward the runway, crazed soldiers standing on the tarmac fired their rifles and threw grenades at the plane. One exploding grenade jammed the flaps on the left wing of the 727. Because a stalled VNAF A-37 jet fighter with bombs slung under its wings blocked the main runway, Healy was forced to gun the 727 into the air by using the short taxi strip. As the overloaded plane struggled into the air, observers on the ground could see bodies hanging from the plane's undercarriage and wheel wells. Ninety minutes later, the plane delivered its payload of patriots safely in Saigon.[31]

Almost ten years to the day after the first U.S. Marines hit the beaches near Danang to initiate the American Vietnam war, South Vietnam's second largest city was occupied by the Communists. Within less than a month, South Vietnam had been shorn of half its territory, half its armed forces, and millions of its people. These calamities occurred mainly because General Thieu had made a desperate decision to surrender half his country to try to save the other half.

During the first week of April 1975, the coastal cities of Quang Ngai, Qui Nhon, Tuy Hoa, and Nha Trang fell to the NVA attackers as they advanced down the South China seacoast of South Vietnam toward Saigon. PAVN forces also occupied Cam Ranh, formerly the site of the largest U.S. logistics facility in South Vietnam. Hanoi, sensing that final victory was near, ordered General Dung to marshal all his forces for one big offensive against Saigon. As the Communist leaders planned the final campaign destined to bring their thirty-year war for independence and national unity to a victorious climax, they named it the Ho Chi Minh Offensive, in honor of Vietnam's greatest revolutionary leader.

By mid-April advance elements of the North Vietnamese army were approaching Saigon. The last major battle of the postwar war occurred at Xuan Loc, a strategic crossroads that formed the center of Saigon's forward defenses. At Xuan Loc, located about thirty miles west of the capital city astride Route 1, the main Vietnamese north-south highway, the 18th ARVN Division under the command of General Le Minh Dao made a gallant stand against four NVA divisions that were reinforced with tank and artillery regiments. In an epic struggle, the defenders of Xuan Loc held their positions for a week against vastly superior numbers and firepower. Although the heroic defenders of Xuan Loc could delay the North Vietnamese advance, they could not stop it. After the fall of Xuan Loc, the road to Bian Hoa airport and Saigon lay open. "After Xuan Loc, it was a slide into the abyss for the South Vietnamese."[32]

As the end of the Republic of South Vietnam approached, the civil war in neighboring Cambodia that had been going on for five years played itself out. With the defensive perimeter around the besieged capital of Phnom Penh shrinking daily, the hapless leader of the Khmer Republic, Lon Nol, was forced to resign on April 1. Efforts by Secretary of State Kissinger to arrange an eleventh-hour peace settlement were spurned by Prince Sihanouk and his Chinese patrons. On April 10, Congress refused to support a bill calling for $222 million in emergency military aid for the dying Khmer Republic. Two days later, the American evacuation of Phnom Penh began. After five years, at a cost exceeding a billion dollars, the U.S. effort to prevent a Communist takeover in Cambodia had failed. On April 17, the Khmer Rouge forces entered the city. An eyewitness, New York *Times* reporter Sydney Schandberg, described Phnom Penh's conquerors as "grim, robotlike, brutal."[33] They immediately began evacuating the 1.5 million people crammed into the city. The Cambodian holocaust was about to begin.

Washington had known for months that the Khmer Republic was doomed, but the sudden collapse of the South Vietnamese armies in the central highlands and northern provinces in the spring of 1975 had stunned American officials. Intelligence reports had given them no indication that Hanoi had planned a major offensive for 1975. American officials had assumed that South Vietnam's defenses were adequate to withstand any attacks that the Communists were likely to mount that year. But it soon became clear, even in the face of mounting disaster in southern Vietnam, that the Ford administration had no plans for any further U.S. military intervention in that region. Both Ford and Kissinger understood that it would be politically impossible for the United States to send in the B-52s, as Nixon had done in 1972, to try to save the South Vietnamese armed forces from another NVA offensive.

On April 10, in a televised speech to the nation, Ford asked Congress to appropriate $722 million in emergency military assistance for General Thieu's imperiled government. To support his proposal, Ford sounded the familiar themes. He pleaded with the Congress to honor a sacred U.S. commitment. He spoke of America's "profound moral obligation" to the South Vietnamese people. He told the legislators and the American people that the United States would dishonor the sacrifices made by the thousands of American soldiers who had died in Vietnam if it failed to help the people of South Vietnam in their hour of mortal danger. He raised the specter of a bloodbath in which thousands of South Vietnamese, particularly Catholics, would be slaughtered by the victorious Communists. Few congressional leaders on either side of the aisle responded to Ford's emotional appeal with any enthusiasm. Most congressional leaders, viewing the cause in Vietnam as already lost, were more concerned about assuring the evacuation of all Americans from Saigon than they were about sending General Thieu's failing government any more weapons. On April 17, the same day that Xuan Loc fell and the Khmer Rouge entered Phnom Penh, Congress rejected Ford's request for military aid for South Vietnam.[34] Kissinger observed fatalistically, "The Vietnam debate has run its course."[35]

Most Americans, suffering from severe domestic economic and energy problems, and concerned about important foreign policy matters elsewhere, had long since lost their crusading enthusiasm for saving South Vietnam from Communist aggression. Opinion polls taken in April 1975 showed that a large majority of Americans opposed any further U.S. military action in South Vietnam even if the failure to take such action resulted in a Communist takeover. Most Americans were unhappy with the prospect of a Communist victory in Vietnam, but they were resigned to its occurrence. Many Americans also believed that their country had already sacrificed far too much of its blood and treasure in Indochina, and they were loath to contribute more.

General Thieu resigned on April 21, convinced at last that the Americans were not going to send South Vietnam any more military aid, nor would they attempt an eleventh-hour military intervention to save his country. That evening Thieu spoke for the last time to his countrymen. Most of his ninety-minute televised speech amounted to a bitter attack on his longtime ally and patron, the United States. He denounced American officials for having forced him to sign the Paris Accords and then refusing to honor former President Nixon's pledges of support when North Vietnam renewed its aggression. He bitterly denounced the American betrayal of his imperiled nation. He stated that, "Refusing to aid an ally and abandoning it is an inhumane act."[36]

Thieu's successor was elderly and feeble Tran Van Huong, the GVN vice president, who, during his few days of power, tried futilely to seek a negotiated settlement of the war. The North Vietnamese, positioning their forces for a final assault, had no time for desperate proposals for a political solution to a war that they were about to win. On April 22,

General Dung signed the order to commence the Ho Chi Minh Campaign to conquer Saigon. At that moment, ten NVA divisions encircled the virtually defenseless city. On April 23, speaking to a large audience at the Tulane University field house, President Ford made U.S. abandonment of South Vietnam official. He urged Americans to forget about the Vietnam war and to avoid arguments about who was to blame for its disastrous outcome. He told the crowd:

> America can regain the sense of pride that existed before Vietnam. But it cannot be achieved by refighting a war that is finished as far as America is concerned.[37]

As Ford uttered the magic word, "finished," the predominantly student audience of 4,500 erupted with frenzied whistling, cheering, clapping, foot-stomping, and shouting that lasted for several minutes. The president had given voice to the American national mood that existed at the moment when the PAVN forces readied themselves to win the final victory of the Vietnam war.

With the NVA forces surrounding the doomed city, thousands of Vietnamese tried desperately to escape. Everywhere Americans were accosted by Vietnamese brandishing letters, documents, and assorted papers, pleading for a way out of their country. To facilitate the evacuation of South Vietnamese nationals, the U.S. Congress hastily approved legislation waiving entry restrictions for 130,000 Indochinese aliens, including 50,000 high-risk Vietnamese. Each day, thousands of Vietnamese flew out of Tan Son Nhut airport on board C-141s and C-130s that formed a round-the-clock airlift to freedom.

On April 27, the Communists launched their first attack on Saigon, a rocket barrage that they deliberately aimed at densely populated areas of the city: downtown Saigon and Cholon. The rockets killed and wounded hundreds of people. On the same day, the hapless Tran Van Huong resigned the GVN presidency. The South Vietnamese Assembly then replaced Troung with General Doung Van Minh, the man who had briefly headed the military directorate that had replaced Ngo Dinh Diem in November 1963. The Assembly charged Minh with the task of restoring peace to South Vietnam. Lest there be any doubt on this matter, the Communists quickly made it unmistakably clear that the only political settlement that they would consider accepting from General Minh would be unconditional surrender.[38]

On April 28, fighting erupted along the outskirts of Saigon. Late in the day, the only Communist air strike of the entire Vietnam war hit Tan Son Nhut air base. Five American-built A-37s, in a perfectly executed operation that fooled the defenders, destroyed or damaged several aircraft parked along the main runways and disrupted the U.S. airlift for several hours. The attack had been led by a VNAF defector, Lieutenant Nguyen Thanh Trung. Now a captain in the North Vietnamese Air Force, Trung had trained a group of MIG pilots to fly the A-37s that had been captured from the South Vietnamese earlier in the 1975 offensive.[39]   After a three-hour delay, the airlift resumed.

Early on the morning of April 29, the NVA launched a rocket attack on Tan Son Nhut airport. The first rockets slammed into a Marine guard post. They killed Lance Corporal Darwin Judge and Corporal Charles McMahon, Jr.. Corporals Judge and McMahon were the last U.S. fatalities of the Vietnam war, the last of more than 58,000. Shortly after the first rocket barrages struck, long-range artillery shells began falling on the air base. The rocket and artillery barrages shut down the fixed-wing airlift operations.

Ford then ordered the final phase of the Saigon evacuation, code-named Operation FREQUENT WIND, to begin. It was a massive helilift designed to remove the remaining Americans and eligible Vietnamese from the surrounded city and to fly them to a large fleet of U.S. naval ships anchored some forty miles out to sea. Buses navigated the crowded city streets to designated pick-up sites, gathered the evacuees, and hauled them to Tan Son Nhut and the waiting helicopters. At every assembly site, the number of people waiting to board the buses vastly exceeded their carrying capacities. Many eligible Vietnamese never got evacuated.[40]   By afternoon, the entire city had dissolved into chaos. Frenzied mobs roamed the streets. Vandals overturned cars and set fire to buildings. Looters ransacked homes and apartments. Thousands converged on the U.S. embassy either in the hope of finding a way out or else to vent their rage at the departing Americans. Marine security guards, standing atop the compound walls, had to use their rifle butts and boots to beat back hundreds of Vietnamese trying to climb over, while at the same time helping stranded Americans to get inside and to join the estimated 2,000 people already on the embassy grounds.

By 8:00 p. m., the evacuation from Tan Son Nhut had been completed. The last Americans to depart the airport were a detachment of Marine security guards who had been assisting the evacuees. Before the Marines boarded the last helicopter, they prepared the Defense Attache Office complex for destruction. Formerly the headquarters of the United States Military Assistance Command in Vietnam (MACV), the buildings had symbolized for a decade the U.S. commitment to defend South Vietnam. From their vantage point aboard the helicopter ascending into the night, the departing Marines watched the structures that had housed sophisticated communications equipment, secret documents, and a vault containing $3.5 million dollars in U.S. currency collapse into rubble.[41]

During the early morning hours of April 30, helicopters flying from the American embassy made the last evacuations of the Vietnam war. Just before 5:00 A.M., Ambassador Martin and his senior staff members departed the embassy. But there were not nearly enough places on board the

South Vietnamese evacuees lined up on the flight deck of USS *Hancock* (CVA-19) after being helilifted from Tan Son Nhut air base during Operation FREQUENT WIND April 29 and 30, 1975. *Source*: U.S. Marine Corps Photo.

available helicopters to evacuate all the remaining Vietnamese and third-country nationals. Between 400 and 500 people were left behind on the embassy grounds. Looking down at the stranded people milling about helplessly as his helicopter headed for the open sea, one of the U.S. officials could think "of no word in any language adequate to describe the sense of shame that swept over me."[42] The last Americans to leave were the Marine security forces who had barricaded themselves on the embassy rooftop to await the final helicopters that would take them to the waiting ships. As the last

American helicopter lifted off, Sergeant Juan Valdez observed Vietnamese evacuees trying to push their way through the still-barricaded door, waving papers at the sky to show that they too should be allowed to leave Vietnam.

A few hours after the last U.S. Marine had left Saigon, the thirty-year Indochina War ground to its end. About noon, North Vietnamese tanks rumbled by the American embassy, headed for Independence Palace, the South Vietnamese capitol and official residence of President Minh. Alongside the tanks rolled trucks crammed with young PAVN soldiers. All headed for the heart of the city. As it approached the palace grounds, the lead tank barreled through the steel front gate, smashing it down. The tanks gathered in a semi-circle facing the entrance to the palace. In a gesture of triumph, a lone soldier, waving a huge blue and red flag with the yellow star of the National Liberation Front, raced up the steps of the palace. Provisional Revolutionary Government officials announced over radio Saigon that the city had been liberated. In Paris, Communist envoys announced that Saigon had been renamed Ho Chi Minh City. Inside Independence Palace, President Minh tried to surrender to the Communists, but he was curtly informed that all power had already passed into the hands of the revolution, and then he was taken into custody.[43] The final North Vietnamese offensive that had caused the Republic of South Vietnam's collapse had required fifty-five days.

Some of Saigon's inhabitants welcomed their conquerors. The vast majority of the population greeted their "liberators" with indifference and in many cases with fear and uncertainty. On May 8, a large crowd gathered in front of the presidential palace to hear the head of the new South Vietnamese provisional government, General Tran Van Tra, proclaim the success of the Vietnamese revolution. Even before the cheering stopped, the victorious North Vietnamese began rounding up many categories of Saigonese residents for "reeducation" at camps being set up in the countryside. The Republic of South Vietnam was swept into the dustbin of history. The American limited war fought in Indochina in order to contain the expansion of Communism had failed. Kissinger observed, "We should never have been there at all. But now it's history."[44]

AFTER THE FALL

The American effort to preserve South Vietnam was probably destined to fail. The Republic of South Vietnam never became, probably could never have become, a viable nation-state. From Ngo Dinh Diem's to Nguyen Van Thieu's, every one of the succession of inept, weak, and usually corrupt governments supported by the United States failed to develop a popular base of support and failed to achieve political stability. Those governments also failed to develop programs enabling the southern Vietnamese to modernize their society and economy. The most fundamental failures of these governments was that they never acquired the ability to defend themselves from the revolutionary war waged unrelentingly against them for nearly twenty years. With or without U.S. backing, there probably never was a viable political alternative to the revolutionary nationalism that swept Vietnam after 1945. The United States and its succession of clients could never solve the essential South Vietnamese conundrum: how to achieve a stable political order without supporting revolutionary changes.

U.S. officials defended the long American Vietnam involvement primarily as an effort to maintain political stability in Southeast Asia. The domino correlative to America's containment ideology magnified the significance of the endeavor to create a pro-Western and non-Communist alternative to revolutionary nationalism in southern Vietnam: The larger U.S. mission in Indochina always was defined as preventing the spread of Chinese and Soviet influence throughout Southeast Asia. Vietnam was perceived as a conduit of Communist expansionism that had to be closed to keep southern Vietnam, the rest of Indochina, and the nations of Southeast Asia within the Western orbit.

But the outcome of the American Indochina war invalidated its prime ideological justifications and suggested that the containment ideology itself rested upon dubious assumptions. American security was not threatened. American alliances elsewhere were not weakened nor were American allies disheartened by the outcome. After the fall of Saigon, there was no deluge of Communist takeovers in Southeast Asia. Outside of Cambodia and Laos, countries that had become involved in the Second Indochina war, the dominoes never fell. In fact, within Indochina, the Communist dominoes soon clashed among themselves. Military victory only accentuated the internal divisions within the Communist world. In Cambodia, the Khmer Rouge leadership implemented a savage reign that cost at least a million lives. The Vietnamese, nursing an imperialistic agenda of their own, invaded Cambodia in 1978 and overthrew the Khmer Rouge regime that it had previously helped come to power. Hanoi established a replacement regime, a puppet government in Phnom Penh supported by Vietnamese troops. China, which had close ties with Cambodia, then sent its forces into northern Vietnam in 1979 to punish Vietnam for its aggression in Cambodia. The United States, which had gone to war in Vietnam in 1965 to contain Chinese expansionism found itself quietly backing China's efforts to contain Vietnamese expansionism in 1979. In these intramural Communist wars, the Soviets backed the Vietnamese against the Chinese and their Cambodian allies. Clashing perceptions of national interest consistently overrode ideological considerations in guiding the actions of Communist political leaders in Indochina during the wars of the late 1970s.

In the aftermath of the Communist takeover in Indochina, the elaborate edifice of international economic and political relations that the United States had constructed in the Far East during the 1950s and 1960s did not become unhinged. In the years since the end of the Indochina War, the non-Communist nations of Southeast Asia have enjoyed unprecedented stability and prosperity. Their energetic populations and vibrant economies contrasted starkly with the Communist-controlled nations of Vietnam, Cambodia, and Laos, which remained grim islands of poverty and repression amid a sea of prosperity.

Within Vietnam itself the costs of the long war were horrendous: catastrophic human loss and suffering, and extensive damage to a fragile pre-industrial economy struggling to escape the legacies of French colonial exploitation. Millions of acres of forest and croplands were destroyed; millions of South Vietnamese were turned into refugees. Since the Communist conquest, an estimated 1.5 million South Vietnamese have fled poverty, oppression, and discrimination. About half of these refugees have come to the United States. The only positive outcome of the Vietnam war for the United States has been the acquisition of a large new ethnic minority. Since fleeing their homeland, many Vietnamese-Americans have established themselves as loyal and productive citizens.

Vietnam remains one of poorest countries in the world. Per capita annual income is about $150. Both unemployment and inflation remain chronically high. Rice production is stagnant, the population is growing rapidly, and living standards are declining. Vietnam has become an economic dependency of the Soviet Union. Thousands of Soviet advisers and technical specialists administer an elaborate range of Vietnam aid programs that cost the USSR about $2 billion per year. The Vietnamese have great need of American technology and economic aid, but U.S. assistance waits upon its establishing normal relations with their former adversaries. Efforts to normalize relations between American and Vietnam have failed since the war because of mutual hostility and distrust, Vietnamese insensitivity to the American MIA issue, and the Vietnamese invasion of Cambodia.

Within the United States, there was no bitter "who lost Vietnam?" debate or a resurgence of McCarthyite red-baiting following the fall of Saigon. Instead, historical amnesia set in, symptomatic of moral and political exhaustion. Most Americans did not want to think or talk about Vietnam for years, much less fight about it or indulge in recriminations.

The fallacies of U.S. Cold War ideology may have been exposed by the internecine Communist wars in Indochina and by the absence of a McCarthyite backlash at home. Vital American foreign policy interests in the Far East may have suffered no permanent setbacks following the U.S. withdrawal and defeat. However, the harm done to the United States by the Vietnam experience was nevertheless severe and lasting. George Kennan, the principal theorist of the American containment policy, has called the Vietnam War "the most disastrous of all America's undertakings over the whole two hundred years of its history."

The fall of Saigon in April 1975 was a severely damaging blow to the pride and self-confidence of a nation whose fondest boast had been that it had never lost a major war. The tragic outcome of the long war on the eve of the Bicentennial dampened many Americans' enthusiasm for celebrating their nation's two-hundredth birthday. The Vietnam war had consumed over 58,000 American lives and left another 300,000 soldiers wounded. In addition to the human costs of the war, the economic and financial costs were high. The Vietnam war cost more than any other war in American history except World War II, an estimated $150 billion. President Johnson's efforts to finance simultaneously a major war and Great Society reform programs ignited inflation, lowered the value of the dollar, and brought economic decline.

There were other costs of war. A bitter controversy erupted over whether hundreds of thousands of draft evaders and resisters, and deserters, should be granted amnesty or severely punished for their violations of Selective Service laws. The debate perpetuated the war-sown divisions between doves and hawks. The Vietnam War was the most controversial and least popular war in United States history. It divided Americans more deeply than any conflict since their own Civil War a hundred years earlier. Most Americans had become disillusioned with the national crusade to save South Vietnam from Communism and had stopped supporting the U.S. war effort long before it ended.

The war undermined public faith in the competency and honesty of elected officials and forced two strong presidents out of office prematurely. Military service was discredited for years. The Vietnam War shattered the bipartisan consensus that had guided U.S. foreign policy since the late 1940s and inaugurated an era of confusion and conflict that has never been entirely resolved. The losing war also proved that America's vast wealth and powerful military technology could not defeat a poor Third World nation determined to prevail, nor could the United States support forever an ineffective regime. Americans also discovered that there were limits to American power and there were limits to the burdens Americans would bear in pursuit of foreign policy objectives. For the first time since the Cold War began, many Americans questioned the validity of their global mission to contain Communism.

The specter of Vietnam lurked in the background of every American foreign policy debate of the 1970s and 1980s. There was a manifest unwillingness to intervene militarily in Third World countries for fear of being sucked into another Vietnam quagmire. An arrogance about the uses of American military power that existed before the Vietnam intervention had been succeeded by a diffident neo-isolationist yearning to avoid all military involvement in the world.

The gravest damage done to America by the Vietnam war occurred in the realm of the spirit. The ultimate domino was America's mythic conception of itself. Before Vietnam, America's most cherished vision of itself was expressed in the famed metaphor of the city upon a hill. America's mission in the world was to redeem history. In secular terms, America's mission was to set a democratic example to guide and to inspire the rest of the world. America's post–World War II foreign policy was founded upon the principle of thwarting the spread of Communism to preserve the sphere of freedom, the empire of liberty, in the world. The redeemer-nation sent its citizen-soldiers to southern Vietnam to save its inhabitants from the evil embrace of expanding Communism. But once launched upon their errand into the wilderness of Vietnam, Americans made the horrible discovery that the red-white-and-blue alternative to revolutionary nationalism was only destruction and, ultimately, defeat for their soldiers and for the Vietnamese people that they tried so hard so long to help. The lofty American conception of itself as the world's redeemer civilization perished in the jungles, swamps, and rice paddies of Vietnam.

NOTES

1. Quoted in Lipsman and others, *The False Peace*, p. 51.
2. Isaacs, *Without Honor*, pp. 173–180.
3. *Ibid.*, pp. 217–240; Lipsman and others, *The False Peace*, pp. 53–57, 118–122, 124–133, 171–172.
4. Kissinger linked the return of the POWs to the departure of the final contingents of U.S. ground forces to ensure that these provisions of the Paris agreements were carried out.
5. Terry, Wallace (ed.), *Bloods: An Oral History of the Vietnam War By Black Veterans*, (New York: Ballantine, 1984), pp. 281–283.
6. Frey-Wouters, Ellen, and Laufer, Robert S., *Legacy of a War: The American Soldier in Vietnam*, (Armonk, N.Y.: M. E. Sharpe, 1986), pp. 39–72; Lifton, Robert J., *Home from the War: Vietnam Veterans: Neither Victims nor Executioners* (New York: Simon and Schuster, 1973).
7. The most extensive survey of the mental health of Vietnam war veterans was funded by the Veterans Administration in 1986–1988. A team of psychiatrists and clinical psychologists conducted in-depth interviews of more than 1,600 Vietnam veterans. From their studies, researchers concluded that approximately 15 percent of all Vietnam combat veterans still suffered from PTSD. The researchers also discovered that higher proportions of black and Hispanic veterans continued to suffer from PTSD symptoms.
8. Lipsman and others, *The False Peace*, pp. 76–79; New York *Times*, August 30, 1988, p. A6.
9. New York *Times*, August 31, 1988, p. A6. The official number of MIAs in Indochina is very low compared to America's previous wars. Most officials who have studied the Vietnam MIA issue assumed that all the missing soldiers had perished; their physical remains may never be recovered.
10. Herring, *America's Longest War*, p. 257.
11. Turley, *The Second Indochina War*, pp. 162–165.
12. Szulc, *The Illusion of Peace*, pp. 672–676; Duiker, *The Communist Road*, pp. 301–302.

13. Porter (ed.), "Statement by the Provisional Revolutionary Government Foreign Ministry," Nov. 2, 1973, *Vietnam Documents*, vol. 2, Document 345, pp. 642–645; Duiker, *The Communist Road*, pp. 302–305.

14. Porter, (ed.), "Fulbright-Aiken Amendment—Public Law 93-52, Section 108, July 1, 1973," *Vietnam Documents*, vol. 2, Document 341, p. 639; Isaacs, *Without Honor*, pp. 143, 226–228, 234–237.

15. Davidson, *Vietnam at War*, pp. 741–742; Turley, *The Second Indochina War*, pp. 173–174.

16. Herring, *America's Longest War*, pp. 261–262.

17. In mid-1974, total RVNAF forces numbered about 1.1 million. The Vietcong and PAVN forces, both regulars and guerrillas, totaled about 240,000.

18. Lipsman and others, *The False Peace*, p. 138.

19. Turley, *The Second Indochina War*, pp. 173–174; Lipsman, and others, *The False Peace*, pp. 140–141. South Vietnam's trade deficit for 1974, most of it with America, totaled $750 million. The value of the country's exports, mostly food-stuffs and raw materials, totaled less than $100 million.

20. Lipsman and others, *The False Peace*, pp. 142–144.

21. Isaacs, *Without Honor*, pp. 313–321; Lewy, *America in Vietnam*, pp. 207–209.

22. Snepp, Frank, *Decent Interval: An Insider's Account of Saigon's Indecent End Told by the CIA's Chief Strategy Analyst in Vietnam* (New York: Vintage, 1977), pp. 116–124.

23. Porter (ed.), "General Dung's Account of the October Political Bureau Conference," *Vietnam Documents*, vol. 2, Document 351, (Extract), pp. 658–659. Dung conceded that U.S. intervention remained a possibility, but he also stated that even if the Americans did reenter the war they could not possibly save Thieu's regime from collapse. See also Duiker, *The Communist Road*, pp. 306–308.

24. Lipsman and others, *The False Peace*, pp. 182–183.

25. Duiker, *The Communist Road*, pp. 308–309; Davidson, *Vietnam at War*, pp. 762–764; Isaacs, *Without Honor*, pp. 331–335.

26. Isaacs, *Without Honor*, pp. 345–352; Davidson, *Vietnam at War*, pp. 770–774; Dougan, Clark; Fulghum, David, and the editors of Boston Publishing Company, *The Fall of the South* (Boston: Boston Publishing Co., 1985), pp. 48–52.

27. Davidson, *Vietnam at War*, pp. 774–777; Isaacs, *Without Honor*, pp. 353–356; Turley, *The Second Indochina War*, pp. 179–181.

28. Davidson, *Vietnam at War*, pp. 777–779; Dougan and others, *Fall of the South*, pp. 56–63.

29. Herring, *America's Longest War*, p. 265.

30. Dougan and others, *Fall of the South*, p. 83.

31. Isaacs, *Without Honor*, pp. 366–371; Dougan and others, *Fall of the South*, pp. 81–82; CBS television documentary, "Vietnam: A War that is Finished," August, 1975.

32. Davidson, *Vietnam at War*, p. 790. See Davidson's account of the epic Battle of Xuan Loc. The ARVN soldiers fought with a kind of desperate ferocity. For at least this battle, no one could fault either their tenacity or their valor. The rifle companies of the 18th ARVN Division were all decimated at Xuan Loc, but they took 5,000 Communist KIAs with them.

33. Quoted in Isaacs, *Without Honor*, pp. 281–282. Isaacs has a riveting account of the final days of the Khmer Republic. See his chap. 8, "Fall of the Khmer Republic," pp. 241–289. Schandberg and two other American journalists were taken prisoner by the Khmer Rouge, who threatened to execute them. Schandberg's

Cambodian assistant, Dith Pran, persuaded their captors not to shoot them. Although the U.S. journalists soon got out of Cambodia, Dith Pran did not. Four years later, Pran managed to escape from Cambodia to Thailand. He later rejoined Schandberg in the United States, where he works as a photojournalist.

34. *Ibid.*, pp. 407–413; Dougan and others, *Fall of the South*, pp. 107–108, 118–121, 127–129. Although rejecting the president's request for $722 million, Congress authorized a final $300 million that Ford had requested to provide humanitarian aid and to pay the costs of the American evacuation from South Vietnam.

35. Quoted in Herring, *America's Longest War*, p. 266.

36. Quoted in Isaacs, *Without Honor*, p. 420; Snepp, *Decent Interval*, pp. 392–397.

37. Recorded on CBS film, "Vietnam: A War that is Finished."

38. Dougan and others, *Fall of the South*, pp. 154–155.

39. *Ibid.*, pp. 157–158.

40. *Ibid.*, pp. 163–164.

41. Isaacs, *Without Honor*, pp. 447–468. The evacuations carried out Tuesday, April 29, from Tan Son Nhut were successful; 6,236 people, including 819 Marines assisting the evacuees, were flown out in 122 evacuation sorties.

42. Quoted in Dougan and others, *Fall of the South*, p. 171.

43. Isaacs, *Without Honor*, pp. 477–483; Hosmer, Stephen T., Kellen, Konrad, and Jenkins, Brian M., *The Fall of South Vietnam: Statements by Vietnamese Military and Civilian Leaders* (New York: Crane, Russak, 1980), pp. 252–253.

44. Quoted in Isaacs, *Without Honor*, p. 485.

STATISTICS

TABLE A. United States Military Personnel Serving in South Vietnam

December 31, 1960	900
December 31, 1961	3,205
December 31, 1962	9,000
December 31, 1963	16,500
December 31, 1964	23,300
December 31, 1965	184,300
June 30, 1966	267,500
December 31, 1966	385,300
June 30, 1967	448,800
December 31, 1967	485,600
June 30, 1968	534,700
December 31, 1968	536,100
April 30, 1969	543,400
June 30, 1969	538,700
December 31, 1969	475,200
June 30, 1970	414,900
December 31, 1970	334,600
June 30, 1971	239,200
December 31, 1971	156,800
June 30, 1972	47,000
December 31, 1972	24,200
March 30, 1973	240

Source: U.S. Department of Defense official records.

TABLE B.   Casualties, from January 1, 1961 to January 28, 1973

United States	
Killed in action	45,941
Wounded	300,635
Missing	2,330
Killed or died, noncombat-related	10,420
South Vietnam	
Military: Killed in action	220,357
Military: Wounded	499,026
Civilian: Killed	415,000
Civilian: Wounded	935,000
Vietcong/North Vietnam	
Military: Killed	851,000
Civilian: North Vietnam	65,000
Third-Country Forces	
Military: Killed in action	
Korea	4,407
Australia/New Zealand	469
Thailand	351

Sources: Lewy, Gunther, *America in Vietnam*; O'Ballance, Edgar, *The Wars in Vietnam*; Thayer, Thomas C., *War Without Fronts: The American Experience in Vietnam*.

TABLE C.   U.S. Combat Deaths Year by Year

Prior to 1965	267
1965	1,369
1966	5,008
1967	9,378
1968	14,592
1969	9,414
1970	4,221
1971	1,380
1972	312
Total	45,941

Source: Thayer, *War Without Fronts.*

TABLE D.   Statistical Portrait of U.S. Casualties in Indochina

1. Killed in combat	45,941
2. Wounded in combat	300,635
3. Died in non-combat situations	10,420
4. 90% of combat deaths were enlisted men	41,003

TABLE E.   Statistical Portrait of U.S. Casualties in Indochina (*cont'd.*)

5. 10% of combat deaths were officers	4,938
6. 60% of combat deaths were aged 19–21	26,931
7. 22% of combat deaths were aged 22–25	10,421
8. 18% of combat deaths were aged 26+	8,589
9. 33% of the dead had served less than 1 year	14,995
10. 33% of the dead had served between 1 and 2 years	14,853
11. Blacks accounted for 12% of the combat deaths	5,662
12. Other non-whites accounted for 1% of the combat deaths	469
13. Whites accounted for 87% of the combat deaths	39,827
14. Draftees accounted for 33% of the combat deaths	15,404

Source: Thayer, *War Without Fronts.*

TABLE F.   Causes of Combat and Non-Combat Deaths

Combat Deaths	45,941
Aircraft loss	4,178
Gunshot or small arms fire	18,385
Artillery/rocket/other explosion	12,350
Multiple fragmentation wounds	8,465
Other causes/unknown	2,563
Non-Combat Deaths	10,420
Accidents	8,483
Illness	929
Murder	190
Suicide	379
Other	439

Source: Thayer, *War Without Fronts.*

TABLE G.   A Statistical Portrait of U.S. Vietnam Veterans

Service during Vietnam era, 1964–1975	8,700,000
Service in South Vietnam	2,700,000
Combat in South Vietnam	870,000

Vital Statistics, (1978)

Median age	32 years
Median education	12.9 years
Median income, ages 20–39	$12,680
Unemployment rate, ages 20–34	5.5%
In VA hospitals	9,652

Source: Veterans Administration and Department of Defense official reports.

TABLE H.   Defoliation and Crop Destruction Coverage, 1962–1970

Year	Defoliation (acres)	Crop Destruction (acres)	Total
1962	4,940	741	5,681
1963	24,700	247	24,947
1964	83,486	10,374	93,860
1965	155,610	65,949	221,559
1966	741,247	103,987	845,144
1967	1,486,446	221,312	1,706,758
1968	1,267,110	63,726	1,330,836
1969	1,198,444	64,961	1,263,405
1970	220,324	32,604	252,928

Totals:	5,182,307 acres defoliated
	563,901 acres of crops destroyed
	5,746,208 acres defoliated and crops destroyed

Source: Lewy, *America in Vietnam.*

GLOSSARY

AK-47: A Russian and Chinese assault rifle used extensively by the Vietcong and by the PAVN forces.

Annam: Central section of Vietnam, a French protectorate from 1883 to 1954.

APC: Armored personnel carrier.

ARVN: Army of the Republic of Vietnam. The regular South Vietnamese national forces.

A Teams: Twelve-man Special Forces units.

Attrition Warfare: A strategy with the objective of destroying enemy personnel and materiel faster than they can be replenished until the enemy's ability to wage war is exhausted.

Binh Xuyen: A criminal army led by Bay Vien, a.k.a. Le Van Vien, that controlled portions of Saigon in 1954–1955.

Can Lao: The Can Lao Nhan Vi Cach Mang Dang, or Personalist Labor Revolutionary Party. Ngo Dinh Nhu's secret political party and police force.

Cao Dai: A religious sect formed in 1925 in southern Vietnam.

Charlie: GI slang for the Vietcong, a short version of Victor Charlie, from the U.S. military phonetic alphabet for VC.

Chinook: CH-47 transport helicopter.

CIA: Central Intelligence Agency.

CIDG: Civilian Irregular Defense Groups, teams devised by CIA operatives that combined defense functions with social and economic development programs designed to win the allegiance of the Montagnards.

CINCPAC: Commander-in-Chief, United States Pacific Command.

Cobra Bell: AH-1G fast attack helicopter, armed with machine guns, grenade launchers, and rockets.

Cochin China: The southern section of Vietnam, a French colony from 1863 to 1954.

COMUSMACV: Commander, United States Military Assistance Command, Vietnam.

CONUS: Military acronym for the Continental United States.

CORDS: Civil Operations and Revolutionary Development Support.

Corps: Two divisions assigned to defend a military region.

COSVN: Central Office, South Vietnam, the headquarters controlling all Vietcong political and military operations in southern Vietnam.

Counterinsurgency: The guiding doctrine of U.S. military forces in Vietnam during the early 1960s; its fundamental purpose was to win the allegiance of the people, not to destroy the enemy's armed forces. Inspiration for the phrase, "winning hearts and minds."

CTZ: Corps Tactical Zone.

DAO: Defense Attache Office, an agency that was part of the U.S. mission sent to South Vietnam following the January 1973 Accords that ended the American war. It was a replacement for MACV; DAO administered the U.S. military assistance program to the GVN, 1973–1975.

DEROS: Date eligible for return from overseas. The date a soldier's tour of duty in Vietnam ended, usually one year after arriving in the country.

Dien Bien Phu: Site in northwestern Vietnam next to the Laotian border where the French suffered a major defeat that led to the end of their power in Vietnam.

DMZ: Demilitarized Zone.

DOD: Department of Defense.

DRV: Democratic Republic of Vietnam (North Vietnam), created by Ho Chi Minh, September 2, 1945.

EAGLE PULL: Code-name of the U.S. evacuation of Phnom Penh in April 1975.

FAC: Forward Air Controller, a forward spotter who coordinated air strikes, usually airborne.

FMFPAC: Fleet Marine Force, Pacific Command.

Fragging: The murder of a commissioned or non-commissioned officer by an enlisted man of lower rank, usually with a fragmentation grenade.

Free-fire Zones: Territory considered completely under enemy control. South Vietnamese officials authorized the use of unlimited firepower in such zones.

FREQUENT WIND: Code-name of the U.S. evacuation of Saigon in April 1975.

FSB: Fire support base, a protected forward artillery base.

Green Berets: Famed nickname of soldiers serving in the U.S. Army Special Forces trained for counterinsurgency operations. The named derived from the green berets worn by these elite forces.

Grunt: The most frequent nickname given Army and Marine ground combat forces.

GVN: The Government of Vietnam (South Vietnam).

Hoa Hao: A religious sect formed in 1939 in southern Vietnam by Huynh Phu So.

Huey: Nickname given the UH-1 series helicopter.

ICC: International Control Commission, created by the Geneva Accords (1954) to supervise implementation of the agreements.

ICCS: International Commission of Control and Supervision, Agency responsible for administering the January 1973 Paris agreement.

JCS: Joint Chiefs of Staff.

JGS: Joint General Staff, the South Vietnamese equivalent of the U.S. Joint Chiefs.

JMC: Joint Military Commission, consisting of members from North Vietnam, South Vietnam, the PRG, and the United States, responsible for implementing the military provisions of the 1973 Paris Agreement.

JMT: Joint Military Team, consisting of members from North Vietnam, South Vietnam, the PRG, and the United States, responsible for accounting for all prisoners of war and MIAs.

Kampuchea: The name given Cambodia in 1975 by the victorious Khmer Rouge.

Khmer Rouge: Members of the Pracheachon, a left-wing revolutionary movement that came to power in Cambodia in April 1975.

KIA: Killed in action.

Lao Dong: The Vietnamese Worker's Party, the North Vietnamese Communist party founded in 1951. The ruling party of North Vietnam until 1975; thereafter it ruled the entire country.

LINEBACKER I: Code-name for U.S. bombing of North Vietnam resumed in April 1972 in response to the Nguyen Hue offensive.

LINEBACKER II: Code-name for the U.S. bombing of North Vietnam during December 1972, the Christmas Bombing.

LST: Landing Ship Tank, a large, shallow-draft cargo-hauling and landing craft.

LZ: Landing Zone, for helicopters.

MAAG: Military Assistance Advisory Group, the forerunner of MACV, 1955–1964.

MACV: Military Assistance Command, Vietnam, formed in 1962, lasted until 1973.

Main Force: Regular army forces of the North Vietnamese and Vietcong.

Medevac: Helicopters with the mission of transporting wounded soldiers quickly from the battlefield to forward hospitals.

MENU: Code-name for the secret B-52 bombing missions in Cambodia.

MIA: Missing in Action.

Montagnards: (Mountain dwellers) Indigenous tribal populations of Vietnam, who generally inhabit hilly and mountainous terrain.

MR: Military Region; formerly a CTZ, Corps Tactical Zone.

Napalm: A jellied incendiary weapon used by the French and the Americans during the Indochina wars. It could be dropped from aircraft in cannisters or fired from flamethrowers. Used as both a defoliant and antipersonnel weapon.

NCO: Noncommissioned Officer.

NLF: The National Liberation Front, formed December 20, 1960.

NSAM: National Security Action Memorandum.

NSC: National Security Council.

NVA: North Vietnamese Army.

NVN: North Vietnam or North Vietnamese.

OB: Order of Battle, a comprehensive arrangement and disposition of military units deployed in battle.

OCS: Officers' Candidate School.

Operation VULTURE: A planned U.S. operation to relieve the siege at Dien Bien Phu in April 1954. It was never implemented.

OPLAN: Operations Plan.

OSS: Office of Strategic Services, a World War II intelligence organization, forerunner of the CIA.

PACAF: United States Pacific Air Force.

PACFLT: United States Pacific Fleet.

Pacification: South Vietnamese and U.S. programs designed to win the allegiance of the South Vietnamese people and to eliminate Vietcong influence.

Pathet Lao: Laotian Communist insurgents who came to power in 1974–1975.

PAVN: People's Army of Vietnam, the North Vietnamese army.

Pentagon Papers: Secret Department of Defense studies of U.S. involvement in Vietnam, 1945–1967. The papers were stolen by Daniel Ellsberg and Anthony

Russo in 1971 and given to the New York *Times*, which published them that same year.

PF: Popular Forces.

PHOENIX: A joint U.S./South Vietnamese program to detect and to neutralize the Vietcong infrastructure.

PLA: People's Liberation Army of South Vietnam, the military arm of the Vietcong.

PLAF: People's Liberation Armed Forces of South Vietnam, a.k.a. the PLA.

Politburo: The executive committee of the Lao Dong; members were responsible for making all government policies.

POW: Prisoner of War.

PRG: Provisional Revolutionary Government, formed by NLF in 1969.

PRP: People's Revolutionary Party, the Communist Party apparatus that controlled the National Liberation Front, founded in 1962.

PTSD: Post-Traumatic Stress Disorder.

RD: Revolutionary Development Cadres, teams of South Vietnamese pacification workers trained to carry out various missions.

RF: Regional Forces.

ROTC: Reserve Officer Training Corps.

RVN: Republic of Vietnam (South Vietnam).

RVNAF: Republic of Vietnam Armed Forces, all South Vietnamese military forces including ARVN, Regional Forces, and Popular Forces.

SA-2: Medium-range Communist surface to air missile, effective up to 60,000 feet, speed about Mach 2.5.

SAC: Strategic Air Command.

SAM: Surface-to-air missile.

SANE: Committee for a Sane Nuclear Policy, an organization opposed to the nuclear arms race active in the late 1950s and early 1960s.

SDS: Students for a Democratic Society, the largest radical student organization in the country during the 1960s, led antiwar activities on many college campuses.

SEATO: Southeast Asia Treaty Organization.

17th Parallel: Temporary dividing line separating northern and southern Vietnam, created by Geneva Accords (1954), pending unification elections scheduled for July, 1956, which were never held.

Sortie: An operational flight by one aircraft.

Special Forces: U.S. Army personnel trained to carry out counterinsurgency operations, often covert and unconventional. They also trained Montagnards and South Vietnamese Special Forces.

Strategic Hamlets: A South Vietnamese program begun in 1962 that concentrated rural populations into fortified villages to gain their allegiance and to both separate and protect them from Vietcong guerrillas.

SVN: South Vietnam.

Tet: The Vietnamese lunar New Year and their most important holiday.

Third Countries: U.S. Allies that furnished military forces for the Vietnam war: South Korea, Thailand, the Philippines, Australia, and New Zealand.

Tonkin: The northern section of Vietnam, a French protectorate from 1883 to 1954.

USAID: United States Agency for International Development.

VC: Vietcong, a derogatory contraction meaning a Vietnamese who is a Communist.

VCI: Vietcong infrastructure, the political leaders of the Vietcong, also responsible for logistic support of the military forces.

Vietminh: A coalition political party formed by Ho Chi Minh in 1941 dominated by Vietnamese Communist leaders; it came to power in Hanoi September 2, 1945.

Vietnamization: The word was coined by Secretary of Defense Melvin Laird to describe Nixon's policy, inherited from Johnson, of withdrawing U.S. forces from Vietnam and transferring their responsibilities to the RVN forces.

VNAF: Vietnamese Air Force (the South Vietnamese Air Force).

WIA: Wounded in action.

CHRONOLOGY
OF U.S. INVOLVEMENT
IN VIETNAM,
1942–1975

1942
U.S. pilots attached to the Flying Tigers fly combat missions in Vietnam against Japanese military installations.

1943–1945
The OSS funds Vietminh actions against the Japanese in Vietnam. OSS operatives work with the Vietnamese to rescue downed U.S. flyers and go on espionage and sabotage missions with them.

September 1945
America supports the French efforts to reimpose colonialism in Vietnam.

May 8, 1950
The United States signs an agreement with France to provide the French Associated States of Vietnam with military assistance.

August 3, 1950
A U.S. Military Assistance Advisory Group (MAAG) of thirty-five men arrives in Vietnam to teach troops receiving U.S. weapons how to use them.

September 7, 1951
The Truman administration signs an agreement with Saigon to provide direct military aid to South Vietnam.

September 30, 1953
President Eisenhower approves $785 million for military aid for South Vietnam.

April 7, 1954
At a news conference, President Eisenhower, stressing the importance of defending Dien Bien Phu, enunciates the domino theory.

July 21, 1954
The American observer at Geneva, General Walter Bedell Smith, issues a unilateral declaration stating that the United States will refrain from the threat or the use of force to prevent implementation of the Geneva Accords.

September 8, 1954
The Manila Treaty is concluded creating SEATO. A separate protocol extends the SEATO umbrella to include Laos, Cambodia, and "the free territory under the jurisdiction of the State of Vietnam" (South Vietnam).

October 24, 1954
President Eisenhower sends a letter to the new leader in southern Vietnam, Ngo Dinh Diem, pledging U.S. support and agreeing to send $100 million to build up Diem's military forces. Eisenhower begins the U.S. commitment to maintaining a non-Communist government in South Vietnam.

April 28, 1955
Under severe pressure from a coalition of political enemies, Diem's fledgling regime almost falls. He is saved by the actions of Air Force Colonel Edwin Landsdale, who is also a CIA operative.

October 26, 1955
Diem, after defeating Bao Dai in a rigged election, declares himself to be president of the Republic of South Vietnam. His government is instantly recognized by the United States.

July 20, 1956
The deadline for holding reunification elections in accordance with the Geneva Accords passes. America supports Diem's refusal to hold elections.

May 8, 1957
Diem makes a triumphant visit to the United States. Eisenhower praises him lavishly and reaffirms American support for his government.

October, 1957
Small-scale civil war begins in South Vietnam between Diem's forces and cadres of Vietminh who have remained in South Vietnam after the partition at Geneva.

April 4, 1959
Eisenhower delivers a speech in which he links American vital national interests to the survival of a non-Communist state in South Vietnam.

December 20, 1960
The National Liberation front is formed. It is the Vietminh reborn. The Communist-controlled NLF takes charge of the growing insurgency against the Diem regime. Diem dubs the NLF the "Vietcong," meaning Vietnamese who are Communists.

January 6, 1961
Soviet Premier Khrushchev announces support for all "wars of national liberation" around the world. His speech influences the incoming Kennedy administration's decision to support counterinsurgency in Vietnam.

April 1961
The Kennedy administration confronts a crisis in Laos. Kennedy considers military intervention, then decides to seek a political solution.

May 1961
Kennedy approves sending Special Forces to South Vietnam. He also authorizes clandestine warfare against North Vietnam and a secret war in Laos.

June 1961
Kennedy and Khrushchev, meeting in Vienna, agree to support a neutral and independent Laos. Kennedy rejects neutrality for Vietnam.

November 1961
Special Forces are deployed to the central highlands in the vicinity of Pleiku to work with Montagnards, and they begin developing the CIDGs.

December 1961
The New York *Times* reports that some of the 3,200 U.S. advisers are operating in battle areas and are authorized to fire back if fired on.

January 1962
The Air Force launches Operation RANCH HAND, the aerial spraying of defoliating herbicides to deny cover to the Vietcong and to destroy their crops.

February 8, 1962
MACV is established in Saigon; its first commander is General Paul D. Harkins.

December 1962
There are now about 9,000 U.S. advisory and support personnel in South Vietnam; 109 Americans were killed or wounded in 1962.

January 2, 1963
At Ap Bac in the Mekong delta, the ARVN 7th Division, equipped with American weapons and accompanied by U.S. advisers, cannot defeat a lightly armed Vietcong battalion of 300 soldiers. The battle demonstrates that government troops cannot match the tactics or the fighting spirit of the insurgents.

May 8, 1963
In Hue, 20,000 Buddhists celebrating the birthday of Gautama Siddhartha Buddha are fired on by government forces. This action begins a series of events that will bring the downfall of the Diem regime.

June 11, 1963
Thich Quang Duc, an elderly Buddhist monk, immolates himself by fire at a busy Saigon intersection to protest Diem's suppression of the Buddhists.

August 21, 1963
Military forces loyal to Diem and to his brother Nhu attack Buddhist temples. President Kennedy denounces these actions. Meanwhile, a coup to overthrow Diem is being planned by dissident ARVN generals.

September 2, 1963
President Kennedy strongly reaffirms the American commitment to Vietnam. He also criticizes Diem's attacks on the Buddhists and calls for reform.

November 1, 1963
A coup, led by General Tran Van Don and General Duong Van Minh, with the foreknowledge and encouragement of American officials, overthrows the Diem regime. A military directorate, led by General Minh, succeeds Diem.

November 24, 1963
President Lyndon Johnson affirms U.S. support of the new South Vietnamese government.

December 31, 1963
There are about 16,500 U.S. soldiers in South Vietnam at year's end; 489 have been killed or wounded during 1963.

January 2, 1964
President Johnson approves covert military operations against North Vietnam to be carried out by South Vietnamese and Asian mercenaries. Called OPLAN 34A, they include espionage, sabotage, psychological warfare, and intelligence gathering.

January 30, 1964
Minh's government is overthrown in a bloodless coup by General Nguyen Khanh.

March 8–12, 1964
Secretary of Defense Robert McNamara visits South Vietnam. He affirms that America will remain in South Vietnam for as long as it takes to win the war.

April 1964
North Vietnam decides to infiltrate units of the NVA into South Vietnam.

June 20, 1964
General Harkins is succeeded by General William C. Westmoreland as COM-USMACV. Three days later, Henry Cabot Lodge resigns as the U.S. ambassador to the GVN, and is replaced by General Maxwell Taylor.

July 1964
Both sides are engaged in covert warfare in violation of the 1954 Geneva Accords. North Vietnam is using the Ho Chi Minh trail to infiltrate NVA troops south and to supply the Vietcong. America implements the OPLAN 34A operations. One OPLAN 34A operation uses U.S. destroyers to conduct surveillance missions off the North Vietnamese coast. These operations are called DESOTO Missions.

August 2, 1964
North Vietnamese patrol boats attack the U.S.S. *Maddox*, which was on a DESOTO Mission in waters near the North Vietnamese coast.

August 3, 1964
South Vietnamese PT boats carry out OPLAN 34A raids, attacking North Vietnamese radar installations in same area.

August 4–5, 1964
Both U.S.S. Maddox and another destroyer, U.S.S. *Turner Joy*, which has joined the *Maddox*, report that they are under attack at sea. Carrier-based U.S. naval aircraft fly reprisal raids ordered by President Johnson against North Vietnamese targets.

August 7, 1964
At Johnson's request, Congress enacts the Gulf of Tonkin resolution granting President Johnson the power to "to take all necessary measures to repel any armed attack against the forces of the United States and to prevent further aggression...including the use of armed force...." Johnson will later use this resolution as a postdated declaration of war.

October 1964
General Khanh resigns and is replaced by a civilian, Tran Van Huong.

December 31, 1964
About 23,000 Americans are now serving in South Vietnam. There is now a full-scale undeclared war raging in South Vietnam, and there is also fighting in Laos and Cambodia. There have been 1278 U.S. casualties for the year.

January 4, 1965
In his State of the Union address, President Johnson reaffirms the American commitment to South Vietnam. He states that American security is tied to peace in Southeast Asia.

January 27–28, 1965
Tran Van Huong is ousted and General Khanh returns to power.

February 7, 1965
The Vietcong attack a U.S. helicopter base and other installations near Pleiku in the central highlands. Eight Americans are killed and 126 wounded. Johnson orders retaliatory air strikes on targets in North Vietnam.

February 13, 1965
Johnson orders a sustained bombing campaign against North Vietnam that has been long-planned by his advisers. Called Operation ROLLING THUNDER, it will continue, with occasional pauses, until October 31, 1968. The American air war against North Vietnam begins on March 2.

February 25, 1965
General Khanh is forced out by Air Marshal Nguyen Cao Ky.

March 8, 1965
The first U.S. combat troops arrive in Vietnam.

April 6, 1965
President Johnson authorizes U.S. forces to take the offensive to support ARVN forces.

June 19, 1965
Air Marshal Ky becomes premier of the eighth South Vietnamese government since Diem was overthrown.

June 28–30, 1965
U.S. forces undertake the first major American offensive against the Vietcong in War Zone D, twenty miles northeast of Saigon.

July 21–28, 1965
President Johnson makes a series of decisions that amount to committing the United States to a major war in Vietnam. Among the decisions he makes: draft calls will be raised to 35,000 per month, 50,000 additional troops will be sent to Vietnam with additional increases as the situation demands, and the air war against North Vietnam is expanded. Johnson also makes it clear that he wants these decisions implemented in low-key fashion so as not to excite or alarm either the Congress or the American people. These decisions began the seven-and-a half-year U.S. war in Indochina.

August 7, 1965
The Chinese government warns the United States that it will send troops to fight in Vietnam if necessary.

October 23 to November 20, 1965
In the largest battle of the war to date, the U.S. 1st Air Cavalry defeats NVA forces in the Ia Drang valley, in a remote corner of Pleiku province.

December 31, 1965
This was a pivotal year of the war. America began a sustained air war against North Vietnam. It also committed large numbers of forces to ground combat operations in South Vietnam. At year's end, there are 184,000 U.S. troops in South Vietnam. U.S. casualties for the year, 1369 KIA and 5300 WIA; 1965 is Year One of the American war in Vietnam.

March 9, 1966
The U.S. Department of State issues a White Paper claiming that American intervention in Vietnam is legal under international law, the UN Charter, and the U.S. Constitution.

June 29, 1966
U.S. aircraft strike North Vietnamese petroleum storage facilities near Haiphong and Hanoi.

October 15 to November 26, 1966
U.S. forces are involved in one of the biggest operations of the war in Tayninh Province near the Cambodian border, fifty miles northwest of Saigon.

December 31, 1966
The Vietnam war has become the dominant event in world affairs. During the year the United States increased its forces in Vietnam from 184,000 to 385,000. The air war

against North Vietnam has been expanded significantly; 5,008 Americans were killed and 30,093 wounded during the year.

January 8–26, 1967
American troops are involved in the largest offensive of the war. About 16,000 American troops participate in Operation CEDAR FALLS to disrupt Vietcong operations in the Iron Triangle region northeast of Saigon.

February 22 to April 1, 1967
The largest Allied offensive of the war to date takes place, Operation JUNCTION CITY, involving thirty-four U.S. battalions. Its goal is to smash the VC stronghold in War Zone C near the Cambodian border and ease pressure on Saigon.

March 10–11, 1967
U.S. aircraft bomb the Thainguyen steel works near Hanoi; they are the first bombing raids on a major industrial target.

May 14–16, 1967
A U.S. newspaper reports that Chinese Premier Chou En-lai threatened to send Chinese troops into North Vietnam if the United States invaded that country.

May 19–24, 1967
McNamara sends a memo to President Johnson arguing against widening the war and proposes curtailing the air war against North Vietnam. Responding to McNamara's dovish memo, the Joint Chiefs call for expanding the air war against North Vietnam and for sending 200,000 additional troops to South Vietnam.

July 7–12, 1967
A compromise is worked out between Johnson's dovish and hawkish advisers. McNamara recommends a troop increase of 55,000. The president accepts it.

July 30, 1967
A Gallup poll shows that 52 percent of Americans disapprove of Johnson's Vietnam war policy; 56 percent believe that America is in a stalemate.

October 16–21, 1967
Antiwar activists hold anti-draft demonstrations throughout the United States. The largest occurs at the Army Induction Center in Oakland, California.

October 21–23, 1967
Fifty thousand demonstrate against the Vietnam War in Washington, D.C.

October 25–30, 1967
The air war against North Vietnam intensifies. Sustained attacks are carried out on targets near Hanoi and Haiphong.

November 2, 1967
President Johnson meets privately with a group of distinguished former leaders. Dubbed the "wise men," they generally support his war policy.

November 3–22, 1967
One of the bloodiest and fiercest battles of the war between American and North Vietnamese troops occurs at Dak To in the central highlands.

November 22, 1967
President Johnson brings General Westmoreland home to rally support for the war. Westmoreland tells his audiences that the United States is winning the war.

November 30, 1967
Senator Eugene J. McCarthy announces that he will challenge President Johnson for the Democratic presidential nomination in 1968. He will run on a platform calling for a negotiated settlement of the Vietnam war.

December 31, 1967
At year's end, there are about 500,000 U.S. troops in Vietnam. For the year, the war cost taxpayers about $21 billion. Casualties, 9,353 KIA and 99,742 WIA.

January 20 to April 14, 1968
One of the most famous battles of the war takes place at Khe Sanh, an American Marine base located just south of the DMZ. NVA forces besiege Khe Sanh. It is feared that Khe Sanh will become an American Dien Bien Phu. But U.S. airpower eventually breaks the siege, and the Communists are forced to withdraw.

January 30 to February 10, 1968
On the first day of the Tet truce, Vietcong forces, supported by NVA troopers, launch the largest offensive of the war. Simultaneous attacks are mounted in South Vietnam's largest cities and many provincial capitals. The offensive is crushed by American and GVN forces. Tet is a decisive military victory for the Allies, but turns out to be a psychological and political disaster.

February 28, 1968
General Earle Wheeler, chairman of the Joint Chiefs, tells Johnson that General Westmoreland needs an additional 206,000 troops. A crucial point in the war has been reached. If Johnson does not send the troops, he will be conceding that the United States cannot win a military victory. But if he sends the troops, it will require a reserve call-up, and significantly raise the costs and casualties of war. Johnson delays a decision and asks his new secretary of defense, Clark Clifford, to conduct a thorough reappraisal of U.S. Vietnam policy.

March 12, 1968
Senator Eugene McCarthy, in the New Hampshire primary, makes a strong showing in a hawkish state. Four days later, Senator Robert Kennedy announces that he too will seek the Democratic nomination and run on an antiwar platform.

March 16, 1968
In what will become the most notorious atrocity committed by American soldiers during the Vietnam war, a platoon of troopers slaughter hundreds of unarmed villagers in the hamlet of My Lai-4.

March 25–26, 1968
Johnson reconvenes the "wise men." Most advise against any more troop increases and recommend that the United States seek a negotiated peace in Vietnam.

March 31, 1968
Johnson announces a unilateral halt to all U.S. bombing north of the DMZ and that he will seek to get negotiations started with North Vietnam. He also stuns the nation with an announcement that he will not seek reelection.

April 22, 1968
Clifford announces that GVN is going to take responsibility for more and more of the fighting. This is the first announcement of a policy that under President Nixon will be called Vietnamization.

May 3, 1968
America and North Vietnam agree to begin formal negotiations in Paris on May 10.

June 10, 1968
General Creighton W. Abrams succeeds General Westmoreland as COMUSMACV.

August 5–8, 1968
The Republican National Convention, meeting in Miami, nominates Richard M. Nixon for president. The Republican platform calls for an honorable negotiated peace in Vietnam and for the progressive "de-Americanization" of the war.

August 26–29, 1968
The Democratic National Convention meets in Chicago. Democrats adopt a platform endorsing the administration's war policy and nominate Vice President Hubert H. Humphrey for president. On the evening of August 28, there is a full-scale riot in the streets between Chicago police and antiwar radicals.

October 31, 1968
In a televised address to the nation, President Johnson announces a complete bombing halt over North Vietnam.

November 5, 1968
Richard Nixon is elected president of the United States.

December 31, 1968
The major turning point of the American Vietnam war occurred in 1968. After Tet, Johnson had to abandon his policy of measured escalation in search of military victory and replace it with an early version of Vietnamization looking to a negotiated settlement. Richard Nixon was elected president, and the general sense at the time was that he had a plan for bringing the war to an early end. 1968 is the largest and costliest year of the American war, 14,314 KIAs and 150,000 WIAs. Cost, about $30 billion.

January 25, 1969
The first plenary session of the four-way Paris peace talks among the Americans, the North Vietnamese, the South Vietnamese, and the National Liberation Front occurs.

March 18, 1969
President Nixon orders the secret bombing of Communist base camps and supply depots in Cambodia to commence.

May 10–20, 1969
The battle for Hamburger Hill takes place near the A Shau valley. In ten days of intense fighting and heavy casualties, Allied forces take the hill. The hill is abandoned soon thereafter.

June 8, 1969
President Nixon announces that 25,000 U.S. troops will be withdrawn by the end of August and that they will be replaced by South Vietnamese forces. The gradual phase-out of the American war in Vietnam has begun.

June 10, 1969
The NLF announces the formation of a Provisional Revolutionary Government (PRG) to rule in South Vietnam. It amounts to a formal challenge to the Thieu regime for political control of South Vietnam.

August 4, 1969
Secret negotiations began in Paris between U.S. special envoy Henry Kissinger and North Vietnam's Xuan Thuy.

August 17–26, 1969
During a major battle between U.S. and NVA forces in the Queson valley about thirty miles south of Danang, the first combat refusal by U.S. troops occurs.

September 23, 1969
Eight antiwar leaders go on trial in Chicago for their part in organizing the antiwar demonstrations occurring in Chicago at the time of the Democratic convention, August 26–29, 1968.

October 15, 1969
The largest antiwar demonstrations in American history take place at many sites across the country.

November 3, 1969
President Nixon makes his most successful speech in defense of his Vietnam war policies. Congress and public opinion overwhelmingly support Vietnamization as he successfully blunts the efforts of the antiwar movement.

November 15, 1969
More than 250,000 come to Washington, D.C., to protest the Vietnam war. It is the largest single antiwar demonstration to date.

December 31, 1969
At year's end, there are 479,000 U.S. troops in Vietnam. GVN forces have increased and now number over 900,000. Fighting continued during the year on a large-scale. American KIAs totaled 9,414 for the year. The U.S. forces are showing signs of declining morale, discipline, and fighting spirit.

February 19–20, 1970
All defendants in the Chicago trial are convicted of conspiracy to incite rioting and receive maximum sentences of five years in prison and $5,000 fines. All will be acquitted on appeal.

March 18, 1970
In a bloodless coup in Cambodia, pro-Western General Lon Nol ousts neutralist Prince Norodom Sihanouk as head of state.

April 11, 1970
Polls show that only 48 percent of Americans support Vietnamization, down from 70 percent in November 1969.

April 20, 1970
President Nixon promises to withdraw 150,000 more U.S. troops over the next year if Vietnamization continues to make progress.

May 1, 1970
American forces totaling about 30,000 invade the Fishhook region of Cambodia. The Cambodian incursion is the last major offensive of the Indochina war involving U.S. ground combat forces.

May 4, 1970
National Guards fire into a group of student demonstrators on the campus of Kent State University, killing four and wounding eleven.

May 6, 1970
More than a hundred colleges and universities across the nation shut down because of student protests and rioting in response to the Cambodian invasion and the killings at Kent State.

May 8–20, 1970
In New York City, construction workers attack antiwar demonstrators on Wall Street. An estimated 80,000 young people, mostly college students, demonstrate peacefully in the nation's capital. They protest the "Kent State Massacre" and call for the immediate withdrawal of all U.S. troops from Indochina. In New York City, more than 100,000 workers march in support of Nixon's war policies.

June 24, 1970
The Senate, by a vote of 81-10, repeals the Gulf of Tonkin resolution. President Nixon states that the legal basis for the American war in Vietnam is not the Gulf of Tonkin resolution, but the constitutional authority of the president as commander-in-chief to protect the lives of U.S. military forces in Vietnam.

August 19, 1970
America signs a pact with Cambodia to provide Lon Nol's government with military aid.

November 9, 1970
The Supreme Court refuses to hear a case brought by the state of Massachusetts challenging the constitutionality of the Vietnam war.

November 11, 1970
On this day, for the first time in more than five years, no American soldier is killed in Vietnam.

December 31, 1970
The U.S. war in Vietnam is winding down. At year's end there are about 335,000 U.S. troops in South Vietnam. U.S. KIAs for the year number 4,221. But the war has spread to Cambodia, and no progress is reported at the Paris peace talks.

January 1, 1971
Congress forbids the use of U.S. ground troops in either Laos or Cambodia.

March 6–24, 1971
ARVN forces invade Laos to interdict enemy supply routes down the Ho Chi Minh trail complex. Communist counterattacks drive the invaders out of Laos and inflict heavy casualties. It is a major defeat for the GVN.

April 19–23, 1971
Vietnam Veterans Against the War stage a demonstration in Washington, D.C. It ends with veterans throwing combat ribbons and medals at the Capitol steps.

April 20, 1971
The Pentagon reports that fragging incidents are increasing. There were ninety-six incidents in 1969 and 209 in 1970.

June 13, 1971
The New York *Times* begins publication of the leaked portions of the forty-seven–volume Pentagon analysis of the U.S. involvement in Vietnam through 1967.

July 1, 1971
The 26th Amendment to the Constitution, granting the vote to eighteen to twenty-one year-olds, is ratified.

July 15, 1971
In a surprise announcement, President Nixon tells the American people that he will be visiting China before May 1972.

December 31, 1971
The American war in Vietnam is ending; 156,800 U.S. troops remain. There were 1,380 KIAs that year. As the Americans withdraw, the Communists intensify their attacks in Laos, Cambodia, and parts of South Vietnam. U.S. morale continues to deteriorate. Vietnamization is not working, and the Paris talks remained stalled.

February 21–27, 1972
President Nixon makes his historic visit to China. The North Vietnamese fear that China and the United States will make a deal behind their backs; Taiwan calls for peace in Vietnam.

March 30 to April 8, 1972
A major NVA offensive begins as Communist forces attack South Vietnamese towns and bases just south of the DMZ. The Communists open a second front with a drive into Binh Long province about seventy miles north of Saigon. Communists forces open a third front with drives into the central highlands. The fighting in South Vietnam between GVN and Communist forces is the most intense of the entire war.

April 10, 1972
America responds with air attacks. B-52s strike targets in North Vietnam for the

first time since November 1967. B-52s and tactical bombers also strike targets in South Vietnam. America is waging an air war over all of Vietnam.

May 8, 1972
Nixon announces that he has ordered the mining of all North Vietnamese ports.

May 20, 1972
The summit conference between President Nixon and Leonid Brezhnev takes place on schedule in Moscow. Both sides are unwilling to risk detente over the Vietnam war. Nixon's Soviet visit is the first ever by a U.S. president.

June 28, 1972
President Nixon announces that no more draftees will be sent to Vietnam unless they volunteer.

August 11, 1972
The last U.S. combat unit is withdrawn from South Vietnam. There are now 44,000 American servicemen in South Vietnam.

August 16, 1972
U.S. aircraft fly a record 370 sorties against North Vietnam. Most American aircraft fly from carriers in the Gulf of Tonkin or from bases in Thailand.

September 15, 1972
ARVN forces recapture Quang Tri City. The fighting destroys most of the city, which formerly had a population of 300,000. Most of these people now reside in squalid refugee camps.

October 8–11, 1972
Lengthy secret meetings in Paris between Henry Kissinger and Le Duc Tho produce a tentative settlement of the war. The substance of the agreement is a cease-fire, to be followed by both sides working out a political settlement.

October 22, 1972
President Thieu rejects the proposed settlement.

November 7, 1972
Richard Nixon is reelected president by a landslide margin. He promises that he will achieve "peace with honor" in Vietnam.

November 11, 1972
The U.S. Army turns over its giant headquarters base at Long Binh to the South Vietnamese, symbolizing the end of the direct American participation in the war after more than seven years.

December 14, 1972
The U.S. breaks off peace talks with the North Vietnamese that have been going on since Nixon's reelection.

December 18–31, 1972
President Nixon announces the resumption of the bombing and mining of North Vietnam. The most concentrated air offensive of the war begins, mostly aimed at targets in the vicinity of Hanoi and Haiphong.

December 28, 1972
Hanoi announces that it is willing to resume negotiations if the United States will stop bombing above the 20th Parallel. The bombing ends on December 31.

December 31, 1972
At year's end there are about 24,000 U.S. troops remaining in South Vietnam; 312 Americans were killed in action.

January 8–18, 1973
Henry Kissinger and Le Duc Tho resume negotiations in Paris, and they reach an agreement that is similar to the one that had been rejected by General Thieu.

January 19–26, 1973
There is heavy fighting in South Vietnam between GVN and Communist forces as both sides try to gain as much territory as they can before the cease-fire.

January 23, 1973
Nixon announces that the Paris Accords will go into effect at 7:00 p. m. EST, January 27, 1973. He says that "peace with honor" has been achieved.

January 27, 1973
The draft ends. For the first time since 1949, America has no conscription.

February 12–27, 1973
American POWs begin to come home.

February 21, 1973
A cease-fire formally ends the 20-year war in Laos.

March 29, 1973
The last U.S. troops leave South Vietnam. Only a DAO contingent and Marine embassy guards remain. About 8,500 U.S. civilian officials stay on.

June 4 to August 15, 1973
The Senate blocks all funds for any U.S. military activities in Indochina. The House concurs. The Nixon administration works out a compromise agreement with the Congress to permit continued U.S. bombing in Cambodia until August 15. The cessation marks the end of twelve years of American military action in Indochina.

November 7, 1973
Congress enacts the War Powers Act over President Nixon's veto. It requires the president to report to Congress within forty-eight hours after committing American forces to combat on foreign soil. It also limits to sixty days the time that the President can commit soldiers to foreign combat without congressional approval.

December 31, 1973
The war in Vietnam continues without U.S. involvement. Most of the provisions of the Paris agreements are not observed by either side. During the year, there were 13,788 RVNAF KIAs and 45,057 Communist KIAs.

August 5, 1974
Congress makes sharp cuts in the amount of military aid going to the South Vietnamese government.

December 31, 1974
During 1974, 80,000 people, both civilians and soldiers, have been killed in the war. This is the highest total for any year of the wars that began in 1945.

January 6, 1975
NVA forces overrun Phuoc Long province. When the Americans do not react, Hanoi concludes that America will not reintroduce its military forces to save the GVN.

January 28, 1975
President Ford requests an additional $722 million in military aid for South Vietnam. Congress refuses his request.

March 1975
NVA forces launch an offensive in the central highlands. In a desperate effort to save the southern half of his country, General Thieu orders his forces to abandon their central highlands positions.

March 24, 1975
Hanoi launches its Ho Chi Minh Campaign to "liberate" South Vietnam before the rains begin.

April 8–21, 1975
The last major battle of the Vietnam war is fought at Xuan Loc, about thirty miles from Saigon. After hard fighting, the Communists win.

April 16, 1975
The Cambodian government surrenders to the Khmer Rouge, who promptly occupy the capital city of Phnom Penh.

April 23, 1975
President Ford pronounces the Vietnam war "finished as far as America is concerned."

April 29–30, 1975
The last Americans and eligible South Vietnamese are evacuated from Saigon.

April 30, 1975
The Communists conquer Saigon. The Vietnam war ends in victory for the VC/NVA forces. The long American effort to create a non-Communist state in southern Vietnam fails.

Major sources for the chronology:

BOWMAN, JOHN, General Editor, *The World Almanac of the Vietnam War* (New York: Bison Books, 1985).

DAVIDSON, PHILLIP B., *Vietnam at War: The History 1946–1975* (Novato, Calif.: Presidio, 1988).

GRAVEL, MIKE (ed.), *The Pentagon Papers: The Defense Department History of U.S. Decision Making in Vietnam*, 4 vols. (Boston: Beacon, 1971).

SUMMERS, HARRY G., JR., *The Vietnam War Almanac* (New York: Facts on File, 1985).

BIBLIOGRAPHY

BOOKS

AMBROSE, STEPHEN E., *Eisenhower*, vol. 2: *The President*. New York: Simon and Schuster, 1984.
———, *Nixon: The Education of a Politician*. New York: Simon and Schuster, 1987.
———, *Rise to Globalism: American Foreign Policy Since 1938*. 2nd rev. ed. New York: Penguin, 1985.
ARLEN, MICHAEL J., *The Living Room War*. New York: Viking, 1969.
BAIN, CHESTER A., *Vietnam: The Roots of Conflict*. Englewood Cliffs, N. J.: Prentice Hall, 1967.
BAKER, MARK (ed.), *NAM: The Vietnam War in the Words of the Soldiers Who Fought There*. New York: Berkeley, 1981.
BALL, GEORGE, *Diplomacy for a Crowded World*. Boston: Little, Brown, 1976.
———, *The Past Has Another Pattern*. New York: W. W. Norton, 1982.
BARITZ, LOREN, *Backfire: A History of How American Culture Led Us into Vietnam and Made Us Fight the Way We Did*. New York: Ballantine, 1985.
BARNET, RICHARD J., *The Roots of War*. New York: Atheneum, 1972.
———, *Intervention and Revolution*. New York: New American Library, 1972.
BASKIR, LAWRENCE M.; and STRAUSS, WILLIAM A., *Chance and Circumstance: The Draft, the War, and the Vietnam Generation*. New York: Vintage, 1978.
BATOR, VICTOR M., *Vietnam: A Diplomatic Tragedy*. Dobbs Ferry, N. Y.: Oceana, 1965.
BERGER, CARL (ed.), *The United States Air Force in Southeast Asia, 1961–1973*. Washington, D.C.: U.S. Government Printing Office, 1977.
BERMAN, LARRY, *Lyndon Johnson's War*. New York: W. W. Norton, 1989.
———, *Planning a Tragedy*. New York: W. W. Norton, 1982.
BERMAN, WILLIAM C., *William Fulbright and the Vietnam War: The Dissent of a Political Realist*. Kent, Ohio: Kent State University Press, 1988.
BECKET, IAN F. W.; and PIMLOTT, JOHN (eds.), *Armed Forces and Modern Counter-Insurgency*. London: Croom Helm, 1985.
BECKETT, BRIAN, *The Illustrated History of the Vietnam War*. New York: Gallery, 1985.
BILLS, SCOTT, L. (ed.), *Kent State/May 4: Echoes Through a Decade*. Kent, Ohio: Kent State University Press, 1982.

BLAKELEY, SCOTT, *Prisoner at War: The Survival of Commander Richard A. Stratton*. Garden City, N. Y.: Doubleday, 1978.

BLAUFARB, DOUGLAS S., *The Counterinsurgency Era*. New York: The Free Press, 1977.

BLUM, ROBERT, *Drawing the Line: The Origins of the American Containment Policy in East Asia*. New York: W. W. Norton, 1982.

BODARD, LUCIEN, *The Quicksand War: Prelude to Vietnam*. (Boston: Little, Brown, 1967.

BORNET, VAUGHN, *The Presidency of Lyndon Johnson*. Lawrence, Kansas: University Press of Kansas, 1983.

BOETTCHER, THOMAS D., *Vietnam: The Valor and the Sorrow*. Boston: Little, Brown, 1985.

BOUSCAREN, ANTHONY TRAWICK, *The Last of the Mandarins: Diem of Vietnam*. Pittsburgh: Duquesne University Press, 1965.

BOWMAN, JOHN S. (ed.), *The World Almanac of the Vietnam War*. New York: Bison Books, 1985.

BRAESTRUP, PETER, *Big Story*, 2 vols. Boulder, Colo.: Westview, 1977.

BRAESTRUP, PETER, (ed.), *Vietnam as History*. Washington, D.C.: University Press of America, 1984.

BRANDON, HENRY, *The Retreat of American Power*. Garden City, N. Y.: Doubleday, 1973.

————, *The Anatomy of Error*. Boston: Bambit, 1969.

BRANFMAN, FRED, *Voices from the Plain of Jars*. New York: Harper and Row, 1970.

BRODIE, BERNARD, *War and Politics*. New York: Macmillan, 1973.

BRYAN, C. D. B., *Friendly Fire*. New York: G.P. Putnam's Sons, 1976.

BUCKINGHAM, WILLIAM A., JR., *Operation Ranch Hand: The Air Force and Herbicides in Southeast Asia, 1961–1971*. Washington, D.C.: U.S. Government Printing Office, 1982.

BURCHETT, WILFRED G., *Vietnam North*. New York: International Publishers, 1966.

BURNS, RICHARD DEAN; and LEITENBERG, MILTON, *The Wars in Vietnam, Cambodia, and Laos, 1945–1982: A Bibliographic Guide*. Santa Barbara, Calif.: ABC-Clio Information Services, 1984.

BUTLER, DAVID, *The Fall of Saigon*. New York: Simon and Schuster, 1985.

BUTTINGER, JOSEPH, *A Dragon Defiant: A Short History of Vietnam*. New York: Praeger, 1972.

————, *The Smaller Dragon: A Political History of Vietnam*. New York: Praeger, 1958.

————, *Vietnam: A Dragon Embattled*. 2 vols. New York: Praeger, 1967.

————, *Vietnam: The Unforgettable Tragedy*. New York: Horizon, 1977.

CABLE, LARRY E., *Conflict of Myths: The Development of Counterinsurgency Doctrine and the Vietnam War*. New York: New York University Press, 1988.

CADY, JOHN F., *The Roots of French Imperialism in Eastern Asia*. Ithaca, N.Y.: Cornell University Press, 1954.

————, *Southeast Asia: Its Historical Development*. New York: McGraw-Hill, 1964.

CAIRNS, JAMES F., *The Eagle and the Lotus: Western Intervention in Vietnam, 1847–1968*. Melbourne, Australia: Landsdowne, 1969.

CAPPS, WALTER H., *The Unfinished War: Vietnam and the American Conscience*. Boston: Beacon, 1982.

CASH, JOHN A., *Seven Firefights in Vietnam*. Washington, D.C.: U.S. Government Printing Office, 1970.

CHEN, KING C., *Vietnam and China, 1938–1954*. Princeton, N. J.: Princeton University Press, 1969.

CHINH, TRUONG, *The Resistance Will Win*. Hanoi: Foreign Language Publishing House, 1960.

CINCINNATUS, *Self-Destruction: The Disintegration and Decay of the United States Army During the Vietnam Era*. New York: W. W. Norton, 1981.

COEDES, GEORGE, *The Making of Southeast Asia*. Berkeley, Calif.: University of California Press, 1966.

COHEN, STEVEN (ed.), *Vietnam: Anthology and Guide to A Television History*. New York: Knopf, 1983.

COHEN, WARREN, *Dean Rusk*. New York: Cooper Square, 1980.

COLBY, WILLIAM; and FORBATH, PETER, *Honorable Men: My Life in the CIA*. New York: Simon and Schuster, 1978.

COLE, ALLAN B. (ed.), *Conflict in Indochina and International Repercussions: A Documentary History, 1945–1955*. Ithaca, N. Y.: Cornell University Press, 1956.

COLLINS, JOHN M., *The Vietnam War in Perspective*. Washington, D.C.: Strategic Research Group, 1972.

COOPER, CHESTER L., *The Lost Crusade: America in Vietnam*. New York: Dodd, Mead, 1970.

Cornell University Study Group, *The Air War in Vietnam*. Ithaca, N. Y.: Cornell University Press, 1972.

CORSON, WILLIAM R., *The Betrayal*. New York: W. W. Norton, 1968.

————, *Consequences of Failure*. New York, W. W. Norton, 1974.

CURREY, CECIL B., *The Unquiet American*. Boston: Houghton Mifflin, 1988.

DAVIDSON, PHILLIP B., *Vietnam at War: The History 1946–1975*. Novato, Calif.: Presidio, 1988.

DAWSON, ALAN, *55 Days: The Fall of South Vietnam*. Englewood Cliffs, N. J.: Prentice Hall, 1977.

DEBENEDETTI, CHARLES, *The Peace Reform in American History.* Bloomington, Ind.: Indiana University Press, 1984.

DEVILLERS, PHILIPPE, *Histoire du Viet-Nam, de 1940 à 1952.* Paris: Editions du Seuil, 1952.

———; and LACOUTURE, JEAN, *The End of A War: Indochina, 1954.* New York: Praeger, 1969.

DIEM, BUI; with CHANOFF, DAVID, *In the Jaws of History.* Boston: Houghton Mifflin, 1987.

DIETZ, TERRY, *Republicans and Vietnam, 1961–1968.* New York: Greenwood, 1986.

DIVINE, ROBERT A. (ed.), *Exploring the Johnson Years.* Austin, Texas: The University of Texas Press, 1981.

DOUGHAN, CLARK; FULGHUM, DAVID; and the editors of Boston Publishing Company, *The Fall of the South.* Boston: Boston Publishing Co., 1985, a volume in the series, *The Vietnam Experience,* a 26-volume series on the Vietnam war.

DOYLE, EDWARD; LIPSMAN, SAMUEL; and the editors, *America Takes Over.* Boston: Boston Publishing Co., 1982, a volume in the series *The Vietnam Experience.*

———; LIPSMAN, SAMUEL; and the editors, *Setting the Stage.* Boston: Boston Publishing Co., 1981, a volume in the series, *The Vietnam Experience.*

———; LIPSMAN, SAMUEL; MAITLAND, TERRENCE; and the editors, *The North.* Boston: Boston Publishing Co., 1982, a volume in the series, *The Vietnam Experience.*

———; LIPSMAN, SAMUEL; WEISS, STEPHEN; and the editors, *Passing the Torch.* Boston: Boston Publishing Co., 1981, a volume in the series, *The Vietnam Experience.*

———; MAITLAND, TERRENCE; and the editors, *The Aftermath, 1975–1985.* Boston: Boston Publishing Co., 1985 a volume in the series, *The Vietnam Experience.*

DRACHMAN, EDWARD R., *United States Policy Toward Vietnam, 1940–1945.* Rutherford, N. J.: Fairleigh-Dickinson University Press, 1970.

DRAPER, THEODORE, *Abuse of Power.* New York: Viking, 1967.

DRENDEL, LOU, *The Air War in Vietnam.* New York: Arco, 1968.

DUIKER, WILLIAM J., *The Rise of Nationalism in Vietnam, 1900–1941.* Ithaca, N. Y.: Cornell University Press, 1975.

———, *The Communist Road to Power.* Boulder, Colo.: Westview, 1981.

———, *Vietnam: Nation in Revolution.* Boulder, Colo.: Westview, 1983.

———, *Vietnam Since the Fall of Saigon.* Athens, Ohio: Ohio University, Center for International Studies, 1980.

DUNCAN, DAVID D., *War Without Heroes.* New York: Harper and Row, 1970.

DUNG, VAN TIEN, *Our Great Spring Victory: An Account of the Liberation of South Vietnam.* New York: Monthly Review Press, 1977.

DUNN, PETER M., *The First Vietnam War.* New York: St. Martin's Press, 1985.

EDELMAN, BERNARD (ed.), *Dear America: Letters Home from Vietnam.* New York: Pocket Books, 1985.

EISENHOWER, DWIGHT DAVID, *The White House Years: Mandate for Change, 1953–1956.* Garden City, N. Y.: Doubleday, 1963.

ELLSBERG, DANIEL, *Papers on the War.* New York: Simon and Schuster, 1972.

EMERSON, GLORIA, *Winners and Losers: Battles, Retreats, Gains, Losses, and Ruins from a Long War.* New York: Harcourt, Brace, 1976.

ENNIS, THOMAS E., *French Policy and Developments In Indochina.* Chicago: University of Chicago Press, 1956.

ENTHOVEN, ALAIN C.; and SMITH, K. WAYNE, *How Much Is Enough: Shaping the Defense Program, 1961–1968.* New York: Harper & Row, 1971.

EPSTEIN, EDWARD JAY, *News from Nowhere: Television and the News.* New York: Vintage, 1973.

FAIRLIE, HENRY, *The Kennedy Promise: The Politics of Expectation.* New York: Doubleday, 1973.

FALL, BERNARD, *Hell in a Very Small Place: The Siege of Dien Bien Phu.* New York: Lippincott, 1967.

——— (ed.), *Ho Chi Minh on Revolution, Selected Writings, 1920-1966.* New York: Harper Colophon, 1971.

———, *Street Without Joy.* Harrisburg, Penn.: The Stackpole Co., 1967.

———, *The Two Vietnams: A Political and Military Analysis.* New York: Praeger, 1964.

———, *Vietnam Witness, 1953–1966.* New York: Praeger, 1966.

FERBER, MICHAEL; and LYND, STAUGHTON, *The Resistance.* Boston: Beacon, 1971.

FISHEL, WESLEY R. (ed.), *Vietnam: Anatomy of a Conflict.* Itasca, Ill., F. E. Peacock, 1968.

FITZGERALD, FRANCES, *Fire in the Lake: The Vietnamese and the Americans in Vietnam.* New York: Random House, 1972.

FRANKLAND, NOBLE; and DOWLING (eds.) *Decisive Battles of the Twentieth Century.* London, 1976.

FREY-WOUTERS, ELLEN; and LAUFER, ROBERT S., *Legacy of a War: The American Soldier in Vietnam.* Armonk, N. Y.: M. E. Sharpe, 1986.

FULBRIGHT, J. WILLIAM, *The Arrogance of Power.* New York: Random House, 1967.

FULGHUM, DAVID; MAITLAND, TERRENCE; and the editors, *South Vietnam on Trial.* Boston: Boston Publishing Co., 1984, a volume in the series, *The Vietnam Experience.*

FURGUSON, ERNEST B., *Westmoreland: The Inevitable General.* Boston: Little, Brown, 1968.

GABRIEL, RICHARD; and SAVAGE, PAUL, *Crisis in Command.* New York: Hill and Wang, 1978.

GALLUCCI, ROBERT L., *Neither Peace nor Honor: The Politics of American Military Policy in Vietnam.* Baltimore: Johns Hopkins University Press, 1975.

GARDNER, LLOYD C., *Approaching Vietnam: From World War II through Dienbienphu.* New York: W. W. Norton, 1988.

GELB, LESLIE; with BETTS, RICHARD, *The Irony of Vietnam: The System Worked.* Washington, D.C.: The Brookings Institution, 1979.

GETTLEMAN, MARVIN E., (ed.), *Viet Nam: History, Documents, and Opinions on a Major World Crisis.* Greenich, Conn.: Fawcett, 1965.

———; FRANKLIN, JANE; YOUNG, MARILYN; and FRANKLIN, H. BRUCE (eds.), *Vietnam and America: A Documentary History.* New York: Grove Press, 1985.

GEYELIN, PHILIP, *Lyndon B. Johnson and the World.* New York: Praeger, 1966.

GIAP, VO NGUYEN, *Big Victory, Great Task.* New York: Praeger, 1967.

———, *People's War, People's Army.* Hanoi: Foreign Language Publishing House, 1961.

GIBBONS, WILLIAM CONRAD, *The U.S. Government and the Vietnam War.* 2 vols., Princeton, N. J.: Princeton University Press, 1986.

GIBSON, JAMES WILLIAM, *The Perfect War: The War We Couldn't Lose and How We Did.* New York: Vintage, 1986.

GITLIN, TODD, *The Sixties: Years of Hope: Days of Rage.* New York: Bantam, 1987.

———, *The Whole World Is Watching: Mass Media in the Making and Unmaking of the New Left.* Berkeley, Calif.: University of California Press, 1980.

GOLDMAN, ERIC, *The Tragedy of Lyndon Johnson.* New York: Dell, 1968.

GOLDSTEIN, MARTIN E., *American Policy Toward Laos.* Teaneck, N. J.: Fairleigh-Dickinson University Press, 1986.

GOODMAN, ALLEN E., *The Lost Peace: America's Search for a Negotiated Settlement of the Vietnam War.* Stanford, Calif.: Hoover Institution Press, 1978.

GOULDEN, JOSEPH C., *Truth Is the First Casualty.* Chicago: Rand McNally, 1969.

GOULDING, PHIL G., *Confirm or Deny: Informing the People on National Security.* New York: Harper and Row, 1969.

GRAEBNER, NORMAN (ed.), *Nationalism and Communism in Asia.* Lexington, Mass.: Heath, 1977.

GRAFF, HENRY, *The Tuesday Cabinet: Deliberation and Decision on Peace and War under Lyndon B. Johnson.* Englewood Cliffs, N. J.: Prentice Hall, 1970.

GREENE, GRAHAM. *The Quiet American.* New York: Penguin, 1980 [novel].

GRIFFITHS, PHILIP JONES, *Vietnam Inc.* New York: Macmillan, 1971.

HACKWORTH, DAVID H; and SHERMAN, JULIE, *About Face.* New York: Simon and Schuster, 1988.

HALBERSTAM, DAVID, *The Best and the Brightest.* New York: Random House, 1964.

———, *The Making of a Quagmire: America and Vietnam during the Kennedy Era.* New York: Random House, 1964.

———, rev. ed. New York: Knopf, 1988.

———, *The Powers that Be.* New York: Dell, 1979.

HALDEMAN, HARRY R., *The Ends of Power.* New York: New York Times Book, 1978.

HALL, DANIEL G. E., *Atlas of Southeast Asia.* New York: Macmillan, 1964.

———, *A History of Southeast Asia,* 2nd ed. New York: MacMillan, 1963.

HALLIN, DANIEL C., *The Uncensored War: The Media and Vietnam.* New York: Oxford University Press, 1986.

HAMMER, ELLEN J., *A Death in November: America in Vietnam, 1963.* New York: E. P. Dutton, 1987.

———, *The Struggle for Indochina, 1940–1955.* Palo Alto, Calif.: Stanford University Press, 1966.

———, *Vietnam, Yesterday and Today.* New York: Holt, Rinehart, and Winston, 1966.

HANH, NHAT, *Vietnam: Lotus in a Sea of Fire.* New York: Hill and Wang, 1962.

HANNAH, NORMAN B., *The Key to Failure: Laos and the Vietnam War.* Madison Books, 1988.

HARRIMAN, AVERELL, *America and Russia in a Changing World: A Half Century of Personal Observation.* New York: Doubleday, 1971.

HARRISON, JAMES PINCKNEY, *The Endless War: Fifty Years of Struggle in Vietnam*. New York: Free Press, 1982.

HARVEY, FRANK, *Air War Vietnam*. New York: Bantam, 1967.

HASKINS, JAMES, *The War and the Protest: Vietnam* New York: Doubleday, 1971.

HAVENS, THOMAS R. H., *Fire Across the Sea: The Vietnam War and Japan, 1965–1975*. Princeton, N. J.: Princeton University Press, 1987.

HELLER, CHARLES E.; and STOFFT, WILLIAM A., *America's First Battles*. Lawrence, Kansas: University Press of Kansas, 1986.

HELLMAN, JOHN, *American Myth and the Legacy of Vietnam*. New York: Columbia University Press, 1986.

HELMER, JOHN, *Bringing the War Home: The American Soldier in Vietnam and After*. New York: Free Press, 1974.

HERRING, GEORGE C., *America's Longest War: The United States and Vietnam, 1950–1975*. 2nd ed. New York: Knopf, 1986.

———, ed., *The Secret Diplomacy of the Vietnam War: The Negotiating Volumes of the Pentagon Papers*. Austin, Texas: The University of Texas Press, 1983.

HERRINGTON, STUART A., *Peace with Honor?: An American Reports on Vietnam, 1973–1975*. Novato, Calif.: Presidio, 1983.

HERSH, SEYMOUR M., *Cover-up: The Army's Secret Investigation of the Massacre at My-Lai 4*. New York: Random House, 1972.

———, *My Lai 4: A Report on the Massacre and Its Aftermath*. New York: Vintage, 1970.

———, *The Price of Power: Kissinger in the Nixon White House*. New York: Summit, 1983.

HERZ, MARTIN F., *The Prestige Press and the Christmas Bombings, 1972*. Washington, D.C.: Ethics and Public Policy Center, 1980.

HESS, GARY R., *The United States' Emergence as a Southeast Asian Power, 1940–1956*. New York: Columbia University Press, 1987.

HILSMAN, ROGER, *To Move a Nation: The Politics of Foreign Policy in the Administration of John F. Kennedy*. New York: Doubleday, 1967.

HOBART, MARK; and TAYLOR, ROBERT H. (eds.), *Context, Meaning, and Power in Southeast Asia*. Ithaca, N. Y.: Cornell University Press, 1986.

HODGSON, GEOFFREY, *America in Our Time: From World War II to Nixon, What Happened and Why*. New York: Vintage, 1976.

HOOPES, TOWNSEND, *The Limits of Intervention: An Inside Account of How the Johnson Policy of Escalation in Vietnam was Reversed*, rev. ed., New York: McKay, 1973.

HORNE, A. D. (ed.), *The Wounded Generation*. Englewood Cliffs, N. J.: Prentice Hall, 1986.

HOSMER, STEPHEN, and others, *The Fall of South Vietnam*. Santa Monica, Calif.: Rand Corporation, 1978.

HUMPHREY, HUBERT H., *The Education of a Public Man: My Life and Politics*. New York: Doubleday, 1976.

IRVING, R. E. M., *The First Indochina War: French and American Policy, 1945–1954*. London: C. Helm, 1975.

ISAACS, ARNOLD, *Without Honor: Defeat in Vietnam and Cambodia*. Baltimore: The Johns Hopkins University Press, 1983.

ISAACS, HAROLD, *No Peace for Asia*. New York: MacMillan, 1947.

JANIS, IRVING, *Victims of Groupthink: A Psychological Study of Foreign Policy Decisions and Fiascos*. Boston: Houghton-Mifflin, 1972.

JOHNSON, LADY BIRD, *A White House Diary*. New York: Holt, Rinehart, and Winston, 1970.

JOHNSON, LYNDON, *The Vantage Point: Perspectives of the Presidency, 1963–1969*. New York: Holt, Rinehart, and Winston, 1971.

KAHIN, GEORGE, *Intervention: How American Became Involved in Vietnam*. New York: Knopf, 1986.

———, *Nationalism and Revolution in Indonesia*. Ithaca, New York: Cornell University Press, 1952.

———; and LEWIS, JOHN, *The United States in Vietnam*. New York: Delta, 1967; rev. ed., 1969.

KALB, MARVIN; and ABEL, ELIE, *Roots of Involvement, The United States in Asia, 1784–1971*. New York: W. W. Norton, 1971.

KARNOW, STANLEY, *Vietnam: A History*. New York: Viking, 1983.

KATTENBURG, PAUL M., *The Vietnam Trauma in American Foreign Policy*. New Brunswick, N. J.: Transaction, 1980.

KEARNS, DORIS, *Lyndon Johnson and the American Dream*. New York: Signet, 1976.

KENDRICK, ALEXANDER, *The Wound Within: America in the Vietnam Years, 1954–1974*. Boston: Little, Brown, 1974.

KENNEDY, PAUL, *The Rise and Fall of the Great Powers: Economic Change and Military Conflict from 1500 to 2000*. New York: Random House, 1987.

KHOI, LE TRANH, *Le Viet-Nam: Historie et Civilisation*. Paris: Editions de Minuit, 1955.

KINNARD, DOUGLAS, *The War Managers*. Hanover, N. H.: University Press of New England, 1977.

KIRK, DONALD, *Wider War*. New York: Praeger, 1971.

KISSINGER, HENRY A., *Nuclear Weapons and Foreign Policy*. New York: Doubleday, 1957.

———, *The White House Years*. Boston: Little, Brown, 1979.

———, *Years of Upheaval*. Boston: Little, Brown, 1982.

KNIGHTLEY, PHILLIP, *The First Casualty: From the Crimea to Vietnam: The War Correspondent as Hero, Propagandist, and Myth Maker*. New York: Harcourt, Brace, Jovanovich, 1975.

KOLKO, GABRIEL, *Anatomy of a War: Vietnam, the United States, and Modern Historical Experience*. New York: Pantheon, 1985.

KOMER, ROBERT, *Bureaucracy Does Its Thing: Institutional Constraints on U.S.-GVN Performance in Vietnam*. Santa Monica, Calif.: RAND Corp., 1973.

KOWET, DON, *A Matter of Honor*. New York: Macmillan, 1984.

KNOLL, ERWIN; and McFADDEN, JUDITH NIES (eds.), *War Crimes and American Conscience*. New York: Holt, Rinehart, and Winston, 1970.

KRASLOW, DAVID; and LOORY, STUART H., *The Secret Search for Peace in Vietnam*. New York: Random House, 1968.

KREPINEVICH, ANDREW F., JR., *The Army and Vietnam*. Baltimore: The Johns Hopkins University Press, 1986.

LACOUTURE, JEAN, *Ho Chi Minh: A Political Biography*. New York: Random House, 1968.

———, *Vietnam Between Two Truces*. New York: Viking, 1966.

———; and DEVILLERS, PHILIPPE, *La Fin d'une Guerre: Indochine, 1954*. Paris: Editions du Seuil, 1960. There is an English translation of this book: *End of a War: Indochina, 1954*. New York: Praeger, 1969.

LAFEBER, WALTER, *America, Russia, and the Cold War, 1945–1975*. 3rd ed., New York: John Wiley, 1976.

LAKE, ANTHONY (ed.), *The Vietnam Legacy*. New York: New York University Press, 1976.

LANCASTER, DONALD, *The Emancipation of French Indo-China*. London: Oxford University Press, 1961.

LANDSDALE, EDWARD GEARY, *In the Midst of Wars: An American's Mission to Southeast Asia*. New York: Harper and Row, 1972.

LE GRO, WILLIAM E., *Vietnam from Cease-Fire to Capitulation*. Washington, D.C.: U.S. Army Center of Military History, 1981.

LEUCHTENBURG, WILLIAM, *A Troubled Feast*. Boston: Little, Brown, 1983.

LEWIS, CHESTER; HODGSON, GODFREY; and PAGE, BRUCE, *An American Melodrama: The Presidential Campaign of 1968*. New York: Viking, 1969.

LEWY, GUENTHER, *America in Vietnam*. New York: Oxford University Press, 1978.

LIFTON, ROBERT L., *Home from the War: Vietnam Veterans: Neither Victims nor Executioners*. New York: Simon and Schuster, 1973.

LIPSMAN, SAMUEL; DOYLE, EDWARD; and the editors, *Fighting for Time*. Boston: Boston Publishing Co., 1983, a volume in the series, *The Vietnam Experience*.

———; WEISS, STEPHEN; and the editors, *The False Peace*. Boston: Boston Publishing Co., 1985, a volume in the series, *The Vietnam Experience*.

LITTAUER, RAPHAEL; and UPHOFF, NORMAN (eds.), *The Air War in Indochina*, rev. ed. Boston: Beacon, 1972.

LODGE, HENRY CABOT, JR., *The Storm Has Many Eyes: A Personal Narrative*. New York: W. W. Norton, 1973.

LOMPERIS, TIMOTHY J., *Reading the Wind*. Durham, N. C.: Duke University Press, 1987.

McCARTHY, EUGENE J., *The Year of the People*. New York: Doubleday, 1969.

MacDONALD, J. FRED., *Television and the Red Menace: The Video Road to Vietnam*. New York: Praeger, 1985.

MACLEAR, MICHAEL, *The Ten Thousand Day War: Vietnam, 1945–1975*. New York: Avon, 1981.

McALEAVY, HENRY, *Black Flags in Vietnam: The Story of Chinese Intervention*. London: Allen and Unwin, 1968.

McALISTER, JOHN T. JR., *Vietnam: The Origins of Revolution*. New York: Knopf, 1969.

———; and MUS, PAUL, *The Vietnamese and Their Revolution*. New York: Harper & Row, 1970.

McCOY, ALFRED W.; with READ, CATHLEEN B.; and ADAMS, LEONARD P., II, *The Politics of Heroin in Southeast Asia*. New York: Harper & Row, 1972.

McPherson, Harry, *A Political Education*. Boston: Little, Brown, 1971.

Maitland, Weiss; and the editors, *Raising the Stakes*. Boston: Boston Publishing Co., 1982, a volume in the series, *The Vietnam Experience*.

Marolda, Edward J.; and Fitzgerald, Oscar P., *The United States Navy and the Vietnam Conflict*, vol. 2: *From Military Assistance to Combat, 1959–1965*. Washington, D.C.: Government Printing Office, Naval Historical Center, 1986.

Marr, David G., *Vietnamese Anti-Colonialism, 1885–1925*. Berkeley, Calif.: University of California Press, 1971.

Marshall, Kathryn, *In the Combat Zone*. New York: Penguin, 1987.

Marshall, S. L. A., *Vietnam: Three Battles*. New York: Da Capo Press, 1971.

Matthews, Lloyd J.; and Brown, Dale E. (eds.), *Assessing the Vietnam War*. Washington, D.C.: Pergamon-Brassup, 1987.

Maurer, Harry, *Strange Ground: Americans in Vietnam, 1945–1975*. New York: Holt, 1988.

May, Ernest R., *"Lessons" of the Past: The Use and Misuse of History in American Foreign Policy*. New York: Oxford University Press, 1973.

———; and Neustadt, Richard E., *Thinking in Time: The Uses of History for Decision-Makers*. New York: The Free Press, 1986.

Mead, Walter Russell, *Mortal Splendor: The American Empire in Transition*. Boston: Houghton Mifflin, 1987.

Mersky, Peter B.; and Polmar, Norman, *The Naval Air War in Vietnam*. New York: Kensington, 1981.

Meyerson, Harvey, *Vinh Long*. Boston: Houghton Mifflin, 1970.

Michener, James, *Kent State: What Happened and Why*. New York: Random House, 1971.

Millett, Allan R.; and Maslowski, Peter, *For the Common Defense: A Military History of the United States of America*. New York, The Free Press, 1984.

Millett, Allan R. (ed.), *A Short History of the Vietnam War*. Bloomington, Ind.: Indiana University Press, 1978.

Minh, Ho Chi, *Prison Diary*. Hanoi, Foreign Language Publishing House, 1966.

Miroff, Bruce, *Pragmatic Illusions: The Presidential Politics of John F. Kennedy*. New York: David McKay, 1976.

Moise, Edwin E., *Land Reform in China and North Vietnam*. Chapel Hill, N. C.: University of North Carolina Press, 1983.

Morris, Roger, *An Uncertain Greatness: Henry Kissinger and American Foreign Policy*. New York: Harper & Row, 1977.

Morrocco, John; and the editors, *Thunder from Above*. Boston: Boston Publishing Co., 1984, a volume in the series, *The Vietnam Experience*.

———, *Rain of Fire: Air War, 1969–1973*. Boston: Boston Publishing Co., 1985, a volume in the series, *The Vietnam Experience*.

Moss, George, *America in the Twentieth Century*. Englewood Cliffs, N. J.: Prentice Hall, 1989.

Mueller, John E., *War, Presidents, and Public Opinion*. New York: John Wiley, 1973.

Newfield, Jack, *Robert Kennedy: A Memoir*. New York: E.P. Dutton, 1969.

Nguyen, Cao Ky, *Twenty Years and Twenty Days*. New York: Stein and Day, 1976.

Nguyen, Gregory Tien Hung, *Economic Development of Socialist Vietnam, 1955–1980*. New York: Praeger, 1977.

———; and Schechter, Jerrold L., *The Palace File*. New York: Harper & Row, 1986.

Nixon, Richard, *RN: The Memoirs of Richard Nixon*. New York, Grosset & Dunlap, 1978.

———, *No More Vietnams*. New York: Avon, 1985.

———, *1999: Victory Without War*. New York, Pocket, 1988.

———, *The Real War*. New York: Warner, 1980.

O'Ballance, Edgar, *The Indo-China War, 1945–1954*. London: Faber and Faber, 1964.

———, *The Wars in Vietnam*. New York: Hippocrene, 1981.

Oberdorfer, Don, *Tet! The Turning Point in the Vietnam War*. Garden City, N. Y.: Doubleday, 1971.

O'Donnell, Kenneth P.; and Powers, David F.; with Joe McCarthy, *Johnny, We Hardly Knew Ye: Memories of John Fitzgerald Kennedy*. Boston, Little, Brown, 1972.

Olson, James S., (ed.), *Dictionary of the Vietnam War*. New York: Greenwood, 1988.

O'Neill, Robert J., *General Giap: Politician and Strategist*. Australia: Cassell, 1969.

O'Neill, William, *Coming Apart: An Informal History of America in the 1960s*. New York: Quadrangle, 1971.

Osgood, Robert E., *America and the World: From the Truman Doctrine to Vietnam*. Baltimore: Johns Hopkins University Press, 1970.

————, *Limited War Revisited*. Boulder, Colo.: Westview, 1979.

PALMER, BRUCE, JR., *The 25-Year War: America's Military Role in Vietnam*. New York: Simon and Schuster, 1985.

PALMER, DAVE RICHARD, *Summons of the Trumpet: A History of the Vietnam War from a Military Man's Vietpoint*. New York: Ballantine, 1978.

PALMER, GREGORY, *The McNamara Strategy and the Vietnam War: Program Budgeting in the Pentagon, 1960–1968*. Westport, Conn.: Greenwood, 1978.

PALMER, LAURA, *Shrapnel in the Heart: Letters and Remembrances from the Vietnam Veterans Memorial*. New York: Vintage, 1987.

PARET, PETER; and SHY, JOHN W., *Guerrillas in the 1960s*, rev. ed. New York: Praeger, 1962.

PARMET, HERBERT, *JFK: The Presidency of John F. Kennedy*. New York: Penguin, 1983.

PATERSON, THOMAS G.; and others, *American Foreign Policy*. Lexington, Mass: D.C. Heath, 1977.

PATTI, ARCHIMEDES L., *Why Vietnam? Prelude to America's Albatross*. Berkeley, Calif.: University of California Press, 1980.

PEARSON, WILLIARD, *The War in the Northern Provinces, 1966–1968*. Washington, D.C.: Department of the Army, 1975.

PEERS, WILLIAM R., *My Lai Inquiry*. New York: W. W. Norton, 1979.

PERRIN, LINDA, *Coming to America: Immigration from the Far East*. New York: Dell, 1980.

PETTIT, CLYDE EDWIN, *The Experts*. Secaucus, N. J.: Lyle Stuart, 1975.

PIKE, DOUGLAS, *History of Vietnamese Communism, 1925–1976*. Stanford, Calif.: Hoover Institution Press, 1978.

————, *PAVN: People's Army of Vietnam*. Novato, Calif.: Presidio, 1986.

————, *Vietcong: The Organization and Technique of the National Liberation Front of South Vietnam*. Cambridge, Mass.: MIT Press, 1966.

————, *The Vietcong Strategy of Terror*. Cambridge, Mass.: MIT Press, 1970.

————, *War, Peace, and the Vietcong*. Cambridge, Mass.: MIT Press, 1969.

PILGER, JOHN, *The Last Day: America's Final Hours in Vietnam*. New York: Vintage, 1975.

PISOR, ROBERT, *The End of the Line: The Siege of Khe Sanh*. New York: W. W. Norton, 1982.

PODHORETZ, NORMAN, *Why We Were in Vietnam*. New York: Simon and Schuster, 1982.

POLNER, MURRAY, *No Victory Parades: The Return of the Vietnam Veterans*. New York: Holt, Rinehart, and Winston, 1971.

POOLE, PETER A., *America in World Politics*. New York: Praeger, 1975.

POPKIN, SAMUEL, *The Rational Peasant: The Political Economy of Rural Society in Vietnam*. Berkeley, Calif.: University of California Press, 1979.

PORTER, GARETH, *The Myth of the Bloodbath: North Vietnam's Land Reform Program Reconsidered*. Ithaca, N. Y.: Cornell University Press, 1972.

————, *A Peace Denied: The United States, Vietnam, and the Paris Agreements*. Bloomington, Ind.: Indiana University Press, 1975.

POWERS, THOMAS, *Vietnam: The War at Home*. Boston: G. K. Hall, 1984.

PRADOS, JOHN, *The Sky Would Fall: Operation Vulture: The U.S. Bombing Mission in Indochina*. New York: Dial, 1982.

RACE, JEFFREY, *War Comes to Long An: Revolutionary Conflict in a Vietnamese Province*. Berkeley, Calif.: University of California Press, 1972.

RANDLE, ROBERT, *Geneva 1954: The Settlement of the Indochinese War*. Princeton, N.J.: Princeton University Press, 1969.

RAPPAPORT, ARMIN (ed.), *Sources in American Diplomatic History*. New York: Macmillan, 1966.

RASKIN, MARCUS G.; and FALL, BERNARD B., (eds.), *The Viet-nam Reader: Articles and Documents on American Foreign Policy and the Vietnam Crisis*. New York: Vintage, 1965.

REEDY, GEORGE E., *Lyndon B. Johnson, A Memoir*. New York: Andrews and McMeel, 1982.

————, *The Twilight of the Presidency*. New York: World, 1970.

REISCHAUER, EDWIN O., *Beyond Vietnam: The United States and Asia*. New York: Vintage, 1967.

RESTON, JAMES, JR., *Sherman's March and Vietnam*. New York: Macmillan, 1984.

DE RIENCOURT, AMAURY, *The American Empire*. New York: Dell, 1968.

ROBBINS, CHRISTOPHER, *Air America*. New York: Avon, 1979.

ROBERTS, STEPHEN H., *History of French Colonial Policy: 1870–1925*, two vols. London: P. S. King and Son, 1929.

ROGERS, BERNARD W., *Cedar Falls-Junction City: A Turning Point*. Washington, D.C.: U.S. Government Printing Office, 1974.

ROSTOW, WALT W., *The Diffusion of Power: An Essay in Recent History*. New York: Macmillan, 1972.

ROTH, ANDREW J., *The Path to Vietnam: Origins of The American Commitment to Southeast Asia.* Ithaca, N. Y.: Cornell University Press, 1987.

ROY, JULES, *The Battle of Dienbienphu.* New York: Harper & Row, 1965.

RUST, WILLIAM J., *Kennedy in Vietnam: American Vietnam Policy 1960–1963.* New York: Da Capo, 1985.

SAFIRE, WILLIAM, *Before the Fall: An Insider's View of the Pre-Watergate White House.* New York: Doubleday, 1975.

SAINTENY, JEAN, *Histoire d'une paix manque.* Paris: Amoit Dumont, 1953.

SALE, KIRKPATRICK, *SDS.* New York: Vintage, 1973.

SALISBURY, HARRISON, *Behind the Lines: Hanoi, Dec. 23, 1966 to January 7, 1967.* New York: Harper & Row, 1967.

———, (ed.), *Vietnam Reconsidered: Lessons from a War.* New York: Harper & Row, 1983.

SANTOLI, AL, *To Bear Any Burden.* New York: Ballantine, 1985.

———, *Everything We Had.* New York: Random House, 1981.

SCHANDLER, HERBERT Y., *The Unmaking of a President: Lyndon Johnson and Vietnam.* Princeton, N. J.: Princeton University Press, 1977.

SCHEER, ROBERT, *How the United States Got Involved in Vietnam.* Santa Barbara, Calif.: Center for the Study of Democratic Institutions, 1965.

SCHELL, JONATHAN, *The Real War.* New York: Pantheon, 1988.

———, *The Time of Illusion.* New York: Knopf, 1976.

———, *The Village of Ben Suc.* New York: Knopf, 1967.

SCHEMMER, BENJAMIN, *The Raid.* New York: Harper and Row, 1976.

SCHLESINGER, ARTHUR M., JR., *The Bitter Heritage: Vietnam and American Democracy 1941–1966.* New York: Fawcett, 1966.

———, *The Imperial Presidency.* Boston: Houghton Mifflin, 1973.

———, *Robert Kennedy and His Times.* Boston: Houghton Mifflin, 1978.

———, *A Thousand Days: John F. Kennedy in the White House.* Boston: Houghton Mifflin, 1965.

SCHOENBAUM, THOMAS J., *Waging Peace and War: Dean Rusk in the Truman, Kennedy, and Johnson Years.* New York: Simon and Schuster, 1988.

SCIGLIANO, ROBERT, *South Vietnam: Nation Under Stress.* Boston: Houghton Mifflin, 1964.

SHAPLEN, ROBERT, *The Lost Revolution: The U.S. in Vietnam, 1946–1966,* rev. ed. New York: Harper & Row, 1966.

———, *The Road from War: Vietnam, 1965–1971.* New York: Harper & Row, 1970.

———, *Time Out of Hand: Revolution and Reaction in Southeast Asia.* New York: Harper & Row, 1969.

SHARP, ULYSSES S. GRANT, *Strategy for Defeat.* San Rafael, Calif.: Presidio, 1978.

SHAWCROSS, WILLIAM, *Sideshow: Kissinger, Nixon and the Destruction of Cambodia.* New York: Simon and Schuster, 1979.

SHEEHAN, NEIL, *A Bright Shining Lie: John Paul Vann and America in Vietnam.* New York: Random House, 1989.

SHULIMSON, JACK, *U.S. Marines in Vietnam: 1966.* Washington, D.C.: U.S. Marine Corps, 1982.

SIDEY, HUGH, *A Very Personal Presidency: LBJ in the White House.* New York: Atheneum, 1968.

SMITH, RALPH BERNARD, *An International History of the Vietnam War.* New York: St. Martin's, 1983.

SMITH, R. HARRIS, *OSS: The Secret History of America's First Central Intelligence Agency.* New York: Delta, 1973.

SNEPP, FRANK, *Decent Interval.* New York: Random House, 1977.

SORENSEN, THEODORE C., *Kennedy.* New York: Harper & Row, 1965.

SPECTOR, RONALD H., *United States Army in Vietnam: Advice and Support: The Early Years, 1941–1960.* Washington, D.C.: Center for Military History, 1984.

———, *Researching the Vietnam Experience* Washington, D.C.: Analysis Branch of the U.S. Army Center of Military History, 1984.

STANTON, SHELBY L., *The Rise and Fall of An American Army: U.S. Ground Forces in Vietnam, 1965–1973.* New York: Dell, 1985.

———, *Vietnam Order of Battle.* New York: Galahad, 1987.

STEEL, RONALD, *Pax Americana: The Cold War Empire and the Politics of Counter-Revolution.* rev. ed. New York: Viking, 1970.

STEVENS, ROBERT W., *Vain Hopes, Grim Realities: The Economic Consequences of the Vietnam War.* New York: New Viewpoints, 1976.

STEVENSON, CHARLES A., *The End of Nowhere: American Policy Toward Laos Since 1954.* Boston: Beacon, 1972.

STOCKDALE, JAMES B. and SYBIL, *In Love and War.* New York: Harper & Row, 1984.

STOESSINGER, JOHN, *Crusaders and Pragmatists*. New York: W. W. Norton, 1979.

SUGNET, CHRISTOPHER L.; and HICKEY, JOHN T., *Vietnam War Bibliography*. Lexington, Mass: D. C. Heath, 1983.

SUMMERS, HARRY G., JR., *On Strategy: A Critical Analysis of the Vietnam War*. New York: Dell, 1982.

——, *Vietnam War Almanac*. New York: Facts on File, 1985.

SZULC, TAD, *The Illusion of Peace: Foreign Policy in the Nixon-Kissinger Years*. New York: Viking, 1979.

TAYLOR, MAXWELL D., *Swords and Ploughshares*. New York: W. W. Norton, 1972.

——, *The Uncertain Trumpet*. New York: Harper & Row, 1959.

TAYLOR, TELFORD, *Nuremberg and Vietnam: An American Tragedy*. New York: Quadrangle, 1967.

THAYER, THOMAS C., *War Without Fronts: The American Experience in Vietnam*. Boulder, Colo.: Westview, 1985.

THEOHARIS, ATHAN, *Spying in America: Political Surveillance from Hoover to the Huston Plan*. Philadelphia: Temple University Press, 1978.

THIES, WALLACE J., *When Governments Collide: Coercion and Diplomacy in the Vietnam Conflict, 1964–1968*. Berkeley, Calif.: University of California Press, 1980.

THO, TRAN DINH, *The Cambodian Incursion*. Washington, D.C.: U.S. Army Center of Military History, 1983.

THOMPSON, JAMES CLAY, *Rolling Thunder: Understanding Policy and Program Failure*. Chapel Hill, N. C.: University of North Carolina Press, 1980.

THOMPSON, ROBERT G. K., *No Exit from Vietnam*. New York: David McKay, 1969.

——, *Peace Is Not at Hand*. New York: David McKay, 1974.

THOMPSON, VIRGINIA M., *French Indochina*. London: Allen and Unwin, 1937.

THOMPSON, W. SCOTT; and FRIZZELL, DONALDSON D. (eds.), *The Lessons of Vietnam*. New York: Crane, Ruzzak, 1977.

TRA, TRAN VAN, *Vietnam: History of the Bulwark B-2 Theater*, vol. 5: *Concluding the 30-Years' War*. Ho Chi Minh City: Van Nghe Publishing Plant, 1982.

TRAGER, FRANK N. (ed.), *Marxism in Southeast Asia*. Palo Alto, Calif.: Stanford University Press, 1959.

TREGASKIS, RICHARD B., *Vietnam Diary*. New York: Holt, Rinehart, and Winston, 1963.

TREWHITT, HENRY L., *McNamara: His Ordeal in the Pentagon*. New York: Harper & Row, 1971.

TRUONG, NGO QUANG, *The Easter Offensive of 1972*. Washington, D.C.: U.S. Army Center of Military History, 1980.

TUCHMAN, BARBARA, *The March of Folly*. New York: Ballantine, 1984.

TURLEY, WILLIAM S., *The Second Indochina War: A Short Political and Military History, 1954–1975*. New York: New American Library, 1986.

TURNER, KATHLEEN, *Lyndon Johnson's Dual War: Vietnam and the Press*. Chicago: University of Chicago Press, 1985.

Twentieth Century Fund, *Battle Lines*. New York: Priority Press, 1985.

ULACK, RICHARD; and others, *Atlas of Southeast Asia*. New York: Macmillan, 1988.

UNGER, IRWIN, *The Movement: A History of the American New Left 1959–1972*. New York: Dodd, Mead, 1974.

VALENTI, JACK, *A Very Human President*. New York: W. W. Norton, 1975.

VAN DYKE, JOHN M., *North Vietnam's Strategy for Survival*. Palo Alto, Calif.: Stanford University Press, 1972.

VIEN, CAO VAN, *The Final Collapse*. Washington, D.C.: U.S. Army Center of Military History, 1982.

——; and KHUYEN, DONG VAN, *Reflections on the Vietnam War*. Washington, D.C.: U.S. Army Center of Military History, 1980.

VO, NGUYEN GIAP, *People's War, People's Army*. New York: Praeger, 1962.

VON CLAUSEWITZ, KARL, *On War*, edited by Michael Howard and Peter Paret. Princeton, N. J.: Princeton University Press, 1976.

WALT, LEWIS W., *Strange War, Strange Strategy*. New York: Funk and Wagnalls, 1969.

WALTON, RICHARD J., *Cold War and Counter-Revolution: The Foreign Policy of John F. Kennedy*. Baltimore: Penguin, 1972.

WARNER, DENIS, *The Last Confucian*. New York: Macmillan, 1963.

WEIGLEY, RUSSELL, *The American Way of War: A History of United States Military Strategy and Policy*. New York: Macmillan, 1973.

WESTMORELAND, WILLIAM C., *A Soldier Reports*. New York: Dell, 1976.

WHALEN, RICHARD, *Catch the Falling Flag*. Boston: Houghton Mifflin, 1972.

WHEELER, JOHN, *Touched with Fire: The Future of the Vietnam Generation.* New York: Avon, 1984.
WHITE, RALPH K., *Nobody Wanted War: Misperceptions in Vietnam and Other Wars.* New York: Doubleday, 1968.
WHITE, THEODORE H., *Breach of Faith: The Fall of Richard Nixon:.* New York: Atheneum, 1975.
———, *The Making of the President 1960.* New York: Atheneum, 1961.
———, *The Making of the President 1964.* New York: New American Library, 1965.
———, *The Making of the President 1968.* New York: Atheneum, 1969.
———, *In Search of History.* New York: Harper & Row, 1978.
WICKER, TOM, *JFK and LBJ: The Influence of Personality on Politics.* New York: William Morrow, 1968.
WILLENSON, KIM, *The Bad War: An Oral History of the Vietnam Conflict.* New York: New American Library, 1987.
WILLIAMS, WILLIAM APPLEMAN; MCCORMICK, THOMAS; GARDNER, LLOYD; and LAFEBER, WALTER (eds.), *America in Vietnam: A Documentary History.* Garden City, N. Y.: Doubleday, 1985.
WILLS, GARRY, *The Kennedy Imprisonment: A Meditation on Power.* Boston: Little, Brown, 1982.
WILSON, JAMES C., *Vietnam in Prose and Film.* Jefferson, N.C.: McFarland, 1982.
WINDCHY, EUGENE, *Tonkin Gulf.* New York: Doubleday, 1971.
WITCOVER, JULES, *85 Days: The Last Campaign of Robert F. Kennedy.* New York: Atheneum, 1969.
WOODSIDE, ALEXANDER, *Community and Revolution in Modern Vietnam.* Boston: Houghton Mifflin, 1976.
———, *Vietnam and the Chinese Model: A Comparative Study of Vietnamese and Chinese Government in the First Half of the Nineteenth Century.* Cambridge, Mass.: Harvard University Press, 1971.
WOODWARD, BOB; and BERNSTEIN, CARL, *All the President's Men.* New York: Warner, 1974.
———, *The Final Days.* New York: Avon, 1976.
The World Almanac of the Vietnam War, John S. Bowman, General Editor, with introduction by Fox Butterfield. New York: Bison, 1985.
YARMOLINSKY, ADAM, *The Military Establishment: Its Impact on American Society.* New York: Harper & Row, 1971.
ZAROULIS, NANCY; and SULLIVAN, GERALD, *Who Spoke Up? American Protest Against the War in Vietnam.* Garden City, N. Y.: Doubleday, 1984.
ZASLOFF, JOSEPH J., *Origins of the Insurgency in South Vietnam, 1954–1960: The Role of the Southern Vietminh Cadres.* Santa Monica, Calif.: RAND Corporation, 1968.

ARTICLES

ADAMS, SAMUEL, "Vietnam Cover-up: Playing with Numbers," *Harper's Magazine* (May 1975), p. 41.
BADILLO, GILBERT; and CURRY, G. DAVID, "The Social Incidence of Vietnam Casualties: Social Class or Race?" *Armed Forces and Society,* vol. 2 (Spring 1976), pp. 397–406.
BAILEY, GEORGE A., "Television War: Trends in Network Coverage of Vietnam 1965–1970," *Journal of Broadcasting,* vol. 20 (Spring 1976), pp. 147–157.
BALL, GEORGE, "The Light that Failed," *Atlantic Monthly* (July 1973), pp. 33–49.
———, "Top Secret: The Prophecy the President Rejected," *Atlantic,* vol. 230 (July 1972), pp. 35–49.
BELLHOUSE, MARY L.; and LITCHFIELD, LAWRENCE, "Vietnam and the Loss of Innocence: An Analysis of the Political Implications of the Popular Literature of the Vietnam War," *Journal of Popular Culture,* vol. 16 (Winter 1982), pp. 157–174.
BRODIE, BERNARD, "Why We Were So (Strategically) Wrong," *Foreign Policy,* (Winter 1971–1972), pp. 151–162.
CADY, JOHN F., "The French Colonial Regime in Vietnam," *Current History,* vol. 50 (1966) pp. 72–78, 115.
CHEN, KING C., "Hanoi's Three Decisions and the Escalation of the Vietnam War," *Political Science Quarterly,* vol. 90 (Summer 1975), pp. 239–259.
CHESNEAUX, JEAN, "The Historical Background of Vietnamese Communism," in *Government and Opposition,* vol. 4 (Winter 1969), pp. 119–135.
CLIFFORD, CLARK, "A Vietnam Reappraisal," *Foreign Affairs,* vol. 47 (July 1969), pp. 601–622.

CONVERSE, PHILIP E.; MILLER, WARREN E.; RUSK, JEROLD G.; and WOLFE, ARTHUR C., "Continuity and Change in American Politics: Parties and Issues in the 1968 Election," *American Political Science Review*, vol. 63 (December 1969), pp. 1,083–1,105.

————; and SCHUMAN, HOWARD, "'Silent Majorities' and the Vietnam War," *Scientific American*, vol. 222 (June, 1970).

COOPER, CHESTER L., "The Complexities of Negotiations," *Foreign Affairs*, vol. 46 (April 1968), pp. 454–466.

DEBENEDETTI, CHARLES, "A CIA Analysis of the Anti-Vietnam War Movement: October, 1967," *Peace and Change*, vol. 9 (Spring 1983), pp. 31–42.

————, "On the Significance of Citizen Peace Activism: America, 1961–1975," *Peace and Change*, vol. 9 (Summer 1983), pp. 6–20.

DUNN, PETER M., "The American Army: the Vietnam War, 1965–1973," in *Armed Forces and Modern Counter-insurgency*, edited by Ian F. W. Beckett and John Pimlott. London: Croom Helm, 1985.

ELEGANT, ROBERT, "How to Lose a War: Reflections of a Foreign Correspondent," *Encounter* (August 1981).

EPSTEIN, EDWARD J., "The War in Vietnam, What Happened Vs. What We Saw," *TV Guide* (October 6, 1973).

ESZTERHOZ, JOSEPH; and others, "The Massacre at My Lai," *Life* (December 5, 1969).

GELB, LESLIE, "The Essential Domino: American Politics and Vietnam," *Foreign Affairs*, vol. 50 (April 1972), pp. 459–472.

————, "The System Worked," *Foreign Policy*, vol. 3 (Summer 1971), pp. 140–167.

HALBERSTAM, DAVID, "The Ugliest American in Vietnam," *Esquire*, vol. 62 (November 1964), pp. 37–40.

————, "Getting the Story in Vietnam," *Commentary*, vol. 39 (January 1968), pp. 30–34.

————, "Vietnamese Reds Gain in Key Area" in New York *Times*, August 15, 1963, pp. A1, A3.

HEINL, ROBERT, "The Collapse of the Armed Forces," *Armed Forces Journal*, vol. 19 (June 1971), pp. 30–38.

HERRING, GEORGE C., "American Strategy in Vietnam: The Postwar Debate," *Military Affairs*, vol. 46 (April 1982), pp. 57–63.

————, "The 1st Cavalry and the Ia Drang Valley, 18 October-24 November 1965," in Heller, Charles E.; and Stofft, William A., *America's First Battles*, pp. 300–326. Lawrence, Kansas: University Press of Kansas, 1986.

————, "The Nixon Strategy in Vietnam," in *Vietnam as History*, edited by Peter Braestrup, Washington, D.C.: University Press of America, 1984.

————, "The Truman Administration and the Restoration of French Sovereignty in Indochina," *Diplomatic History*, vol. 1 (Spring 1977), pp. 97–117.

————, "Vietnam, El Salvador, and the Uses of History," in *The Central American Crisis*, edited by Kenneth Coleman and George C. Herring. Wilmington, Del.: 1985.

————; and IMMERMAN, RICHARD H., "Eisenhower, Dulles, and Dienbienphu: 'The Day We didn't Go to War' Revisited," *Journal of American History*, vol. 71 (September 1984), pp. 343–363.

HESS, GARY R., "Franklin D. Roosevelt and Indochina," *Journal of American History*, vol. 59 (September 1972), pp. 353–368.

JACOBS, JAMES B.; and MCNAMARA, DENNIS, "Vietnam Veterans and Agent Orange," *Armed Forces and Society*, vol. 13 (Fall 1986), pp. 57–79.

————, "The Pentagon Papers: A Critical Evaluation," *American Political Science Review*, vol. 69 (June 1975) 675–684.

KARNOW, STANLEY, "The Newsmen's War in Vietnam," *Nieman Reports*, vol. 17 (December 1963), pp. 3–8.

KATTENBURG, PAUL M., "Vietnam and U.S. Diplomacy, 1940–1970," *Orbis*, vol. 15 (Fall 1971), pp. 818–841.

KIMBALL, JEFFREY P., "The Stab-in-the-Back Legend and the Vietnam War," *Armed Forces and Society*, vol. 14 (Spring 1988), pp. 433–458.

KISSINGER, HENRY A., "The Viet Nam Negotiations," *Foreign Affairs*, vol. 47 (January 1969), pp. 211–234.

LAFEBER, WALTER, "The Rise and Fall of American Power, 1963–1975," in Williams, William Appleton; McCormick, Thomas; Gardner, Lloyd; and LaFeber, Walter (eds.), *America in Vietnam: A Documentary History*. Garden City, N. Y.: Doubleday, 1985.

———, "Roosevelt, Churchill, and Indochina, 1942–1945," *American Historical Review*, vol. 80 (December 1975), pp. 1277–1289.

LICHTY, LAWRENCE W., and BAILEY, GEORGE A., "Violence in Television News: A Case Study of Audience Response," *Central States Speech Journal*, vol. 23 (Winter 1972), pp. 225–229.

LINDEN, EUGENE, "Fragging and Other Withdrawal Symptoms," *Saturday Review* (January 8, 1972), pp. 12–17, 55.

MANDELBAUM, DAVID, "Vietnam: The Television War," *Daedalus*, vol. 111 (Fall 1982), pp. 157–169.

MOISE, EDWIN E., "Land Reform and Land Reform Errors in North Vietnam," *Pacific Affairs*, vol. 49 (Spring 1976), pp. 70–92.

MOSKOS, CHARLES C., "Success Story: Blacks in the Army," *Atlantic Monthly* (May 1986), pp. 64–72.

MUELLER, JOHN E., "Reflections on the Vietnam Antiwar Movement and the Curious Calm at War's End," in *Vietnam as History*, edited by Peter Braestrup. Washington, D.C.: The University Press of America, 1984, pp. 151–157.

———, "The Search for the 'Breaking Point' in Vietnam: The Statistics of a Deadly Quarrel," *International Studies Quarterly*, vol. 4 (December 1980), pp. 497–519.

———, "A Summary of Public Opinion and the Vietnam War," in *Vietnam as History*, edited by Peter Braestrup. Washington, D.C.: University Press of America, 1984, appendices.

NIXON, RICHARD M., "Asia after Vietnam," *Foreign Affairs*, vol. 46 (October 1967), pp. 111–125.

PARKER, MAYNARD, "Vietnam: The War that won't End," *Foreign Affairs*, vol. 53 (January 1975), pp. 352–374.

PATERSON, THOMAS G., "Bearing the Burden: A Critical Look at JFK's Foreign Policy," *Virginia Quarterly Review*, vol. 54 (Spring 1978), pp. 193–212.

PATTERSON, OSCAR, III, "An Analysis of Television Coverage of the Vietnam War," *Journal of Broadcasting*, vol. 28 (Fall 1984), pp. 397–404.

PELZ, STEPHEN, "John F. Kennedy's 1961 Vietnam War Decisions," *Journal of Strategic Studies*, vol. 4 (December 1981), pp. 356–385.

POPKIN, SAMUEL, "Pacification: Politics and the Village," *Asian Survey*, vol. 10 (August 1970), pp. 662–671.

PROSTERMAN, ROY L., "Land-to-the-Tiller in South Vietnam: The Tables Turn," *Asian Survey*, vol. 10 (August 1970), pp. 751–764.

RACE, JEFFREY, "How They Won," *Asian Survey*, vol. 10, (August 1970), pp. 628–650.

———, "The Origins of the Second Indochina War," *Asian Survey*, vol. 10, (May 1960), pp. 359–382.

ROBERTS, CHALMERS, "Foreign Policy and a Paralyzed Presidency," *Foreign Affairs*, vol. 52 (July 1974).

SALTER, MACDONALD, "The Broadening Base of Land Reform in South Vietnam," *Asian Survey*, vol. 10 (August 1970), pp. 724–737.

SAVAGE, PAUL; and GABRIEL, RICHARD A., "Cohesion and Disintegration in the American Army," *Armed Forces and Society*, vol. 2 (Spring 1976), pp. 340–376.

SCHANDLER, HERBERT Y., "America and Vietnam: The Failure of Strategy, 1964–1967," in *Vietnam as History*, Braestrup, Peter (ed.). Washington, D.C.: University Press of America, 1984.

SCHUMAN, HOWARD, "Two Sources of Antiwar Sentiment in America," *American Journal of Sociology*, vol. 78 (November 1972), pp. 519–535.

SHEEHAN, NEIL, "In Vietnam, the Birth of the Credibility Gap," New York *Times*, Oct. 1, 1988, p. A15.

———, four articles about the life, military career, and Vietnam service of John Paul Vann appeared in consecutive issues of the *New Yorker* under the general title of "Annals of War: An American Soldier in Vietnam," vol. 44, Nos. 19–22, June 20, June 27, July 4, and July 11, 1988.

SMALL, MELVIN, "The Impact of the Antiwar Movement on Lyndon Johnson, 1965–1968," *Peace and Change*, vol. 10 (Spring 1984), pp. 1–22.

SUMMERS, HARRY G., JR., "The Bitter Triumph of Ia Drang," *American Heritage* (January–February 1984), pp. 51–58.

SZULC, TAD, "Behind the Vietnam Cease Fire Agreement," *Foreign Policy*, vol. 15 (Summer, 1974), pp. 21–69.

THOMSON, JAMES C., "How Could Vietnam Happen?" *Atlantic*, vol. 22 (April 1968), pp. 47–53.

U.S. News and World Report, "'The Phantom Battle' that Led to War," (July 23, 1984), pp. 56–67.

WARD, RICHARD, "The Origins of United States Interest in Vietnam," Vietnam Quarterly, No. 1 (Winter 1976).

WARNER, GEOFFREY, "The United States and the Fall of Diem," 1, "The Coup That Never Was," Australian Outlook, vol. 28 (December 1974), pp. 245–258; 2, "The Death of Diem," Australian Outlook, vol. 29 (March 1975), pp. 3–17.

WOODSIDE, ALEXANDER, "Decolonization and Agricultural Reform in Northern Vietnam," Asian Survey, vol. 10 (August 1970), 705–723.

———, "Some Southern Vietnamese Writers Look At the War," Bulletin of Concerned Asian Scholars, vol. 2 (October 1969) pp. 53–58.

PUBLIC DOCUMENTS

Citizen's Commission of Inquiry (eds.), The Dellums Committee Hearings on War Crimes in Vietnam. New York: Vintage, 1972.

GRAVEL, MIKE, (ed.), The Pentagon Papers: The Defense Department History of U.S. Decisionmaking in Vietnam. Boston: Beacon, 1971.

JOHNSON, LYNDON B., Public Papers of Lyndon B. Johnson, 1968–1969. Washington, D.C.: U.S. Government Printing Office, 1970.

NIXON, RICHARD M., Public Papers, Richard Nixon, 1969 and 1970. Washington, D.C.: U.S. Government Printing Office, 1971.

PORTER, GARETH, Vietnam: The Definitive Documentation of Human Decisions. Stanfordville, N. Y.: Earl M. Coleman, 1979.

SHEEHAN, NEIL; SMITH, HEDRICK; KENWORTHY, E. W.; and BUTTERFIELD, FOX, The Pentagon Papers: The Secret History of the Vietnam War. New York: Bantam, 1971.

United States, Department of State, Foreign Relations of the United States, 1955–1957, vol. 3, John P. Glennon general editor. Washington, D.C.: U.S. Government Printing Office, 1971.

OTHER SOURCES

Accuracy in Media (AIM), "Television's Vietnam. Part 1: The Real Story; Part 2: The Impact of Media," 1984 and 1985, television documentary transcripts.

AMBROSE, STEPHEN, "Nixon and Vietnam: Vietnam and Electoral Politics," No. 3 in a lecture series, "The Dwight D. Eisenhower Lectures in War and Peace," given at Kansas State University in Manhattan, Kansas, Oct. 24, 1988.

"Apocalypse Now," fiction film.

CAPUTO, PHILLIP, A Rumor of War. New York: Ballantine, 1977, Novelistic memoir.

CBS News, "The Uncounted Enemy: A Vietnam Deception," January 23, 1982, television documentary transcript.

CBS News, "Vietnam: A War That is Finished," July, 1975, television documentary transcript.

CBS News, "The World of Charlie Company," television documentary transcript.

"Coming Home," fiction film.

The Congressional Medal of Honor Library, Vietnam. New York: Dell, 1984.

"The Deer Hunter," fiction film.

DEL VECCHIO, JOHN M., The 13th Valley. New York: Bantam, 1982. Novel.

"Full Metal Jacket," fiction film.

GREENE, GRAHAM, The Quiet American. New York: Penguin, 1977. Novel.

"Hamburger Hill," fiction film based on the Battle of Dong Ap Bia, fought along the rim of the A Shau valley, May 11–20, 1969.

HARKINS, PAUL D., "Oral History." 1974, U.S. Army Military History Institute Archives, Carlisle Barracks, Penn.

KAIKO, TAKESHI; translated by Cecilia Segawa Seigle, Into a Black Sun. Tokyo: Kadansha, 1980. Distributed in the United States by Kadansha through Harper & Row, 1980, Novel.

"The Killing Fields," fiction film based on the experiences of Sydney Schrandberg and Dith Pran.

KOVIC, RON, Born on the Fourth of July. New York: McGraw-Hill, 1976. Novelistic memoir.

LEDERER, WILLIAM, J.; and BURDICK, EUGENE, *The Ugly American*. New York: W. W. Norton, 1958. Novel.

Los Angeles *Times*, various issues.

MAILER, NORMAN, *Armies of the Night*. Cleveland: World, 1968. Novelistic journalism.

MASON, BOBBIE ANN, *In Country*. New York: Harper and Row, 1985. Novel.

MASON, ROBERT, *Chickenhawk*. New York: Penguin, 1983. Novelistic memoir.

————, "News or Nemesis: Did Television Lose the Vietnam War?" Unpublished essay, 1988.

————, "The Vietnam Generation: The Impact of the War and the Draft on the Generation Called to Fight in Southeast Asia." Unpublished essay, 1984.

The 'Nam Magazine, vol. 1, nos. 3 and 4, (October, November 1988), Comic books.

Newsweek, July 10, 1967, pp. 20–24.

New York *Times*, various issues.

NIXON, RICHARD M., transcript of televised speech November. 3, 1969.

O'BRIEN, TIM, *Going after Cacciato*. New York: Delacorte, 1978. Novel.

————, *If I Die in a Combat Zone*. New York: Dell, 1969. Novelistic memoir.

OFFNER, ARNOLD A., "The Truman Myth Revealed: From Parochial Nationalist to Cold Warrior." Unpublished essay, 1988.

O'KEEFE, KEVIN, "Media Coverage of Gulf of Tonkin." Unpublished essay, 1988.

"Platoon," fiction film based on the Vietnam experiences of Oliver Stone.

SMITH, STEVEN PHILLIP, *American Boys*. New York: Avon, 1978. Novel.

STONE, ROBERT, *Dog Soldiers*. Boston: Houghton Mifflin, 1974. Novel.

PEERS, WILLIAM R., "Oral History," U.S. Army Military History Institute Archives, Carlisle Barracks, Penn.

Time, various issues.

VANN, JOHN PAUL, papers, Archives of the U.S. Army Military Institute, Carlisle Barracks, Penn.

Vietnam Veterans Against the War, *The Winter Soldier Investigations*. Boston: Beacon, 1972.

Washington *Post*, various issues.

WEBB, JAMES, *Fields of Fire*. Englewood Cliffs, N. J.: Prentice Hall, 1978.

Winter Soldier Archive, *Soldiering in Vietnam: The Short-Timer's Journal*. Berkeley, Calif.: Winter Soldier Archive, 1980.

ZAIS, MELVIN, Oral History Interview, pp. 575–583, Archives of the U.S. Army Military History Institute, Carlisle Barracks, Penn.

INDEX